Online Multimedia Advertising:

Techniques and Technologies

Xian–Sheng Hua
Microsoft Research Asia, China

Tao Mei
Microsoft Research Asia, China

Alan Hanjalic
Delft University of Technology, The Netherlands

INFORMATION SCIENCE REFERENCE

Hershey · New York

Senior Editorial Director:	Kristin Klinger
Director of Book Publications:	Julia Mosemann
Editorial Director:	Lindsay Johnston
Acquisitions Editor:	Erika Carter
Typesetters:	Michael Brehm, and Milan Vracarich, Jr.
Production Coordinator:	Jamie Snavely
Cover Design:	Nick Newcomer

Published in the United States of America by
Information Science Reference (an imprint of IGI Global)
701 E. Chocolate Avenue
Hershey PA 17033
Tel: 717-533-8845
Fax: 717-533-8661
E-mail: cust@igi-global.com
Web site: http://www.igi-global.com/reference

Library of Congress Cataloging-in-Publication Data

Online multimedia advertising : techniques and technologies / Xian-Sheng Hua, Tao Mei and Alan Hanjalic, editors.
      p. cm.
   Includes bibliographical references and index.
   Summary: "This book unites recent research efforts in online multimedia advertising and includes introductions to basic concepts and fundamental technologies for online advertising, basic multimedia technologies for online multimedia advertising, and modern multimedia advertising schemes, theories and technologies"--Provided by publisher.
   ISBN 978-1-60960-189-8 (hbk.) -- ISBN 978-1-60960-191-1 (ebook) 1. Internet advertising. 2. Internet marketing. 3. Multimedia systems. I. Hua, Xian-Sheng, 1973- II. Mei, Tao, 1978- III. Hanjalic, A.
   HF6146.I58O56 2011
   659.14'4--dc22
                              2010051809

British Cataloguing in Publication Data
A Cataloguing in Publication record for this book is available from the British Library.

All work contributed to this book is new, previously-unpublished material. The views expressed in this book are those of the authors, but not necessarily of the publisher.

Xuerui Wang, *Yahoo! Labs, USA*
Xiao Wu, *Southwest Jiaotong University, China*
Jun Yan, *Microsoft Research Asia, China*
Bruce Zhang, *Yahoo! Lab, USA*
Dan Zigmond, *Google, USA*

Table of Contents

Preface xv

Section 1
Traditional Text/Banner Advertising Techniques

Chapter 1
Click-Through Rate Estimation for Rare Events in Online Advertising 1
Xuerui Wang, Yahoo! Labs, USA
Wei Li, Yahoo! Labs, USA
Ying Cui, Yahoo! Labs, USA
Ruofei Zhang, Yahoo! Labs, USA
Jianchang Mao, Yahoo! Labs, USA

Chapter 2
Reinforcement Learning for Online Optimization of Banner Format and Delivery 13
Benoit Baccot, Sopra Group, France & University of Toulouse, France
Romulus Grigoras, University of Toulouse, France & Devatics, France
Vincent Charvillat, University of Toulouse, France

Chapter 3
Utilizing Sentiments in Online Contextual Advertising 32
Tanveer J. Siddiqui, University of Allahabad, India

Section 2
Image Advertising

Chapter 4
In-Image Advertising 49
Lusong Li, Beihang University, China
Xian-Sheng Hua, Microsoft Research Asia, China

Chapter 5

Argo: Intelligent Advertising Made Possible from Images 67

    Xin-Jing Wang, Microsoft Research Asia, China
    Mo Yu, Harbin Institute of Technology, China
    Lei Zhang, Microsoft Research Asia, China
    Wei-Ying Ma, Microsoft Research Asia, China

Chapter 6

The Advent of Play and Pursuit 84

    Yasmin Ibrahim, Queen Mary University of London, UK

Section 3
Video Advertising

Chapter 7

Content and Attention Aware Overlay for Online Video Advertising 101

    Huazhong Ning, Google Inc., USA
    Junxian Wang, Microsoft Corporation, USA
    Xu Liu, Microsoft China Co. Ltd., China
    Ying Shan, Microsoft Corporation, USA

Chapter 8

An Explorative Study of the Virtual Product Placement: Take ViSA as an Example 122

    Chia-Hu Chang, National Taiwan University, Taiwan
    Ja-Ling Wu, National Taiwan University, Taiwan

Chapter 9

Adapting Online Advertising Techniques to Television 148

    Sundar Dorai-Raj, Google Inc., USA
    Yannet Interian, Google Inc., USA
    Igor Naverniouk, Google Inc., USA
    Dan Zigmond, Google Inc., USA

Chapter 10

Linking Traditional TV Advertising to Internet Advertising 166

    Ling-Yu Duan, Peking University, China
    Jinqiao Wang, Chinese Academy of Sciences, China
    Wen Gao, Peking University, China
    Hanqing Lu, Chinese Academy of Sciences, China
    Jesse S. Jin, The University of Newcastle, Australia
    Changsheng Xu, Chinese Academy of Sciences, China

Chapter 11
Contextual In-Stream Video Advertising 194
Tao Mei, Microsoft Research Asia, China
Shipeng Li, Microsoft Research Asia, China

Section 4
Behavior Targeting/Personalized Ads/Audience Intelligence

Chapter 12
Behavioral Targeting Online Advertising 213
Jun Yan, Microsoft Research Asia, China
Dou Shen, Microsoft Corporation, USA
Teresa Mah, Microsoft Corporation, USA
Ning Liu, Microsoft Research Asia, China
Zheng Chen, Microsoft Research Asia, China
Ying Li, Microsoft Corporation, USA

Chapter 13
Distributed Technologies for Personalized Advertisement Delivery 233
Dorothea Tsatsou, Informatics and Telematics Institute, Greece
Symeon Papadopoulos, Informatics and Telematics Institute, Greece
Ioannis Kompatsiaris, Informatics and Telematics Institute, Greece
Paul C. Davis, Motorola Applied Research Center, USA

Chapter 14
Audience Intelligence in Online Advertising 262
Bin Wang, Microsoft Corporation, China

Section 5
Mobile Advertising

Chapter 15
Targeted Mobile Advertisement in the IP Multimedia Subsystem 279
C. Tselios, University of Patras, Greece
H. Perkuhn, Ericsson Research, Germany
K. Vandikas, Ericsson Research, Germany
M. Kampmann, Ericsson Research, Germany

Compilation of References 301

About the Contributors 319

Index 329

Detailed Table of Contents

Preface xv

Section 1
Traditional Text/Banner Advertising Techniques

Chapter 1
Click-Through Rate Estimation for Rare Events in Online Advertising 1

Xuerui Wang, Yahoo! Labs, USA
Wei Li, Yahoo! Labs, USA
Ying Cui, Yahoo! Labs, USA
Ruofei Zhang, Yahoo! Labs, USA
Jianchang Mao, Yahoo! Labs, USA

In online advertising campaigns, to measure purchase propensity, click-through rate (CTR), defined as a ratio of number of clicks to number of impressions, is one of the most informative metrics used in business activities such as performance evaluation and budget planning. No matter what channel an ad goes through (display ads, sponsored search or contextual advertising), CTR estimation for rare events is essential but challenging, often incurring with huge variance, due to the sparsity in data. In this chapter, to alleviate this sparsity, the authors develop models and methods to smoothen CTR estimation by taking advantage of the natural data hierarchy or by clustering and data continuity in time to leverage information from data close to the events of interest. In a contextual advertising system running at Yahoo!, the authors demonstrate that their methods lead to significantly more accurate estimation of CTRs.

Chapter 2
Reinforcement Learning for Online Optimization of Banner Format and Delivery 13

Benoit Baccot, Sopra Group, France & University of Toulouse, France
Romulus Grigoras, University of Toulouse, France & Devatics, France
Vincent Charvillat, University of Toulouse, France

This chapter deals with three main problems a web marketer can be confronted with: the right format among those available (e.g. text, image, video, interactive, etc.), the right time to display a banner during a user browsing session (e.g. at the beginning, at the end or when salient events are detected, etc.)

and the right sequence of banners to display (that takes into account the format and the time problem). The authors show that these problems share common points. These points fit well within the reinforcement learning framework: a "trial-and-error" process can be used to dynamically determine an advertising policy that optimizes a criterion based on an impact measure (e.g. the click-through rate or the session duration of a user). Two stochastic models based on Markov Decisional Processes and Multi-Armed Problems are presented in order to solve the three problems.

Chapter 3

Utilizing Sentiments in Online Contextual Advertising 32
Tanveer J. Siddiqui, University of Allahabad, India

Ever increasing number of internet users has attracted many of the companies on the internet for promoting their product and services. This has led to the development of new age of advertising called online or web advertising. The objective of this chapter is two-fold. First, it introduces concepts involved in online advertising. Second, it proposes a novel conceptual framework for contextual online advertising which attempts to utilize local context and sentiment for identifying relevant ads. Contextual advertising is an important class of online advertising in which ads are displayed automatically on web pages based on their content. The proposed framework works in two stages. The first stage retrieves ads for placement. The second stage uses sentiment analysis to filter out ads that do not agree with the sentiments (positive or negative polarity) being expressed in the document. The polarity is identified using SentiWordNet and context-based heuristics.

Section 2
Image Advertising

Chapter 4

In-Image Advertising 49
Lusong Li, Beihang University, China
Xian-Sheng Hua, Microsoft Research Asia, China

The daunting volumes of images on the Web have become one of the primary sources for online advertising. This work presents a contextual in-image advertising strategy driven by images, which automatically associates relevant ads with an image and seamlessly inserts the ads in the nonintrusive areas within each individual image. In in-image advertising platform, the ads are selected based on not only textual relevance but also visual similarity. The ad insertion positions are detected based on image salience, as well as face detection, to minimize intrusiveness to the user. In addition to general in-image advertising, the authors also provide a special game-like in-image advertising model dedicated to image on the basis of gaming form, called GameSense, which supports creating a game from an online image and associates relevant ads within the game. The authors evaluate in-image advertising model on a large-scale real-world images, and demonstrate the effectiveness of in-image advertising platform.

Chapter 5

Argo: Intelligent Advertising Made Possible from Images 67

Xin-Jing Wang, Microsoft Research Asia, China
Mo Yu, Harbin Institute of Technology, China
Lei Zhang, Microsoft Research Asia, China
Wei-Ying Ma, Microsoft Research Asia, China

This chapter introduces the Argo system which provides intelligent advertising made possible from user generated photos. Based on the intuition that user-generated photos imply user interests which are the key for profitable targeted ads, Argo attempts to learn a user's profile from his shared photos and suggests relevant ads accordingly. To learn a user interest, in an offline step, a hierarchical and efficient topic space is constructed based on the ODP ontology, which is used later on for bridging the vocabulary gap between ads and photos as well as reducing the effect of noisy photo tags. In the online stage, the process of Argo contains three steps: 1) understanding the content and semantics of a user's photos and auto-tagging each photo to supplement user-submitted tags (such tags may not be available); 2) learning the user interest given a set of photos based on the learnt hierarchical topic space; and 3) representing ads in the topic space and matching their topic distributions with the target user interest; the top ranked ads are output as the suggested ads. Two key challenges are tackled during the process: 1) the semantic gap between the low-level image visual features and the high-level user semantics; and 2) the vocabulary impedance between photos and ads. The authors conducted a series of experiments based on real Flickr users and Amazon.com products (as candidate ads), which show the effectiveness of the proposed approach.

Chapter 6

The Advent of Play and Pursuit 84

Yasmin Ibrahim, Queen Mary University of London, UK

Multimedia advertising on the internet has demanded that advertisers and marketers become more creative and adventurous in their pursuit of consumers. This chapter argues that the notions of play and pursuit are intrinsic components of persuading consumers to interact and engage with advertising. On-line advertising is also simulating game environments to reach consumers through an alternate reality. These techniques elevate play as a persuasive tool to entice consumers and to capture data for advertisers. It tacitly thwarts the assumption that the internet is a space of consumer empowerment and control. Instead it reinforces the hand of capital and uses the architectures and features of the internet to make virtual environments a productive space for advertisers.

Section 3
Video Advertising

Chapter 7

Content and Attention Aware Overlay for Online Video Advertising.. 101

Huazhong Ning,Google Inc., USA
Junxian Wang, Microsoft Corporation, USA
Xu Liu, Microsoft China Co. Ltd., China
Ying Shan, Microsoft Corporation, USA

Recent proliferation of online video advertising brings new opportunities and challenges to the multimedia community. A successful online video advertising system is expected to have the following essential features: effective targeting, scalability, non-intrusiveness, and attractiveness. While scalable systems with targeting capability are emerging, few have achieved the goal of being both non-intrusive and attractive. To the authors' knowledge, this work is the first attempt to generate video overlay ads that balances the two conflicting characteristics. The authors achieve the goal by jointly optimizing a non-intrusive metric and a set of metrics associated with video ad templates designed by UI experts. The resulting system is able to dynamically create a video overlay ad that effectively attracts user attention at the least intrusive spatial-temporal spots of a video clip. The system is also designed to enable a scalable business model with effective targeting capabilities, and later will be tested with live traffic on a major video publisher site. In this work, the authors conducted intensive experiments and user studies on the samples of a large-scale video dataset. The results demonstrate the effectiveness of this approach.

Chapter 8

An Explorative Study of the Virtual Product Placement: Take ViSA as an Example........................ 122

Chia-Hu Chang, National Taiwan University, Taiwan
Ja-Ling Wu, National Taiwan University, Taiwan

With the aid of content-based multimedia analysis, virtual product placement opens up new opportunities for advertisers to effectively monetize the existing videos in an efficient way. In addition, a number of significant and challenging issues are raising accordingly, such as how to less-intrusively insert the contextually relevant advertising message (what) at the right place (where) and the right time (when) with the attractive representation (how) in the videos. In this chapter, domain knowledge in support of delivering and receiving the advertising message is introduced, such as the advertising theory, psychology and computational aesthetics. The authors briefly review the state of the art techniques for assisting virtual product placement in videos. In addition, they present a framework to serve the virtual spotlighted advertising (ViSA) for virtual product placement and give an explorative study of it. Moreover, observations about the new trend and possible extension in the design space of virtual product placement will also be stated and discussed. The authors believe that it would inspire the researchers to develop more interesting and applicable multimedia advertising systems for virtual product placement.

Chapter 9

Adapting Online Advertising Techniques to Television 148

Sundar Dorai-Raj, Google, USA
Yannet Interian, Google, USA
Igor Naverniouk, Google, USA
Dan Zigmond, Google, USA

The availability of precise data on TV ad consump¬tion fundamentally changes this advertising medium, and allows many techniques developed for analyzing online ads to be adapted for TV. This chapter looks in particular at how results from the emerging field of online ad quality analysis can now be applied to TV.

Chapter 10

Linking Traditional TV Advertising to Internet Advertising 166

Ling-Yu Duan, Peking University, China
Jinqiao Wang, Chinese Academy of Sciences, China
Wen Gao, Peking University, China
Hanqing Lu, Chinese Academy of Sciences, China
Jesse S. Jin, The University of Newcastle, Australia
Changsheng Xu, Chinese Academy of Sciences, China

Web-based technologies and interactive TV had rapidly penetrated the advertising mainstream and displace traditional forms of advertising. As most television advertising goes unnoticed, more and more advertisers attempt to communicate their stories across media platforms. The consistent spikes in usage statistics on television, Internet and mobile devices dedicatedly support the three-screen advertising in a cross media environment. Maximizing opportunities for traditional TV ads in collaborating with Internet ads will continuously improve the impact of a mass media campaign. The authors present the current research efforts in the field of analyzing TV ads as well as linking TV ads with relevant Internet ads. While our relationship with TV remains strong and durable, consuming media from anywhere, at any time, is a crucial part of the much broader picture of consumers utilizing rich media. How to collect correlated advertisements across multiple media platforms such as TV and Internet would see significant growth potential in cross-media marketing campaigns.

Chapter 11

Contextual In-Stream Video Advertising 194

Tao Mei, Microsoft Research Asia, China
Shipeng Li, Microsoft Research Asia, China

With Internet delivery of video content surging to an unprecedented level, online video advertising is becoming increasingly pervasive. In this chapter, the authors present a new advertising paradigm for online video, called contextual in-stream video advertising, which automatically associates the most relevant video ads with online videos and seamlessly inserts the ads at the most appropriate spatiotemporal positions within each individual video. Different from most current video-oriented sites that only display the ads at the predefined locations in a video, this advertising paradigm aims to embed more contextually relevant ads at less intrusive positions within the video stream nonlinearly. The authors introduce the following key techniques in this paradigm: video processing for ad location detection, text analysis for ad selection, and optimization for ad insertion. They also describe two recently developed systems as showcases, i.e., VideoSense and AdOn which support in-stream inline and overlay advertising, respectively.

Section 4
Behavior Targeting/Personalized Ads/Audience Intelligence

Chapter 12

Behavioral Targeting Online Advertising 213
Jun Yan, Microsoft Research Asia, China
Dou Shen, Microsoft Corporation, USA
Teresa Mah, Microsoft Corporation, USA
Ning Liu, Microsoft Research Asia, China
Zheng Chen, Microsoft Research Asia, China
Ying Li, Microsoft Corporation, USA

With the rapid growth of the online advertising market, Behavioral Targeting (BT), which delivers advertisements to users based on understanding of their needs through their behaviors, is attracting more attention. The amount of spend on behaviorally targeted ad spending in the US is projected to reach $4.4 billion in 2012. BT is a complex technology, which involves data collection, data mining, audience segmentation, contextual page analysis, predictive modeling and so on. This chapter gives an overview of Behavioral Targeting by introducing the Behavioral Targeting business, followed by classic BT research challenges and solution proposals. The authors also point out BT research challenges which are currently under-explored in both industry and academia.

Chapter 13

Distributed Technologies for Personalized Advertisement Delivery 233
Dorothea Tsatsou, Informatics and Telematics Institute, Greece
Symeon Papadopoulos, Informatics and Telematics Institute, Greece
Ioannis Kompatsiaris, Informatics and Telematics Institute, Greece
Paul C. Davis, Motorola Applied Research Center, USA

This chapter provides an overview on personalized advertisement delivery paradigms on the web with a focus on the recommendation of advertisements expressed in or accompanied by text. Different methods of online targeted advertising will be examined, while justifying the need for channeling the appropriate ads to the corresponding users. The aim of the work presented here is to illustrate how the semantic representation of ads and user preferences can achieve optimal and unobtrusive ad delivery. The authors propose a set of distributed technologies that efficiently handles the lack of textual data in ads by enriching ontological knowledge with statistical contextual data in order to classify ads and generic content under a uniform, machine-understandable vocabulary. This classification is used to construct lightweight semantic user profiles, matched with semantic ad descriptions via fuzzy semantic reasoning. A real world user study, as well as an evaluative exploration of framework alternatives validate the system's effectiveness to produce high quality ad recommendations.

Chapter 14

Audience Intelligence in Online Advertising.. 262
Bin Wang, Microsoft Corporation, China

This chapter introduces the fundamentals of audience intelligence's important aspects. The goal is to present what are related to audience intelligence, how online audience intelligence could be done, and some representative methods. In this chapter, the author will first address the fundamentals of the audience intelligence, including the brief introduction of the online ad eco-system, the relationship between audience intelligence and existing online ad types, performance measures and the challenges in this field. Next, some classical methods of audience intelligence on end-users will be introduces, namely, demographic, geographic, behavioral targeting and online commercial intent (OCI) detection. Then, audience intelligence on advertisers will be presented. Finally, related topics of online advertising, such as the privacy issue, will be addressed.

Section 5
Mobile Advertising

Chapter 15

Targeted Mobile Advertisement in the IP Multimedia Subsystem 279
C. Tselios, University of Patras, Greece
H. Perkuhn, Ericsson Research, Germany
K. Vandikas, Ericsson Research, Germany
M. Kampmann, Ericsson Research, Germany

This chapter provides an overview on targeted advertisement in the IP Multimedia Subsystem (IMS). A new entity called Personalization and Advertisement Insertion Logic (PAIL) is introduced, which enables a mobile network operator to exploit contextual data stored in its network for personalized advertisement selection. PAIL combines location information with user profile information in order to select the best match from a pool of advertisement clips. This selection is based on the Vector Space Model. For the evaluation of this framework a series of tests with users were executed. These tests show that using contextual information from the IMS network a subjective better match of advertisement clips with user interests is achievable.

Compilation of References 301

About the Contributors 319

Index.. 329

Preface

Advertising provides financial support for a large portion of today's Internet ecosystem. Compared to traditional means of advertising, such as a banner outside a store or textual advertisements in newspapers, multimedia advertising has some unique advantages: it is more attractive and more salient than plain text, it is able to instantly grab users' attention and it carries more information that can also be comprehended more quickly than when reading a text advertisement. Rapid convergence of multimedia, Internet and mobile devices has opened new opportunities for manufacturers and advertisers to more effectively and efficiently reach potential customers. While largely limiting itself to radio and TV channels currently, multimedia advertising is about to break through on the web using various concepts of *online multimedia advertising*.

This book aims at bringing together recent insights from the research on online multimedia advertising that addresses the theoretical fundamentals, solution concepts, and the issues related to the development of modern multimedia advertising schemes. As the first book in this field, we are also aiming at stimulating the developments of this emerging and promising direction. The book is organized into five sections and contains fifteen chapters.

Section 1 introduces conventional text- and banner-based advertising techniques. In the first chapter, Wang *et al.* discuss the click-through rate estimation for rare events in online advertising. In the second chapter, Grigoras *et al.* propose a reinforcement learning method for online optimization of banner format and delivery, where contextual ads are delivered using rich media banners to display motion and exploit sensory information. Finally, Siddiqui introduces in the third chapter some basic concepts of online advertising and proposes a new framework for contextual online advertising, which attempts to utilize local context and sentiment for identifying relevant ads.

Section 2 describes techniques for image advertising. The first chapter, by Li and Hua, presents a contextual in-image advertising system in which the product information selected via multimodal relevance is embedded non-intrusively within each individual image. Then, Wang *et al.* present in the second chapter an intelligent image advertising system called Argo. Argo learns a user's profile from his/her shared photos and suggests relevant ads accordingly. The third chapter in this section, by Ibrahim, discusses concepts of "pursuit" and "play" in the multimedia advertising. It is concluded that the role of play and pursuit situate consumers in the online environments as both agents and consumers in creating value for marketers.

Section 3 focuses on video advertising which has become a hot research topic and a key strategy for monetizing media contents. In the first chapter, Ning *et al.* propose an intelligent overlay video advertising system which is characterized by content and human attention awareness. The second chapter, by Chang and Wu, provides an explorative study on the virtual product placement in a sports video, which is another angle on video advertising. The third chapter, by Zigmond *et al.*, focuses on how the results on quality analysis of online advertising can be applied to the TV domain. In the fourth chapter, Duan *et al.* present an online video service that can link relevant advertisements with traditional TV programs. The last chapter, by Mei and Li, describes an in-stream video advertising system which can insert commercial video clips non-intrusively into a source video program. The advertisements are selected by multimodal content relevance, while the optimal ad locations are automatically detected by video content analysis.

Section 4 addresses the user-related issues in online advertising. The first chapter, by Yan *et al.*, provides a survey on behavior targeting, where the inferred information on a user's behavior serves to understand his or her needs and deliver advertisements accordingly. Then, Tsatsou *et al.* discuss in the second chapter the distributed technologies for personalized advertisement delivery. The third chapter, by Wang, introduces the fundamentals of understanding the users in an online advertising eco-system. Classical methods, among which those relying on demographic and geographic information, as well as behavioral targeting and online commercial intent detection, are discussed.

Section 5 focuses on recent technologies for mobile multimedia advertising. Tselios *et al.* provide an overview on targeted advertisement in an IP multimedia subsystem. A new entity called personalization and advertisement insertion logic is introduced, which enables a mobile network operator to exploit contextual data stored in its network for personalized advertisement selection.

The book is well suited for both graduate students and senior researchers working in the field of multimedia and/or online advertising, but also for practitioners, such as those working in the field of search engine development, video/image content providers, developers of video/image sharing portals and IPTV providers.

Our interactions with many exceptional colleagues made significant impact on the development of this book. We would like to thank all the authors for their contributions. We would also thank the editorial advisory board members, Kiyoharu Aizawa, Alberto Del Bimbo, Shih-Fu Chang, Chang Wen Chen, Tat-Seng Chua, Shipeng Li, Ying Li, and Ming-Ting Sun, for their encouragements and advices on publishing this book. We are also thankful to a number of reviewers who provided insightful and valuable comments to improve the quality and readability of this book. These reviewers are Chia-Hu Chang, Ying Cui, Lingyu Duan, Winston Hsu, Zhigang Hua, Yannet Interian, Shuqiang Jiang, Yuan Liu, Qiaozhu Mei, Huazhong Ning, Dou Shen, Jialie Shen, Ja-Hwung Su, Yongqing Sun, Christos Tselios, Bin Wang, Jingdong Wang, Jinqiao Wang, Xin-Jing Wang, Xuerui Wang, Xiao Wu, Jun Yan, Bruce Zhang, and Dan Zigmond.

Finally, we are deeply indebted to our wives, Shu Miao, Yali Liu, and Tatjana Ulicevic, and our children, Ziyan Hua, Yuting Mei, Miran and Anja Hanjalic for their patience and understanding while we were busy with creating this book.

We wish you a pleasant reading.

Xian-Sheng Hua
Microsoft Research Asia, China

Tao Mei
Microsoft Research Asia, China

Alan Hanjalic
Delft University of Technology, The Netherlands

Section 1
Traditional Text/Banner Advertising Techniques

Chapter 1
Click–Through Rate Estimation for Rare Events in Online Advertising

Xuerui Wang
Yahoo! Labs, USA

Wei Li
Yahoo! Labs, USA

Ying Cui
Yahoo! Labs, USA

Ruofei Zhang
Yahoo! Labs, USA

Jianchang Mao
Yahoo! Labs, USA

ABSTRACT

In online advertising campaigns, to measure purchase propensity, click-through rate (CTR), defined as a ratio of number of clicks to number of impressions, is one of the most informative metrics used in business activities such as performance evaluation and budget planning. No matter what channel an ad goes through (display ads, sponsored search or contextual advertising), CTR estimation for rare events is essential but challenging, often incurring with huge variance, due to the sparsity in data. In this chapter, to alleviate this sparsity, we develop models and methods to smoothen CTR estimation by taking advantage of the natural data hierarchy or by clustering and data continuity in time to leverage information from data close to the events of interest. In a contextual advertising system running at Yahoo!, we demonstrate that our methods lead to significantly more accurate estimation of CTRs.

DOI: 10.4018/978-1-60960-189-8.ch001

INTRODUCTION

The Internet revolution has driven a transformation of how people experience information, media and advertising. Web advertising did not even exist twenty years ago, but nowadays it has become a vital component of the modern Internet, where advertisements are delivered from advertisers to users through different channels such as display ads, sponsored search and contextual advertising. Based on a recent study by Interactive Advertising Bureau and PricewaterhouseCoopers International, online advertising revenue in the first half of 2009 reached over 10.9 billion US dollars (IAB & PwC, 2009). Recent trends have also witnessed that larger and larger share of advertisers' budgets are devoted to the online world, and online advertising spending growth has greatly outpaced some of the traditional advertising media, such as radio and magazine.

There are many pricing models for online advertising. For example, in a pay-per-impression campaign, the advertisers pay for the number of ad exposures. This is a very popular model in display ads. Another example is pay-per-action, where the advertisers pay only if the ad leads to a sale or similar transaction. Both models have their own limitations. The pay-per-impression model does not consider ad performance while the pay-per-action model often has difficulty in tracking user transactions. Therefore, the success and effectiveness of online advertising campaigns is prevalently measured by whether users click on ads. This pricing model is called pay-per-click, where the advertisers pay a certain amount for every click. As a result, the click-through rate (CTR), defined as a ratio of number of clicks to number of impressions of an ad for a query or on a page, is one of the most useful and informative metrics to measure user response in online advertising. The use of CTR in online advertising is everywhere. For many advertising systems, CTR is one important factor to determine what advertisements to be displayed and in what order.

In addition, advertisers often plan their budget based on historical CTRs or predicted CTRs.

In online advertising, a serving event refers to the showing of an ad in response to a user query, which can be a search query in sponsored search or a Web page in display and contextual advertising. The serving frequency varies for different queries and ads. Some popular ones account for a large fraction of Internet traffic while the overwhelming counterparts are extremely rare events, whose behaviors follow a typical power-law pattern. Even being infrequent, the revenue from the rare events generates a several-billion-dollar business, which makes estimating CTR for such rare events an extremely important and practical problem. Unfortunately, due to the sparseness, the CTR estimation for rare events is notoriously challenging and extremely unreliable, often with huge variance. There are two scenarios that are especially difficult to deal with. The first one is when we observe a click out of only few serving events. A direct estimation of the CTR is often much higher than the true CTR. Another case is when we observe no clicks at all out of thousands of serving events. This is very common in contextual advertising because many page/ad CTRs are on the magnitude of 0.1% or even lower. Again, a direct estimation is not desirable here. In order to address these issues, we need to take into account that rare events are not strictly independent to each other. Instead, the existing correlations or associations among events can be leveraged into the CTR estimation for rare events.

First, in many scenarios, attributes in event data are naturally organized in hierarchies, and/or can be clustered via data-driven methods. An illustrative example of a page to publisher hierarchy is shown in Figure 1. As we can see, the publisher "yahoo_food_specialday" (special day site for Yahoo! Food) contains many pages that are similar to each other, such as foods for birthday and anniversary. These pages differ in content but share some common themes in the big picture, and we would imagine CTRs on these

Figure 1. An illustrative example of a page to publisher hierarchy

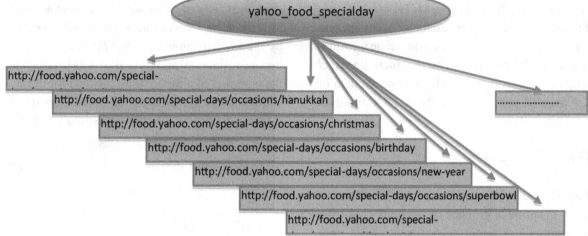

pages should be closer than the one on a random page. In general, events close in data hierarchy or in the same cluster share certain commonality compared to the events far in hierarchy or in different clusters. Information from "close" events can be utilized to enrich what we can learn from rare events themselves.

Second, most event data are often collected over time and advertising campaigns run over a certain period. Even though such dynamics make the patterns lying in the data earlier generally disappear later, the continuation in short-term still provides us with more reliable information about the events we are interested in. For example, an exponential smoothing technique can be employed to gather information from events closer in time to the events of interest, and at the same time, events far away play less significant role due to the dynamic changes in patterns.

It is worth pointing out that the two ideas described above can be employed either together or separately to estimate CTRs for rare events more robustly in most cases, since they exploit data commonality from two different angles. And we find their benefits are additive instead of being cancelled out by each other.

In this chapter, we develop models and methods to smoothen CTR estimation by taking advantage of the data hierarchy and data continuity in time to leverage information from data close to the events of interest. We use contextual advertising as an example to illustrate our approaches, but the models and methods discussed in this chapter could be well and easily extended to other online advertising channels such as display ads and sponsored search. Further more, the concept of smoothing comes into play handily as well when other ratios (such as conversion-rates) are under investigation, for which, the sparseness concern is even more severe, and therefore we expect more effectiveness.

BACKGROUND

The problem of CTR estimation in contextual advertising could be formalized as follows: for a given page/ad pair (p, a), with the number of impressions (I) and clicks (C), we want to estimate the CTR associated with this pair. For rare pairs, which drive the vast majority of impressions and clicks online, the standard estimation of CTR as C/I is inevitably unreliable. For example, if we only get one impression of a page/ad pair, and a click is recorded from that impression, the naïve calculation (C/I) would give a CTR = 1, which is a totally unrealistic estimate for most advertising campaigns. However, if we can leverage information from the data hierarchy to which the page/ad pair belongs to and/or the time series data of the page/ad pair, more reliable CTR estimation could be obtained.

Data Hierarchies

Pages and ads can be either associated with hierarchies in nature or grouped by applying clustering techniques in different metric spaces. On the page side, there is a natural hierarchy indicated by the URL path. For example, many pages belong to the same domain and further to the same publisher. On the ad side, an advertiser can have multiple accounts that roughly partition the ads. Furthermore, each account can have multiple ad groups where the ads in one group are closely related to each other. One could take advantage of the hierarch on the ad side, or on the page side, or both. To illustrate the idea, for simplicity, we describe the hierarchy (from ad to account) on the ad side in details, and the similar hierarchy on the page side (e.g., from page to publisher) also exists.

Assume that we have N ads in the same account $(a_1, a_2, ..., a_N)$ and a page p, and we are interested in the CTR of the page/ad pair (p, a_i). A two-stage empirical Bayes method is employed to estimate this CTR by combining information from empirical measurements on ad a_i and all other ads in the same account on page p. In our setting, the observed clicks $(C_1, C_2, ..., C_N)$ are assumed to be generated from an underlying set of CTR $(r_1, r_2, ..., r_N)$, according to a probability distribution, for instance, Binomial (I, r_i), where I_i is the number of impressions for the page/ad pair (p, a_i). The parameters r_i in turn can be considered as samples drawn from a population of the account characterized by further hyperparameters, according to a probability distribution, for instance, Beta (α, β).

Information about r_i therefore comes not only from (I_i, C_i) which directly depends on it, but also from the CTRs of other ads in the same account inferred from the data as a whole, summarized by the hyperparameters α and β. The conjugacy between Binomial and Beta allows us to compute the marginal likelihood of all the data for the account and to estimate the hyperparameters α and β using maximum likelihood estimate (MLE). Once α and β are estimated (denoted by $\hat{\alpha}$ and $\hat{\beta}$, respectively), the posterior estimate of r_i could be calculated as

$$\hat{r_i} = (C_i + \hat{\alpha}) / (I_i + \hat{\alpha} + \hat{\beta}),$$

which is considered as a smoothed CTR with smaller variance and more stability than C/I_i. As we discussed earlier, other hierarchies (such as page to domain) and multiple hierarchical levels (such as page to domain to publisher) can be included as well easily, and other compound distributions (such as Gamma-Poisson) can be possibly chosen based on the modeling need.

Data Continuity

In many cases, we are more interested in the trend of CTRs more than just a snapshot of the absolute values. For rare page/ad pairs, at any time point, the CTR estimation could be very noisy. By acknowledging some kind of data continuity, we treat impressions and clicks as discrete sets of repeat measurements, and an exponential smoothing technique is adopted to smoothen these measurements, and at the end we calculate a smoothed CTR.

Assume that, for a page/ad pair, we have M consecutive days of measurements of impressions $(I_1, I_2, ..., I_M)$ and clicks $(C_1, C_2, ..., C_M)$, and we want to estimate the CTR on the Mth day. Denote the smoothed impressions and clicks as $\hat{I}$ and $\hat{C}$ respectively, and we can calculate the smoothed

CTR as $\widehat{C} / \widehat{I}$ in contrast to C/I. $\widehat{C}$ is defined as follows ($\widehat{I}$ is defined similarly):

$$\widehat{C}_j / C_j \qquad j = 1$$

$$\widehat{C}_j / \gamma C_j + (1 - \gamma)\widehat{C}_{j-1} \qquad j = 2, ..., M$$

where γ is the smoothing factor, and $0 < \gamma < 1$ (the value of γ controls how much history we want to include in the smoothing: when γ is close to 0, we get very heavy smoothing from historical values; when γ is close to 1, little information in history is used for smoothing). In other words, as time passes the smoothed $\widehat{C}_j$ becomes the exponentially decreasing weighted average of its past observations. One could apply exponential smoothing directly on CTR instead of impressions and clicks respectively, but we find that is often less effective. In addition, it is not easy to interpret from probability distribution perspective. On the contrast, smoothing impression and click separately can be interpreted as imposing a Beta prior

$$Beta(\frac{1-\gamma}{\gamma}\widehat{C}_{j-1}, \frac{1-\gamma}{\gamma}\left(\widehat{I}_{j-1} - \widehat{C}_{j-1}\right)).$$

As we pointed out earlier, the above two smoothing methods can be $Beta\left(-\right)$ combined together with ease, for example, we can first do exponential smoothing on impressions and clicks before leveraging the data hierarchy.

SMOOTHING CTR ESTIMATION

In this section, we present the details of the smoothing methods discussed in the previous section, and their mathematical foundations.

Leveraging Data Hierarchies with Empirical Bayes Methods

In statistics, with empirical Bayes methods, the integrals over conditional probability distributions are substituted by the empirical statistics in the observed data, which allows us to estimate the posterior probabilities (such as CTRs) about one page/ad pair by leveraging the information from all page/ad pairs that are close to the page/ad pair of interest in the hierarchy.

There are multiple hierarchies that we could take advantage of in online advertising, and for illustration, we choose the hierarchy from page/ad pairs to publisher/account pairs. In another word, every page belongs to a publisher, and every ad is associated with an account, and in combination, every page/ad pair is mapped to a publisher/account pair.

Considering the hierarchical nature of the empirical Bayes methods, two assumptions are made in our experimental setting: 1) for each publisher/account pair, there is an underlying/unknown probability distribution of CTR, and the CTR of every page/ad pair in the publisher/account pair could be regarded a stochastic outcome of the distribution; and 2) for every page/ad pair, we observe the impressions and clicks generated from a distribution of the CTR of this pair. To parameterize the generative process, we use Beta and Binomial distributions, respectively in the above two assumptions. Essentially, we have a Beta-Binomial compound distribution for the observed data. The generative process of this hierarchical Bayesian model is described as follows:

- Given a publisher/account pair that has N page/ad pairs, we have a distribution $Beta(\alpha, \beta)$.
- For every page/ad pair belonging to the publish/account pair:

- ◦ Sample CTR $r \sim \text{Beta}(\alpha,\beta)$,

$$p(r \mid) = \frac{\Gamma(\alpha + \beta)}{\Gamma(\alpha)\Gamma(\beta)} r^{\alpha-1}(1 - r)^{\beta-1}$$

- ◦ Sample clicks $C \sim \text{Binomial}(I, r)$,

$$P(C \mid I, r) \propto r^{C}(1 - r)^{1-C}$$

The graphical model representation is shown in Figure 2. Shaded variables are observed, and others are hidden. Plate denotes replicates.

The resulting data likelihood over all the clicks of all page/ad pairs is

$$P(C_1, C_2, \ldots, C_N \mid I_1, I_2, \ldots, I_N, \alpha, \beta) =$$
$$\prod_{i=1}^{N} P(C_i \mid I_i, \alpha, \beta) =$$
$$\prod_{i=1}^{N} \int_{r_i} P(C_i, r_i \mid I_i, \alpha, \beta) dr_i =$$
$$\prod_{i=1}^{N} \int_{r_i} P(C_i \mid I_i, r_i) p(r_i \mid \alpha, \beta) dr_i \propto \prod_{i=1}^{N} \int_{r_i} r_i^{C_i} (1 - r_i)^{I_i-C_i} r_i^{\alpha-1} (1 - r_i)^{\beta-1} dr_i =$$
$$\prod_{i=1}^{N} \frac{(\alpha + \beta)}{(I_i + \alpha + \beta)} \frac{(C_i + \alpha)}{(\alpha)} \frac{(I_i - C_i + \beta)}{(\beta)}$$

The gradient of the log-likelihood is

$$\frac{d\log P(C_1, C_2, \ldots, C_N \mid I_1, I_2, \ldots, I_N, \alpha, \beta)}{d\alpha} =$$
$$\sum_{i=1}^{N} [(\alpha + \beta) - (I_i + \alpha + \beta) + (C_i + \alpha) - (\alpha)]$$

$$\frac{d\log P(C_1, C_2, \ldots, C_N \mid I_1, I_2, \ldots, I_N, \alpha, \beta)}{d\beta} =$$
$$\sum_{i=1}^{N} [(\alpha + \beta) - (I_i + \alpha + \beta) + (I - C_i + \alpha) - (\beta)]$$

where

$$\Psi(x) = \frac{d}{dx} \ln \Gamma(x)$$

Figure 2. The graphical model representation of the CTR estimation with the empirical Bayes methods

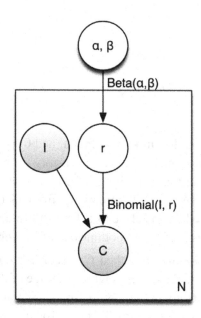

is the digamma function, and can be calculated quickly using the Bernardo's algorithm (Bernardo, 1976).

The maximum can be calculated through the fixed-point iteration (Minka, 2003)

$$\alpha^{new} = \alpha \frac{\sum_{i=1}^{N} [\Psi(C_i + \alpha) - \Psi(\alpha)]}{\sum_{i=1}^{N} [\Psi(I_i + \alpha + \beta) - \Psi(\beta)]}$$

$$\beta^{new} = \beta \frac{\sum_{i=1}^{N} [\Psi(I_i - C_i + \beta) - \Psi(\beta)]}{\sum_{i=1}^{N} [\Psi(I_i + \alpha + \beta) - \Psi(\alpha + \beta)]}$$

The stopping criterion we use is either 1000 iterations or the changes in both α and β are smaller than *1E-10*. Once α and β are estimated (denoted by $\hat{\alpha}$ and $\hat{\beta}$, respectively), the posterior estimate of r_i could be calculated as

$$r_i = (C_i + \widehat{\alpha}) / (I_i + \widehat{\alpha} + \widehat{\beta}).$$

It is a common practice to smoothen an estimate with some background estimate, however, a combining parameter needs to be carefully tuned to get desirable performance. Our method avoids such hassle, and requires little to no human interaction.

Utilizing Event History with Exponential Smoothing

In statistics, with exponential smoothing, the time series data, as a sequence of noisy observations of an underlying random process, can be used to produce smoothed data for processing.

Directly substituting the recursively defining equation in the previous section for exponential smoothing back into itself, we can find that

$$\widehat{C}_M =$$
$$\gamma C_M + \left(1 - \gamma\right)\widehat{C}_{M-1} =$$
$$\gamma C_M + \left(1 - \gamma\right)(\gamma C_{M-1} + \left(1 - \gamma\right)\widehat{C}_{M-2}) =$$
$$\gamma C_M + \gamma\left(1 - \gamma\right)C_{M-1} + \gamma\left(1 - \gamma\right)^2 C_{M-2} + ... +$$
$$\gamma\left(1 - \gamma\right)^j C_{M-j} + ... + \gamma(1 - \gamma)^{M-1}C_1$$

In another word, as time passes, the smoother estimate $\widehat{C}_j$ becomes a weighted average of more and more past observations in the history, and the weights assigned to the historical observations are exponentially discounted as shown above, i.e., the weighting factors give more weight to the most recent measurements in the time series and less weight to older data.

Technically speaking, exponential smoothing can be regarded as an ARIMA model with one non-seasonal difference and an MA(1) coefficient, and no constant term, that is, an ARIMA(0,1,1) model with no constant term in statistics. The MA(1) term come from the quantity 1-γ. Therefore, one could take advantage of this to calculate confidence intervals for the exponential smoothing model.

Combining Data Hierarchies and Temporal Smoothing

We discussed that the two smoothing techniques discussed in this chapter can be combined together to achieve better performance than each individual model alone. For example, after exponential smoothing of the event data, it is straightforward to exploit the data hierarchies to further alleviate the sparsity concern.

One would think about conducting empirical Bayes with data hierarchy first, and then do temporal smoothing with CTR instead of impressions and clicks. Preliminary experiments show that directly smoothing CTR usually leads to large fluctuation and ends up with inferior results than smoothing impressions and clicks separately. For this reason, we do not pursue this direction further, and only show results with empirical Bayes first, and then exponential smoothing. From now on, we refer to this as the combined smoothing strategy.

EXPERIMENTAL RESULTS

In this section, we discuss the evaluation metrics we adopted, and the corresponding experimental results for the methods that were laid out in the previous section: empirical Bayes, exponential smoothing and the combined smoothing.

Evaluation Metrics

We use the mean squared error (MSE) between the estimated CTR and the true CTR to measure the performance of our methods. The MSE is defined as

$$MSE(\hat{r}) = E[(\hat{r} - r)^2] = \sum_{i=1}^{N} (\hat{r}_i - r_i)^2 \, / \, N$$

MSE is always non-negative, and a zero MSE means that the estimator $\hat{r}$ predicts observations of the parameter r with a perfect accuracy. Note that, in this particular measurement, the constraint that $0 \leq \hat{r} \leq 1$ **is not utilized.**

On the other hand, the CTR we estimate is essentially parameterized with a Bernoulli probability distribution, thus, we can use the Kullback-Leibler (KL) divergence (Kullback&Leibler, 1951) to measure how the estimated CTR differs from the "true" CTR in the data. For probability distributions $P(r)$ and $Q(\hat{r})$, **where** r **and** $\hat{r}$ are the true CTR and the estimated CTR respectively, the KL divergence of $Q(\hat{r})$ from $P(r)$ is defined as

$$D_{KL}(P(r) \,||\, Q(\hat{r})) = r \log \frac{r}{\hat{r}} + (1-r) \log \frac{1-r}{1-\hat{r}}$$

$D_{KL}(P(r) \,||\, Q(\hat{r}))$ is also always non-negative, and 0 when $\hat{r} = r$. Unfortunately, as we can see when r and $\hat{r}$ are in extreme values (such as 0 and 1), $D_{KL}(P(r) \,||\, Q(\hat{r}))$ is not well defined, we ignore such cases in our KL divergence evaluation. However, a big trunk of the data does have extreme CTRs (e.g., $\hat{r} = 0$ or r=0), and, not like the MSE, the KL divergence evaluation only provides results on a portion of data under investigation. Nevertheless, we have found that MSE and the average KL divergence in general agree with each other based on our experiments.

Experiments

We collect event samples from a contextual advertising system at Yahoo! from Aug. 1 to Nov.

20, 2009 to provide the ground truth of the CTR of the page/ad pairs we are interested in. To make sure that we indeed have a relatively reliable ground truth, all the page/ad pairs we consider in this chapter have at least 10,000 impressions. We also eliminate non-Yahoo! publishers. This is done primarily for the following reason: the publisher outside of Yahoo! can be arbitrarily defined, there is no guarantee that the pages under one publisher are generally more similar than the pages from other publishers. To measure the effectiveness of the hierarchical smoothing with empirical Bayes, we also exclude the publisher/account pairs that do not have at least 10 page/ad pairs.

In the ground truth data, we have 30 billion impressions, 30K pages, 80K ads, 20K accounts and a little more than 100 publishers. Note that not every page/ad is a valid combination due to the sparsity nature of the data or our previous filtering, and we have 260K page/ad pairs that are mapped to 49K publisher/account pairs.

To test our methods against different sparsity settings, we uniformly sample S, S/10 and S/100 of the event data described above to get our test data (S is the base sampling rate). The statistics of the sampled test data are summarized in Table 1. As we can see, even with the lowest sampling ratio (S/100), we still have a large data set with more than 1M impressions.

Results on Smoothing with Data Hierarchies

In Table 2, we report the MSE and the average KL divergence for the test data we collected with different sampling ratios using the empirical Bayes method, where the baseline method is not involved with any smoothing.

From Table 2, we can find that both the MSE and the KL divergence become worse when the data are sparser (smaller sampling ratios) in both baseline and empirical Bayes, which indicates the CTR estimation indeed becomes more challenging when data are sparser as expected. On the

Table 1. Statistics of sampled data set with different sampling ratios

Sampling ratio	S	S/10	S/100
Impressions	136.37M	13.58M	1.34M
Publishers	73	73	71
Accounts	1,245	1,245	1,102
Pages	27,739	27,739	25,316
Ads	30,922	30,922	26,400
Publisher/account pairs	2,588	2,588	2,249
Page/ad pairs	176,389	176,389	149,121

Table 2. Smoothing with data hierarchies on different levels of sparsity

Sampling ratio	Methods	MSE (%improvement)	Avg KL divergence (%improvement)
S	Baseline	9.46041e-7	0.00141036
	Empirical Bayes	8.43402e-7 (10.85%)	0.00138567 (1.75%)
S/10	Baseline	1.09668e-5	0.0157694
	Empirical Bayes	9.05408e-6 (17.44%)	0.0146967(6.80%)
S/100	Baseline	6.45237e-5	0.103176
	Empirical Bayes	3.18008e-5 (50.71%)	0.070434 (31.73%)

other hand, the improvement with smoothing is more and more dramatic when the data are sparser. With the S/100 sampling ratio, we achieve 50% deduction in MSE and 30% deduction in average KL divergence.

Results on Temporal Exponential Smoothing

As to exponential smoothing, it puts more emphasis on observations in recent history than in earlier history. For example, with $\gamma=0.7$, the contribution weight from ten days ago only accounts for *2E-6* of the overall observations. In our experiments, with the sampled events (sampling ratio = S) on Sep. 10-30, we apply the exponential smoothing technique, and compare the estimated daily CTR accuracy on Sep 26-30, in comparison to the one of the baseline method that does not have smoothing at all. Theoretically, the effect of smoothing can be

controlled by the value of γ, and we experimented 3 different values of γ.

For temporal smoothing, the MSE and the average KL divergence with different values of γ are shown in Table 3. At first glance, no matter what value of γ we used, the exponential smoothing significantly outperform the baseline in both MSE and the average KL divergence. Also as expected, different values of γ have significant influence on the smoothing performance. As γ decreases, the more historical information that gets incorporated into the estimation, the more improvement we obtain.

Results on the Combined Smoothing

As we discussed before we can combine the two different smoothing techniques to further improve the estimates because they utilize different information to deal with sparsity. In our experiment, we first employ the exponential smoothing on

Table 3. (Temporal) exponential smoothing with different smoothing factors

Methods	Smoothing factor (γ)	MSE (%improvement)	Avg KL divergence (%improvement)
Baseline	N.A.	1.97448e-5	0.0623606
Exponential smoothing	0.9	1.62459e-5 (17.72%)	0.0519508 (16.69%)
	0.7	1.34620e-5 (31.82%)	0.0459063 (26.39%)
	0.5	1.14469e-5 (42.03%)	0.0408431 (34.51%)

Table 4. Comparison of different smoothing techniques

Smoothing factor (γ)	Methods	MSE (%improvement)	Avg KL divergence (%improvement)
N.A.	Baseline	1.97448e-5	0.0623606
	Empirical Bayes	1.07309e-5 (45.65%)	0.0459972 (26.24%)
0.9	Exponential smoothing	1.62459e-5 (17.72%)	0.0519508 (16.69%)
	Combined smoothing	8.30497e-6 (57.94%)	0.0371832 (40.37%)
0.7	Exponential smoothing	1.34620e-5 (31.82%)	0.0459063 (26.39%)
	Combined smoothing	6.15689e-6 (68.82%)	0.0304852 (51.11%)
0.5	Exponential smoothing	1.14469e-5 (42.03%)	0.0408431 (34.51%)
	Combined smoothing	4.63981e-6 (76.50%),	0.0241584 (61.26%)

the test data we experimented for Table 3, and then utilize the empirical Bayes method on the temporally smoothed data to get the final CTR estimates. The experimental results are listed in Table 4, with some results copied from Table 3 for comparison purpose. To study the advantage of combing two different smoothing techniques, the results from each technique alone are also listed in Table 4.

First of all, both empirical Bayes alone and exponential smoothing individually have significantly outperformed the baseline that does not conduct smoothing. Second, the advantages we get from two different smoothing techniques are additive as expected, since they utilize different perspective of the data. Third, when the effect from temporal smoothing gets improved (while decreasing the value of γ), the performance from the combined model is increased as well. In another word, even if we improve one of the models alone, a significant boost in the combined model

is still demonstrated in Table 4. This is a strong indicator that we should combine the two different and orthogonal techniques whenever it is possible to do so.

RELATED WORK

Click-through rate is one of the most studied topics in online advertising. Historically, the majority of methods deals with events with high frequency, and ignores rare events or aggregates them to higher frequency. More recently, researchers have paid more attention to CTR estimation for rare events. Richardson et al. (2007) discussed a method of learning CTRs of new ads in sponsored search using a logistic regression model. They carefully designed features such as top unigrams, how many words in the title, the fraction of images in the landing page, etc. The CTRs reported in their work is higher than ours because the user intention in sponsored search is much clearer than in other channels where CTRs are generally lower, and event data are sparser.

Agarwal et al. (2007) mapped pages and ads into a hierarchy that is derived from contextual information. However, the coverage in the hierarchy is very unbalanced, and for most regions of the hierarchy, the sparsity is still a concern. They designed a sampling mechanism and a two-stage model to overcome the sparsity problem: the first stage adjusts the sampling bias and the second stage incorporates correlation among sibling nodes through a tree-structured Markov model. Agarwal et al. (2009) designed a spatio-temporal model to estimate CTRs in the context of content recommendation. They employed a dynamic Gamma-Poisson model to track CTR over time at specific locations and combined information from correlated locations through dynamic linear regressions. Large-scale experiments showed that their model provided very encouraging results.

CONCLUSION

Estimating CTRs for rare events are extremely important but very challenging. We designed two different smoothing techniques to deal with the sparsity problem lying in the rare events. The first technique utilizes the natural data hierarchy with an empirical Bayes method, and the second takes advantage of temporal continuity in certain period. Both techniques leverage information from events that are closely related to the one of interest, but from orthogonal perspectives. Thus we also experiment a combined model that achieves more than 70% reduction in mean squared error and more than 60% deduction in average KL divergence against the baseline without smoothing.

In this chapter, we have demonstrated the effectiveness of estimating CTRs in a contextual advertising system, but the same techniques could be easily extended to other advertising channels or other ratios of interest. Also, the ad ranks are not considered in this chapter, while rank has a

decisive role in CTR in many online advertising circumstances due to user attention capture. However, breaking-down the events that are already rare by rank will increase the severity of sparseness, and we believe that the smoothing techniques discussed here could be more effective to deal with that problem.

The contextual information of pages and ads provides very useful information in CTR estimation as demonstrated in Richardson et al. (2007) and Agarwal et al. (2007), and we believe that this is another orthogonal dimension we can potentially enhance our model additively.

REFERENCES

Agarwal, D., Broder, A. Z., Chakrabarti, D., Diklic, D., Josifovski, V., & Sayyadian, M. (2007). Estimating rates of rare events at multiple resolutions. In *Proceedings of the 13th ACM SIGKDD international Conference on Knowledge Discovery and Data Mining* (pp. 16-25).

Agarwal, D., Chen, B., & Elango, P. (2009). Spatio-temporal models for estimating click-through rate. In *Proceedings of the 18th international Conference on World Wide Web* (pp. 21-30).

Bernardo, J. M. (1976). The Psi (Digamma) function: An algorithm. *Applied Statistics*, *25*, 315–317. doi:10.2307/2347257

Interactive Advertising Bureau (IAB) & PricewaterhouseCoopers International. (PwC). (2009). Internet ad revenues at $10.9 billion for first half of '09. Retrieved December 15, 2009, from http://www.iab.net/about_the_iab/recent_press_releases/press_release_archive/press_release/pr-100509

Kullback, S., & Leibler, R. A. (1951). On Information and Sufficiency. *Annals of Mathematical Statistics*, *22*(1), 79–86. doi:10.1214/aoms/1177729694

Minka, T. P. (2003). Estimating a Dirichlet distribution. Retrieved from http://research.microsoft.com/en-us/um/people/minka/papers/dirichlet/

Richardson, M., Dominowska, E., & Ragno, R. (2007). Predicting clicks: estimating the click-through rate for new ads. In *Proceedings of the 16th international Conference on World Wide Web* (pp. 521-530).

KEY TERMS AND DEFINITIONS

Contextual Advertising: a form of targeted advertising for advertisements appearing on websites or other media based on the content displayed to the user.

CTR: click through rate

Data Hierarchy: the systematic organization of data, often in a hierarchical form.

Empirical Bayes Methods: procedures for statistical inference in which the prior distribution is estimated from the data.

Exponential Smoothing: a technique that can be applied to time series data, either to produce smoothed data for presentation, or to make forecasts.

Kullback-Leibler Divergence: a non-symmetric measure of the difference between two probability distributions P and Q. It measures the expected number of extra bits required to code samples from P when using a code based on Q, rather than using a code based on P.

Machine Learning: a scientific discipline that is concerned with the design and development of algorithms that allow computers to evolve behaviors based on empirical data.

Chapter 2
Reinforcement Learning for Online Optimization of Banner Format and Delivery

Benoit Baccot
Sopra Group, France & University of Toulouse, France

Romulus Grigoras
University of Toulouse, France & Devatics, France

Vincent Charvillat
University of Toulouse, France

ABSTRACT

In our Internet-connected world, online advertising has grown into one of the most successful advertising channels, since users spend an important amount of time browsing the web. Among the different types of online advertising (emails, games, etc.), we are particularly interested in contextual ads using rich media banners that display motion and exploit sensory information such as video, audio, animation etc. Once the various banners of an ad campaign are produced, a legitimate question arises for a web marketer: among various options, and for the same banner content, what is the optimal banner format and delivery policy?

In this chapter, we deal with three main problems a web marketer can be confronted with: the right format among those available (e.g. text, image, video, interactive, etc.), the right time to display a banner during a user browsing session (e.g. at the beginning, at the end or when salient events are detected, etc.) and the right sequence of banners to display (that takes into account the format and the time problem). We show that these problems share common points. These points fit well within the reinforcement learning framework: a "trial-and-error" process can be used to dynamically determine an advertising policy that

DOI: 10.4018/978-1-60960-189-8.ch002

optimizes a criterion based on an impact measure (e.g. the click-through rate or the session duration of a user). Two stochastic models based on Markov Decisional Processes and Multi-Armed Problems are presented in order to solve the three problems.

Results, showing the power and the efficiency of the two models to solve our problems, are also given. By comparing to a "ground truth" acquired by observing user browsing session on a test site, we conclude that our models are able to determine optimal advertising policies concerning banner formats and delivery.

INTRODUCTION

Today, online advertising has grown into one of the most successful advertising channels, since browsing the web has become a daily activity for a majority of users. Website owners call on the experience of marketers or online advertising agencies in order to design, produce and deploy ad campaigns (see for example (Marketing Sherpa, 2008) or (McCoy et al., 2007) if you are interested in this process).

Among the different types of online advertising (emails, games, etc.), we are particularly interested in contextual ads using rich media banners. In fact, on a commercial website, contextual ads are used to drive users and transform their navigation into a transaction. Traditionally, the banner's content has been presented in the form of text and hyperlinks. Recent studies such as (Rosenkrans, 2009) have shown the benefits of using rich media for displaying motion and exploit sensory information such as video, audio, animation etc. Rich media content is considered more attractive since it can grab users' attention easily and can also leave stronger memories (Mei et al., 2007). Rich media naturally fights the banner blindness problem, when users tend to completely ignore banners. These are some of the reasons that made rich media advertising very popular.

Unfortunately, some sites make excessive use of it, leading to the commonly called *ad overload problem*. The overabundance of banners or the poor targeting of ad campaigns make sometimes the user navigation on a web site difficult or unenjoyable. Moreover, users tend to learn (by

reinforcement...) how to avoid clicking on banners, since they can lead to unwanted content, which is clearly contrary to the aim of the ad campaign.

Once the various banners of an ad campaign are produced, a legitimate question arises (Baccot et al., 2009): among various options, and for the same banner content, what is the optimal banner format and delivery policy?

In this chapter, we intentionally put aside the banner content issue and consider it (as other authors, like Hauser et al. in 2009) as a separate question. Thus, the problem is how to take into account three classical dimensions of a banner seen as a hypermedia document:

- the logical and spatial layout. The logical layout includes the different elements (and their links) that can be inserted in a banner (e.g. an image, or an image with a caption, a video etc.) whereas the spatial layout gives the way these elements are presented (e.g. a caption above or below the image).
- the level of interactivity of banners. Basic or more complex banners may be available, enabling users to click, scroll, type etc.
- the timing of delivery: the instants when banners are added. Adding them at very specific times (e.g. when the user level of interest falls) can increase their effectiveness and therefore their click-through rate (CTR).

A variety of options for designing and delivering the banners are available. Obviously, the various possibilities do not have the same impact, therefore what should we (or should we not) do, what are the criteria that allow us to choose?

The remaining of this chapter is organized in three sections. The first one (section 2) introduces the three banner problems we will deal with: the right format for a banner, the right time to display it and the right sequence of banners. While presenting these problems, we will introduce step by step all the ingredients that enable us to work in the reinforcement learning framework. In the next section (section 3), we formalize these problems and present more precisely the reinforcement learning framework. Two stochastic models that will help to solve the previous problems are also detailed. The third section (section 4) presents results obtained by solving the banner problems using reinforcement learning. The results prove the strength and the efficiency of the models. Finally, a discussion about the benefits of reinforcement learning is conducted. The chapter ends with a conclusion and some perspectives.

1,2,3... BANNERS PROBLEMS

Among the various possible use cases related to banner optimization of format and delivery, we choose to address three problems. These problems are important to solve, since they handle essential aspects of the banners: the right format, the right time to insert and the right sequence of banners.

The Right Banner Format

Today advertisers produce a wide variety of banner formats that compete for capturing users' attention and fulfill advertisers' requirements... This includes various banners sizes (from leaderboard to skyscraper), rich in interactivity or not, or using various technologies (from standard text or images to a complex highly "dynamic" Flash application).

Marketers are confronted with a difficult question (Cole et al., 2009): among this large variety

of banner formats, which one to use? The answer is not straightforward, since many parameters impact the effectiveness of a banner. Obviously, the usage context is important, since the same banner cannot be deployed on terminals or browsers with very different characteristics: mobile access requires small and lightweight banners whereas rich media banners can be easily displayed on a desktop computer. Marketers have also stressed the importance of fine targeting the banners according to users by taking into account users preferences, intentions and various other behavior parameters.

In brief, this first problem is to decide the right banner format according to what is generally called *context*. It is actually an instantiation of a more general multimedia adaptation problem: how to adapt a multimedia document (in our case the banners) to the context of usage (taking into account both human and non-human factors)?

Commonly, the problem is solved empirically by defining rules (expressed by marketers) which provide adaptation instructions (banner formats) upon detection of a salient event during users' navigation on a website. In order to pretest the campaign (the set of advertising rules), multivariate or A/B testing is used: different versions of the banner (i.e. different formats) are deployed to selected distinct groups of visitors and their effectiveness is measured, using an impact measure (various examples of such measures are given in (Cole, 2008)). When the test period is finished, the format which gave the best results is chosen. Obviously, this is a tedious process, made even more complicated if the set of banners is large.

A major drawback of this solution is that suboptimal versions waste advertising efficiency during the tests. The testing phase can be called exploration, since the various possibilities are explored, even the ones that will be revealed as inefficient later. Once the best format is identified, a second phase starts: the exploitation phase. Clearly, the exploration phase should be as short as possible in order to rapidly put the system into effective operation.

Instead of having the exploration and exploitation periods in a sequence, a better solution would be to combine them. This means that we may mix exploration and exploitation and make a trade-off between them: *explore* more in the beginning and *exploit* more and more with time.

In order to model the banner impact problem, it is natural to consider the following elements:

- a set of states representing the state of the context at instants when a decision about the banner can be issued,
- a set of actions that reflect these decisions,
- an impact measure that allows to evaluate the result of the actions.

In any state of the system an action (inserting a banner in a predefined format) can be taken and its impact is measured in the form of a reward. By trying the various possible actions, an optimal mapping between a state and an action may be learnt. This mapping is called an *optimal policy*. Later in this chapter we will formalize this problem within the reinforcement learning framework as a Multi-Armed Bandit Problem. For now, we only provide a quick intuition: it is like going to the casino and using slot machines. You try to optimize the revenues by choosing the machine that provides you with the best money return.

The Right Time to Insert

Banner effectiveness is not only about the format, but also about timing. When should a banner be displayed during a user's browsing session?

Once again, the answer is not obvious. Displayed too early (in the beginning of a browsing session), the banner can be ignored by the user since his or her attention is much more focused on the content of the website than on ads. The phenomenon is called the "blindness problem" (e.g. it is studied in (Calisir & Karaali, 2008)). Displayed too late, the impact can be null, since the user may have already left the site. Therefore,

if we are able to detect the precise moment during a user navigation to insert a banner, the impact will be more important.

In our previous work (Baccot et al., 2009), we have shown that adding a banner close to the end of a browsing session can lead to an increase of users' interest levels and lengthen sessions' duration.

Thus, our second problem is to choose the optimal instant for inserting the banner. Trying various instants (chosen at the beginning of a user browsing session) is a natural solution. After each try the system observes the impact and dynamically learns which action is the best. Therefore the system operates in a closed-loop.

Figure 1 generalizes this idea. The system is composed of a learning agent and its environment. The agent observes the context (i.e. users' preferences, terminals, network conditions etc.). Based on this observation, it builds a state. By following a policy, it decides whether or not to add a banner. After the banner is inserted, the system observes the impact of this action and collects a reward, measuring the effectiveness of the action. The policy is updated continuously according to the reward: fruitful actions are reinforced, whereas unfruitful ones are avoided. By following this trial-and-error process, the system is able to dynamically learn an optimal time insertion policy.

The level of dynamism goes further than the previous problem. However, the three main ingredients are still present: states, actions and rewards.

The Right Sequence

Another advertisers' need is to decide the sequence of banner formats to be displayed during a user browsing session. At each step, the format of a banner that can be displayed needs to be chosen.

Intuitively, the sequence counts, since it may be counterproductive to visually stimulate heavily (and too much) the user with the first banner. Instead, an increasing power of stimulus may result in a better absorption of the advertisements

Figure 1. A decision-taking agent operating in a closed-loop

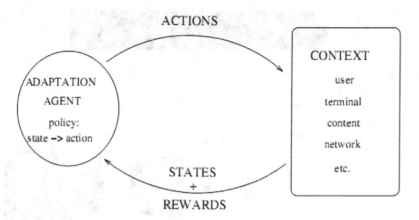

message. Section 3 presents results from an experiment we led. The experiment was carried out on a real web site using three types of banner formats (Figure 2):

- the basic version, only composed of a text (including links to recommended content),
- the video/avatar version. In that case, an avatar in a video serves as a teaser,
- the animated version. It uses a ``carousel''. Recommendations are included in the different facets.

For this experiment, we choose to determine which banner format sequence (basic, animated, video or video, animated, basic or etc.) is best according to various impact criteria.

More generally, we can state our third problem as a problem of sequentially deciding a set of banners. Like in the previous problems we propose to identify the states, the actions (insert a banner of a certain format) and the rewards (the CTR or the session duration). Users' navigations are closely monitored (the context is observed) and, at particular navigation moments, various banner format sequences are tested (possible actions are tried). Naturally, observed rewards (e.g. session duration) influence the subsequent taken

actions and make the system learnt in a closed-loop manner.

Expressing a problem as a closed-loop system (see Figure 1 previously presented) of such states, actions and rewards, fits well within the reinforcement learning (RL) framework, as we will see later.

Wrap Up

The three problems have common ingredients. In each problem, states are defined. In a given state, different actions are available and one of them is chosen. The impact of the action is measured and rewards are obtained. Moreover, by using the closed-loop framework (Figure 1) and a "trial-and-error" process, an optimal mapping between actions and states (called policy) can be dynamically learnt. The closed-loop also enables to take decision in sequence, allowing us to deal with the third problem.

All these elements are at the heart of the reinforcement learning framework. In the next section, we will present more precisely this framework and see how it can help to solve the three problems.

Figure 2. The different types of banner formats available for our test site

STOCHASTIC MODELS FOR BANNER OPTIMIZATION

As previously suggested, the dynamics of the web navigation context are heavily influenced by the variability of human and non-human factors. These dynamics are stochastic. In this section, we first introduce the reinforcement learning framework. Then we present two stochastic models that will be used to solve the banner problems.

The Reinforcement Learning Framework

According to (Sutton & Barto, 1998), reinforcement learning is "learning what to do (i.e. how to map situations to actions) so as to maximize a numerical reward signal". An agent, in a given situation, should try every possible action and discover by itself which are the ones that yield the most important reward. Action taking process is really important since actions affect immediate

rewards, and, by modifying the environment, the next situations the agent will be in, and therefore, the subsequent rewards. Therefore the agent is able to maximize the long term (cumulative) reward.

Reinforcement learning is a sub-area of machine learning. Supervised and unsupervised learning are the two main types of machine learning. Reinforcement learning is close to unsupervised learning in that solutions do not necessarily need help from a human expert, nor sub-optimal actions are explicitly corrected. Further, there is a focus on on-line performance, which involves finding a balance between exploration (of uncharted territory) and exploitation (of current knowledge). The exploration vs. exploitation trade-off in reinforcement learning has been mostly studied through the multi-armed bandit problem.

Reinforcement learning has been successfully used in many applications, from robotics and control to game playing (the survey (Kaelbling et al., 1996) gives more details about the possible uses of RL).

In the context of the Web, we propose here to solve our banner problems using two stochastic models that make use of reinforcement learning: Markov Decision Processes (MDP) and Multi-Armed Bandit Problems (MABP). At some moments during a Web navigation, the system needs to decide "advertising actions" that maximize the utility criteria defined by a web marketer. A MDP sequentially decides of an advertising action at each step in the navigation. Bandit models are simpler and lighter, since only specific navigation states are considered and advertisement actions can only be computed for those states.

Markov Decision Processes

Markov Decision Processes are commonly used for solving sequential decision problems under stochastic conditions. A sequence of decisions is called a policy. In our case, users' interactions and network's performance are unpredictable, making our rich media banners operate under stochastic conditions.

A MDP is a stochastic controlled process that assigns rewards to transitions between states (Sutton & Barto, 1998). It is defined as a quintuple $(S; A; T; p_t; r_t)$ where S is the state space, A is the action space, T is the discrete temporal axis of instants when actions are taken, $p_t()$ are the probability distributions of the transitions between states and $r_t()$ is a given function of reward on the transitions. We rediscover in a formal way the previous ingredients (Figure 1): at each instant $t \in T$, the decisional agent (the advertising controller component) observes its state $\sigma \in S$, applies on the system the action $a \in A$ that brings the system (randomly, according to $p_t(\sigma'|\sigma,a)$) to a new state σ', and receives a reward $r_t(\sigma,a)$.

In this framework, we are looking for the best policy with respect to the accumulated rewards. A policy is a function π that associates an action $a \in A$ with each state $\sigma \in S$. Our aim is to find the best one, π^*. In each state σ, the optimal action $\pi^*(\sigma)$ maximizes the expected cumulated reward

on the remaining temporal horizon. This cumulated reward may be defined as the sum of local rewards associated with the actual transitions. Other similar cumulative measures such as discounted sum or mean value are possible as well. In our case, since the model probabilities (i.e. $p_t()$) are not known, a reinforcement learning algorithms such as Q-learning can be used to find π^*.

In the Q-learning algorithm, Q-values are defined: $Q(\sigma,a)$ corresponds to the expected cumulated reward in state σ when action a is chosen. The principle of Q-learning (algorithm 1) is the following: after each observed transition $(\sigma_n, a_n, \sigma_{n+1}, r_n)$ the current value function Q_n for the couple (σ_n, a_n) is updated, where σ_n represents the current state, a_n the chosen and applied action, σ_{n+1} the resulted state, r_n the immediate reward and R_n the accumulated reward for this experience.

The updating formula trades off previous estimation of Q_n and accumulated reward R_n for the current experience. The learning rate $\alpha_n(\sigma,a)$ is particular to each pair state-action and controls how fast we modify our estimates. One expects to start with a high learning rate (e.g. 1), which allows fast changes, and lowers the learning rate as time progresses.

In this algorithm, N_{tot} is an initial parameter that represents the number of iterations. The function *simulate* returns a new state and its associated reward according to the dynamics of the system. The choice of the current state and of the action to execute is made by the functions *chooseState* and *chooseAction*. The function *initialize* is used most of the time to initialize the Q_0 values to 0.

After N_{tot} iterations, it is easy to determine the best policy π^*: in each state σ, the action to take is the one that maximizes the Q-values, i.e. $\max_a(Q(\sigma,a))$.

A Markov Decisional Process is a good model for our banner problems, since:

Algorithm 1. The Q-learning algorithm.

```
Initialize Q₀ for n = 0 to N_tot - 1 do
        σ_n = chooseState
        a_n = chooseAction
        (σ'_n, r_n) = simulate(σ_n,a_n)
        /* update Q_{n+1} */
        Q_{n+1} ← Q_n
        /* compute the current expectation reward R_n */
        R_n = r_n + γ max_b Q_n(σ'_n,b)
        Q_{n+1}(σ_n,a_n) ← (1 - α_n(σ_n,a_n))Q_n(σ_n,a_n) + α_n(σ_n,a_n)R_n
end for
returnQ_Ntot
```

- we can define a set of decisional states, representing states in the browsing session context,
- in each state we can choose among different banner actions (e.g. choice of the banner format),
- rewards are given by an impact/utility measure defined by a marketer (e.g. the session duration). The reward is cumulative: the impact of each banner format decision influences the user behavior and adds up to the total session duration.

Using a trial and error mechanism, Q-learning can be iteratively used to try the various banner actions and compute the optimal policy.

Multi-Armed Bandit Problems

A Multi-Armed Bandit Problem (MABP) is named by analogy to a slot machine. For example, in the K-Armed Bandit Problem, a gambler has to choose which of the K slot machines to play with. At each time step, he pulls the arm of one machine and receives a reward. His aim is to maximize the sum of rewards he perceives over time. This clearly shows the "exploration vs. exploitation" dilemma: the purpose of the gambler is to find,

as rapidly as possible, the arm that gives the best expected reward.

In order to solve a Bandit problem (i.e. to find the best arm to play), various strategies can be used (Sutton & Barto gives a good overview in their book). Recent research has proposed various solutions to solve optimally and online this dilemma, minimizing the number of errors over time. One of the most efficient is called Upper Confidence Bound (UCB, by Auer et al., 2003). At each play, it computes a priority index for each arm, based on the previous rewards and the number of times it has already been invoked. The index p_j for arm j is given by

$$p_j = \overline{x}_j + \sqrt{\frac{2\ln(n)}{n_j}} \qquad (1)$$

where $\overline{x}_j$ is the average rewards obtained from arm j, n_j the number of times arm j has been chosen and n the overall number of plays done so far. The best arm to choose is the one with the highest priority.

In equation 1, $\overline{x}_j$ can be seen as the exploitation term (it uses the previous observed information about the arm) whereas the second term is an exploration term since it takes into account the

Figure 3. The adaptation platform that allows us to deploy both MDP and MABPs based models

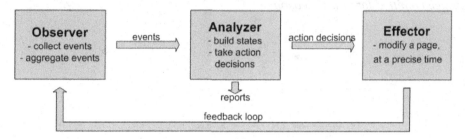

number of times an arm has already been played with respect to the others.

For our banner problems, we can use MABPs as follows:

- we strategically define a set of decisional states,
- we associate one MABP to each state of the context,
- each arm corresponds to a possible advertising action in a given state,
- rewards are given by an impact/utility measure, defined by a marketer.

Figure 9 depicts a 6-armed Bandit problem associated to a state. Pushing arm *i* at a play means performing action *i* at this step.

As a result, we get a collection of independent multi-armed Bandit problems. Each MAPB can be solved independently using the UCB technique. One can notice that, compared to the MDP, this is done at the expense of neglecting potential relations between states.

EXPERIMENTS

A set of experiments was conducted on a website to test the various proposed models, focusing on the three banner problems.

In order to conduct these test rounds, we have built a generic software platform (Figure 3). Our system is able to dynamically adapt website pages during a browsing session, and deploy either heuristic (fixed) policies or MDP/MABPs based model.

It has three main components. First, the user behavior is observed and his interactions with the web browser are collected (Observer). Interactions (mouse clicks, mouse movements...), called events, are sent back to a server and are analyzed in order to decide whether an adaptation should be done or not (Analyzer). The last component (Effector) performs the web page adaptation as decided by the Analyzer. The system works in a closed loop: when an adaptation is performed by the Effector, the user continues to be observed and the effect of the adaptation is measured by the Analyzer.

In this section, we describe how to use reinforcement learning techniques on a real website using this software platform. The site we choose is a showcase for a company that sells "Collaborative Business Solutions". The website has a section/subsection structure; each subsection presents a product or know-how of the company.

Case Study 1: The Right Time to Insert a Banner

In this section, we study the problem of the right time when a banner should be inserted in a page. In this set of experiments, we look for the optimal instants for insertion during a user browsing session.

Concerning the displayed banner, we choose to focus on the delivery problem only and put aside the content problem. However, in order to

Figure 4. A MDP model to solve the optimal time problem. Rewards are written in red, actions in blue. Action Φ has been omitted for clarity reason

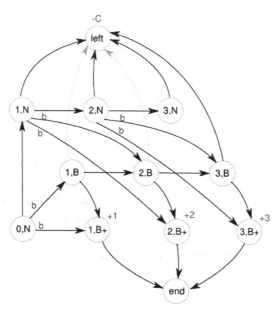

present the users with consistent banners, we use the existing RSS feed of the test site as content provider (the feed is composed of links to the new products or white papers; these links are included in the banners). We also deliberately choose one banner format, by taking the basic one (presented in Figure 2).

We first conduct a round of experiments where banners were inserted at different instants during the navigation. We used 170 testers and collected the insertion instants and their browsing session duration. What we realized is that adding the banner close to the end of the session can lengthen the session duration.

Then, we exploited these data to seed a simulator that was used to test our models. We can also use these data as "ground-truth" and compare them with the results obtained with the models.

A MDP Solution

A MDP to model the problem is shown in Figure 4.

The first thing we have to do is to model the different states. We chose each state to be com-

posed of two variables: T and s. The state is therefore denoted as $<T,s>$. T is a positive integer that represents the current session duration time for a given user, after choosing a quantization for the browsing time of a user. s can have three values: N when the banner has not been displayed yet, B when the banner has been displayed but has not been followed (clicked on) by the user yet and $B+$ when the banner has been displayed and has been followed by the user.

Two states have a particular definition: *left*, reached when a user left the site without having seen or followed a banner and *end*, reached when a user has followed a banner.

Concerning the transitions between the states, there are three types, presented in Figure 5. When the banner is not displayed at time i, it can be not displayed at time $i+1$ (N), displayed (B) or directly followed by the user ($B+$). The user can also leave the website.

As for the actions, they are of two types: b, the action that consists in adding the banner and Φ, an action that corresponds to the null action (nothing is done).

Figure 5. The three "generic" types of transition at time i

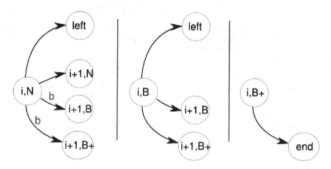

Table 1. Average session duration obtained for the different sequences of the PDM

Sequence	Average session duration
Φ, Φ, Φ	102s
b, Φ, Φ	120s
Φ, b, Φ	121s
Φ, Φ, b	146s

Thus, for example, being in state *<i,N>* means that the user has spent *i* time units on the website, and that the banner has not been displayed yet. In that state, two actions can be taken: adding a banner (*b*) that leads to *<i+1,B>, <i+1,B+>* or *left*, and *Φ* that leads to *<i+1,B>* or *left*.

Finally, let us present the rewards:

- $r(<i,B+>,a)=i$, for all actions *a*.
- $r(left,a)=-C$, for all actions *a*, where *C* is a positive integer.
- $r(s,a)=0$ otherwise.

The rewards, that are higher if the banner is inserted at the latest possible instant, encourage the agent to try to insert the banner just before the end of the session, in order to get the maximum rewards. However, this is balanced by the fact that if the user prematurely left the website, the reward will be negative.

The model is not deterministic since when an action is taken in a given state, the resulting state does not only depend on the chosen action.

In fact, the user can leave the site in any states, whatever the chosen action.

Table 1 shows the results (by setting the value of *C* to 4, which corresponds to the highest reward). They were obtained using the simulator and 10.000 Q-learning iterations. Only the actions taken at time 1, 2 and 3 are mentioned.

These results confirm the preliminary observed results and our intuition: adding the banner at the end of the user browsing session leads to longer session duration. Practically, it allows the system to identify the optimal, latest moment for the banner insertion.

A MABP Solution

We choose to use a very simple model, based on a single state. The associated Bandit problem has two arms (Figure 6): *0s* and *120s*.

We choose an arm to pull at the beginning of user navigation. When arm *0s* is chosen, the ad is included immediately in the page (i.e. at the beginning of a user session) whereas when the other one is chosen, it is inserted 120 seconds after the beginning of the session. 120 seconds is chosen based on our preliminary results: average session duration was about 140 seconds.

In Table 2, the values of the priority indexes (computed according the UCB method, equation 1) for the two arms are presented at different iterations. The chosen action is the one with the greatest index, that is to say *120s* most of the time.

Table 2. Priority indexes for the two arms of the Bandit problem

iteration	0s	120s
0	∞	∞
10	1.22	1.58
20	1.14	1.38
100	0.85	1.12

In Figure 7, the percentage of optimal chosen action is depicted in function of the number of times the Bandit has been invoked. Quickly, after a few dozen browsing sessions, the chosen action is optimal (120 seconds), showing the efficiency of this Bandit problem.

Again, results confirm what we already know: adding a banner at the end of a user browsing session leads to an increase in the session duration. This proves that MABPs may be used to solve such problems.

Comparison

The MDP solution to model the right insertion time is more complex than the Bandit Problem, but it allows a finer time granularity, at the expense of an increase in the number of states. If the number of states gets too large, it will be difficult to solve the MDP using methods such as Q-Learning (it requires an important amount of memory and needs a lot of training data, i.e. user navigations on the web site).

On the contrary, the Bandit based model is very simple but much more static since the decision to insert the banner is taken at the beginning of the session. Nevertheless, it is easy to add other arms corresponding to other instants of insertion.

Case Study 2: The Right Sequence of Banners

During navigation, a user may be presented, sequentially, with a set of banners. This is the

Figure 6. A Bandit model to solve the optimal time problem

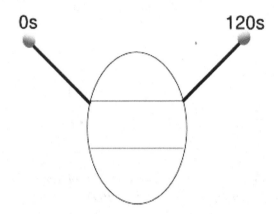

third problem exposed in the introduction of this chapter. For each banner, we only focus on the format of the banner and put aside the content problem. Like in the previous section, in order to get an appropriate content for our test users, we choose to use the existing RSS feed of the web site as the content provider for recommendations.

Concerning the format of the banner, three types of banner formats are available (see Figure 2):

- the basic version, only composed of a text (including links to recommended content),
- the video/avatar version. In that case, an avatar in a video serves as a teaser,
- the animated version. It uses a "carousel" component written in Adobe Flash. Recommendations are included in the different facets.

We choose to display banners in a sequence. A sequence contains exactly one banner of each format. Therefore, six sequences are available (basic/video/animated, video/basic/animated, etc.). Thus, adaptations will consist in displaying the banners in a certain order.

Among many possibilities, we chose to use as an objective/target of the adaptation to get users stay longer on the site, i.e. increase their session

Figure 7. Percentage of optimal action chosen

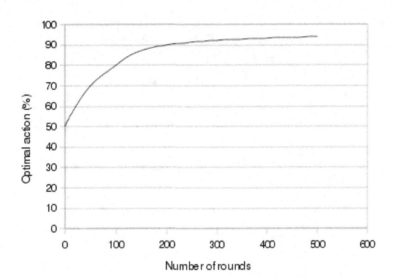

duration. We use the session duration as an impact measure (reward) for a given sequence.

In order to experimentally validate our approach, like in the previous case study, we use a navigation simulator that has been seeded with the data collected from 170 users from our previous work (Baccot et al., 2009) in which we also have sequences of three similar banner types. We have already concluded which sequence of banners is the best (basic/animated/video). Using this "ground truth", we want to determine whether our stochastic models rediscover or not this conclusion.

A MDP Solution

We define a simple Markov Decision Process in order to model the problem (Figure 8).

17 states are defined. Each state is composed of the previously added banner format. For instance, when state *<ABV>* is reached, an animated banner (*A*), a basic banner (*B*) and a video banner (*V*) have been displayed, in this order. There are also 2 specific states: *init* and *end*. At the beginning of a user session, the agent is in the state *init* and will reach the state *end* when a se-

quence of 3 banner formats have been displayed or when the user has prematurely left the website.

As for the adaptation actions, they consist in displaying a banner in a specific format. 3 actions are defined: *a* consists in adding an animated banner to the web page currently visited by a user, *b* a basic banner and *v* a video banner.

This model is also non-deterministic since knowing the chosen action is not sufficient to determine the next state (e.g. the user can leave the site whatever the action is).

Concerning the temporal axis, actions are taken when the user activity decreases. The user activity on the website corresponds to the number of events (mouse clicks, moves, scroll, etc...) done in a given time slot. We choose to add banners on activity decreases since users may be more receptive at these instants.

The last element to define concerns the rewards. When state *end* is reached, the given reward corresponds to the session duration of the user.

We apply the Q-Learning algorithm (algorithm 1) to solve the problem and use our simulator. Table 3 presents the Q-values obtained after 10.000 iterations.

Figure 8. A PDM to solve the optimal banner format sequence problem

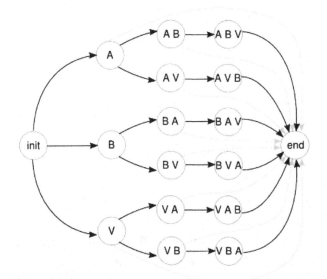

In a given state, the chosen action is the one with the highest Q-value. When we look more precisely at the table, the first action to choose (in the *init* state) is *b*. As a result, state *<B>* is reached, the action to choose is *a*; state *<BA>* is reached and the final action to choose is *v*, leading to *state <BAV>*.

Thus, the optimal sequence of banner format to choose is basic (*b*), animated (*a*) and video (*v*). This confirms the results we drew while studying the data collected during the preliminary experiment.

A MAPB Solution

First, we need to define the different states and the associated Bandit problems.

For the state, the simplest solution is to use a single state. It only contains an inferred information: the user "activity" (the number of events produced by the user in a given time window) on the website.

When the user activity decreases, a banner is displayed on the site according to the chosen sequence of banners.

As for the associated Bandit problems, actions are the different sequences to display, and thus we consider a 6-armed Bandit problem (Figure 9).

The (stochastic) reward is given by the session duration.

Figure 10 presents the evolution of priority indexes values for each arm of the associated Bandit. As the number of times the Bandit is invoked gets higher, priority indexes decreases. However, if we zoom into, we notice that the one for the sequence video/animated/basic (bold black line) is often greater than the others. It means that the associated arm is pulled more frequently. Using the ground truth, we realize that, indeed, this adaptation action is better that the others with respect to the session duration.

Figure 11 shows the percentage of the optimal action the Bandit has chosen as a function of the number of plays. Let us recall that we know which action is the best thanks to the original dataset. As the number of plays gets higher, the percentage increases, indicating the efficiency of the Bandit strategy. Interesting results are reached after around *10.000* sessions. On our test website, ac-

Table 3. Q-values obtained after 10.000 iterations of the Q-Learning algorithm. In a given state, the optimal action to choose is the one with the highest Q-value

	0	a	b	v
init	0	140	**209**	170
A	37	0	145	176
B	65	**328**	0	145
V	39	173	167	0
AB	60	0	0	132
AV	95	0	35	0
BA	53	0	0	**423**
BV	54	166	0	0
VA	0	0	145	0
VB	136	165	0	0
ABV	230	0	0	0
AVB	115	0	0	0
BAV	**277**	0	0	0
BVA	112	0	0	0
VAB	230	0	0	0
VBA	148	0	0	0

cording to its popularity, this can be realized in less than a month.

Bandit problems allow us to draw a conclusion similar to the preliminary results: the usefulness of considering sequence for improving the effectiveness of banners. These results demonstrate the power and simplicity of a Bandit-based adaptation strategy.

Figure 9. A Bandit-based model to solve the optimal banner format sequence problem. The six arms describe the possible six actions that can be done

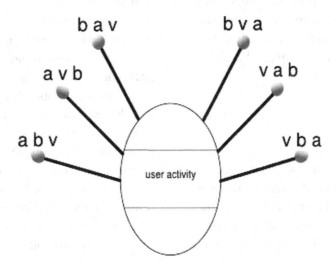

Figure 10. Evolution of priority indexes for each arm of the Bandit problem

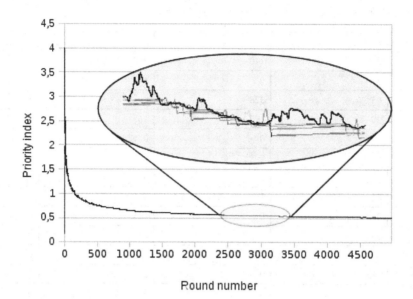

Comparison

The two models give similar results, but they are different in the approach. The MDP allows to issue a decision at each navigation step whereas the MABP-based model simply choses the whole set of actions at the beginning of the session. In other words, on the contrary of the MABPs, MDPs can adjust the advertising strategy in real-time during the navigation. Nevertheless, MDPs are more expensive to implement and solve, since their number of states is significantly larger. Both MDPs and MABPs realize a compromise between exploration and exploitation. In the MDP case, Q-learning allows to mix the two, while in the MABP case, UCB does the job.

DISCUSSION

We proposed in this chapter models that are able to provide a fully dynamic delivery policy using the reinforcement learning framework. During a user browsing session, states define instants when an action can be taken. The impact of the action

is measured and has an effect in the subsequently taken actions. This is opposed to the classic policies that are static: in ad servers such as OpenX[1], delivery parameters and format for banners are chosen at the beginning of a user navigation.

Moreover, using the reinforcement learning, framework the policy can be learnt **online**, using a "trial-and-error" process. In a given situation, different actions are tested, their impact measured and the policy is updated using these measures. It goes a step further than policies that are set up offline.

One key problem is to deal with the "**exploration vs. exploitation**" trade-off. In widely used tools such as Google Website Optimizer[2], these two phases are separated: first the exploration is done (it generally consists in testing different versions of a delivery parameter), then an expert (a web marketer) decides to end the process, chooses a policy and starts the exploitation phase. Using the reinforcement learning framework, the trade-off can be naturally done by taking into account the rewards given by the impact measure.

Moreover, if there is a need to also provide recommendation content, reinforcement learning

Figure 11. Percentage of optimal action chosen

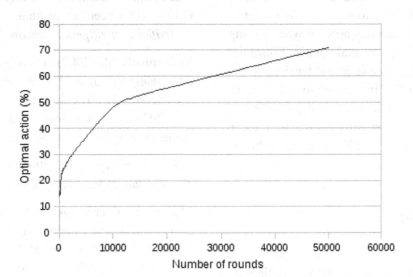

has also proved useful for providing recommendations on a websites (e.g. Shani et al., 2005).

While many authors focus solely on spatial optimization (banner format and position, e.g. Calisir et al.), we proposed to integrate in the models a full spatio-temporal control by adding the time dimension and taking into account the sequence of banners. In previous work, premises of this general idea have also been suggested by other authors. For example, Takashi et al., in 2002, used it in the context of streaming video and Madambath in 2009 mentioned it in a personal blog.

Finally, while currently fully empirical optimization based on marketers is used for banners delivery, we are able to propose a model-driven simulation and optimization, using any of previously presented stochastic models.

CONCLUSION

Rich-media banners on the web are probably the most demanding ad content, since they are more difficult to design, deploy and evaluate. Even if the approaches presented in this paper are tailored to meet such requirements, they can naturally be applied to classic text-based ad. Therefore we believe that applications such as keyword advertising can greatly benefit from using reinforcement learning methods.

The models we used have confirmed what we get while off-line analyzing data collected from some experiments. This underlines the power of the models. Moreover, they can easily be implemented and tested on-line using our platform, previously presented in Figure 3. Thus, using such platform, web marketers can choose between:

- a set of fixed policies and conduct A/B tests to get feedback on their effectiveness.
- relaxing:) while the system computes automatically (online) an optimal policy using RL.

In many real-world environments, it will not be possible for the agent to have perfect and complete perception of the state of the environment. Unfortunately, complete observability is necessary for learning methods based on MDPs. In the future, we will consider the case in which the agent makes observations of the state of the environment, but these observations may be noisy and provide incomplete information. For example, subjective, implicit factors such as user's interest level can be taken into account when issuing a decision about the optimal banner. Therefore, future work needs to consider extensions to the basic MDP or MABP framework for solving partially observable problems. The resulting formal models are called Partially Observable Markov Decision Processes (POMDP) or Bandit Problems with side information.

REFERENCES

Auer, P., Cesa-Bianchi, N., Freund, Y., & Schapire, R. E. (2003). The Nonstochastic Multiarmed Bandit Problem. *SIAM Journal on Computing, 32*(1), 48–77. doi:10.1137/S0097539701398375

Baccot, B., Choudary, O., Grigoras, R., & Charvillat, V. (2009). On the impact of sequence and time in rich media advertising. In *Proceedings of the Seventeen ACM international Conference on Multimedia* (Beijing, China, October 19 - 24, 2009) (pp. 849-852). New York: ACM.

Calisir, F., & Karaali, D. (2008). The impacts of banner location, banner content and navigation style on banner recognition. *Computers in Human Behavior, 24*(2), 535–543. doi:10.1016/j.chb.2007.02.019

Cole, S. (2008). *Creative insights on rich media (Tech Rep)*. DoubleClick Research.

Cole, S. G., Spalding, L., & Fayer, A. (2009). *The brand value of rich media and video ads (Tech Rep)*. DoubleClick Research.

Hauser, J. R., Urban, G. L., Liberali, G., & Braun, M. (2009). Website Morphing. *Marketing Science, 28*(2), 224–224. doi:10.1287/mksc.1080.0459

Kaelbling, L. P., Littman, M. L., & Moore, A. W. (1996). Reinforcement learning: a survey. *Journal of Artificial Intelligence Research, 4*, 237–285.

Madambath, M. (2009). The idea of sequential advertising - moving beyond the context. Retrieved May 2, 2010 from http://www.watblog.com/2009/01/30/the-idea-of-sequential-advertising-moving-beyond-the-context

Marketing Sherpa (Ed.). (2008). *Online Advertising Handbook*. Marketing Sherpa.

McCoy, S., Everard, A., Polak, P., & Galletta, D. F. (2007). The effects of online advertising. *Communications of the ACM, 50*(3), 84–88. doi:10.1145/1226736.1226740

Mei, T., Hua, X., Yang, L., & Li, S. (2007). VideoSense: towards effective online video advertising. In *Proceedings of the 15th ACM International Conference on Multimedia* (Augsburg, Germany, September 25 - 29, 2007) (pp. 1075-1084). New York: ACM.

Oshiba, T., Koike, Y., Tabuchi, M., & Kamba, T. (2002). Personalized advertisement-duration control for streaming delivery. In *Proceedings of the Tenth ACM International Conference on Multimedia* (Juan-les-Pins, France, December 01 - 06, 2002) (pp. 21-28). New York: ACM.

Rosenkrans, G. (2009). The creativeness and effectiveness of online interactive rich media advertising. *Journal of Interactive Advertising, 9*(2), 18–31.

Shani, G., Heckerman, D., & Brafman, R. I. (2005, Dec.). An MDP-Based Recommender System. *Journal of Machine Learning Research, 6*, 1265–1295.

Sutton, R. S., & Barto, A. G. (1998). *Reinforcement learning: an introduction*. Cambridge, MA: MIT Press.

ENDNOTES

[1]   OpenX Ad Server, http://www.openx.org
[2]   Google Website Optimizer, http://www.
       google.com/websiteoptimizer

Chapter 3
Utilizing Sentiments in Online Contextual Advertising

Tanveer J. Siddiqui
University of Allahabad, India

ABSTRACT

Ever increasing number of internet users has attracted many of the companies on the internet for promoting their product and services. This has led to the development of new age of advertising called online or web advertising. The objective of this chapter is two-fold. First, it introduces concepts involved in online advertising. Second, it proposes a novel conceptual framework for contextual online advertising which attempts to utilize local context and sentiment for identifying relevant ads. Contextual advertising is an important class of online advertising in which ads are displayed automatically on web pages based on their content. The proposed framework works in two stages. The first stage retrieves ads for placement. The second stage uses sentiment analysis to filter out ads that do not agree with the sentiments (positive or negative polarity) being expressed in the document. The polarity is identified using SentiWordNet and context-based heuristics.

1. INTRODUCTION

Traditionally newspapers, bill boards, radio and television have been preferred media for advertisement. The advent of Internet has led to the new way of advertising, on-line advertis-

ing (also known as web /Internet advertising). Its wide coverage and low cost as compared to traditional form of advertising mediums makes it quite attractive. Many organizations are spending significant amount of their advertisement budget on it. As mentioned in Broder et al. (2007) the total advertisement cost was estimated over 17 billion dollars in United States alone in 2006 with yearly

DOI: 10.4018/978-1-60960-189-8.ch003

growth rate of 20%. It is major source of funding for many of the Internet companies. Earlier on-line advertising was in the form of banner, pop-up and e-mail, now it appears in various forms like sponsored search, pay-per-click, pay-per-action, behavioral targeting, contextual advertising, video advertising, in-line text, etc. The impact of on-line advertisement can be understood from the fact that it had forced Google to change their advertisement policies. Earlier Google restricted ads up to a dozen words only on results from its web search engine. Now it has started putting videos on pages of search results. New ad formats with images, interactive maps and other features are being developed. However, textual advertising still remains the primary business model behind web search. Most of the Ad networks like Yahoo!, Google, MSN, etc. use textual advertising in which contextually relevant ads are displayed alongside search results. They find relevant ads by matching ads in a large inventory with query or web page content and deliver them at certain position on web pages. Yahoo! and YouTube rely on text only for on-line media advertising also. One step further is in-line advertising used in Vibrant media (Vibrant, 2010). Instead of delivering ads around content, in-line advertising embeds them inside the media content. ImageSense (2010) and VideoSense (2010) use this approach. ImageSense and VideoSense are contextual advertising system for online images and video services which embeds contextually relevant ads at appropriate positions within the image and video. These systems consider both textual relevance and visual similarity into account in ad selection process. This is unlike conventional ad networks such as Google AdWords (2010) and AdSense (2010) which treat image and video advertising as general text advertising and display ads relevant to query or web page based on textual relevance only. The increasing amount of images and videos on the internet has made image and video advertising an important research topic. However, in this chapter, we restrict to textual advertising only.

On-line advertising can be considered as search problem over a corpus of ads. The results retrieved should be relevant for display in a particular context. In this way it is similar to information retrieval (IR) system. However, there are some differences between them. One important distinction is that unlike IR system which always returns some results, in on-line advertising it is acceptable and even desirable not to return any result if it is not relevant (Ribeiro-Neto et al. 2005).

Ad Networks and publishers are continually looking for new and innovative advertising solutions that will increase their ad revenue and provide advertisement with a variety of options to choose from to reach their target audience. Several approaches to select ads based on content or keywords have been proposed (Broder et al., 2007; Lacerda et al. 2006; Ribeiro-Neto et al. 2005; Yih et al., 2006). In this chapter we will review some of these approaches. These approaches may end up in selecting inappropriate ads. This causes poor user experience and unnecessarily wastes space in displaying ads that don't earn any revenue. For example, on a blog site if a blogger is complaining about a product then it is quite likely that a keyword-based approach returns an ad on the same product as relevant one. Displaying this ad will irritate the blogger. Likewise, it will be useless to give an ad of a product which the blogger is using and is satisfied with it. This problem occurs because existing approaches neglect the sentiments or opinions being expressed in the document in deciding relevant ads. In this chapter, we propose a novel two-stage framework for online contextual advertising which uses both local context as well as sentiments for retrieving ads. The proposed framework first retrieves a set of ads based on local context defined by co-occurring text. In the second stage, it uses sentiment analysis to identify the polarity of opinionated expressions. This information is used to decide ads for promotion on a web page. In the second stage, we also make use of heuristics based on local context. The sentiment being conveyed by a word is often dependent on the context. Negation, conjunctions also add to difficulties. For example, the polarity being expressed on both sides of 'but' is usually opposite as in the following example:

This camera takes *great* pictures but takes *long* time to focus.

These heuristics help in correct identification of polarity in this and similar cases.

The motivation behind this framework is the fact that relevancy can not be decided objectively based on keywords. It is subjective in nature. Only the user can tell the true relevance; however, it is extremely difficult to measure this "true relevance". Words may mean differently in different context. Further ads cannot be targeted uniformly for all sorts of web pages. Particularly on blog and social websites, which contain personalized and opinionated expressions, we cannot get relevant ads for display by retrieving merely on the basis of matching contents. Local context along with sentiment analysis can help identifying user's intent to some extent. Ad selection mechanisms that use local context and sentiment analysis in selecting ads are expected to deliver contextually appropriate ads. The rest of the chapter is organized as follows:

The next Section introduces basic concepts involved in online advertising. This includes the key issues involved in web advertising, the important categories of web advertising namely sponsored search and contextual advertising, the elements of online advertising and the auction process. In Section 3, a vector space model for content-based advertising has been presented and existing approaches for contextual advertising have been briefly reviewed. Section 4 presents a framework for contextual advertising that combines sentiment analysis and context to improve relevancy of ads. Finally, in Section 5 conclusions have been made and some of the future directions have been suggested.

2. ONLINE ADVERTISING BASICS

Before we discuss specific approaches to contextual advertising and present our framework, let us identify the important categories of online advertising and discuss some of the basic concepts involved in it. In particular, we identify major issues and key elements involved in online textual advertising and briefly discuss the commonly used auction process. These concepts are applicable to contextual advertising as well and are important from the point of view of developing a clear understanding of contextual online advertising. We begin the discussion with a note on important categories of online textual advertising.

A. Types of Online Advertising

Online advertising has many forms. We can categorize it in a number of ways: on the basis of underlying method used in ad retrieval and distribution channel (keyword match vs. content-match), on the basis of pricing model used (pay-per-click, pay-per-action, pay-per-impression, etc.), on the basis of display format used (pop-up, banner, inline text, etc.) and on the basis of objective (direct marketing vs. brand advertising). The most important categories of web advertising are keyword match, also known as sponsored search, or paid listing and content match, also called content-targeted advertising, or contextual advertising.

1. Sponsored Search: In sponsored search paid ads are displayed alongside web search results in the sponsored links section if the search query includes keywords specified by advertisers as in Figure 1. Sponsored search is predominant business model for web search engines and is critical to the success of many online businesses (Jansen & Mullen, 2008). All major current web search engines, e.g. Google, Yahoo!, Microsoft, etc., support paid listing. An overview of factors that led to the development of sponsored search can

Figure 1. Sponsored search

be found in (Battelle, 2005). A brief history of sponsored search and concept and technology involved in it has been provided by Lacerda et al. (2006).

2. *Content-targeted Advertising or Contextual Advertising*: Instead of showing advertisements alongside search results, it can be shown in different contexts. For example, relevant ads can be shown to users directly on the third party website as shown in Figure 2. This type of advertising is termed as content-targeted advertising. Content-based advertising takes advantage of user's immediate information interests at browsing time. In it ads to be displayed are selected on the basis of content of web page instead of user supplied keywords. It is also termed as contextual advertising i.e. advertising in context with its environment. It is a major source of revenue for publishers ranging from individual bloggers, news papers, etc. Contextual advertising is dynamic. If user refreshes the web page an entirely new set of ads are displayed. An ad network crawler uses the text of the web page and the title of the article to retrieve ads related to the web page and then dynamically inserts them. Google's Ad Sense (AdSense, 2010), Yahoo Publish Network(2010) and Microsoft Ad Center (2010) are major contextual text advertisers besides numerous other participants like Peer39 (2010), ad pepper (2010), iSense (2010), etc.

B. Issues in ONLINE Textual Advertising

The key issues involved in on-line advertising are:

1. Keyword Selection: On-line advertising requires advertiser to submit keywords related to their ads. These keywords, termed as bid phrases, play an important role in deciding which ad to display and the amount to be paid by advertisers. Selecting accurate and approximate keyword is crucial to running an optimized keyword targeted ad campaign. If keywords are quite broad then the ads may not be relevant. On the other hand, if keywords are too specific then the ad server may fail in getting any ad.

Figure 2. A portion of gardening website with content-based ads by Google

2. Relevance: As the advertisers have to pay for advertisement, they would like their ads to be displayed to potential customers of their product. Therefore, relevancy of the ads to the content of the web page and/ or queries becomes an important issue in deciding when and where to display ads. Experimental investigations suggest that higher relevance increases the number of clicks (Chatterjee et al., 2003; Wang et al. 2002). The language of the advertising is quite rich and complex. The text is limited to few phrases or sentences. It may not contain keywords that are directly related to product being advertised. This makes it difficult to get relevant ads.

3. Efficiency: The ads need to be displayed in runtime. Relevant ads have to be identified quickly and efficiently from a huge ads database. The task is particularly difficult for contextual advertising where ads are selected based on content of web pages. The communication and latency cost does not permit analysis of the whole body of the web page in run time. Hence, usually web pages are fetched and analyzed offline and results are applied when these pages are requested by users.

4. Personalization: Traditional Media (TV, radio, news papers, and billboards) advertise products to people non-selectively. In online advertising, user preferences / interests can be learned automatically by tracking their surfing or search behavior and relevant and personalized ads can be delivered to them. For example, someone who frequently visits gardening site would be served ads on gardening tools. This type of advertising is not much useful for mass market consumer goods but can be very effective for specialized products. Advertising systems allow advertisers to target ads based on demographic information. For example, Microsoft adCenter (2010) allows an advertiser to target users based on gender and age.

5. Payment model: In order to bill content provider's some method has to be devised. The most common method is pay-per-click model. Other methods such as pay-per-action, pay-per-impression and pay-per-call are also in use. In pay-per impression the advertiser has to pay a flat fee to show their ads for a fixed number of times, typically for one thousand showings or impressions. This model has its roots in traditional offline advertising model known as cost per mille (CPM) where advertisements were sold per thousand impressions. CPM model was quite common in early banner advertising on internet. This model is more profitable for search engine owner. Advertiser will prefer a situation where they have to pay for a direct response, e.g. when an ad leads to a sale of their product. This situation corresponds to pay-per-action pricing model. In this model, advertiser has to pay only if the ad leads to some action such as user purchases an item listed on the website, gets register on the landing page (advertiser's web page), sign up at the website, or make a phone on a number listed on the website. Pay-per-action

model is profitable for advertisers but not for search engine owner because most of the ad will not result in any revenue. Quite often a potential buyer uses sponsored links to get information about the product or service and then switches to offline way to purchase a product or hire a service. In this case the search engine owner will not get any revenue even though the advertisers are being benefitted by the ads being shown on the search engine result pages. Pay-per-click model takes a middle ground by considering the interests of both the parties involved. In it advertiser has to pay for each click that leads the user to advertiser's web page. Over the years pay-per-click model has almost become a standard for on-line advertising. One of the problems associated with pay per click model is that of click fraud. Click fraud takes place when a company's employee repeatedly clicks on a competitor's link. These false clicks will unnecessarily consume competitor's advertising budget thus wasting their ad campaign. Pay per action model reduces such frauds by linking payments with actions that are costly to perform than click.

C. Elements of Online Advertising

Online advertising is interplay among advertiser, search engine (SE), publishers and users. Let us have look at the key elements involved in this game. The elements listed below are mainly from the point of view of sponsored search model but are applicable to contextual advertising also with little variation.

1. Advertiser: The person or organization interested in bringing user traffic to a particular website.

2. Advertiser provided content: The advertisement or the sponsored link provided by the

advertiser. It consists of a set of keywords along with the associated hyperlinks, titles and descriptors. The keywords submitted by provider are called bid phrases. An appropriate bid phrase is one that is likely to be included in the search query, is relevant to the intent of the searcher and is applicable to the web content. This content is referred to as sponsored listing in order to differentiate it from non-sponsored content on search engine result pages.

3. Advertiser provided bids: The advertiser bids for specified keywords. These bids specify the advertiser's monetary valuation of traffic to a particular website by a provider. A bid usually include a maximum price of a keyword and other constraints such as position, period of activation, age, gender, language and geographical location of searcher. As there are a number of advertisers bidding for a phrase, the amount to be paid are determined by an auction process (Edleman et al., 2007) discussed in section II-D.

4. Search engine: A search engine that displays advertisement in response to user queries on search engine result pages.

5. Searcher: The person performing the search who actually clicks on a sponsored link that is deemed relevant. The content providers select keywords that they believe will match with searcher's information need.

In contextual advertising ads are displayed on third party website instead of search engine result pages. It involves an additional element, namely ad network which is responsible for selecting ads to display on the web page. Ad network automatically analyzes the content of the web page dynamically and provide relevant ads to serve there without any explicit specification from publisher or the advertiser. Where and how these ads are displayed is controlled by the publisher of the website. The ad network may be a search engine or it may be some other ad agency, Google's Ad Sense being the most popular. The revenue is shared between the ad network and the website owner.

D. Search Engine Auction

Search engines have limited space for showing ads. The ads are displayed in some order. As the ads being shown at the top have greater potential to get user's attention than those being shown at the bottom, the advertisers are willing to pay more for higher positions. This leads to a competition for higher position in SE paid listing section. Search engine use an auction process for deciding the order of display. A separate auction is set up for each bid phrase. SE auctions are unique in the sense that there is no closing time and purchase of clicks on different prices goes on continuously. For example, the advertiser with highest bid on a given phrase will be listed as first sponsored link at that instant. Other advertisers can revise their bid amount at any time resulting in a different order and price at another instant. This process continues. Advertisers outbid each other unless one of them drops their bid and the other one follows by revising its bid to a small amount higher than the competitor's bid. This leads to a bidding war cycle as shown in Table 1.

Google noticed this problem and introduced generalized second price auction (GSP) in its own pay-per-click system, Adwords select introduced in 2002, to solve it. Google realizes the fact that a bidder in any position will never like to pay a minimum amount more than the bid of the advertiser in the next position and used this in the auction process. In GSP auction, an advertiser in position i pays a price per click equal to the bid of an advertiser in position $(i+1)$ plus a minimum increment. GSP makes the market more stable, user friendly and less amenable to gaming (Edleman et al., 2007; Jansen and Mullen 2008).

Table 1. Bidding cycle for a phrase by advertisers A, B, C

Date	Time	Position		
		1	**2**	**3**
4/4/2010	10:30:30	A $2.20	B $2.1	C $1.8
4/4/2010	10:40:30	A $2.28	B $1.9	C $1.8
4/4/2010	11:30:30	A $2.0	B $1.9	C $1.8
4/4/2010	11:50:10	B $2.1	A $2.0	C $1.8
4/4/2010	12:10:10	B $2.1	C $2.1	A $2.0
4/4/2010	12:30:00	A $2.2	B $2.1	C $2.1

3. APPROACHES TO CONTEXTUAL ADVERTISING

The basic approaches to contextual advertising can be broadly categorized into keyword match (sponsored search) approach and IR approach.

A. Keyword Match Approach

The keyword match approach reduces contextual advertising problem to sponsored search advertising problem. This is done by extracting a list of keywords or phrases from the web page and matching them with bid phrases. The ads with bid phrases (keywords supplied by the advertisers) matching with extracted keywords are selected for display.

An exact match approach which identifies relevant ads merely on the basis of matching bid phrases within the web page has several limitations. First, it may fail to get any relevant ad. As the advertisers have limited number of keywords to specify their ads, it may happen that the bid phrases do not match with the content of web page. Instead of using only bid phrases in the matching process we can consider larger context by including keywords appearing in the title, abstract and landing page in the matching process. Second, it can result in displaying inappropriate ads. For example, it can result in display of ads on 'Safari suitcase' on a web page containing news about drug found in suitcase of a foreigner. Third, it fails

Figure 3. Vector space model for contextual ad placement

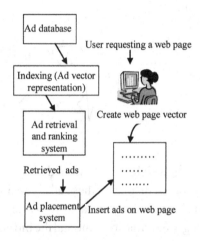

to match with web pages containing synonyms of ad keywords. For example, advertisement with bid phrase 'mobile phone' will fail to match with a web page containing 'cell phone'. One solution to this problem is to extend the ad representation by adding synonyms of the bid phrases and words appearing in its title and abstract.

B. IR Approach

The IR approach views the ad retrieval process as an information retrieval process. Hence, well established IR models can be used for this task. A basic model following vector space retrieval model for contextual ad placement is shown in Figure 3.

The ad retrieval system uses traditional information retrieval concepts such as cosine similarity and *tf-idf* (term frequency- inverse document frequency) features to compute a similarity value between the ad vector and the web page vector. The features used in ad vector may include the bid phrase, the title words, synonyms of these words, the target URL, the displayed abstract, the semantic category, etc. Similarly, the web page vector uses features such as words appearing in the title, words in content of the web page, URL, category, synonyms, etc. The cosine similarity between the ad vector a_k and web page vector d_j can be computed as:

$$sim(d_j, a_k) = \frac{(d_j, a_k)}{\|d_j\|\|a_k\|} = \frac{\sum_{i=1}^{m} W_{ij} \times W_{ik}}{\sqrt{\sum_{i=1}^{m} W_{ik}^2 \times \sum_{i=1}^{m} W_{ij}^2}}$$

where, w_{ij} is weight of ith term in d_j.

The order of display of these ads is decided by their rank. For ranking ads, a score is assigned to ad a_k using the similarity value and the bid amount of ad a_k such as:

Score $(d_j, a_k) = sim(d_j, a_k) \times bid(a_k)$

The ad network places the ad that maximizes this score in the order determined by this score.

C. Related Work

Extracting appropriate keywords is important from the perspective of users as well as advertisers. For user it will result in displaying ads she may be interested in and for advertisers it results in increased click-through-rate resulting in increased revenue for web page provider and increased revenue and profit for advertiser. The work by Yih et al. (2007) focuses on learning good advertising keywords from web pages. They used a supervised learning algorithm which uses pages hand annotated with important phrases for training. The learning algorithm uses a number of features based on tf-idf, HTML meta tag, location of meta tags, search query logs, etc. During evaluation each phrase up to length 5 was considered as potential result and evaluated against the trained classifier.

One of the problems with web advertising is that content providers usually select quite general terms to describe their product. The web page on a specific topic may fail to contain matching vocabulary. Existing literature attempt to handle this problem mainly in two ways: by considering broader context as in (Ribeiro-Neto et al., 2005) and by incorporating semantics as in (Broder et al., 2007) in the matching process. Esuli and Sebastiani (2006) extended the idea of matching phrases extracted from web page and bid phrases by considering the ad text and the landing page in the matching process. They proposed five different matching strategies for associating ads with a web page. The ads were ranked using cosine similarity between vector representing web page and the ad vector. The best performing case – AAK (ads and keywords) - uses text associated with ads and the keywords declared by the advertisers in the matching process and require the presence of ad keywords in the web page. In order to handle the problem of low vocabulary match between ads and web pages they proposed five impedance coupling strategies similar to query expansion strategies used in information retrieval. The underlying idea behind impedance coupling is to expand web page with terms extracted from similar documents on the web with a hope to reduce the vocabulary impedance. The best impedance coupling strategy improves precision roughly by 50% relative to AAK strategy. Murdock et al. (2007) used machine translation techniques to overcome vocabulary mismatch problem. They considered ad as a noisy version of the text in the ad landing page and used features derived from statistical machine translation technology to re-rank set of ads retrieved by ad server so that best ads are displayed on higher positions. Their results confirm the findings of Rebeiro Neto et al.(2005) that the ad landing page provides useful information for matching pages. Their approach is language independent and does not use any external knowledge source. However, their results are biased by the initial ad retrieval algorithm. Lacerda et al. (2006) used machine learning approach to find good ranking function for ads. Using genetic programming they selected a ranking function that maximizes the average precision on the training data. Their ranking function is a non-linear combination of simple components based on frequency of ad terms in the target page, document frequencies, document length and size of the collection. They compared the performance of their ranking function with the work by Rebeiro Neto et al.(2005) and find it more accurate.

Broder et al. (2007) proposed an approach for combining syntactic and semantic matching for ranking ads relevance. They used taxonomy of approximately 6000 nodes developed by Yahoo! US for commercial queries. The taxonomy provides sufficient differentiation between the common commercial topics. Both the ads and web page were classified into this taxonomy. The proximity of the ad and page classes was used to define a semantic score. The relevance between ads and web page was defined by combining syntactic (keyword) score and semantic score. The results indicate that semantic score improves ad relevance significantly. Use of taxonomy helps in generalizing ad search space. This makes it possible to get topically relevant ads in cases where keyword matching may fail to get relevant ads. For example, even if it fails to get ads on "LG RD2330" model of mobile it will still be able to get ads on mobile.

In contextual advertising, ads are returned by ad network after a user requests a new page. This leaves very small amount of time with ad network to respond. Due to low latency requirement web pages are usually fetched and analyzed offline and the results are applied whenever users request

to view these pages. However, this approach is not applicable for pages that are dynamically created. The communication and latency cost prohibits on–the–fly analysis of whole body of such pages. Anagnostpolous et al. (2007) used text summarization technique for contextual advertising in real time for dynamic pages which can not be accessed ahead of time. They created a short extractive summary of the web page and used it for ad retrieval. They supplemented these summaries with information from the page and referrer URLs, and summary class information obtained by classifying summaries with respect to a large taxonomy of commercial topics. Empirical investigation show that carefully selected 5% extractive summaries act as good replacement for the page.

4. SENTIMENTS IN CONTEXTUAL ADVERTISING

Most of the existing approaches do not consider opinionated expression present on the web page while selecting ads for display. This results in inappropriate ads being displayed on the web page which might irritate user. Such ads do not have potential to invite a user click and thus leading to a non-profitable situation for both the publisher and the advertiser. Web site owner would like to display ads which are positively related to contents of web page or blog post. This can be achieved by analyzing the content of the web page to get opinionated expressions, determining semantic orientation of these expressions and then selecting ads that are related to the positive (or neutral) aspects of it. We propose a framework for contextual advertising (Figure 4) to meet this objective.

Only a few published literature report work in this direction (Fan and Chang, 2009; Liu et al., 2007). The SemanticMatch™ algorithm used by online semantic advertising company Peer39 (2010) uses natural language processing and machine learning to understand the content, mean-

Figure 4. Two stage framework for contextual advertising

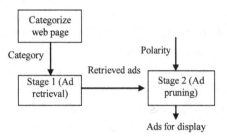

ings, topics, categories and sentiment of web page in real time to deliver relevant and effective advertising. Fan and Chang (2009) proposed a sentiment oriented contextual framework. The framework attempts to combine sentiment analysis and contextual advertising matching to select ads that are related to the positive (and neutral) aspects of a web page and then ranks them according to their relevance. Liu et al. (2008) proposed dissatisfaction oriented advertising framework (DASA). The framework uses sentiment analysis to identify consumer's attitudes and uses it to supply ads that meet the user's underlying needs. They first extracted opinion sentences and then find topics in these sentences using a set of syntactic relationships. Consumer's attitude towards topics is determined using polarity score of sentiment word with contextual information taken into account. Appropriate ads are then selected that are relevant to the topic and meets user's need as well. For example, if a user complains about the image quality of mobile camera of a particular model of blueberry then ads of model with better image quality would be promoted. On the other hand if the user is satisfied with the features provided in the mobile phone then it would be better not to promote any ads of mobile phone. They have evaluated their framework against a strategy, called TE-ALL, which is similar to DASA except that it does not consider customer's attitudes. A subjective evaluation has been made in which volunteers were asked to comment on products (features of cars) and then

ads are retrieved using DASA and TE-ALL. Volunteers were presented with both the lists and were asked to tell which list better meets their needs and is less annoying. In 61% of the cases volunteers found the list retrieved by DASA better than TE-ALL.

A. The Proposed Framework

As shown in Figure 4 our framework consists of two stages. The first stage uses vector space retrieval model, as discussed in Section 3, to retrieve contextually relevant ads. We assume existence of taxonomy into which ads have been categorized. Additionally, the ad vector is enriched by adding synonyms of bid phrases, semantic category and keywords appearing in the title. The retrieval process uses co-occurring text as a representation of local context of the web page. For simplicity, we assume that the target page contains opinion about a product.

Stage 1:
The steps involved in this stage are listed below:

1. Categorize web page using the ad taxonomy.
2. Create ad vector
    a. Extract keywords from title and abstract of ad description.
    b. Extract synonyms of bid phrases, semantic category of the ad and keywords extracted from title of the ad.
    c. Create an ad vector using bid phrases and set of keywords identified in (ii) and (iii).
3. Create web page vector using the content of the web page.
4. Using web page vector as a query retrieve a set of ads from the category identified in stage 1.

Stage 2:
The second stage uses semantic orientation of document to filter out those ads selected in the

first stage that do not positively relate to it. For example, if the first stage selects an ad about a model xxx of mobile phone of brand Y and the web page has a negative opinion about it then second stage will filter out this ad. The steps in stage 2 are summarized below:

1. Determine brand/model name of the product being commented in the web page
2. Determine semantic orientation (polarity) of the opinions being expressed in the web page
3. Drop ads retrieved in stage 1 that do not agree with the sentiments identified in step 2.

B. Detecting Semantic Orientation

In order to identify the semantic orientation (polarity) of the document an approach based on SentiWordNet and a set of heuristics can be used as in Agarwal and Siddiqui (2009). These heuristics make use of context to determine the correct polarity of the opinions being expressed in a sentence. SentiWordnet is a lexical resource designed by Esuli and Sebastiani (2006) for each synset (different senses of each term defined in the WordNet 2.0). Each sysnset is assigned three scores - a positive score, a negative score and an objective score - indicating its degree of positivity, negativity and objectivity. Each score ranges from 0.0 to 1.0 and their sum is 1 for each synset. Instead of using terms, synsets have been used with the assumption that the different senses of terms may have different sentiment polarity. A synset may have nonzero scores for all the three categories. In order to define these scores, Esuli and Sebastiani (2006) used gloss analysis of each synset in the WordNet and applied semi supervised method for classification of terms.

The steps involved in detecting semantic orientation of document are:

1. Pre-processing
   The web page is pre-processed to assign part of speech to terms appearing in it, to remove stop words and to reduce morphological variants to their stems during this step. Stop words like 'very', 'much', 'not' etc. may intensify or modify the opinion being expressed in a sentence but they themselves do not express opinion. Hence, we drop them from word scoring. We use heuristics to modify the sentence score in order to take care of their modifying effect. The SentiWordNet is also pre-processed to stem synset terms and to remove sense number information from it.

2. Word Scoring
   The opinion bearing words in the document are assigned positive and negative scores as defined in SentiWordNet. A word may have more than one part of speech. SentiWordNet lists multiple senses of words for each of its part of speech. Instead of using the average score of term over all senses across different part of speech we use term score of the sense 1 of the same POS only. Sense 1 represents most common sense. For example, if the word 'good' occurs as noun in a sentence then only score of the noun sense of "good" is used. Sentence score is computed by combining scores of individual words appearing in it. Each sentence is assigned a positive score, a negative score and an objective score.

$$senPosScore(S) = \frac{1}{n} \sum_{i=1}^{n} posScore(i)$$

$$senNegScore(S) = \frac{1}{n} \sum_{i=1}^{n} negScore(i)$$

$$senObjScore(S) = \frac{1}{n}\sum\nolimits_{i=1}^{n} objScore(i)$$

where, senPosScore(S), senNegScore(S), senObjScore(S) are the positive, negative, objective score respectively of sentence S.

posScore(i), negScore(i), objScore(i) are the positive, negative, objective score respectively of ith word in sentence S and n = Total number. of words in S.

3. Heuristics

Following heuristics were used to modify the sentence scores (Agarwal & Siddiqui, 2009):

    a. If there is a word like not or any other negative word present in the sentence then we change the score *(now positive score will be negative score and vice versa)* of its next word and recalculate sentence scores.

    b. If intensifiers like 'very', 'more', etc. are present in the sentence then the larger score (positive or negative) of next word is incremented by 'x' (i.e. if positive score is greater than negative score then larger score is positive score and vice versa).

    c. Three additional heuristics were used to change the polarity of a sentence based on context sensitive words.

Intra-sentence conjunction rule.

Opinion on both sides of "and, not only - but also etc" should be the same, e.g., "This camera takes *great* pictures and has a *long* battery life".

It is not likely to say:

"This camera takes *great* pictures and has a *short* battery life."

Opinion on both sides of "but, yet, or etc" should be opposite. E.g. in the sentence

"This camera takes *great* pictures but takes *long* time to focus."

    ▪ Intra Sentence Comma Rule.

Opinion on both sides of comma should be same, e.g., "The camera has a *long* battery life that's *good*"

    ▪ Inter sentence Similarity Rule.

People usually express the same opinion across sentences, unless there is an indication of opinion change using words such as "but" and "however". e.g. "The picture quality is amazing. The battery life is long"

It is not common to say:

"The picture quality is amazing. The battery life is short".

4. Document Scoring

Positive, Negative and Objective scores for whole document is calculated by using average score over all sentences.

$$docPosScore(S) = \frac{1}{n}\sum\nolimits_{S=1}^{n} senPosScore(i)$$

$$docNegScore(S) = \frac{1}{n}\sum\nolimits_{S=1}^{n} senNegScore(i)$$

$$docObjScore(S) = \frac{1}{n}\sum\nolimits_{S=1}^{n} senObjScore(i)$$

where, docPosScore(D), docNegScore(D), docObjScore(D) are the positive, negative, objective score respectively of document D, senPosScore(S), senNegScore(S), senObjScore(S) are the positive, negative, objective score respectively of sentence S and n = Total number of sentences in the document.

5. Polarity Classification

The three scores computed in step 4 are used to classify document as positive, negative and neutral. The semantic orientation of the document is considered positive if docPosScore(D) greater than docNegScore(D) and docObjScore(D). The overall web page is classified as negative if docNegScore(D) is largest, otherwise the document is classified as neutral.

Maximum accuracy observed using this approach is 85.5%, as compared to 58.1% baseline performance, on movie review dataset[1]. The baseline used by Agarwal and Siddiqui (2009) is similar to SentiWordNet average scoring approach used by Devitt and Ahmad (2007) in which the score of each term is calculated by taking average score of all of its synsets listed in SentiWordNet. The investigations made by them suggest that this huge gain in performance is mainly due to the heuristics being used and restricting synsets belonging to same syntactic class for contributing term score.

The ads retrieved in stage 1 are dropped if they do not agree with the polarity identified by sentiment analysis. Thus only ads that have potential to be clicked by user as indicated by the polarity qualify for display.

5. CONCLUSION AND FUTURE WORK

The huge number of internet users has attracted advertiser on the web. More and more companies are now switching to online advertising to promote their product or services and brand building. In order for the system to be beneficial for all the three parties involved, namely the advertiser, the publisher (web site owner) and the ad network, it is required that the ads be delivered to potential customer. This means that ads being displayed should meet user's immediate need. However, the task of inferring user's mind based on content of web page is far from trivial. Quite often a potential customer relies on the reviews on products in order

to decide whether to purchase a product or hire a service or not. Web pages containing user generated content contain opinionated expression that can provide useful information on deciding which ad to display. Contextual advertising systems that select ads only on the basis of content of such web pages may result in displaying inappropriate ads. This leads user frustration besides no win situation for all the parties involved. We propose a two stage model for contextual online advertising that attempts to take advantage of local context and opinionated expressions to get appropriate ads for displaying on a web page. Stage 1 of the proposed model retrieves ads from ad database. Stage 2 uses sentiment analysis to identify the polarity of the web page and uses this information to filter out ads that do not agree with the sentiment being expressed in it. Thus, resulting in ads that lead to a profitable situation for advertiser, publisher and ad- network and better user experience.

The sentiment detection approach used in this framework has shown promising results on movie review dataset. Use of sentiments in online advertising is still less investigated in general. Little amount of published work available on this topic indicate positive results. Before making any claim on the performance of our framework, we would like to evaluate it on standard datasets. It is expected that based on the results of evaluation the framework can be improved. One possible direction of improvement is to handle the ambiguities present on the web page. Another direction is to use an information extraction framework in sentiment detection part in order to get views expressed on specific features of a product and using this information to promote ads.

ACKNOWLEDGMENT

I would like to thank Prof. Uma Shanker Tiwary, IIITA and annoynymous reviewers for commenting and providing useful suggestions on previous version of this chapter.

REFERENCES

Ad pepper the e-advertising network. (n.d.). Retrieved from http://www.adpepper.com/home/

Agarwal, S., & Siddiqui, T. J. (2009). Using syntactic and Contextual Information for Sentiment Polarity Analysis. *ICIS 2009*, November 24-26, Seoul. *Korea & World Affairs*, 620–623.

Anagnostopoulos, A., Broder, A. Z., Gabrilovich, E., Josifovski, V., & Riedel, L. (2007). Just-in-Time Contextual Advertising. In *Proceedings of the sixteenth ACM conference on Conference on information and knowledge management* (pp. 331–340). New York: ACM.

Battelle, J. (2005). *The Search: How Google and Its Rivals Rewrote the Rules of Business and Transformed Our Culture*. New York: Penguin Group.

Broder, A., Ciaramita, M., Fontoura, M., Gabrilovich, E., Josifovski, V., Metzler, D., et al. (2008). To swing or not to swing: Learning when (not) to advertise. In *Proceedings of 17th International Conference on Information and Knowledge Management* (pp. 1003–1012).

Broder, A., Fontoura, M., Josifovski, V., & Riedel, L. (2007). A semantic approach to contextual advertising. In *Proc. 30th Ann. Intl. ACM SIGIR Conf. on Research and Development in Information Retrieval* (pp. 559–566).

Chatterjee, P., Hoffman, D. L., & Novak, T. P. (2003). Modeling the clickstream: Implications for web-based advertising efforts. *Marketing Science*, 22(4), 520–541. doi:10.1287/mksc.22.4.520.24906

Devitt, A., & Ahmad, K. (2007). Sentiment Polarity Identification in Financial News: A Cohesion-based Approach. In *Proceedings of the 45th Annual Meeting of the Association of Computational Linguistics*, Prague, Czech Republic (pp. 984–991).

Edelman, B., Ostrovsky, M., & Schwarz, M. (2007). Internet advertising and the generalized second price auction: Selling billions of dollars worth of keywords. *The American Economic Review*, 97(1), 242–259. doi:10.1257/aer.97.1.242

Esuli, A., & Sebastiani, F. (2006). Sentiwordnet: A publicly available lexical resource for opinion mining. In *Proceedings of LREC-06, the 5th Conference on Language Resources and Evaluation*, Genova, Italy.

Fan, T.-K., & Chang, C.-H. (2009). Sentiment-Oriented Contextual Advertising. In *Proceedings of the 31th European Conference on IR Research on Advances in Information Retrieval* (pp. 202–215).

Google AdSense. (2010). Retrieved from http://www.google.com/adsense

Google AdWords. (2010). Retrieved from http://www.adwords.google.com

iSense (n.d.). Retrieved from http://www.isense.net/home/

Jansen, B. J., & Mullen, T. (2008). Sponsored search: an overview of the concept, history, and technology. *International Journal of Electronic Business*, 6(2), 114–131. doi:10.1504/IJEB.2008.018068

Lacerda, A., & Cristo, M. Gonsalves., M. A., Fan, W., Ziviani, N., & Ribeiro-Neto, B. (2006). Learning to advertise. In *Proceedings of the 29th Annual International ACM SIGIR Conference on Research and Development in Information Retrieval* (pp. 549–556). New York: ACM.

Liu, K., Qiu, Q., Wang, C., Bu, J., Zhang, F., & Chen, C. (2008). Incorporate Sentiment Analysis in Contextual Advertising. In *Proceedings of the First Workshop on Targeting and Ranking for Online Advertising* (In conjunction with WWW'08).

Mei, T., Hua, X.-S., & Li, S. (2007). Contextual in-image advertising. In *Proceedings of the 15th International conference on multimedia* (pp. 439–448). New York: ACM.

Mei, T., Hua, X.-S., Yang, L., & Li, S. (2007). VideoSense: towards effective online video advertising. In *Proceedings of the 15th International conference on multimedia* (pp. 1075–1084). New York: ACM.

Microsoft advertising adCenter (2010). Retrieved from http://www.adcenter.microsoft.com

Murdock, V., Ciaramita, M., & Plachouras, V. (2007). A noisy channel approach to contextual advertising. In *Proceedings of the 1st International Workshop on Data Mining and Audience Intelligence for Advertising (ADKDD'07)* (pp. 21–27).

Peer39 Semantic advertising solution (2010). Retrieved from http://www.peer39.com/

Ribeiro-Neto, B., Cristo, M., Golgher, P. B., & de Moura, E. S. (2005). Impedance coupling in content-targeted advertising. In *Proceedings of the 28th annual international ACM SIGIR conference on Research and development in information retrieval* (pp. 496–503). New York: ACM.

Vibrant (2010). Retrieved from http://www.vibrantmedia.com

Wang, C., Zhang, P., Choi, R., & Eredita, M. D. (2002). Understanding consumer's attitude toward advertising. In *Proceedings of Americas Conference on Information Systems* (pp. 1143–1148).

Yahoo. Publisher Network. (n.d.). Retrieved from http://advertising.yahoo.com/publisher

Yih, W., Goodman, J., & Carvalho, V. R. (2006). Finding Advertising Keywords on Web Pages. In *Proceedings of the 15th international conference on World Wide Web* (pp. 213–222).

ENDNOTE

[1]   http://www.cs.cornell.edu/people/pabo/movie-review-data/review_polarity.tar.gz

Section 2
Image Advertising

Chapter 4
In–Image Advertising

Lusong Li
Beihang University, China

Xian-Sheng Hua
Microsoft Research Asia, China

ABSTRACT

The daunting volumes of images on the Web have become one of the primary sources for online advertising. This work presents a contextual in-image advertising strategy driven by images, which automatically associates relevant ads with an image and seamlessly inserts the ads in the nonintrusive areas within each individual image. In in-image advertising platform, the ads are selected based on not only textual relevance but also visual similarity. The ad insertion positions are detected based on image salience, as well as face detection, to minimize intrusiveness to the user. In addition to general in-image advertising, we also provide a special game-like in-image advertising model dedicated to image on the basis of gaming form, called GameSense, which supports creating a game from an online image and associates relevant ads within the game. We evaluate in-image advertising model on a large-scale real-world images, and demonstrate the effectiveness of in-image advertising platform.

INTRODUCTION

Nowadays we live in a advertising world where advertisements come at us from all directions, such as billboards, print ads, television ads, radio ads, ads on subways and buses. Most of us may probably ignore these ads, because they are not applicable to what we're doing at the moment we see the advertising. However, online contextual advertising has been become an express and effective way for delivering marketing messages to attract customers, because it links advertising to

DOI: 10.4018/978-1-60960-189-8.ch004

the information it supports. In another word, on-line webpage advertising displays text or graphic advertisements that correspond to the content of Web page on which the ad is shown. For example, when a Chinese student is browsing a Web page about English grammar, he or she may need some help to improve his or her English. If there are some ads about English training displayed in the same page, the student may be willing to click the ads to find some English courses provided by the advertisers. Another method is to embed keyword hyperlinks in the page which are sponsored by an advertiser. When users follow the link, they are sent to a sponsor's website. These advertisements are believed to have a chance of attracting a user, because they may tend to share a similar context as the user's browsing intention. There usually needs to be an advertising network which connects Web sites (also called publishers) that want to host advertisements with advertisers who want to run advertisements.

Since digital capture devices and community-contributed photo sites have become widely popular, countless images are constantly accumulated in social image-share sites and shared among individuals and community members. Like the large amount of Web pages, the explosive growth of images also brings huge opportunities for advertisers to deliver commercial messages. That's to say, images can be another powerful information carrier for advertising.

Advertising is a form of communication intended to persuade potential customers to purchase or to consume more product or service of a particular brand. Generally, in the field of advertising, there exist two kinds of advertising, informative advertising and image advertising. Informative advertising is when advertising is carried out in an informative manner. It is a promotional effort at generating interest and credibility in a product, service, or organization by providing consumers with information. For example, alcohol producers run advertisements with the general message being "don't drive drunk." As a comparison, im-age advertising is used for promoting the image, or general perception, of a product or service, rather than promoting its functional attributes. However, being different to the one defined in the field of general advertising, image advertising in this article refers mainly to image-driven advertising. In another word, it uses images as the commercial information carrier. One important point we want to make here is that we focus on the online image advertising which uses web images to carry advertisements, do not discuss the image advertisements which are image banners/rectangles created by advertisers manually that will be laid on a Web page, or product logos/images that will be inserted into a source image or video.

Many existing ad-networks such as Google Ad-Sense, Yahoo! and BritePic, can provide contextual advertising services around images. However, the conventional advertising methods primarily use text content rather than image content to match relevant ads. There is no existing system to automatically monetize the opportunities brought by individual images. As a result, the ads are only generally relevant to the entire Web page rather than specific to images it contained. Moreover, the ads are embedded at a predefined position in a Web page adjacent to the image, which normally destroys the visually appealing appearance and structure of the original web page. It could not grab and monetize users' attention aroused by these compelling images.

What we want to argue is that the ads should be dynamically embedded at the appropriate positions within each individual image (i.e., in-image) rather than around image like traditional advertising, so that no predefined ad blocks are to be preserved. Furthermore, the ads can also be promoted by the salient appearance of the image. The more compelling the image contents, the more audience will view them, then the more revenue will be generated.

Figure 1 gives an example of in-image advertising. It is observed that an exemplary advertisement (i.e., our ImageSense logo) has been inserted into

Figure 1. An example of in-image advertising. The highlighted rectangle area indicates the associated ad

the region with less information within this image. Compared with unattractive text, image is more salient than text. It can grab users' attention instantly, naturally becomes the region of interest (ROI) in a web page. Now that users' attention is on the images, by embedding the ads within images, the ads will in turn get more attention. Therefore, the ad embedded in the image can leave audience a much deeper impression due to the salience of images in human perception. Based on this claim, it is reasonable to assume the embedded ads should be mostly image logos, rather than just textual descriptions, which are more suited to be inserted into images. If the ad information is precisely relevant to the image content, the audiences who are interested in this image probably have similar interests to the relevant product or service advertised in it.

BACKGROUND

Online Advertising Industry

The advertising industry is a rapidly growing industry, and functions as an intermediate between the manufacturers and the customers. Commer-

cial advertisers often seek to generate increased consumption of their products or services through branding, which associates qualities with the brand in the minds of consumers and improves the repetition of the name of a product or service. Different types of media can be used to deliver these messages, including traditional media such as newspapers, magazines, television, radio, movie, shopping bags, wall paintings, bus stop benches, sides of cars, billboards, or direct mails; or new media such as Web pages, video in some media share websites. Nowadays the Internet has become a powerful tool for delivery of commercial messages. We have witnessed a fast and consistently growing online advertising market in recent years. Jupiter Research forecasted that online advertising spending will surge to $18.9 billion by 2010---up about 60% from that in 2005. Motivated by the huge business opportunities in the online advertising market, people are now actively investigating new Internet advertising models.

From the perspective of industry, most of current ad-networks have mainly focused on text advertising. Even they are trying to associate an image with advertisements; they match advertisements with image only based on textual information of the whole Web page which contains the image, without considering the intrinsic characteristics of the visual content, so that the ads are not always contextually relevant to image content. It is well known that surrounding text is usually very poor, either too few or too noisy, to precisely describe an embedded image. Second, the ads are typically embedded at a fixed or predefined position around the image in a Web page, so that the visual appearance and structure of the Web page is usually broken. Therefore, it is desirable to find a more effective image-driven advertising model taking these into account.

Online Advertising Research

The most important thing in online advertising is to increase the advertisement relevance, which may not detract from user experience and may get the reaction from users, for example, clicking the ads and checking out more information on the ads' web sites (Mccoy, Everard, Polak, & Galletta, 2007). Typical online advertising systems analyze a Web page or query to find prominent keywords or categories, and then match these keywords or categories against the words for which advertisers bid. If there is a match, the corresponding ads will be displayed to the user through the Web page (Yih, Goodman, & Carvalho, 2006) (Li, Zhang, Hu, Zeng, & Chen, 2007) (Shen, Sun, Yang, & Chen, 2006). Research on ad relevance has proceeded along three directions from the perspective of what the advertisements are matched against: (1) "sponsored search" advertising in which the ads are matched against the originating query (Joshi & Motwani, 2006) (Mehta, Saberi, Vazirani, & Vazirani, 2007), (2) "contextual advertising" advertising in which the ads are associated with the Web page content rather than the keywords (Broder, Fontoura, Josifovski, & Riedel, 2007) (Lacerda, Cristo, Goncalves, Fan, Ziviani, & Ribeiro-Neto, 2006) (Murdock, Ciaramita, & Plachouras, 2007) (Ribeiro-Neto, Cristo, Golgher, & de Moura, 2005), and (3) "audience intelligence" advertising in which the ads are driven based on

user profile and demography (Hu, Zeng, Li, Niu, & Chen, 2007), or behavior (Dai, Zhao, Nie, Wen, Wang, & Li, 2006) (Richardson, Dominowska, & Ragno, 2007).

Recently, researchers have invented context-aware video advertising technologies that can automatically insert video ads into video clips using intelligent video content analysis techniques (Kastidou & Cohen, 2006) (Liao, Chen, & Hsu, 2008) (Mei, Hua, Yang, & Li, 2007) (Srinivasan, Sawant, & Wadhwa, 2007). Some researchers realized the emergence of image-driven advertising, however they only focused on delivering the advertisements during image buffering on the Web (Li, Zhang, & Ma, 2008). Specifically, a product logo will appear in the middle of display area before a full version of image is downloaded from server side and displayed at local side.

It is observed that most related work is focused on general text advertising or video advertising in particular, while very few publications deal with image-driven advertising, despite the pervasiveness of images over the Internet and the importance of this area. Since the problem of image-driven advertising is posed differently from that of either text or video advertising, the techniques in the domain of text and video cannot be directly applied to image. Therefore, an advertising system dedicated to image domain is much desired. We believe that the problem of image-driven advertising should be posed differently from that of either text or video-driven advertising. The techniques in the domain of text and video cannot be directly applied to image. Therefore, an advertising system dedicated to image domain is much desired, in which the following problems should be effectively addressed: (1) how to find nonintrusive ad insertion positions within images, (2) how to match ads to image content and embeds relevant ads into nonintrusive positions, and (3) how to deliver the ads in an impressive way.

ONLINE SERVICE FOR IN-IMAGE ADVERTISING

Framework

Basically, in image-driven contextual advertising, there are three main roles in the ecosystem of this in-image advertising, including publishers, advertisers, and service provider which is an intermediary commercial ad-network entity (between the publisher and advertiser) in charge of optimizing the ad selection and display aiming at the two often conflicting goals of increasing the revenue (shared between the publisher and the ad-network) and improving user experience. It is always preferable to the publishers and profitable to the advertisers to do target ads, that is, distribute ads relevant to the image content rather than unrelated generic ads. By adopting a solid image-driven contextual advertising strategy into an existing content delivery chain, publishers and advertisers can deliver more effective advertisements carried through compelling image contents, reach a much larger online audience, and eventually generate more additional revenue from online images.

Figure 2 shows the general framework of online service for in-image advertising and a piece of code for applying this service in publishers' pages. Through the online service for in-image advertising, both publishers and advertisers can register and subscribe in-image advertising service. In-image advertising platform builds an index based on ad database for ad ranking. Meanwhile, the Web pages on publishers' websites are crawled and processed by page segmentation module. The extracted images' surrounding texts are then used to rank candidate ads based on multimodal relevance matching. At the same time, the crawled images are analyzed by "image analyzer" module to detect a set of candidate advertisement insertion positions. Then "image-ad matching" module will optimize the matching between the insertion positions and ads. Finally, the XML description file containing the URLs of selected ads and ad insertion positions will be delivered to the publishers.

The publisher is usually a social photo sharing website. The user can earn some money just by uploading and sharing photos with friends on the Internet via the in-image advertising platform. For example, a user took a beautiful photo by his Nikon D50 camera and uploaded it onto a social site which has subscribed the in-image advertising service. The user also provided some tags about his photo, such as "Nikon D50", "Nikon", "Beautiful scene" and so on. When the Web page which contains this photo is shown, a relevant advertisement, e.g. Nikon Company's logo, will be seamlessly embedded into the non-salient region of the image because this photo contains "Nikon" tag. The person who uploaded it can get some revenue from Nikon Company each time when the photo is viewed. He or she may earn more money if the viewers click the ads and go to the website of Nikon Company. It is well known that many people especially young people usually like to upload and share beautiful photos with their friends. The more appealing the photos are, and the more attention the viewers will pay to the embedded ads. Therefore, this online service for in-image advertising should be very effective.

Problem Formulation

In general, ad relevance and ad position are two most important problems in an in-image advertising system (Li, Edwards, & Lee, 2002) (Mccoy, Everard, Polak, & Galletta, 2007).

- **Relevance**—which ads should be selected for an image? Since relevance increases advertising revenue (Chatterjee, Hoffman, & Novak, 2003), in-image advertising model performs multimodal relevance matching by considering high-level topic relevance, low-level visual relevance, as well as user relevance.

Figure 2. The general framework of online service for in-image advertising

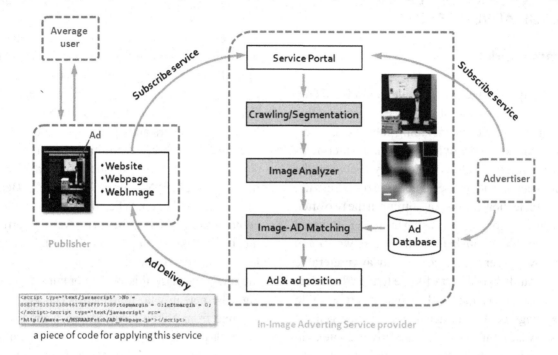

- **Position**—where should the selected ads be inserted? Ad position will certainly affect user experience when an image or a Web page is viewed (Mccoy, Everard, Polak, & Galletta, 2007). In in-image adverting models, the ads are inserted into the most non-intrusive positions within the image. These positions are detected based on image saliency analysis.

An effective advertising system is able to maximize contextual relevance while minimizing content intrusiveness at the same time. Therefore, it should be formulated as an optimization problem with each of the above rules as a constraint.

Without of loss of generality, the task of advertising optimization can be defined as the association of ads with insertion points in an image. Suppose we have an ad database A which contains N_a ads, represented by $A = \{a_i\}_{i=1}^{N_a}$, and we also have a set of candidate ad insertion points B which contains N_b points, represented by $B = \{b_j\}_{j=1}^{N_b}$. Let $R(a_i, b_j)$ denote the contextual relevance between each ad a_i and point b_j, while $I(a_i, b_j)$ denote the content intrusiveness. The objective of contextual advertising is to maximize the overall contextual relevance $R(A, B)$ while minimizing the overall intrusiveness $I(A, B)$. The following design variables can be introduced for problem formulation, i.e., $x \in R^{Nb}$, $y \in R^{Na}$, $x = [x_1, ..., x_{Na}]^T$, $x_i \in \{0,1\}$, and $y = [y_1, ..., y_{Nb}]^T$, $y_j \in \{0,1\}$, where x_i and y_j indicate whether a_i and b_j are selected ($x_i = 1$, $y_j = 1$) or not ($x_i = 0$, $y_j = 0$) in A and B. Given the number of ads N to be inserted in an image, the above expectation can be formulated as the following nonlinear 0-1 integer programming problem (NIP):

$$\max_{\{(x_i, y_j)\}} f(x, y) = \alpha \sum_{i=1}^{N_a} \sum_{j=1}^{N_b} x_i y_j R(a_i, b_j) - \beta \sum_{i=1}^{N_a} \sum_{j=1}^{N_b} x_i y_j I(a_i, b_j)$$
$$= \alpha x^T R y - \beta x^T I y$$

$s.t.$

$$\sum_{i=1}^{N_a} x_i = N, \qquad x_i \in \{0,1\},$$
$$\sum_{j=1}^{N_b} y_j = N, \qquad y_j \in \{0,1\},$$

$$(1)$$

where $\mathbf{R} \in R^{Na \times Nb}$, $\mathbf{R} = [\ R_{ij}\ ]$, $R_{ij} = R(a_i,\ b_j)$, and $\mathbf{I} \in R^{Na \times Nb}$, $\mathbf{I} = [\ I_{ij}\ ]$, $I_{ij} = I(a_i,\ b_j)$, α and β are two weights for linear combination.

KEY PROBLEMS

Since the ads are embedded within an image automatically, how to alleviate the intrusiveness is one of the most important things for in-image advertising. If the users feel the ads are intrusive when they are viewing the image, they will be very unhappy, and hate the ads, the ad-networks, and even the advertisers. In order to alleviate the intrusiveness, we should seamlessly embed the ads into the non-salient region of the image, and the ads will disappear after a while. Furthermore, the ads should keep the relevance to the images as much as possible. So that audiences who are actually interested in this photo may have the same interest on the embedded product or service.

In the following sections, we will discuss how to alleviate the intrusiveness and improve the ad relevance.

Insertion Point Detection

Note that in-image advertising system will embed the contextually relevant ads at certain spatial positions within an image. We aim to find the non-intrusive ad positions within an image and select the ads whose logos are visually similar or have similar visual style to the image, in order to minimize intrusiveness and improve user experience. Specifically, the candidate ad insertion positions are detected based on the combination of image saliency map and face detection, while visual similarity is measured on the basis of HSV color feature.

Given an Image $\mathbf{I}$ which is represented by a set of blocks $\boldsymbol{B} = \{b_i\}_{i=1}^{N_b}$, a saliency map $\mathbf{S}$ representing the importance of the visual content is extracted for image $\mathbf{I}$, by investigating the effects of contrast in human perception (Ma & Zhang, 2003). Figure 3 (d) shows an example of the saliency map of an image. The brighter the pixel in the salience map, the more salient or important it is. However, saliency map predominantly focuses on modeling visual attention while neglects face in images. In fact, face usually presents informative content in an image. A product logo should not overlay the areas with face. Motivated by this assumption, we perform face detection (Li, Zhu, Zhang, Blake, Zhang, & Shum, 2002) for each image and obtain the face areas. We then overlay the saliency map $\mathbf{S}$ with detected face areas by a *max* operation. In this way, a combined saliency map $\mathbf{C}$ is obtained in which the value of each pixel indicates the overall salience for ad insertion. Figure 3 (c) shows the combined saliency map of the original image in Figure 3 (a).

Intuitively, the ads should be embedded at the most non-salient regions in the combined saliency map $\mathbf{C}$, so that the informative content of the image will not be occluded and the users may not feel intrusive. Meanwhile, the image block set $\mathbf{B}$ is obtained by partitioning image $\mathbf{I}$ into $M \times M$ grids. Each grid corresponds to a block b_i ($i=1, 2, \ldots, N_b$) where $N_b = M^2$, and also a candidate ad insertion point. Consequently, there are N_b candidate ad insertion points in total. For each block b_i, a combined saliency energy c_i ($0 \leq c_i \leq 1$) is computed by averaging all the normalized energies of the pixels within b_i. As the combined saliency map $\mathbf{C}$ does not consider the spatial importance for ad insertion, a weight map $\mathbf{W} = \{w_i\}$ ($i=1, 2, \ldots, N_b$) is designed to weight the energy c_i, so that the ads will be inserted into the corners or sides rather than center blocks. Figure 3 (d) and (e) show an example of the weight map and $w_i \times (1-c_i)$, respectively. Therefore, $w_i \times (1-c_i)$ indicates the suitability of block b_i for embedding an ad.

Figure 3. An example of detecting candidate ad positions in an image. (a) **I***: original image, (b) face detection result, (c)* **C***: combined saliency map, (d)* **W***: weight map, (e) final saliency map, (f) the most nonintrusive candidate ad position. The brighter the pixel in the saliency map (c), the more important or salient it is; while the brighter each block in (e), the more likely it is a candidate ad position. The highlighted rectangle in (f) is obtained from (e). We use 5×5 for illustration in this figure*

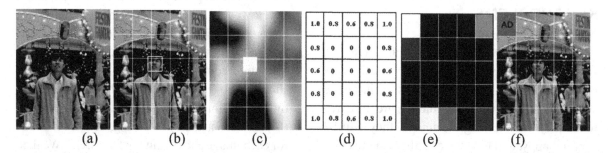

| (a) | (b) | (c) | (d) | (e) | (f) |

Multimodal relevance

In general, people won't like the ads shown on the images, but if the ads are relevant to the images, the viewers may feel them useful and follow the links to get more information from the advertisers. In order to find the most relevant ads, we adopt multimodal relevance measure including topical, visual and user relevance.

Topical Relevance

In order to fully utilize the textual information and alleviate the noises, we adopt a LDA-based topic-level model to perform the topic matching between ads and images. Latent Dirichlet Allocation (LDA) is a generative probabilistic model of a corpus. The documents D are represented as random mixtures over latent topics, where each topic is characterized by a distribution over words.

Let a word w be a unit-basis vector with the i-th component equal to one and all other components equal to zeros, if it is the i-th word in the vocabulary. A document $d \in D$ is now considered to be a sequence of n words denoted by $\mathbf{d}=(w_1, w_2, \ldots, w_n)$, where w_i is the i-th word in the sequence. LDA assumes the following generative process for each document $\mathbf{d}$ in a corpus D:

1. Choose $n \sim \text{Poisson}(\xi)$
2. Choose $\theta \sim \text{Dir}(\alpha)$
3. For each of the n words w_i
   a. Choose a topic $z_i \sim \text{Multinomial}(\theta)$
   b. Choose a word w_i from $p(w_i|z_i, \beta)$, a multinomial probability conditioned on the topic z_i

The probability density of a k-dimensional Dirichlet distribution is defined as:

$$Dir(\theta; \alpha) = \frac{\Gamma(\sum_{i=1}^{k} \alpha_i)}{\prod_{i=1}^{k} \Gamma(\alpha_i)} \prod_{i=1}^{k} \theta_i^{\alpha_i - 1} \qquad (2)$$

where $\alpha = (\alpha_1, \ldots, \alpha_k)$ is the parameter of this density. Given the parameters α and β, the joint distribution of a topic mixture θ, a set of n topic $\mathbf{z}$, and a set of n words $\mathbf{d}$ is given by:

$$p(\theta, \mathbf{z}, \mathbf{d} \mid \alpha, \beta) = p(\theta \mid \alpha) \prod_{i=1}^{n} p(z_i \mid \theta) p(w_i \mid z_i, \beta) \qquad (3)$$

Integrating over θ and summing over z, we obtain the marginal distribution of a document:

$$p(\mathbf{d} \mid \alpha, \beta) = \int p(\theta \mid \alpha)(\prod_{i=1}^{n}\sum_{z_i} p(z_i \mid \theta)p(w_i \mid z_i, \beta))d\theta \tag{4}$$

Thus, the posterior distribution of the hidden variables given a document is:

$$p(\theta, \mathbf{z} \mid \mathbf{d}, \alpha, \beta) = \frac{p(\theta, \mathbf{z}, \mathbf{d} \mid \alpha, \beta)}{p(\mathbf{d} \mid \alpha, \beta)} \tag{5}$$

Although Equation (5) computationally intractable, the variational inference can provide a close approximation to the model parameters. Through the inference, each document $d_i \in D$ is finally represented by a Dirichlet distribution over the mixture of latent topics, with the optimized posterior parameter γ_i

In this topic-level model, a query and a document are considered to be relevant if they have similar distributions over latent topics. Here, we use the Kullback-Leibler (KL) divergence (Kullback & Leibler, 1951) to measure the similarity of two distributions. The KL divergence of two k-dimensional Dirichlet distributions (i.e., $Dir(\theta; \gamma q)$ and $Dir(\theta; \gamma d)$) is define as

$$KL_{Dir}(\gamma^q; \gamma^d) = \log \frac{\Gamma(\sum_{i=1}^{k}\gamma_i^q)}{\Gamma(\sum_{i=1}^{k}\gamma_i^d)}$$
$$+\sum_{i=1}^{k}\log\frac{\Gamma(\gamma_i^d)}{\Gamma(\gamma_i^q)} + \sum_{i=1}^{k}[\gamma_i^q - \gamma_i^d][\Psi(\gamma_i^q) - \Psi(\sum_{j=1}^{k}\gamma_j^q)] \tag{6}$$

where $\Gamma(x)$ is the Gamma function. $\Psi(x)$ is the first derivative of $\log\Gamma(x)$, which can be approximated via Taylor expansion. As the KL divergence is asymmetry, the semantic similarity between q_i and d_j is finally defined as:

$$sim(i,j) = \exp\left(-\frac{1}{2}\left(KL_{Dir}\left(\gamma^i; \gamma^j\right) + KL_{Dir}\left(\gamma^j; \gamma^i\right)\right)\right) \tag{7}$$

The estimated parameters α, β and document-specific parameters $\gamma^i(i=1,\dots,N)$ are kept in the text model for calculating the similarity between the query and the document.

Let $\mathbf{I}^{(T)}$ denote the textual information of Image $\mathbf{I}$, the topic relevance $R_t(\mathbf{I}, a_j)$ is given by

$$R_t(\mathbf{I}, a_j) = sim(\mathbf{I}^{(T)}, a_j^{(T)}) \tag{8}$$

By considering $\mathbf{I}^{(T)}$ as the query and $a_j^{(T)}$ as the document, we can rank the ads with regard to the image $\mathbf{I}$.

Visual Relevance

The ads are assumed to have similar appearance with the neighboring blocks around the insertion position, so that the users may perceive the ads as a natural part of original image. To measure the visual similarity between the ad a_j and ad insertion position b_i, we compute the L_1 distance between $a_j^{(V)}$ and the neighboring block set B_i of b_i.

The distance is defined in a HSV color space which has been widely adopted in visual content retrieval and search systems, given by

$$d(B_i, a_j^{(V)}) = \frac{1}{|B_i|}\sum_{b_i \in B_i} L_1\left(f^{(b_i)} - f^{(a_j)}\right) =$$
$$\frac{1}{|B_i|}\sum_{b_i \in B_i}\sum_{k=1}^{K}\left|f^{(b_i)}(k) - f^{(a_j)}(k)\right| \tag{9}$$

where $|B_i|$ denotes the number of blocks adjacent with b_i, $f^{(b_i)}(k)$ and $f^{(a_j)}(k)$ denote the k-th color feature of block b_i and ad a_j, respectively. K is the feature dimension. For example, if we use a 64-dimensional HSV color histogram to describe the visual content, then $K=64$. As a result, the local content relevance $R_c(b_i, a_j)$ between a candidate ad insertion point b_i and ad a_j is given by

$$R_c(b_i, a_j) = w_i \times (1 - c_i) \times \left(1 - d\left(B_i, a_j^{(V)}\right)\right) \quad (10)$$

User Relevance

Because users who are looking at the images and the associated ads are the potential customers, delivering user-targeted ads for in-image advertising is believed as an effective way. Therefore, the rank of ads is decided not only by the topic matching between the tags of image and the ad's text information, but also by the topic matching between the user's interests and the ad's topics. The users are assumed to be grouped into a set of predefined interest groups or provide their profile in advance, and then the ads falling into the users' interest will be delivered based on classification techniques. It may be formalized:

$$\Phi : P \times C \rightarrow \{T, F\} \quad (11)$$

Where $C = c_i (i=1,2,..,N_c)$ is a predefined set of categories and P is a set of user preference $p_j \in P$. The task should be a multi-label task, i.e. any number $0 \leq n_j \leq N_c$ categories may be assigned to a user preference. We can learn a classifier trained by text categorization techniques based on Support Vector Machine (SVM). Therefore, $R_u(p,x)$ is given by

$$R_u(p, x) = sim(p^{(T)}, x^{(T)}) \quad (12)$$

where $p^{(T)}$ is the text information in user profiles.

Based on user relevance, the ads are expected to be relevant to user profile, interest, location, click-through, historical behavior (e.g., travel traces), and so on.

EXEMPLARY SYSTEMS

ImageSense

Figure 4 illustrates the system framework of ImageSense. Given a Web page which contains some images, a vision-based page segmentation algorithm is applied to partition the page into several blocks each with consistent content. The images suitable for advertising are then selected by an image filtering module and then represented by visual content and surrounding text (such as titles and descriptions) within the corresponding page blocks. A textual relevance matching module ranks the ads based on a LDA model according to the textual relevance between the ads and the content of Web page and images. The textual information of each image comes from the text of the Web page, the surrounding text in the corresponding page block, the expansion words of the surrounding text, and automatically recognized concepts (a set of predefined categories) based on visual content analysis. Meanwhile, the candidate ad insertion positions are detected in each image through visual salience analysis and face detection. Intuitively, the ads are to be embedded in the unimportant areas within the image. The relevant ads will be reranked by simultaneously considering local content relevance which is derived from the visual similarity between each ad and ad insertion position, as well as the intrusiveness of ad insertion position. Finally, the most contextually relevant ads will be embedded at the most non-intrusive position within each image by an ad displaying module.

GameSense

In addition to the standard in-image advertising, we also provide a game-like in-image advertising

Figure 4. System framework of ImageSense

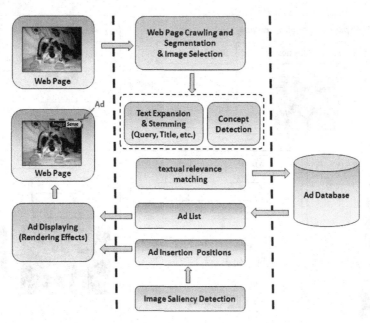

model dedicated to image on the basis of gaming form, called GameSense, which supports creating a game from an online image and associates relevant ads within the game. Compared with other media forms such as text, image, and video, games are more attractive and can deliver much more enjoyable experience to users. Using game as an advertising carrier, users can get more involved with image contents so that ad impression can be significantly promoted at the same time. If the ads related to image content can be embedded during the game, it would be a new perspective for advertising. We use "sliding puzzle" game as a demonstration in GameSense.

GameSense usually consists of four major components: Web page processing engine, ad ranking engine, ad insertion point detection, and game engine. Figure 5 illustrates the overview framework of GameSense. Web page processing engine selects suitable images and extracts surrounding text by Web page layout analysis. Ad insertion point detection component detects the most non-salient area for ad insertion through visual salience analysis, face, and caption detec-

tion. The ranking engine ranks the ads according to textual and visual relevance between the ads and the images. The game engine creates a Flash or Silverlight game and delivers it to client browser.

To create a "sliding puzzle" from an image, the image is partitioned into 4×4 or 5×5 pieces in a random order with one missing as the empty space. The objective of the game is to place the pieces in order by making sliding moves with the empty space. The last piece will be displayed automatically once the other pieces have been lined up. A relevant ad is embedded in this empty space when gamers slide the pieces to figure out the whole image. Inspired by Google Image Labeler, besides the single-player mode, the game can run in the two-player mode which allows gamers to form pairs randomly and compete to solve the same sliding puzzles. Client games interact with a Web Service on the GameSense server to update the playing status. The gamers can see their score for the game and their individual cumulative score to date. These are compared to the daily top scores and the all-time high scores. Gamers' competitiveness to rack

Figure 5. System framework of GameSense

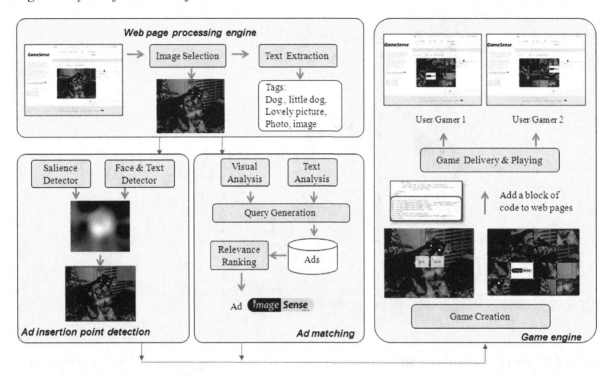

up high scores will make them spend more time in the game which can increase the effect of the advertising campaign.

EXPERIMENTS

Because GameSense is a special case of in-image advertising, we only evaluated the effectiveness of general in-image advertising model, i.e. ImageSense from the perspective of ad relevance.

Data and Methodology

In ImageSense, we set $M = 5$ so that there are 16 candidate ad insertion points. Note that the blocks with the weight "0" are neglected. In conventional evaluations on textual relevance (Broder, Fontoura, Josifovski, & Riedel, 2007) (Ribeiro-Neto, Cristo, Golgher, & de Moura, 2005), the number of relevant ads is usually fixed to three (i.e., $N = 3$), while we have set $N = 5$ for evaluat-

ing ad relevance in ImageSense, as well as $N_{a'} = 100$. For concept text, we only selected the top five concept words according to the confidence scores as current performance of concept detection is still not satisfying. A large-scale and general concept ontology rather than the one used in TRECVID will help improve relevance matching within the same framework. As there are currently very few ad-networks supporting real collection of ads with product logos, we have collected around 7,285 unique ad product logos from innovativeclipart.com. We invited 20 subjects to annotate each product logo (i.e., *title*, *keywords*, *description*, and *hyperlink*).

We prepared three photo-sharing sites with around one million high-quality photos in total. To evaluate ad relevance, the 100 representative top image queries from Live image search were put to the three sites as the queries and the top 10 images were returned for each query. As a result, there are 1,000 images and the corresponding surround texts.

In addition, similar to text advertising (Broder, Fontoura, Josifovski, & Riedel, 2007) (Lacerda, Cristo, Goncalves, Fan, Ziviani, & Ribeiro-Neto, 2006) (Ribeiro-Neto, Cristo, Golgher, & de Moura, 2005), we quantified the effect of ImageSense supporting Web page-based advertising using a set of 100 Web pages. These pages were selected from the most recent news in several major news web sites, such as Yahoo!, CNN, MySpace, as well as the popular pages in several major photo-sharing web sites, such as Flickr, photoSIG. Consequently, there were 1,100 triggering pages including 1,000 images and 100 pages used as the test bed. For each triggering page, we returned the top five ad logos by the following advertising strategies for evaluation, which is similar to the experimental settings for general Web page advertising (Lacerda, Cristo, Goncalves, Fan, Ziviani, & Ribeiro-Neto, 2006) (Ribeiro-Neto, Cristo, Golgher, & de Moura, 2005).

Usually, user's interest and profile are not easy to obtain. We conduct the evaluation only based on the topical and visual relevance. In order to contrast with conventional online advertising which matches ads with image only based on textual information of the whole web page without considering the intrinsic characteristics of the image content, we extend the general relevance items(i.e. topical relevance and visual relevance), and introduce the following three relevance items for each advertisement.

- **Global textual relevance** $R_g(\mathbf{P}, a_j)$—the textual relevance between the Web page $\mathbf{P}$ and ad a_j, which is given by the cosine similarity in the vector space model, as in most of conventional advertising systems. Since $\mathbf{P}$ is always given, we can drop $\mathbf{P}$ and rewrite such relevance as $R_g(a_j)$.
- **Local textual relevance** $R_l(\mathbf{I}, a_j)$—the textual relevance between the image $\mathbf{I}$ and ad a_j, where the text associated with $\mathbf{I}$ comes from not only the surrounding text in the corresponding page block, but also the hidden concepts recognized by visual content analysis. Since $\mathbf{I}$ is always given, we can also drop $\mathbf{I}$ and rewrite such relevance as $R_l(a_j)$.
- **Local content relevance** $R_c(b_i, a_j)$—the combination of content-based visual similarity between the ad insertion block b_i and ad a_j and the non-intrusiveness of b_i for inserting the ads. To minimize intrusiveness to the user, the ads are to be inserted into the most non-intrusive positions, and to be similar to the corresponding neighboring image blocks.

According to the general equation (1), we have the following nonlinear 0-1 integer programming problem (NIP) for ImageSense. Suppose we introduce the following design variables $x \in \mathbf{R}^{Nb}$, $y \in \mathbf{R}^{Na}$, $x = [x_1, \ldots, x_{Nb}]^T$, $x_i \in \{0,1\}$, and $y = [y_1, \ldots, y_{Na}]^T$, $y_j \in \{0,1\}$, where x_i and y_j indicate whether b_i and a_j are selected ($x_i=1$, $y_j=1$) or not ($x_i=0$, $y_j=0$). The above expectation can be formulated as:

$$\max_{\{(x_i, y_j)\}} f(\mathbf{x}, \mathbf{y})$$

$$= w_g \sum_{j=1}^{N_a} y_j R_g(a_j) + w_\ell \sum_{j=1}^{N_a} y_j R_\ell(a_j) + w_c \sum_{i=1}^{N_b} \sum_{j=1}^{N_a} x_i y_j R_c(b_i, a_j)$$

$$= w_g \mathbf{y}^T \mathbf{R}_g + w_\ell \mathbf{y}^T \mathbf{R}_\ell + w_c \mathbf{x}^T \mathbf{R}_c \mathbf{y}$$

$$s.t.$$

$$\sum_{i=1}^{N_b} x_i = N,$$

$$x_i \in \{0,1\},$$

$$\sum_{j=1}^{N_a} y_j = N,$$

$$y_j \in \{0,1\},$$

$$(13)$$

where $\mathbf{R}_g = [R_g(a_1), R_g(a_2), \ldots, R_g(a_{Na})]^T$, $\mathbf{R}_l = [R_l(a_1), R_l(a_2), \ldots, R_l(a_{Na})]^T$, $\mathbf{R}_c \in \mathbf{R}^{Nb \times Na}$. The parameters (w_g, w_l, w_c) control the emphasis on global and local textual relevance, as well as local content relevance, and satisfy the constraints: $0 \leq w_g, w_l, w_c \leq 1$ and $w_g + w_l + w_c = 1$. The parameters of (w_g, w_l, w_c) can be empirically set to $w_c < w_g < w_l$, as it is reasonable to assume that textual relevance is more important than image content relevance (He, Cai, Wen, Ma, & Zhang, 2007). Alternatively, the parameters can be trained by cross-validation experiments.

Note that the following results were produced according to different settings of the parameters in equation (13).

- **I: Global textual relevance** (w_g=1, w_l=0, w_c=0). This is similar to conventional contextual advertising in which the ads are selected according to the generic content of the Web page (Ribeiro-Neto, Cristo, Golgher, & de Moura, 2005). This is used as the baseline for comparison.
- **II: Global and local textual relevance without concept** (w_g=0.3, w_l=0.5, w_c=0, $\mathbf{I}^{(T)}=\mathbf{I}^{(T1 \cup T2)}$). In addition to global textual relevance, local textual relevance based on Web page segmentation and image block detection is also taken into account, while concept text is neglected.
- **III: Global and local textual relevance** (w_g=0.3, w_l=0.5, w_c=0, $\mathbf{I}^{(T)}=\mathbf{I}^{(T1 \cup T2 \cup T3)}$). Both global and local textual relevance is linearly combined for ad ranking, with concept text included in the computation of local textual relevance.
- **IV: Global and local textual relevance, as well as local content relevance, with different weights to IV** (w_g=0.33, w_l=0.33, w_c=0.33). All the relevance including global and local textual relevance, as well as local content relevance, is linearly combined. The weights are empirically set to be equal for comparison, as we aim to investigate the different contributions of the multimodal relevance for in-image advertising.
- **V: Global and local textual relevance, as well as local content relevance** (w_g=0.3, w_l=0.5, w_c=0.2). All the relevance including global and local textual relevance, as well as local content relevance, is linearly

combined. Note that the weights are set different according to different contributions from the multimodal relevance. Intuitively, the local textual relevance is more important than global relevance as it is derived from the page block near to the image, while global relevance is more important than local content relevance as the low-level content features cannot preserve the semantics of image. This strategy is the optimal setting of ImageSense.

Evaluation on Ad Relevance

According to the above five settings, there were totally 27,500 (1100×5×5) page-ad pairs. Fifteen subjects including 7 males and 8 females, with different background were invited to manually judge the page-ad relevance. The human subjects are university students, teachers, medical people, IT people and finance people. All the subjects' ages range from 19 to 40. These subjects did not know by which among the above five strategies the current results were produced. Each page-ad pair has been judged by three or more subjects on a 1-3 scale, that is, irrelevant (1), somewhat relevant (2) and relevant (3) (Broder, Fontoura, Josifovski, & Riedel, 2007). We assumed that the page-ad pairs judged with "2" or "3" are positive and those judged with "1" are negative.

Figure 6 shows the precision-recall curves of the five strategies. We used 11-point average figures to quantify the precision (Ribeiro-Neto, Cristo, Golgher, & de Moura, 2005). We can also see that strategy III and V achieved the best performance in terms of relevance, while strategy IV underperformed V. This has proved the assumption on different contributions from different kinds of textual information---the local surround texts of the images and their expansion words are more important than the general Web page content and visual content from the perspective of ad relevance. We believe an optimal set

Figure 6. Precision-recall curves

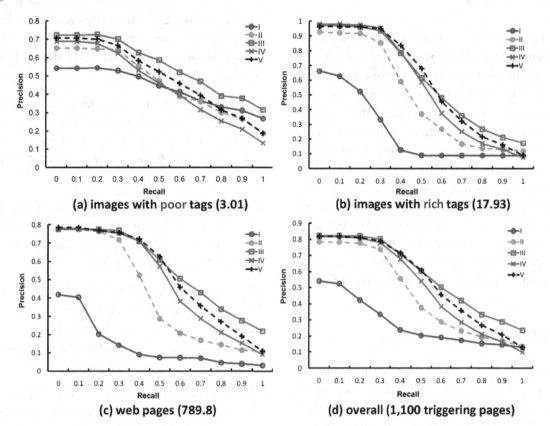

(a) images with poor tags (3.01)

(b) images with rich tags (17.93)

(c) web pages (789.8)

(d) overall (1,100 triggering pages)

of parameters of (w_g, w_p, w_c) can further improve the advertising performance.

FUTURE RESEARCH DIRECTIONS

Image has become one of the most compelling aspects of online media properties. With the right strategy and the right technology for advertising, we can start using the power of image to build value in any Web site, page, and image. In this work, we have gone one step further from existing online advertising and proposed ImageSense and GameSense as the ones of first attempts towards in-image advertising. To the best of our knowledge, this is one of the first works showing how visual content analysis at different levels (i.e., low-level appearance and high-level semantic) can yield more effective image advertising, especially

from the perspectives of ad position detection and multimodal relevance. We believe that there is rich potential for future research. From the point of view of ad relevance, future work includes: 1) selecting the ads not only visually similar to the surrounding image blocks but also with the similar style to the Web page, so that the intrusive experience can be further minimized, 2) leveraging more visual concepts for ad matching, especially an ontology dedicated for advertisements, 3) making the ads user-targeted in terms of demographic (Hu, Zeng, Li, Niu, & Chen, 2007), geo-location (Ahlers & Boll, 2008) (Chen, Lee, & Chang, 2006) (Kennedy, Naaman, Ahern, Nair, & Rattenbury, 2007), social context (Adams, Phung, & Venkatesh, 2006) (Aroyo, Nack, Schiphorst, Schut, & KauwATjoe, 2007), user behavior (Chatterjee, Hoffman, & Novak, 2003), and so on.

CONCLUSION

We have presented an innovative platform for in-image advertising. The platform is able to automatically decompose the Web page into several coherent blocks, select the suitable images from these blocks for advertising, detect the nonintrusive advertisement insertion positions within the images, and associate the relevant advertisements with these positions. In contrast to conventional ad-networks, in-image advertising is fully dedicated to image and aims to monetize the visual content rather than surrounding text. We formalize the association of advertisements with images as an optimization problem and show a practical solution over a large-scale of real-world data.

REFERENCES

Adams, B., Phung, D., & Venkatesh, S. (2006). Extraction of social context and application to personal multimedia exploration. In *Proceedings of the 14th annual ACM international conference on Multimedia* (pp. 987-996). New York: ACM.

Ahlers, D., & Boll, S. (2008). oh web image, where art thou? *International Conference on Multi-Media Modeling*.

Aroyo, L., Nack, F., Schiphorst, T., Schut, H., & KauwATjoe, M. (2007). Personalized ambient media experience: move.me case study. In *Proceedings of Conference on Intelligent User Interfaces* (pp. 298-301).

Broder, A., Fontoura, M., Josifovski, V., & Riedel, L. (2007). A semantic approach to contextual advertising. In *Proceedings of the 30th annual international ACM SIGIR conference on Research and development in information retrieval* (pp. 559-566). New York: ACM.

Chatterjee, P., Hoffman, D. L., & Novak, T. P. (2003). Modeling the clickstream: Implications for web-based advertising efforts. *Marketing Science*, *22*(4), 520–541. doi:10.1287/mksc.22.4.520.24906

Chen, W.-Y., Lee, B. N., & Chang, E. Y. (2006). Fotowiki: distributed map enhancement service. *Proceedings of the 14th annual ACM international conference on Multimedia* (pp. 803-804). New York: ACM.

Dai, H., Zhao, L., Nie, Z., Wen, J.-R., Wang, L., & Li, Y. (2006). Detecting online commercial intention. In *Proceedings of International World Wide Web Conference*. ACM.

He, X., Cai, D., Wen, J.-R., Ma, W.-Y., & Zhang, H.-J. (2007). Clustering and searching WWW images using link and page layout. *ACM Transactions on Multimedia Computing, Communications, and, 3*(2).

Hu, J., Zeng, H.-J., Li, H., Niu, C., & Chen, Z. (2007). Demographic prediction based on user's browsing behavior. In *Proceedings of the 16th international conference on World Wide Web* (pp. 151-160). New York: ACM.

Joshi, A., & Motwani, R. (2006). Keyword generation for search engine advertising. In *Proceedings of the Workshops of IEEE International Conference on Data Mining*.

Kastidou, G., & Cohen, R. (2006). An approach for delivering personalized ads in interactive tv customized to both users and advertisers. In *Proceedings of European Conference on Interactive Television*.

Kennedy, L., Naaman, M., Ahern, S., Nair, R., & Rattenbury, T. (2007). How flickr helps us make sense of the world: context and content in community-contributed media collections. In *Proceedings of the 15th international conference on Multimedia* (pp. 631-640). New York: ACM.

Kullback, S., & Leibler, R. A. (1951). On information and sufficiency. *Annals of Mathematical Statistics*, 79–86. doi:10.1214/aoms/1177729694

Lacerda, A., Cristo, M., Goncalves, M. A., Fan, W., Ziviani, N., & Ribeiro-Neto, B. (2006). Learning to advertise. In *Proceedings of the 29th annual international ACM SIGIR conference on Research and development in information retrieval* (pp. 549-556). New York: ACM.

Li, H., Edwards, S. M., & Lee, J.-H. (2002). Measuring the intrusiveness of advertisements: scale development and validation. *Journal of Advertising*, *31*(2), 37–47.

Li, H., Zhang, D., Hu, J., Zeng, H.-J., & Chen, Z. (2007). Finding keyword from online broadcasting content for targeted advertising. *International Workshop on Data Mining and Audience Intelligence for Advertising.*

Li, S. Z., Zhu, L., Zhang, Z., Blake, A., Zhang, H.-J., & Shum, H. (2002). Statistical learning of multi-view face detection. In *Proceedings of European Conference on Computer Vision* (pp. 67-81). Copenhagen, Denmark.

Li, Z., Zhang, L., & Ma, W.-Y. (2008). Delivering online advertisements inside images. In *Proceedings of ACM Multimedia* (pp. 1051-1060). ACM.

Liao, W.-S., Chen, K.-T., & Hsu, W. H. (2008). Adimage: video advertising by image matching and ad scheduling optimization. In *Proceedings of ACM SIGIR conference on Research and Development in Information Retrieval* (pp. 767-768). ACM.

Ma, Y.-F., & Zhang, H.-J. (2003). Contrast-based image attention analysis by using fuzzy growing. In *Proceedings of ACM Multimedia* (pp. 374-381). ACM.

Mccoy, S., Everard, A., Polak, P., & Galletta, D. F. (2007). The effects of online advertising. *Communications of the ACM*, *50*(3), 84–88. doi:10.1145/1226736.1226740

Mehta, A., Saberi, A., Vazirani, U., & Vazirani, V. (2007). Adwords and generalized on-line matching. *Journal of the ACM*, *54*(5). doi:10.1145/1284320.1284321

Mei, T., Hua, X.-S., Yang, L., & Li, S. (2007). Videosense: Towards effective online video advertising. In *Proceedings of ACM Multimedia* (pp. 1075-1084). ACM.

Murdock, V., Ciaramita, M., & Plachouras, V. (2007). A noisy channel approach to contextual advertising. *International Workshop on Data Mining and Audience Intelligence for Advertising.*

Ribeiro-Neto, B., Cristo, M., Golgher, P. B., & de Moura, E. S. (2005). Impedance coupling in content-targeted advertising. In *Proceedings of the 28th annual international ACM SIGIR conference on Research and development in information retrieval* (pp. 496-503). New York: ACM.

Richardson, M., Dominowska, E., & Ragno, R. (2007). Predicting clicks: Estimating click-through rate for new ads. In *Proceedings of International World Wide Web Conference*. ACM.

Shen, D., Sun, J.-T., Yang, Q., & Chen, Z. (2006). Building bridges for web query classification. In *Proceedings of ACM SIGIR conference on Research and Development in Information Retrieval*. ACM.

Srinivasan, S. H., Sawant, N., & Wadhwa, S. (2007). vadeo: Video advertising system. In *Proceedings of ACM Multimedia* (pp. 455-456). ACM.

Yih, W.-T., Goodman, J., & Carvalho, V. R. (2006). Finding advertising keywords on web pages. *Proceedings of International World Wide Web Conference* (pp. 213-222). ACM.

KEY TERMS AND DEFINITIONS

Ad Insertion Point: It is a position where the advertisement will be associated and inserted.

Advertisement (ad): It is a public notice or announcement for attracting attention of the public, especially by paid announcements. It takes a variety of forms, including text, image, video, animation, or a combination of these forms.

Advertising: It is a form of communication that typically attempts to persuade potential customers to purchase or to consume more of a particular brand of product or service.

Image Advertisement: It is an image banner or rectangle created by advertisers manually that will be laid on a Web page, or product logos that will inserted into a source image or video.

Image Advertising: It is used for promoting the image, or general perception, of a product or service, rather than promoting its functional attributes. However, being different to the one defined in the field of general advertising, image advertising in this book chapter refers mainly to image-driven advertising which uses images as the commercial information carrier.

Informative Advertising: It is when advertising is carried out in an informative manner. It is a promotional effort at generating interest and credibility in a product, service, or organization by providing consumers with information.

Multimodal Relevance: It can be measured by the similarity between two documents in terms of various modalities including low-level aspects of visual data (such as the color and textures), some mid-level visual concept categories, high-level textual descriptions associated with the documents (such as user-provided tags, automatically recognized captions on the image), and so on.

Chapter 5
Argo:
Intelligent Advertising Made Possible from Images

Xin-Jing Wang
Microsoft Research Asia, China

Mo Yu
Harbin Institute of Technology, China

Lei Zhang
Microsoft Research Asia, China

Wei-Ying Ma
Microsoft Research Asia, China

ABSTRACT

In this chapter, we introduce the Argo system which provides intelligent advertising made possible from user generated photos. Based on the intuition that user-generated photos imply user interests which are the key for profitable targeted ads, Argo attempts to learn a user's profile from his shared photos and suggests relevant ads accordingly. To learn a user interest, in an offline step, a hierarchical and efficient topic space is constructed based on the ODP ontology, which is used later on for bridging the vocabulary gap between ads and photos as well as reducing the effect of noisy photo tags. In the online stage, the process of Argo contains three steps: 1) understanding the content and semantics of a user's photos and auto-tagging each photo to supplement user-submitted tags (such tags may not be available); 2) learning the user interest given a set of photos based on the learnt hierarchical topic space; and 3) representing ads in the topic space and matching their topic distributions with the target user interest; the top ranked ads are output as the suggested ads. Two key challenges are tackled during the process: 1) the semantic gap between the low-level image visual features and the high-level user semantics; and 2) the vocabulary impedance between photos and ads. We conducted a series of experiments based on real Flickr users and Amazon.com products (as candidate ads), which show the effectiveness of the proposed approach.

DOI: 10.4018/978-1-60960-189-8.ch005

1. INTRODUCTION

Due to the popularity of digital cameras and mobile phones in human life, billions of user-generated images were and are being uploaded to the Web. Photo sharing has become an everyday behavior of users. Using Flickr[1] as an example, as of November 2008, it claims to host more than 3 billion images. The availability of the huge amount of user-generated content (*UGC*) has motivated many interesting data mining researches and applications (Crandall, & Backstrom, et al., 2009; Plangprasopchok & Lerman, 2009).

Despite such a precious media format which glues people, how to monetize user-generated photos is still a seldom-touched question, which leaves the photos as well as photo sharing websites an uncovered gold mine. Li et al. (2008) proposed a method to deliver online ads along with Web images utilizing the downloading time of Web images, particularly when a Web image has a large file size and the network bandwidth is limited. The focus of this work is to develop an innovative way to non-intrusively embed ads into images in a visually pleasant manner, but it does not touch the relevance problem of advertising. Hua et al. (2008), on the other hand, proposed a so-called image Adsense approach. However, their main focus is intelligent placement of ads, which identifies an unimportant region of an image and displays an ad photo/logo in this region. The relevant ads, in their approach, are identified simply by matching the ads descriptions with the surrounding texts of the carrying image.

Motivated by the huge potential of monetizing user-generated photos on the Web, we attempt to develop an effective approach for intelligent advertising. The contribution of this chapter is twofold: Firstly, it is the first work which takes image visual content into account and attempts to suggest relevant ads based on both image content analysis and tag mining. It is known that many Web photos do not have any user-submitted tags or surrounding texts, therefore text-based ads selection (Hua, Mei, & Li, 2008) can only handle a very small portion of Web photos. Although image auto-annotation has been studied for decades, the problem of image understanding for advertising has many new challenges (Li, Zhang, & Ma, 2008). For example, even if users have tagged their photos, many tags are still not ready for use: not only there are many typos or unparsed phrases which are typical in UGC data, but also users prefer to use personal vocabulary to summarize the same main concepts, which results in the sparseness of tags. Moreover, the vocabulary of user-submitted tags is different from the vocabulary of ads, which is typically called *vocabulary impedance* (Ribeiro-Neto, & Cristo, M., et al., 2005), so that the recall of ads matching tends to be very low. Secondly, it suggests targeted ads based on user interest modeling from image content features rather than directly based on content or context analysis (Hua, Mei, & Li, 2008; Murdock, Ciaramita, & Plachouras, 2007; Lacerda, Cristo, M., et al., 2006).

In fact, user-generated photos tell about user interest either explicitly or implicitly. Generally people are unwilling to share their interest publicly by typing keywords and filling forms; however, the photos they took reveal their interest, because people tend to capture various objects or scenes that attract them. Figure 1 shows the screen shots of part of the photo galleries of three Flickr users, which illustrates that different users have very diverse interest.

We believe that users' interest is the key for targeted advertising which associates ads with user-generated content, and propose the *Argo* system which automatically detects a user's interest from his shared photos and suggests user-targeted ads. To our knowledge, though user interest discovery has been investigated in many previous work, most of them were targeting at the problems of personalized Web search (Trajkova & Gauch, 2004; Zhou, & Wu, S.-T., et al., 2006; Ma, Pant, & Sheng, 2007; Evans, & Fernandez, M., et al., 2006; Kim & Chan, 2003), browsing

Figure 1. Photos shared by three Flickr users, which shows that different users have different interest

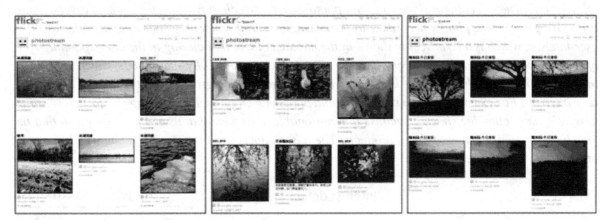

(Gunduz & Ozsu, 2003; Grcar, Mladenic, & Grobelnik, 2005), news articles or scientific paper finding (Chen, Chen, & Sun, 2002; Middleton, De Roure, & Shadbolt, 2001), etc., and none of them ever explored the market possibility of the user interest in query, document, or image monetization[2].

In this study, we focus on the problem of monetization of images and attempt to answer a challenging question: Can we automatically detect a user's interest from his shared photos and advertise accordingly? Figure 2 illustrates the mission. Given a user and his photo gallery, we discover his interest and suggest relevant ads. For example, user A uploaded a series of photos on lotus, so it is reasonable to assume that this user likes photography or flowers and hence we suggest photography-related products to him. Since user B shares many photos of children, most probably she will be interested in buying things for the children. Thus, it is profitable to suggest her related products. On the other hand, intuitively, a user may have various interests, e.g. user A uploaded diverse photos about lotus, snow mountain climbing and sculptures, so it is necessary to cluster the photos into different interest group and show adaptive ads for each group, as shown in Figure 2. However, we do not discuss the image grouping problem in this chapter for two reasons: 1) typically users will create albums

or photo streams when they upload their photos, which automatically provide a semantic grouping, and 2) in our implementation, we narrow down "a group of photos" to be "a page of photos (for a certain author)" and show adaptive ads based on each page, so that when a user browses though different pages, alternative ads may be shown even if the images on the current page share the same semantic concepts with the previous page. Such a strategy is advantageous not only in that it avoids the difficult and low-performance image clustering problem, but also it provides the opportunity for showing more ads. Meanwhile, it coincides with the browsing behavior supported by current photo sharing websites, e.g. Flickr. com, which displays users' photo collections in successive pages.

It is worth noting that we emphasize to learn a user interest from a set of photos because a user interest can be more reliably discovered from a group of semantically relevant photos than from one single photo. This is another variance to the previous image advertising approach (Li, Zhang, & Ma, 2008; Hua, Mei, & Li, 2008). We use an example to explain this point: If only one photo of a white cat is given, it is hard to tell whether the user is interested in white cats, cats, or pets. However, if photos about white cats and puppies are given simultaneously, it would be more con-

Figure 2. Sketch of the goal of Argo --- to detect a user's interest from his shared photos, and suggest relevant ads. The left column shows a user's photo gallery, which may contain photos of diverse concepts. We group these photos according to their semantics and for each group we detect the specific user interest, which is a term vector shown in the middle column associating to the corresponding row of grouped photos. According to a specific user interest, we automatically suggest ads, which are shown in the last column; each row of ads is associated to a corresponding group of photos (and its embedded user interest). For example, for the snow mountain photos taken by user A, we suggest "jacket", "snow glasses", and "climbing shoes", because it is reasonable to assume that user A likes sports so that he may be interested in buying related products. The ads products are from Amazon.com, which are real output of the Argo system

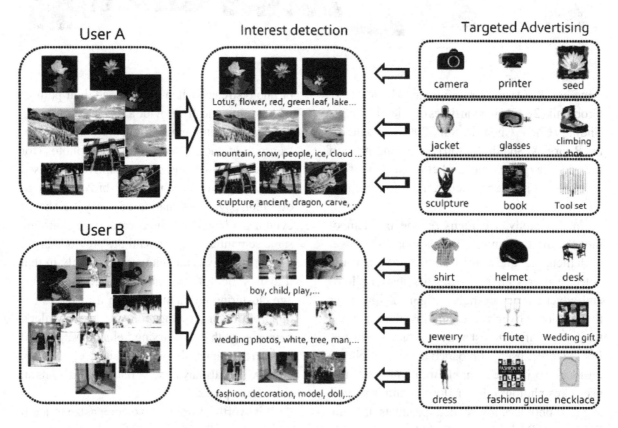

fident for us to conclude that the user is interested in pets.

The open question now is how to represent a user interest. Previous work defines a user interest in a variety of ways, e.g. Letizia et al. (1995) produced a bookmark-like list of Web pages; some researchers (Middleton, De Roure, & Shadbolt, 2001; Li, Guo, & Zhao, 2008) created a list of concepts or tags, while most researchers (Trajkova & Gauch, 2004; Kim & Chan, 2003;

Grcar, Mladenic, & Grobelnik, 2005; Ma, Pant, & Sheng, 2007; Zhou, & Wu, S.-T., et al., 2006) adopted a hierarchically-arranged collection of concepts, or ontology, with each node of the ontology representing a certain interest. We follow the method of Evans et al. (2006) which defines a user interest as a distribution, i.e. a vector of weights (numbers from 0 to 1), on the category nodes of an ontology. Each element of the vector shows the degree of interest for the corresponding category.

However, the differences of our method to (Evans, & Fernandez, M., et al., 2006) lie in that: 1) we only keep a few numbers of category nodes corresponding to the largest weights rather than the whole weight vector to represent a user interest. This intuitively will reduce noise. 2) Evans et al. (2006) used the domain-specific ontology of multimedia with the goal of personalized multimedia search, while we use a general ontology to tackle the problem of targeted advertising. Adopting a general ontology is important not only because ads themselves cover a large variety of concepts, but also because the concept space covered by user-generated photos is very rich and is large enough to describe the natural concepts of the webpage content (Li, Guo, & Zhao, 2008). 3) We use different method to represent a category node. We adopt the ontology of the Open Directory Project (ODP, http://dmoz.org/), and represent each node as a term distribution which is learnt from the web pages assigned to this node by human experts. Each category node is therefore called a "topic". In short, a user interest in our approach is defined as a topic distribution, while each topic is again a term distribution which represents certain semantics or concepts. We will detail this step in Section 3.2.2.

The entire approach of user interest learning and ads suggestion is conducted as follows: In an offline step, we learn a hierarchical topic space which supports real-time matching of textual queries. Then in the online stage, given a group of images (in one webpage), firstly we adopt a data-driven image annotation approach to automatically annotating each image. Secondly, we combine the generated annotations with user-submitted tags (if they are available) and use the combination as a query to match the hierarchical topic space. The output is a topic distribution to represent a user interest. Thirdly, a ranking model is applied to rank ads by their relevance to the user interest, and the top-ranked ads are returned as the suggestions. Figure 3 illustrates the process.

Note that we focus only on ads relevance while do not discuss the bidding problem in this research. Relevance is very important because current online advertising revenue is mainly based on user behaviors (Pay-Per-Click or Pay-Per-Action). Thus, the key to attract a user's click is to suggest ads which are relevant to either the user's information need or interest (Broder & Fontoura, et al., 2007; Chen, Xue, & Yu, 2008).

The remainder of this chapter is organized as follows. In Section 2 we detail the offline topic space learning method. In Section 3 the online advertising approach is described, which contains the entire process of image understanding (Section 3.1), user interest modeling (Section 3.2) and ads ranking (Section 3.3). We evaluate the proposed approach in Section 4 and draw the conclusion in Section 5.

2. LEARNING EFFICIENT TOPIC SPACE

Previous work has proven the effectiveness of a hierarchical ontology in learning user interest. Some researchers learnt ontology from users' browsing history, click-through data, or bookmarks, etc. (Kim & Chan, 2003; Grcar, Mladenic, & Grobelnik, 2005; Zhou, & Wu, S.-T., et al., 2006). Broder et al. leveraged the commercially built taxonomy by Yahoo!US (2007). And many other researchers adopted the publicly available ontology provided by ODP (Ma, Pant, & Sheng, 2007; Trajkova & Gauch, 2004; Chen, Xue, & Yu, 2008).

ODP is a manually edited directory. Currently it contains 4.6 million URLs that have been categorized into 787,774 categories by 68,983 human editors. A desirable feature is that for each category node of ODP, there is a large amount of manually chosen webpages that are freely available to be used for either learning a topic or categorizing a document at the query time. Therefore we build our hierarchical topic space based on the ODP tree

Figure 3. Argo system overview. Given a page of user photos, we adopt a data-driven annotation approach to auto-tagging each photo to supplement the user-generated tags. We combine these two types of tags and map the result to a hierarchical topic space learnt offline; the resulted topic distribution is assumed as the user interest. We map the ads textual descriptions to the same topic space, and rank them by measuring their relevance to the learnt user interest. The top-ranked ones are output as suggested ads. The suggested baby shampoo and clothes are real output of Argo

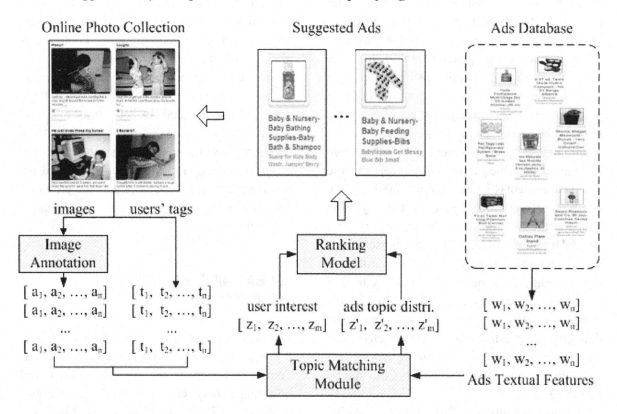

and learn a topic for each category node based on its associated webpages.

A straightforward way to learn such a topic is to represent each webpage attached to the corresponding category node in the vector space model (weighted by TF-IDF, for example), and average the weight vectors on all the webpages belonging to this category. The resulted feature vector thus defines a topic. However, this simple method has two disadvantages: 1) intuitively, many terms in the webpages are not related to the semantic concept of the target category. Therefore to reduce noise and ensure the locality of a topic (i.e. different topics have distinct term distributions), it is necessary to differentiate salient terms (or topic-specific terms) with noisy terms. 2) since there are nearly a million nodes in the ODP tree, if a query had to be matched sequentially with all the topics, it would be too time consuming and impractical for online advertising. Hence to support real-time matching between queries and topics, it is necessary to find an efficient solution.

To build a hierarchical topic space based on ODP which satisfies the above two requisitions is not a trivial task. In this work, we tackle the first difficulty by block-wise topic identification, and solve the second problem by building an inverted index based on the ODP tree.

2.1 Block-Wise Topic Identification

In the ODP tree, the webpages under the same node were chosen by human experts because they are about the same topic. It is reasonable to assume that there are two types of sentences among the webpages: topic-related sentences and topic-unrelated sentences. Typically, topic-related sentences will cover a small vocabulary with similar terms because they are similar to each other while topic-unrelated ones will have a much large and diverse term vocabulary. Motivated by this intuition, we propose a sentence importance measure to weight sentences according to their importance scores in interpreting the topic of the corresponding ODP category.

2.1.1 Sentence Importance

We call a sentence s_i is similar to sentence s_j if their cosine similarity is larger than a predefined threshold ε, and a sentence s is similar to a webpage d if at least one sentence of d is similar to s. We use $S(s,d)$ to denote this relationship, and we have $S(s,d)=1$ if s is similar to d, and $S(s,d)=0$ otherwise.

Based on this notation, we define a sentence frequency (SF) measure for the ith sentence s_i as Eq.(1):

$$SF_i = \sum\nolimits_{j=1}^{n} S(s_i, d_j) \tag{1}$$

where $\underline{n}$ is the total number of webpages associated with the ODP category under consideration, and d_j is the jth webpage.

Fundamentally, SF measures to what extent a sentence is consistent with the topic-related webpages in the feature space. Intuitively, the larger the frequency, the more important the sentence is in representing the topic of the corresponding category.

On the other hand, if a sentence s_i is also similar to webpages of other categories, then intuitively

this sentence is not important or even noisy to reflecting the topic, or topic-unrelated. We define an inverse webpage frequency (IWF) to quantify such an idea, which gives Eq.(2):

$$IWF_i = \log \frac{N}{\sum_{j=1}^{N} S\left(s_i, d_j\right)} \tag{2}$$

where N is the number of webpages randomly sampled from the ODP categories.

Based on these two measures, we define the sentence importance (SI) of a sentence s_i to be:

$$SI_i = \frac{SF_i \times IWF_i}{\sum_{j=1}^{n} SF_j \times IWF_j} \tag{3}$$

which is the normalized SF-IWF score. The higher the SI score, the more important the sentence is for a certain topic. The underlying idea is that a sentence is important for a certain category if it has a localized distribution, i.e. it has many near-duplicates in this category while has few in other categories. This formulation is very similar to the TF-IDF weighting scheme typically used in text search and mining area, which measures the importance of a term with respect to a document, whose basic idea is to assign a high weight to a term if it has a high frequency in this document and meanwhile a low frequency in the whole corpus. The same idea was adopted in the region importance learning method proposed by Jing et al. (2002) for region-based image retrieval, whose intuition is that a region is important if it is similar to many regions in other positive images, while it is less important if it is similar to many regions in both positive and negative images.

2.1.2 Topic Learning

Based on the proposed sentence importance score, we are able to separate topic-related sentences from topic-unrelated ones, and learn specific topics from the topic-related sentences.

To achieve this goal, we adopt a simple yet efficient block-wise topic identification method as below:

Firstly, we separate the content of each web-page into sentences[3] and represent each sentence in the vector space model. Secondly, for each category node, we cluster all the sentences in the webpages associated with this node using k-means algorithm. We define the cluster importance (CI) of the kth cluster CI_k as the average sentence importance:

$$CI_k = \frac{1}{M} \sum_{i=1}^{M} SI_i \qquad (4)$$

where M is the number of sentences in this cluster.

Since topic-related sentences tend to have a smaller vocabulary than topic-unrelated ones, they are more likely to be grouped into one cluster. Moreover, since they tend to have higher sentence importance scores, the corresponding cluster is more likely to have a higher cluster importance score, so that we rank the clusters based on their CI scores and keep the top one cluster for simplicity. Sentences in this cluster are thus assumed as isolated topic-related ones, and we build a new vector space model based on these sentences; the resulted TF-IDF-weighted vector is therefore the corresponding topic. We iterate such a process over all ODP categories [4], which results in a hierarchical topic space.

2.2 Efficient Topic Space Indexing

As aforementioned, to enable online usage of the topic space, we borrow the idea from general Web search to build an efficient topic index. Specifically, since each topic is represented as a TF-IDF-weighted term vector, we treat each topic as a document and upon which we build an inverted index to index all the topics, so that given a query term, all the topics that contain this term can be instantly fetched. When a query has multiple terms, exactly the same technique of general Web search is applied which outputs the ranked list of the intersection of the topics indexed by individual query terms.

In this way, we obtain a hierarchical topic space which supports large-scale topic indexing and matching.

3. ADVERTISING BY USER INTEREST MINING

This section details the online stage of image advertising, which contains three steps: 1) image content understanding, 2) user interest mining, and 3) ads matching and ranking.

3.1 Image Content Understanding

We adopt the data-driven approach, *Arista*, proposed by Wang et al. (2008) to annotate an image. Torralba et al. (2008) proposed a similar approach, but they did not leverage the available surrounding texts but use example images to recognize a new one. Unlike previous model-based image auto-tagging methods, this approach has two special advantages: 1) it annotates an image in real time, and 2) it supports open vocabulary.

Its basic idea is: If a large-scale image database is available so that for each new image we can find a duplicate in the database, then to annotate the new image, what we need to do is simply to copy the duplicate's textual descriptions. While in reality, since it is infeasible to obtain such a database, we instead find for a new image a set of visually and semantically similar images, or near-duplicates, and infer the annotations from their descriptions.

This, fundamentally, coincides with the idea of statistical image auto-annotation as shown in Eq.(5). The aim of image auto-annotation is to find a group of keywords $\mathbf{w}^*$ that maximizes the conditional distribution $p(\mathbf{w}|I_q)$, as described in Eq.(5a), where I_q is the uncaptioned query image and $\mathbf{w}$ are terms or phrases in the vocabulary. Applying the Bayesian rule, we obtain Eq.(5b), where Θ_q denotes the set of image search results, and $p(\mathbf{w}|\Theta_q)$ investigates the correlation between Θ_q and $\mathbf{w}$. If we assume that there is a hidden layer of "image topics" so that an image are represented as a mixture of the topics, and it is from these topics that terms are generated, we obtain Eq.(5c), where $\mathbf{t}$ represents a topic in the topic space.

$$
\begin{aligned}
w^* &= \operatorname*{argmax}_{\mathbf{w}} p\left(\mathbf{w}|I_q\right) \ldots (a) \\
&= \operatorname*{argmax}_{\mathbf{w}} p\left(\mathbf{w}|\Theta_q\right) \cdot p\left(\Theta_q|I_q\right) \ldots (b) \\
&\sim \operatorname*{argmax}_{\mathbf{w}} \left[\max_{\mathbf{t}} p\left(\mathbf{w}|\mathbf{t}\right) \cdot p\left(\mathbf{t}|\Theta_q\right)\right] \cdot p\left(\Theta_q|I_q\right) \ldots (c)
\end{aligned}
$$
$$(5)$$

Interestingly, this equation simulates exactly the process of "image search plus text mining". Since both these two steps have mature technologies to be finished in real time, this annotation approach can also be used online[5].

In summary, Arista (2008) works in the following way: 1) given an uncaptioned image, retrieving its similar images; 2) mining salient terms from the surrounding texts of the retrieval results; and 3) rejecting noisy terms and returning the remaining terms as the suggested annotations. This approach is based on 2.4 million high-quality web images crawled from a few photo forum websites, which generally have meaningful surrounding texts. For more details, please refer to Wang, X.-J., & Zhang, L., et al. (2008).

A typical character of user-generated photos is that they may also be tagged by the users. Fortunately this feature is also supported by Arista. The only change is in the image retrieval step. In this case, an image and some tags are given together as the query, and image search results are produced by first performing text-based image search given the query tags, followed with a visual-based re-ranking step to find both semantically and visually relevant images. The

$$
w^* = \operatorname*{argmax}_{\mathbf{w}} \left[\max_{\mathbf{t}} p\left(\mathbf{w}|\mathbf{t}\right) \cdot p\left(\mathbf{t}|\Theta_q\right)\right] \cdot p\left(\Theta_q|I_q, w_q\right)
$$
$$(6)$$

where $w_q w_q$ denote the query tags.

We call annotations resulted from Eq.(5) as *c-tag* (i.e. image content-based tag, which are auto-annotated tags using an image as a query) and those from Eq.(6) as *ck-tag* (i.e. image content plus keywords-based tag, which are auto-annotated tags using an image and its user-generated tags as query), and compare the quality of the two in the evaluation (see Section 4). To differentiate, we denote the user-submitted tags as *u-tags*. Note that not all photos have u-tags, and when such tags are available, we adopt Eq.(6) to annotate each image, otherwise we use Eq.(5).

3.2 User Interest Mining

3.2.1 Query Processing

Given an image, we construct a query (i.e. a term list) as follows: we combine its c-tags or ck-tags with the u-tags (if available), and remove the stopwords and do stemming, then we weight each remaining term with its TF-IDF score so that each image is represented in a textual feature vector. The DF score is given by taking all the images in the target page into consideration.

The reason that we make one query for each image rather than using all the images in a page is to avoid the long-query problem[6] (which will result in an inefficient search) and ensure enough topic search results. Recall that the general Web search technique is used to retrieve relevant topics.

3.2.2 User Interest Mining

We propose two methods to model the user interest given a page of his photos, namely the term distribution model and the topic distribution model.

3.2.2.1 Term Distribution Model

This is a naïve model which simply uses the TF-IDF-weighted term vector generated from the query to represent a user interest. It serves as the baseline method.

However, there are at least two key problems that will greatly degrade the effectiveness of the term distribution model. The first is the noisy tag problem. It is known that user-generated tags are usually noisy, while image annotation is still a challenging research topic which can neither provide 100 percent accurate tags. Since it is not able to differentiate noisy tags from accurate tags, the term distribution model is inevitably biased. The second problem is known as "vocabulary impedance" (Broder & Fontoura, et al., 2007; Ribeiro-Neto, & Cristo, M., et al., 2005; Chen, Xue, & Yu, 2008). It is known that there is not only a lexical gap but also a semantic gap between the vocabulary of ads and the vocabulary of general images. As an example of the lexical gap, a user tags his dog photo with his dog's name, while such a term is out of the ads' vocabulary. The semantic gap between ads and photos, however, is more complex. For example, it is reasonable to show advertisements from insurance companies when a photo collection contains car photos and car-related tags and meanwhile we do not know the car brand. Obviously, the term distribution model is not able to bridge the two types of gaps and hence degrades the relevance of ads matched to the learnt interest.

3.2.2.2 Topic Distribution Model

Topic distribution model, on the other hand, maps a query into a pre-learnt topic space and represent the query by a linear combination of the topics in this space. The coefficient vector thus represents the topic distribution of the query.

Many previous works have been proposed to tackle the vocabulary impedance. Some of them attempt to suggest additional keywords or refine the available ones. For example, Google's Adwords tool (2010) suggests new terms based on query logs and advertisers' logs. The WordTracker (2010) finds relevant keywords which co-occur in meta tags. Joshi et al. (2006) made use of near-by phrases in search results. Chen et al. (2008) leveraged the ontology structure to suggest relevant keywords. A few researchers adopted machine learning techniques to build the bridge between ads and documents. For example, Lacerda et al. (2006) associated ads with web pages via Genetic Programming. Broder et al. (2007) trained SVM and logistic regression classifiers to categorize both web pages and ads to a manually built taxonomy. Murdock et al. (2007) proposed a machine translation model to translate between ads and target pages. Intuitively, this type of methods also helps on handling the noisy tag problem.

In our approach, we leverage the ODP-based hierarchical topic space (see Section 2) to handle both the noisy tag problem and vocabulary impedance; it also allows an image to be assigned to multiple topics so that a user interest is represented as a topic distribution. The advantage of representing an image as a concept distribution rather than categorizing it to a certain concept as some previous work did (Grcar, Mladenic, & Grobelnik, 2005) is twofold. Firstly, the soft membership effectively handles textual ambiguities, e.g. "apple" can either represent a fruit or a computer brand. Secondly, it solves the semantic mismatch problem to a certain extend. For example, a photo on soccer matches is labeled as "soccer" and one of its suggested ads is "FIFA champion watch" since both of them have high weights on the concept "sports".

Now we describe the details of the topic distribution model. Its basic idea is to map a query to the hierarchical topic space and represent the user interest by a ranked list of the topics. Specifically, given a page of I_i be an image, and θj be the j-th topic. $T(Ii_j)$ is represented as the feature vector whose nonzero elements are the normalized similarity scores of the retrieved topics, i.e.

$$T\left(I_i\right) = [w_j\left(\theta_j\right) | \sum_j w_j\left(\theta_j\right) = 1, 0 \le w_j\left(\theta_j\right) \le 1]$$

(7)

where $w_j(\theta j_j)$ is the normalized score of θj. Such a feature vector represents the topic distribution of a photo. We iterate this process for each photo in the target page and then aggregate the topic distributions by summing ·their topic distribution vectors. We remove those topics whose weights are under a certain threshold; the resulted normalized topic distribution is used to represent the user interest.

Fundamentally, this ODP tree introduces a super-vocabulary, which is a superset of both the vocabulary of general images and that of ads, and therefore it enlarges the possibility that ads are matched to images which have semantically similar but lexically dissimilar textual descriptions. This explains why it can be used to solve vocabulary impedance. Moreover, this vocabulary is structuralized to define a semantic topic space; either an image or an ad is represented as a data point in this space.

3.3 Ads Matching and Ranking

Corresponding to the user interest models, we propose two ranking method to identify relevant ads. Moreover, a mixture model is presented based on these two models.

3.3.1 Direct Match Model (COS)

The direct match model (COS) is widely adopted (Ribeiro-Neto, & Cristo, M., et al., 2005; Hua, Mei, & Li, 2008). In this model, an ad is represented in the vector space model and COS simply measures the cosine similarity between the term distributions of photos and ads. This is used as a baseline method.

3.3.2 Topic Bridging Model (TB)

In this model, an ad is also mapped to the topic space and represented as a topic distribution. Then we score it by its cosine similarity to the user interest query which is also represented as a topic distribution. We rank all the ads in the descending order of their scores and the top ranked ones are returned for display. The entire process is shown in Figure 4.

3.3.3 Mixture Model

The TB model may be inferior to the COS model if the textual descriptions of photos and ads already suggest a good match. In this case, mapping the terms to an intermediate taxonomy may bring additional noise.

To address this issue, we propose a mixture model which performs a convex combination of the above two models. In particular, we measure the relevance of an ad ad_i to the query user interest q by Eq.(8):

$$Score_{mix(ad_i,q)} = \alpha * tb\left(ad_i, q\right) + \left(1 - \alpha\right) * \cos\left(ad_i, q\right)$$

(8)

where $tb(\cdot)$ and $\cos(\cdot)$ are the relevance scores output by TB and COS respectively. α is an empirically determined parameter which shows the confidence in $tb(\cdot)$. When α is set to zero, the model shrinks to COS, and when α is set to one, it is exactly TB.

4. EVALUATIONS

A series of experiments were conducted to evaluate the performance of the proposed approach, the

Figure 4. Given the learnt ODP-based topic space, we are able to build semantic connections between images and ads: Both user interests and ads are matched with the leaf topics, so that they are represented as topic distributions. The dotted lines suggest relevant matching with the leaf ODP topics, and the thickness suggests the relevance score. Ads ranking is then based on such representations

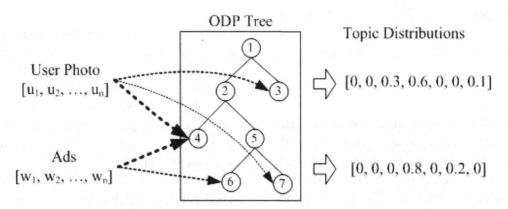

effect of auto-annotated tags, and the impact of the coefficient α in the mixture model.

We used 5,000 photos from Flickr.com to evaluate our method, which were uploaded by 25 Flickr users and are distributed in 420 pages. A large Amazon product set in July 2008 was downloaded for the evaluation, which contains about 20 million products belonging to 6,500 Amazon product categories. Each category is used as an ad campaign. We aggregate the title of each product in each *leaf* category as the corresponding ads description and construct one feature vector for that leaf category based on such a pseudo-document.

Given a query page of Flickr photos, we rank each leaf category and keep maximally the top three ones whose score is above a certain threshold; then we randomly select at most three products from each of the categories as the suggested ads. Comparing with the approach that matching photos directly with individual products, the intuition behind this method is that the products in the same leaf category have very close descriptions (e.g. the pants of the same brand, style and color but of different size). If we rank individual products, most probably the suggested ads will be dominated by a single category, which will result in poor user satisfaction.

Three volunteers were asked to mark each suggested ad as irrelevant, relevant or perfect. "Irrelevant" means an ad is a false-alarm. "Relevant" means an ad is somewhat relevant, and "perfect" means strong relevance.

Two metrics were used for the evaluation. One is Average Precision (AP) @ N which is the mean fraction of correct answers (i.e. relevant or perfect ads) in the top N results. Contrarily, to differentiate "perfect" suggestions from relevant ones for better understanding of the performance, the Weighted Average Precision (WAP) metric is adopted which is defined as Eq.(9):

$$WAP = (p + 0.5r) / (p + r + w) \qquad (9)$$

where p, r, w denote the number of "perfect", "correct" and "wrong" ads respectively.

4.1 The Performance

Figure 5 illustrates the average precision of the three ranking models versus the top N outputs on the evaluation groups of photos. Textual features used are the combinations of u-tags with ck-tags (i.e. "u-tag+ck-tag"). The mixture model was tuned to its best performance.

Figure 5. AP performance of the three ranking models on u-tag+ck-tag features vs. the top N ads. The mixture model performs the best

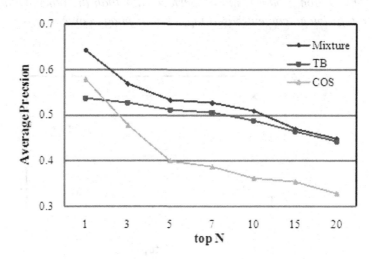

From Figure 5, it can be seen that the mixture model performs the best, while the TB model generally outperforms the COS model except for the top one result. This is probably because the vocabulary mismatch problem is not very severe in the top one result. This suggests that the image annotation system is effective so that the ck-tags had caught the semantics of the query images.

4.2 Effect of Different Textual Descriptions

Figure 6 illustrates the effect of different types of textual features of the images, namely "c-tag", "ck-tag", "u-tag plus c-tag", and "u-tag plus ck-tag". "c-tag", "ck-tag" and "u-tag" respectively stand for the annotation result that using an image only as the query, using both an image and a keyword as a query, and being provide by the user. The former two are purely based on Arista output, while the latter two combine the Arista output with the user-submitted tags. Note that when no u-tags are available for an image, we have equal c-tag and ck-tag. We ignore the case of "u-tag only" since some photos do not have

any u-tags. In this case, no ads will be suggested and the approach is meaningless.

From Figure 6, we can see that: 1) u-tag can help image understanding and hence improve the performance. 2) ck-tag is more effective than c-tag. Recall that a ck-tag is generated by leveraging the available u-tags in the annotation process, which helps bridge the semantic gap. This conclusion is consistent with the discoveries in Wang, X.-J., & Zhang, L., et al (2008). 3) The u-tag+ck-tag combination produces more "perfect" ads than the u-tag+c-tag combination and the rest since it significantly surpasses the others in terms of the WAP metric while they are comparable in terms of the AP metric.

4.3 Effect of Parameter α

Figure 7 shows the effect of the coefficient α on the mixture model at the top N results. WAP and the u-tag+ck-tag combination are used for this evaluation. The model obtains its best performance when α is between zero and one, which means that the mixture model performs the best. Moreover, when α is larger than 0.5, the performance drops

Figure 6. The effect of different types of tags on the TB model. The effectiveness of u-tag+ck-tag is comparable to u-tag+c-tag with the AP metric, but is significantly superior with the WAP metric. This means that such a combination produces more "perfect" ads than the other methods. (Note: u-tag: user-submitted tag, c-tag: image content-based tag, ck-tag: image content plus keywords-based tag. See Section 3.1.)

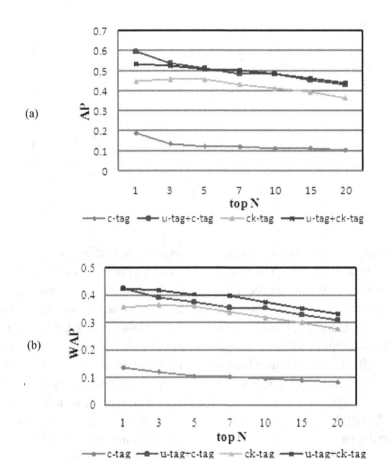

(a)

(b)

slowly as α increases, which suggests that TB is superior to COS.

5. CONCLUSION

Though image advertising market has turned to be non-negligible as photo sharing becomes popular, image monetization is still left as an isolated topic: No commercial search engines or photo sharing websites ever monetized such a media format, and even in the research area, few previous work has been proposed for image-based advertising.

We attempt to fill in this blank by this work. We have observed that user-generated photos imply user interests which are the fundamental basis for intelligent advertsing. Therefore we try to answer one question with this work: Can we learn a user's interest from his shared photos and apply targeted ads?

To answer this question, two key challenges must be addressed: 1) how to understand the

Figure 7. The effect of on the mixture model vs. the top N results. The "u-tags+ck-tags" features were used. It shows that the mixture model is the most effective, and BT generally works better than COS

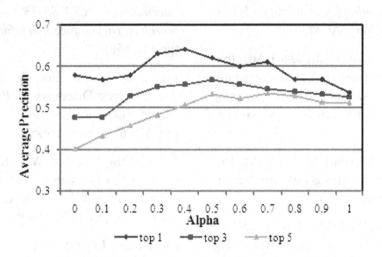

content and semantics of an image so that the user interest can be further discovered? and 2) how to bridge the vocabulary gap between user interests and ads?

We solved the first problem by adopting a search-based annotation method to understand each photo and learning a hierarchical topic space to model a user interest. An interest is represented as a topic distribution based on the learnt topic space, which is obtained by mapping the tags of the target set of photos onto the topic space. Moreover, to support efficient mapping, we indexed all the topics using the inverted index technique.

We addressed the second problem by representing both user interests and ads in the topic space and matching their similarities in this space. Each ad is then ranked by its topic similarity to the target user interest. Furthermore, a mixture model which combines topic matching and keyword matching was also proposed, which achieves the best performance. We evaluated our proposed approach on real Flickr photos and Amazon.com products, which have proven the effectiveness of the proposed method.

6. ACKNOWLEDGMENT

We thank Feng Jing and Xingrong Chen for the idea and implementation on the ODP-based topic space learning method.

7. REFERENCES

Badi, R. (2005). *Recognition and Representation of User Interest*. Unpublished master dissertation. Texas A&M University.

Broder, A., Fontoura, M., et al. (2007). A Semantic Approach to Contextual Advertising. In *Proceedings of the 30th annual international ACM SIGIR conference on Research and development in information retrieval* (pp. 559-566). New York: ACM.

Chen, C., Chen, M., & Sun, Y. (2002). PVA: A Self-Adaptive Personal View Agent. *Journal of Intelligent Information Systems*, 173–194. doi:10.1023/A:1013629527840

Chen, Y., Xue, G.-R., & Yu, Y. (2008). Advertising Keyword Suggestion Based On Concept Hierarchy. In *Proceedings of the international conference on Web search and web data mining* (pp. 251-260). New York: ACM.

Crandall, D., Backstrom, L., et al. (2009). Mapping the World's Photos. In *Proceedings of the 18th international conference on World Wide Web* (pp.761-770). New York: ACM.

Evans, A., Fernandez, M., et al. (2006). Adaptive Multimedia Access: From User Needs Semantic Personalization. In *Proceedings of IEEE International Symposium on Circuits and Systems* (pp. 2097-2100).

Google AdWords Keyword Tool. (2010). Retrieved from https://adwords.google.com/select/ *KeywordToolExternal*.

Grcar, M., Mladenic, D., & Grobelnik, M. (2005). User Profiling for Interest-focused Browsing History. In *Proceedings of SIKDD 2005 at Multiconference IS 2005*.

Gunduz, S., & Ozsu, M. (2003). A User Interest Model for Web Page Navigation. In *Proc. of Int. Workshop on Data Mining for Actionable Knowledge* (pp. 46-57).

Hua, X.-S., Mei, T., & Li, S. P. (2008). When Multimedia Advertising Meets the New Internet Era. *Intl Workshop on Multimedia Signal Processing.* (pp. 1-5).

Jing, F., Li, M., et al. (2002). Learning Region Weighting from Relevance Feedback in Image Retrieval. In *Proc. of IEEE Int. Conf. on Acoustics Speech and Signal* (Vol. 4, pp. 4088-4091).

Joshi, A., & Motwani, R. (2006). Keyword Generation for Search Engine Advertising. In *Proc. of the 6th IEEE Int. Conf. on Data Mining – Workshops.* (pp. 490-496).

Kim, H. R., & Chan, P. K. (2003). Learning Implicit User Interest Hierarchy for Context in Personalization. In *Proc. of International Conference on Intelligent User Interface* (pp. 101-108).

Lacerda, A., Cristo, M., et al. (2006). Learning to Advertise. In *Proceedings of the 29th annual international ACM SIGIR conference on Research and development in information retrieval.* (pp.549-556).

Li, X., Guo, L., & Zhao, Y. (2008). Tag-based Social Interest Discovery. In *Proceedings of the 17th international conference on World Wide Web* (pp. 675-684). New York: ACM.

Li, Z., Zhang, L., & Ma, W.-Y. (2008). Delivering Online Advertisements inside Images. In *Proceeding of the 16th ACM international conference on Multimedia* (pp. 1051-1060). New York: ACM.

Lieberman, H. (1995). Letizia: An Agent That Assists Web Browsing. In *Proc. of the International Joint Conference on Artificial Intelligence.* (pp. 924-929). Morgan Kaufmann Publishers Inc.

Ma, Z., Pant, G., & Sheng, O. (2007). Interest-Based Personalized Search. *ACM Transactions on Information Systems, 25*(1). doi:10.1145/1198296.1198301

Middleton, S., De Roure, D., & Shadbolt, N. (2001). Capturing Knowledge of User Preferences: Ontologies in Recommender Systems. In *Proceedings of the 2nd international conference on Knowledge capture* (pp. 62-69). New York: ACM.

Murdock, V., Ciaramita, M., & Plachouras, V. (2007). A Noisy-Channel Approach to Contextual Advertising. In *Proceedings of the 1st international workshop on Data mining and audience intelligence for advertising* (pp.21-27). New York: ACM.

Plangprasopchok, A., & Lerman, K. (2009). Constructing Folksonomies from User-Specified Relations on Flickr. In *Proceedings of the 18th international conference on World wide web.* (pp. 781-790). New York: ACM.

Ribeiro-Neto, B., Cristo, M., et al. (2005). Imped-ance Coupling in Con-tent-targeted Advertising. In *Proceedings of the 28th annual international ACM SIGIR conference on Research and development in information retrieval* (pp. 496-503).

Torralba, A., Fergus, R., & Weiss, Y. (2008). *Small codes and large databases for recognition* (pp. 1–8). IEEE Computer Vision and Pattern Recognition.

Trajkova, J., & Gauch, S. (2004). Improving Ontology-Based User Profiles. In *Proceedings of 4th international conference on Adaptivity, Personalization and Fusion of Heterogeneous Information.* (pp. 380-389).

Wang, X.-J., & Zhang, L. (2008). Annotating Images by Mining Image Search Results. *IEEE Transactions on Pattern Analysis and Machine Intelligence, 30*(11), 1919–1932. doi:10.1109/TPAMI.2008.127

WordTracker. (2010). Retrieved from http://www.wordtracker.com.

Zhou, X., Wu, S.-T., et al. (2006). *Utilizing Search Intent in Topic Ontology-based User Profile for Web Mining. In Proceedings of the 2006 IEEE/WIC/ACM International Conference on Web Intelligence.* (pp.558-564). IEEE Computer Society.

ENDNOTES

[1] http://www.flickr.com

[2] Current commercial text search engines such as Google, Live Search, generally adopt relevance-driven advertising which suggest ads without modeling a user's interest. Commercial image search engines, on the other hand, even do not monetize their search results. We discovered that Flickr.com recently show sponsored ads in image search results by matching query keywords and bid keywords of advertisers, which is exactly the same technique adopted by commercial text search engines and wastes the informative image content. This, again, shows that image monetization is still an unexplored market.

[3] In our current implementation, we define a block as a sentence. Any other block definition can be used, e.g. a paragraph, or a sliding window, and we can formulate similar importance score to weight a block.

[4] We did not differentiate leaf categories from medium ones, but for each category, we use its corresponding webpages to learn the *SF* score while ignore those belonging to its child categories.

[5] In fact, the authors reported that an image is annotated in less than 1 second based on a 2.4 million image database. But in the advertising scenario, it is reasonable to auto-tag user photos offline.

[6] The search strategy generally adopted by current commercial search engines is like this: given a query, the search engine retrieves the documents indexed by each valid term of this query, and computes their intersection. Then documents remained in the intersection are ranked and the top ones are presented to the user. Therefore, in the case that a query contains tens or even hundreds of terms (e.g. the query is a document), the document indexing step will be less efficient, and the intersection tends to contain few documents, which is called a "long-query" problem.

Chapter 6
The Advent of Play and Pursuit

Yasmin Ibrahim
Queen Mary University of London, UK

ABSTRACT

'Multimedia advertising on the internet has demanded that advertisers and marketers become more creative and adventurous in their pursuit of consumers. This chapter argues that the notions of play and pursuit are intrinsic components of persuading consumers to interact and engage with advertising. Online advertising is also simulating game environments to reach consumers through an alternate reality. These techniques elevate play as a persuasive tool to entice consumers and to capture data for advertisers. It tacitly thwarts the assumption that the internet is a space of consumer empowerment and control. Instead it reinforces the hand of capital and uses the architecture and features of the internet to make virtual environments a productive space for advertisers.'

The Web 2.0 experience (and beyond) is constructed through the notion of interactivity, and equally through the multimedia environment encompassing audio, video and textual platforms enabling a multitude of communication formats. Whilst conventional advertising used to employ the notion of dedicated space and slots to advertise product and services, the Web 2.0 and future online environments carry advertising as a concept that can be embedded anywhere without the user

having an idea of where it might be. The notion of advertising space is then problematised through its ability to leap marked and traditional boundaries that used to keep advertising and editorial apart in printed pages. Advertising on the internet conceals an invisible economy where pop-up adverts can be triggered through the movements of the cursor without the realization of the user. The concealment through design and architecture then become a form of play. As Johan Huizinga (1971) contends play is central to cultural life, however

DOI: 10.4018/978-1-60960-189-8.ch006

it takes various manifestations in the digital environment.

This paper argues that advertising on the internet works on the principle of 'ubiquitous pursuit' where advertising can be present at the tip of the cursor without warning and through a multitude of strategies which have gone beyond simple banner advertising and pop-ups. This pervasive pursuit of the user means that online advertising works against some of the conventional principles of print and television advertising. Online advertising, unlike conventional advertising, employs both visibility and non-visibility where invisible elements can constantly surveil and monitor consumer behaviour. This notion of the advertiser monitoring the consumer while she interacts with the advertising component means that pursuit becomes an activity in which consumer behaviour is converted into data and this data mining makes consumer activity productive for the advertiser.

The online environment challenges firstly the notion of the conventional dedicated advertising space. Secondly, it intuitively challenges the notion of self-empowerment on the internet where consumers are often given the impression that they are in control of their environment. In the new media environment advertising can be hidden from the eye but activated through the movement of the cursor and through modes and techniques of interactivity. The internet throughout its inception has been narrated as a space where the user can assert choice and a degree of control in choosing, navigating and interacting with content unlike traditional broadcasting. The unrelenting pursuit of the user's attention through creative advertising prolongs the notion that the user is in control. The internet, however, is a space overrun with commercial intent where the hand of capitalism is dominant but partially invisible. More importantly, online advertising works through the notion of not completely instilling strict boundaries between advertising and non-advertising content. Whilst this may be somewhat distinct in print and television advertising (and perhaps increasingly contested), the blurring of the boundaries between advertising and editorial in the online environment enables advertising to inhabit a new liminal space where it cannot be firmly categorised but can obfuscate the user about the origins of a source. The idea of pursuit on the internet also means that advertising can physically move with the cursor in its endeavour to capture the attention of the user. Thus interactivity, moving images and the overarching concept of movement in the Web 2.0 environment makes 'pursuit' an intrinsic part of online engagement. Web 2.0 technologies allow the creation of networks where consumer participation is seen as important in creating and adding value for companies and brands. With banner advertising and pop-ups increasingly categorised as clutter by consumers, advertisers are adapting more to interactive strategies to bind the consumer and to create experiential value in advertising spaces.

Besides the notion of pursuit, this chapter builds on the idea of play in the new media environment. This idea of play can seemingly make the insidious notion of ubiquitous pursuit much more palatable and less intimidating as it is often in academic literature and human cultures associated with frivolity. The idea of 'play' employs humour, intertextuality and interactivity to make the pursuit of the user light-hearted but also consensual where the user may not completely block off advertising once made aware of it. The use of clever graphics, design and sound makes play a professional and persuasive technique to entice the audience and to deliver millions to the advertiser. The notion of 'play' in the online environment takes various formats where interactivity makes the audiences complicit in engaging with advertising material whilst blurring the boundaries between advertising and non-advertising. The employment of playfulness or the 'ludic' in online advertising means that as an entity it can leap off anywhere whilst giving a false perception to the user that he is in charge of his destiny without perhaps an intimate understanding of the architecture or the code of the internet. Designers in tandem are increasingly designing pages which give audiences less agency to be divorced from advertising content.

Additionally, this chapter argues that whilst we are socialised into identifying advertising in most forms of media, the internet inverts some of the social codes of advertising. The increasing embedding of advertising in interactive content calls for new forms of media literacy where every movement and consumption on the internet can be turned into opportunities for advertising or mining personal data. This data mining and tracking of movement becomes part of the phenomenon of 'pursuit' where audiences' behaviours are predicted and written into programmes and in the design of websites. In this sense, pursuit and play become an intrinsic part of the advertising architecture of the internet.

THE GROWTH OF ONLINE ADVERTISING

The internet is increasingly used as an advertising medium and despite the digital divide there has been a vast expansion in internet-based marketing. A worldwide internet advertising spending report by IDC projects that advertising on the internet will total US$106.6 billion in 2011 or 13.6% of the total expenditure across all media (www.marketingcharts.com). The United States is expected to lead the world with regard to the total advertising expenditure as well as spending on online advertising with the latter totalling US$45 billion. The report reiterates that most companies recognise that the internet must be incorporated into any comprehensive advertising strategy and presently the mix between traditional and online media involves a high degree of experimentation as marketers test the results of mixing media. Beyond the US, central and eastern Europe, the Middle East and Africa are predicted to experience the fastest growth in online advertising from 2008 till 2011, according to this report.

Similarly, the United Kingdom is the first major economy where advertisers spent more on internet than television advertising in 2009 (Sweney 2009). The Internet Advertising Bureau (IAB) reveals that this amounted to advertisers spending £1.75 billion in the first six months of 2009 on internet advertising, representing 23.5% of all advertising money spent in the country. This commitment to internet advertising means that it took just a little more than a decade for the internet to become the biggest advertising sector in the UK. Denmark was another country whose advertising revenue on the internet surpassed that of television in early 2009, although the UK remains the only major economy in which this trend has been observed.

Traditional and conventional spaces are seen as struggling to maintain consumer attention in an increasingly mediated world. The media industry is characterised by both monopoly of ownership and by fragmentation of consumer choice. The fragmentation of the television audience and the rise of niche channels and programming have made advertisers review the ways they reach consumers. With a saturation of advertising in different kinds of media consumers view much of these advertisements as 'clutter' or 'junk'. The ability to switch channels and to install filtering software to stop advertising and promotions on the web means marketers have to rise to the challenge of advertising in the world of ubiquitous marketing. Straightforward commercial advertising on television or print has given way to a complex and strategic mix of integrated marketing techniques where a combination of media is used to reiterate messages and reach consumers.

Unlike traditional media new media, including the internet, afford consumers more control with a non-linear access to differentiated content whilst enabling varied forms of sense simulation due to their characteristics (Hoffman & Novak 1995). Such characteristics include interactivity, telepresence, hypermedia and network mobility. Hoffman and Novak (1995: 29) argue that the hypermedia computer-mediated environment signifies a 'fundamentally different environment for marketing activities compared to traditional media due to the manner in which consumers can exercise unprecedented control over content they interact with'.

The web experience with regard to the consumer is defined as the 'consumer's total impression of a website and may entail elements such as searching, browsing, finding, selecting, comparing and evaluating information and would additionally include exposure to a combination of virtual marketing tools which is likely to influence consumer behaviour' (Constantinides 2004: 113). The web experience itself can be influenced by the design, creative, aesthetic and interactive elements within a website. Undoubtedly, a key element in the success of online marketing is user involvement where involvement is defined as 'an observable state of motivation, arousal or interest' (Rothschild 2004: 216). A testimony to experimentation amongst corporate brands is Coca Cola's strategy to move away from television advertising into video games and DVDs (Grover et al. 2004). Even though the level of online advertising and consumer interaction and trust with online commerce can vary globally, the necessity to experiment with the internet via social networks and virtual domains has increased the need to be creative and playful with online spaces.

PERSUASION, PLAY AND ADVERTISING

Throughout the history of advertising the concept of persuasion has been an intrinsic part of academic scrutiny. Persuasion here is defined as 'human communication designed to influence the autonomous judgements and decisions of others. As a form of attempted influence persuasion seeks to alter the ways in which people think or act' (Simon et al. 2001: 21). As Simon et al. (2001) reiterate, it does not coerce but seeks to predispose individuals such that it can influence their sense of the real, the probable, their sense of judgement of ideas, people and events and perhaps more fundamentally their belief systems and values.

With the advent of mass media, industrialization, modernisation and the increase in leisure much of modern political history and political enquiry has centred on the idea of how mass media has worked as a medium of persuasion. The techniques of persuasion mediated through technology and the increasing interest in the psychology of persuasion resulted in business schools recruiting psychologists to study consumer behaviour from the 1950s onward. The end of World War II and the increasing commercialization of culture along with consumerism brought increased focus on the theories of persuasion where consumers were seen as being lured into making purchasing decisions through clever marketing techniques. The shift from modernity to postmodernity is marked by cultural transformations where developments in communications are accelerating these changes in leisure, communication and consumption patterns.

Within this theorem of persuasion, the notions of play, pleasure and enticing consumer engagements through fun and humour have always been an integral part of marketing (See Sternthal & Craig 1973; Weinberger & Gulas 1992). Advertising has often leveraged on humour, parody and intertexuality between everyday life, popular culture and screen culture to draw in consumers. The notions of play and humour often often reside within the insidious side of persuasion and seek to influence consumer behaviour through media messages.

Mark Bartholomew (2007) points out that in the late 1800s there was a shift towards the primacy of persuasion in advertising. Whilst advertising prior to that was centred on imparting information, the dominance of persuasion was palpable with the infusion of affect and aesthetics. The role of emotions was evident where advertising increasingly focused on consumer anxieties such as social advancement, mortality, and vanity (Bartholomew 2007: 751). The role of emotions in influencing consumer behaviour has been an area of increasing analysis and study by both psychologists and marketers with an acceptance that beyond rationality, the irrational and subconscious feelings can also shape and mediate consumer behaviour.

Holbook et al. (1984: 728), in examining the notion of playful consumption, point out that the category belongs to a broad range of motivated consumer behaviour which includes leisure activities, hobbies, games and aesthetic appreciation. Additionally it involves the consumer expending time on activities which yield enjoyable experiences. Holbrook et al. conclude that elements such as satisfaction, enjoyment, fun and other hedonic aspects of the consumption experience can be classified under the rubric of play.

The embracing of Taylorism (i.e. the breaking down of tasks into smaller segments) before World War II and the rise of the bureaucratic state meant that play was often conflated with the frivolous and the irrational and was seen as entirely antithetical to the rational pursuit of order. Brian Sutton-Smith (1997), in writing about the construction of play as a juxtaposition to the productive and rational in historical contexts, asserts that the absence of the term in books of human behaviour constituted a form of intellectual denigration both in its omission and conflation with frivolity. While research on humour was burgeoning in social psychology, marketing and political theory, play was entrapped into a binary dualism against utilitarianism. This puritanical and even polemic positioning of play meant it was not fully explored as a form of cultural practice embedded into our daily lives. With the advent of digital technologies and platforms and with increasing interest in digital gaming and its attendant culture play has been the subject of renewed scholarship in the last decade where its notions have been deconstructed in order to understand the psychology of the postmodern media consumer and the architecture of the internet.

The conjoining of an interactive and simulated environment on the internet brings both literal and sensory applications to the notion of play in online environments compared with television or film. Whilst the notion of audience passivity (or 'active' engagement) in communication and media studies has been amenable to shifting approaches of what it can constitute with regard to the ability to interpret text, messages and images, in the internet environment the concept of play can encompass both cognitive and physical agency. These interactive environments are starting to replace television viewing and radio listening especially among younger consumers (Chaney 2004: 37).

Beyond the normative notion of play the internet is intimately entwined with the concept of empowerment where it is deemed to empower consumers through increased creativity as well as socio-economic and political benefits (Bonsu & Darmody 2008: 356). However the internet, whilst propagating more control and power for the consumer, is a space of interface between global capital flows and consumer cultures. The flow of capital on the internet means that commercial forces become dialectical to the notion of consumer agency and empowerment, creating spaces where commerce and consumer culture constantly comingle to create new forms of partnerships, both tacit and overt.

These constant interfaces between consumers and companies mean that products are constantly redefined through these engagements, hence the internet delineates product value through these consumer inputs. In effect, it challenges the rigid dichotomy between production on the one hand and consumption on the other. These freedoms may be enabled through new media technologies and marketing strategies, but there is nevertheless a 'commodification of consumer creativity and colonization of consumer collectivity' to perform in the interest of capital (Bonsu & Darmody 2008: 365). The new media environment is seen as presenting a false economy of consumer empowerment when the immaterial labour of the consumer is used to produce new forms of meaning and value for producers and advertisers.

As digital consumption practices lack materiality (Molesworth & Denegri-Knott 2007: 115) the postmodern consumer is constructed as less concerned about material values and more engaged in experiential values (Firat & Dholakia 2006: 140).

The notion of play is much more manifest in game environments on the internet. Mattias Svahn (2009: 1) defines play as 'a state of mind surrounding and relating to the artefact of a game.' Svahn contends that the appropriation of play into advertising and persuasive communications can be a viable tool in marketing. The concept of play is seen as pleasure, fun or entertainment and hence is deemed to constitute a positive experience (Malaby 2007). Ian Bogost (2007: ix) points out that the most significant aspect of using game environments is that they deploy techniques of persuasion not in the conventional sense of spoken or written words, images or moving pictures. Instead persuasion is used through rule-based representations and interactions. In this sense, Bogost's contention is that games should be perceived as persuasive devices and their power lies in their procedural form where it is not purely verbal, discursive or visual but may in fact have a preconceived logic about how things can work. This positions the participant as an active player who enacts the claims of the game by experiencing and partaking in it (Bogost 2007:9). Thus persuasion works through this ability to partake in a preconceived logic as a participant in the process. The virtual game environment on the internet thus re-positions the centrality of the concept of play to online multimedia marketing.

Evidently, marketing in the postmodern world has developed as a consumer-centric paradigm and this change reflects the way it has evolved with the dynamics of capitalism in postmodernity (Bonsu & Darmody 2008: 356). With the rise of user-generated content and different models of communication (i.e. one-to-one and one-to-many) there is an emphasis on the co-creation of value as a shared agenda between marketers and consumers to produce new consumption experiences where these can be measured and tracked. As Bonsu & Darmody reiterate this co-creation involves the building of a mutually beneficial relationship between marketers and consumers where the latter are seen as creative collaborators and participants (without complete knowledge or consent) in the production process. The internet as a space of many paradoxes - but mainly that between control and autonomy and between individual freedom and the capitalist agenda – is encrypted as a contested space where corporations seek to influence consumers through an illusion of empowerment whilst exploiting them for their own profit-driven goals.

HARNESSING THE CHARACTERISTIC OF THE VIRTUAL

The internet, often dubbed a virtual environment, is strongly associated with voyeurism, avatarism and the ability to make believe through the real and the unreal, simulation and animation. The concepts of play and pursuit become elements that can be suspended into this virtual environment where there is both a connection with offline realities and the ability to create new online realities disembbeded from the real. The internet's duality; which binds the offline and online worlds and creates a reality of its own (through the virtual environment and the architecture of the internet), makes the internet ripe for a multitude of activities. These can range from commercial pursuits, surveillance, social networking, the exchange of information and communication to the ordering of information through new typologies and the mining of information to create consumer demographics and patterns. As advertisers use the internet for both interacting with consumers and as a platform for advertising and promoting their products there is an increasing imperative to be more creative and innovative with their approaches to lure users' attention and interactivity. The notion of pursuit in the internet is much more complex as many commercial players and agents vie for consumer attention and time.

Whilst digital television and targeted advertising through SMS messages by mobile phone may enable interactive advertising, the internet offers unlimited potential for advertisers to reach out to consumers in imaginative ways. Creativity has always been important in marketing and advertising but with the internet the emphasis on creativity has become the key to success for many marketing campaigns. With an avalanche of information and numerous actors and activities vying for the attention of the user and consumer, directing the attention of the user becomes paramount for marketers (Mathieu 2010). Marketers are using a combination of strategies to maximise the reach to their audience which go beyond banner advertising to include email and social media, the pursuit of consumer attention and the element of play become intrinsic to the digital environment. The notion of creativity is not just determined through clever ideas or presentation but the ability to draw even the apathetic to experiment and lose some of their inhibitions.

Like television and to some extent radio, the internet has the ability to transport audiences through both visual and simulated environments especially in the realms of video games where the ability to create fictional environments and to experience different scenarios and assume different personalities are made possible through role play and gaming. Whilst the early text-based and discursive environments of the internet laid less emphasis on graphics and mobile images, the Web 2.0 environment and beyond positions graphics and mobile images as quite central to the imagination and experience of the users. Thus the ability to transport and view images non-stop is a distinctive characteristic of the internet today. In view of this, advertising on the internet seeks to both manipulate the senses as well as to pursue the user's attention through creative online advertising.

Chuan-Fong Shih (1998) highlights two seminal experiences in cyberspace to comprehend consumer behaviour: telepresence and bricolage. Telepresence refers to the degree in which consumers feel their existence in the virtual sphere. This entails being transported across time and space to a virtual realm. The consequence of telepresence mediated by technology means that the user is projected into a sensory world which can involve fantasy and make-believe where elements of fun and playfulness can be invoked. Shih suggests that the telepresence that emerges from new media technologies, namely interactivity and the stimulation of sense, promotes the notion of play through interaction with the medium. Bricolage, on the other hand, refers to the manipulation of objects around one's immediate surroundings.

Whilst Sherry Turkle (1995) appropriates bricolage to refer to the ability to learn through play in the online environment, Shih extends it to consumer behaviour on the internet where consumers can use links and virtual objects to experience play. As a result the user's engagement with the text or spaces of advertising would differ from conventional media. Users can defy the linearity of presentation to consume information as per consumer preference. In combining the concepts of telepresence and bricolage, Shih postulates that these capture the experiential and cognitive components of consumer behaviour. But more significantly, they complement the notion of play where immersion into the environment comes through a sensory existence in a virtual sphere and through the possibility of interacting with virtual objects and links which can transport users to different spaces and mediate the user experience.

Similarly, Kar Yan Tam and Shuk Ying Ho (2005: 272) argue that websites' characteristic elements can be deemed as a 'stimuli-based decision making environment' where stimuli can be manifest through text, audio, animations or video. In terms of customizing the web for one's audience they assert that these become persuasive techniques to influence user behaviour. Persuasive messages within these environments can be used to divert attention, reallocate cognitive resources and to invoke affective responses and behaviour (Tam & Ho 2005: 272). They contend that the internet can be used as a personalization tool and this in itself can be persuasive. Nevertheless new media technologies have not in themselves created new strategies for persuasion but they enable old strategies to be introduced in new ways and become part of a wider ecology of persuasion technologies in society such as television (King & Tester 1999: 1999: 37). The internet allows for not just the customization of experience but also role play, interactions with virtual communities, simulated experiences, as an environment for discovery (or bricolage) as well as surveillance and the tracking of consumer activities.

THE PHILOSOPHY OF PLAY

Whilst there has been limited attention given to play in political thought and marketing literature it has nevertheless been a subject of theoretical scrutiny for over 50 years in various fields and disciplines ranging from anthropology to digital game cultures which sought to conceptualise paradigms to explain human motivation and cognitive agency especially in the last decade where the online gaming environment has emerged as a research domain in its own right (Mathwick & Rigdon 2004). In the field of learning and teaching play as a philosophy emanating from Aristotelian traditions holds much currency and provokes much debate. For psychologists play reduces penalties whilst increasing the opportunities for experimentation (Lieberman 1977).

As Malaby (2007: 100) points out play, in Western thought, is often contrasted with work as a means of distinguishing between productive activity and unproductive action where it is set apart as a state in which nothing happens. This is visible in Roger Caillois' (2001: 5) assertion of play as an 'occasion of pure waste; waste of time, energy, ingenuity, skill and often money.' Johan Huizinga (1971), on the other hand, con-

structed play as a central part of human culture and experience rather than subordinate to another activity. In his book, *Homo Ludens,* Huizinga constructed human culture as originating out of play. In analysing the notion of play in different cultures Huizinga drew out the subtle variations of this term in these cultures. For Huizinga play constitutes 'a free activity standing quite consciously outside 'ordinary' life as being 'not serious' but at the same time absorbing the player intensely and utterly' (cf. Lastowka 2009: 383). According to Greg Lastowka (2009) both Caillois and Huizinga disembedded play from productive pursuits but Huizinga nevertheless elevated play to the sublime and sacred and often equated it with ritual. Huizinga's notion of play as inhabiting an irrational domain was also echoed by Bernard Suits (1978) who like Huizinga classifies play as separate and distinct from productive activity. In his book *Grasshopper*, Suits (1978) contends that the rules of play often are designed to make participants act according to its own intrinsic logic which entails behaving in a less efficient manner which rational thought might not entertain.

Others such as Jean Baudrillard wrote about games and play in synonymous terms and through the course of his lifetime of writing, games came to embody the world and life both as metaphor and as a form of intrinsic logic and process (See Galloway 2007:376). Veering away from these philosophical positions of viewing play as a form of metaphor to capture the social relationships and the dichotomies between life routines which can be divided into work and play, the paper employs the notion of play as an experiential dimension. As Malaby (2008:5) points out this dimension is often underexplored in anthropological literature. Malaby, in citing Mihalyi Csikszentmihalyi, defines play as 'a state of experience in which the actor's ability to act matches the requirements for action in his environment' (2008:5) This experiential dimension of play has been applied to the consumption experience and tangentially to relationship-building and the marketing domain

(See Deighton & Grayson 1995; Holt 1995; Holbrook et al. 1984). This chapter thus situates play as a form of experiential value in the online marketing environment.

The notion of playfulness in the computer-mediated environment is also often conjoined with the concept of flow where it encapsulates the consumer's ability to have a sense of control over their agency in interactive environments thus affording some cognitive enjoyment and gratification whilst enabling focus on the interactive component (See Hoffman & Novak 1995: 12). This conjoining of agency and consciousness centralises the focus, leaving out what may be considered irrelevant to the experience. This web experience which induces an optimal mental state is termed as 'flow' by Csikszentmihalyi (1990). Csikszentmihalyi (cf. Hsu & Lu 2004: 856) elaborates his original concept of flow as 'the holistic experience that people feel when they act with total involvement'. Hsu and Lu (2004: 857), in analysing the concept of flow and surveying the academic literature, concur that the characteristics of flow may well include 'control, concentration, enjoyment, curiosity, intrinsic interest' amongst others.

The immersion of consciousness into the experience signifies a fusing of self, temporality and the cognitive environment (Csikszentmihalyi 1990: 72). Research has found that high levels of playfulness or flow in computer-mediated interactions correlate with higher experimentation (See Hoffman & Novak 1995: 25; Katz 1987; Ghani et al. 1991). The degree of involvement of the consumer means that they not only seek to increase their product knowledge but to experience pleasure (Mathwick & Rigdon 2004: 326). The web experience of the user can also be intimately tied to the degree of decisional control or perception of choice and as such it may positively influence outcome and behaviour if people feel they can assert more control over their environment (See Ghani & Deshpande 1994; Czikszentmihalyi 1990).

For marketers this relationship reiterates the fact that a hypermedia environment may initiate exploratory behaviour among consumers. According to Webster et al. (1993) higher playfulness can also lead to a higher level of positive mood and satisfaction and may lead to consumers spending more quality time with certain environments. In relation to consumer behaviour the flow experience can draw consumers, mediate price sensitivity and may influence consumer attitudes and behaviour in a positive manner (Mathwick & Rigdon 2004: 324). Charla Mathwick and Edward Ridgon (2004: 330) studying the experiential value of online information searches found that 'attitudes toward a firm's Web site and its brands appear enhanced' when consumers partake in 'enjoyable and engaging online experiences'. They note that this is encouraging news for marketers where web experiences can be enhanced through good web design. As such online advertising has to strive for sustained engagement to defy the click-through mentality and such engagements can be cultivated by exploiting the hypermedia environment of the internet in innovative ways.

PUTTING PLAY INTO ONLINE PLATFORMS

With the focus on play and pursuits as central elements marketers are increasingly exploiting the virtual features of the internet. One important trend which captures the novel ways in which advertisers and marketers use play and pursuit is through the creation of virtual worlds. Virtual worlds are not synonymous with virtual reality. The latter is a more generic term to refer to environments created through computer-mediated communication. Virtual worlds, on the other hand, refer to a type of computer application that lets users navigate and interact with a three-dimensional, computer-generated (and computer-maintained) environment in real time (cf. Taylor 1997). These virtual worlds are seen as spaces for commodification and increased capitalism. Virtual worlds must possess certain salient elements to qualify as such: they must be interactive, must simulate a physical environment and must be sustained or prolonged even after a user has stopped using it. The thematic content of virtual worlds can differ dramatically, entail gaming activities and be described as next-generation chat rooms (Bartle 2003). A study by University of Bochum in Germany reveals that gamers could recall a brand they saw in advertised game much more easily and be empathetic to advertisement in games (cf. Giordano & Hummel 2005:225).

Play can be a serious element when advertisers create 'virtual worlds' (such as *Second Life* and *Sims*) to enhance consumer brand awareness and recall. It creates an environment where users can lose their inhibitions whilst fostering experimentation. This trend in transcending and recognising the virtual world as an environment in its own right has also seen the proliferation of specialised marketing and advertising agencies which cater to advertising in virtual environments. Whilst there has been friction between virtual communities and advertisers these specially built virtual environments provide lots of opportunities to understand and re-negotiate consumer behaviour. Virtual worlds are not new in themselves and can be traced to text-based multi-user environments first developed nearly thirty years ago (Bartholomew 2007: 741).

According to Paul Hemp (2006) marketers can exploit the avatarism element on the internet where people can appropriate new and different personalities from their offline selves when they enter different environments on the internet. Virtual worlds such as *Second Life*, which offer game-like elements and opportunities for social interaction, provide different types of opportunities for online marketing. In 2006 the creators of *Second Life*, Linden Lab, had around 65,000 paid and 100,000 unpaid subscribers respectively. As Hemp points out, in such environments people have more than one persona and these offer vast

potential for virtual commerce as users of the environment make virtual transactions in the buying and selling of commodities and services.

The blurring of boundaries between offline and online worlds mean real marketers can create awareness and engagements through these spaces. There has also been a recognition of games as a means of persuasion (See Frasca 2007; Bogost 2007). The importing of real brands and logos into virtual worlds opens up new ways to create and promote visibility of brands and their associations with lifestyle. Creative advertising on the internet in recent years has also included adverworlds (sometimes used synonymously with advergaming) or branded virtual worlds. These environments don't often use advertising in the traditional sense and instead such self-contained platforms resemble online multi-player environments which entail custom-made experiences to promote branding of goods and services (Shwartz 2006). The user engagements involve personalizing their 'habitat' within the environment, opting for avatars (or online identities) and even making purchasing decisions. This means pursuing the consumer's time and attention in terms of hours as opposed to seconds where these engagements involve play, pleasure and emotional experiences which conventional advertising techniques such as banners or pop-ups may not deliver.

Similar to adverworld is advergaming which involves companies building a custom-made game around the attributes of a brand (Kanth 2010). An advergame has also been defined as a game whose main purpose is to boost sales of a product or service through a combination of methods to boost brand recognition (Smith & Just 2009: 54). In line with this the objective is to influence post-player behaviour. In this environment the brand becomes the protagonist and consumer experiences are shaped around the brand. Advergaming can include sweepstakes, knowledge-based quizzes or video contests with a complete virtual world. Advergaming often invites users to register their personal details to play the game and this means companies can measure and use their demographics to further refine their marketing strategies. The more complex the advergaming environment the more it can cost companies to engage their audiences in play and companies have been known to invest in six-figure sums (Buss 2003).

This marketing tool often involves role-playing and initiates interactivity with the brand through fun, pleasure and control. Jason Chambers (2005), writing on advergaming, postulates that this process can be likened to product placement within movies and television programmes. But unlike movies and games Chambers (2005: 4) points out that 'game playing is an active process where the brand can be integrated into the plot thus directing the user experiences'. This inserts both pleasure and control within the experience and has been proven successful in automobile advertising (See Chaney et al. 2004; Nelson 2002). Research by Nelson (2002) confirms there is higher brand recall when users recalled the car they were using in the game even though the ability to recall after five months diminished for the users. The positive experience a user feels in playing a game is then transferred to the brand. According to a study by Chaney et al. (2004: 43) virtual world billboards for both high and low value products have a higher recall than in real-life situations. Other empirical studies such as that done by Winkler and Buckner (2006) show that advergames are more effective when the user is already familiar with the brand and as such there is a positive increase in brand recall. Martin Lindstorm (2004) illustrates that games are potent tool in luring young and youthful consumers around the world.

The domains of digital games and online marketing are no longer mutually exclusive on the internet. There is an increased degree of intertextuality between the two where virtual environments can conjoin with life experiences from real-life brands. Nevertheless whilst these techniques are used to pursue consumer interests there may be age and gender disparities in gaining audience attention. According to Rajani Kanth (2010), writing on the market in India, men and children are more likely to get involved compared to women. More significantly, the objective behind advergaming is not necessarily a direct increase in revenue but rather the need to create awareness through engagement. Advergaming allows advertisers to generate response and data from user engagement. Similarly the US Army used gaming platforms as a recruiting tool in 2002 and has increasingly incorporated the gaming environment for training purposes as well (van Der Graaf & Nieborg 2003).

With concepts such advergames and virtual worlds there is a sense that capitalist motives can infiltrate every corner of the internet even when there has been protest or discontent from the virtual world communities (See Chambers 2005; Book 2004: 12). Whilst virtual worlds may be too expensive for marketers without big budgets like Coca Cola, Nike or McDonalds, which have all experimented with such formats, the concept of using games and play to pursue consumers is an integral part of online advertising. According to a study done by Phoenix Marketing International, Coke, Nike, Pepsi and Adidas were the top brands recalled by consumers when playing games with advertising (cf. Jenkins 2006). Global spending in video game advertising is expected to reach $1bn by 2011.

The targeting of virtual communities and social networks also means that advertisers are drawing from a ready pool of target consumers where peer participation and engagement can shape individual behaviour and response. The increasing encroachment of advertising into spaces which people consider private such as those on social networking sites reveal the permeability of capital and its ability to pursue target consumers and to provide experiential value through creative design. Consumers are no longer active or passive audiences but co-creators of shared meanings and values which can in turn affect the perceptions of brands (See Bonsu and Darmody 2008; Terranova 2000; Vargo and Lusch 2004).

Sutton-Smith (1997) views such environments as play providing game-based rules for consumers to be co-opted as labour for a capitalist agenda. Such environments may evoke feelings of community, control, empowerment and enjoyment for the consumer whilst extracting immaterial labour through these interactions. Bonsu and Darmody (2008: 364) assert that the co-creation of value is an important strategy of the capitalistic agenda to manage consumer independence in the digital age.

CONCLUSION

This chapter looked at the dual concepts of pursuit and play in the multimedia environment where the need to pursue consumer attention through play was situated through the postmodern media economy characterised by increasing fragmentation of the audience and their ability to block out advertising. Play was constructed through the notion of flow where there is a direction of focus which provides the user control, enjoyment and gratification and where it can positively affect consumer behaviour. Additionally, marketers are able to impart experiential value to the consumers and thus instead of vying for a fraction of their time and attention, techniques of immersion and enticement in the multimedia environment seek to use elements of telepresence and bricolage to engage the consumer in the virtual environment. Even though the notion of play is often juxtaposed against productive labour, for marketers it is an instrumental concept in enabling the emergence of a dynamic relationship between consumers and producers and one that challenges this dichotomy in the age of user-generated content. The co-creation of value in the multi-media environment becomes a collaborative enterprise between the producer and consumer and the latter are co-opted to produce meaning, knowledge and valuable experiences which become a form of social capital for producers in these online spaces. Whilst this collaboration is done through meticulous pursuit

and play the consumer becomes a complicit participant in value creation in such marketing techniques. The role of play and equally pursuit situate consumers in the online environments as both agents and consumers in creating value for marketers.

REFERENCES

Bartholomew, M. (2007). Advertising in the Garden of Eden. *Buffalo Law Review, 55*(3), 737–775.

Bartle, R. (2003). *Designing Virtual Worlds*. Indianapolis, IN: New Riders Press.

Bogost, I. (2007). *Persuasive Games: The Expressive Power of Video Games*. Cambridge, MA: MIT Press.

Bonsu, S., & Darmody, A. (2008). Co-creating Second Life: Market-Consumer Cooperation in Contemporary Economy. *Journal of Macromarketing, 24*(4), 355–368. doi:10.1177/0276146708325396

Book, B. (2004). These Bodies are Free, So Get One Now!' Advertising and Branding in Social Virtual Worlds. *Virtual Worlds Review*. Retrieved February 14, 2010 http://www.virtualworldsreview.com/papers/adbrand.pdf

Buss, D. (2003, February 24). Advergaming Scores. *Brand Channel*. Retrieved February 15, 2010 from http://www.brandchannel.com/print_page.asp?ar_id=145&section=main

Caillois, R. (2001). *Man, Play and Games* (Barash, M., Trans.). Urbana: University of Illinois Press.

Chambers, J. (2005). The Sponsored Avatar: Examining the Present Reality and Future Possibilities of Advertising in Digital Games. In *Proceedings of DiGRA 2005 Conference: Changing Views – Worlds in Play*, Vancouver, Canada.

Chaney. I., Lin, K., & Chaney, J. (2004). The Effect of Billboards Within the Gaming Environment. *Journal of Interactive Advertising*, 37-45.

Constantinides, E. (2004). Influencing the Online Consumer's Behaviour: the Web Experience. *Internet Research, 14*(2), 111–126. doi:10.1108/10662240410530835

Czikszentmihalyi, M. (1990). *Flow: The Psychology of Optimal Experience*. New York: Harper and Row.

Deighton, J., & Grayson, K. (1995). Marketing and Seduction: Building Relationships in Managing Social Consensus. *The Journal of Consumer Research, 21*, 660–676. doi:10.1086/209426

Firat, F., & Dholakhia, N. (2006). Theoretical and Philosophical Implications of Postmodern Debates: Some Challenges to Modern Marketing. *Marketing Theory, 6*(2), 123–162. doi:10.1177/1470593106063981

Frasca, G. (2007). *Play the Message: Play, Game and Videogame Rhetoric*. Unpublished PhD Thesis. Copenhagen: University of Copenhagen.

Galloway, A. (2007). A Radical Illusion (A Game Against). *Games and Culture, 2*(4), 376–391. doi:10.1177/1555412007309532

Ghani, J., & Deshpande, S. (1994). Task Characteristics and Experience of Optimal Flow in Human-Computer Interaction. *The Journal of Psychology, 128*(4), 381–391. doi:10.1080/00223980.1994.9712742

Giordano, M., & Hummel, J. (2005). *Mobile Business*. Germany: Springer Science.

Hemp, P. (2006, June). Avatar-Based Marketing. *Harvard Business Review*, 48–57.

Hoffman, D., & Novak, T. (1995). Marketing in Hypermedia Computer Mediated Environments: Conceptual Foundations. Working Paper no 1. Retrieved February 14, 2010 from http://www2000.ogsm.vanderbilt.edu

Holbrook, B., Chestnut, R., Oliva, T., & Greenleaf, E. (1984). 'Play as Consumption Experience: The Roles of Emotions, Performance and Personality in the Enjoyment of Games. *The Journal of Consumer Research, 11*(2), 728–739. doi:10.1086/209009

Holt, D. (1995). How Consumers Consume: A Typology of Consumption Practices. *The Journal of Consumer Research, 22*, 1–16. doi:10.1086/209431

Hsu, C., & Lu, H. (2004). Why Do People Play On-line Games? An Extended TAM with Social Influences and Flow Experiences. *Information & Management, 41*, 853–868. doi:10.1016/j.im.2003.08.014

Huizinga, J. (1971). *Homo Ludens*. New York: Boston.

Jenkins, D. (2006, Nov 6) 'Coke, Pepsi, Nike and Adidas Top-in Advertising Survey', *Gamasutra*. Retrieved February 14, 2010 from http://www.gamasutra.com/php-bin/news_index.php?story=11631

Katz, J. (1987). Playing at Innovation in the Computer Revolution. In M. Frese, E.Ulich, & W. Dzida (Eds.), *Psychological Issues of Human Computer Interaction in the Work Place* (pp 97-112). Amersterdam: North-Holland.

King, P., & Tester, J. (1999). The Landscape of Persuasive Technologies. *Communications of the ACM, 42*(5), 31–38. doi:10.1145/301353.301398

Lastowska, G. (2009). Rules of Play. *Games and Culture, 4*(4), 379–395. doi:10.1177/1555412009343573

Lieberman, N. (1977). *Playfulness: the Relationship to Imagination and Creativity*. New York: Academic Press.

Lindstorm, M. (2004). Branding is no Long Child's Play. *Journal of Consumer Marketing, 21*(3), 175–182. doi:10.1108/07363760410534722

Malaby, T. (2007). Beyond Play: A New Approach to Games. *Games and Culture, 2*(2), 95–113. doi:10.1177/1555412007299434

Malaby, T. (2008). Anthropology and Play: The Contours of Playful Experience. Retrieved February 14, 2010 from http://papers.ssrn.com/sol3/papers.cfm?abstract_id=1315542

Mathieu, B. (2010, January 18). Online Marketing Trends for 2010. *Marketing Daily Commentary.* Retrieved February 14, 2010, from http://www.mediapost.com/publications/?fa=Articles.showArticle&art_aid=120798

Mathwick, C., & Rigdon, E. (2004). Play, Flow and the Online Search Experience. *The Journal of Consumer Research, 31,* 324–332. doi:10.1086/422111

Molesworth, M., & Denegri-Knott, J. (2007). Digital Play and the Actualization of Consumer Imagination. *Games and Culture, 2*(2), 114–133. doi:10.1177/1555412006298209

Nelson, M. (2002). Recall of Brand Placements in Computer/Video Games. *Journal of Advertising Research, 42*(2), 80–92.

Rajani Kanth, K. (2010, January 7). Catch them Young with Advergaming. *Business Standard.* Retrieved February 14, 2010, from http://www.business-standard.com/india/news/catch-them-youngadvergaming/381926/

Rothschild, M. (1984). Perspectives on Involvement: Current Problems and Future Directions. In Kinnear, T. C. (Ed.), *Advances in Consumer Research* (*Vol. 11,* pp. 216–217). Provo, UT: Association for Consumer Research.

Schwartz, J. (2006, March 10). Bold New Opportunities in Virtual World. *iMediaConnection.* Retrieved February 14, 2010, from http://www.imediaconnection.com/content/8605.asp

Shih, C. (1998). Conceptualising Consumer Experiences in Cyberspace. *European Journal of Marketing, 32*(7/8), 655–663. doi:10.1108/03090569810224056

Simon, H., Morreale, J., & Gronbeck (2001). *Persuasion in Society.* London: Sage Publications.

Smith, J., & Just, S. (2009). Playful Persuasion. *Nordicom Review, 2,* 53–68.

Sternthal, B., & Craig, S. (1973). Humor in Advertising. *Journal of Marketing, 37*(4), 12–18. doi:10.2307/1250353

Suits, B. (1978). *The Grasshopper: Games, Life, and Utopia.* Toronto, ON: University of Toronto Press.

Sutton-Smith, B. (1997). *The Ambiguity of Play.* Cambridge, MA: Harvard University Press.

Svahn, M. (2009). Processing Play, Perceptions of Persuasion. Breaking New Ground: *Innovation in Games, Play, Practice and Theory, Proceedings of DiGra 2009.*

Sweney, M. (2009, September 30). Internet Overtakes Television to Become Biggest Advertising Sector in the UK. *The Guardian.* Retrieved February 14, 2010, from http://www.guardian.co.uk/media/2009/sept/30/internet-biggest-uk-advertising-sector/

Tam, K., & Ho, S. (2005). Web Personalization as a Persuasion Strategy: An Elaboration Likelihood Model Perspective. *Information Systems Research, 16*(3), 271–292. doi:10.1287/isre.1050.0058

Taylor, J. (1997). The Emerging Geographies of the Virtual World. *Geographical Review, 87*(2), 172–192. doi:10.2307/216004

Terranova, T. (2000). Free Labour: Producing Culture for the Digital Economy. *Social Text, 18*(2), 33–58. doi:10.1215/01642472-18-2_63-33

Turkle, S. (1995). *Life on the Screen*. New York: Simon & Schuster.

Van Der Graaf, S., & Nieborg, D. (2003). 'Together We Brand America's Army', Level Up: Digital Games Research Conference, Utrecht, Holland, Universiteit Holland.

Vargo, S., & Lusch, R. (2004). Evolving to a New Dominant Logic for Marketing. *Journal of Marketing, 68*, 1–17. doi:10.1509/jmkg.68.1.1.24036

Webster, J., Trevino, L., & Ryan, L. (1993). The Dimensionality and Correlates of Flow in Human Computer Interactions. *Computers in Human Behavior, 9*(4), 411–426. doi:10.1016/0747-5632(93)90032-N

Weinberger, M., & Gulas, C. (1992). The Impact of Humour in Advertising: A Review. *Journal of Advertising, 21*(4), 35–59.

World Wide Internet Advertising Spending to Surpass $106 Billion in 2011 (2008, June 25). marketingcharts.com. Retrieved February 14, 2010, from http://www.marketingcharts.com/television/worldwide-internet-advertising-spending-to-surpass-106-billion-in-2011-5068/

ADDITIONAL READING

Biocca, F., & Levy, M. R. (1995). *Communication in the age of virtual reality*. Hillsdale, NJ: Lawrence Erlbaum.

Holzwarth, M., Janiszewski, C., & Neumann, M. M. (2006). The Influence of Avatars on Online Consumer Shopping Behavior. *Journal of Marketing, 70*(4), 19–36. doi:10.1509/jmkg.70.4.19

Kleeberger, J. (2002). *Online-Gaming as a Marketing and Sales Catalyst*. Gallen, Switzerland: Department of Media and Communication, University of St.

Li, H., Daugherty, T., & Biocca, F. (2002). Impact of 3-D Advertising on Product Knowledge, Brand Attitude, and Purchase Intention: The Mediating Role of Presence. *Journal of Advertising, 31*(4), 43–57.

Suler, J. (n.d.). The Psychology of Avatars and Graphical Space in Multimedia Chat Communities. Retrieved from http://www.rider.edu/~suler/psycyber/psyav.html

Taylor, T. L. (2002). Living Digitally: Embodiment in Virtual Worlds. In Shroeder, R. (Ed.), *The Social Life of Avatars: Presence and Interaction in Shared Virtual Environments*. London: Springer-Verlag.

KEY TERMS AND DEFINITIONS

Avatars: In computer and gaming environments avatar refers to self representations and identity through texts and graphics or a combination of these.

Interactivity: assumes communication patterns entail response from recipients who receive a message or information. Interactivity is used to refer to the shift in communication pattern from one-way flow to one in which audience can interact with messages.

Multimedia Advertising: advertising through the interactive environment of the web using audio, visual and textual features which capitalise on movement and engagement of the senses.

Persuasion: Drawing initially from the art of rhetoric, persuasion in the interactive environment is used as a pull towards becoming part of a community through new rules and game playing.

Play: is used here to refer to the gaming and interactive environment of the internet where users interact through the given rules of engagement. It also refers to techniques where humour and light-hearted game playing is employed as a technique to encourage participation and interaction of the audience.

Second Life: A virtual world created by Linden Lab where users become residents and create a virtual presence through avatars. Residents can socialize, trade virtual property, travel and build virtual objects.

Virtual World Advertising: the utilization of gaming environments to engage users in multimedia worlds which simulate and/or recreate new worlds where users can assume new identity and agency.

Section 3
Video Advertising

Chapter 7
Content and Attention Aware Overlay for Online Video Advertising

Huazhong Ning
Google Inc, USA

Junxian Wang
Microsoft Corporation, USA

Xu Liu
Microsoft China Co. Ltd., China

Ying Shan
Microsoft Corporation, USA

ABSTRACT

Recent proliferation of online video advertising brings new opportunities and challenges to the multimedia community. A successful online video advertising system is expected to have the following essential features: effective targeting, scalability, non-intrusiveness, and attractiveness. While scalable systems with targeting capability are emerging, few have achieved the goal of being both non-intrusive and attractive. To our knowledge, this work is the first attempt to generate video overlay ads that balances the two conflicting characteristics. We achieve the goal by jointly optimizing a non-intrusive metric and a set of metrics associated with video ad templates designed by UI experts. The resulting system is able to dynamically create a video overlay ad that effectively attracts user attention at the least intrusive spatial-temporal spots of a video clip. The system is also designed to enable a scalable business model with effective targeting capabilities, and later will be tested with live traffic on a major video publisher site. In this work, we conducted intensive experiments and user studies on the samples of a large-scale video dataset. The results demonstrate the effectiveness of our approach.

DOI: 10.4018/978-1-60960-189-8.ch007

Figure 1. An overlay ad placed on a low attentive region (bottom), which has animations in the video. The text ads relevant to the video content are graphically rendered at the right time and place in the video, through an optimization algorithm that balances the intrusiveness and attractiveness

1 INTRODUCTION

Recently, consumption of online video has grown dramatically. A survey conducted by LiveRail (*State of the Industry—LiveRail's Q4 2008 Review of Online Video Advertising*, 2009) in December 2008 shows that, the viewers, especially the valuable 18-24 year old demographic, are increasingly spending more time watching internet-distributed video content than traditional broadcast television. Consequently, the online video advertising market also grows dramatically from $214 million in 2006 to $565 million in 2008, and is expected to reach $1,226 million in 2010 (*State of the Industry—LiveRail's Q4 2008 Review of Online Video Advertising*, 2009). This in turn attracts more attention in the research community of online video advertising.

Among the existing advertising formats for online video, four of them are the most popular ones: in-stream (pre/mid/ post roll), banner, virtual content insertion (VCI), and overlay ad. In-stream ad (Mei, Hua, Yang, & Li, 2007) is an ad format that inserts an ad video clip before/after the video or in-between with the original video stream stopped.

It is a direct copy of the traditional TV-style ad format, used for online business. But this format is intrusive to users because it interrupts the users' viewing experiences. The banner ad is less intrusive since it is placed around the video. But it is also less attractive and more probable to be avoided by viewers because the viewers are more focusing on the video window. What's more, both in-stream and banner ad are not suitable for the small and mid-tier advertisers because of the high entry cost of creating the professional ad video clips or ad images. Virtual content insertion (H. Liu, Jiang, Huang, & Xu, 2008) produces impressive results but only works for high quality videos in specific domains such as sports.

Overlay ad is a technology to deliver text ads to online videos by overlaying text information on the video window (see Figure 1 for an example that is a snapshot produced by our system). Recent trend seems to favor overlay ad over the above three ad formats because of its supreme advantages. (1) Overlay ad is *scalable* to a wide range of advertisers and video content, because it is generated with zero cost for advertisers and applicable to both premium and user generated videos. (2) It can use any existing paid search and content ad platforms that serve text ads, and therefore reduce the cost for the video publishers. Our work is based on the overlay advertising framework to take these advantages.

Existing overlay advertising systems tend to ignore the intrusiveness of ad placement. For example, YouTube[1] and AdImage (Liao, Chen, & Hsu, 2008) insert overlay ads at fixed temporal and/or spatial locations without considering the video content blocked by the overlays. *Intrusiveness* is "the degree to which advertisement in a media vehicle interrupts the flow of an editorial unit(Ha, 1996)." Neglecting intrusiveness may result in ad irritation and ad avoidance (H. Li, Edwards, & Lee, 2002). There exist some methods (H. Liu et al., 2008, Mei, Hua, & Li, 2008) to tackle the intrusiveness issue for other ad formats, by detecting *low attentive regions* (LAR) in video frames and assuming that ads placed on LAR are less intrusive to users than those placed on other locations. But these methods use handcrafted models. In this work, we use a machine learning algorithm to simulate how neurons respond to low attentive stimuli so that the results are consistent with human judgment.

From advertiser's perspective, the overlay ad has to be *attractive* to draw viewer's attention. However, to the best of our knowledge, the existing overlay advertising systems also often neglect the *attractiveness* issue[2]. This problem hasn't been addressed even by YouTube, where text ads are rendered on half-transparent white rectangles that lack of attraction. In this work, a set of animate overlay templates designed by UI experts is used to emphasize the ad content and to attract user attention (see Figure 1). Each template is associated with a set of parameters controlling the font size, color of ad text and other template components. Selecting the most suitable template for a given ad and adjusting the appearance of its graphical components are formulated into an optimization problem, with the consideration of intrusiveness

as well as targeting effectiveness described below. The overlay ads can be dynamically created and placed by solving the optimization problem.

Another important issue is *targeting* that is the ability to deliver the right ad to the right person at the right time. There are two categories of targeting methods including *content-based* and *user-based* targeting. Content-based targeting is to associate the video with the ads relevant to the video content, which has been deeply studied and widely used in both online text (Yih, Goodman, & Carvalho, 2006, Lacerda et al., 2006) and video (Mei et al., 2007) advertising. User-based targeting uses information collected on an individual's web-browsing behavior (Hu, Zeng, Li, Niu, & Chen, 2007) to select which advertisements to be displayed to that individual. It is also widely used in the text advertising[3], while it is rarely mentioned in the literature of video advertising. In this work, both targeting methods are enabled to achieve high performance.

The contributions of this work can be summarized as below

1. A set of expert-designed overlay templates that improves the *attractiveness* of overlay ads, and enables scalable implementation and adoption.

2. An algorithm that balances non-intrusiveness and attractiveness in the creation of overlay ads.

3. An LAR detector and the corresponding non-intrusive metric that approximates human judgment.

This work is organized as follows. The related work is given in the next section. Section 3 overviews the system framework and processing pipeline. Section 4 describes low attentive region detection. Our algorithm to create overlay ads is elaborated in Section 5. The last section provides the experimental results and user study report.

2 RELATED WORK

The research topic in this work is closely related to salience /LAR detection, overlay ad for online video, virtual content insertion, and ad relevance.

Salience/LAR detection: Salience of an object is its state or quality of standing out relative to neighboring objects, *e.g.*, a red flower among green leaves. Salience detection is often studied in the context of visual systems, and researchers in psychology and computer vision communities have proposed several computational models to quantify salience in images and videos. Back to 1998, Itti *et al.* (Itti, Koch, & Niebur, 1998) proposed a visual attention system that combines multiscale image features, including color, intensity, and orientation, into a single topographical salience map. This model was deeply studied and largely improved by the succedent work (Walther, Riesenhuber, Poggio, Itti, & Koch, 2002, Itti & Koch, 2001). Liu *et al.* (T. Liu, Sun, Zheng, Tang, & Shum, 2007) also use a machine learning algorithm (conditional random field) to train a salience model but it is more applicable to object detection. Salience and attention models are also extended to videos. Ma *et al.* (Ma, Hua, Lu, & Zhang, 2005) define viewer attention through multiple perceptions including visual and aural stimuli as well as semantic understanding and then apply the attention model to video summarization.

In video advertising, LAR detection can be regarded as a similar problem of visual salience. Liu *et al.* (H. Liu et al., 2008) calculate a salience map for each video frame based on contrast and density information and insert the ads into LARs. Mei *et al.* (Mei et al., 2008) obtains a salience map for in-image advertising.

Overlay ad for online video: It is arguable who invented this technology. CrunchBase[4] claims that "VideoEgg[5] was the first to *commercialize* interactive advertising overlays onto video." Currently, this technology has been widely adopted by major players in the industry such as YouTube and BrightCove[6]. However, all of these systems place overlay ads on fixed positions, usually over the lower fifth of the video window after the video is playing for a fixed period (*e.g.*, 10 seconds). This may result in intrusiveness to video viewers.

Virtual content insertion (VCI): VCI for advertisement (Wan & Xu, 2006, Y. Li, Wan, Yan, & Xu, 2005, Tamir, Sharir, & Wilf, 2002, Deshpande, Naphade, Rao, Bhadada, & Rangan, 2007, H. Liu et al., 2008) refers to the technology that inserts the advertisement segment such as logo or other motion images into video streams and usually aligns the insertion with regular shapes (*e.g.*, billboard and central circle of a court) in the video. This advertisement is similar to overlay ad in terms of content insertion. VCI advertisement makes ad appear natural in video so as to reduce the intrusiveness to users. Existing VCI approaches are often tested on sports videos which have high quality and contain many regular shapes such as court. However, for general videos, especially user generated videos that are popular on video sharing web sites, detecting smooth region and aligning the insertion by geometric transformation is very challenging.

Ad relevance: Targeting relevant ads according to video content is related to the paid search and content ads technologies: *content-targeted advertising* (Ribeiro-Neto, Cristo, Golgher, & Moura, 2005), *keyword-targeted advertising* (Weideman & Haig-Smith, 2002) where query items or keywords in web pages are associated with ads possessing the same or similar bidding keywords. Keyword extraction from web page has been well studied and widely adopted by the industry. Well known extraction algorithms are logistic regression model (Yih et al., 2006), GenEx (Turney, 2000), and KEA (Frank, Paynter, Witten, Gutwin, & Nevill-Manning, 1999). Ribeiro-Neto *et al.* (Ribeiro-Neto et al., 2005) also proposed other strategies, referred to as *impedance coupling strategies*, for associating ads with web pages, which focused not on finding keywords on web pages, but on directly matching ads to those web pages (Yih et al., 2006).

Figure 2. A snapshot of an animate template designed by UI experts. A template has a close button, a link button, and text boxes for ad title and description

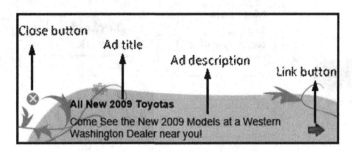

For video content, visual and audio understanding are being experimented by (Barnard et al., 2003, X. Li, Chen, Zhang, Lin, & Ma, 2006, Liao et al., 2008, Ballan, Bertini, & Jain, 2008), and Blinkx[7], but no concrete reports on the accuracy and effectiveness for targeting.

3 SYSTEM OVERVIEW

When a user clicks on a video, the video id and user id are sent to the system, where keywords are extracted from video metadata and user profile. The keywords target the individual user as well as the video content. Then the keywords are queried against the ad delivery engine that returns a set of relevant text ads. The system selects the optimal templates, text ads, and placement location, and dynamically creates and places overlay ads on the clicked video. To improve the efficiency, a major portion of computations are done offline. Hence, the system consists of a back-end responsible for offline processing and a front-end for online requests. We start the overview by introducing the concept of an ad template, which is a key constituting component of the overall system.

3.1 Ad Template

The *template* in this work refers to a flash or silverlight animation consisting of two text boxes associated with the ad title and description, and of a close button and a link button that enable interactions with users. Figure 2 gives a snapshot of an animate template designed by expert. The system can dynamically generate the so called *overlay ad creative* by associating the text ad to the text boxes.

The attractiveness of our overlay ads depends on two factors. One is the animations and shapes of graphical components designed by UI experts, and the other is the compatibility between the template, the text ad, and the video. The former is determined by the designers while the latter can be controlled by our system. Each template is associated with a set of parameters such as font size/color of text boxes and color configuration. Given the text ads, video, and selected template, the system can adjust the font size/color and adapt its color configuration to the video content, to allow better visual compatibility, by solving an optimization problem in Section 5.

3.2 Back-End System

The back-end system provides offline data of LAR information, keywords, and templates. The offline data are stored in databases that can be queried by the front-end system. This can largely improve the efficiency of the front-end system. As shown in Figure 3 the back-end system consists of three modules including keyword extraction, LAR detection, and template design.

Figure 3. Framework of the back-end system. LAR: low attentive region. LAS: low attentive score

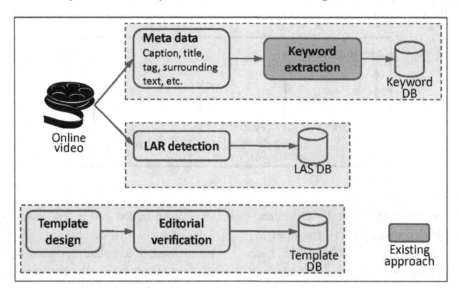

Keyword extraction: Videos shared on internet usually have rich meta data such as title, description, tag, surrounding text, *etc.* For those videos that contain captions and speech, we obtain the caption texts by OCR and transcripts by speech recognition. Although the caption and speech text are noisy due to recognition errors, they are helpful when other meta data are missing or too sparse. The video keywords are extracted from the meta data and stored in the keyword database. We use existing extraction algorithms that focus on the keywords that have high monetization values.

LAR detection: A machine learning algorithm is used to train a model that estimates a *low attentive score* (LAS) for every possible ad placement region (see Section 4 for details). The scores are pre-computed and stored in a database.

Template design: The templates are designed by UI experts and, after editorial verification, are stored in the template database.

3.3 Front-End System

The font-end system is a web service that delivers overlay ads to each online video. Figure 4 illus-

trates its framework, whose modules are briefly described as follows.

Targeting keywords and re-weighting: When a user clicks on an online video, the video id and user id is sent to the front-end system. The content-based keywords are obtained by querying the video id against the keyword database. The user-based keywords are obtained by querying the user id against the user-profile database. Each keyword is associated with a confidence score. Because content and user-based keywords come from two different pipelines, re-weighting is applied to ensure that confidence scales are consistent.

Ad delivery engine: This is where the re-weighted keywords are matched against keywords bided by advertisers. The matched text ads are ranked based on the relevance between the keywords as well as on the value the advertisers willing to pay. The top ranked ads are returned.

Dynamic overlay ad: This module receives the top ranked ads and obtains the video LAR score and template information from the databases. Based on these inputs, it selects the optimal ad, template, template parameters, and ad placement location by solving an optimization problem detailed in Section 5.

Figure 4. Framework of the font-end system. LAS: low attentive score

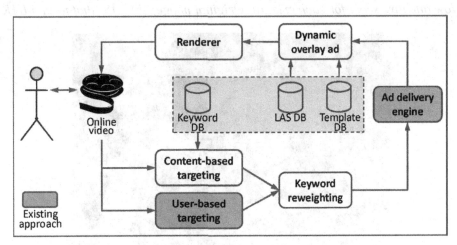

Renderer: This is where the result from the previous step is sent back to the user end, where the selected template and the text ad are dynamically rendered into an animation which is overlaid on the optimal placement region in the video.

It is important to note that the above system can leverage on any existing paid search and content ads platforms that serving targeted text ads with scalability. By automatically converting text ads into video ads, mid-tier and small advertisers are given the opportunity to access video audience without extra cost.

4 LOW ATTENTIVE REGION DETECTION

We expect that overlay ads placed on the low attentive regions (LAR) are less *intrusive* than those placed elsewhere. As mentioned in Section 2, LAR detection may share the same technologies with salience detection. But the inverse of a salience map itself may be not an appropriate LAR map. The filters used for salience detection are usually simulating neurons that may amplify the most salient signals while inhibiting the less salient and low attentive stimuli. This makes it difficult

to differentiate the lowest attentive regions from relative low attentive regions.

On the other hand, existing approaches to both salience and LAR detection assume that salience is a filter response to a set of low level visual features in a receptive field. And detectors often utilize hand-crafted filters whose performance heavily relies on the designer's experience. Such design suffers from the problem that "a machine estimated map is inconsistent with human perception." In this work, the parameters of filters are obtained by a machine learning algorithm. So it is expected that the filter is consistent with the human labeled training data, *i.e.*, human perception if the data are general enough.

4.1 Low Level Visual Features

We partition each video frame into non-overlapping grids, as shown in Figure 5(a). The size of a grid is large enough so that human can decide its attentiveness but a coarse partition may affect the accuracy of LAR detection. We choose 32×32 in this work. The low level visual feature is computed on each grid, instead of on individual pixels.

Contrast: It is straightforward that an LAR is often more smooth or less contrastive than a salient area. Contrast based attention analysis

Figure 5. LAR map. The original image is partitioned into non-overlapping grids, and the SVM model estimates a low attentive score for each grid. (a) Original image; (b) LASs that form a LAR map

a

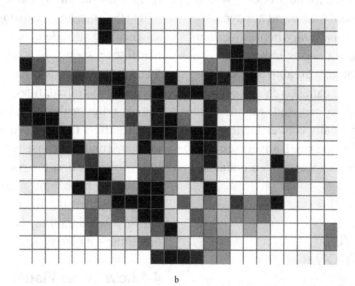

b

shows that human vision system is sensitive to feature contrast of center-surround structure in receptive field (Itti et al., 1998, Ma et al., 2005, H. Liu et al., 2008). A typical approach to contrast analysis is to convolve the *difference of Gaussian* (DOG) with the original video frame, as it was used in (H. Liu et al., 2008). A DOG filter is defined by subtracting a wide Gaussian from a narrow Gaussian:

$$D(x,y) = \frac{1}{\sigma\sqrt{2\pi}} \exp\left(-\frac{x^2 + y^2}{2\sigma^2}\right) - \frac{1}{k\sigma\sqrt{2\pi}} \exp\left(-\frac{x^2 + y^2}{2(k\sigma)^2}\right) \tag{1}$$

The contrast map is the convolution of a original video frame $I(x,y)$ and a DOG filter $D(x,y)$

$$c(x,y)=I(x,y)*D(x,y). \tag{2}$$

Then in each grid, we calculate the mean and variance of the pixel contrasts, denoted as m_c and ςc.

Motion information: Motion is a strong spatial-temporal cue to detect attentive region (Ma et al., 2005, H. Liu et al., 2008). It is expected that an LAR consists of less motion. Optical flow is probably the most widely used method to obtain motion information and its accuracy has been largely improved recently (Xiao, Cheng, Sawhney, Rao, & Isnardi, 2006). The method using cone-shaped Motion Vector Space can even estimate object motion under moving camera (Duan, Xu, Yu, & Tian, 2002). In this work, a general purpose optical flow approach is adopted since additive motion effect of video objects and camera serves our purpose. For each grid, we compute the mean m_m and variance ςm of the motion magnitude. We also build an 8-bin orientation histogram in the range from 0 to π. Each pixel softly votes with respect to its motion orientation, weighted by the motion magnitude. Suppose Hm is the histogram, the motion entropy

$$E_m = \int_0^\pi -H_m(\theta)\log H_m(\theta)d\theta, \qquad (3)$$

reflects the information of pixel motions and is also used as a feature.

Gradient information: we can imagine that a smooth region often contains less information than a region with many lines and edges. In other words, a region with small gradients is more likely to be an LAR. Like we did for motion information, we compute mean m_{gd} and variance ςg_d of the gradient magnitudes, build a gradient orientation histogram, and obtain an entropy Eg_d. The entropy reflects statistics of line/edge directions, and to some extent the existence of textures.

Color information: given a video frame, suppose the pixel colors has a distribution $p(r,g,b)$ where (r,g,b) is a point in the RGB color space. For a specific pixel of color (r_0,g_0,b_0), a small $p(r_0,g_0,b_0)$ often means a large probability of the pixel belonging to foreground. By information

theory, $-\log p(r_0,g_0,b_0)$ represents the information contained by this pixel. The total information over a grid is the color entropy given as below:

$$E_{ci} = \sum_{v\in\mathcal{R}} -\log p(r_v, g_v, b_v), \qquad (4)$$

where R is the grid region and (r_v,g_v,b_v) is the color of pixel v. Besides the entropy, we also compute the mean and variance of each color channel in the grid, denoted by m_r, ςr, mg, ςg, mb, and ςb.

We use the vector

$$\mathbf{v} = \{m_c, \sigma_c, m_m, \sigma_m, E_m, m_{gd}, \sigma_{gd}, E_{gd}, E_{ci}, m_r, \sigma_r, m_g, \sigma_g, m_b, \sigma_b\}$$

to represent the low level visual features of a grid. To enable fast convergence in the learning stage, all feature dimensions are normalized to zero mean and unit variance.

4.2 Learning the LAR Detector

Theoretically, the *low attentive score* (LAS) of a grid should be a real number. However, it is impractical for the human labelers to assign a real number to a sample. Instead, to make the labeling task more realistic and efficient, the labelers classify each sample as either 1:*low attentive* (LA) or -1:*high attentive* (HA).

Given a human labeled training set $\mathcal{D} = \{(\mathbf{v}_i, u_i)\}_{i=1}^N$ where $u_i \in \{-1,1\}$ is the label of the i-th sample and $\mathbf{v}_i$ is the low level feature vector extracted from this sample grid. We need to learn a mapping $u=f(\mathbf{v},\Phi)$ from the training data where Φ is a set of parameters. The mapping predicts a label u for each new grid given its feature vector $\mathbf{v}$, simulating how a visual neuron responds to the low attentive stimuli in the receptive field.

It is natural to use a neural network to simulate the visual neuron response. But a standard neural network training needs to solve a non-convex, unconstrained minimization problem (Mandal, Majumdar, & Wu, 2007). Support Vector Machine

(SVM) models are similar to classical multilayer perception neural network in many aspects. An SVM using kernel function provides an alternate training method for multilayer perception neural network in which the network weights are obtained by solving a quadratic programming problem with linear constraints. Therefore, we apply a kernel SVM to our problem with radial basis function

$$k(\mathbf{v}_1, \mathbf{v}_2) = \exp(-\gamma \, \| \, \mathbf{v}_1 - \mathbf{v}_2 \, \| \, 2, \gamma > 0$$

(5)

where $\mathbf{v}_i$ is a low level visual feature vector. Instead of using the binary classification results, LAS is represented by the confidence scores output from the SVM model. A confidence score indicates the distance from an individual sample to the haperplane separating the two classes. Figure 5 gives an example of estimated LASs of a video frame.

4.3 LAR Map

Given a video frame, the LASs form an LAR map. Suppose the size of an specific overlay template is $n \times m$ grids and the display duration is t frames. The average LAS over this $n \times m \times t$ volume can be used to represent the *non-intrusiveness* (NI) of the overlay ad placed in this region.

To facilitate efficient computation of non-intrusiveness in both spatial and temporal domains, we build a 3D integral image (Viola & Jones, 2004) over the LAR map of the entire video. With the integral image, averaging over an $n \times m \times t$ volume is reduced to 8 arithmetic operations. The integrate image will be used for ad placement optimization discussed in the next section.

5 JOINT OPTIMIZATION FOR OVERLAY ADS

This section provides an optimization framework to fit a video overlay ad into a given video. The goal is to balance the following key factors:

1. The *non-intrusiveness* of the ad placements.
2. The *attractiveness* of the overlay ad, which is defined by a set of compatibility metrics between ad text and ad template, as explained in Section 5.3.
3. The *relevance* of selected ads. As mentioned in Section 3.3, the ad delivery engine returns a list of top ranked ads for each video. This provides additional opportunity of selecting only a few ads in the list to maximize the first two objectives, without affecting ad relevance.
4. The time interval between any two ad insertion points. This is set to be longer than a pre-defined threshold to avoid frequent ad showing.

5.1 Formulation

Let $\mathcal{A}$ denote the set of most relevant text ads returned by the ad delivery engine, with each ad $a \in A$ having a rank score r_a. The set of expert designed templates is denoted as T. Each template has a couple of text boxes, and the ad title and description can be dynamically fitted to the text boxes in rendering. We use $\varphi(a,t)$ to represent how well the text of the ad a can be fitted to the template t, and it is called ad-template compatibility and will be described in detail in Section 5.3. Suppose a template t is placed at location $l=(p,\mathbf{x})$ where p is the time location and $\mathbf{x}$ the space location, the *non-intrusiveness* (NI) of this ad placement is defined as the average LAS over the entire placement region and duration, denoted as $\psi\big(t, p, \mathbf{x}\big)$ or $\psi\big(t, l\big)$. Let

$$\mathcal{L}_t = \{p, \mathbf{x}\} \mid \psi(t, p, \mathbf{x}) > \mu \,,$$

i.e., $\mathcal{L}_t$ is the set of all locations at which the NI of placing an ad with template t is greater than a threshold μ. To generate and place an overlay ad, we need a template t (and the template parameters adjusted and included in t), a text ad a, and the placement location $(p,\mathbf{x})$. In other words, an overlay ad can be represented by a quadruplet $o=(t,a,p,\mathbf{x})$. Suppose it is expected to place at most K overlay ads on a video, which forms a set $\mathcal{O} = \{o_i\}_{i=1}^{K}$. Here K depends on the length of the video. To make sure that no repeated overlay ads irritate the viewers, any two ads in O are completely different, *i.e.*, $o_i \neq o_j$, $\forall o_i, o_j \in O, i \neq j$. Here $o_i \neq o_j$ is defined as $t_i \neq t_j$, $a_i \neq a_j$, $p_i \neq p_j$, and $\mathbf{x}_i \neq \mathbf{x}_j$. The set O can be found by maximizing the following objective function

$$\max_{\mathcal{O}} R(\mathcal{O}) = \sum_{o \in \mathcal{O}} \alpha \psi(t, p, \mathbf{x}) + \beta \phi(a, t) + \gamma r_a \tag{6}$$

$$s.t. \mid pi - pj \mid > \kappa, o_i \neq o_j, \forall o_i, o_j \in \mathcal{O}, i \neq, i \neq j \tag{7}$$

Here the parameters (α, β, γ) control the strength of each constraint, and are non-negative satisfying $(\alpha + \beta + \gamma) = 1$. And κ is the minimal time interval between any two overlay ads.

5.2 Solution

Suppose the average size of $\mathcal{L}_t$ is $\overline{N}_\mathcal{L}$, $|\mathcal{T}| = N_T$, and $|\mathcal{A}| = N_A$, the solution space of the optimization problem in Eqn. 6 has $\overline{N}_\mathcal{L}^K \binom{N_T}{K}\binom{N_A}{K}$ combinations, exponentially growing with K, the number of required overlay ads. Even though usually $K \leq 5$ and $N_A \leq 10$ in real applications, the number of templates N_T can amount to hundreds. This is very challenging for a online system. To reduce the computational cost, we propose a greedy searching algorithm for Eqn. 6 (see Algorithm 1). The basic idea is to greedily find the best overlay ad one by one, instead of finding the optimal combinations simultaneously. In Algorithm 1, the time complexity of Step 5 and 9 is $O(\overline{N}_\mathcal{L} N_T)$ and that of Step 6 is $O(N_T N_A)$. So the total time complexity of Algorithm 1 is

$O(KN_T(\overline{N}_\mathcal{L} + N_A))$ that is acceptable for our online system.

A time consuming part is to obtain $\mathcal{L}_t$ for each template t, which involves computing an average LAS at each spatial-temporal location and sifting out the locations with low scores. This computational cost can be largely reduced by playing the following tricks. (1) As mentioned in Section 4.3, calculation of a average LAS can be reduced to several arithmetic operations by using a 3D integral image. (2) By design, each template is expected to be placed in one of the eight areas: four corners and four sides (the central area of the video window is never touched by overlay ads), but it can be fine adjusted within the area. So for each template, we only need to compute the average LAS in one area. (3) The templates can be grouped by their placing areas and then by their sizes. Then one $\mathcal{L}$ is needed for all templates in the same group. This is practical due to the design requirement of standardized template size. And (4) very close candidates in $\mathcal{L}_t$ can be consolidated using a neighborhood suppression algorithm such as (Agarwal & Triggs, 2004). This trick largely reduces the size of $\mathcal{L}_t$, *i.e.*, $\overline{N}_\mathcal{L}$, subsequently reduces the time complexity of Algorithm 1.

Figure 6 gives two optimization results for the same video but at different user-click times. The difference between the two results is due to that the text ads returned by the ad delivery engine are changing over time, even for the same video, to allow opportunities for more advertisers. This also means that the optimization problem must be solved online.

5.3 Ad-Template Compatibility

As mentioned above, the ad text should be fitted to an appropriate template so as to enhance the viewing experience, *e.g.*, a short ad prefers a template with small text boxes as in Figure 6.

Algorithm 1. Greedy searching algorithm for Eqn. 6

1. **Input:** $\mathcal{L}_t, \phi(a,t), \psi(t,p,\mathbf{x}), \forall \in \mathcal{T}, \mathcal{A} \in$ and $\forall (p,\mathbf{x})$
2. **Output:** $\mathcal{O}$
3. $k=0$, $\mathcal{O} \neq \varnothing$
4. Repeat
5. For $\forall t \in \mathcal{T}$, select $l_t \in \mathcal{L}_t$ that has max NI value among all the locations in $\mathcal{L}_t$
6. Select $t^* \in \mathcal{T}$ and $a^* \in \mathcal{A}$ to maximize $\max\limits_{t,a} \alpha\, \psi(t,l_t) + \beta\phi(a,t) + \gamma r_a$
7. $k \leftarrow k+1, \mathcal{O} \leftarrow \mathcal{O} \cap \{o^*\}$ where $o = (t^*, a^*, l_{t*})$
8. $\mathcal{T} \leftarrow \mathcal{T} - t^*, \mathcal{A} \leftarrow \mathcal{A} - a^*$
9. $\forall l = (p,\mathbf{x}) \in \mathcal{L}_t \leftarrow \mathcal{L}_t - l$ if $|p - p^*| \leq \kappa$
10. Until $k=K$ or all $\mathcal{L}_t$ are empty
11. Return $\mathcal{O}$

So, an ad-template compatibility is needed to measure how well an ad is fitted to a template. The compatibility needs to consider three objective constraints

1. Bigger font size is preferable as long as it is in the acceptable range (the range is suggested by the UI designers).
2. Smaller unfilled space of the text boxes is preferable if the ad text is very short.
3. If the ad text is too long to be fitted into a text box, fewer cut-off letters are preferable.

Considering a simple case where a string s is fitted to a text box. Let $\mathcal{F}$ denote the set of allowable font sizes and $|\mathcal{F}| = N_{\mathcal{F}}$. Given a font size $z \in F$, assume n_z characters can be exactly fitted into the text box. Then the difference $\delta_z = |n_z - |s||$ indicates the length of unfilled space or the number of cut-off letters. We use the following objective function to measure how well the string s is fitted to the text box using font size z:

$$\rho_s(z) = e^{-\eta|z-\tilde{z}|} + \omega e^{\xi\delta_z} \tag{8}$$

where $\tilde{z}$ is the max font size in $\mathcal{F}$, η and ξ are positive coefficients, and ω is the weight.

For a template with two text boxes that are for ad title τ and ad description d respectively, the font size for d should be slightly smaller than that for τ, i.e., $z_\tau - \varsigma \leq z_d \leq z_\tau$. Considering this constraint, the ad-template compatibility for an ad $a = (\tau, d)$ and template t is defined as the maximum of the objective function:

$$\phi(a,t) = \max_{\substack{z_\tau \in \mathcal{F}, z_d \in \mathcal{F} \\ z_\tau - \varsigma \leq z_d \leq z_t}} \rho_\tau(z_\tau) + \rho_d(z_d) \tag{9}$$

The solution to the above maximum problem also gives optimal font sizes as by product that are necessary to generate attractive overlay ads. To improve efficiency, the compatibilities can be calculated offline, since the size of F and the length of ad text are in a limited range.

Also note that each template has a set of parameters, such as font size/color and entire color configuration, which are dynamically program-

Figure 6. Two optimization results for the same video but at different user-click times. The selected templates and locations may vary even for the same video because the text ads are changing. (a) Short text ad prefers a small template; (b) Long text ad prefers a large template

a

b

mable. But currently only the font size is optimized while adjustment of other parameters is left for future work.

6 EXPERIMENTAL RESULTS

We have performed extensive experiments to evaluate the performance of the proposed LAR detector, and verify if the corresponding low attentive score is indeed consistent with human judgment. User studies are also given to gauge the quality of the output from ad placement optimization. Results provide strong evidence for the effectiveness of the proposed approach.

6.1 Data Collection

We crawled from a major video publisher site over 20,000 legal videos with various sizes, qualities, and lengths. The videos also cover categories including news, sports, indoor /outdoor activity, natural scene, and cartoon. Among them, 100 videos are randomly selected for training the LAR detector and another 100 videos are chosen for user study on ad placement. And the rest are processed by the back-end system and will be used for testing with live traffic in this video publisher site.

The training data is prepared by showing the labelers a square 32×32 region in a video frame selected from a random video. The labeler is asked to assign the region a label of either 1:*low attentive* (LA) or -1:*high attentive* (HA). The labeling tool allows the access of neighboring frames to provide the motion context of the region being labeled.

6.2 Performance of LAR Detector

We collect 2000 labeled regions, among which 80% is used for training and the rest for testing. The low level visual features are obtained from each labeled region. Then the SVM models with radial basis kernel function are trained as LAR detectors. In the testing stage, the SVM models predict an LA/HA label for each testing sample based on the confidence score s:

$$s \geq \zeta, \ LA$$
$$s < \zeta, \ HA \tag{10}$$

where ζ is a discrimination threshold.

We measure the performance using a *receiver operating characteristic* (ROC) curve, where a plot of *true positive rate* vs. *false positive rate* is presented as the threshold ζ varying from minimum to maximum. We compare LAR detectors that are trained on a single feature category (contrast, motion, gradient, or color information) to the LAR detector that is trained on a combination of the features. The ROC curves are plotted in Figure 7. The LAR detector using combined feature vectors has a significant improvement over those trained on a single feature category.

Table 1 gives the average accuracy of five-folder cross validation, for each of the five LAR detectors. It also shows that combining the features improves the performance, by about 14%. Note that we are using the average LAS over the entire ad placement region, instead of using individual scores of grids, to measure the intrusiveness of

Figure 7. ROC curves of the LAR detectors that are trained on a single feature category (contrast, motion, gradient, or color information) and of the LAR detector that is trained on a combination of them

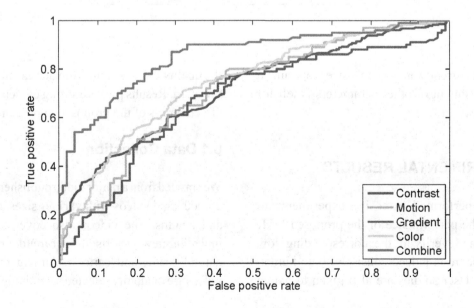

ad placement. This can further reduce errors caused by LAR detectors for individual grids.

6.3 User Study on Ad Placement

It is hard to objectively evaluate a video advertising system due to multiple factors including ad placement location, duration, content, appearance, and ad relevance. To simplify the problem while still obtaining meaningful results, we designed two user studies to evaluate the ad placement and ad-template compatibility, respectively. In each user study, our system is controlled to allow only a single-variable and then is compared to a baseline system.

We invite 18 users to participate in the user study on ad placement. For each of the 100 selected videos, two ad placements are selected. The first placement has a fixed location at the bottom of the video and starts at the 10-th second from the

beginning of the video. This setting represents most of the existing video advertising systems in industry using overlay ad. The second placement is provided by our algorithm described in Section 5. To avoid the distraction of template animations, the overlay ad is replaced by half-transparent white rectangles that have typical sizes representing each template group. Each time a short clip containing a single faked overlay ad (white rectangle) is cut from the original video and shown to the user. At the end of each clip, the user is asked to give a score: 1 (*intrusive*), 2 (*normal*), and 3 (*non-intrusive*). The video clips are presented to users in a random order so that the users cannot guess whether the ad placement is fixed or selected by our algorithm.

We first study the relationship between the human evaluation score and the algorithm generated LAS. The algorithm makes sense only if the scores are consistent. At each evaluated location,

Table 1. Average accuracy over five-folder cross validation, for each of the five LAR detectors

	Contrast	Motion	Gradient	Color	Combine
Acc	66.1%	68.0%	67.0%	69.5%	79.1%

Figure 8. Histograms of low attentive scores for each human evaluation score group

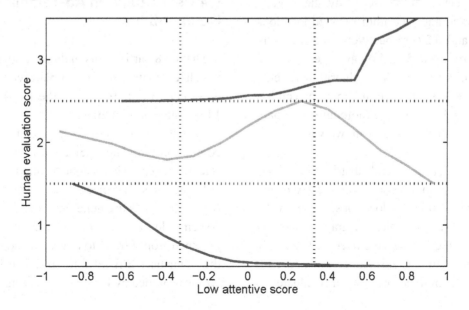

Table 2. Percentage of the histograms over each interval. It is equal to the area under the histogram curve in each interval in Figure 8

	[-1, -1/3)	[-1/3, 1/3)	[1/3, 1]
3 (non-intrusive)	0.8%	14.2%	85.0%
2 (normal)	29.2%	43.1%	27.7%
1 (intrusive)	86.8%	11.9%	1.3%

we use the algorithm to compute an LAS. These LASs are separated into three groups with respect to the human scores. Then a histogram of the LASs is obtained for each group. Figure 8 plots the three histograms, where the range of LASs is divided into intervals of $[-1,-1/3)$, $[-1/3,1/3)$, and $[1/3,1]$, respectively. These intervals correspond to the three human evaluation scores of 1, 2, and 3, respectively. The percentage of a histogram over each interval is given in Table 2, which is similar to a confusion matrix. Both Figure 8 and Table 2 show that our algorithm is consistent with human perception. Note that the histogram corresponding to the human evaluation score 2 (*normal*) spreads in a large region. This is because human can easily tell an extreme case while harder to decide on a moderate one.

From the above, the higher LAS of an ad placement location, the higher human evaluation score is expected. In the user study, the average LASs of fixed and algorithm selected locations are -0.49 and 0.27, respectively, and the users scored them 1.56 and 2.24 on average.

To quantify how much the algorithm selected locations are less intrusive in human perception than the fixed locations, we thoroughly compare the human evaluation scores in two ways.

1.   We inspect the overall distribution of human evaluation scores, for the fixed and algorithm selected locations, respectively. Figure 9(a) gives the bar graph where the percentage numbers are over the bars. 75% of algorithm selected locations, compared to only 38% of fixed locations, are evaluated as

non-intrusive or *normal*. Note that a small portion of the selected locations are also evaluated as *intrusive*. We inspected those video clips and found that the users are usually prone to be critical to the ad placement. They felt that the placements are intrusive even overlay ads block informative areas in only a few frames.

2.   We analyze how the same user evaluates the same video on average. In the user study, the users evaluated both a fixed and a selected location for each individual video. We compute the percentages of comparisons with respect to the three cases: the fixed location is better, the selected better, or they tie. The percentages are given in Figure 9(b). The users felt that the selected locations are better in about 87% comparisons.

6.4 User Study on Ad-Template Compatibility

We have 18 participants in the second user study which evaluates the ad-template compatibility described in Eqn. 9. Among the 18 participants, 14 are male and 4 female.

The user study is designed such that the most compatible template is selected given a randomly selected text ad. This is done by maximizing Eqn. 9. Using the same selected text ad and template, two overlay ads are generated and displayed on screen side-by-side. One ad uses the font size obtained from Eqn. 9 to render the ad text while the other uses a fixed font size. The fixed font size is provided by UI experts in designing stage

Figure 9. Comparing human evaluation scores between fixed ad placement locations and algorithm selected locations. (a) Percentage of the locations with respect to human evaluation scores. (b) Percentage of selected locations (Sel) that have higher, equal, or lower human evaluation scores than fixed locations (Fix)

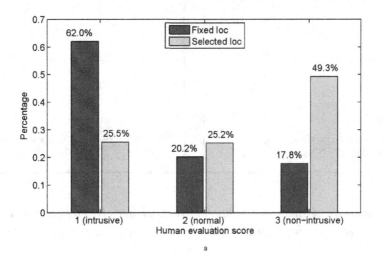

a

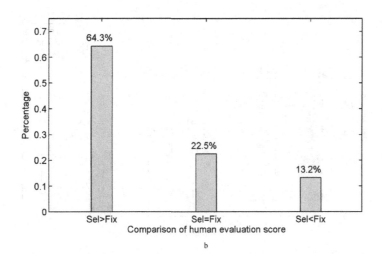

b

by default and is not optimal for a specific text ad. To avoid the distractions from the video, the generated overlay ads are placed on a uniform background, instead of on videos. Figure 10 gives a snapshot of two side-by-side overlay ads.

The user is asked to compare the two ads and choose from three options including: algorithm selection is better, fixed selection is better, or tie. Figure 11 gives the percentage of each category.

The users felt that the algorithm selection is equal or better than fixed selection in 77% pairs. We also calculate the percentage for male and female, respectively. The difference between male and female participants is significant: the female is more critical to ad placement. But, the fact of the unbalanced male/female participants probably weakens this statement.

Figure 10. A snapshot of two side-by-side overlay ads. Left: an overlay ad using the font size obtained from Eqn. 9; Right: an overlay ad using a fixed font size provided by UI experts in designing stage. Users are asked to compare these two ads

 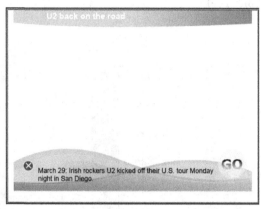

Figure 11. Evaluation on the ad-template compatibility. Each bar gives a percentage of the comparison pairs that are marked by users as: algorithm selection is better (A>F), fixed selection is better (A<F), or tie (A=F)

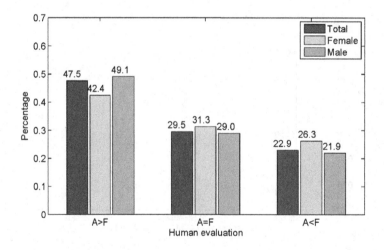

7 CONCLUSION AND FUTURE WORK

We propose a system of content and attention aware overlay for online video advertising. The key contribution is an algorithm that balances attractiveness and non-intrusiveness in a unified framework. Specifically, we introduce animate templates designed by UI experts to improve the attractiveness of overlay ad and reduce the ad-vertisers' cost. The constraints between text ads, templates, and online video are formulated into an optimization problem. To reduce the intrusiveness, we use a machine learning algorithm to learn a model that simulates human perception to detect low attentive region. The experimental results as well as the user study report provide strong evidence to the effectiveness of our approach.

A debatable issue is whether the ads should be placed on/at "interesting" video shots. Many researchers (H. Liu et al., 2008, Mei et al., 2007) support this argument. This is probably true for the TV style in-stream ads, because the absorbed viewers cannot skip the ads and some of them get used to be patient to wait for video/TV coming back. However, if an overlay ad is placed on a very interesting video shot, the ad may be avoided or even closed by the viewers because the viewers are completely attracted by the video content itself. While the overlay ads placed on less interesting video shots may attract the viewers' attention, as long as the overlay ads themselves are attractive enough, since the viewers are less absorbed by the video content. But these statements still need further evaluation using live traffic. That is why we did not consider this in our optimization formulation. We leave this evaluation for future work.

To further improve the attractiveness of the overlay ads, a future work is to adjust the color of the template and the ad text such that they are visually compatible with the background video.

REFERENCES

Agarwal, A., & Triggs, B. (2004). *Learning to track 3D human motion from silhouettes*. ICML.

Ballan, L., Bertini, M., & Jain, A. (2008). A system for automatic detection and recognition of advertising trademarks in sports videos. In *Proceedings of the 16th ACM International Conference on Multimedia*.

Barnard, K., Duygulu, P., de Freitas, N., Forsyth, D., Blei, D., & Jordan, M. I. (2003). Matching words and pictures. *Journal of Machine Learning Research*, 3, 1107–1135. doi:10.1162/153244303322533214

Deshpande, S., Naphade, P., Rao, C. V. K., Bhadada, K., & Rangan, P. V. (2007). *Method and apparatus for including virtual ads in video presentations* (Nos. 7,158,666).

Duan, L., Xu, M., Yu, X., & Tian, Q. (2002). A unified framework for semantic shot classification in sports videos. In *Proceedings of the Tenth ACM International Conference on Multimedia*.

Frank, E., Paynter, G. W., Witten, I. H., Gutwin, C., & Nevill-Manning, C. G. (1999). Domain-specific keyphrase extraction. In *Proceedings of the Sixteenth International Joint Conference on Artificial Intelligence*.

Ha, L. (1996). Advertising clutter in consumer magazines: dimensions and effects. *Journal of Advertising Research*, 36.

Hu, J., Zeng, H., Li, H., Niu, C., & Chen, Z. (2007). Demographic prediction based on user's browsing behavior. In *Proceedings of the 16th International Conference on World Wide Web*.

Itti, L., & Koch, C. (2001, Mar). Computational modelling of visual attention. *Nature Reviews. Neuroscience*, 2(3), 194–203. doi:10.1038/35058500

Itti, L., Koch, C., & Niebur, E. (1998, Nov). A model of saliency-based visual attention for rapid scene analysis. *IEEE Transactions on Pattern Analysis and Machine Intelligence*, 20(11), 1254–1259. doi:10.1109/34.730558

Lacerda, A., Cristo, M., Gonçalves, M. A., Fan, W., Ziviani, N., & Ribeiro-Neto, B. (2006). *Learning to advertise*. SIGIR.

Li, H., Edwards, S. M., & Lee, J. (2002). Measuring the intrusiveness of advertisements: scale development and validation. *Journal of Advertising*.

Li, X., Chen, L., Zhang, L., Lin, F., & Ma, W. (2006). Image annotation by large-scale content-based image retrieval. In *Proceedings of the 14th Annual ACM International Conference on Multimedia*.

Li, Y., Wan, K. W., Yan, X., & Xu, C. (2005). Real time advertisement insertion in baseball video based on advertisement effect. In *Proceedings of the 11th ACM International Conference on Multimedia* (pp. 343–346).

Liao, W. S., Chen, K., & Hsu, W. H. (2008). Ad-image: video advertising by image matching and ad scheduling optimization. In *SIGIR*.

Liu, H., Jiang, S., Huang, Q., & Xu, C. (2008). A generic virtual content insertion system based on visual attention analysis. In *Proceeding of the 16th ACM International Conference on Multimedia* (pp. 379–388). New York: ACM.

Liu, T., Sun, J., Zheng, N., Tang, X., & Shum, H. (2007). *Learning to detect a salient object*. CVPR.

Ma, Y., Hua, X., Lu, L., & Zhang, H. (2005). A generic framework of user attention model and its application in video summarization. *IEEE Transactions on Multimedia, 7*(5), 907–919. doi:10.1109/TMM.2005.854410

Mandal, T., Majumdar, A., & Wu, Q. (2007). Face recognition by curvelet based feature extraction. In *Image Analysis and Recognition* (LNCS 4633, pp. 806-817).

Mei, T., Hua, X., & Li, S. (2008). Contextual in-image advertising. In *Proceeding of the 16th ACM International Conference on Multimedia* (pp. 439–448). New York: ACM.

Mei, T., Hua, X., Yang, L., & Li, S. (2007). Videosense: towards effective online video advertising. In *Proceedings of the 15th International Conference on Multimedia* (pp. 1075–1084). New York: ACM.

Ribeiro-Neto, B., Cristo, M., Golgher, P. B., & Moura, E. Silva de. (2005). Impedance coupling in content-targeted advertising. In *SIGIR. State of the industry—liverail's q4 2008 review of online video advertising* (Tech. Rep.). (2009). Live Research Department.

Tamir, M., Sharir, A., & Wilf, I. (2002). *Method and apparatus for automatic electronic replacement of billboards in a video image* (Nos. 6,384,871).

Turney, P. D. (2000). Learning algorithms for keyphrase extraction. *Information Retrieval, 2*(4), 303–336. doi:10.1023/A:1009976227802

Viola, P., & Jones, M. (2002). Robust real-time object detection. *International Journal of Computer Vision, 57*(2), 137–154. doi:10.1023/B:VISI.0000013087.49260.fb

Walther, D., Riesenhuber, M., Poggio, T., Itti, L., & Koch, C. (2002, Apr). Towards an integrated model of saliency-based attention and object recognition in the primate's visual system. *Journal of Cognitive Neuroscience, B14*(S), 46-47.

Wan, K., & Xu, C. (2006). Automatic content placement in sports highlights. In *IEEE International Conference on Multimedia & Expo* (pp. 1893–1896).

Weideman, M., & Haig-Smith, T. (2002). *An investigation into search engines as a form of targeted advert delivery*. SAICSIT.

Xiao, J., Cheng, H., Sawhney, H., Rao, C., & Isnardi, M. (2006). Bilateral filtering-based optical flow estimation with occlusion detection. In *European Conference on Computer Vision*.

Yih, W. T., Goodman, J., & Carvalho, V. R. (2006). Finding advertising keywords on web pages. In *Proceedings of WWW*.

KEY TERMS AND DEFINITIONS

Ad relevance: a metric to measure the relevance between the advertisements and advertised videos or the veiwers.

Ad template: in this work it refers to a flash or silverlight animation consisting of two text boxes associated with the ad title and description, and of a close button and a link button that enable interactions with users.

Attractiveness: the degree to which advertisement in a media vehicle attacts the viewers.

Intrusiveness: the degree to which advertisement in a media vehicle interrupts the flow of an editorial unit.

Low attentive region: regions of videos where viewers pay little attention.

Overlay ad: a technology to deliver text ads to online videos by overlaying text information on the video window

Targeting: the ability to deliver the right ad to the right person at the right time.

ENDNOTES

[1]   http://www.youtube.com

[2]   Some previous work (Mei et al., 2007, H. Liu et al., 2008) improve the ad attractiveness for other ad formats by inserting ads in the most "interesting" shots. We will discuss its pros and cons in the Section 7.

[3]   http://en.wikipedia.org/wiki/Behavioral_targeting

[4]   http://www.crunchbase.com

[5]   http://www.videoegg.com

[6]   http://www.brightcove.com

[7]   http://www.blinkx.com/

Chapter 8
An Explorative Study of Virtual Product Placement:
Take ViSA as an Example

Chia-Hu Chang
National Taiwan University, Taiwan

Ja-Ling Wu
National Taiwan University, Taiwan

ABSTRACT

With the aid of content-based multimedia analysis, virtual product placement opens up new opportunities for advertisers to effectively monetize the existing videos in an efficient way. In addition, a number of significant and challenging issues are raising accordingly, such as how to less-intrusively insert the contextually relevant advertising message (what) at the right place (where) and the right time (when) with the attractive representation (how) in the videos. In this chapter, domain knowledge in support of delivering and receiving the advertising message is introduced, such as the advertising theory, psychology and computational aesthetics. We briefly review the state of the art techniques for assisting virtual product placement in videos. In addition, we present a framework to serve the virtual spotlighted advertising (ViSA) for virtual product placement and give an explorative study of it. Moreover, observations about the new trend and possible extension in the design space of virtual product placement will also be stated and discussed. We believe that it would inspire the researchers to develop more interesting and applicable multimedia advertising systems for virtual product placement.

DOI: 10.4018/978-1-60960-189-8.ch008

INTRODUCTION

Over the years, the rapid technical advances in video coding and broadband network delivery have led a huge amount of video content distribution. In addition, with dramatically boosted online video services, people can easily create, share, and watch tremendous videos in their daily lives. Either the traditional broadcasting or webcasting, the considerable population of the audiences brings forth great advertising boom indeed. Therefore, it has created phenomenal opportunities for advertisers and content owners to seek to monetize the video assets of the media industry and online video services. The multimedia advertising dramatically draws a lot of attention due to its potential commercial benefits (Hua et al., 2008; Wang, X. et al., 2009; Wang, J. et al., 2008, 2009).

In the field of advertising and marketing, lots of advertising strategies (Moriarty, 1991) were developed and widely adopted in practice based on the *advertising theory* and *psychology*. There are various media for conveying the advertising message to people, for example, texts, images, and videos. In order to grab and keep audiences' attention in a pleasing manner, advertisers usually bring together creativity into advertisements according to the principle of design and the *applied media aesthetics* (Zettl, 1999). Traditionally, *product placement* and the *30-second commercials* are commonly used in well-organized TV programs or movies. Product placement is a paid advertising message aimed at influencing audiences by bringing branded products or images into videos in a planned and unobtrusive way. On the other hand, the 30-second commercials are usually placed in the breaks of TV programs.

The traditional advertising model for broadcast videos is based mainly on the 30-second commercials. In order to watch the videos without missing the highlights, most audiences may find some of these commercials, which regularly interrupt video programs, boring and intrusive, but they were forced to endure them. With the growing popularity of IPTV and the advent of intelligent digital video recorder (DVR), video viewers are no longer passive audiences. Users can not only fast-forward through the videos but can also easily skip all or most of the commercials with the introduction of DVR technology. Such uncontrollable ability of gaining more technical power for users to avoid advertisements decreases the effectiveness of the 30-second commercials in videos. The advertising messages would not easily be delivered to the consumers unless the advertisements are very impressive or attractive to them. Facing diminished passive audiences, advertisers have to revise or reinvent their advertising strategies and promote their products in other ways. Therefore, product placement receives more and more attention and its importance rises in recent years.

According to the essential characteristic of advertising media, the advertisements can be divided into two categories: the physical advertisement and the virtual advertisement. By taking sports videos as an example, the trademarks or slogans which appeared on the billboards or printed on the court in reality are physical advertisements. On the other hand, the virtual advertisements are those which are inserted fictionally into videos by using computer-aided blending techniques. For example, the overlaid logos on the screen or the virtually projected logos on the court in the tennis videos are virtual advertisements (Yu et al., 2006, 2007, 2009). Generally, since physical advertisements originally appeared on the billboard at the fringes of the court, audiences do not feel disturbed while watching sports videos. However, with fixed content and locations of advertising, people usually adapt to the presence of physical advertisements and easily filter them out of their vision, which is the so-called *ad-blindness effect*. Thus, the advertising effectiveness produced in this way is limited. In contrast, the virtual advertisement is paid more attention due to its capability of permitting dynamic and switchable content for advertising. Since the additional contents, which are inserted into the videos virtually, can be considered as the virtual content compared to the original content, such insertion techniques are also called *virtual content insertion* (VCI). By using the VCI techniques, virtual product placement replaces specific objects or regions in the video with the branded products or images as seamlessly as possible after the program is complete. Generally, advertisers would hire professional editors to produce virtual product placement by manually post-processing videos. In order to achieve the goal of making virtual product placement vivid, they would carefully analyze the characteristics of each video and attentively implant the branded products or images into videos. Although professional editors could make the inserted branded products or images seem really a part of the original video and even create a variety of fancy animation effects for each case, such production of virtual product placement is very labor-intensive and inefficient. In addition, it may be very time-consuming and expensive for rapid productions on monetizing videos in this way. Fortunately, with the aid of content-based multimedia analysis, virtual product placement would become even more powerful and also considerably cheaper.

Currently, virtual product placement is mainly used in specific videos where the geometrical relationships can be easily estimated, such as sports videos which contain flat surfaces and detectable features. Based on the practical consideration to sacrifice partial generality as a tradeoff, advertisers attempt to preliminarily replace specific regions in the videos with advertisements (e.g., logos) to support the *image advertising* (Parker, 1992). Here, the image advertising is a tactic for promoting an *overall brand perception* of a company, a product or a service instead of its specific attributes. It is still a big challenge to automatically insert advertisements into videos with maximum capacity of visual communication in a virtually 3D projected way without artifacts. The size, placement locations, and the representation of advertisements are the critical factors that have significant impact on both the recognition effectiveness and the perceived intrusiveness. Accordingly, how to elaborately present the advertisement in videos for improving the advertising effectiveness is an important and challenging problem in the field of virtual product placement. In this chapter, we present a framework to serve the *virtual spotlighted advertising* (Chang et al., 2008, in press) by taking tennis videos as the target media for virtual product placement.

REVIEW OF THE LITERATURE

Product placement is a promotional tactic for increasing audiences' interest in a specific product. In 1957, a marketing researcher James Vicary conducted a subliminal advertising study in a movie theater for six weeks. During the movie, he projected the words "eat popcorn" and "drink Coca-Cola" on a movie screen for 1/3,000 of a second. Since the flashing messages subliminally directed audiences to eat popcorn and drink Coca-Cola, the sales of popcorn and cola in the movie theater increased 58% and 18% respectively. Product placement usually attempts to take advantage of such *subliminal perception* to influence audiences' brand choice and purchase behavior without letting them be aware that any advertising communication has taken place. For this reason, product placement is considered as a kind of *subliminal advertising* (Broyles, 2006).

Generally, the design space of product placement can be divided into three dimensions: *screen placement, script placement,* and *plot placement* (Russell, 1998), as shown in Figure 1. For screen placement, there are two ways to show branded products or the advertising message on the screen. One is *creative placement*, for example, it shows the scene where the billboards appear by artfully controlling the camera path; the other is *on-set placement*, it means the product is directly and dully placed in the environment of the scene. For script placement, the actor is asked to mention

Figure 1. The three dimensions of product placement

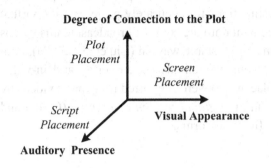

the brand or the product in the script. As for plot placement, the product becomes a part of the storyline by constructing a semantically or visually relevant connection between the product and the video content.

Nowadays, a considerable amount of multimedia content with product placement gain lots of commercial values. Although product placement is popular and nearly mature, there are many challenging issues that need to be addressed in designing strategies and mechanisms for virtual product placement. Specifically, how to less-intrusively insert the contextually relevant advertisements (what) at the right place (where) and the right time (when) with the attractive representation (how) in the videos are significant and challenging problems. In the following paragraphs, we will review the existing work which is relevant to virtual product placement. According to the research problems, they are classified into three major categories: advertisement selection (what), insertion points detection (where and when), and advertisement adaption (how). Meanwhile, we will discuss the roles of each category in the field of advertising.

Advertisement Selection

Before applying virtual advertisement insertion to multimedia, a proper advertisement should be selected first. The target advertising, which as-

sociates relevant candidate advertisements based on the audiences' preference, demographics or observed behaviors, was an effective method to be used for IPTV (Lim et al., 2008). On the other hand, *Mei et al.* proposed an online video advertising system (2007, 2009) in which contextually relevant advertising videos are selected for inserting at detected less intrusive time instances within video streams. In addition to videos, the contextual in-image advertising was proposed in (Mei et al., 2008) by considering the texture relevance and visual similarity between the advertising images and the target images.

Insertion Point Detection

The appropriate insertion point for temporal frames and spatial regions should be identified cautiously. A number of prior works have been conducted to analyze suitable insertion points for inserting advertisements into videos. Based on the domain knowledge of sports videos, the regions for virtual content replacement can be identified by detecting prescribed landmark targets in videos. For example, *Wan et al.* (2003) selected the region above the goal-mouth bar for placing virtual contents by exploiting the goal-mouth detection in soccer videos. Moreover, besides the goal mouth, *Xu et al.* (2004) detected and utilized the predefined static regions, the central ellipse, and the field boundaries to provide more opportunities for virtual content insertion in soccer videos.

The generic approaches (Wan et al., 2004, 2006; Li et al., 2005) were proposed for selecting the insertion regions in sports videos. In order to limit the clutter caused by additionally overlaying advertisements, the regions with crowded clutter and moving background are identified as suitable locations on each of the frames (Wan et al., 2004, 2006). On the other hand, based on the idea of making the advertisements inserted video more informative and abundant, the *less informative region* (LIR) at consecutive frames with less camera motion are selected in (Li et al., 2005). In recent years, lots of methods had been proposed attempting to identify the insertion regions by conducting the *human visual system* (HVS) analysis. Based on the results of visual attention modeling, less salient regions or unimportant regions of images are considered as non-intrusive positions for embedding the advertisements in (Mei et al., 2008). In addition, *Liu et al.* (2008) proposed the *lower attention region* (LAR) detection to automatically identify the spatial positions for inserting virtual contents into general videos by using the visual attention analysis. It is still an open issue that where is an effective region, which could be spatially replaced with the advertisement, on multimedia content.

In addition to the region, the timing for delivering the advertising message is also an important issue. The highlights of sports videos, which are highly relevant to game moments, are considered as suitable video segments to attract more viewers' attention for inserted advertisements. According to the estimation of the *viewer relevance measure* (VRM) (Wan et al., 2004, 2006), the temporal frames with low viewer relevance within the extracted highlights are selected as the timing instances to do virtual content exposure. For general videos, the *higher attractive shots* (HAS) (Liu et al., 2008a, 2008b) are automatically detected based on the visual attention analysis. In (Mei et al., 2007, 2009), the most relevant video advertisements were inserted at the time between two source video shots, which are with high discontinuity and low attractiveness content, to avoid interrupting the audience's viewing experience.

Advertisement Adaption

Generally, the type of virtual advertisement placement can be divided into two types: overlay and in-video placement. The in-video placement needs the knowledge of the geometry of the scene in the video to manipulate the inserted advertisement to make it like a part of the original video, while overlays can be done by simply placing the original

advertisement on the plane of video frames. *Yu et al.* (2006, 2007, 2009) proposed camera parameter estimations for accurately projecting the virtual content onto the court of broadcast tennis videos in a more stable way. In (Liu et al., 2008a), both placement methods (i.e., overlay and in-video placement) were supported for general videos by using the *global motion estimation* (GME) and affine transforms.

VIRTUAL SPOTLIGHTED ADVERTISING

As mentioned in the previous section, most existing related works have proposed various solutions to handle the problems about what, where, and when, but how to elaborately present the virtual advertisement is rarely touched. In other words, they focus on camera calibration, selection of insertion points and relevant advertisements, rather than the representation of advertisements. In this section, we present an alternative solution to the critical issues and show the way to extend virtual product placement from *screen placement* toward *plot placement* in the design space of product placement. We introduce a distinctive framework, which incorporates a top-down approach with a defined effectiveness measurement in terms of visual acuity. This framework shares similar goals as the inline advertising but emphasize more on the construction of the advertising representation and the virtually visual interactions between advertisements and video contents. Compared with the existing research, this framework has the following distinguishing features:

1. The foveation model, which is one of the HVS models, and the color harmonization are firstly explored to improve the visual cognition process of receiving the advertising message.
2. Important domain knowledge in support of delivering and receiving the advertising mes-

sage for virtual product placement is used, such as advertising theory, psychology, and computational aesthetics.

3. The framework, which elaborately supports virtual spotlighted advertising in tennis videos, can flexibly incorporate with the existing techniques of content-based video analysis and a variety of the contextual advertising to further improve the effectiveness.

Essential Ideas

In the field of advertising and marketing, AIDMA model, which was developed by Merrill Devoe (Barry & Howard, 1990), is a well-known fundamental model for sales promotion and for creating any advertising or marketing communications. AIDMA represents the psychological process that consumers respond to the advertisement communication and stands for a hierarchy of *Attention, Interest, Desire, Memory*, and *Action*, as shown in Figure 2. This process can be broken up into three stages: *Cognition, Affect*, and *Action*. Over these three stages the consumers first pay attention to the advertisements in the Cognition stage, and then they become interested in the corresponding brands or products, crave for the product and remember the brand or products in the affect stage. Finally, the consumers decide to take action to purchase the related product in the action stage. Notice that *interest, desire* and *action* are generally referred to viewers' personal preference and the attributes of products/services or the image of companies. In other words, evoking these three psychological reactions usually depends on the individuals' mind or need and the success of advertising campaigns. Nevertheless, it had shown that people instinctively prefer an item they have previously seen (Aaker, 1996) and such item memory provides a convenient cue for their purchase choice (Hoyer et al., 1990). Therefore, we usually identify the objectives of virtual product placement in terms of *attention* and *memory* on the basis of AIDMA-inspired advertising message

Figure 2. The AIDMA model. The arrow indicates the order of the psychological processes that consumers respond to the communication of advertising messages

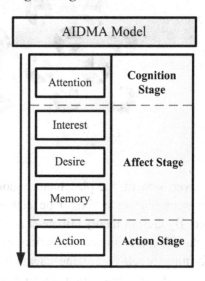

communication to fundamentally serve the general audiences and advertisers.

Intuitively, a simple but effective way to ensure the advertisement being noticed is to directly emplace it on the salient region especially at the time when people concentrate on watching. As for sports videos, the important play events are mainly produced by attractive objects (such as players or balls) and occur frequently at the court during the game proceeding. This is also the reason why the studies of the sports video summarization (Tjondronegoro et al., 2004) take shots with court view as part of highlights. The frames within the court view shots represent the audiences' main focus instances in the temporal domain; on the other hand, the associated locations of players or balls are the corresponding attractive areas in the spatial domain. Therefore, such regions in the court view frames could be considered as candidate insertion points in both temporal and spatial domains to let audiences naturally see the inserted advertisement.

In order to further increase audiences' awareness and reinforce their memory about the in-

Figure 3. An example shows the self-organizing tendency for human brains based on Gestalt theory. (a) It can be seen as a cube floating in front of black circles. (b) A cube without masking. (c) A cube without black circles

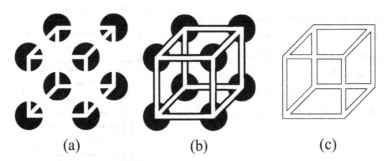

(a)   (b)   (c)

serted advertisement, the placement region and the representation style should be elaborately designed. By Gestalt theory (Bruce et al., 1996) of psychology, the human sensation has the form-forming (or self-organizing) capability with respect to the visual recognition of an incomplete pattern, which is composed of simple lines and curves. Specifically, humans visually perceive an object as a "whole" pattern instead of parts or components and recognize it according to their experience or imagination. Such perceptual organizing capability of human senses is the key concept of Gestalt theory. Since more personal experience and imagination would be involved in the Gestalt-based recognition process for an incomplete pattern, presenting an object in the way of partially masking would be more attractive and impressive to viewers. As an illustrative example given in (Bradley & Petry, 1977), we are capable of forming a cube while looking at the image shown in Figure 3(a) and feel it more attractive than the clear and complete cube shown in Figure 3(b), and Figure 3(c). Such representation styles inspired by Gestalt theory are widely used to arouse people's curiosity and grab their attention among artists and designers in the design of esthetic arrangement for posters, magazines, and advertisements. Since the moving attractive object (e.g., player) attracts much audiences' attention and directs audiences' sight subconsciously, inserting the advertisement at the moving region of the player makes the advertisement more attentive. Also, the moving player sporadically covers the advertisement. This coverage also causes the audiences' curiosity about the inserted advertisement. Therefore, audiences will be repeatedly impressed with the inserted advertisement by seeing it unconsciously or consciously without interruption.

Generally, if the inserted advertisement could be looked like as a part of the scene in the video, audiences would see it with higher acceptability. Thus, instead of simply overlaying the advertisements on the screen without considering the geometry of the scene, we should make the advertisement insertion more visually compelling by blending it on the court, i.e., in-video placement. In this way, audiences could not adapt to the advertisement, which is blended on the player moving region of the court, and filter it out of their vision, especially at the moment of sports highlights. Furthermore, since the surroundings of advertisement are monotone court color and smooth texture, blending the advertisement on the court can also easily catch audiences' attention. But if it is visually or contextually irrelevant to the sports, audiences may feel intrusive and thus result in negative impact on the viewing experience. Therefore, the size and color distribution of the projected advertisement should be carefully adjusted based on the human visual model and computational aesthetics. Furthermore, we can dynamically control the transparency of advertise-

Figure 4. The framework for the presented virtual spotlighted advertising in tennis videos

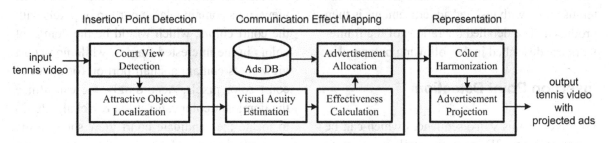

ments in a non-uniform manner according to its distance from certain attractive object to construct a virtual interaction between the inserted advertisement and the video content. In this way, the visual interference of inserted advertisements would be reduced and the introduced intrusiveness could be further limited. Furthermore, the position movement of the attractive object gracefully spotlights the inserted advertisement. Consequently, audiences would unconsciously reinforce their memory of the inserted advertisements without missing the details of the game proceeding.

Based on the above observations and concepts, the virtual spotlighted advertising was developed. Its benefit is twofold. First, the effect of *subliminal perception* (Smith & Rogers, 1994) is exploited for the viewers, who concentrate on the game proceeding, to influence their brand choice. The concept of ViSA can be regarded as a variation of the *subliminal advertising* (Broyles et al., 2006; Tsai et al., 2007), but with no legal problems. Second, the inattentive viewers will be attracted to watch the projected advertisements because of the *Gestalt effect* (Bruce et al., 1996). In this ingenious way, ViSA could efficiently deliver the advertising message to the diverse audiences of tennis videos.

The Framework of ViSA

Figure 4 illustrates the overview of the framework, which consists of three phases, including: insertion point detection, communication effect mapping,

and representation. First, given an input tennis video, the court view shots of the video, which people pay more attention to, are detected automatically in the insertion point detection phase. A predefined attractive object on the court which implicitly leads viewers to see the advertisement is then localized via the attractive objects localization module.

In the communication effect mapping phase, the human visual foveation model (Geisler & Perry, 1998) is adopted for estimating extraneous visual acuity (i.e. spatial resolving capacity) while watching the attractive object. And then, a saliency map in terms of visual acuity is constructed for each corresponding court view shot. The effectiveness of candidate regions on the court for advertisement insertion is quantified according to the salience strength. With the information of effectiveness for candidate regions, the appointed advertisement which is selected from the advertisement database is resized and allocated to a proper region.

Finally, in the representation phase, the color harmonization is applied to the selected advertisement to harmonize it with the background i.e., the video frames with court view. After that, the transparency of advertisement is tuned on the basis of a non-uniform distribution, obtained from the human visual foveation model for reducing the visual intrusiveness and enhancing the advertising effect simultaneously. According to camera calibration parameters, the well-processed advertisement is projected onto the most effective region of video frames with court view for a duration measured in video shots. After all prescribed processes, the tennis video with inserted advertisements is then produced. The detailed operations of the framework are described in the following paragraphs.

Insertion Point Detection

For given tennis video sequences which can be represented as a 3D space-time volume, so as to provide the information for finding candidate insertion points in both temporal and spatial domains, the spatiotemporal attention analysis is needed. Note that the basic temporal unit here is a video shot and the spatial unit is a set of pixels of the video frames. Compared with other videos, such as news and movies, sports videos have well-defined content structures and domain-specific rules. Because of the finite number of typical views, scenes, and production rules, the sports video has a predictable temporal syntax. For example, different types of views presented in a tennis video can be generally divided into two principal classes: court view and non-court view. In other words, tennis videos, generally, are composed of court view shots and non-court view shots. In a tennis video production, court views contain much of the pertinent information, since from a serve starts to a break which momentarily stops the game, the scenes are usually shown with the court views. Furthermore, the important play events which most viewers naturally focused on occur frequently within the court view shots. Since court shots represent viewers' main focus of game proceeding, we first determine whether a video shot is in court view or not.

Court View Detection

A common approach to identify the court view shots within the input sports video is to use visual features, such as ground colors, court lines and positions of players. In most of the methods that use color information, the court color has to be evaluated first, because it can largely vary from one shot to another. In tennis videos, the court view shots contain a large portion of pixels with the court colors, which would be the dominant colors in the interested frames, while non-court view shots contain a small portion (or none) of court color pixels. Accordingly, we can utilize the dominant color ratio (Ekin & Tekalp, 2003) to locate the candidate court view shots in the temporal domain. However, the color of court surface varies in different tennis matches or in different lighting and viewing angles. In order to avoid the use of predefined court color, by adaptively determining the color characteristics, the adaptive court detection method proposed in (Liu, 2005) is adopted. Before detecting the court view shots, the input tennis video is first decomposed into shots by using the color-based method given in (Zhang et al., 1993). For each shot, we extract the middle frame as its key-frame to do court view detection. According to the ratio of the amount of dominant-color pixels in a video frame, we can identify possible candidate court view shots.

For the candidate court view shots, we detect the court lines based on the techniques of line detection and camera calibration (Yu et al., 2008; Farin et al., 2004). We first extract white pixels in frames, and accordingly apply a standard Hough transform line detector to find the white lines. We can obtain the court position if all court lines are perfectly detected. However, because of the noises caused by players or the characteristic of different stadiums, court lines are often unclear, and many misses or false alarms occur in line detection. Fortunately, the specification of a tennis court is fixed in all matches. Therefore, a court verification model is also applied to reduce false positives. Based on the intersections of detected lines, we can map them with a pre-defined court model (i.e., real-world court) and find the camera parameters. Since this mapping is plane-to-plane, it can be viewed as an eight-parameter perspective transformation (Hartley & Zisserman, 2003) and can be estimated easily. To solve these eight parameters, we choose at least four line intersections

Figure 5. The relationships between the video frame coordinate system and the pre-defined court model coordinate system. The circle represents the court line intersections and the solid circles are the ones utilized to perform camera calibration

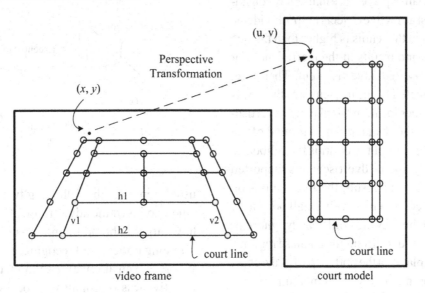

in video frames to map the corresponding ones in the pre-defined court model. Figure 6 shows the line intersections utilized to obtain the parameters of camera calibration. Not only real intersections but also the ones caused by extensions of lines are utilized. Totally twenty-five points are possibly used in camera calibration. Generally, the horizontal lines h1 and h2 and the vertical lines v1 and v2 are the most robustly detected lines. Therefore, we can use their four intersections for camera calibration at the first frame of a shot. After calibration, we can map the real-world court onto the displayed plane and obtain all court lines according to the estimated camera parameters. Details of the camera calibration can be found in (Farin et al., 2004). Since the camera motion of tennis videos will not change too much in two successive frames, the court positions in the next few frames would be similar to the current one. Therefore, with the previously estimated camera parameters, we can map the real-world court to the next few frames and search for possible intersections around the mapped ones. Then, the court verification model can be applied again

to adjust the camera parameters. This tracking method facilitates robust selection of referred intersections. The errors caused by line detection can therefore be filtered out. By this method, only parts of court lines should be correctly detected for robust court detection. Furthermore, this line-based camera calibration can be applied to other sports videos (for example, volleyball and soccer) with little modification. With the so-obtained court information, we can filter out the outliers. That is, if no court is detected, the shot should be filtered out even if it contains large amounts of dominant color pixels.

Note that the mapping between the coordinates $q=(u,v)$ of the points at the pre-defined court model and the coordinates $p=(x,y)$ of the pixels at video frames can be represented as $q=J\{p\}$, where J is the widely used perspective transformation matrix (Hartley & Zisserman, 2003). In this way, the corresponding coordinates of each pixel in a pre-defined court model can uniquely be determined on the video frame, as shown in Figure 5.

Attractive Object Detection

Generally, the ball or players are intuitively considered as the most attractive objects in sports videos. The ball speed in the tennis is higher than the one in other sports and results in the inefficiency for scanning the inserted advertisement. Therefore, the region projected by the trajectory of the tennis ball is not a proper location for placing advertisements. On the other hand, the background of the player at the top part of the court is the billboard, which is usually full of advertisements supported by the sponsors. As a result, the free regions on the billboard occupy a relatively small portion of the screen and the viewers could easily ignore or avoid seeing the advertisements on these regions. Therefore, the player at the bottom part of the court would be a comparatively good medium to scan the inserted advertisement in tennis videos. By combining the results of the court view detection and the camera calibration, the player position at the bottom part of the court in each frame can be located easily. The essential idea of the player detection is to find a region with non-dominant-color pixels and which is surrounded by dominant-color areas. Details of the player detection please refer to (Farin et al., 2004).

To sum up, with the insertion point detection, we obtain the spatiotemporal information for determining the candidate timing and locations to place the advertisements. Specifically, in the temporal domain, we identify court view shots, which game viewers are mostly interested in. In the spatial domain, the position of the attractive object (i.e., the player), which is one of the main attractive areas in court view shots, is located and tracked.

Communication Effect Mapping

The visual communication effect is a critical issue in advertising field but rarely discussed in virtual product placement. The relevant problems

Figure 6. The geometric relationships between the eccentricity, the foveation point, and the fovea under a specific viewing distance

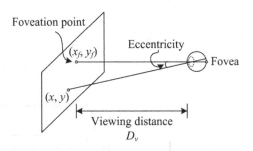

usually include the following two points: one is where to insert the advertisement and the other is how large it should be in terms of effectiveness for being noticed and recognized. In this section, we present an alternative solution to quantify the effectiveness of cognitive process and estimate the most effective replacement space.

Visual Acuity Estimation

According to the anatomy of the human eyes, it is found that the sensor neurons such as photoreceptors (cones and rods) and ganglion cells are non-uniformly distributed in the retina. The densities of cone receptors and ganglion cells determine the ability of our eyes to resolve the perceived visual stimulus. Spatially, the density of cone cells is the highest at the fovea and drops rapidly away from that point. Therefore, when a human gazes at a point, a variable resolution image is perceived by the human visual system. Specifically, only the region around the point of fixation (or foveation point) is projected onto the fovea, sampled with the highest density, and then perceived with the maximum resolution. For regions that are away from foveation point, the perceived resolution decreases progressively with increasing eccentricity (i.e., the viewing angle with respect to the foveation point). Human visual foveation model was thus developed to describe the inability of HVS to perceive an entire visual stimulus at full resolution.

Giesler et al. (1998) derived a contrast sensitivity model by giving a fit to the sensitivity data from rigid psychological experiments. Accordingly, the minimum contrast threshold of human eyes required to perceive a sinusoid of spatial frequency at an eccentricity can be computed as follows:

$$T\left(f, \theta_e\right) = T_0 \cdot \exp\left(f_0 \cdot f \frac{\theta_0 + \theta_e}{\theta_0}\right), \qquad (1)$$

Where f is the spatial frequency (in cycles per degree–cpd), θ_e is the eccentricity (in degrees), T_0. T_0 is the minimum possible observable contrast by HVS, f_0 is the spatial frequency decay constant (in degrees), and θ_0 is the half resolution eccentricity constant (in degrees). Note that the contrast threshold (within the range of [0.0, 1.0]) is the reciprocal of the contrast sensitivity.

For any given point **p** at the image coordinate (x,y), the corresponding eccentricity (see Figure 6) with respect to the foveation point $\mathbf{p_f}$ at the image coordinate (x_f, y_f) can be calculated as

$$\theta_e(\mathbf{p}, \mathbf{p_f}) = \tan^{-1}\left(\frac{\|\mathbf{p} - \mathbf{p_f}\|}{D_v}\right), \qquad (2)$$

Where D_v is the viewing distance (in pixels) and $\|\cdot\|$ refers to the Euclidian distance. Note that this model assumes that the eyes are equally sensitive at all orientations, but using chessboard distance instead of Euclidian distance for eccentricity estimations could further reduce the computational cost.

Based on the foveation model, for any given point **p** with respect to the fixation point $\mathbf{p_f}$ in the image, the corresponding normalized maximum detectable frequency $F(\mathbf{p}, \mathbf{p_f})$ (Sheikh, 2003) can be written as

$$F(\mathbf{p}, \mathbf{p_f}) = \min\left\{1, \frac{2\ln(T_r)}{f_0 \cdot D_v \left(1 + \hat{\theta}_e \cdot \theta_0^{-1}\right) \cdot \sec^2(\hat{\theta}_e)}\right\}, \qquad (3)$$

where T_r is the contrast threshold ratio and $\hat{\theta}_e$ is the general eccentricity in degrees. The general eccentricity $\hat{\theta}_e$ in eqn. (3) is given by

$$\hat{\theta}_e(\mathbf{p}, \mathbf{p_f}) = \max\left\{0, \ \theta_e - \theta_f\right\}, \qquad (4)$$

Where θ_f is the full resolution eccentricity (in degrees) which corresponds to the region where the actual fixation point lies circular around the assumed fixation point. The best fitting parameters reported in (Sheikh, 2003) are f_0=0.106, θ_0=2.3°, T_r=4, and θ_f=0.5°. For general viewing scenarios, the viewing distance D_v is suggested to be set as 2.6 times the display image width. Note that this calculation is still valid when the image is scaled with a fixed aspect ratio.

In order to quantify the extraneous visual acuity while watching the attractive object, we define the visual acuity $V_k(\mathbf{p})$ of a pixel **p** at the k-th video frame in the court view shot as

$$V_k(\mathbf{p}) = \sum_{\mathbf{p_f} \in \Lambda_k} l_k(\mathbf{p}) \cdot \hat{F}(\mathbf{p}, \mathbf{p_f}), \qquad (5)$$

where $l_k(\mathbf{p})$ indicates the points of the detected player region Λ_k at the k-th video frame, that is

$$l_k(\mathbf{p}) = \begin{cases} 0, & \mathbf{p} \in \Lambda_k \\ 1, & otherwise \end{cases}. \qquad (6)$$

$\hat{F}(\mathbf{p}, \mathbf{p_f})$ in eqn. (5) is the approximated normalized maximum detectable frequency and is given by

$$\hat{F}(\mathbf{p}, \mathbf{p_f}) = \max\left\{f_c, \ F(\mathbf{p}, \mathbf{p_f})\right\}, \qquad (7)$$

where f_c is the maximum cut-off frequency as a simple condition for thresholding. In the implementation, the maximum cut-off frequency f_c can empirically set to 0.9. That is, almost only the fixation region which is perceived by HVS with maximum resolution is included to construct the visual acuity map.

For each video frame in the same court view shot, we map the visual acuity of each point onto a pre-defined court image and integrate all the visual acuity values into a unique saliency map. Thus, the visual acuity $V(\mathbf{q})$ of a point $\mathbf{q}$ on the saliency map, which is named as the *visual acuity map*, can be computed as

$$V(\mathbf{q}) = \frac{1}{N} \sum_{k=1}^{N} \gamma_k \cdot V_k (J^{-1}\{\mathbf{q}\}), \qquad (8)$$

where N is the total number of frames in the court view shot, and γ_k is a weighting factor for linear combination. For simplicity, γ_k can be set to 1 for all video frames within the court view shot.

Effectiveness Calculation

Let a rectangular space be defined by a left-top corner point $\mathbf{q}_r$ of a rectangle together with an associated dimension $\mathbf{d}_r = (h_r, w_r)$, where h_r and w_r are the height and the width of the rectangle, respectively. Let's denote the rectangular space as $(\mathbf{q}_r, \mathbf{d}_r)$. Note that the boundaries of the rectangular spaces are parallel to the sides of the visual acuity map image. All the rectangular spaces, which have different attributes and reside inside the sets of pixels with non-zero value in the map, can be regarded as *candidate replacement spaces*, as shown in Figure 7.

A *candidate replacement space* with higher visual acuity can be intuitively considered as an effective region for emplacing the advertisement in terms of recognition. Since the value of each point in the map stands for the strength of visual acuity, we define a function $E(V, (\mathbf{q}_r, \mathbf{d}_r))$ to measure the effectiveness of the *candidate replacement space* $(\mathbf{q}_r, \mathbf{d}_r)$ in V as follows:

Figure 7. The defined rectangular spaces

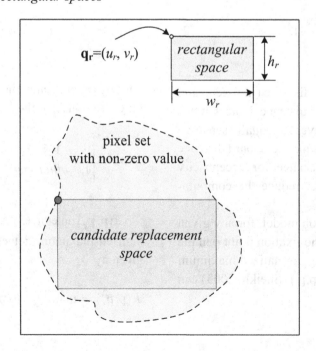

$$E(V,(\mathbf{q_r},\mathbf{d_r})) = \sum_{u=u_r}^{u_r+w_r-1} \sum_{v=v_r}^{v_r+h_r-1} V(u,v). \qquad (9)$$

In this way, the effectiveness of each *candidate replacement space* on the tennis court can be simply quantified as the index for the advertisement allocation.

Advertisement Allocation

A few online advertising services, such as Google's AdWord and AdSense, select the relevant advertisements according to the user's profile, preference, or searched keywords. Some related work (Mei, et al., 2008; Liao et al., 2008) had developed such contextual-based or content-targeted advertising and reported encouraging results after performance investigation. This framework could flexibly incorporate with the techniques of advertisement selection according to some suitable business model in practice.

The placement of advertisements in tennis videos can be regarded as the advertisement allocation with or without considering the court lines. Without court lines consideration, the projected advertisement on the tennis court may be segmented by court lines. On the other hand, the advertisement allocation with court lines consideration would be well-regulated and can be considered as an aesthetic based allocation. For the advertisement allocation with court lines consideration, the image pixel value at the court line position in the map is replaced by zero, thus forming separate sets of pixels from those pixels with non-zero value in the map.

For efficiency, the *candidate replacement space* with the largest effectiveness is selected as the most adequate emplaced region (i.e., *replacement space*) in the map. Thus, given a visual acuity map V, the *replacement space* $R(V)$ is determined by maximizing the E function, defined in eqn. (9), over all *candidate replacement spaces* $(\mathbf{q_r},\mathbf{d_r})$, that is

$$R(V) = (\mathbf{q_R},\mathbf{d_R}) \text{ s.t. } (\mathbf{q_R},\mathbf{d_R}) = \arg\max_{(\mathbf{q_r},\mathbf{d_r})} E(V,(\mathbf{q_r},\mathbf{d_r})). \qquad (10)$$

An example of different replacement spaces corresponding to two types of advertisement allocations is shown in Figure 8.

Once the replacement space is determined, an appointed advertisement will be selected from the advertisement database (Ads DB) and be resized to fit this region. The scaling factor β of the selected advertisement I_M with a side length $\mathbf{d}_m$ is then given by

$$\beta = \min(\frac{h_R}{h_m}, \frac{w_R}{w_m}). \qquad (11)$$

In order to avoid shape distortion, the aspect ratio of the selected advertisement is kept fixed, and then the same scaling factor is applied to its dimension $\mathbf{d}_m$. The dimension of the resized advertisement I_M is then given by

$$\mathbf{d_M} = (h_M, w_M) = \beta \cdot (h_m, w_m). \qquad (12)$$

After that, the replacement spot $S(V)$, at map V, for inserting the advertisement I_M is determined by:

$$S(V) = (\mathbf{q_M},\mathbf{d_M}) \text{ such that } \mathbf{q_M} = \arg\max_{\mathbf{q_m}} E(V,(\mathbf{q_m},\mathbf{d_M})), \qquad (13)$$

where $\mathbf{q_M}$ is the left-top corner point of the rectangle which is the so-called replacement spot. Figure 9 shows a specificity of defined regions for the advertisement allocation.

So far, we can ensure that the selected advertisement which is placed on the replacement spot will automatically get noticed and attended with relatively larger probability. In addition to considering the effectiveness of the advertising message communication, the induced intrusiveness should be limited by representing the selected advertisement in a more elaborate way.

Representation

Since the advertisements, which are selected for projecting onto the scene in sports videos, are extrinsic to the original video content, the representation of projected advertisements plays an important role in attaining realistic object assimilation. To ensure that the virtual spotlighted advertising is effective and less intrusive in terms of representation styles, we present a novel representation mechanism for projected advertisements. Before projecting the selected advertisement onto the replacement spot as seamlessly as possible, the color scheme of the advertisement is adjusted for providing visual aesthetics and the sense of

harmony according to empirical harmony theories of colors. On the other hand, the transparency of the projected advertisement elaborately varies with the moving attractive objects for further reducing the visual intrusiveness in each court view shot. Furthermore, the advertising effect is enhanced by the virtually induced interaction between the projected advertisement and the moving attractive object.

Color Harmonization

For fans of sports videos, the projected advertisements with a large amount of color stimuli (i.e.,

Figure 9. An example shows the determined replacement space and the replacement spot at the court for tennis videos. The white bounding rectangles represent the candidate replacement spaces with the highest effectiveness in each subregion of the tennis court because of considering the court lines

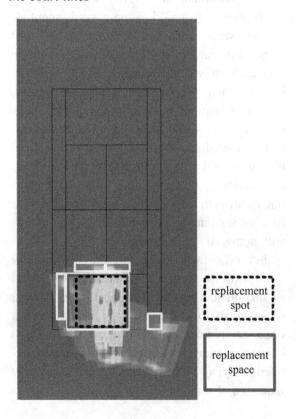

Figure 8. An example shows the candidate replacement spaces (i.e., white bounding rectangles) from two types of advertisement allocations in tennis videos. (a) Advertisement allocation with court lines consideration, and (b) Advertisement allocation without court lines consideration. In order to show the distribution of the visual acuity on the tennis court, the court lines are superimposed on each of the visual acuity map. In this map, warm colors mean higher values and cold colors represent smaller ones

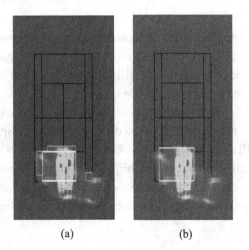

(a) (b)

degree of colorfulness) and stimuli variations (i.e., contrast) may cause visual disturbances and difficulties in concentrating on the game proceeding. These visually intrusive effects may provoke audiences and reduce the accessibility of the image advertising. However, advertisements with monotonous color schemes would be less impressive to the inattentive audience. Therefore, how to effectively represent inserted advertisements for diverse audiences is a very challenging task.

Color scheme is an important characteristic of advertisements because it is usually noticed first than other attributes. Therefore, advertisers generally utilize well-designed color schemes to make advertisements effectively grab viewers' attention. If we directly use the advertisements without adjusting their color schemes, it may create a pop-out effect in terms of color after inserting advertisements into the videos. The visually pop-out advertisements would supplant the role of attractive objects in the original sports videos and result in visual disturbances. On the other hand, the color scheme of advertisements is usually inharmonic with the host video frame and it may lead to a displeasing visual perception or a severe visual fatigue. There are two ways to improve the visual balance or the harmony between the advertisement (i.e., the foreground) and the corresponding court view frames (i.e., the background), where the advertisement will be inserted. Certainly, the target for the color adjustment is either the foreground or the background image. Since the background is the main role of the sports video and contains relatively large pixels and color information, its colors would not be suitable to be changed. Therefore, we should aesthetically adjust the color scheme of the selected advertisement to harmonize it with the corresponding court view frame for providing a pleasant visual perception. Note that since some colors are formed with certain feelings that advertisers want to convey, the color schemes may be critical for viewers to recognize the advertisements and link it to a brand. Therefore, the process

of color harmonization should be only applied to those advertisements which have permissions to change their colors.

In order to ensure the foreground be in harmony with the background, the task is to adjust the color distribution of the selected advertisement by using a proper harmonic color scheme, while fixing the color distribution of the corresponding video frame where the advertisement will be projected. Therefore, a good choice of the harmonic color scheme for the projected advertisement is the one that minimize the color disharmony degree of the corresponding video frame. There are eight types of hue distributions defined as the harmonic hue templates by *Tokumaru et al.* (2002). Each harmonic hue template is described by the degrees of sectors and their separation angle over the hue channel of the HSV color wheel. The hues that fall within sectors are sets of colors with harmonic relationships and the colors have been found to be pleasing to the human visual perception. Based on the empirical harmony theories of colors, *DanielCohen-Or et al.* (2006) proposed a method for the color adjustment in an unsupervised manner and the optimal harmonic color scheme can be easily estimated.

With the information of the best harmonic color scheme, we can adjust the color distribution of the advertisement to ensure that all the hues fall within sectors of the harmonic hue template. That is, we harmonize the colors of advertisements with respect to the best-fitting harmonic scheme of the key-frame of the court view shot. Since each frame of a court view shot contains similar color distribution, we estimate the optimal harmonic color scheme from the key-frame of the court view shot. The reason why we do not harmonize the advertisements with each corresponding frame of the court view shot individually is to avoid the flickering effect which results from the color variation within the same shot and reduce the computational cost on the color harmonization process. Instead of using the whole key-frame as the reference to harmonize with, we only use the pixel collection in the detected court area for estimating the proper harmonic color scheme. As a result, the re-colored advertisement would be in more harmony with the surroundings of the replacement spot. Note that the color harmonization is a full automatic process, but it can only be enabled with advertisers' permissions.

Advertisement Projection

According to the camera calibration parameters, we integrate the advertisement with the original frames at the corresponding replacement spot within the court view shot. Although there are some effective blending methods for the seamless image composition, such as the Poisson editing (Gangnet et al., 2003) and α-Poisson image blending (Rother et al., 2006), we adopt a modified alpha-blending method while considering the time efficiency. Let $I_{\hat{M}}$ be the selected advertisement with harmonized color schemes (if re-colored) for projecting on the considered frame. The color value $I'(\mathbf{p})$ of each pixel $\mathbf{p}$ in the replacement spot at the frame can be determined by

$$I'(\mathbf{p}) = (1 - \alpha \cdot \tilde{l}_k) \cdot I(\mathbf{p}) + \alpha \cdot \tilde{l}_k \cdot I_{\hat{M}}(\mathbf{p}),$$

(14)

where $I(\mathbf{p})$ is the original color value in the replacement spot at the frame, α is the normalized opacity, $I_{\hat{M}}(\mathbf{p})$ is the color value of the pixel $\mathbf{p}$ in the advertisement image, and the replacement indicator $\tilde{l}_k(\mathbf{p})$ is

$$\tilde{l}_k(\mathbf{p}) = \begin{cases} 0, & \mathbf{p} \in \Phi_k \\ 1, & otherwise \end{cases},$$

(15)

where Φ_k denotes pixels of the detected attractive objects and court lines in the k-th frame within the court view shot. Note that the replacement indicator is used to avoid projecting advertisements onto the pixels of the attractive object and

court lines. Therefore, the projected advertisement would not obstruct the attractive object and make it look more natural.

Based on the contract sensitivity function (Geisler & Perry, 1998), we derive the normalized opacity $\alpha(\mathbf{p}, \mathbf{pf})$ as

$$\alpha(\mathbf{p}, \mathbf{p}_f) = A \cdot \exp(f_0 \cdot f \cdot \frac{-\hat{\theta}_e(\mathbf{p}, \mathbf{p}_f)}{\theta_0}),$$

(16)

where A is the amplitude tuner and f is the spatial frequency of the contract sensitivity function. The range of normalized opacity is [0, 1]. Note that the amplitude tuner A and the spatial frequency f are user-defined parameters for controlling the advertising stimuli. For example, a lower value of amplitude tuner A could let the inserted advertisement operate below a threshold of consciousness but can be perceived subconsciously by audiences. On the other hand, different settings of the spatial frequency f contribute different curvatures (see Figure 10(a)) which represent the sensitivity of the transparency variation. In the implementation, A and f can empirically set to 0.7 and 8 cycles per degree, respectively. In addition, the fixation point $\mathbf{p}_f$ is set to the center point of the detected attractive object (i.e., the player at the bottom of the tennis court) for providing better viewing experience. The corresponding curve for $\alpha(\mathbf{p}, \mathbf{pf})$ with respect to the distance from p to the fixation point pf is shown in Figure 10(b).

In this way, how the attractive object moves along the time axis will further affect the advertisement representation in terms of the transparency. This can be considered as a virtual interaction between the projected advertisement and the original attractive object in sports videos. Furthermore, it would be an efficient delivery for advertising messages by gradually revealing the pixels which could be resolved by the extraneous visual acuity of viewers while watching the attractive object. It could also reduce the visual disturbances since the inserted extrinsic object

Figure 10. The normalized opacity with different parameters. (a) The comparisons of different curvatures for a range of spatial frequencies, and (b) The curve of normalized opacity with respect to the distance measured in pixels by setting the parameter values to A=0.7, f=8cpd and $D_v = 3328$ pixels

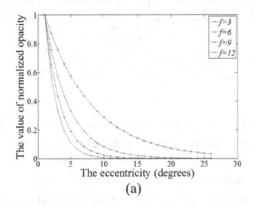

(a)

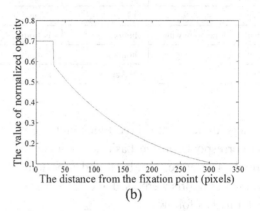

(b)

(i.e., advertisement) would not pop out at the position far from the attractive object and attract viewers' attention.

EVALUATION RESULTS

We followed the mainstream approaches in the field of advertising to investigate the performance of the virtual spotlighted advertising by taking a subjective evaluation. First of all, we randomly selected five segments, which consist of plays and breaks, from a recorded broadcast tennis video with 1280x720 resolution. The detailed information of the five court view shots among the segments is listed in Table 1. Then, we cascaded the five segments with different orders to produce two video sequences, V1 and V2, for evaluation and comparison. For the advertisements database, a number of commercial logos, such as Starbucks, Coca-Cola, Merrill Lynch, etc, were collected. These collected commercial logos were divided into two groups to ensure that each group contains the same number of famous and unfamiliar commercial logos. Finally, after feeding the two video sequences (i.e., V1 and V2) into the system, four videos with projected commercial logos are produced according to different settings, such as

different advertisement allocations and the switch of the color harmonization. We applied the color harmonization to all the projected advertisements and compare their advertising effect with the ones that retain the original color distribution. In addition, twenty subjects were randomly invited from our campus to join our user study. They are in the ages of 22 to 55, all with Chinese as their native language and love tennis games. Before joining the study, they have no idea about the virtual spotlighted advertising. Video sequences were presented to the subjects by projecting onto a 60-inch screen at the average viewing distance of 2.6 times the display image width.

Effectiveness

In order to investigate the effectiveness of the framework and compare the different advertisement allocations, two video sequences (i.e., V1-A and V2-A) were individually presented to the subjects. The subjects were asked to answer some questions, such as what are the events occurred in videos and who wins the point in a play after watching the video, to ensure that viewers concentrate on cognizing the content. We analyzed 532 plays in different tournaments and observed that the pattern of player moving regions can

Table 1. The information of selected plays for the evaluation

Source Video	2007 US Open Men's Singles – Final: Roger Federer vs. Novak Djokovic				
Court view shot ID	1	2	3	4	5
Duration	13 sec.	7 sec.	14 sec.	10 sec.	12 sec.
The position of the point winner	bottom	bottom	top	bottom	bottom
The position of the serving side	bottom	bottom	bottom	top	bottom
Event type	Net approach	Ace	Rally	Rally	Rally

be generally divided into three types and each of them corresponds to the basic tennis events respectively. Therefore, three basic and important events in tennis sports were used and each event type is defined as follows.

1. *Rally*: A player successfully serves and the opponent successfully returns and they then stroke until one of them fails to return.
2. *Net approach*: A player successfully serves and the opponent successfully returns. One or both of them once approach the net to stroke.
3. *Ace*: A player successfully serves, and the opponent is not able to touch the ball and therefore fails to return.

For the unaided recall measurement, the subjects were asked to write down the brand names of each remembered commercial logo. Note that drawing down the pattern of commercial logos was also acceptable in case the weak brand awareness affects the results. Then, the subjects were asked to select the corresponding commercial logos from a list of 10 items for the aided recall measurement. Unaided recall or aided recall is computed as the percentage of commercial logos correctly recalled or selected, respectively. The average recalls for the two video sequences are listed in Table 2.

Overall, it is obvious that ViSA is effective in terms of memory-based measurements, no matter how the advertisement allocations are used. In addition, the higher aided recall rate can be con-

sidered as one of the practical evidence (Schacter, 1987) to support the benefits of the subliminal advertising. Most subjects commented that ViSA unobtrusively attracts them to look at the commercial logo in their free time without disrupting the viewing experience. That is, the viewers would pay attention to the commercial logos because the representation style is interesting for them, and remember the commercial logos subliminally.

Visual Intrusiveness

We further evaluated the visual intrusiveness of the virtual spotlighted advertising. Similar to the definition of the intrusiveness described by *Li et al.* (2002), we define the visual intrusiveness as a sensation that occurs when the cognitive processes are interfered by the visual disturbance. Note that the visual disturbance may be resulted from the locations and behaviors or colors of projected advertisements. To evaluate the visual intrusiveness in terms of locations and behaviors of projected advertisements, we applied different advertising mechanisms to a selected court view shot to produce four video clips, such as VI-1, VI-2, VI-3, and VI-4. Video clips VI-1 and VI-2 were produced by the ViSA system. The way of advertisement allocations in video clip VI-1 is to take court lines into consideration and video clip VI-2 is not. In video clip VI-3, the commercial logo was projected on the outside of the central court, which can be considered as a traditional and conservative advertising mechanism. Such

Table 2. The average results of memory measurements

Video Sequence	Duration	Recall (unaided)	Recall (aided)
V1-A	101 sec.	67%	99%
V2-A	101 sec.	66%	98%

selected regions in VI-3 are similar to the *unimportant regions* utilized by *Mei et al.* (2008). We also adopted an advertising mechanism, in which the commercial logo is projected onto the *less informative region* (Li et al., 2005) at the court, and produced video clip VI-4. Note that the position of the projected commercial logo in video clip VI-4 would dynamically change during the play to ensure the region against the cover of the ball or players. The concept of the advertising mechanism adopted in video clip VI-4 is commonly used in the related work. Intuitively, the advertising mechanism used in video clip VI-3 is relatively less visual intrusive, thus it can be regarded as a baseline for the visual intrusiveness evaluation. We presented the four video clips to the subjects and ask them to answer the following questions.

- **Q1:** Please compare the visual intrusiveness between the four video clips, while concentrating on watching the video clips to recognize events occurred in the plays.
- **Q2:** Please compare the appropriateness of each logo's location in the four video clips, while giving consideration to recognize events and the projected logos simultaneously.

The evaluation result shows that 75% of the subjects think the visual intrusiveness introduced by ViSA is higher than that of the case shown in video clip VI-3 and lower than that of the case shown in video clip VI-4. Furthermore, 80% of the subjects agree that the replacement spots determined by the ViSA system are much more effective than the others in terms of visual communication in advertising because it requires less

effort to look at the projected logos and the content of sports videos at the same time. Both in Q1 and Q2, most subjects think that the advertisement allocation in video clip VI-1 is better than that in video clip VI-2. Therefore, we believe that it is important to take court lines into consideration for the advertisement allocation to further limit the induced visual intrusiveness.

Visual Acceptability

To further evaluate the visual acceptability in terms of colors, we compared two video sequences (i.e., V1-A and V1-B), in which commercial logos were with and without color harmonization, respectively. The video sequence V1-B was produced by keeping the original color distribution of projected logos in the video sequence V1-A. The subjects were asked to answer the following questions for video sequences V1-A and V1-B:

- **Q1:** Which one is more visually pleasant in terms of the color harmony?
- **Q2:** Which one is more impressive in terms of projected commercial logos?
- **Q3:** Which one is more visually intrusive in terms of colors?
- **Q4:** Overall, which one provides higher visual acceptability?

For each of the questions, three given options were allowed for subjects to choose as their answers. The options for each question are listed in Table 3. As shown in Table 3, most subjects felt the projected commercial logos comfortable and less intrusive after color harmonization. However, since some commercial logos are designed to

Table 3. The relative preference of harmonized logos in V1-A with regard to the original logos in V1-B

Shot ID	The color harmony			The visual intrusiveness			The impressiveness		
	Worse	No Diff.	Better	Lower	No Diff.	Higher	Less	No Diff.	More
1	15.0%	25.0%	**60.0%**	**45.0%**	**45.0%**	10.0%	**90.0%**	10.0%	0.0%
2	**70.0%**	25.0%	5.0%	15.0%	**60.0%**	25.0%	40.0%	**60.0%**	0.0%
3	5.0%	10.0%	**85.0%**	**70.0%**	25.0%	5.0%	**85.0%**	15.0%	0.0%
4	20.0%	25.0%	**55.0%**	**40.0%**	35.0%	25.0%	**80.0%**	20.0%	0.0%
5	0.0%	**95.0%**	5.0%	5.0%	**95.0%**	0.0%	5.0%	**95.0%**	0.0%

Table 4. The relative preference of the overall visual acceptability for V1-A and V1-B

V1-B is better	No Diff.	V1-A is better
30%	35%	35%

impress people more deeply by their colors than their patterns or other attributes, changing the color distribution of such commercial logos may let the viewers harder to recognize and memorize them. From the results in Table 4, the overall visual acceptability of VI-A is slightly better than that one of VI-B. In other words, the overall visual acceptability is almost no difference between the two video clips. The results imply that applying the color harmonization process only to those advertisements that are with advertiser s' permissions would be practicable.

Comparative Evaluation

To our best knowledge, although some research about virtual product placement for tennis videos is proposed, there is rare exactly relevant work can be directed used for fairly comparison from the view point of advertising effect. Therefore, we compared ViSA with an intuitive advertising scheme to further investigate the performance of ViSA.

Three clips each with 6 plays and breaks, were randomly extracted from the broadcast tennis video, which was recorded from "2007 US Open Tennis 3rd Round Federer vs Isner" with 1280x720 resolution. Famous commercial logos such as BMW, Apple, etc. were randomly selected for the first 3 plays and different flags, which are unfamiliar to the subjects, were randomly selected for the others. We inserted both famous commercial logos and unfamiliar flags into the videos and produced three video clips, M1, M2 and M3. We manually projected the original commercial logos and flags on the corner of the tennis court in video clip M1 to avoid obstructing the audiences' view of the player. Such advertising strategy used in M1 can be considered as the trivial and simplified mechanism. Note that the selected regions in M1 are similar to the less-informative regions and the unimportant regions. On the other hand, video clips M2 and M3 were with ViSA. The way of advertisement allocations in M3 was to take court lines into consideration while M2 was not. Fifteen tennis video fans with ages of 22 to 25 were invited to join this user study and each of them was assigned a 19-in LCD at the viewing distance of 60 cm to watch the produced video sequences. To ensure that viewers concentrate on cognizing the content, they are asked to answer series of questions, such as the event type, who wins the

Table 5. The average results of the comparative evaluation

Video Clip	Intrusiveness	Unaided Recall (logos)	Aided Recall (flags)
M1	1.3	23%	11%
M2	3.9	65%	63%
M3	3.1	62%	61%

point and the number of hits after watching the video. They were then asked to write down the commercial logos for the unaided recall measurement and to select the flags from a list of eight items for the aided recall measurement. Besides, they were also asked to give a score from 1 to 10 to show the intrusiveness level. Recall rate is computed as the percentage of commercial logos or flags correctly recalled.

The average results are shown in Table 5. Although the intrusiveness induced in M1 is less than that of M2 and M3, the effectiveness of remembering the commercial logos projected on the court is suffered. The subjects commented that the ad-blindness effect occurred while concentrating on watching the game to count the number of hits. It is interesting that the unaided recall rate of famous commercial logos is similar to the aided recall rate of unfamiliar flags in the case of the produced video clips with ViSA, because remembering the unfamiliar flags would be more difficult than remembering the famous commercial logos. On the other hand, the intrusiveness induced in M2 is larger than the one in M3 due to the large size of projected logos and somehow a kind of clutter.

The experiments and evaluation results show that ViSA is advantageous to advertisers in several ways. Viewers cannot bypass this advertising because of its ingenious integration with the tennis videos, unless they skip the whole game. It is less intrusive to the audiences and the viewing experience on-screen may be more enriched than just watching games live. ViSA can be used for promoting the brand perception of products or companies and to overcome the decline of the efficacy of the 30-second commercials in tradi-

tional tennis videos. In addition, it allows content owners to sell the same placement spots to multiple advertisers, and then create different versions of showcases for the different advertisements. In addition, advertisements can be dynamically switched based upon the behavioral information and demographics, which are customized to suit local requirements. Advertisers can use both the 30-second commercials and ViSA as part of a comprehensive marketing strategy to reach more viewers for tennis videos. More experimental results are available at http://www.cmlab.csie.ntu. edu.tw/~chchang/visa.

FUTURE RESEARCH DIRECTIONS

Under the presented framework, there are many issues that can be further explored to improve the advertising effectiveness. To prevent the jerkiness effect resulted from the camera calibration errors, more accurate and stable camera calibration techniques would be worthy of further study. For choosing a medium in sports videos to induce a virtual interaction, taking the ball instead of players into account during the play may make the considered situations closer to the way viewers watch the game. For the visual acuity map construction, we can give different weights to different moments in a play on the basis of the information theory or using the results of semantic event detection in tennis videos (Tien et al., 2008). In this way, the visual acuity map can further increase the accuracy in quantifying the strength of being noticed and recognized for regions. Moreover, it would enhance the accessibility and the effectiveness of ViSA by inserting relevant advertisements (e.g., players' endorsements) into sports videos to virtually interact with the moving player. For the representation issues in terms of colors, since the re-colored advertisement and original advertisement should be as similar as possible for brand identification, how to minimally modify the original colors of the advertisement with the lightness-preserving color harmonization (Wang, L. et al., 2008) is worthy of further investigation. Furthermore, we can try to develop more interesting and applicable advertising mechanisms to other sports videos besides tennis by following the idea of ViSA, and investigate the corresponding advertising effect.

The next generation of virtual product placement is to place the contextually relevant product or brand into general videos with vivid presentation styles for different target customers. For example, according to the concept of the applied media aesthetics, animating the inserted ads would engage audience with interesting and impressive interactions between ads and the video content (Chang et al., 2009; Chiang et al., 2009). It would benefit the research of virtual product placement with more different viewpoints and other relevant domain knowledge. All the efforts along the directions mentioned above would make virtual product placement extend from the screen placement toward to the plot placement in the design space of product placement and become more effective and acceptable.

CONCLUSION

In this chapter, we presented a framework that performs the virtual spotlighted advertising and introduced the domain knowledge in support of delivering and receiving the advertising message, such as advertising theory, psychology and computational aesthetics. In addition, observations about the new trend and possible extensions for virtual product placement in the design space of product placement was also stated and discussed. By utilizing more relevant domain knowledge and bringing together the originality would create more impressive advertising strategies for virtual product placement. With the development of content-based multimedia analysis, computer graphics and context reasoning, virtual product placement would become more effective and substantially increase the advertising revenue for multimedia content.

REFERENCES

Aaker, D. A. (1996). *Building strong brands*. New York: Free Press.

Barry, T., & Howard, D. (1990). A review and critique of the hierarchy of effects in advertising. *Journal of Advertising*, *9*(2), 121–135.

Bradley, D. R., & Petry, H. M. (1977). Organizational determinants of subjective contour: The subjective Necker cube. *The American Journal of Psychology*, *90*(2), 253–262. doi:10.2307/1422047

Broyles, S. (2006). Subliminal advertising and the perpetual popularity of playing to people's paranoia. *The Journal of Consumer Affairs*, *40*(2), 392–406. doi:10.1111/j.1745-6606.2006.00063.x

Bruce, V., Green, P. R., & Georgeson, M. A. (1996). *Visual perception: physiology, psychology, and ecology* (3rd ed.). U.K.: Psychology Press.

Chang, C.-H., Chiang, M.-C., & Wu, J.-L. (2009). Evolving Virtual Contents with Interactions in Videos. In *The 1st ACM International Workshop on Interactive Multimedia for Consumer Electronics* (pp. 97-104).

Chang, C.-H., Hsieh, K.-Y., Chiang, M.-C., & Wu, J.-L. (in press). Virtual Spotlighted Advertising for Tennis Videos. *Journal of Visual Communication and Image Representation*.

Chang, C.-H., Hsieh, K.-Y., Chung, M.-C., & Wu, J.-L. (2008). ViSA: Virtual Spotlighted Advertising. In *the 16th ACM International Conference on Multimedia* (pp. 837-840).

Chiang, M.-C., Chang, C.-H., & Wu, J.-L. (2009). Evolution-based Virtual Content Insertion. In *The 17th ACM International Conference on Multimedia* (pp. 995-996).

Cohen-Or, D., Sorkine, O., Gal, R., Leyvand, T., & Xu, Y.-Q. (2006). Color harmonization. *ACM Transactions on Graphics, 25*(3), 624–630. doi:10.1145/1141911.1141933

Ekin, A., & Tekalp, A. (2003). Robust dominant color region detection and color-based applications for sports video. In *The 2003 IEEE International Conference Image Processing, Vol. 1* (pp. 21-24).

Farin, D., & Krabbe, S., & With, Peter H.N. de, & Effelsberg, W. (2004). Robust camera calibration for sport videos using court models. *SPIE: Storage and Retrieval Methods and Applications for Multimedia, 5307,* 80-91.

Gangnet, M., Perez, P., & Blake, A. (2003). Poisson image editing, In *The ACM SIGGRAPH'03* (pp. 313-318).

Geisler, W., & Perry, J. (1998). A real-time foveated multiresolution system for low-bandwidth video communication. *SPIE: Human Vision and Electronic Imaging, 3299*(1), 294–305.

Hartley, R., & Zisserman, A. (2003). *Multiple view geometry in computer vision.* U.K.: Cambridge University Press.

Hoyer, W. D., & Brown, S. P. (1990). Effects of brand awareness on choice for a common, repeat-purchase product. *The Journal of Consumer Research, 17*(2), 141–148. doi:10.1086/208544

Hua, X., Mei, T., & Li, S. (2008). When multimedia advertising meets the new Internet era. In *The 10th IEEE Workshop on Multimedia Signal Processing* (pp. 1-5).

Li, H., Edwards, S., & Lee, J. (2002). Measuring the intrusiveness of advertisements: scale development and validation. *Journal of Advertising, 31*(2), 37–47.

Li, Y., Wan, K., Yan, X., & Xu, C. (2005). Real time advertisement insertion in baseball video based on advertisement effect. In *The 13th ACM International Conference Multimedia* (pp. 343-346).

Liao, W., Chen, K., & Hsu, W. (2008.) AdImage: video advertising by image matching and ad scheduling optimization. In *The 31th ACM International Research and Development in Information Retrieval* (pp. 767- 768).

Lim, J., Kim, M., Lee, B., Kim, M., Lee, H., & Lee, H. (2008). A target advertisement system based on TV viewer's profile reasoning. *International Journal on Multimedia Tools and Applications, 36*(1), 11–35. doi:10.1007/s11042-006-0079-2

Liu, H., Jiang, S., Huang, Q., & Xu, C. (2008a). A generic virtual content insertion system based on visual attention analysis. In *The 16th ACM International Conference Multimedia* (pp. 379-388).

Liu, H., Jiang, S., Huang, Q., & Xu, C. (2008b). Lower attentive region detection for virtual content insertion. In *The 2008 IEEE International Conference Multimedia and Expo* (pp. 1529-1532).

Liu, Y., Jiang, S., Ye, Q., Gao, W., & Huang, Q. (2005). Playfield detection using adaptive GMM and its application. In *The 2005 IEEE International Conference Acoustics, Speech, and Signal Processing, Vol. 2* (pp. 837- 840).

Mei, T., Hua, X., & Li, S. (2008). Contextual In-image advertising. In *The 16th ACM International Conference Multimedia* (MM'08) (pp. 439-448).

Mei, T., Hua, X., & Li, S. (2009). VideoSense: A Contextual In-Video Advertising System. *IEEE Transactions on Circuits and Systems for Video Technology, 19*(12), 1866–1879. doi:10.1109/TCSVT.2009.2026949

Mei, T., Hua, X., Yang, L., & Li, S. (2007). VideoSense: towards effective online video advertising. In *The 15th ACM International Conference Multimedia* (pp. 1075-1084).

Moriarty, S. E. (1991). *Creative advertising: Theory and practice*. USA: Prentice-Hall.

Parker, G. R. (1992). *Institutional change, discretion, and the making of modern Congress: An economic interpretation*. USA: University of Michigan Press.

Rother, C., Bordeaux, L., Hamadi, Y., & Blake, A. (2006). Autocollage. *ACM Transactions on Graphics, 25*(3), 847–852. doi:10.1145/1141911.1141965

Russell, C. A. (1998). Toward a framework of product placement: theoretical propositions. *Advances in Consumer Research. Association for Consumer Research (U. S.), 25*(1), 357–362.

Schacter, D. (1987). Implicit memory: history and current status. *Journal of Experimental Psychology. Learning, Memory, and Cognition, 13*(3), 501–518. doi:10.1037/0278-7393.13.3.501

Sheikh, H. R., Evans, B. L., & Bovik, A. C. (2003). Real-time foveation techniques for low bit rate video coding. *Real-Time Imaging, 9*(1), 27–40. doi:10.1016/S1077-2014(02)00116-X

Smith, K., & Rogers, M. (1994). Effectiveness of subliminal messages in television commercials: two experiments. *The Journal of Applied Psychology, 79*(6), 866–874. doi:10.1037/0021-9010.79.6.866

Tien, M.-C., Wang, Y.-T., Chou, C.-W., Hsieh, K.-Y., Chu, W.-T., & Wu, J.-L. (2008). Event detection in tennis matches based on video data mining. In *The 2008 IEEE International Conference Multimedia and Expo* (pp. 1477-1480).

Tjondronegoro, D., Chen, Y., & Pham, B. (2004). Highlights for more complete sports video summarization. *IEEE MultiMedia, 11*(4), 22–37. doi:10.1109/MMUL.2004.28

Tokumaru, M., Muranaka, N., & Imanishi, S. (2002). Color design support system considering color harmony. In *The IEEE Fuzzy Systems, Vol. 1.* (pp. 378-383).

Tsai, M., Liang, W., & Liu, M. (2007). The effects of subliminal advertising on consumer attitudes and buying intentions. *Journal of Management, 24*(1), 3–14.

Wan, K., Wang, J., Xu, C., & Tian, Q. (2004). Automatic sports highlights extraction with content augmentation. In *The Pacific-Rim Conference Multimedia* (pp. 19-26).

Wan, K., & Xu, C. (2006). Automatic content placement in sports highlights. In *The 2006 IEEE International Conference Multimedia and Expo* (pp. 1893-1896).

Wan, K., Yan, X., Yu, X., & Xu, C. (2003). Robust goal-mouth detection for virtual content insertion. In *The 11th ACM International Conference Multimedia* (pp. 468-469).

Wang, J., Duan, L., Wang, B., Chen, S., Ouyang, Y., Liu, J., et al. (2009). Linking video ads with product or service information by web search. In *The 2009 IEEE International Conference Multimedia and Expo* (pp. 274-277).

Wang, J., Fang, Y., & Lu, H. (2008). Online video advertising based on user's attention relavancy computing. In *The 2008 IEEE International Conference Multimedia and Expo* (pp. 1161-1164).

Wang, L., & Mueller, K. (2008). Harmonic colormaps for volume visualization. In *The 7th IEEE/EG Symposium on Volume Graphics* (pp. 33-40).

Wang, X., Yu, M., Zhang, L., Cai, R., & Ma, W. (2009). Argo: intelligent advertising by mining a user's interest from his photo collections. In *The 3rd International Workshop on Data Mining and Audience Intelligence for Advertising* (pp. 18-26).

Xu, C., Wan, K., Bui, S., & Tian, Q. (2004). Implanting virtual advertisement into broadcast soccer video. In *The Pacific-Rim Conference Multimedia* (pp. 264-271).

Yu, X., Jiang, N., & Cheong, L. (2007). Accurate and stable camera calibration of broadcast tennis video. In *The 2007 IEEE International Conference Image Processing* (pp.93-96).

Yu, X., Jiang, N., Cheong, L., Leong, H., & Yan, X. (2009). Automatic camera calibration of broadcast tennis video with applications to 3D virtual content insertion and ball detection and tracking. *Computer Vision and Image Understanding, 113*(5), 643–652. doi:10.1016/j.cviu.2008.01.006

Yu, X., Yan, X., Chi, T., & Cheong, L. (2006). Inserting 3D projected virtual content into broadcast tennis video. In *The 14th ACM International Conference Multimedia* (pp. 619-622).

Zettl, H. (1999). *Sight, sound, motion: Applied media aesthetics*. USA: Wadsworth.

Zhang, H., Kankanhalli, A., & Smoliar, S. (1993). Automatic partitioning of full-motion video. *Multimedia Systems, 1*(1), 10–28. doi:10.1007/BF01210504

ADDITIONAL READING

Chang, C.-H., Chiang, M.-C., & Wu, J.-L. (2009). Evolving Virtual Contents with Interactions in Videos. In *The 1st ACM International Workshop on Interactive Multimedia for Consumer Electronics* (pp. 97-104).

Chang, C.-H., Hsieh, K.-Y., Chiang, M.-C., & Wu, J.-L. (in press). Virtual Spotlighted Advertising for Tennis Videos. *Journal of Visual Communication and Image Representation*.

Chang, C.-H., Hsieh, K.-Y., Chung, M.-C., & Wu, J.-L. (2008). ViSA: Virtual Spotlighted Advertising. In *The 16th ACM International Conference on Multimedia* (pp. 837-840).

Chiang, M.-C., Chang, C.-H., & Wu, J.-L. (2009). Evolution-based Virtual Content Insertion. In *The 17th ACM International Conference on Multimedia* (pp. 995-996).

KEY TERMS AND DEFINITIONS

Ad-Blindness Effect: An effect stands for adapting to the presence of advertisements and filtering them out of the vision.

AIDMA Model: A model represents the psychological process that consumers respond to advertisement communication.

Image Advertising: A tactic for promoting an overall brand perception of a company, product or service instead of the specific attributes of a product or service.

Product Placement: A paid advertising message aimed at influencing audiences by bringing branded products or images into videos in a planned and unobtrusive way.

Subliminal Advertising: An advertising strategy uses stimuli that operate below the threshold of consciousness but that can be perceives subconsciously.

Subliminal Perception: A stimulation which is so weak that people almost can't aware of it.

Virtual Content Insertion: A technique inserts additional contents into multimedia content.

Virtual Product Placement: A post-processing technique replaces specific regions in the video with brands or products to make brands or products like a part of the original video.

Chapter 9
Adapting Online Advertising Techniques to Television

Sundar Dorai-Raj
Google Inc., USA

Yannet Interian
Google Inc., USA

Igor Naverniouk
Google Inc., USA

Dan Zigmond
Google Inc., USA

ABSTRACT

The availability of precise data on TV ad consumption fundamentally changes this advertising medium, and allows many techniques developed for analyzing online ads to be adapted for TV. This chapter looks in particular at how results from the emerging field of online ad quality analysis can now be applied to TV.

INTRODUCTION

As online advertising has exploded in the past decade, it has often been contrasted with traditional media such as television, print, and radio. The inherently connected nature of online content has enabled unprecedented tracking and analysis of online advertising, and the resulting explosion of data has allowed Internet companies to develop ever more sophisticated algorithms for allocating and pricing advertising inventory. Using user-initiated signals (like "clickthrough"), these companies can indirectly measure the relevance of ads in specific contexts, and build models to predict which ads will most interest future users and maximize revenues for online publishers (Richardson et al., 2007).

In contrast, traditional television measurement has typically relied on relatively small panels of pre-selected households to report their viewing

DOI: 10.4018/978-1-60960-189-8.ch009

behavior. This approach often has meant that reliable measurements took days or weeks to produce, and could not be produced at all for niche programming that appealed to very small audiences. These methods also did not generate enough data to build determine which TV ads were most appealing to viewers, nor to predict which ads would be most appealing in the future.

However, a new source of TV-related data has emerged in recent years, one that is closer to Internet scale. The set-top boxes (STBs) used by most cable and satellite TV subscribers are often capable of collecting data on viewing behavior. These data can then be stripped of personally-identifiable information and anonymously aggregated, allowing for very detailed measurement of television viewing behavior. While previous panels collected data from thousands or perhaps tens of thousands of households, set-top box data are available from many million US households and similar numbers in other countries.

With these data in hand, it is now possible for television to adopt many of the analytical techniques pioneered in online advertising. In particular, ads can be scored for relevance or quality based on statistical models that predict how viewers are likely to respond. Ad inventory can then be allocated so as to maximize relevance, and to compensate publishers for any loss of audience due to ads.

This chapter will explore this emerging discipline. We will introduce the basic statistical techniques underlying the approach, and give examples for how such models can be implemented in software. We will also discuss applications of these models to television advertising, and some of the issues raised in the application of these techniques.

TV Audience Measurement

Panel-based audience measurement has a long history. In the US, Arthur Nielsen began measuring television audiences in 1950 based on a nationwide sample of 300 households (Nielsen, 2009a). Because there were only 48 commercial television stations in the US at the time and no more than a handful of viewing choices in any one local area, the audience of any given station could be adequately estimated with such a small sample. The Nielsen Company continues measuring TV audiences today, now with a sample of over 9,000 households (Nielsen, 2009b). Understanding and using these audience ratings has evolved into a discipline unto itself (see, for example, Webster et al., 2006).

Even the modern, expanded panel, however, is at times unable to measure the increasing fragmented TV audience flocking to niche programming (Bachman, 2009). For television ads (as opposed to programs), this bias is further compounded: attempts to judge the reaction of TV audiences to ads have focused on only the most popular programming. For the 2009 Super Bowl, for example, Nielsen published a likeability score and a recall score for the top ads [1]. The scores were computed using 11,466 surveys, and Nielsen reported only on the top 5 best-liked ads and most-recalled ads.

Several companies have started using data from STBs to measure TV audiences. In addition to Google, TNS, CANOE, Retrak, Tivo, and The Nielsen Company itself are using STB data (Mandese, 2009). Several of these companies will make such data available to media researchers on a subscription basis.

Measuring Ad Quality

In the world of online advertising, the term "ad quality" has taken on a very specific meaning. Roughly speaking, an ad quality is "a measure of how relevant an ad is" (Yahoo, 2009); in the context of Internet keyword search ads, ad quality scores "measure how relevant [the] keyword is to [the] ad text and to a user's search query" (Google, 2009). In other words, ad quality represents a judgment on an ad primarily from a user's or viewer's perspective. It asks, to what extent is the ad the viewer would most like to see.

Ad quality is not, in other words, a measure of cost effectiveness from an advertiser's perspective. It is easy to imagine ads that viewers consider highly enjoyable and relevant, but which are ineffective at meeting the goals of the advertisers themselves. Similarly, it is not hard to find examples of ads that viewers may dislike, but nevertheless seem to be cost-effective. (Much "junk mail" and the online equivalent – email spam – might fall into this second category.)

However, there are reasons to predict a synergy between ad quality (as defined above) and ad effectiveness, at least in the long run. If viewers become accustomed to seeing relevant ads, they may pay more attention and thus increase the effectiveness of ads generally. Furthermore, TV programmers have a vested interest in keeping viewers from changing the channel and so may reap an economic benefit from increasing viewer-perceived ad quality.

SOLUTIONS AND RECOMMENDATIONS

Precise television usage data is now available from several sources. Google aggregates data collected and anonymized by DISH Network L.L.C., describing the precise second-by-second tuning behavior for several million of US television set-top boxes, covering millions of US households, for thousands TV ad airings every day. From this raw material, we have developed several measures that can be used to gauge how appealing and relevant commercials are to TV viewers. One such measure is the percentage initial audience retained (IAR): how much of the audience, tuned in to an ad when it began airing, remained tuned to the same channel when the ad completes.

In many respects, IAR is the inverse of online measures like click-through rate (CTR). For online ads, CTR is a positive action; advertisers

want users to click through. This is somewhat reversed in television advertising, in which the primary action a user can take is a negative one: to change the channel. However, we see broad similarities in the propensity of users to take action in response to both types of advertising. Figure 1 shows tune-away rates (the additive inverse of IAR) for 182,801 TV ads aired in January 2009. This plot looks similar to the distribution of CTRs for paid search ads also ran that month. Although the actions being taken are quite different in the two media, the two measures show a comparable range and variance.

A significant challenge in interpreting TV audience data like this is that many factors appear to impact STB tuning during ads, making it difficult to isolate the effect of the specific ad itself on the probability that a STB will tune away. Rather than using raw measures of tune-away directly, we have developed a "retention score" that attempts to capture the creative effect itself.

Definition

We calculate per airing the fraction of initial audience retained (IAR) during a commercial. This is calculated by taking the number of TVs tuned to an ad when it began which then remained tuned throughout the ad airing as shown in equation (1).

$$IAR = \frac{\text{Audience that viewed whole ad}}{\text{Audience at beginning of the ad}}$$

(1)

The hypothesis behind this measure is that when an ad does not appeal to a certain audience, they will vote against it by changing the channel. By including only those viewers who were present when the commercial started, we hope to exclude some who may be channel surfing. However, even these initial viewers may tune away for other reasons. For example, a viewer may be finished watching the current program on one channel and begin looking for something else to watch.

Figure 1. Density of tune away rate for TV ads, defined by the percentage of watchers who click away from an ad

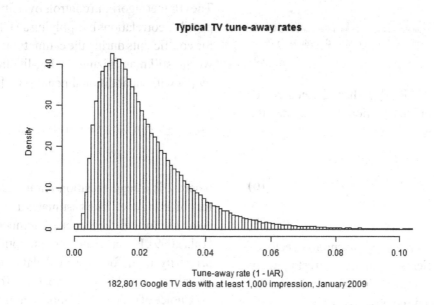

Typical TV tune-away rates

Tune-away rate (1 - IAR)
182,801 Google TV ads with at least 1,000 impression, January 2009

We can interpret IAR as the probability of tuning away from an ad. In order to isolate extraneous factors like the network, day part, and day of the week from the effect of the creative, we define the *Expected IAR* of an airing as

$$I\hat{A}R = E(IAR|\mathbf{x}) \qquad (2)$$

where $\mathbf{x}$ is a vector of features extracted from an airing, which exclude any features that identify the creative itself; for example, hour of the day and TV channel, but not the specific campaign or advertiser. Then we define the *IAR Residual* as in equation 3 to be a measure of the creative effect.

$$\text{IAR Residual} = IAR - I\hat{A}R \qquad (3)$$

There are a number of ways to estimate $I\hat{A}R$, which we will discuss in this chapter. Using equation 3 we can define *underperforming airings* as the airings with IAR residual below the median. We can then formally define the *retention score* (RS) for each creative as one minus the fraction of airings that are underperforming.

$$RS = 1 - \frac{\text{Number of underperforming airings}}{\text{Total number of Airings}} \qquad (4)$$

The remainder of this chapter focuses on methods for obtaining accurate retention scores. We explore four different statistical models based on three different algorithms. We will rank each method by metrics we have constructed to measure its usefulness as a measure of ad quality. We have also conducted extensive experiments to validate the usefulness of retention scores as an ad quality signal. These include comparing retention scores to subjected human evaluations for ads, and the extent to which past retention scores predict future audience retention (Zigmond et al., 2009).

MODEL ESTIMATION

In this section we introduce three estimation algorithms to obtain predictions for IAR. All three approaches are based on logistic regression with

IAR as our response. To motivate the algorithm descriptions, consider the following two events:

C_0 = STB tuned to the beginning of an ad leaves before the ad ends
C_1 = STB tuned to the beginning of an ad remains through the entire ad,

$$(5)$$

where $\Pr(C_1) = 1 - \Pr(C_0)$. Then, given a vector of features $\mathbf{x}_i$ for observation i, we model the log-odds of C_1 as

$$\log\left(\frac{\Pr(C_1|\mathbf{x}_i)}{\Pr(C_0|\mathbf{x}_i)}\right) = \beta_0 + \sum_{j=1}^{k} x_{ij}\beta_j. \qquad (6)$$

where β_0 is the intercept, $\boldsymbol{\beta}$ is a length-k vector of unknown coefficients. We then obtain estimates of $(\beta_0, \boldsymbol{\beta})$ by maximizing the binomial log-likelihood of $\Pr(C_1 \mid \mathbf{x}_i)$ given the observed IAR:

$$\max_{(\beta_0,\boldsymbol{\beta})\in\Re^{k+1}}\left[\frac{1}{N}\sum_{i=1}^{N} n_i\left\{\mathrm{IAR}_i\log(\Pr(C_1|\mathbf{x}_i)) + (1-\mathrm{IAR}_i)\log(\Pr(C_0|\mathbf{x}_i))\right\}\right], \qquad (7)$$

where n_i is the number of viewers at the beginning of the ad for observation i and $\Pr(C_1 \mid \mathbf{x}_i)$ is given by

$$\Pr(C_1|\mathbf{x}_i) = \frac{1}{1 + \exp\{-\beta_0 - \sum_{j=1}^{k} x_{ij}\beta_j\}}. \qquad (8)$$

For this discussion, an "observation" depends on the feature list. At its most basic level, an observation is an individual STB. However, to improve computational efficiency, our algorithms aggregate over STBs with identical feature sets, where each group of STBs is thought of as a single observation. The one exception is the last algorithm, which is efficient enough to handle each STB as a separate observation.

Glmnet Logistic Regression

The Glmnet algorithm controls overfitting and any possible correlations by applying an L1 penalty on the coefficients during the estimation. In essence, we are still maximizing the log-likelihood given by (7) with an additional penalty with the form

$$\max_{(\beta_0,\boldsymbol{\beta})\in\Re^{k+1}}\left[\frac{1}{N}\sum_{i=1}^{N} n_i\left\{\mathrm{IAR}_i\log(\Pr(C_1|\mathbf{x}_i)) + (1-\mathrm{IAR}_i)\log(\Pr(C_0|\mathbf{x}_i))\right\} - \lambda\sum_{j=1}^{k}|\beta_j|\right], \qquad (9)$$

where λ is a regularization parameter. Software for obtaining coefficient estimates using Glmnet is available through the R package glmnet (Friedman et al., 2009). R is an open source scripting language primarily used for statistical data analysis and visualization (R Development Core Team, 2010).

Choice of the regularization parameter λ affects the amount of shrinkage applied to each β_j. The larger λ is, the smaller the resulting β_j's. Some β_j's will be shrunk to zero, implying this coefficient has no impact on IAR or that it is correlated with another feature in the models.

Principal Components Logistic Regression

The next algorithm we tried is based on principal components logistic regression (Aguilera et al., 2006). The algorithm is as follows:

1. Build a model matrix $\mathbf{X}$ of size $n \times p$, where n is the number of rows and p is the number of parameters (columns).
2. Assuming $\mathbf{X}$ has an intercept, drop the first column of $\mathbf{X}$ and center and scale the remaining columns. Call the result $\mathbf{X}^*$.
3. Transform $\mathbf{X}^*$ using singular value decomposition (SVD) into matrix components $\mathbf{U}_{n \times k}$, $\mathbf{d}_{(k \times k)}$, and $\mathbf{V}_{(k \times k)}$, where

$$\mathbf{X}^* = \mathbf{U}\mathbf{d}\mathbf{V} \qquad (10)$$

and $k = p - 1$.

Define $\mathbf{W}$ as

$$\mathbf{W} = \begin{bmatrix} 1 & \mathbf{0}' \\ \mathbf{0} & \mathbf{V} \end{bmatrix}, \tag{11}$$

where $\mathbf{0}$ is a column vector of length k containing all zeros.

Define $\mathbf{Z}$ as

$$\mathbf{Z} = \mathbf{XW}, \tag{12}$$

which is $n \times p$.

6. Keep only the first m columns of $\mathbf{Z}$. There are many published ways for choosing m. See Aguilera et al. (2006), for example.

    Maximize the log-likelihood binomial with response IAR against the first m columns of $\mathbf{Z}$:

$$\max_{\boldsymbol{\beta}^* \in \mathfrak{R}^m} \left[\frac{1}{N} \sum_{i=1}^{N} n_i \left\{ \mathrm{IAR}_i \log(\Pr(C_1 | \mathbf{z}_i)) + (1 - \mathrm{IAR}_i) \log(\Pr(C_0 | \mathbf{z}_i)) \right\} \right]$$
$$, \tag{13}$$

where

$$\Pr(C_1 | \mathbf{z}_i) = \frac{1}{1 + \exp\{-\sum_{j=1}^{m} z_{ij} \beta_j^*\}}, \tag{14}$$

and z_{ij} is the ij[th] element of $\mathbf{Z}$, and β_j^* is the jth regression coefficient based on the jth principal component of $\mathbf{Z}$. Note that (13) and (14) are fundamentally the same to (7) and (8), respectively, except that m is typically much smaller than k.

By maximizing (13) with respect to the β_j^*s and given our observed IAR, we obtain estimates

$\hat{\beta}_j^*$. Since $\hat{\beta}_j^*$ is estimated in the transformed space, we convert back to the original space spanned by $\mathbf{X}$ by performing a matrix multiplication given by:

$$\hat{\boldsymbol{\beta}} = \mathbf{W}_m \hat{\boldsymbol{\beta}}^*, \tag{15}$$

where $\mathbf{W}_m$ contains the first m columns of $\mathbf{W}$ and $\hat{\boldsymbol{\beta}}^*$ a column vector containing the $\hat{\beta}_j^*$s. The resulting vector $\hat{\boldsymbol{\beta}}$ contains coefficients for all features in the model. As with the Glmnet estimators, the estimated coefficients will be shrunk towards zero as more correlations are present in $\mathbf{X}$ and the larger m is.

The latter algorithm is used in the demographics model because of the strong relationship between the makeup of a household and which networks viewers in that household watch.

A Proprietary Logistic Regression Implementation

The last algorithm we tried is based on proprietary logistic regression implementation designed by Google to handle very large data sets. The basic algorithm optimizes over coefficients β_j with respect to the log-likelihood function in (7). However, we apply additional regularization techniques to shrink unimportant or highly correlated coefficients while also merging similar coefficients.

The main advantage of this method is efficiency. The algorithm design allows for significant parallelization, which means we can model more features on a greater number of STBs. In fact, unlike the Glmnet and principal component algorithms, with our proprietary algorithm we model each STB as an individual observation rather than rely on grouping of STBs by feature. Given that we have data for several million STBs, that level of prediction is not possible with most statistical software packages, such as R.

RETENTION SCORE MODELS

We have devised several models for computing retention scores, which help us rank ads based on their quality. In this chapter, we will discuss our findings in the areas of household demographics and user behavior. In addition, we have developed metrics to rank our models based accuracy of predictions and their ability to discriminate ads consistently. In this section we introduce the basic model first developed by Google, along with 3 competing models later designed as possible improvements.

All model comparisons are based on training and test data from October 2009. The primary tool for analysis is the R language, which suffers from fairly severe memory constraints. For this reason, we limited our analysis to the 25 top-viewed networks to improve memory efficiency for the Glmnet and principal components algorithms. For the machine learning algorithm, we used an internal software tool that is much more scalable. However, for comparison purposes, we still limited the analysis to the same networks.

The Basic Model

The first model relates the observed IAR to the Day Part, Weekday, Ad Duration, and Network. Each feature is described in more detail below. All time-based features are EST/EDT.

1. Day Part – a categorical variable with the following levels:
2. Weekday – a Boolean variable determining whether the ad was placed on the weekday (TRUE) versus weekend (FALSE).
3. Ad Duration – the duration of the ad in seconds. Most ads are 15 or 30 seconds, but 45, 60, and 120-second ads are also shown. In the basic model, we treat Ad Duration as a numeric variable and not categorical. Doing so assumes a linear relationship between IAR and Ad Duration.

4. Network – a categorical feature of network id. For the Dish population, this variable has roughly 100 levels.

Each observation used in the Basic Model represents a single airing. We typically use three weeks of data to train a model and estimate coefficients, and predict for only a single week.

Demographics Model

The demographics model is motivated by the fact that households of certain demographic composition tend to watch the same networks. To observe this behavior we first conducted a simple principal components analysis to determine the reduction in dimensionality achieved by modeling variations in household makeup rather than network viewership. In essence, we attempted to determine whether demographics were a proxy for network viewership. This would imply we could subsequently remove or diminish network from our Basic Model as a feature for predicting IAR in return for including certain household conditions.

First let us discuss our findings of the principal components analysis. For the month of October, the percentage of time a given STB was tuned to a particular network was recorded, provided the STB was tuned to that network for at least 60 seconds and under two hours. As mentioned above, only the 25 top-viewed networks were included in the analysis. In addition, the actual names of the networks have been obfuscated. Table 2 contains the demographics we considered in our study.

Figure 2 shows strong correlations between 113 household demographics and viewership for 25 networks. To explain this relationship in further detail, we performed a principal components analysis (PCA) on these percentages. PCA is a dimension reduction technique that allows view the highly correlated data in Figure 2 with just a few uncorrelated variables, or principal components (Shaw, 2003).

Table 2. Table of demographics we considered as a partial proxy for network. Note that Single is not the opposite of married, as there exists households containing unmarried couples. STBs labeled as unknown were removed from the principal components analysis, but are included in the retention score model

Gender	Kids	Married	Single	Age
Male	Yes	Yes	Yes	18-24
Female	No	No	No	25-34
Both	Unknown	Unknown		35-44
Unknown				45-54
				55-64
				65-74
				75 plus+

Figure 3 shows the cumulative percentage of variance for each principal component. As we can see, over 95% of the total variation is explained in the first three principal components. Figures 4 and 5 explore these three dimensions even further. Figures 4 plots each principal component versus the age group and split by presence of children and gender. From the first principal component we see clear variations due to age. However, there also exists a separation due to the presence of children. The second principal component also shows differences due to age, while the third component in particular shows the greatest amount of variation is due to gender. This is seen by the top two dashed lines, which correspond to households that contain either a single female or female head of household.

Figure 5 shows biplots of the first three principal components. Biplots are useful for overlaying the principal components (shown in black) with the rotated data (shown in gray) (Gabriel, 1971). To interpret a biplot, we focus on areas where the data and the principal components are somewhat aligned. For the biplot containing the first and second principal component, we see as strong correlation between older adults without children and viewership of cable news networks such as "News Channel 2" and "News Channel 1". In addition, we also see that younger adults with children tend to watch "Cartoon Network 2"

and "Cartoon Channel 3". The latter observations match very well with our comments about the first and second principal components in Figure 4.

For the biplot containing the second and third principal components shows a relationship of gender and age to network viewership. Note that most of the data for females between the ages of 45 and 64 are in the upper left corner of the plot, relating to networks such as "Women's Network 1", "Women's Network 2", and "DIY Channel 2". In addition, households with males or mixed genders along the bottom of the figure show a strong correlation to the networks "Documentary Channel 2", "Sports Channel 1", and "Mixed Programming Channel 4".

For our demographics model we simply added the 113 different combinations from Table 2 along with the same list of features in the Basic model, which lead to 143 coefficients in the model. Applying the algorithm for principal components regression described above, we reduced the dimensionality to 125 coefficients, or 90% of the total variation. This is considerably more dimensions than the demographics-to-network PCA discussed in this section. However the PCA study described the viewership of networks, while our demographics model describes STB tune-out at ads.

Figure 2. This figure shows the percentage of time over the course of a month that a STB was tuned to a particular network (vertical axis) versus the demographic makeup of the household (horizontal axis). The darker area, the more time a particular household was tuned to that network. For example, older people without kids (upper right) tend to watch "News Channel 2" the most, while younger people with kids (upper right) tend to watch more "Cartoon Channel 2" and "Cartoon Channel 3". This plot shows 25 networks and 113 demographic groups

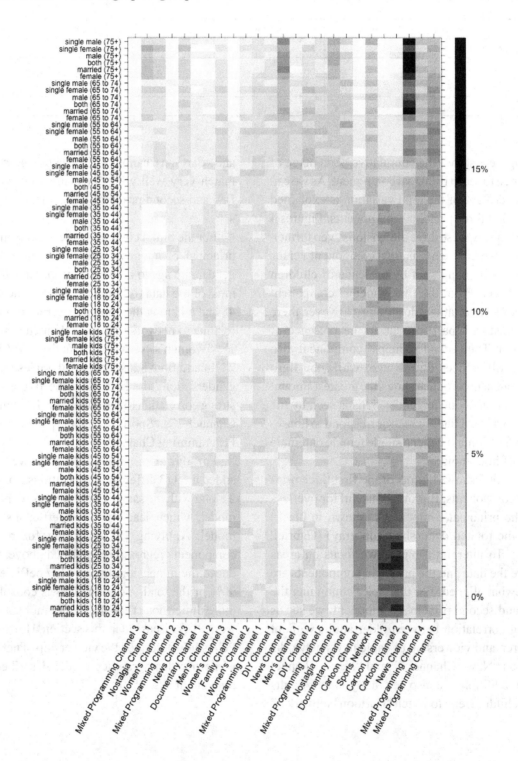

Figure 3. This plot shows the cumulative percentage of variance explained by 25 principal components. The first three principal components explain more than 95% of the total variation

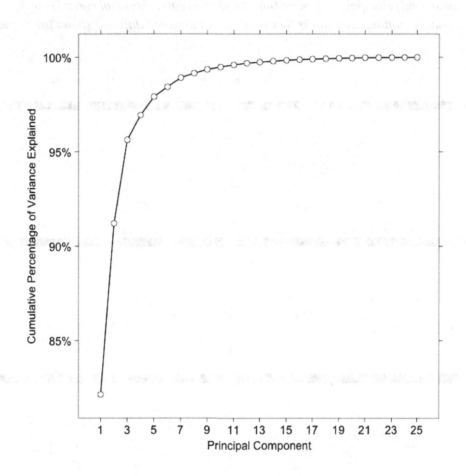

Local User Behavior Model

In this model we monitor STB behavior up to the point of a particular ad. Our hypothesis is that users how have a channel change closer to an ad insertion are more likely to tune away from the ad than users have not had a recent channel change. In essence we are trying to separate "active" users from "passive" users based on recent events.

For this model we define the following features:

1. LastEvent – whether the last event occurred in the previous minute, 10 minutes, 30 minutes, 60 minutes, or greater than 60 minutes.

2. NumberEvents – the number of channel changes in the 60 minutes prior to tuning away from an ad. STBs with 5 or more events are grouped in the same category.
3. MF – Male, Female, Both, or Other.
4. AGE – Over 65, Under 65, or Unknown
5. Network – Limited to the top 25 viewed networks.
6. Ad duration (in seconds).

The first two features separate the active viewers from the passive ones, which helps us predict who is more likely to tune away from an ad. Figure 7 shows the distribution of IAR for the viewers who had an event within the last hour ("Active")

Figure 4. Plots of first 3 principal components vs. age group, split by gender (lines) and presence of children (panels). The first principal component (top row) varies mostly by age differences and presence of children. The second principal component (middle row) reveals additional variation in age. The third principal component (bottom row) shows that women tend to watch different shows from other gender groups

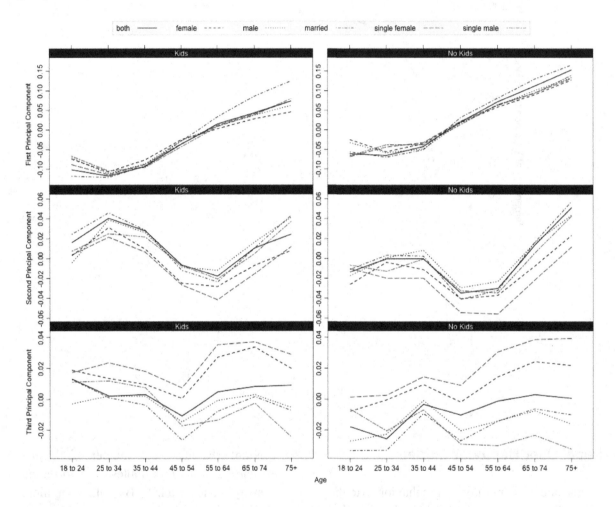

versus the IAR for viewers who had no events in the past hour. Figure 8 is a similar plot for the NumberEvents feature. These two plots clearly show a dependence on how much a viewer is actively watching TV prior to an ad's airing.

We also added two demographic features to help predict IAR: MF and AGE. We chose these two because of the principal components analysis discussed earlier in the chapter. However, due to the memory constraints of the R language we limited the levels of each demographic.

Figure 9 shows the distribution of IAR for the two demographic groups in our model. For the gender demographic we see that men are less tolerant of ads and tend to have a lower IAR than women. Similarly, older adults tend to watch more ads than younger adults.

A Machine Learning Approach

The machine learning approach relies on our proprietary logistic regression implementation. This

Figure 5. This figure shows biplot of principal components 2 vs. 1. From this figure we see that older adults with no children present tend to watch "News Channel 2", "News Channel 1", and "Nostalgia Chanel 1", while younger adults with children tend to watch more "Cartoon Channel 2" and "Cartoon Channel 3"

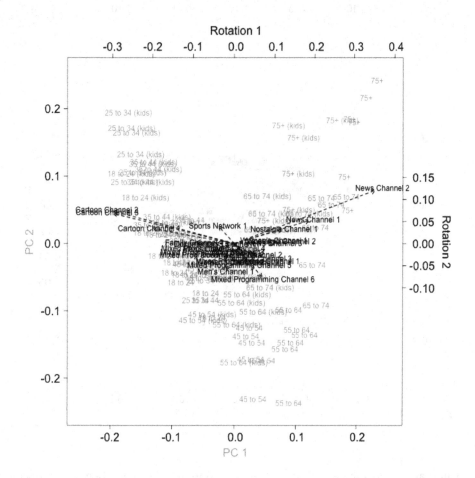

model greatly expands upon the previous models but does not suffer from the memory limitations of R. The main features included in this model are the following:

1. LN(Time to last event) – the natural log of the time to the last event. This is a continuous version of the "LastEvent" in the previous model.

2. DurationSec and sqrt(DurationSec) – the ad duration and its square root. The square root transformation controls for longer ads,

which do not have the same effect on IAR as shorter ads.

3. The genre of the show where the ad was placed (e.g. adventure, comedy, etc.)

4. Five minutes from the end or beginning of show, which models the behavior that viewers tend to have higher tune-away rates at the beginning or ending of a show.

5. The show name (e.g. Phineas and Ferb, Without a Trace, etc.).

6. Network – Not limited to the top 25 networks as in the previous models. However, for comparison purposes we filtered the results

Figure 6. This figure shows biplot of principal components 3 vs. 2. From this figure we see women from aged 45-74 tend to watch "Women's Channel 3", "DIY Channel 2", and "Mixed Programming Channel 5"

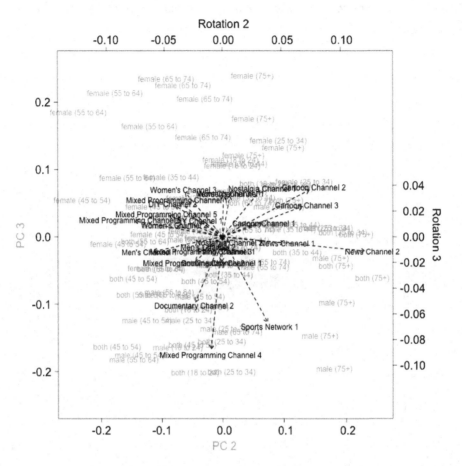

to the same airings as the data used in the first three models.

7. Household demographics, including those in Table 2, as well as ethnicity and occupation.
8. STB time zone and geographic location.
9. Day part (see Table 1).
10. Weekday vs. weekend.
11. Stickiness, which is defined as the total percentage of times a STB tuned away from an ad over a month of time.

All these features are used in the model. Unlike the previous algorithms, this implementation looks at more than just the main effects. Because this approach is extremely memory efficient, we also investigated higher order interactions.

The previous algorithms have no mechanism for updating coefficients that may become stale over time. However, the machine-learning approach automatically recalculates the model coefficients with the introduction of new data, while down weighting the contribution of older data to the estimation.

PREDICTIVE POWER

To compare the models introduced in the chapter, we need a metric that demonstrates their ability

Figure 7. This figure shows the density of IAR for active viewers versus passive viewers. Active viewers changed the channel in the hour prior to an ad, while passive viewers did not

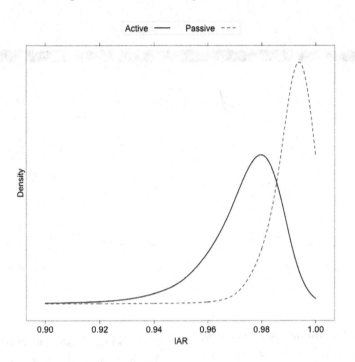

Figure 8. This figure shows the IAR for viewers as number of channel changes increased within the past hour. The plot is truncated for to 5 or more events

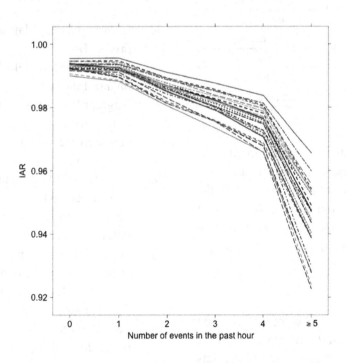

Figure 9. Density plots of IAR by gender and age. Men tend to be tune away from ads more than women. We also see that adults under 65 tend to tune away from ads than older adults

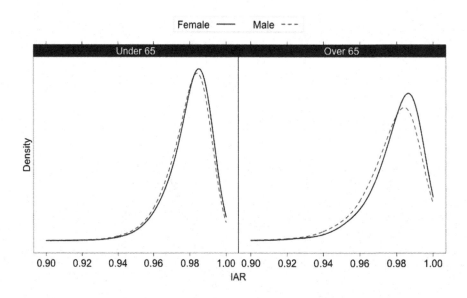

Table 1. Category definition for Day Part. Most networks start and end their broadcasting day at 5 am Eastern time

Day Part	Time
Morning	5am to 10am
Daytime	10am to 2pm
Late Afternoon	2pm to 5pm
Evening	5pm to 8pm
Prime	8pm to 12pm
Overnight	12pm to 5am

to produce accurate retention scores. In this section we discuss a metric that measures a models capability to predict retention scores. For all the algorithms we trained our models on the first 75% of the airings in October 2009 and predicted retention scores the remaining 25% of the airings.

Algorithm

The main metric we use to compare retention score models is called *predictive power*. A model with high predictive power accurately predicts

ad rankings based on current retention scores. We interpret this metric as the total percentage of ads correctly sorted by our retention score algorithm. The following provides the algorithm for our metric:

1. Using a training dataset, build a model to predict IAR.
2. With the fitted model, obtain predicted IARs on a test dataset.
3. Aggregate the observed and predicted IARs to the airing level (i.e. each row in the test dataset represents a single ad placement).
4. For each airing, use (3) to compute a residual.
5. For each creative, obtain a retention score (RS) based on (4).
6. For each airing, determine all other airings within the same commercial break, or *pod*.
7. For each pod, compute the pairwise differences of observed IAR as well as the pairwise differences for the predicted retention scores for each airing.
8. For all ad pairs whose difference in RS is in the interval $(\Delta, \Delta + 0.01)$, where $0 < \Delta <$

Figure 10. Illustration of how we estimate predictive power. Comparisons of ads are only made within a commercial break, or pod, since all factors are essentially the same at this level

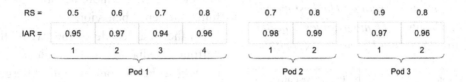

1, determine the proportions of those pairs whose corresponding observed IAR agrees with their respective RS.

9. Define the *predictive power* as the weighted mean of all proportions determined in the previous step, with weights determined from the total number of ad pairs in each interval.

Illustration Of Predictive Power

Figure 10 illustrates the algorithm for computing predictive power. In this example, we have eight airings distributed among three pods. The numbers in each box are the observed IAR for each airing, while the numbers above the box are the retentions scores (RS) of the creative. The RS values are determined from one of the models. In Pod 1, with four airings, we make six comparisons, of

which three of the comparisons have the same sign while three have opposite sign. All comparisons for each pod are shown in Table 3.

Model Comparison

The predictive power for the four models discussed in this paper is shown in Table 4. Their relative performances can be seen more easily in Figure 11. The model that faired the best is the "Local Events + Demographics" model with 76.5% of all ad pair correctly sorted. However, this model is not as scalable as the "Machine Learning" model and thus loses some of its attractiveness. The Machine Learning model is the first of its kind that we tried and is easily expandable to include other features.

Table 3. Table of IAR and RS comparisons for the example shown in Figure 10. The predictive power is the percentage of comparisons where IAR agrees with RS. Comparisons agree when ΔRS and ΔIAR have the same sign. For this example, there are five comparisons that agree (Y) and three comparisons that do not agree (N). The predictive power for this example is 5/8 = 62.5%.

	Pod 1			Pod 2			Pod 3		
	ΔRS	ΔIAR	Agrees	ΔRS	ΔIAR	Agrees	ΔRS	ΔIAR	Agrees
2-1	0.1	0.02	Y	0.1	0.01	Y	-0.1	-0.01	Y
3-2	0.1	-0.03	N						
3-1	0.2	-0.01	N						
4-3	0.1	0.02	Y						
4-2	0.2	-0.01	N						
4-1	0.3	0.01	Y						

Table 4. Predictive power for each of the models. The metric is interpreted as the percentage of all ad pairs within a pod that are correctly sorted by their respective retention scores. The best model is the "Local Events + Demographics" model followed by the "Machine Learning" algorithm

Model	Predictive Power
Basic	72.8%
Demographics	65.8%
Local Events + Demographics	76.5%
Machine Learning	73.8%

CONCLUSION AND FUTURE RESEARCH DIRECTIONS

In this chapter we have introduced three models for predicting ad retention on TV. However, we still have room for improvement, of which the machine-learning algorithm has the greatest potential because of its scalability. This is an area ripe for further innovation. Many new (and perhaps yet-to-be-developed) machine learning algorithms could be applied to this problem, and ever-greater quantities of data can be fed to such models to produce more accurate predictions of future audience behavior.

In the first decade of the twentieth century, "offline" media such as TV, radio, and print were thought to be in conflict with emerging online opportunities, such as Web-based display advertising and paid search ads. In the coming decade, however, the distinction between online and offline is likely to blur considerably. Content will often be available in many forms: traditionally offline media such as newspapers will be read on the Web, while online videos from sites like YouTube will be downloaded to be watched later on possibly disconnected devices.

The online-offline division will soon be replaced by a new distinction, between measured and unmeasured. Data from set-top boxes and similar sources will provide a degree of measurability and accountability to TV and other "offline" advertising that had previously only been available online, and allow the traditional advertising world

Figure 11. Comparison of the four retention score models in terms of predictive power. The curves are logit trend lines with 95% confidence bands. The size of each point is proportional to the number of ad pairs in the denominator of the percentage

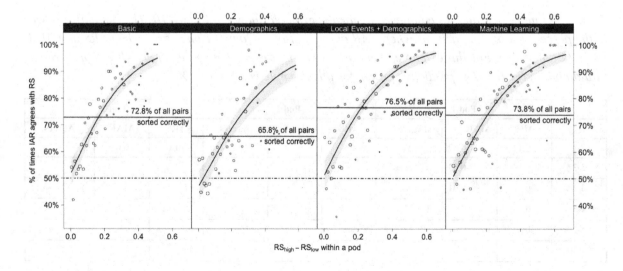

to adopt the quantitative techniques pioneered in online settings. We have described one such application in this chapter: creating ad quality scores for TV ads similar to those first developed for paid search advertising.

Because what can be measured can also be analyzed and optimized, well-measured media will develop a natural efficiency advantage over unmeasured. Advertising budgets will naturally flow to those media that are best able to generate and capitalize on data. Successfully applying the quantitative lessons from online advertising will become essential for the survival of all advertising media.

REFERENCES

Ana, M. A., Manuel, E., & Mariano, J. V. (2006). Using principal components for estimating logistic regression with high-dimensional multicollinear data. *Computational Statistics & Data Analysis*, (50): 1905–1924.

Bachman, K. (2009). Cracking the set-top box code. *AdWeek*, August 17, 2009. Retrieved December 22, 2009, from http://www.adweek.com/aw/content_display/news/e3i8fb28a-31928f66a5893aa9825dee83f2.

Friedman, J., Hastie, T., & Tibshirani, R. (2009). glmnet: Lasso and elastic-net regularized generalized linear models. R package version 1.1-3. http://www-stat.stanford.edu/~hastie/Papers/glmnet.pdf

Gabriel, K. R. (1971). The biplot graphic display of matrices with application to principal component analysis. *Biometrics*, (58): 453–467.

Google. (2009). What is 'Quality Score' and how is it calculated? Retrieved December 23, 2009, from http://adwords.google.com/support/aw/bin/answer.py?hl=en&answer=10215.

Mandese, J. (2009). Research Rivals Nielsen, comScore, Rentrak, TiVo, TNS Agree to Pool TV Set-Top Data. Retrieved January 14, 2009, from http://www.mediapost.com/publications/?fa=Articles.showArticle&art_aid=105217

R Development Core Team. (2010). R: A language and environment for statistical computing. R Foundation for Statistical Computing, Vienna, Austria. Retrieved from http://www.R-project.org

Richardson, M., Dominowska, E., & Ragno, R. (2007). Predicting Clicks: Estimating The Click-Through Rate For New Ads. In *WWW '07: Proceedings of the 16th international conference on World Wide Web*, (pp. 521–530). New York, NY, USA.

Shaw, P. (2003). *Multivariate statistics for the Environmental Sciences*. Hodder-Arnold.

The Nielsen Company. (2009a). The Evolution – and Revolution – of Meters. Retrieved December 22, 2009, from http://www.nielsenmedia.com/lpm/history/History.html

The Nielsen Company. (2009b). Nielsen TV Audience Measurement. Retrieved December 22, 2009, from http://en-us.nielsen.com/tab/product_families/nielsen_tv_audience

Webster, J. G., Phalen, P. F., & Lichty, L. W. (2006). *Ratings Analysis*. Mahwah, NJ: Lawrence Erlbaum Associates.

Yahoo. (2009). Writing ads: Ad Quality and Quality Index. Retrieved on December 23, 2009, from http://help.yahoo.com/l/us/yahoo/ysm/sps/articles/writing_ads4.html.

Zigmond, D., Dorai-Raj, S., Interian, Y., & Naveriouk, I. (2009). Measuring Advertising Quality on Television: Deriving Meaningful Metrics from Audience Retention Data. *Journal of Advertising Research*, *49*(4), 419–428. doi:10.2501/S0021849909091090

Chapter 10
Linking Traditional TV Advertising to Internet Advertising

Ling-Yu Duan
Peking University, China

Jinqiao Wang
Chinese Academy of Sciences, China

Wen Gao
Peking University, China

Hanqing Lu
Chinese Academy of Sciences, China

Jesse S. Jin
The University of Newcastle, Australia

Changsheng Xu
Chinese Academy of Sciences, China

ABSTRACT

Web-based technologies and interactive TV had rapidly penetrated the advertising mainstream and displace traditional forms of advertising. As most television advertising goes unnoticed, more and more advertisers attempt to communicate their stories across media platforms. The consistent spikes in usage statistics on television, Internet and mobile devices dedicatedly support the three-screen advertising in a cross media environment. Maximizing opportunities for traditional TV ads in collaborating with Internet ads will continuously improve the impact of a mass media campaign. We present the current research efforts in the field of analyzing TV ads as well as linking TV ads with relevant Internet ads. While our relationship with TV remains strong and durable, consuming media from anywhere, at any time, is a crucial part of the much broader picture of consumers utilizing rich media. How to collect correlated advertisements across multiple media platforms such as TV and Internet would see significant growth potential in cross-media marketing campaigns.

DOI: 10.4018/978-1-60960-189-8.ch010

INTRODUCTION

With the advent of the Internet and interactive TV, the advertising industry is much better turning to measurability and differentiation (Razorfish, LLC, 2009). Advertising is becoming less wasteful and its values measurable. The Internet enables advertisers to pay only for real and measurable actions by consumers, such as clicking on a web link, an image or a video, placing a call, or buying something. Depending on an advertiser's goal, proven formats include search ad, ad networks, online video and targeted media. In particular, the success of Google search ad formats like AdWords Sitelink (Ad Sitelinks) and AdWords InVideo ads (InVideo Ads) has eventually led to the significant growth of online advertising. On the other hand, differentiation is an important key to increased market share. Good branding should determine who is and who is not the intended audience. Audience fragmentation is driving the development of geographic, demographic, contextual, and behavior targeting in online advertising. The Internet, with its ability to record behavior and acquire demographic information for a geographic location, is largely responsible for the increase in targeted ads. Now more and more advertisers are moving toward targeted advertising by coping with audience fragmentation.

The Internet is overtaking traditional television to become leading advertising sector. For example, the UK has become the first major economy where Internet ad spend overtook TV, with a record £1.75bn online spend in the first six months of 2009 (Sweney, 2009). With the increasing saturation of Internet penetration, a huge long tail of advertisers that even have not advertised have been attracted. The evolving landscape of online video services, e.g., YouTube (YouTube. com), YouKu (Youku.com), Hulu (hulu.com), etc., and interactive TV services, e.g., TiVo (Tivo. com), Sky+ (radioandtelly.co.uk), etc., are offering advertisers new opportunities to reach consumers more effectively and efficiently rather than tradi-

tional forms of advertising on a separate media platform. For example, Green Button Advertising of Sky+ (Green/Red Button advertising), an interactive advertising, can prompt the viewer to join the advertiser in a journey of some sort, allowing consumers to access long-form video advertising or branded content experiences. Moreover, Red Button Advertising of Sky+, can even trigger a viewer action by an on-air call to deliver a wide range of campaign objectives from enhancing a brand, giving more information, extending a TV ad, impulse led purchasing, building a database and market research. Google offers several advertising solutions, e.g., text overlay ads, In-stream video ads, placement targeting, etc., to help advertisers target video content across Google's ad networks, based on the widest reach of YouTube (Video Advertising Solutions).

Television's most outstanding attribute is its ability to reach a vast number of consumers at the same time. TV ads' other advantages are impact, credibility, selectivity, and flexibility (Vilanilam & Varghese, 2004), although the cost of creating, producing, and airing a TV ad are staggering, and most traditional TV advertising goes unnoticed. Critically, interactive television (generally known as iTV) (Kunert, 2009) allows viewers to interact with TV program content and TV-related content. Interactivity with TV related content may provide more information about what is being advertised, and even the ability to buy it. However, as a competitive media from Internet-based content, internet ads continue to fast advance as Internet technology allows advertisers to target by demographics, geographic, contextual, scheduling, behavior, etc. More importantly, Internet ads give us access to a wide range of products or services information such as deals, discounts, reviews, etc. Targeting and interactive capabilities will make it essential and promising to investigate innovative ways to bridge the gap between Internet ads and traditional TV ads (Wang, et al., 2009).

According to The Nielsen Company's latest Three Screen Report (Nielsenwire, 2010), overall media consumption of the average American continue to increase. The rise in simultaneous use of the web and TV gives the viewer a unique on-screen and off-screen relationship with TV programming. Nielsen data shows, nearly 60% of TV viewers go online simultaneously at least once a month, DVRs continue to gain popularity in 35% of American household. More recently, OnDemand Online (comcast.net) and TV Everywhere (timewarnercable.com) initiate to make television programs available online. The goal is to make available TV shows online to authenticated cable subscribers, at no cost, in the format that each show was originally presented on television – the same program, the same national commercials. Though no one knows for sure the consumer adoption of different business models for extended screens, service providers are entering the media business with multimedia content on TV, Internet, and Mobile in order to leverage the various media platforms and channels available to them to target advertisers (Alcatel-Lucent, 2009). Consumers are choosing to add elements to their media experience, rather than to replace them.

Communicators and marketers frequently use multiple communication tools (e.g., advertising, public relations and direct marketing) or channels (e.g., television, magazines and the Web) within a single campaign. The ultimate goal of employing multiple communication vehicles is to have them synergize to create the greatest persuasion effect (Chang & Thorson, 2004). In this chapter, we present some insights on effective collaboration between TV advertising and Internet advertising. *Synergy* is defined as "the interaction of two or more agents or forces so that their combined effect in greater than the sum of their individual effect" (American Heritage College Dictionary, 1997). To take advantage of television-Web synergy, we propose to intelligently digest TV ads and link traditional TV ads to the relevant Internet ads through multimedia content analysis and information retrieval techniques, as illustrated

in Figure 1. When some successful online and interactive TV campaigns like search ad formats and (Green/Red Button advertising) become more interactive, more visual, and perhaps engaging, traditional TV ads enriched with further links and contents from relevant online ads could be used as a powerful advertising medium to communicate with more audience across TV, Internet, and mobile. It doesn't solve the battles between the Internet and TV, but focuses on the integration of television and Web advertising.

BACKGROUND

A wealth of information creates a poverty of attention. There is a need to allocate that attention efficiently among the overabundance of information sources that might consume it. In recent years, the problem of information load (Simon, 1971) has been widely characterized as an economic one. Attention economies is an approach to the management of information that treats human attention as a scarce commodity, and applies economics theory to solve various information management problems (Wikipedia). Today attention economics is primary concerned with the problem of getting consumers to consume advertising. Such an economy is driving a marketplace where consumers agree to receive services, e.g., multimedia content, in exchange for their attention. Service providers sell consumers' attention in the form of time or space to advertisers. Media companies like Comcast Corp., Time Warner and DirecTV Group, have long benefited from such dual revenue streams. There is certainly no better example of efficient attention economy model than search. As user queries follow user interests, be it informational, educational, entertaining, or commercial, search behavior reveals the consumer's attention by which marketers can target ads to specific consumers, eliminating waste and increasing efficiency.

Figure 1. An illustration of digesting TV ads as well as linking TV ads to Internet ads. Content analysis and information retrieval techniques are employed to establish ads links to bridge the gap between traditional television ads and Internet ads, which allows TV viewers to search and browse the TV ads enriched with links to relevant Internet ads. Based on user profiles, summary and recommend can be made to meet the personalized requirements of ads

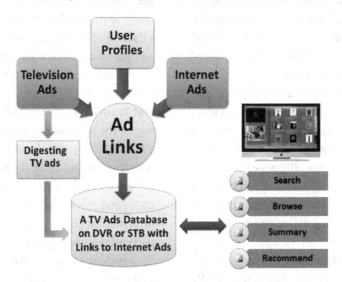

Consumers are increasingly exercising control of how they view, interact with, and filter advertising in a multichannel world (Berman, Battino, Shipnuck, & Neus, 2007). They adopt ad-skipping, ad-sharing, and ad-rating tools, as digital video recorders (DVRs), video on demand (VOD), online sites (like YouTube and MySpace), mobile, games and other emerging entertainment platforms offer the environment – the viewer is in control. The actual growth of interactive advertising formats, such as Internet, interactive television promotions, mobile and in-game advertising, has outpaced forecast by IBM Institute for Business Value (Berman, Battino, Shipnuck, & Neus, 2007). The shift of consumers' attention will eventually be reflected in attention economy. We will review the advent of new ad formats and improved traditional advertising techniques, given the engaging and targeting capabilities of new media platforms, in the context of attention economy.

INTERNET ADVERTISING

Advances in Internet advertising techniques fall into the developments of ad formats and ad targeting.

Internet ad formats are advanced through the use of media authoring, photo- and video-editing tools (like Adobe Flash and Adobe Photoshop) and Web-based technologies (like communities, user-generated content (UGC) sites, social networking sites). The simplest ad format is text ads. One can create simple messages in a standardized format, and place them on a site like Google.com and Yahoo.com in minutes. A standard display ad includes texts with a visual design such as a logo or a graphic. Standard display ads can either be static or animated. With a click on them, one will be taken to a destination site. Display ads can be in formats like JPEG, GIF, SWF and more. In particular, intended to be small enough for publication on the web, SWF files can contain animation or applets of varying degrees of interactivity and function (Adobe Systems Incorporated, 2008).

SWF currently functions as the dominant format for delivering animated vector graphics over the Internet. Flash video content (FLV or F4V formats) may also be embedded within SWF file. Notable users include YouTube, Yahoo! Video, Youku, etc.

Rich media (synonymous for interactive multimedia) technologies are gaining increasing momentum to make the most technically advanced and engaging display ads (Interactive media). Rich media responds to the user's action by presenting content such as vector graphics, text, video, and sound, etc. Rich media capabilities enable a viewer to interact with an ad and learn about a brand without having to leave the page they're on. Ads may expand when users click or roll over, for example, and there are extensive possibilities for interactive content, such as HD video or even the ability to click to make a phone call. Compared with standard text and display formats, rich media ad format has the potentials to clearly and vividly communicate an advertising message via high interactivity, expansion, and more. Interactivity can offer markers opportunities in creating customer-centric brand experience (Djurovic, 2008).

As opposed to mass marketing techniques, online ad-targeting technology continues to advance. Current technology allows advertisers to target by context and behavior. Contextual targeting dominates, while behavioral targeting is relatively new but catching on fast.

Contextual targeting has been used in offline advertising for a long time. You read a magazine article about home decorating ideas and the ads on the page might be for furniture or paint. In new attention economy, the same principle is applied to the websites ranging from individual bloggers and niche communities to large publishers such as major newspapers. Search marketing from major web search engines (Google, Yahoo!, and Microsoft) has established a successful paradigm of placing ads based on dominant keywords or phrases. When a page is visited by a user, the page URL is sent to an advertising system, where the page is crawled and parsed to find relevant ads that will be sent back to be embedded in the webpage which the user is browsing. A Web contextual model relies on informative texts, hyperlinks, anchor tags, metadata, etc. Extensive research efforts in the field of information retrieval (IR) have been made to match the content of a Web page against a dataset of ads to find out relevant text or display ads based on contextual analysis by syntactic or semantic clues found in texts. For example, (Yih, Goodman, & Carvalho, 2006) proposed a system that learns how to extract keywords from web pages for advertising targeting..They examined a wide variety of information sources including words or phrases in a document, meta-tags, title information, and even the words in the URL of the page, and found that the overall query frequency information (from MSN search query logs) of a particular word or phrase on a page was helpful in determining if that word or phrase was relevant to that page. (Jin, Li, Mah, & Tong, 2007) presented a sensitive content (e.g., adult, accident, etc.) classification approach to detect whether a publisher webpage is appropriate for displaying ads on it. (Broder, Fontoura, Josifovski, & Riedel, 2007) developed a hierarchcial taxonomy of around 6000 nodes primarily built for classifying commercial interet queries to classify web pages and ads into a taxonomy of topics, In the ad ranking forumua, the proximity of the ad and page classes, as well as the traditional key word matching, are employed based on a combination of semantic and syntactic features.

Consumers are spending more time consuming images and videos on the Web. Targeting ads based on the context of online images and videos have attracted growing marketing and research interests. (Mei, Hua, & Li, 2008) proposed to locate nonintrusive areas within an image to place a logo or a graphic of an ad, and rank the ads according to the textual relevance between each ad' description, and the global textual content of the Web page and the local surround text. (Li, Zhang, & Ma, 2008) proposed to utilize idle time and the display area, owing to large image size and limited network bandwidth (or progressive downloading), for non-intrusively embedding ads into images. The relevance between ads and images can be measured based on user-generated tags or image annotation. However, contextual advertising solutions from leaders like Google AdSense and BritePic (britepic.com) rely heavily on text-based models, rather than on an automated method that quickly indexes, filers, and classifies images and videos to place targeted ads alongside rich media. Visual content is basically used to locate the less intrusive regions for placing ads (Li, Wang, Yan, & Xu, 2005) (Liu, Jiang, Huang, & Xu, 2008). (Mei T., Hua, Yang, & Li, 2007) tried to detect a set of candidate video ad insertion points by locating the positions with higher content discontinty and lower attrativness within an online video.

Innovative research has tried to associate relevant ads by matching characteristic images like logos (Liao, Chen, & Hsu, 2008) or detecting high-level semantic concepts (Mei T., Hua, Yang, & Li, 2007) (Wang, Fang, & Lu, 2008). For example, "car" in a road scene is clearly related to car ads. A cell-phone video ad can be triggered when the user's mouse moves on the "phone" in a video scene. In a generic sense, the scalability of such advertising systems yet relies much on the success of exiting text based online ads, as automatic image and video annotation has proved to be a very challenging research problem (Wang, Zhang, Jing, & Ma, 2006). Most existing approaches attempt to learn models from a small-scale training set. Unfortunately, those models cannot be applied to large-scale web images. An alternative approach is to impose domain knowledge on visual content analysis (Gong, Lim, & Chua, 1995) (Duan, Xu, Chua, Tian, & Xu, 2003) (Li, Wang, Yan, & Xu, 2005) when scanning through images and videos for appropriateness as well as contextual relevance. For example, (Wan & Xu, 2006) used domain features to compute viewer relevance in soccer and tennis videos, where less intrusive regions like defocused background areas in a close-up shot are

segmented for advertising content placement in sports highlights.

The technology of behavioral targeting delivers relevant ads by tracking user behavior like past search, browsing and clicking. For example, search profiling allows marketers to serve users ads using query history. Targeted ads can associate categories of interest, say sports, gardens, cars, pets, with user browser, based on the types of sites users visit and the pages they view. MSN search query logs were found to be useful in finding advertising keywords on web pages (Yih, Goodman, & Carvalho, 2006). At the heart of behavioral targeting is a learning-based investigation of consumer behaviors over time (Agichtein, Brill, & Dumais, 2006) (Agichtein, Brill, Dumais, & Ragno, 2006). However, behavioral targeting does have a few problems. For the first, it may be effective to target ads to a well motivated audience, whereas lots of potential prospects may not reflect a user' real interest through past behavior. Moreover, some folks never learn about new products unless they are advertised, and advertisers could be missing lots of sales opportunities. In a sense, behavioral targeting has the effect of reducing reach. The second problem is with the privacy issues of behavioral targeting. Popular companies like Google have been struggling to provide transparency, choice, and control around privacy safety (Google Blog, 2009).

TELEVISION ADVERTISING

A television advertisement – often just commercial or TV ad – is span of television programming produced and paid for by an organization that conveys a message (Wikipedia). The vast majority of television advertisements today consist of brief adverting spots, ranging in length from a few second to a few minutes. The average cost of producing a 30-second national TV ad is over $300,000. A 30-second spot may easily run in excess of $100,000. The cost of producing a commercial, and the cost of airing it are clearly prohibitive for small- to medium-sized business owners. But local advertising may fit better with their budgets and marketing goals. Today TV continues to be an important entertainment platform, and a latest Three Screen Report (Nielsenwire, 2010) has revealed the steady trend of increased TV viewership alongside expanded simultaneous usage of TV/Internet. Millions of people are reached by TV ads which modify their living and work habits, if not immediately, at least later. Research shows that most people do not mind TV advertising in general, although they dislike certain commercials; they do not like to be yelled at or treated rudely (Vilanilam & Varghese, 2004).

As Internet marketing brings great revenue success by advertising targeting technologies, there are significant pressures on traditional TV ads via both linear broadcast and on-demand cable networks. Traditional television advertising is shifting to more targeted solutions using the statistics on TV viewing behavior and demographics. The Nielsen ratings system provides over 40% of the world's TV viewing behavior (Nielsen). With two types of electronic meters, Set Meters and People Meters, Nielsen TV research capture what channel is being tuned, as well as who is watching. The viewing information provides a basis for program scheduling and advertising decisions for television stations, cable systems, and advertisers. To mimic Internet advertising, the providers of addressable advertising and interactive television solutions like Navic Networks (navic.tv) and Dish Network (dishnetwork.com) are redoubling their efforts to target ads to selected groups of consumers. For example, Navic Networks aggregates viewer data from multiple satellite and cable TV systems, as well as geographic and demographic data, to determine which ads to serve. With a digital set-top box (STB), Dish Network provides targeting advertising solutions according to specific household viewer geographic and demographic and other viewer metrics like income. In addition, the semantic match of the program content and the ads can be performed by classifying both into a common taxonomy. The taxonomy could be established by using keyword suggestions tools used by ad networks to suggest keywords to internet advertiser. For example, if a view has selected to watch a TV program on a car repair, a car repair ad may appear. These matching, combined with subscriber viewing habits and preferences, allow addressable advertising services.

Interactive television (iTV), in particular, represents a remarkable advance in what television can do for viewers and advertisers. iTV viewers can interact with programs, ads, sponsorship bumper, and even channels, via their remote control to get more information. When the commercial begin, an interactive call to action appears on screen, prompting the viewer to join the advertiser in a journey of some sort. For example, a 30- and 60-second Nike shoe ad on Dish Network in 2007 allowed viewers to zoom in to see a show of San Diego Chargers running back LaDainian Tomlinson's signature "spin" move in different speeds, watch his workout routine, play a remote-control game that tests reflexes, get a 3D demo of the Zoom shoe or click on the store locator. Another example is Green/Red Button advertising (skymedia) with the added functionality of Sky+. In addition to accessing long-form video advertising or branded content experiences, Green Button Advertising enables consumers to book or download TV ads to their set-top boxes, and read more or experience for themselves. Red-button advertising can trigger viewers to action by an on-air call in order to deliver a wide range of campaign objectives such as impulse led purchasing, building a database and market research. In the UK, more than 40 million viewers in Sky or Freeview STB homes can access iTV ads, and over 1,000 interactive campaigns have been run since 2000. More than 70 per cent of advertisers that experiment with red-button campaigns end up coming back for more according to the data (thinkbox.tv) from Sky Media.

INTERNET ADVERTISING VERSUS TELEVISION ADVERTISING

As opposed to purposeful Web customers, the passive TV audience is willing to view irrelevant content as long as it is entertaining enough. In any particular TV audience, only a few have an immediate need for the product or service being advertised. As a sort of impression-based advertising, the traditional form of TV ads is, to some degree, a mixture of substance and amusement. This is why television advertising invests more into having the athlete or star celebrities in a TV ad, in addition to the effect of testimonials. Today the dominant trend in the evolution of online advertising represents a shift from selling audience to selling behavior. As a result, traditional television advertising was ever considered as brand awareness only and usually an unfocused and expensive method of advertising. Nowadays a range of technologies like iTV advertising have been developed to allow advertisers to access extra content of brands, and target viewers in a manner similar to the classic performance-based advertising like Google's AdSense. According to one thinkbox study (Ray), brands that use iTV advertising benefit from added consumer trust compared to online ads, and iTV is thus considered as a source of information and entertainment.

With recent advances in electronics, content is available on multiple platforms. Nielsen reported that the three-screen consumers are choosing to add elements to their media experience, rather than to replace them. Media choices are rarely either/or, and TV and the Internet are particularly complementary. To best leverage the various media platforms to target advertisers and create the greatest persuasion effect, could bring new ad revenues for media companies. One truth is that TV and Internet based media are helping each other grow and develop. For example, TV online initiates of Comcast and Timer Warner are actually helping the Internet by opening it up to wider audiences; on the other hand, Internet

Protocol television (IPTV) systems like (Hulu.com) (Joost.com) are helping the television by integrating live media production with Internet participants in networked scenarios such as social networks and online profiles. In fact, there is strong movement in the industry to roll up forms of three-screen advertising campaign.

A marriage of Internet and Television communication channels is worth being made to have them synergize in advertising to produce attitudinal and behavior effects that are superior to a single media, For example, TiVo, a leading DVR company, has recently teamed up with Google to measure audience reach for Google TV ads with second-by-second television viewing data such as skipping and tuning behaviors, so that Google will use this information to see how many people are watching certain ads and at certain times, in order to improve the measurability and accountability of video ads running on the Google TV Ads platform. On the benefits of employing multiple communication vehicles, several studies have found that engaging TV ads can grasp audiences' attention to Internet communications (Blackwell, Paul, & James, 2001), and the interactive nature of the Web also engages audiences and allows them to be active in the marketing communication process (Allen, Deborah, & Beth, 1998). While high definition programming and flat screen TVs have boosted the quality of the experience, standard television or time shifted television via a DVR are delivering more attractive moving images and sounds than ever before that are effective attention-getting devices, which are often absent in Internet advertising.

LINKING TRADITIONAL TV ADVERTISING TO INTERNET ADVERTISING

In this section, we will look into how to correlate the branded content delivered on television with the relevant information on the Internet platform, maximizing opportunities for advertisers to benefit from the collaboration between traditional TV ad advertising and Internet advertising..Given the strong convergence of the Internet and TV, as well as advertisers' hunger for Web-style measurements for their television ads, there is a good chance regular TV ads are connected to Internet ads, where a "killer" set-top box or an Internet-ready digital video recorder fills that role, The relevance links enable search, discovery, and alert for the availability of ads across media platforms that best fit what TV viewers want.

Information retrieval techniques will be employed to establish the links, where image and video content analysis approaches may facilitate the extraction of syntactic and semantic metadata in television ads. Such automation process reduces an advertising system's operation costs. Based on visual content and metadata of a given TV ad, Internet ads are associated by spotting related advertising keywords on web pages, matching characteristic images or detecting high-level visual concepts in display format ads.

With the growing popularity of household DVRs, time shifted TV ads are delivering more choice to watch ads. Consumers can actively choose to save favorite ads to DVRs for later watching and sharing. When the subscribers' viewing habits or preferences are available, DVRs are able to automatically record TV ads. In addition, extra ad content including texts, images and videos from the Internet, especially E-Commerce Web sites, may be downloaded before TV viewers put requests for link information. As a result, the link process allows TV viewers to enjoy rich media ads over a television screen that involve brilliant and entertaining TV ads, as well as the related internet ads in terms of products or services category, brand, logo and so on. Of course, modeling relevance could involve campaign rules or bidding networks in addition to contextual metadata and visual content. On the other hand, the link can work with the cable companies' video-on-demand, where the central information processing system is

in charge of managing ads, generating metadata, and establishing the contextual links between TV ads and Internet ads. Television VOD systems stream ads information on demand to television through a set-top box.

SYNTACTIC ELEMENTS OF TELEVISION ADS

More and more audience favorite television ads made us smile, think and want more. As the world's biggest celebration of creativity in brand communication, (Cannes Lions International Advertising Festival) annually showcases the most creative television ads from all over the world. Nowadays a 30- or 60-second spot is more like a mini-movie. To attract the viewer attention, innovation arises from a fresh creative treatment and advanced media production, blurring the lines between television advertising and entertainment. To link ads, television ads are first parsed to obtain the syntactic elements. Several studies (Duan, Wang, Zheng, Jin, Lu, & Xu, 2006) have suggested that automated video content analysis is an approach to spot the brand messages from the visual cues in the television advertising, even when the boundaries of entertainment and brand content become more indistinct, which may allow future processing like optical character recognition (OCR).

A subset of video shots, named as Image Frame Marked with Product Information (FMPI) shot, forms a useful syntactic element in television ads (Duan, Wang, Zheng, Jin, Lu, & Xu, 2006). Within an FMPI shot, the images explicitly convey brand messages illustrating products or services being advertised. The visual cues are expressed basically in three ways: texts, graphics, and a live footage of real things or people. Figure 2 shows the frames of selected FMPI shots. The text section may include brand name, store name, address, telephone number, price, etc. Alongside the text section, product images may be placed via computer graphics. As graphics create an abstract,

Figure 2. Key frames of image frame marked with product information shots. (From top to bottom: the simplest yet most popular layouts, the product is projected into the foreground in crisp and clear magnification, and the complex layouts with superimposed texts, graphics, and live footage)

symbolic, or "unreal" universe in which incredible things happen, live footage of real things or people is usually combined with graphics to alleviate the problem of impersonality. FMPI shots often tell the end of each spot within an ad break. Text may be identified using OCR technology to generate metadata for describing TV ads.

Based on FMPI shots, producing a series of picture collages (i.e., daily, weekly, category specific, etc.) for ads may be a useful approach in an interactive television environment. More importantly, content-based image search can be performed to retrieve those display format ads from the Internet that contain visually similar symbols, logos and product images as the query FMPI shot. The surround texts of retrieved display ads may be processed to provide useful information to establish ad links..

In addition, audio scene change indicator (ASCI) is an auditory syntactic element. A spot is usually a combination of music, sound effects, voice-over narration, and storytelling video. (Duan, Wang, Zheng, Jin, Lu, & Xu, 2006) presented ASCI to identify the boundaries of each

spot during TV ad breaks. The assumption is that different spots are basically characterized by dissimilar audio scenes. The metadata on the exact boundaries of each spot are usually unavailable in TV broadcasting streams, whereas effectively extracting this information is significant for establishing links on an individual basis.

SEMANTIC ELEMENTS OF TELEVISION ADS

Favorite television ads involve a collection of memorable images, scenes, or performances. Semantic elements like visual concepts offer an important mean of describing items to locate close match. Either user-supplied or computationally suggested tags allow viewers to search and filter ads. Statistics show that visual concept frequency is potentially useful to reflect the ad categories by products or services (Zheng, Duan, Tian, & Jesse, 2006) (Wang, Duan, Xu, Lu, & Jin, 2007). As illustrated in Figure 3, healthcare ads tend to present more nature scenes, and automobile ads

Figure 3. Example images of visual concepts. (From left to right: road scene v. s. automobile ads, computer graphics v. s. healthcare ads, natural scenes v. s. healthcare ads, and meeting room & skyscraper v. s. finance ads.)

present more road scenes and cars. They used this information to categorize textually unclassified TV ads due to the poor processing results of automatic speech recognition (ASR) and OCR. Generally speaking, a TV ad can be associated with content-based concepts (e.g. keywords, subject matter, visual concepts, etc.) that relates to a service or product associated with both TV ads and Internet ads. Based on extracted concepts, TV ads and Internet ads may be represented as vectors in a vector space. A variety of strategies like the cosine similarity between ads are used to match TV ads to those Internet ads. Moreover, visual concepts can be used as additional information to model user preference in terms of favorite products/services categories, scenes, people, events, etc.

Visual concepts in television ads usually fall into the categories of setting/scene/site (e.g., Indoor/outdoor, office, beach, mountain, sky, road, street, etc.), people (e.g., face, hair, baby, performer, police, spokesperson, beauty, crowd, etc.), objects (e.g., car, bus, boat, animal, airplane, etc.), activities (e.g., walking/running, dancing, etc.), events (e.g. wedding, sports, disaster, explosion, etc.), graphics (e.g., charts, animation, etc), and product/service categories. In recent years, developments of large-scale multimedia concept lexicon have been reported for news videos (Naphade, et al., 2005), consumer videos (Chang, et al., 2007), and general-purpose photographs (Li & Wang, 2008). As opposed to special domains, general-purpose means that pictures are taken in

daily life. Efforts have been made to break down the semantic space using a small number of concepts. For example, (Naphade, et al., 2005) analyzed an expanded lexicon of more than 2000 concepts, with respect to the TRECVID and BBC queries, and came up with 44 concepts along 7 dimensions in news videos. (Li & Wang, 2008) developed a real-time automatic image annotation system where a total of 332 distinct words, e.g., landscape, mountain, ice, lake, are used to annotate each image for 599 semantic concepts by Corel during image acquisition. Since the early 1990s, numerous computation approaches to content-based image/video classification, annotation, and retrieval have been widely studied (TREC Video Retrieval Evaluation). Nowadays researchers in both computer vision and multimedia communities have been actively constructing benchmarking datasets (Caltech 101) (Caltech 256) (Pascal VOC) towards fair evaluation of different features and statistical learning algorithms in object recognition and image/video annotation..

LINKING TELEVISION ADS TO INTERNET ADS VIA SYNTACTIC AND SEMANTIC ELEMENTS

In essence, linking ads is to figure out a sort of meaningful mapping via syntactic and semantic elements between Internet and television ads. When a sufficient amount of elements are available, a

Figure 4. An example scenario of linking TV ads to Internet ads. Syntactic and semantic elements are extracted from TV ads, while display ad images and surround tags are collected from web pages. Information retrieval approaches are employed to link clues across TV and Internet. Recommendation of products or services is provided to TV viewers via either STB or DVR

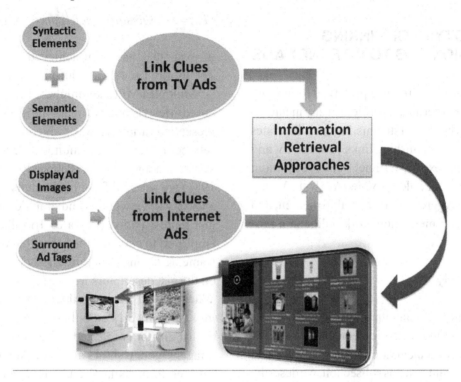

wide range of information retrieval approaches like vector space model and cosine similarity measure (Manning, Raghavan, & Schütze, 2008) can be employed to find the relevant ads, condense the ads' information items and arrange them by some categories. In the subsequent prototype, we will demonstrate how to use content analysis, indexing and retrieval techniques to make a linking solution when TV ads' metadata are not available in broadcasting streams.

To establish ads links, a Web crawler is executed at the central media servers or a set-top box to harvest product/service information from the Internet, such as product or logo image, brand name, price, sales info, etc. A Web crawler is developed to autonomously gather information from Web pages. Many sites, in particular search engines, use a Web crawler as a means of provid-

ing up-to-date data. In this chapter, the prototype will use a customized crawler to collect images and tags from popular E-commerce websites like EBay, Amazon, etc. In future, Semantic Web (Lee, Hendler, & Lassila, 2001) may provide a formal description about the meaning of information and services on the web, so that the tedious workload in gathering and processing Web information would be greatly reduced.

Figure 4 shows an example scenario of linking ads. From elements linking, viewers are offered the opportunity of watching more about a particular product or service, and even accessing related communities on product reviews. When broadcast TV is being librated by new technologies such as IPTV and Web TV, linking ads could probably perform better with TV as the lead medium. In other words, the ability of TV is to start a process, creating the interest or desire to exploit other media, where the links provide a portal service to recommend or decide for viewers.

A PROTOTYPE OF LINKING TELEVISION ADS TO INTERNET ADS

In this section, we present a prototype for linking TV ads to Internet ads, regardless of any metadata on TV ads in broadcast streams. Figure 5 illustrates the process of establishing links between TV and Internet ads. Except Offline Data Preparation, the remaining modules of Video Analysis, Visual Search, Tag Aggregation, Textual Re-search, and Service Recommendation work online in a progressive manner.

Video Analysis

Content analysis is an important approach to extract syntactic and semantic elements from television ads, when metadata are usually unavailable in broadcast streams. In this subsection, we describe two detectors, FMPI and ASCI. Subsequently, we brief our work in detecting visual concepts. The prototype currently emphasizes on how far to go with syntactic elements and basic visual features.

Detecting FMPI Shots

Texture, edge, and color features are combined to represent an FMPI frame. As the layout of graphics, images, and text is significant for distinguishing an FMPI frame, an image is partitioned into sub-regions and spatial constraints are imposed on feature extraction. Based on color histograms, dominant colors are used to approximate color distributions. Gabor filters (Jain & Farrokhnia, 1991) are used to capture rich texture. Canny edge operator (John, 1986) is used to detect stand-alone edges, as opposed to texture. As a result, a 141-d visual feature consisting of 128-d local features and 13-d global ones is constructed (Duan, Wang,

Zheng, Jin, Lu, & Xu, 2006). Support Vector Machines (SVMs) (Cristianini & Taylor, 2000) is used to train the FPMI image recognizer. The F_1 score

$$\left(F_1 = 2 \cdot precision \cdot rcall \big/ \left(precision + recall \right) \right)$$

of over 90% has been achieved (Duan, Wang, Zheng, Jin, Lu, & Xu, 2006).

Multiple FMPI shots might be irregularly interposed in television ads to make the repetition effect, presenting various views of advertised products or services in an ad. To use multiple views for image search, canonical images (Palmer, Rosch, & Chase, 1981) are selected from FMPI shots to represent a variety of viewpoints and graphic overlay. The gist representation (Oliva & Torralba, 2001) is employed to compute the global features of each frame. K-means clustering (Bishop, 2006) is run on the gist descriptors from all the FMPI frames. When one ad has more than one frames falling into the same cluster, only one frame belonging to that cluster is selected to be the canonical ad image. Figure 6 shows a set of canonical images selected from "Nikon" and "iPod" ads.

Modeling ASCI

A proper modeling of ASCI is applied to identify the boundaries of each spot. A mixture Gaussian Hidden Markov Model (HMM) (left-to-right) is utilized to train audio scene change (ASC) recognizers. Diagonal covariance matrix is used to estimate the mixture Gaussian distribution. Suppose we have two HMM models to characterize ASC and Non-ASC, two likelihood values of an observation sequence are generated by the forward-backward algorithm. An unknown audio segment (say 4 seconds in length) is classified by the model that has the highest posterior probability. A series of successive 20 ms analysis frames by shifting the sliding window of 20 ms with an interval of 10 ms are used to extract features. In total 43 audio features are extracted including Mel-

Figure 5. Framework of the prototype of linking television ads to internet ads. Five core modules including Video Analysis, Visual Search, Tag Aggregation, Textual Re-Search, Service Recommendation work in a progressive manner; Preparation for Internet Ads works offline

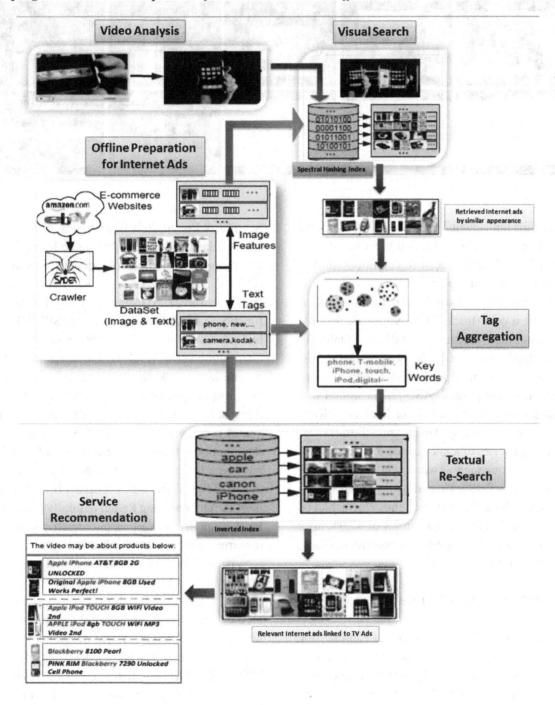

frequency cepstral coefficients (MFCCs) and its first and second derivates, mean and variance of short time energy log measure (STE), mean and variance of short-time zero-crossing rate (ZCR),

Figure 6. The selected canonical images from 'Nikon' camera and 'iPod' video ads. A variety of viewpoints and graphic layouts are usually applied to represent advertised products/services

short-time fundamental frequency (or Pitch), mean of the spectrum flux (SF), and harmonic degree (HD). HTK (HTK Speech Recognition Toolkit) is utilized to train models.

Statistics show that a soundtrack may not synchronize a video track, thus a symmetric window exactly at a shot transition would be unsuitable for extracting features to effectively represent the ASC nearby. An alignment process is thus performed to locate the most possible ASC points around shot change points. Kullback-Leibler divergence (Kullback, 1968) is employed to measure the distances between a series of audio feature distributions of multi-scale overlapping windows. The most likely ASC point is finally located by the highest accumulated values. The ASC recognizer has achieved an overall classification accuracy of 87.9% after performing the alignment process (Duan, Wang, Zheng, Jin, Lu, & Xu, 2006).

Detecting Visual Concepts

Detecting visual concepts involves representing an image by global and local image properties, as well as comparing images by a similarity measure. To extract low- and mid- level features, several state-of-the-art features/kernels are implemented, including patch-based appearance descriptors (i.e., dense-color-SIFT and dense-SIFT (Lazebnik,

Schmid, & Ponce, 2006)), shape descriptors (i.e., self-similarity (SS) (Shechtman & Irani, 2007) and pyramid histogram of orientated gradients (PHOG) (Bosch, Zisserman, & Munoz, 2007), texture features (i.e., Gabor features). Two kernel functions, spatial pyramid kernel (SPK) (Lazebnik, Schmid, & Ponce, 2006) and proximity distribution kernel (PDK) (Ling & Soatto, 2007), are employed. SPK divides an image into cells and performs image matching using the features from the spatially corresponding cells. The resulting kernel is a weighted combination of histogram intersections from coarse-to-fine cells. PDK measures the proximity distributions of vector-quantized local feature descriptors between two images. The resulting kernel naturally combines local geometric as well as photometric information from images at multiple scales.

Visual object recognition is useful to understand what is advertised in TV ads and Internet display ads. A novel discriminative learning method, named Group-Sensitive Multiple Kernel Learning (GS-MKL), was developed to train object classifiers (Yang, Li, Tian, Duan, & Gao, 2009). GS-MKL optimizes the functionality of multiple kernels by introducing an intermediate representation 'group' between images and object categories. GS-MKL attempts to find appropriate kernel combination for each group to get a finer depiction of object categories. As a result, the image-to-image similarity is measured by a weighted combination of multi-kernels, where the weights of each kernel are optimized based on the kernel function, as well as the groups that each pair of comparing images belong to. Compared with a uniform or sample-specific similarity measure, the group-sensitive similarity measure is effective in dealing with intra-class diversity as well as inter-class correlation. GS-MKL has achieved promising results supervisor to the state-of-the-art on benchmarking datasets of Caltech 101, Pascal VOC 2007, and Wikipedia MM.

Image/video data are informative in spatially (and temporally) contextual correlations on both visual cues and semantic concepts. For instance, 'street' and 'building' usually co-occur in a frame or shot, and a concept might be persistent across several neighboring shots. Automatic video annotation is formulated as a sequential multi-labeling (SML) problem accordingly. Beyond individual shots, SML predicts a multi-label sequence for successive shots using spatial and temporal context. A novel discriminative method, named Sequence Multi-label Support Vector Machines (SVMs^{SML}), was proposed to infer the sequence of multi-labels (Li, Tian, Duan, Yang, Huang, & Gao, 2011). In SVM^{SML}, a joint kernel is employed to model three relationships, i.e., dependencies between low-level features and labels, spatial and temporal correlations of labels. A multiple kernel learning (MKL) algorithm was developed to jointly learn the optimal kernel weights and the SVM^{SML} classifier. SVM^{SML} has achieved promising results superior to the state-of-the-art on benchmarking datasets of TRECVID'05,'07, with the resulting Mean Average Precision (MAP) (Manning, Raghavan, & Schütze, 2008) values 50.65% and 38.66%, respectively.

Visual Search

The prototype performs visual search to find the Internet ads with similar image appearance. Based on a few canonical FMPI shots, the most stable key points in key frames are detected to extract local features robust against noise, illumination and viewpoints, followed by Nearest-Neighbor (NN) based image search. To reduce the errors from visual search, the stages of tag aggregation and textual re-search are executed to improve the links between TV and Internet ads.

Visual Features Extraction

Local and global image descriptors are used to compare images. The local descriptors include SURF (Bay, Ess, Tuytelaars, & Gool, 2008), Shape-Context (Mori, Belongie, & Malik, 2005), and Geometric-Blur (Berg & Malik, 2001). A 4x4 region is used to extract 64-d SURF features for 100 selected key points. From Canny edges, 100 key points are randomly sampled to extract Shape-Context features with the quantization of 12 equally spaced angle bins and 6 equally spaced log-radius bins. From Canny edges, 300 key points are randomly sampled to extract Geometric-Blur features, each point being described by a 51×4-d feature vector involving 4 orientation and 51 locations. Two additional global descriptors include color histogram and Gabor texture. Color space transformation from RGB to HSV is applied, with the quantization of 18 hue bins, 3 saturation bins, and 3 value bins. Gabor features with five scales and four orientations are extracted for each sub-image after partitioning an image into 3x4 sub-images.

Naïve Bayes Nearest Neighbor Based Visual Search

Nearest-Neighbor is employed to perform visual search in a nonparametric manner, as NN requires no training time. (Boiman, Shechtman, & Irani, 2008) argued that two practices of descriptor quantization and image-to-image distance actually lead to significant degradation in the performance of nonparametric image classifiers, and

NN distances can achieve leading performance by computing direct image-to-class distances without descriptor quantization in the space of local image descriptors.

In the prototype, Naïve Bayes Nearest Neighbor (NBNN) (Bishop, 2006) is slightly modified to search visually similar images. Given an FMPI image from TV ads, the local descriptors $d_1,...,d_n$ are firstly extracted. Similar ones from the image collection of internet display ads $C = I_1,...,I_{total-displayad-image}$ are ranked by using $\sum_{i=1}^{n} NN_C(d_i, r)$, where $NN_C(d_i, r)$ is the number of descriptors in each image from C, falling into the neighborhood of d_i with radius r (r is currently set to 30 nearest neighbors). To reduce the computation cost of similarity search in the high-dimensional space, spectral hashing (Weiss, Torralba, & Fergus, 2008) is employed to index the huge dataset of local descriptors from Internet images For example, over 1,877,891 SURF points, spectral hashing takes only 42 ms to query one point on a standard PC with CPU 2.33 Giga Hz and 1.0 Giga Byte RAM.

To boost the performance in measuring similarity by local descriptors, dynamically adjusting the weights of different features is applied to NBNN based visual search, provided that the product/service category information of Internet display ads is available in the phase of Web crawling. Suppose that the confident type of descriptor leads to more uniformity of the categories Tag_C of returned similar images C. Entropy is used to measure the tag uniformity of returned images using the type of descriptor t

$$Entropy_t = \sum_{Tag_C} - \frac{|C_{Tag,j}|}{|C|} \ln \frac{|C_{Tag,j}|}{|C|}$$

where $|C|$ is the number of returned images C, $|C_{Tag,j}|$ the number of images with the *jth* tag

category. Consequently, $Entropy_t$ is used to improve the NBNN decision rule by ranking

$$\sum_t \sum_i \frac{1}{Entropy_t} NN_C(d_{i,t}, r)$$

where $d_{i,t}$ denotes the *ith* descriptor with type information t in a query ad image.

Tag Aggregation

Generally speaking, the tags of a display format ad on E-commerce web sites may be classified into several major categories. For example, this prototype tries to categorize tags into three classes, namely, *identification tags*, *attribute tags* and *others*. Identification tags tell the name or brand of a product, e.g., "*Unlocked AT&T T-Mobile 3.0 Touch Screen GSM Quad Band*" (a mobile ad), "*FUJI FinePix S1000 10MP DIGITAL CAMERA+*" (a camera ad). Attribute tags describe the technical details, e.g., "*Output Type: Color; Print Speed (PPM):30-39 ppm*" (a printer ad), "*Rich waterproof leather upper with soft microfiber lining*" (a women shoes ad). Other tags include price, discount, date and other information. An intuitive idea is to take advantage of the contextual tag information of display ads to establish more targeted links between TV ads and Internet ads.

Empirical observation reveals that the surround tags of Internet ads, based on the returned similar images by visual search, tend to form semantic meaningful clusters. Suppose that the aggregation of identification tags can be obtained by those clusters, the results of visual similar images can be re-ranked by their names and brands. In practice, the top clusters of tags are applied to re-rank the returned images.

A K-lines algorithm (Fischer & Poland, 2004) is employed to cluster tags, where the tag elements in each cluster are approximated by a line instead of a spherical for reinforcing the block structure of the affinity matrix. The advantages over the commonly applied K-means can be found in (Fischer & Poland, 2004) A vector space model is used to compute the similarity matrix, where the surround tags of each image are represented as a term vector. For identification tags, the common weighting scheme Term Frequency is applied. In particular, more weights are given to the terms of product brand. The cosine similarity is calculated to measure the distance between two term vectors. With the processes of stemming and stop words removal, there exist some 20 words per Internet ad image. In the prototype, k was set to 15 for K-lines clustering. The resulting clusters are assumed to have put together meaningful keywords and phrases.

Textual Re-search

The majority of product search engines (Google Product Search) (Bing shopping) benefit well from the contextual tags of Internet ads. In a similar way, finding advertising tags on web pages containing Internet ads can be executed to make more targeted ads links. In the phase of textual re-search, the key phrases of identification tags, from the results of tag aggregation, are spotted by ranking the term saliency score as

$$Score_{i,j} = TF_{i,j} \cdot \log \frac{N}{DF_i}$$

where $TF_{i,j}$ is the number of occurrence of term i in the tags of Internet ad j, DF_i the number of Internet ads with term i, and N the number of terms in the tags of entire Internet ads collection. Five top-ranked words are selected as the key phrases in the prototype. Based on the cosine similarity, the key phrases are formed as a query vector to retrieve relevant ads, using the identification tags, of the Internet ads database. Finally, those Internet ad items with higher similarity values are accepted to serve as the ads links.

Empirical Study

The empirical dataset involves TV ads and Internet ads. 13 popular classes of TV ads are collected, each class containing 20~40 video ads. The category details are listed in Figure 8. To demonstrate the functionality of ads link over a large-scale dataset, we attempted to crawl 18 classes of online ads. The majority of Internet ads are collected from http://www.ebay.com. The dataset consists of 40, 000 Internet ad items, each item including product image, brand name, price and other descriptions..Figure 7 gives examples of online ads from EBay. The evaluation criterion is currently on how accurate a TV ad can be linked to Internet ads with correct category of products or services. We will present the results by visual search, tag aggregation, and textual re-search, respectively.

MAP is utilized in evaluating the performance of progressive search. Figure 8 compares the visual search results with single features as well as the fusion strategy. MAP was improved by the fusion stage in 10 classes out of 13 classes of TV ads. There are several factors that may affect the performance of visual search. Firstly, good image quality of FMPI frames is crucial. When the query FMPI frame was seriously blurred, worse results would probably happen. Secondly, the size and texture of product images from Internet ads are influential. Sufficiently large and texture rich images help generate more stable feature points that allows the local descriptors based direct search to work well. Thirdly, the visual characteristics of product/service related appearance are important. It is easy to image, when a class of products/services (e.g., *cell phone*, *chocolate*) are characterized by chief brands and uniform shape, visual search tends to achieve better performance. For instance, the lower search results of *coffee* and *electric shaver* may be attributed to a large variability in shape or appearance of objects or packages. On average, as shown in Figure 8, visual search yields lower MAP ranging from 0.16 to 0.46. For NBNN based visual search, the

Figure 7. Examples of online ads from EBay. The ads information items usually include product image, brand, price, and other technical details. A crawler can be customized to automatically download those items, which are archived and categorized offline

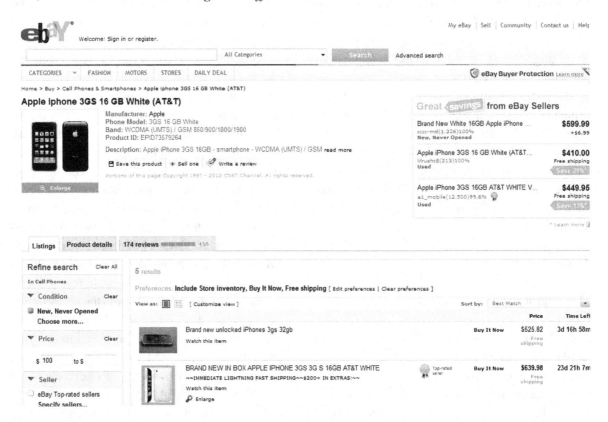

neighborhood radius of local descriptors is an important parameter in practice. We have compared the performances by using different numbers of neighbor points, i.e., NN = 1, 10, 20, 30, 40, 50 and 100, and the NN radius is empirically set to 30 for better visual search.

Figure 9 compares the performances when progressive search undergoes distinct but correlated stages. Tag aggregation is executed to select the top-10 from 15 clusters. The images from visual search are re-ranked in the descending order of the size of a tag cluster. For those ads with tags belonging to the same cluster, their original relative orders from visual search are kept. By extracting the tags as keywords from high-ranked clusters, the textual re-search is executed by using key words. In Figure 9, the textual re-search uses five

keywords. Out of 13 classes, 10 classes have gained improvements in MAP by the progressive search. Overall, the MAP values of all 13 classes for three stages are 0.26, 0.28 and 0.4, respectively, based on the top-50 returned ads. However, with tag aggregation, the search results of *Television* and *Wristwatch* are still worse, while textual re-search unfortunately degrades the performance of visual search. The reasons may be twofold. First, visual search is the kick-off engine of the subsequent tag aggregation and textual re-search. When initial results of visual search were very bad, the progressive search would not obtain desirable or positive MAP gain. On the other hand, the real coherency of ad tags will, of course, have any influence over tag aggregation and textual re-search. Given an ad category, if the tags produce a set of typical

Figure 8. Results of visual search, over 13 popular TV ad categories, with single visual features as well as fusion strategy. MAP is utilized to evaluate the retrieval performance based on the top 100 results from the returned ad images

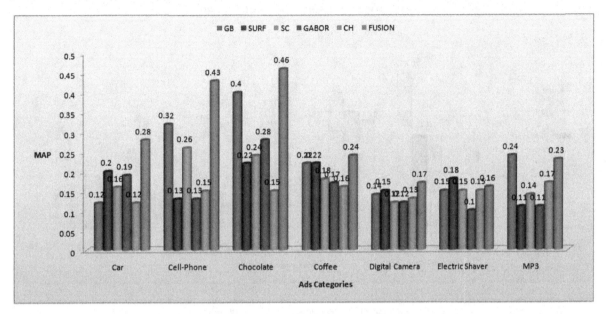

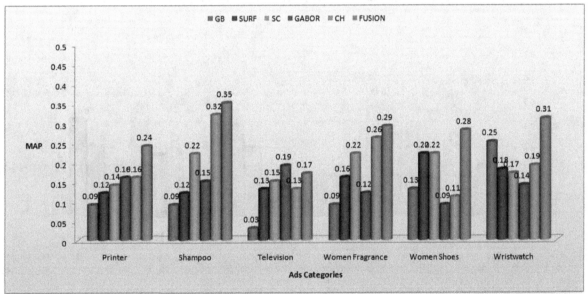

and common words such as t-mobile and Nokia for *Cell Phone*, textual re-search is promising to improve MAP. That is one of the reasons that *Cell Phone*, *MP3*, *Shampoo* and *Digital Camera* have achieved significant MAP improvements by textual re-search.

Figure 10 rearranges the search results by dividing the AP range (from 0.0 to 0.6) of visual search into a series of intervals where each interval length is 0.05. For each query, the visual search AP falls into one of intervals. Within each interval, we compute three types of MAP, namely, visual

Figure 9. Results of the progressive search, with the intermediate ones after executing each distinct stage. Different MAP gains are reflected over 13 ad categories

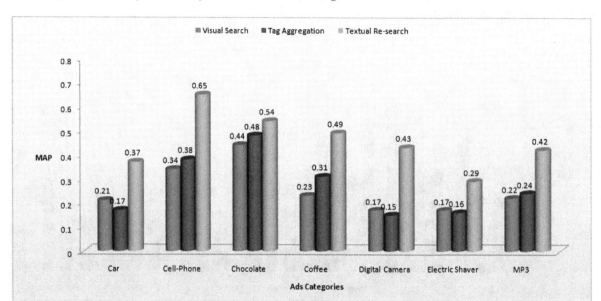

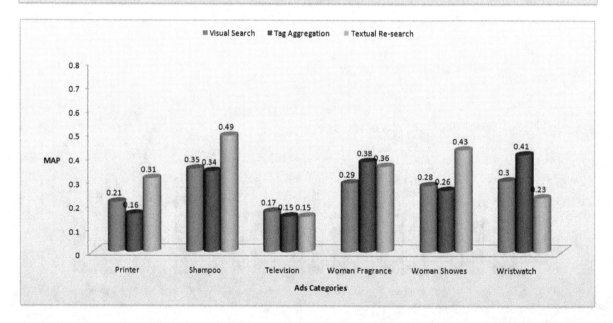

search and the associated tag aggregation and textual re-search, based on the queries whose visual search AP belongs to this interval. It was found that when visual search AP is over 0.3, progressive search is able to consistently obtain MAP improvements after the phases of tag aggregation and textual re-search; on the other hand,

in the case of worse AP less than 0.1, progressive search actually degrades MAP.

The objectives of the present study were to test the existence of synergistic effects of TV ads and Internet ads, as well as to demonstrate the possibility of an information processing approach to establish some kind of synergy link across

Figure 10. Results of the progressive search that are rearranged by dividing the visual search AP of each query into a set of predetermined intervals with the interval length 0.05, and calculating three types of MAP from the set of queries whose visual search AP falls into the same interval

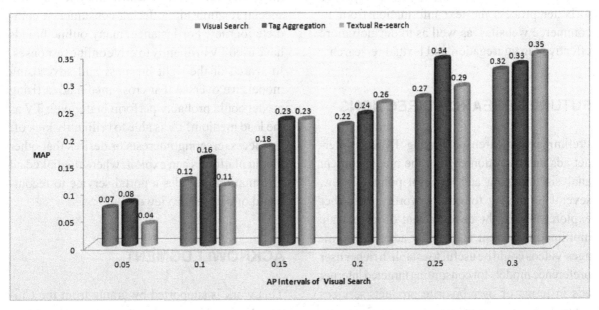

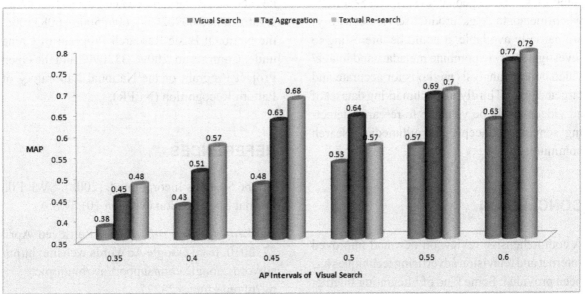

television and Internet platforms. The current prototype worked on the challenging case that TV ads' metadata are totally unavailable in broadcasting streams. Based on visual search results, text-assisted progressive search is expected to satisfy the low-end user requirements. In practice, STB/ DVR service providers or consumers might provide a few metadata such as identification tags or visual concepts, which would undoubtedly enable this prototype to suggest better ad links that are more targeted, relevant and comprehensive, with the support of products/services related taxonomy.

Moreover, in addition to establishing ad links based on pure media content analysis, more information retrieval approaches can be employed to better process the text information from E-commerce websites, as well as to develop more effective tag aggregation and textual re-search.

FUTURE RESEARCH DIRECTIONS

Preliminary research on linking TV and Internet ads has been done. From the media content analysis, indexing and retrieval point of view, several promising topics are worthy to further explore. Firstly, the development of large-scale multimedia concept lexicon for advertising images/videos could be useful to establish richer user preference models for consuming targeted internet ads in terms of user favorite products/services categories, scenes, people, events, etc. Secondly, when metadata (e.g., product/service category) are partially available, it could be interesting to investigate how to combine metadata and image/video content analysis methods for accurate and targeted links. Thirdly, a benchmarking dataset of ad videos might be valuable to research detecting semantic concepts in multimedia research community.

CONCLUSION

A comprehensive review on new and improved Internet and television advertising techniques has been provided. Some kind of integrating Internet and Television advertising may lead to television-Web synergy that brings about higher attention and higher perceived message credibility. To make use of synergy effects, linking ads have been proposed to figure out the meaningful mapping of syntactic and semantic elements between Internet and television ads. A prototype on a number of popular ad categories has empirically demonstrated the capabilities of image/video content analysis in automatically linking ads across two distinct media platforms, regardless of any prior metadata. Television and the Internet exhibit a special relationship, offering consumers a complete journey. For instance, many online brands have used TV brilliantly to drive online responses. In search of the right business and advertising model, we oversee that cross-media advertising model could probably perform better with TV as the lead medium. TV is able to brilliantly kick off a process, creating interests or desires that other media platforms can exploit, where the linked ad information provides a portal service to recommend or decide for viewers.

ACKNOWLEDGMENT

This work is supported by grants from the Chinese National Natural Science Foundation under Contract no. 60902057, 60605008, 60833006, the National Basic Research Program of China under Contract no. 2009CB320902 and the Open Project Program of the National Laboratory of Pattern Recognition (NLPR).

REFERENCES

Adobe Systems Incorporated. (2008). SWF File Format Specification (Version 10). U.S.A.

AdWords InVideo Ads. (n.d.). Retrieved April 27, 2010, from Google AdWords website: http://adwords.google.com/support/aw/bin/topic.py?hl=en&topic=23277

Agichtein, E., Brill, E., & Dumais, S. (2006). Improving web search ranking by incorporating user behavior information. In *Proc. the 29th int. ACM SIGIR conf. on Research and development in information retrieval* (pp. 19-26). Seattle, Washington, USA: ACM.

Agichtein, E., Brill, E., Dumais, S., & Ragno, R. (2006). Learning user interaction for predicting web search result preference. In *Proc. the 29th int.ACM SIGIR conf. on Research and development in information retrieval* (pp. 3-10). Seattle, Washington, USA: ACM.

Alcatel-Lucent. (2009, Jul. 29). Three-Screen Advertising: New Ad Revenues for Service Providers.

Allen, C., Deborah, K., & Beth, Y. (1998). *Internet World:Guide to One-to-One Web Marketing*. New York: Wiley.

(1997). *American Heritage College Dictionary*. Boston: Houghton Mifflin.

Bay, H., Ess, A., Tuytelaars, T., & Gool, L. V. (2008). SURF:Speeded Up Robust Features. *Computer Vision and Image Understanding, 110*(3), 346–359. doi:10.1016/j.cviu.2007.09.014

Berg, A. C., & Malik, J. (2001). Geometric Blue for Template Matching. *Proc. IEEE Conf. on Computer Vision and Pattern Recognition* (pp. 607-613). Kauai, Hawaii: IEEE Computer Society.

Berman, S. J., Battino, B., Shipnuck, L., & Neus, A. (2007). *The end of advertising as we know it*. Somers, NY: IBM Global Services.

Bing shopping. (n.d.). Retrieved May 5, 2010, from Bing shopping: http://cn.bing.com/shopping

Bishop, C. M. (2006). *Pattern Recognition and Machine Learning*. Springer.

Blackwell, R. D., Paul, M. W., & James, E. F. (2001). *Consumer Behavior* (9th ed.). Orlando, FL: Harcourt.

Boiman, O., Shechtman, E., & Irani, M. (2008). In defense of Nearest-Neighbor based image classification. In *Proc. 2008 IEEE conf. on Computer Vision and Pattern Recognition* (pp. 1-8). Anchorage, AK: IEEE Computer Society.

Bosch, A., Zisserman, A., & Munoz, X. (2007). Representing shape with a spatial pyramid kernel. In *Proc. of the 6th ACM int. conf. on Image and video retrieval* (pp. 401-408). Amsterdam, The Netherlands: ACM. *britepic.com*. (n.d.). Retrieved April 29, 2010, from britepic.com: http://www.britepic.com/learnmore.php

Broder, A., Fontoura, M., Josifovski, V., & Riedel, L. (2007). A semantic approach to contextual advertising. In *Proc.of the 30th int. ACM SIGIR conf. on Research and development in information retrieval* (pp. 559-566). Amsterdam, The Netherlands: ACM.

Caltech 101. (n.d.). Retrieved May 4, 2010, from Caltech 101 http://www.vision.caltech.edu/Image_Datasets/Caltech101/

Caltech 256. (n.d.). Retrieved May 4, 2010, from Caltech 256: http://www.vision.caltech.edu/Image_Datasets/Caltech256/

Cannes Lions International Advertising Festival. (n.d.). Retrieved May 2, 2010, from The official website of the international advertising festival: www.canneslions.com/

Chang, S.-F., Ellis, D., Jiang, W., Lee, K., Yanagawa, A., Loui, A. C., et al. (2007). Large-scale multimodal semantic concept detection for consumer video. In *Proc.of the int. workshop on Workshop on multimedia information retrieval* (pp. 255-264). Augsburg, Bavaria, Germany: ACM.

Chang, Y., & Thorson, E. (2004). Television And Web Advertising Synergies. *Journal of Advertising, 33*(2), 75–84.

comcast.net. (n.d.). Retrieved April 27, 2010, from comcast.net: http://www.comcast.net/on-demand-online

Cristianini, N., & Taylor, J. S. (2000). *An introduction to support vector machines and other kernel-based learning*. Cambridge University Press.

dishnetwork.com. (n.d.). Retrieved May 1, 2010, from dishnetwork.com: http://www.dishnetwork.com/

Djurovic, V. (2008, Sep.). *Interactive Media - The New Golden Goose of Branding?* Retrieved Apr. 28, 2010, from http://www.articlesnatch.com/Article/Interactive-Media---The-New-Golden-Goose-Of-Branding-/479306

Duan, L.-Y., Wang, J., Zheng, Y., Jin, J. S., Lu, H., & Xu, C. (2006). Segmentation, categorization, and identification of commercial clips from TV streams using multimodal analysis. In *Proc. the 14th ACM int. conf. on Multimedia* (pp. 201-210). Santa Barbara: ACM.

Duan, L.-Y., Xu, M., Chua, T.-S., Tian, Q., & Xu, C.-S. (2003). A mid-level representation framework for semantic sports video analysis. In *Proc. of the 11th ACM int. conf. on Multimedia* (pp. 33-44). Berkeley: ACM.

Fischer, I., & Poland, J. (2004). *New Methods for Spectral Clustering*. Israel: Hebrew University.

Gong, Y., Lim, T., & Chua, H. (1995). Automatic Parsing of TV Soccer Programs. In *Proc. IEEE Int. Conf. on Multimedia Computing and Systems* (pp. 167-174). IEEE.

Google Blog. (2009, Nov. 5). *Official Google Blog*. Retrieved April 30, 2010, from googleblog: http://googleblog.blogspot.com/2009/11/transparency-choice-and-control-now.html

Google Product Search. (n.d.). Retrieved May 5, 2010, from Google Product Search: http://www.google.com/products

Green/Red Button advertising. (n.d.). Retrieved Apr. 27, 2010, from www.thinkbox.tv: http://www.thinkbox.tv/server/show/nav.1008

HTK Speech Recognition Toolkit. (n.d.). Retrieved May 3, 2010, from http://htk.eng.cam.ac.uk/

Hulu.com. (n.d.). Retrieved from hulu.com: http://www.hulu.com

Interactive media. (n.d.). Retrieved Apr 28, 2010, from Wikipedia: http://en.wikipedia.org/wiki/Interactive_media

Jain, A. K., & Farrokhnia, F. (1991). Unsupervised texture segmentation using Gabor filters. *Pattern Recognition*, 1167–1186. doi:10.1016/0031-3203(91)90143-S

Jin, X., Li, Y., Mah, T., & Tong, J. (2007). Sensitive webpage classification for content advertising. *Proc. The 1st Int. Workshop on Data Mining and Audience Intelligence for Advertising* (pp. 28-33). San Jose, California: ACM.

John, C. (1986). A Computational Approach to Edge Detection. *IEEE Transactions on Pattern Analysis and Machine Intelligence*, 8, 679–714. doi:10.1109/TPAMI.1986.4767851

Joost.com. (n.d.). *joost.com*. Retrieved May 1, 2010, from joost.com: http://www.joost.com/

Kullback, S. (1968). *Information Theory and Statistics*. Mineola, NY: Dover Publication, Inc.

Kunert, T. (2009). *User-Centered Interaction Design Patterns for Interactive Digital Television Applications*. Springer.

Lazebnik, S., Schmid, C., & Ponce, J. (2006). Beyond Bags of Features: Spatial Pyramid Matching for Recognizing Natural Scene Categories. In *Proc. of the 2006 IEEE Conf. Computer Vision and Pattern Recognition* (pp. 2169-2178). Washington, DC: IEEE Computer Society.

Lee, T. B., Hendler, J., & Lassila, O. (2001). The Semantic Web. *Scientific American*.

Li, J., & Wang, J. Z. (2008). Real-time computerized annotation of pictures. *IEEE Trans. Pattern Aanlysis and Machine Intelligence*, 30(6), 985–1002. doi:10.1109/TPAMI.2007.70847

Li, Y., Tian, Y., Duan, L.-Y., Yang, J., Huang, T., & Gao, W. (2011). *Sequence Multi-labeling: A Unified Video Annotation Scheme with Spatial and Temporal Context*. IEEE Trans. Multimedia.

Li, Y., Wang, K. W., Yan, X., & Xu, C. (2005). Real time advertisement insertion in baseball video based on advertisement effects. In *Proc. of the 13th ACM int.conf.on Multimedia* (pp. 343-346). Hilton, Singapore: ACM.

Li, Z., Zhang, L., & Ma, W.-Y. (2008). Delivering online advertising inside images. In *Proc. the 16th ACM int. conf. on Multimedia* (pp. 1051-1060). Vancouver, Canada: ACM.

Liao, W.-S., Chen, K.-T., & Hsu, W. H. (2008). AdImage: video advertising by image matching and ad scheduling optimization. In *Proc. the 31th int. ACM SIGIR conf. on Research and development in information retrieval* (pp. 767-768). Singapore: ACM.

Ling, H., & Soatto, S. (2007). Proximity Distribution Kernels for Geometric Context in Category. In *Proc. 2007 IEEE 11th Int. Conf. on Computer Vision* (pp. 1-8). Rio de Janeiro, Brazil: IEEE Computer Society.

Liu, H., Jiang, S., Huang, Q., & Xu, C. (2008). A generic virtual content insertion system based on visual attention analysis. In *Proc. the 16th ACM int. conf. on Multimedia* (pp. 379-388). Vancouver, Canada: ACM.

Manning, C. D., Raghavan, P., & Schütze, H. (2008). *Introduction to Information Retrieval*. Cambridge University Press.

Mei, T., Hua, X.-S., & Li, S. (2008). Contextual in-image advertising. In *Proc. the 16th ACM int. conf. on Multimedia* (pp. 439-448). Vancouver, Canada: ACM.

Mei, T., Hua, X.-S., Yang, L., & Li, S. (2007). VideoSense:towards effective online video advertising. In *Proc. the 15th int. conf. on Multimedia* (pp. 1075-1084). Augsburg, Germany: ACM.

Mori, G., Belongie, S., & Malik, J. (2005, Nov.). Efficient Shape Matching Using Shape Contexts. *IEEE Transactions on Pattern Analysis and Machine Intelligence, 27*(11), 1832–1937. doi:10.1109/TPAMI.2005.220

Naphade, M. R., Kennedy, L., Kender, J. R., Chang, S.-F., Smith, J. R., & Over, P. (2005). *A Light Scale Concept Ontology for Multimedia Understanding for TRECVID 2005*. IBM Research.

navic.tv. (n.d.). Retrieved May 1, 2010, from navic.tv: http://www.navic.tv/

Nielsen. (n.d.). *Television*. Retrieved May 1, 2010, from en-us.nielsen.com: http://en-us.nielsen.com/tab/measurement/tv_research

Nielsenwire. (2010, March 22). *Americans Using TV and Internet Together 35% More Than A Year Ago*. Retrieved from blog.nielsen.com: http://blog.nielsen.com/nielsenwire/online_mobile/three-screen-report-q409/

Oliva, A., & Torralba, A. (2001). 5). Modeling the Shape of the Scene: A Holistic Representation of the Spatial Envelope. *International Journal of Computer Vision, 42*(3), 145–175. doi:10.1023/A:1011139631724

Palmer, S., Rosch, E., & Chase, P. (1981). *Canonical perspective and the perception of objects* (pp. 135–151). Attention and Performance.

Pascal, V. O. C. (n.d.). Retrieved May 4, 2010, from The PASCAL Visual Object Classes: http://pascallin.ecs.soton.ac.uk/challenges/VOC/

Ray, A. (n.d.). *Interactive TV audiences*. Retrieved May 1, 2010, from thinkbox.tv: http://www.thinkbox.tv/server/show/nav.1188

Razorfish, LLC. (2009). Digital outlook report.

Shechtman, E., & Irani, M. (2007). Matching Local Self-Similarities across Images and Videos. In *Proc. of 2007 IEEE Conf. on Computer Vision and Pattern Recognition* (pp. 1-8). Minneapolis, MN: IEEE Computer Society.

Simon, H. A. (1971). Designing Organizations for an Information-Rich World. In Greenberger, M. (Ed.), *Computers, communications, and the public interest* (pp. 37–72). Baltimore, MD: The Johns Hopkins Press.

skymedia. (n.d.). *Green Button Advertising.* Retrieved May 1, 2010, from skymedia.co.uk: http://www.skymedia.co.uk/greenbutton

SkyPlus. (n.d.). Retrieved from radioandtelly. co.uk: http://www.radioandtelly.co.uk/skyplus.html

Sweney, M. (2009, Sep. 30). *Internet overtakes television to become biggest advertising sector in the UK.* Retrieved from guardian.co.uk: http://www.guardian.co.uk/media/2009/sep/30/internet-biggest-uk-advertising-sector

thinkbox.tv. (n.d.). *Interactive TV - Executive summary, Facts and Figures.* Retrieved May 1, 2010, from thinkbox.tv: http://www.thinkbox.tv/server/show/nav.1009

timewarnercable.com. (n.d.). Retrieved April 27, 2010, from Time Warner: http://www.timewarnercable.com

Tivo.com. (n.d.). Retrieved from Tivo.com: http://www.tivo.com

TREC Video Retrieval Evaluation. (n.d.). Retrieved May 4, 2010, from trecvid.nist.gov: http://trecvid.nist.gov/

Video Advertising Solutions. (n.d.). Retrieved April 28, 2010, from www.google.com: http://www.google.com/ads/videoadsolutions/advertiser.html

Vilanilam, J. V., & Varghese, A. K. (2004). *Advertising basics! A resource guide.* New Delhi: Response Books.

Wan, K., & Xu, C. (2006). Automatic Content Placement in Sports Highlights. In *Proc. of IEEE Int. Conf. on Multimedia and Expo* (pp. 1893-1896). Toronto, Canada: IEEE Computer Society.

Wang, J., Duan, L., Wang, B., Chen, S., Ouyang, Y., Liu, J., et al. (2009). Linking Video Ads with Product or Service Information by Web Search. In *Proc. IEEE Int. Conf. Multimedia & Expo 2009* (pp. 274-277). New York City, USA.

Wang, J., Duan, L., Xu, L., Lu, H., & Jin, J. S. (2007). TV ad video categorization with probabilistic concept learning. In *Proc. of the int. workshop on Workshop on multimedia information retrieval* (pp. 217-226). Augsburg, Bavaria, Germany: ACM.

Wang, J., Fang, Y., & Lu, H. (2008). Online video advertising based on user's attention relevancy computing. In *Proc. of IEEE int. conf. on Multimedia & Expo* (pp. 1161-1164). Hannover, Germany: IEEE.

Wang, X.-J., Zhang, L., Jing, F., & Ma, W.-Y. (2006). AnnoSearch:Image Auto-Annotation by Search. In *Proc. of IEEE Conf. Computer Vision and Pattern Recognition* (pp. 1483-1490). Washington, DC: IEEE Computer Society.

Weiss, Y., Torralba, A., & Fergus, R. (2008). Spectral Hashing. In *Proc. Conf. the Neural Information Processing Systems.*

What are Ad Sitelinks? (n.d.). Retrieved Apr. 27, 2010, from Google AdWords website: https://adwords.google.com/support/aw/bin/answer.py?hl=en&answer=164778

Wikipedia. (n.d.). *Attention economy.* Retrieved April 28, 2010, from Wikipedia: http://en.wikipedia.org/wiki/Attention_economy

Wikipedia. (n.d.). *Television advertisement.* Retrieved April 30, 2010, from Wikipedia.org: http://en.wikipedia.org/wiki/Television_advertisement

Yang, J., Li, Y., Tian, Y., Duan, L.-Y., & Gao, W. (2009). Group-sensitive Multiple Kernel Learning for Object Categorization. In *Proc. of the IEEE 12th int. conf. on Computer Vision* (pp. 436-443). Kyoto, Japan: IEEE Computer Society.

Yih, W.-t., Goodman, J., & Carvalho, V. R. (2006). Finding advertising keywords on web pages. In *Proc. of the 15th Int. Conf. on World Wide Web* (pp. 213-222). Edinburgh, Scotland: ACM.

Youku.com. (n.d.). Retrieved from Youku.com: http://www.youku.com/

YouTube.com. (n.d.). Retrieved from YouTube. com: http://www.youtube.com

Zheng, Y., Duan, L.-Y., Tian, Q., & Jesse, J. S. (2006). TV Commercial Classification Based on Textual and Visual Semantic Features. *Proc. Asia-Pacific Workshop on Visual Information Processing*. Beijing.

Chapter 11
Contextual In-Stream Video Advertising

Tao Mei
Microsoft Research Asia, China

Shipeng Li
Microsoft Research Asia, China

ABSTRACT

With Internet delivery of video content surging to an unprecedented level, online video advertising is becoming increasingly pervasive. In this chapter, we present a new advertising paradigm for online video, called contextual in-stream video advertising, which automatically associates the most relevant video ads with online videos and seamlessly inserts the ads at the most appropriate spatiotemporal positions within each individual video. Different from most current video-oriented sites that only display the ads at the predefined locations in a video, this advertising paradigm aims to embed more contextually relevant ads at less intrusive positions within the video stream nonlinearly. We introduce the following key techniques in this paradigm: video processing for ad location detection, text analysis for ad selection, and optimization for ad insertion. We also describe two recently developed systems as showcases, i.e., VideoSense and AdOn which support in-stream inline and overlay advertising, respectively.

INTRODUCTION

The proliferation of digital capture devices and the explosive growth of online social media (especially along with the so called Web 2.0 wave) have led to the countless private image and video collections on local computing devices, such as personal computers, cell phones, and personal digital assistants (PDAs), as well as the huge yet increasing public media collections on the Internet. Today's online users face a daunting volume of video content. ComScore reports that in March 2006 alone consumers viewed 3.7 billion video streams and nearly 100 minutes of video content per viewer per month (ComScore). The most

DOI: 10.4018/978-1-60960-189-8.ch011

popular video site—Youtube, drew 5 billion U.S. online video views in July 2008 (YouTube).

On the other hand, we have witnessed a fast and consistently growing online advertising market in recently years. Jupiter Research forecasted that online advertising spending will surge to $18.9 billion by 2010-up, which is about 59 percent from an estimated $11.9 billion in 2005 (Jupiter Research). To take the advantages of this increasing market share and effectively monetize video content, video advertising, which associates advertisements with an online video, has become a key online monetization strategy. By implementing a solid online video advertising strategy into an existing content delivery chain, content providers have the ability to deliver compelling content, reach a growing online audience, and generate additional revenue from online media. As reported by Online Publisher Association (Online Publishers), the majority (66%) of Internet users have ever seen video ads, while 44% have taken some action after viewing ads.

Many existing video-oriented sites, such as YouTube (YouTube), Google Video (Google Video), Yahoo! Video (Yahoo! Video), Metacafe (Metacafe), and Revver (Revver), have tried to provide effective video advertising services. However, it is likely that most of them match the ads with online videos only based on textual information and insert ads at the beginning or the end of a video [1]. In other words, contextual relevance in these sites is only based on textual information, while less intrusive insertion points are fixed to the predefined locations, e.g., the beginning or the end of videos. For example, Revver selects one relevant ad (i.e., a static picture or a video clip) for each video clip, and shows it as the first or the last frame or segment of the corresponding video (Revver). Another example is Google's AdSense for video advertising which overlays the ads at a fixed location in the videos (e.g., on the bottom fifth of videos 15 seconds in).

On the other hand, although there are a few systems for overlay advertising proposed recently in the research community (Chang et al., 2008) (Liao et al., 2008) (Liu et al., 2008), they are not practical for real-world application. For example, AdImage predominantly focuses on image-based ad matching while neglects the ad positions (the ads always appear on the right-bottom corner) (Liao et al., 2008). The virtual content insertion (Chang et al., 2008) (Liu et al., 2008) is not practical for user generated videos as these videos are typically with poor visual quality so that detecting smooth area in the frames and aligning the ad by geometric transformation is very challenging.

The following problems that significantly affect advertising effectiveness and impede user experience have not been investigated in existing video advertising:

- We believe ads should be inserted at appropriate locations within video streams rather than any predefined locations. The capability of discovering nonlinear ad locations within videos will lead to embedding not only a greater number of ads but also less intrusive ads within video content.
- We believe ads should be contextually relevant to online video content in terms of multimodal relevance rather than purely based on textual information. For example, when viewing an online music video, users may prefer a relevant ad with the similar editing style or audio tempo style to the video, which cannot be measured just by textual information. This capability will lead to delivering the ads with more relevance.

We present in this chapter a new advertising paradigm for online video, called contextual in-stream video advertising, which automatically associates the most relevant video ads with online videos and seamlessly inserts the ads at the most appropriate spatiotemporal positions within each individual video. Different from most current video-oriented sites that only display the ads at the predefined locations in a video, this advertising paradigm aims to embed more contextually relevant ads at less intrusive positions within the video stream nonlinearly.

The remaining of this chapter is organized as follows. Section II reviews related research on video advertising. Section III describes the approach of the proposed in-stream advertising. Section IV presents two exemplary systems in this paradigm, e.g., VideoSense (Mei et al., 2009) (Mei et al., 2007b) and AdOn (Mei et al., 2010). We conclude this chapter in Section V.

RELATED WORK

Advertising in Text Domain

One of the fundamental problems in online advertising is ad relevance which in studies detracts from user experience and increases the probability of reaction (AAFSurvey,) (Mccoy et al., 2007). The other one is how to pick suitable keywords or Web pages for advertising. The literature review in this paper will focus on two key problems: 1) ad keyword selection, and 2) ad relevance matching.

Typical advertising systems analyze a Web page or query to find prominent keywords or categories, and match these keywords or categories against the words for which advertisers bid. If there is a match, the corresponding ads will be displayed to the user through the web page (Yih et al., 2006) (Li et al., 2007) (Shen et al., 2006).

Yih et al. has studied a learning-based approach to automatically extracting appropriate keywords from Web pages for advertisement targeting (Yih et al., 2006). Instead of dealing with general Web pages, Li et al. proposed a sequential pattern mining-based method to discover keywords from a specific broadcasting content domain (Li et al., 2007). In addition to Web pages, queries also play an important role in paid search advertising. In (Shen et al., 2006), the queries are classified into

an intermediate taxonomy so that the selected ads are more targeted to the query.

Research on ad relevance has proceeded along three directions from the perspective of what the ads are matched against: (1) keyword-targeted advertising (also called "paid search advertising" or "sponsored search") in which the ads are matched against the originating query (Joshi and Motwani, 2006) (Mehta et al., 2007), (2) content-targeted advertising (also called "contextual advertising") in which the ads are associated with the Web page content rather than the keywords (Broder et al., 2007) (Lacerda et al., 2006) (Murdock et al., 2007) (Ribeiro-Neto et al., 2005), and (3) user-targeted advertising (also called "audience intelligence") in which the ads are driven based on user profile and demography (Hu et al., 2007), or behavior (Dai et al., 2006) (Richardson et al., 2007).

Although the paid search market develops quicker than contextual advertising, and most textual ads are still characterized by "bid phrases," there has been a drift to contextual advertising as it supports a long-tail business model (Li et al., 2002a). For example, a recent work (Ribeiro-Neto et al., 2005) examines a number of strategies to match ads to Web pages based on extracted keywords. A follow-up work (Lacerda et al., 2006) applies Genetic Programming (GP) to learn functions that select the most appropriate ads, given the contents of a Web page. To alleviate the problem of exact keyword match in conventional contextual advertising, Broder et al. propose to integrate semantic phrase into traditional keyword matching (Broder et al., 2007). Specifically, both the pages and ads were classified into a common large taxonomy, which was then used to narrow down the search of keywords to concepts. Most recently, Hu et al. propose to predict user demographics from browsing behavior (Hu et al., 2007). The intuition is that while user demographics are not easy to obtain, browsing behaviors indicate a user's interest and profile.

Advertising in Visual Domain

There are three advertising strategies for online videos in terms of ad location, i.e., banner, pre-roll, post-roll, and midroll ads (Mccoy et al., 2007). In banner advertising, advertisers bid for the fixed preserved ad blocks which are usually the most salient parts on a web page. However, this type of advertising is intrusive to users as the ads are not relevant to users at all. The other three strategies, which associate a piece of advertisement with a video at the beginning, end, and middle of video, respectively, are regarded more effective and less intrusive than the traditional banner ads(There is usually an accompany ad around the video at the same time) [2]. Among these three advertising schemes, mid-roll (also called in-video) advertising has attracted a wide attention as it achieves a good balance between the promotion of ad impression and user experience.

According to the ad location in the video, the approaches to video advertising can be further classified into three categories: 1) inline ads, 2) virtual content insertion, and 3) overlay ads. The VideoSense system automatically finds the story breaks as the in-stream ad locations and associates the relevant ads with these locations by textual and visual relevance (Mei et al., 2007b). The vADeo system performs scene detection and inserts the ads by face recognition (Srinivasan et al., 2007). These in-stream ads are similar with traditional commercials in the TV programs and Interactive Digital Television (Kastidou and Cohen, 2006) (Thawani et al., 2004).

To make video content more enriching, virtual content insertion has attempted to replace a specific region with product advertisement (Chang et al., 2008) (Li et al., 2005) (Liu et al., 2008) (Wan et al., 2003). These regions could be the locations with less information in baseball (Li et al., 2005) and tennis (Chang et al., 2008) videos, or the region above the goal-mouth (Wan et al., 2003) or any non-salient region (Liu et al., 2008) in soccer video. However, these domain-specific

approaches such as the detection of line and less-informationregion (Li et al., 2005) (Wan et al., 2003) may not be practical in a general case, especially for online videos.

While region-based product placement is challenging, the personalized ad delivery in IDTV has been a potentially hot application (Kastidou and Cohen, 2006) (Lekakos et al., 2001) (Thawani et al., 2004). Such advertising refers to the delivery of advertisements tailored to individual viewers' profiles on the basis of their preferences (Lekakos et al., 2001) or current and past contextual information (Kastidou and Cohen, 2006) (Thawani et al., 2004). However, most of these systems do not study relevance in terms of video content and the elaborate selection of ad insertion points. In other words, they focus on targeted advertising rather than contextual advertising.

APPROACH

This section will first introduce some preliminary terms for video advertising, the framework for in-stream video advertising, as well as the details for the key components and approaches.

Preliminaries

To clearly present the approach, the following terms are clarified:

- **Video ad**: A video advertisement clip provided by advertisers that can be inserted into or associated with a source video. Although video ads will be associated with video in the proposed in-stream video advertising, they may be in different forms (or a combination of forms) including typical ad clips in TV programs, animations, images, or text. Let A denote the ad database containing N_a ads, represented by $A = \{a_j\}_{j=1}^{Na}$. Let N denote the number of

Figure 1. Framework of video advertising. Please note that the components in the upper dotted-line box correspond to traditional video advertising

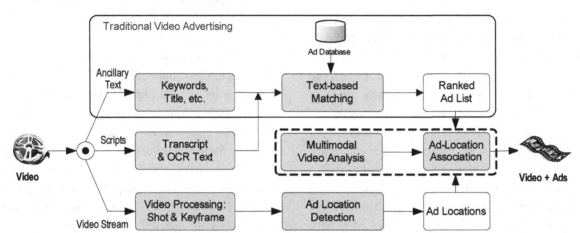

ads for a video. N could be given by the video content owners or publishers.

- **Source video**: Source video is typically produced or owned by content providers, who may be professional videographers or grassroots. Video ads will be embedded at appropriate positions in the source video. The video V consisting of N_s segments (e.g., shots) can be represented by $S = \{s_i\}_{i=1}^{Ns}$.

- **Ad location**: A location/position where a video ad will be associated with the source video. The ad location can be a spot in the timeline of a source video at which one or more ad clips will be inserted (i.e., for in-line video ads), or a spatial position on a particular video frame (i.e., for overlay video ads), as what most of the existing sites do. An ad location could be the boundary of two segments in a video or a spatial region on a video frame. Suppose there are N_p candidate ad insertion locations within video V, then the set of ad locations could be represented by $P = \{p_i\}_{i=1}^{Np}$. For example, in the inline video advertising, $N_p = N_s + 1$, that is, each segment boundary could be a candidate of ad location.

Framework

Figure 1 shows the framework for the proposed contextual in-stream advertising. Given an online video, the system is able to automatically process the video to obtain the structure information (i.e., shots and keyframes), as well as perform text extraction to obtain the textual information embedded in the video. For example, the textual information could include the ancillary text, such as title, keywords, and description; the scripts embedded in the video stream, such as accompany transcript and the caption from optical character recognition (OCR). Based on this information, the candidate ads each consisting of a product logo, product name, description, and link, are selected based on textual relevance. The overlay ad locations are automatically discovered based on video processing to minimize the intrusiveness while maximizing the effectiveness of advertising. Then, the ad-location association component will associate each ad with an appropriate candidate ad location so that the overlay ads yield contextual multimodal relevance to the video content. One point we want to emphasize is that, in the proposed advertising paradigm, the more compelling the content of these segments, the more audience will view them, then the more revenue will be gener-

Table 1. Framework of video advertising. Please note that the components in the upper dotted-line box correspond to traditional video advertising

Advertising paradigm	Ad relevance	Ad location	Exemplary systems
Traditional video advertising	Textual relevance, solely relying on Web page	Predefined ad positions by publishers	AdSense [AdSense], Yahoo! [Yahoo!], BritePic [BritePic], TV commercial
In-stream video advertising	Multimodal relevance (textual, visual, and aural relevance)	Automatically detected ad positions within video	VideoSense [Mei et al., 2009] [Mei et al., 2007b]

ated from these overlay ads. It is worth noting that the bounded portion in Figure 1 corresponds to traditional video advertising, in which only the ancillary text is considered for selecting relevant ads, as well as there is not any component for automatic discovery of ad locations in the video.

We can observe from Figure 1 that the proposed in-stream video advertising framework consists of several key components: 1) contextual relevance for ad selection, 2) video processing for ad location detection, and 3) multimodal analysis for ad-video association. In the next, we will describe the approaches for each component in details.

Key Problems

The comparisons between traditional video advertising and the proposed contextual in-stream advertising in terms of ad relevance and location are listed in Table 1. In general, there are three key problems in an effective contextual multimedia advertising system: ad relevance, ad location, and ad-video association:

- **Ad relevance:** Which ads a_j should be selected from A for a given video V? Since relevance increases advertising revenue (Li et al., 2002a) (Mccoy et al., 2007), contextual multimedia advertising performs multimodal relevance matching by considering both global textual relevance from the entire Web page and local relevance from textual information associated with the video content, as well as low-level vi-

sual and high-level semantic similarity between the ads and ad locations.

- **Ad location:** Where should the selected ads be inserted so that the contextual intrusiveness will be minimized (i.e., how to select N elements from P)? Ad location will certainly affect user experience when a video is viewed (Mccoy et al., 2007). In contextual video advertising, the selected ads are to be inserted into the most non-intrusive positions within the video.

- **Ad-Video association:** Given a ranked list of candidate ads and ad insertion points, how to associate each ad with the ad best insertion point? The objective is to maximize the effectiveness of advertising by simultaneously minimizing the contextual intrusiveness to viewers and maximizing the contextual relevance between the ads and video. The problem is then to associate each select ad a_j with one location p_i.

Contextual Relevance for Ad Selection

An online video is usually accompanied with heterogenous information. For example, users may provide ancillary text (e.g., title, keywords, comments, and so on) to videos when they uploaded them. On the other hand, video can be also regarded as a sequence of images which conveys much visual information. Moreover, there might be accompanied transcript with the video, as well as embedded text (e.g., captions) on the frames and hidden concepts which can be recognized from the visual content. Therefore, the relevance between a video and advertisement should be measured in terms of multimodal relevance. We only focus on two modalities in this work, i.e., textual and visual relevance for ad selection.

Textual Relevance

In contextual video advertising, ads are expected to be relevant to video contents in which the ads will be embedded. Conventional advertising only relies on the ancillary text (i.e., the surrounding text such as title and description of the video) available around the video for ad selection. However, the description power of this text is limited (Yang et al., 2007), which in turn leads to unsatisfying advertising relevance. To enrich the text information for a video, the captions (i.e., the text obtained from OCR) embedded in the video frames and the transcript (if it is available) can be leveraged. The advantages of the OCR text are twofold: first, they can enrich the textual information which describes the video content; second, the aligned OCR text and transcript (associated with certain video segment) can be used to match the ads with video segments rather than the whole video sequence. Therefore, a color-based approach can be first employed to partition the video into a series of shots and detect a keyframe for each shot (Zhang et al., 1993). Then, the edgebased algorithm can be used to detect the text area for each keyframe (Chen and Zhang, 2001). Those detected areas are input to an OCR engine for text recognition [3].

Given the ancillary text and script associated with a video, as well as the keywords associated with each ad, we can adopt the cosine distance in the vector space model (VSM) as the basis of textual relevance between the texts associated with the video and ad (Mei et al., 2007b) (Yang et al., 2007). In the vector model, the relevance

$R(D_x, D_y)$ between two textual documents D_x and D_y is formulated as the *cosine* similarity

$$R\left(D_x, D_y\right) = \frac{\omega\left(D_x\right)\omega\left(D_y\right)}{\omega(D_x) \times \omega(D_y)} \quad (1)$$

where $\omega\left(D_x\right)$ and $\omega\left(D_y\right)$ denote the weight vectors of D_x and D_y, respectively. Each element of the vector indicates the weight of certain keyword in this document. There are many methods to compute the weight vector. A classic algorithm is to use the product of its *term frequency* and *inverted document frequency*, based on the assumption that the more frequently a word appears in a document and the rarer the word appears in all documents, the more informative it is (Baeza-Yates and Ribeiro-Neto, 1999).

In this way, a list of ads can be ranked according to the textual relevance to a given video. Moreover, since we have the closed caption and OCR text for each shot, the ads in this list can be further re-ranked according to the local relevance to an individual shot so that the ads could be relevant to the shots rather than the entire video. Given an ad location p_i and an ad a_j, we can define a global relevance item $R_g\left(a_j\right)$ between the ad a_j and the entire video V, as well as a local relevance item $R_l\left(a_j, p_i\right)$ between the ad a_j and a specific location p_i[4]. Note that the detection of p_i is to be introduced in the next section.

Therefore, the textual relevance $R_T\left(a_j, p_i\right)$ between a_j and p_i is given by the weighted fusion of the global and local textual relevance as follows:

$$R_T\left(a_j, p_i\right) = \omega_g R_g\left(a_j\right) + \omega_l R_l\left(a_j, p_i\right) \quad (2)$$

where $R_g\left(a_j\right)$ and $R_l\left(a_j,p_i\right)$ can be obtained by equation (1) based on the text associated with the ad and the video (or the corresponding segment near to the location). ω_g and ω_l $(0 \leq \omega_g, \omega_l \leq 1, \omega_g + \omega_l = 1)$ are the weights to tune the contribution from each component to the overall relevance, which can be set empirically or by cross-validation. A more complicated usage of text expansion and text categorization techniques for textual relevance could be found in (Yang et al., 2007).

Visual Relevance

In addition to the textual relevance, the visual relevance between each ad and location should be also considered. Since the ads are expected to be with the same style as the video program (Feltham and Arnold, 1994), the visual similarity $R_f\left(a_j,p_i\right)$ between the ad a_j and the location p_i can be integrated into the computation of contextual relevance. The more visually similar the ad and shot, the more relevant the ad is. For example, $R_v\left(a_j,p_i\right)$ could be the visual similarity between the keyframes of a_j and the corresponding segments around p_i based on the HSV color space (Mei et al., 2008), or the similarity in terms of motion (Mei et al., 2007b) (Yang et al., 2007). Note that if we adopt overlay advertising, p_i is then equivalent to s_i.

On the other hand, the high-level concept text (i.e., the hidden text) could also to mined from visual content for computing visual relevance [5]. Specifically, we can perform concept detection over the ad a_j and the ad location p_i, and then compute the conceptual similarity $R_c\left(a_j,p_i\right)$ based on L_1 distance. Then, the visual relevance $R_v\left(a_j,p_i\right)$ can be given by

$$R_v\left(a_j,p_i\right) = \omega_f R_f\left(a_j,p_i\right) + \omega_c R_c\left(a_j,p_i\right)$$
(3)

where ω_f and ω_c $(0 \leq \omega_f, \omega_c \leq 1, \omega_f + \omega_c = 1)$ are the weights.

After we obtain the textual and visual relevance, the overall contextual relevance $R\left(a_j,p_i\right)$ is

$$R\left(a_j,p_i\right) = \omega_T R_T\left(a_j,p_i\right) + \omega_V R_V\left(a_j,p_i\right)$$
(4)

where ω_T and ω_V $(0 \leq \omega_T, \omega_V \leq 1, \omega_T + \omega_V = 1)$ are the weights for tuning the relevance from the textual and visual domain, respectively.

Video Processing for Ad Location Detection

Before the detection of ad locations p_i, a preprocess is supposed to decompose the given video V into shots S, each shot is being represented by a keyframe k_i through the approach described in (Zhang et al., 1993). We will describe the detection of ad location for inline and overlay advertising independently. In the inline advertising, each shot boundary is a candidate ad location. The ads are expected to be inserted in-between two successive segments or shots (Mei et al., 2009) (Mei et al., 2007b). This is analog to TV commercial. In the overlay advertising, the ad locations are visually consistent spatio-temporal regions within video frames (Guo et al., 2009) (Mei et al., 2010). This is similar to virtual content insertion.

Ad Location Detection in Inline Advertising

The detection of ad insertion points is based on content intrusiveness. Li et al. (Li et al., 2002a)

Figure 2. Candidate ad location detection in inline advertising. Suppose there are N_s shot or scene boundaries in a video sequence, then the number of candidate points is N_s+1 (including the beginning and the end of the video), each boundary indicating one candidate location

investigated eight factors that affect consumers' perceptions of the intrusiveness of ads in traditional TV programs. We can excerpt two computable measurements based on these eight factors, i.e., content discontinuity and attractiveness. In fact, different combinations of discontinuity and attractiveness fit the requirements of different roles. For example, it is intuitive that ads are expected to be inserted at the shot boundaries with high discontinuity and low attractiveness from the viewers' perspective. On the other hand, "high discontinuity plus high attractiveness" may be a tradeoff between viewers and advertisers. Then, the detection of ad locations can be formulated as ranking the shot boundaries based on different combinations of content discontinuity and attractiveness. Figure 2 shows the relationship between shots and candidate ad locations.

Content Discontinuity

A soft measure of a shot boundary is assigned to each ad location. As shown in Figure 2, a degree of discontinuity $D(p_i)$ is assigned to each ad location p_i. The higher the discontinuity, the more likely the corresponding insertion point is a boundary of two stories. Therefore, the detection of content discontinuity can be performed similarly to traditional video segmentation. We can use the improved BFMM (so-called "iBFMM") to deal with the interlaced repetitive pattern problem in BFMM (Mei et al., 2007b). In the prepro-

cess step, the most similar shots are merged at different scales to eliminate interlaced repetitive pattern. In the BFMM and normalization step, the merge order is recorded and normalized as the final discontinuity. Any method that generates soft measure for shot boundary can be employed here.

Content Attractiveness

Generally, it is difficult to evaluate how a video clip attracts viewers' attention since "attractiveness" or "attention" is a neurobiological concept. Alternatively, a user attention model is proposed by Ma et al. (Ma et al., 2002) to estimate human's attention by integrating a set of visual, auditory, and linguistic elements related to attractiveness. Another approach to exploring the attention in video sequence is to average static image attention over a segment of frames (Ma and Zhang, 2003). Therefore, we compute an attention value $A(s_i)$ for each shot s_i by the user attention model in (Ma et al., 2002). The content attractiveness of insertion point p_i is highly related to the neighboring shots on both sides of p_i. Therefore, the attractiveness of p_i can be computed by weighted averaging the attention values of its neighboring shots as follows.

$$A(p_i) = \sum_{k=-\delta}^{\delta} \alpha_{|k|} A(s_{i+k}) \qquad (5)$$

where $\sum_k \alpha_k = 1$ and $1 > \alpha_0 > \alpha_1 > \cdots > 0$, since the nearer the neighboring shot, the more effect it has on the attractiveness. The parameters can be empirically set as $\delta = 2$, and $(\alpha_0, \alpha_1, \alpha_2) = (0.4, 0.2, 0.1)$.

Candidate Location Ranking

One way for detecting ad insertion points can be finding the peaks at the combined curve with "discontinuity minus attractiveness," i.e., ranking all locations p_i in terms of "$D(p_i) - A(p_i)$" and selecting the top N locations. However, the detection of ad insertion point could also be based not only on discontinuity and attractiveness, but also on the temporal distribution of these points, as well as the multimodal relevance between the source video and the ad content. In other words, the selected ad insertion points should comply with contextually relevant and less intrusive advertising strategy. This will be detailed in the next.

Ad Location Detection in Overlay Advertising

In overlay advertising, the ads should not occlude the important information in the corresponding frames such as faces, captions, and salient objects. To this end, we detect the candidate ad locations by considering both the content importance and intrusiveness. In other words, the ads are expected to appear at the non-salient portions of frames in the video highlights (Chang et al., 2008) (Liu et al., 2008). As a result, ad impression would be promoted by the highlight content while user intrusiveness would be simultaneously minimized by avoiding the salient areas in the video frames.

Content Importance

The "content importance" $I_m(s_i)$ indicates the "attractiveness" or "highlight" of the content in shot s_i. Ma et al. proposed a generic method to summarize video highlights by visual attention analysis (Ma et al., 2005). However, human attention analysis is not only computationally intensive, but also immature as it is highly subjective. Therefore, we propose to measure the content importance based on shot duration $T(s_i)$ and motion intensity $I(s_i)$ within this shot

$$I_m(s_i) = T(s_i) \cdot I(s_i) \tag{6}$$

where $T(s_i)$ and $I(s_i)$ are the normalized duration and motion intensity of shot s_i. $I(s_i)$ can be computed by averaging the frame differences within shot s_i (Mei et al., 2007b). The above computation is more practical than understanding visual content. Intuitively, the long duration and the intensive motion usually indicate something important happening in this shot. The longer the duration, the higher intensive the motion, the more attractive the shot content would be. It is worth noting that although we propose to compute importance by shot duration and motion intensity here, any other approach to video highlight detection can be also employed.

Content Intrusiveness

The content intrusiveness $I_n(s_i)$ measures whether advertising the upper or bottom fifth areas of video frames are intrusive to users. Figure 3 illustrates the computation of $I_n(s_i)$. For shot s_i, we collect the neighboring frames around its keyframe k_i with the preserved ad duration (e.g., 10 or 15 seconds). Then, several maps are calculated for each frame j, including a text map $M_T(j)$ based on caption detection (Chen and Zhang, 2001), a face map $M_F(j)$ based on face detection (Li et al., 2002b), and an image saliency map $M_S(j)$ based on visual salience analysis (Ma and Zhang, 2003). An intrusive map

Figure 3. Detection of spatio-temporal ad overlay locations

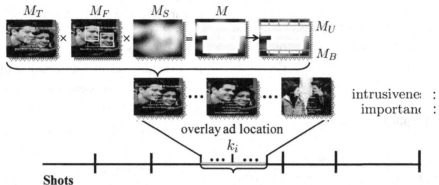

$M(j)$ is then obtained by combining the three maps, i.e., $M(j) = M_t(j) \times M_F(j) \times M_S(j)$. The higher intensity the pixel in $M(j)$, the more intrusive it is to users. We only calculate the energy in the upper and bottom fifth areas (i.e., $M_u(j)$ and $M_B(j)$) as we only consider these two regions for overlay ad. The intrusiveness $I_n(s_i)$ is given by

$$I_n(s_i) = min\{M_u(s_i), M_B(s_i)\} \qquad (7)$$

where $M_u(s_i)$ and $M_B(s_i)$ are the averaged $M_U(j)$ and $M_B(j)$ over the neighboring frames, respectively. As we can see from Figure 3, we can further design block-based computation of $M_u(j)$ and $M_B(j)$, if the ads are to be overlaid over non-salient blocks in the area of top or bottom fifth.

Candidate Location Ranking

As a result, a list of candidate ad locations can be obtained by sorting all the shots according to $I_m(s_i) \cdot (1 - I_n(s_i))$. In this way, the least intrusive regions in the video highlight segments would be advertised to promote the ad impression. It is worth noting that a candidate ad location corresponds to a shot s_i, as the overlay location in this shot is only related to $M_u(s_i)$ and $M_B(s_i)$. If we select a shot s_i, then the overlay ad location will be fixed. Therefore, we use s_i to denote an ad location hereinafter. In the next section, we will show how we can formulate the whole process of ad-location associate in a single framework.

Ad-Video Association

Given a list of ads ranked according to their contextual relevance and a list of ad locations ranked according to their contextual intrusiveness, how to associate each ad with one of locations so that the effectiveness of contextual advertising could be maximized? An effective advertising system is able to maximize contextual relevance while minimizing contextual intrusiveness at the same time. This problem is formulated as a non-linear 0-1 integer programming problem (NIP) in (Mei et al., 2008) (Mei et al., 2007b), with each of the above rules as a constraint.

For example, without of loss of generality, the task of ad-video association can be defined as the association of ads with ad locations in an online video. The contextual relevance $R(a_j, p_i)$ between each ad a_j and ad location p_i can be obtained by the approaches in Section III (i.e., the linear combination of textual and visual relevance), while the contextual intrusiveness $I(a_j, p_i)$ can be obtained in Section III. For example, $I\left(a_j, p_i\right)$ could be given by " $D\left(p_i\right) - A(p_i)$ " in the inline advertising, or given by " $I_m\left(s_i\right) \cdot \left(1 - I_n(s_i)\right)$ " in the overlay advertising. The objective of contextual advertising is to maximize the overall contextual relevance $R(A, P)$ while minimizing the overall contextual intrusiveness $I(A, P)$. The following design variables can be introduced for problem formulation, i.e.,

$$x \in \mathbb{R}^{N_a},\ y \in \mathbb{R}^{N_p},\ x = \left[x_1, \ldots, x_{N_a}\right]^T, x_j \in \{0,1\},$$

and $y = \left[y_1, \ldots, y_{N_p}\right]^T$, $y_i \in \{0,1\}$, where x_j and y_i indicate whether a_j and p_i are selected ($x_j = 1$, $y_i = 1$) in A and P. Given the number of ads N to be inserted in a medium, the NIP formulation (Boyd and Vandenberghe, 2004) is

$$\max_{(x_i, y_i)} f\left(x, y\right) = \alpha \sum_{j=1}^{N_a}\sum_{i=1}^{N_p} x_j y_i R\left(a_j, p_i\right) - \beta \sum_{j=1}^{N_a}\sum_{i=1}^{N_p} x_j y_i I\left(a_j, p_i\right)$$

$$= a x^T R y - \beta x^T I y$$

$$s.t. \qquad \sum_{j=1}^{N_a} x_j = N,\ \sum_{j=1}^{N_p} y_j = N,\ x_j, y_i \in \{0,1\}$$

$$(8)$$

where $R \in \mathbb{R}^{N_a \times N_p}$, $R = \left[R_{ji}\right]$, $R_{ji} = R\left(a_j, p_i\right)$, and $I \in \mathbb{R}^{N_a \times N_p}$, $I = \left[I_{ji}\right]$, $I_{ji} = I\left(a_j, p_i\right)$, α and β are two weights for linear combination. Other constraints such as the uniform distribution of ad insertion points in the source video (Mei et al., 2010) (Mei et al., 2009) (Mei et al., 2007b) can be added in equation (8).

It is observed that there are $C_{N_a}^N C_{N_p}^N N!$ solutions in total to equation (8). As a result, when the number of elements in A and P is large, the searching space for optimization increases dramatically. However, the Genetic Algorithm (GA) (Whitley, 1994) can be employed to find solutions approaching the global optimum. Alternatively, the above problem can be solved by a similar heuristic searching algorithm in practice (Mei et al., 2008) (Mei et al., 2009) (Mei et al., 2007b). In this way, the number of possible solutions can be significantly reduced to $C_{N_a}^1 C_{N_p}^1 N!$. Note that equation (8) is a general formulation for advertising. In fact, it can be easily extended to various advertising strategies from different perspectives. The authors in (Mei et al., 2009) have given detailed discussions on supporting diverse advertising scenarios based on this framework.

EXEMPLARY SYSTEMS: VIDEOSENSE AND ADON

VideoSense

A snapshot of VideoSense is shown in Figure 4. VideoSense is an in-inline advertising system that is able to elaborately detect a set of appropriate ad insertion points (i.e., shot breaks) based on content discontinuity and attractiveness, and associate the most relevant video ads to these points, according to not only global textual relevance but also local visual-aural relevance (Mei et al., 2009) (Mei et al., 2007b).

The performance of ad location detection is shown in Figure 5. 10 long videos were used for this evaluation. The results of ad location detection between iBFMM (Mei et al., 2009) (Mei et al., 2007b) and BFMM (Zhao et al., 2001) were compared. Five annotators were invited to label the confidence of scene boundary (i.e., the probability that a detected boundary is a ground truth) on the set of long videos. The performance is validated by a non-interpolated average precision (AP), which is widely used as a measure of retrieval effectiveness (TRECVID). Suppose the boundaries are ranked according to content discontinuity, the AP is given by

$$AP\left(n\right) = \frac{1}{R_n} \sum_{j=1}^{n} \left(\frac{R_j}{j} I_j\right) \qquad (9)$$

Figure 5. Evaluation of ad location detection in VideoSense, in terms of mean average precision (MAP)

Where R_n is the number of true boundaries in a size of n, $I_j = 1$ if the j-th boundary is true and 0 otherwise. The AP results among all videos are averaged as mean average precision (MAP). It is observed that iBFMM outperforms BFMM in all settings of n.

The other evaluation is given by a subjective evaluation of user experience, in which 12 subjects were invited. When viewing the videos embedded with ads, the evaluators are asked to give a score from 1 to 5 (higher score indicating better satisfaction) to show their satisfactions level based on the following aspects:

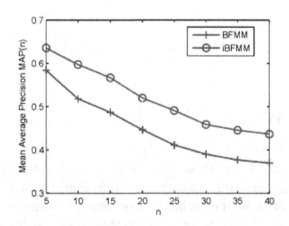

- **Ad relevance** For each inserted ad, how did you feel about the local relevance between the ad and its surround content?

- **Ad location** For each inserted ad, did you feel comfortable as you viewed the ad?
- **Ad satisfaction** For each source video, what was your level of overall satisfaction in how the ads were inserted?

Table 2. Evaluation of VideoSense in terms of user experience on short videos

Results	Ad relevance	Ad location	Ad satisfaction
TV Commerical	2.85	3.07	3.07
VideoSense	3.10	3.54	3.70

Figure 6. An example of a video subscribing AdOn service (Guo et al.,2009) (Mei et al., 2010). The highlighted yellow rectangle indicates that an ad is overlaid on this video shot, while the yellow spots on the timeline indicate the overlay ads in the video stream. The relevant ads are embedded at the non-salient positions (bottom or top) on the suitable frames, while the corresponding accompany ads appears beside the video player (on the right)

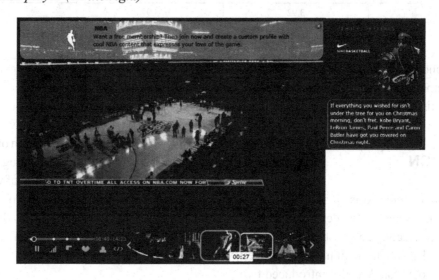

The results of the above three questions are listed in Table 2. In general, the evaluations of VideoSense achieve better than traditional TV commercial.

AdOn

In addition to in-line advertising, the overlay video advertising can be supported based on the same framework (Guo et al., 2009) (Mei et al., 2010). Figure 6 shows the example of a video subscribing AdOn advertising service. Unlike most of current ad-networks such as Youtube (YouTube,) and Revver (Revver,) that overlay the ads at fixed positions in the videos (e.g., on the bottom fifth

of videos 15 seconds in), the ads in (Guo et al., 2009)(Mei et al., 2010) are automatically overlaid.

Table 3 and4 list the subjective evaluations of AdOn, in terms of user experience (Mei et al., 2010). 12 subjects were asked to give a score on 1-5 scale for each video in terms of the overall satisfaction of ad relevance, ad locations, and viewing experience (i.e., whether this kind of advertising is intrusive). The higher the score, the more satisfying the user. 100 videos were selected by the top 20 queries from a commercial search engine in the evaluation. 7,285 product logos were used as the ad database. The AdOn was compared with the advertising approach adopted by AdSense in which the ads are displayed in the 15 seconds and selected only by global

Table 3. Evaluation of AdOn in terms of user experience on short videos

	Ad relevance	Ad location	Ad satisfaction
AdSense	3.63	2.27	2.52
AdOn	3.79	3.46	3.64

Table 4. Evaluation of AdOn in terms of user experience on long videos. Note that the ads in AdSense appear together in 15 sec

	Ad relevance	Ad location	Ad satisfaction
AdSense	3.43	2.13	1.92
AdOn	3.92	3.97	4.08

textual relevance (AdSense,). It can be observed that AdOn outperforms the traditional rule-based overlay advertising.

CONCLUSION

We have introduced contextual in-stream advertising system in this chapter. We described the key techniques for selecting relevant ads, detecting nonintrusive ad locations within video, as well as ad-video association. We also introduced two recently developed exemplary systems in this advertising paradigm.

There are several interesting research topics in the contextual in-stream advertising. First, we can leverage the automatic video categorization (Yuan et al., 2006) and video event detection (Evangelopoulos et al., 2009) techniques to classify the video into a set of predefined categories (e.g., sports, surveillance, movie, etc.), so that we can investigate specific advertising strategy for each category. Second, we can integrate user profile and browsing behavior into this system for user-targeted advertising. For example, the relevance feedback technique (Rui et al., 1998) could be integrated into the proposed system to improve user relevance. Third, the emotion or affective models could be used to compute the emotional involvement of video program (Zhang et al., 2008). This kind of involvement information has been proved to be a key effect on selecting advertisement (Coulter, 1998). Fourth, the advertising strategy for the visual relevance between the ad and program still remains an open problem (Feltham and Arnold, 1994). Although we adopted the strategy from the perspective of viewers (i.e., keeping the ads visually similar to the program) in this paper, it is tunable to satisfy different roles (e.g., advertisers) in different scenarios.

REFERENCES

AdSense. (n.d.). Retrieved from http://www.google.com/adsense/

Baeza-Yates, R., & Ribeiro-Neto, B. (1999). *Modern Information Retrieval*. Addison Wesley.

Boyd, S., & Vandenberghe, L. (2004). *Convex Optimization*. Cambridge University Press.

BritePic. (n.d.). Retrieved from http://www.britepic.com

Broder, A., Fontoura, M., Josifovski, V., & Riedel, L. (2007). A semantic approach to contextual advertising. In *Proceedings of ACM SIGIR conference on Research and Development in Information Retrieval*.

Chang, C.-H., Hsieh, K.-Y., Chung, M.-C., & Wu, J.-L. (2008). ViSA: Virtual spotlighted advertising. In *Proceedings of ACM Multimedia* (pp. 837–840).

Chen, X., & Zhang, H.-J. (2001). Text area detection from video frames. In *Proceedings of the IEEE Pacific Rim Conference on Multimedia* (pp. 222–228).

ComScore. (n.d.). Retrieved from http://www.comscore.com/

Coulter, K. S. (1998). The effects of affective response to media context on advertising evaluations. *Journal of Advertising, XXVII*(4), 41–51.

Dai, H., Zhao, L., Nie, Z., Wen, J.-R., Wang, L., & Li, Y. (2006). Detecting online commercial intention. In *Proceedings of International World Wide Web Conference*.

Evangelopoulos, G., Zlatintsi, A., Skoumas, G., Rapantzikos, K., Potamianos, A., Maragos, P., & Avrithis, Y. (2009). Video event detection and summarization using audio, visual and text saliency. In *Proceedings of IEEE International Conference on Acoustics, Speech and Signal Processing*.

Feltham, T. S., & Arnold, S. J. (1994). Program involvement and ad/program consistency as moderators of program context effects. *Journal of Consumer Psychology, 3*(1), 51–77. doi:10.1016/S1057-7408(08)80028-9

Google Video. (n.d.). Retrieved from http://video.google.com/

Guo, J., Mei, T., Liu, F., & Hua, X.-S. (2009). AdOn: An Intelligent Overlay Video Advertising System. In *Proceedings of ACM SIGIR conference on Research and Development in Information Retrieval* (pp. 628–629).

Hu, J., Zeng, H.-J., Li, H., Niu, C., & Chen, Z. (2007). Demographic prediction based on user's browsing behavior. In *Proceedings of International World Wide Web Conference*.

Joshi, A., & Motwani, R. (2006). Keyword generation for search engine advertising. In *Proceedings of the Workshops of IEEE International Conference on Data Mining*.

Jupiter Research. (n.d.). Retrieved from http://www.jupiterresearch.com/

Kastidou, G., & Cohen, R. (2006). An approach for delivering personalized ads in interactive TV customized to both users and advertisers. In *Proceedings of European Conference on Interactive Television*.

Lacerda, A., Cristo, M., Goncalves, M. A., et al. (2006). Learning to advertise. In *Proceedings of ACM SIGIR conference on Research and Development in Information Retrieval*.

Lekakos, G., Papakiriakopoulos, D., & Chorianopoulos, K. (2001). An integrated approach to interactive and personalized TV advertising. In *Proceedings of Workshop on Personalization in Future TV*.

Li, H., Edwards, S. M., & Lee, J.-H. (2002a). Measuring the intrusiveness of advertisements: scale development and validation. *Journal of Advertising, 31*(2), 37–47.

Li, H., Zhang, D., Hu, J., Zeng, H.-J., & Chen, Z. (2007). Finding keyword from online broadcasting content for targeted advertising. In *International Workshop on Data Mining and Audience Intelligence for Advertising*.

Li, S. Z., Zhu, L., Zhang, Z., Blake, A., Zhang, H.-J., & Shum, H. (2002b). Statistical learning of multi-view face detection. In *Proceedings of European Conference on Computer Vision* (pp. 67–81). Copenhagen, Denmark.

Li, Y., Wan, K., Yan, X., & Xu, C. (2005). Advertisement insertion in baseball video based on advertisement effect. In *Proceedings of ACM Multimedia* (pp. 343–346).

Liao, W.-S., Chen, K.-T., & Hsu, W. H. (2008). AdImage: video advertising by image matching and ad scheduling optimization. In *Proceedings of ACM SIGIR conference on Research and Development in Information Retrieval* (pp. 767–768).

Liu, H., Jiang, S., Huang, Q., & Xu, C. (2008). A generic virtual content insertion system based on visual attention analysis. In *Proceeding of the ACM International Conference on Multimedia* (pp. 379–388).

Ma, Y.-F., Hua, X.-S., Lu, L., & Zhang, H.-J. (2005). A generic framework of user attention model and its application in video summarization. *IEEE Transactions on Multimedia, 7*(5), 907–919. doi:10.1109/TMM.2005.854410

Ma, Y.-F., Lu, L., Zhang, H.-J., & Li, M. (2002). A user attention model for video summarization. In *Proceedings of ACM Multimedia* (pp. 533–542).

Ma, Y.-F., & Zhang, H.-J. (2003). Contrast-based image attention analysis by using fuzzy growing. In *Proceedings of ACM Multimedia* (pp. 374–381).

Mccoy, S., Everard, A., Polak, P., & Galletta, D. F. (2007). The effects of online advertising. *Communications of the ACM, 50*(3), 84–88. doi:10.1145/1226736.1226740

Mehta, A., Saberi, A., Vazirani, U., & Vazirani, V. (2007). Adwords and generalized on-line matching. *Journal of the ACM, 54*(5). doi:10.1145/1284320.1284321

Mei, T., Guo, J., Hua, X.-S., and Liu, F. (2010). AdOn: Toward contextual overlay in-video advertising. Multimedia Systems.

Mei, T., & Hua, X.-S. (2010). Contextual internet multimedia advertising. In *Proceedings of the IEEE*.

Mei, T., Hua, X.-S., Lai, W., & Yang, L. (2007a). 2007: High-level feature extraction and search. In *TREC Video Retrieval Evaluation Online Proceedings*. MSRA-USTC-SJTU at TRECVID.

Mei, T., Hua, X.-S., & Li, S. (2008). Contextual inimage advertising. In *Proceedings of ACM Multimedia* (pp. 439-448). Vanconver, Canada.

Mei, T., Hua, X.-S., & Li, S. (2009). VideoSense: A contextual in-video advertising system. *IEEE Trans. on Circuits and Systems for Video Technology, 19*(12), 1866–1879. doi:10.1109/TCSVT.2009.2026949

Mei, T., Hua, X.-S., Yang, L., & Li, S. (2007b). VideoSense: Towards effective online video advertising. In *Proceedings of ACM Multimedia* (pp. 1075–1084). Augsburg, Germany.

Metacafe. (n.d.). Retrieved from http://www.metacafe.com/

Murdock, V., Ciaramita, M., & Plachouras, V. (2007). A noisy channel approach to contextual advertising. In *International Workshop on Data Mining and Audience Intelligence for Advertising*.

Online Publishers. (n.d.). Retrieved from http://www.online-publishers.org/

Revver. (n.d.). Retrieved from http://one.revver.com/revver

Ribeiro-Neto, B., Cristo, M., Golgher, P. B., & Moura, E. S. (2005). Impedance coupling in content-targeted advertising. In *Proceedings of ACM SIGIR conference on Research and Development in Information Retrieval*.

Richardson, M., Dominowska, E., & Ragno, R. (2007). Predicting clicks: Estimating click-through rate for new ads. In *Proceedings of International World Wide Web Conference*.

Rui, Y., Huang, T. S., Ortega, M., & Mehrotra, S. (1998). Relevance feedback: A power tool for interactive content-based image retrieval. *IEEE Trans. on Circuits and Video Technology, 8*(5), 644–655. doi:10.1109/76.718510

Shen, D., Sun, J.-T., Yang, Q., & Chen, Z. (2006). Building bridges for web query classification. In *Proceedings of ACM SIGIR conference on Research and Development in Information Retrieval*.

Srinivasan, S. H., Sawant, N., & Wadhwa, S. (2007). vADeo: Video Advertising System. In *Proceedings of ACM Multimedia* (pp. 455–456).

Thawani, A., Gopalan, S., & Sridhar, V. (2004). Context aware personalized ad insertion in an interactive TV environment. In *Proceedings of Workshop on Personalization in Future TV*.

TRECVID. (n.d.). Retrieved from http://www-nlpir.nist.gov/projects/trecvid/

Wan, K., Yan, X., Yu, X., & Xu, C. (2003). Robust goal-mouth detection for virtual content insertion. In *Proceedings of ACM Multimedia* (pp. 468–469).

Whitley, D. (1994). A genetic algorithm tutorial. *Statistics and Computing, 4*, 65–85. doi:10.1007/BF00175354

Yahoo. (n.d.). Retrieved from http://www.yahoo.com/

Yahoo. Video (n.d.). Retrieved from http://video.yahoo.com/

Yang, B., Mei, T., Hua, X.-S., Yang, L., Yang, S.-Q., & Li, M. (2007). Online video recommendation based on multimodal fusion and relevance feedback. In *Proceedings of ACM International Conference on Image and Video Retrieval* (pp. 73–80). Amsterdam, The Netherlands.

Yih, W.-T., Goodman, J., & Carvalho, V. R. (2006). Finding advertising keywords on web pages. In *Proceedings of International World Wide Web Conference*.

YouTube. (n.d.). Retrieved from http://www.youtube.com/

Yuan, X., Lai, W., Mei, T., Hua, X.-S., & Wu, X.-Q. (2006). Automatic video genre categorization using hierarchical svm. In *Proceedings of IEEE International Conference on Image Processing*, Atlanta, USA.

Zhang, H.-J., Kankanhalli, A., & Smoliar, S. W. (1993). Automatic partitioning of full-motion video. *Multimedia Systems, 1*(1), 10–28. doi:10.1007/BF01210504

Zhang, S., Tian, Q., Jiang, S., Huang, Q., & Gao, W. (2008). Affective mtv analysis based on arousal and valence features. In *Proceedings of ICME* (pp. 1369–1372).

Zhao, L., Qi, W., Wang, Y.-J., Yang, S.-Q., & Zhang, H.-J. (2001). Video shot grouping using best first model merging. In *Proceedings of Storage and Retrieval for Media Database* (pp. 262–269).

ENDNOTES

[1] Typical examples for textual relevance matching are the keyword-targeted (e.g., Google's AdWords) and content-targeted advertising (e.g., Google's AdSense).

[2] There is usually an accompany ad around the video at the same time.

[3] We used Scansoft which has been integrated into Microsoft Office.

[4] $R_g\left(a_j\right) \triangleq R_g\left(a_j, V\right)$. We drop V for the sake of simplicity.

[5] We select 16 concepts appearing frequently from TRECVID 2006 (TRECVID,), including "Building," "Car," "Entertainment," "Face," "Government-Leader," "Meeting," "Military," "Mountain," "Office," "Person," "Road," "Sky," "Sports," "Studio," "Vegetation," and "Waterscape-Waterfront." The concept models are built based on the work in TRECVID 2007 (Mei et al., 2007a). The 16-dimensional concept probabilities constitute a feature vector.)

Section 4
Behavior Targeting / Personalized Ads / Audience Intelligence

Chapter 12
Behavioral Targeting Online Advertising

Jun Yan
Microsoft Research Asia, China

Dou Shen
Microsoft Corporation, USA

Teresa Mah
Microsoft Corporation, USA

Ning Liu
Microsoft Research Asia, China

Zheng Chen
Microsoft Research Asia, China

Ying Li
Microsoft Corporation, USA

ABSTRACT

With the rapid growth of the online advertising market, Behavioral Targeting (BT), which delivers advertisements to users based on understanding of their needs through their behaviors, is attracting more attention. The amount of spend on behaviorally targeted ad spending in the US is projected to reach $4.4 billion in 2012 (Hallerman, 2008). BT is a complex technology, which involves data collection, data mining, audience segmentation, contextual page analysis, predictive modeling and so on. This chapter gives an overview of Behavioral Targeting by introducing the Behavioral Targeting business, followed by classic BT research challenges and solution proposals. We will also point out BT research challenges which are currently under-explored in both industry and academia.

DOI: 10.4018/978-1-60960-189-8.ch012

INTRODUCTION

Nowadays, all media is starting to move online. The traditional offline mediums of print (newspapers, magazines), radio, TV are all transpiring into online counterparts such as news and magazine portals, customized radio stations, and on-demand television. Advertising, which is always bonded with media, is moving online accordingly. One of the major advantages of online advertising over traditional advertising is the transparency and tracking capability. Online advertising offers advertisers a unique opportunity to achieve higher ROI (Return on Investment) (Phillips, 2003) and effectiveness than with offline advertising. Specifically, due to the fact that online behavior is relatively easy to track, and a person receiving an advertising message is now identifiable, online advertising allows us to get closer to the promise of true one on one targeting. In any advertising campaign, an advertiser has a target audience they want to reach. For instance, the audience in an advertiser's mind may be "Working Moms". If we try to reach these audiences through an offline medium like TV, the only choice is to present the ads on TV shows that are known to attract Working Moms, or on TV shows that attract people of similar age and gender demographics as that of Working Moms, i.e., "25-45", "Female". Clearly, this type of approximate targeting (or no targeting at all) introduces waste in advertising effectiveness, as many other people could be watching the same TV shows who are not Working Moms. In the online space though, there is much more data available, such as users' individual browsing and querying behaviors (White, & Morris, 2007; Hölscher, & Strube, 2000). From these and other types of behavioral data, we can accurately derive a user's demographics, interests, and attitudes, which allow us to provide advertisers with the exact users they are looking for.

To do behaviorally targeted advertising online, there are several key challenges. First, we need to answer the question of how to represent users, which is used for computing relevance between users and ads. Second, after the users are well understood, how to group users with similar intents (or segment users) for advertisers to target against is also a key question to answer. Last but not least, we have to address the challenge of matching user groups with ads to optimize both relevance and revenue.

This chapter of the book provides a brief overview of the Behavioral Targeting online advertising business, presenting existing solutions to the aforementioned challenges. In terms of user representation, there are generally three types of user profiles - static user profiles such as age and gender of users, behavioral profiles such as the recent Web browsing behaviors of users, and semantic user profiles such as the user intent mined from user behaviors. Details about user representation research will be introduced in the following subsections.

In terms of methodologies for creating Behavioral Targeting user segments, the straight-forward option is to create rules that define users in a particular segment. For example, to define a Gamers segment, we can choose the users who have visited some pre-defined gaming *websites* or issued *search queries* like 'xbox', 'ps3', or 'wii' at least *five* times in the *last two days*. One of the pros of this approach is that the rules are simple to understand and easy to explain to advertisers. However, these rules can be subjective depending on the person who creates the rules and how well she/he understands what users in the segment would be interested in. Such a methodology is also not optimized for performance on CTR (click-through rate) or conversion rate, which are the metrics DR (direct-response) advertisers use to measure campaign effectiveness. The quality of a segment defined in such a fashion is bounded by the breadth and depth of the data that publishers/ad networks have to populate segment rules or models (i.e., many publishers do not have access to a broad view of a user's behavior online). Therefore, we foresee that only a few major players will exist in the BT market, since only a few companies in the industry today have the capital and the resources to collect and maintain the amount of data needed to generate accurate and valuable user segments.

Another more advanced methodology commonly used in the marketplace today to create BT segments is look-alike modeling. A look-alike modeling approach uses classification or clustering techniques from data mining and machine learning to automatically optimize against a response variable. It considers both segmentation (group users into segments) and matching (match user segments to ads) simultaneously. Given a set of users who have responded (i.e., clicked or converted) to an online ad and all of their online behaviors, look-alike modeling can then automatically identify the behavioral attributes that distinguish respondents from non-respondents, and generate a model which can run regularly to select users belonging to the segment under consideration.

While we have discussed mainly the methodologies to create explicit segments that are subsequently offered to advertisers, there is a whole other area of exploiting user-level behavioral data for other purposes. For example, we can use behavioral data to optimize ranking and relevance in other online ad delivery channels such as Sponsored Search and Text-Based Contextual Advertising (such as Google's AdSense program) (Davis, 2006). Many companies, even though they may not sell a formal BT product to advertisers, do use user-level behavioral information to optimize or personalize text-based ads that show up when a user is doing a search or browsing web pages.

The rest of this chapter is organized as follows. In the next section, we introduce some background about Behavioral Targeting, including providing a more formal definition of the product and science, and a discussion on companies doing Behavioral Targeting. After that, we introduce the main part of this Chapter, which explains the major challenges of BT, with some solution proposals. In the next section, we introduce some other research

challenges for BT. In the last section, we present a summary to conclude this chapter and list some additional readings.

BACKGROUND

Targeting products are offered by almost all major publishers and ad networks, with the promise to fulfill the basic purpose of advertising – connecting an advertiser to the right consumer, and providing all the necessary algorithms and tools to do so. In online advertising, there are different types of targeting. Most widely used is demographic targeting, where the advertiser specifies the age or gender ranges of users it wants to target its campaign against. Location targeting is also very popular as well, with location attributes generally starting at the country level, and down to the DMA or even zip code level. Behavioral Targeting (BT), the focus of this chapter, is targeting users based on their online behaviors such as users' browsing history or search queries. It is generally offered to advertisers in the form of segments, such as "Auto Researchers", "Home Buyers", "Fashion & Beauty Enthusiasts", "Working Moms", etc. While the data for demographic or location targeting generally comes from either self-reported or third party sources, the challenge with Behavioral Targeting is how a publisher or network can take large scale amounts of online behaviors to derive accurate segments describing their end users. When we take into account the complexity of different advertisers' goals (Branding versus Direct Response) and different requirements for the targeted audience from different advertisers, we see the challenge in optimizing BT. However, it is because of the flexibility of Behavioral Targeting (albeit at the cost of complexity), and its promise of true one on one targeting, that BT is becoming more and more attractive to advertisers. As reported in eMarketer's "Behavioral Targeting: Marketing Trends" (Hallerman, 2008), US Behaviorally Targeted Online Advertising Spending in 2010 will be 1.7B and will reach 4.4B by 2012. The growth is substantial in years to come.

Besides advertisers, Behavior targeting is also attractive to publishers and ad networks, due to its targeting capabilities. A majority of the big players in the online advertising industry have invested in behavioral targeting technologies. Yahoo, Microsoft, and AOL all have behavioral targeting products, as well as the major ad networks such as 24/7, BlueLithium, SpecificMedia, etc, with all offerings in the neighborhood of hundreds to thousands of segments for advertisers to purchase. From publishers and ad networks' point of view, behavioral targeting can generally command a higher eCPM (cost per thousand impressions rate) than untargeted inventory or other forms of targeting and better user experience in term of relevancy. While BT on contextual inventory may not provide as much value add to the advertiser (i.e., targeting an Auto Researchers segment on an Auto-related site), publishers and networks instead package BT capabilities with their remnant inventory that is non-contextual (i.e., on sites such as Mail or Instant Messaging services) to increase the yield from this inventory. Sometimes it can boost multiple fold eCPM lifts when targeting is applied on an impression compared to when no targeting is available, with the sales pitch being that an advertiser's audience can be found across a publisher's entire network.

According to the definition of "Behavioral Targeting" in Wikipedia, which is a good summary of BT related articles, "BT uses information collected on an individual's web-browsing behavior, such as the pages they have visited or the searches they have made, to select which advertisements to display to that individual. Practitioners believe this helps them deliver their online advertisements to the users who are most likely to be influenced by them." In our problem configuration, each individual is defined as an Internet user. According to this definition, BT is generally used for improving the influence of online advertising by targeting the most relevant users with related ads.

From an engineering perspective, after collecting user behaviors (that represent user interests), there are generally two steps in the behavioral targeting process: (1) user segmentation and (2) user segment ranking. The first step aims to segment users according to their behaviors and the second step aims to rank user segments for an ad.

Recently, there are a large number of commercial systems proposed for targeted advertising. For instance, Yahoo! SmartAds collects around 169M registered users for behavioral targeting; besides user behaviors, they integrate demographic and geographic data into their targeting as well. Adlink uses the search information from user sessions for behaviorally targeted advertising. DoubleClick utilizes some extra features such as browsing type and the operating system of users for user segmentation. Specific Media proposes to assign a score for predicting interest and purchase intent of each targeted user. Besides these examples, there are many other popular commercial BT systems developed by companies such as TACODA, Audience Science, Phorm, Blue Lithium, Almond Net, NebuAd, Burst, etc. Although an increasing number of commercial BT systems appear, there have only been a few publications in academia to address BT research challenges and solutions. The work of Yan et al. is the first published work, which aims to answer the question on how much behavioral targeting can help online advertising (Yan, Liu, Wang, Zhang, Jiang, & Zheng, 2009). Soon after that, Chen et al. published the solution for large scale Behavioral Targeting (Chen, Pavlov, & Canny, 2009). However, none of these works have systematically presented the full conceptual map of behavioral targeting research, which is the focus of this chapter.

BEHAVIORIAL TARGETING

In this section, we introduce some feasible solutions for behavioral targeting from three perspectives: (1) user representation, (2) user segmentation and

Figure 1. A flowchart of Behavioral Targeting research to be introduced in this chapter. (R&R: relevance and revenue)

Figure 1. A flowchart of Behavioral Targeting research to be introduced in this chapter. (R&R: relevance and revenue)

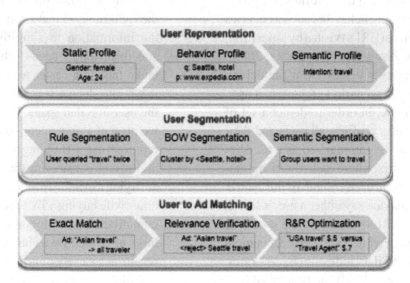

(3) user segment to ad matching. Figure 1 shows the three aspects with examples for explanation purposes. In terms of user representation, there are generally three types of user profiles - static user profiles such as age and gender of users, behavioral profiles taken from behavioral activity such as recent Web browsing behaviors, and semantic user profiles such as the user intent mined from user behaviors. In terms of user segmentation, there are also three types of user segmentation strategies we have identified: (1) rule-based user segmentation, i.e., users who have searched "travel" more than twice in the past week may fall into a Travel Planner segment; (2) Bag of Words (BOW) user segmentation by first representing users in the vector space and then performing clustering or classification in the numerical vector space; (3) and semantic user segmentation by using advanced data mining/machine learning algorithms. For user to ad matching, we introduce a general solution starting from an exact keyword match scenario to automatic optimization. The following subsections will provide more detailed explanations of the below chart.

User Representation

User representation and understanding is a key problem of BT, which will greatly affect the final quality of any BT solution. In this section, we briefly review three classic user representation strategies for BT, which are: demographic and geographic profiling, behavioral user profiling and semantic user profiling.

1. Demographic and geographic profiling
    Demographic and geographic profiling means using the demographic and geographic information of users to build user profiles. Research problems here include how to predict user demographic and geographic data based on a user's behavioral history (that is, not using self-reported data), as well as how to match users with ads based on their demographic and geographic information. This is not the focus of this chapter, and please refer to (Hu, Zeng, Li, Niu, & Zheng, 2007) for more details.

2. Behavioral profiling Behavioral profiling is the idea of building user profiles composed of Web browsing behaviors such as queries issued or pages (URLs) visited by a user (Yan, Liu, Wang, Zhang, Jiang, & Zheng, 2009). The classic Bag of Words (BOW) model can be used in this scenario to represent a user. As an example, in order to depict a set of behavioral user profiles, all users and their behavior can be summarized as a user-by-behavior matrix, where each row of this matrix is a user and each column of this matrix is a user behavior, say either a user's search query or a URL browsed by the user. The classic Term Frequency Inverse Document Frequency (TFIDF) indexing (Baeza-Yates, & Ribeiro-Neto, 1999) can be applied here by considering each user as a document and considering each URL/query as a term for mathematical user representation. As a result, all users are represented by a real valued matrix $U \in R^{g \times l}$, where g is the total number of users and l is the total number of user behaviors that have been used in the dataset. A user is a row of behaviors in the matrix U, which is a real valued vector. For simplicity, if we just consider visited URLs as user behaviors, each entry in the matrix can be calculated as follows,

$$u_{ij} = \left(\log\left(\text{\# times user } i \text{ clicked URL } j\right) + 1\right)$$
$$\times log \frac{l}{\text{\# user clicked URL } j}$$

where $i = 1, 2, ..., g; j = 1, 2, ... l$.

3. Semantic User Profiling A semantic user profile goes further to infer a user's true need at a certain period of time, and can consist of derived attributes such as location, mined from existing attributes such as demographic information or behaviors. As we have discussed in the introduction, the goal of Behavioral Targeting is to deliver the right information to the right user at the right time, so that the user can leverage the information to simplify his/her tasks and fulfill one's needs. Therefore, it will make targeting easier to achieve this goal if we introduce a task/need space and put the user into that space. In order to do this, we present a new intent-based approach to represent users. Building a task/need space is non-trivial, considering that billions of users are trying to achieve millions of goals, from a housewife buying a TV to scientists sending human beings to the moon. Clearly, different tasks have their own characteristics, which results in a variety of information needed to complete the tasks. Buying a TV is totally different from buying a house; also, buying a TV is different from repairing a TV in that they are about different actions. Even for the same task, say, buying a TV, people prefer to do it in different ways. Someone wants to buy it in a local store and therefore wants to get the location and office hours of the store to know when to stop by, while the other tends to buy it online and therefore wants to know which online stores can offer free delivery. These examples illustrate that there are many different aspects to tasks and that due to this, we cannot cover all the tasks in the world. In the Behavioral Targeting field, companies will focus on the tasks which are popular and have high commercial value.

After building the task/need space, we can treat it as a feature space, as we do in the "document/term" space and represent a user's need through one or more dimensions in the space. However, the advantage of the task space is that tasks are associated or linked together. For example, knowing a person is buying a house provides strong clues that she is very likely to buy furniture soon. Given the rich information about users' demographics, locations, time of the day/day of the week visiting patterns, and their online content consumed including search and pages views, the problem of mapping users to a set of dimensions in the space becomes a traditional machine learning problem. After we represent users through the task space, we can apply any of the common targeting techniques to target the user with the right information.

User Segmentation

After users are represented by their profiles and behavioral information, we will group users who have similar interest on (or intent to respond to, i.e., click) the same group of ads. The end product is segments that advertisers can select to advertise to and have highest probability of responding to their ads. In this section, we use some examples to discuss three types of user segmentation strategies, which are

- Rule based user segmentation
- BOW user segmentation
- Semantic user segmentation

Information sources used for deciding how to create a rule-based segment definition can come from marketing surveys or psychographic/behavioral studies that determine what types of behaviors a certain audience of interest may have online. We can then use this information to define a segment, i.e., of Digital Camera Enthusiasts, as "all the users who have searched digital camera related queries more than 5 times in the past two weeks". The major advantage of rule based user segmentation is that it is straightforward and understandable by advertisers. However, when there is no external information available for identifying traits of a certain audience, it is hard to define the optimal rules for user segmentation and it is hard to scale up to a large number of user segments simultaneously.

BOW user segmentation algorithms can be generally categorized into two classes, based on supervised learning and unsupervised learning. There are many classical machine learning algo-

rithms that could be used in this user segmentation scenario. For example, the work of Jun et al. utilized clustering algorithms such as k-means (Kanungo, Mount, Netanyahu, Piatko, Silverman, & Wu, 2000) and CLUTO (Karypis, n.d) to group users according to their behavioral user profiles. The work Chen, Pavlov, & Canny (2009) utilized a regression strategy to group users who were most likely to click on a group of ads. There are also many other machine learning algorithms that could be applied in this scenario, but we will not be diving into all the different options available in this chapter.

In this section, we introduce a semantic user segmentation algorithm -- Probabilistic Latent Semantic Analysis (PLSA) (Deerwester, Dumais, Furnas, Landauer, & Hashman, 1990; Brants, Chen, & Tsochantaridis, 2002). PLSA, which can discover the latent relationship between two objects, is widely studied in document classification and clustering problems. According to the work of Yan et al. (2009), users' behaviors can be represented by their historical queries. Notice the fact that queries consist of terms, thus we can treat each query as one set of terms. Through this way, each user can be represented by a bag of words first, which is the same as the representation of text document.

Inspired by the work in (Wu, Yan, Liu, Yan, Chen, & Zheng, 2009), let $u_i \in U = \{u_1, u_2, ..., u_n\}$ stand for a user, where U represents the set of all users available for BT ad delivery; suppose $t_j \in T = \{t_1, t_2, ..., t_m\}$ is a term, where T represents the vocabulary of all terms used by all users. We define T_{u_i} as the set of all terms used by u_i, thus,

$$T = \bigcup_{u_i \in U} T_{u_i}$$

Then, we define the co-occurrence matrix $N = \{n(u_i, t_j)\}$, where $n(u_i, t_j)$ describes the number of times t_j is used by u_i.

Figure 2. Graph of the aspect model

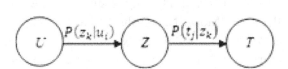

Figure 3. Graph of the PLSA

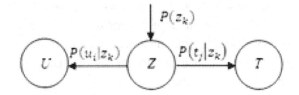

To semantically segment users, we introduce the latent variable $z_k \in Z = \{z_1, z_2, ..., z_l\}$ which represents the topics, i.e., semantic intentions of users. These latent variables represent relationships between users and queries, which are transformed into terms. From the user's perspective, a topic z_k implies a hidden interest of the user. On the other hand, from the term's perspective, terms in one topic may be gathered with some specified field. Here, we assume that for a given topic variable z_k, users and terms are independent to each other. We adopt the classical aspect model (Hofmann, 1999) here. The graph of the aspect model is given by Figure 2.

In the BT scenario, each user has the probability $P(z_k \mid u_i)$ to generate a topic z_k, and then z_k has the probability $P(t_j \mid z_k)$ to generate term t_j. Given the basic model,

$$P(u_i, t_j) = P(u_i)P(t_j \mid u_i)$$

$$P(t_j \mid u_i) = \sum_{z_k \in Z} P(t_j \mid z_k)P(z_k \mid u_i)$$

Notice that, this model contains the probability $P(z_k \mid u_i)$ and $P(u_i)$ which are not convenient to compute. Thus, we transform this model into another equivalent form:

$$P(u_i, t_j) = \sum_{z_k \in Z} P(z_k)P(u_i \mid z_k)P(t_j \mid z_k),$$

where $P(z_k)$ represents the probability that z_k is observed in Z, $P(u_i \mid z_k)$ is the probability that

u_i is relevant to the given topic z_k and $P(t_j \mid z_k)$ is the probability that t_j is related to the given topic z_k. The graphical representation is shown in Figure 3.

Similar to PLSA in the field of text mining, we aim to maximize the likelihood defined as,

$$L = \sum_{i=1}^{n} \sum_{j=1}^{m} n(u_i, t_j) \log P(u_i, t_j)$$

$$= \sum_{i=1}^{n} \sum_{j=1}^{m} n(u_i, t_j) \log \sum_{k=1}^{l} P(z_k)P(u_i \mid z_k)P(t_j \mid z_k)$$

In order to maximize L, we adapt the classical Expectation Maximization (EM) approach. The EM approach is widely used in computing maximum likelihood in latent variable models. EM is an iterative method which alternates between performing two steps. (1) Expectation step (E step) - using the current estimates of parameters, we compute the posterior probabilities $P(z_k \mid u_i, t_j)$ for the latent variable. (2) Maximization step (M step) - aiming to maximize complete likelihood $E[L^c]$, we update $P(z_k)$, $P(u_i \mid z_k)$ and $P(t_j \mid z_k)$.

After finishing EM computation, we aim to segment users with the model obtained. Since a topic has a close relationship with the user and term, a topic can be considered a user segment. In this way, the semantic attributes become the dominant factors in user segmentation. Thus, we aim to solve the question of how to segment users into different topics. To address this question, we focus on an important probability $P(z_k \mid u_i)$ which presents the topic (user segment) z_k is observed with a given user u_i. It can describe how close the relationship between z_k and u_i is. $P(z_k \mid u_i)$ can be computed by the following:

$$P(z_k \mid u_i) = \frac{\sum_{j=1}^{m} n(u_i, t_j) P(z_k \mid u_i, t_j)}{\sum_{j=1}^{m} \sum_{k'=1}^{l} n(u_i, t_j) P(z_{k'} \mid u_i, t_j)}.$$

Intuitively, the easiest way to segment users into topics, i.e., user intents, is that, by computing all $P(z_k \mid u_i)$, $z_k \in Z$ for each u_i, we can then put u_i into the topic with the highest $P(z_k \mid u_i)$. However, this approach of user segmentation cannot handle the following circumstance: If a user is interested in both sports and cooking while there are two topics which exactly imply sports and cooking, this segmentation method will choose only one topic for a user at most. Using this approach, we may lose a user's interest in other important categories. In order to get over this deficiency, we present a novel approach for segmenting users based on the probability $P(z_k \mid u_i)$. Here, we apply a *threshold* for user segmentation. Let S be the set of user segments and $s_k \in S$ as the segment with topic z_k, thus the user segmentation approach is,

$$u_i \in s_k \;\; if \; P(z_k \mid u_i) > threshold,$$
$$u_i \notin s_k \qquad\qquad otherwise$$

Comparing with traditional clustering methods, this simple method allows one user to belong to multiple segments. After users are segmented, the next question to answer is how to match user segments with ads.

Though this semantic approach can semantically segment users in an unsupervised manner, it still has limitations in real application. For example, from a business perspective, many user segments are driven by advertiser demand. However, the problem of how to semantically segment users in the supervised and semi-supervised manner is still underexplored in academia. This encourages us to propose more user segmentation algorithms to help industry applications.

User Segment to Ad Matching

Behavioral targeting has been applied in different online advertising business models such as display ads, contextual ads and paid search, etc. Different online advertising models have different user to ad matching strategies. In this section, we do not explicitly distinguish these models and introduce some common methods as examples. To answer the question of how to match user segments with ads, one approach is to allow advertisers to directly purchase or bid on user segments which requires the advertiser to directly select their preferred user segments among hundreds of user segments. This is common in the Display Advertising area where advertisers explicitly indicate what segments they want to buy. Another method to match ads with user segments is by keyword matching. Specifically, both user segments and advertisers' requirements are represented by a set of keywords. This method is generally more viable for the Contextual Advertising scenario (such as Google AdSense, or adCenter Content Ads), where advertisers specify keywords they want to bid on and the matching of the advertiser to the user segment is done implicitly behind the scenes through these keywords. In this Chapter, we focus on technical challenges and a proposed solution for the latter option. Clearly, the automatic keyword matching strategy tends to involve noise when delivering ads to end users due to the ambiguity of keywords and the underexplored keywords bidded on by advertisers. To overcome these limitations, relevance verification could be considered to verify whether the keyword matching results are correct. Since the final goal of targeted ad delivery is to optimize ad relevance and ad revenue simultaneously, in this section, we

Table 1. Feature description for user/user segment ranking

No.	feature name	Description
Relevance features		
#1	'query history + ad title' similarity	BM25 score computed between a user's query history and the title of the given ad.
#2	'query history + ad desc' similarity	BM25 score computed between a user's query history and the description of the given ad.
#3	'query history + ad whole' similarity	BM25 score computed between a user's query history and the whole content of the given ad.
#4	'click query history + ad whole' similarity	BM25 score computed between a user's query history (queries with ad click) and the whole content of the given ad.
#5	'no-click query history + ad whole' similarity	BM25 score computed between a user's query history (queries without ad click) and the whole content of the given ad.
#6	'clicked ad history + ad whole' similarity	BM25 score computed between a user's ad click history and the whole content of the given ad.
Topic-based relevance features		
#7	'query history + whole page' topic similarity	cosine similarity of topic patterns between query history and the whole content of the given ad.
#8	'clicked ad history + whole page' topic similarity	cosine similarity of topic patterns between ad click history and the whole content of the given ad.
Priori behavioral statistics features		
#9	user global CTR	user's global ad click CTR in the log.
#10	topic-specific CTR	user's ad click CTR when inputting queries which have the same topic with the given ad.
#11	topic-specific %query	the percentage of queries having the same topic with the given ad.
#12	topic-specific %ad-click	the percentage of clicked ads having the same topic with the given ad.
#13	# user query topic	the number of query topics a user has submitted.
#14	# user ad-click topic	the number of ad topics a user has clicked.

introduce a learning approach, which is known as Learning to Rank (Liu, 2009), to optimize the relevance between ads and users for ad delivery.

Suppose an advertiser from a certain industry wants to run his ad campaign online and comes to an online publisher (e.g., a search engine or an ad network). He knows his products well, but has no idea about the best online audience his ads should be delivered to. There are many different types of audiences on the Internet, and it is wasteful to deliver his ads to all of them, considering the ROI and user relevance issues. To optimally find one or more segments of users for this advertiser, we consider an extreme case by considering each user as an independent segment and introducing a user ranking mechanism according to the advertiser's ad campaigns. Similar to document retrieval, the key idea in the user ranking problem is as follows: we treat the advertiser (or his ads) as the query

and use it to retrieve a subset of users as the top audience for the advertiser.

Analogous to learning to rank documents in document retrieval, in the user ranking problem, there should be queries, document repositories, label definitions and feature sets. In our scenario, the query is the advertiser, or, more precisely, the ad composed by the advertiser. An online user is treated as a document, with the label representing whether this user has clicked on the given ad or not. Here, we make use of two types of behavioral data: user search query history and user ad click history. Features are extracted from the ad and this behavioral data. In summary, the goal of learning to rank users is to obtain a ranking model which can identify the users/user segments with the highest probability of interest in an ad. In this section, we introduce 14 example features (listed in Table 1) based on ad content and user behavioral data. We divide the 14 features into three types and introduce each of them in the following subsections.

Relevance Features

In our user ranking problem, user profiles and ads can be represented as word vectors after stemming and indexing (Baeza-Yates, & Ribeiro-Neto, 1999). Therefore, classical features in document retrieval can be employed to indicate the relevance level between users and ads. From the user's perspective, we have the query history together with the ad click history which is recorded by the URL of the ad's landing page. We extract the page title as an abstract of the landing page. Thus, a user can be profiled by the queries he/she ever submitted and the titles of landing pages of the ads he/she ever clicked. From the ad's perspective, we make use of the ad title and description, which we believe to have the most impact on a user's interest. As reported in (Yan, Liu, Wang, Zhang, Jiang, & Zheng, 2009), user query and page view records have strong association with a user's ad click behavior. Users who submitted similar queries or viewed pages with similar content will show the same intent in clicking certain ads. Inspired by this, we extracted 6 relevance features based on the user profile and the ad content. We choose Okapi BM25 (Robertson, Walker, Jones, Hancock-Beaulieu, & Gatford, 1994; Robertson, Walker, & Hancock-Beaulieu, 1998) as the relevance measure due to its excellent performance in various applications. Details about these features are listed in the top category of Table 1.

Topic-Based Relevance Features

Considering the vocabulary mismatch when matching the user behavioral data with the ad content, we additionally match them at the semantic level by analyzing the topic information. In particular, we make use of the Open Directory Project[1] (ODP). The top 16 categories are crawled

Table 2. Top Categories from ODP

category name	category ID	category name
Arts	9	Recreation
Business	10	Reference
Computers	11	Regional
Games	12	Science
Health	13	Shopping
Home	14	Society
Kids and Teens	15	Sports
News	16	World

together with their descriptions. Then, we calculate the relevance score (cosine similarity based on TFIDF (Baeza-Yates, & Ribeiro-Neto, 1999) representation) between the user behavioral data (or the ad) and each category description. Through this way, we can get a 16-dimensional relevance vector called as *topic pattern*. The cosine similarity (Garcia, 2006) of topic patterns is employed to measure the topic overlap. We calculate two such values, one between a user's query history and the ad content and the other between a user's ad click history and the ad content. These two features are listed in the second category of Table 1. In addition, we list the 16 top categories of ODP in Table 2.

Priori Behavioral Statistics Features

The above two types of features consider the content relevance between user behavioral data and given ads. We gathered further insights into some statistics of a user's behavior history. For example, a higher CTR history indicates that the user has a strong tendency to click on some ads (regardless of his/her interest or not), while a lower CTR implies that the user tends to ignore the displayed ads. We believe that such statistics can effectively reflect a user's habits when searching information online or browsing some pages. Moreover, the statistics based on long-term observation of a user is thought to be reliable in predicting such a user's

Box 1.

$$\text{user global CTR} = \frac{\text{total ad click frequency}}{\text{total query frequency}}$$

$$\text{topic-specific CTR} = \frac{\text{ad click frequency following queries of given ad's topic}}{\text{query frequency of given ad's topic}}$$

$$\text{topic-specific \% query} = \frac{\text{query frequency of given ad's topic}}{\text{total query frequency}}$$

$$\text{topic-specific \% ad-click} = \frac{\text{ad click frequency following queries of given ad's topic}}{\text{total ad click frequency}}$$

\#user query topic= number of query topics a user submitted

\#user ad-click topic= number of ad topics a user clicked

future behavior. We calculate 6 different statistics of a user's behavior record in the log data. These features are listed in the third category of Table 1 and are defined as shown in Box 1.

Note the CTR defined here is different from the classical definition for ad CTR. They are only used to define some features for learning. After all the features in Table 1 are extracted, we employ a learning to rank method to automatically learn a ranking model using a training data set. The training data consists of individual ads and each ad is associated with a set of users with binary labels indicating whether a user is interested in an ad, where the interest in an ad is defined as "would like to click an ad". The user is represented as a feature vector. Among various learning to rank methods, we choose Ranking SVM (Cao, Xu, Liu, Li, Huang, & Hon, 2006) as our main method due to its proven efficacy in prior research. We use the default linear kernel function of Ranking SVM. Running Ranking SVM is equivalent to solving the following optimization problem.

$$\min_{\omega, \xi_{ij}} \frac{1}{2} \|\omega\|^2 + C \sum \xi_{ij}$$

$$s.t. \ \langle \omega, x_i - x_j \rangle > 1 - \xi_{ij}, \forall x_i \succ x_j, \xi_{ij} > 0$$

Where $\|\omega\|$ is l_2 norm of ω and ξ_{ij} is a slack variable. (x_i, x_j) denotes a pair of users according to an ad where x_i is a user having interest while x_j is a user without interest. Suppose the solution of this optimization problem is ω^* and a series of ξ_{ij}, the obtained ranking model is

$$f(x) = \omega^*, x$$

In addition, we also use a listwise learning to rank method SVM^{map2} which is implemented based on the Ranking SVM. The difference is that SVM^{map} aims to optimize Mean Average Precision (MAP) rather than pair precision in Ranking SVM. Note though that we only discuss user ranking in this Section; it is easy to extend this to ranking user segments if the features are extracted from user segments.

EVALUATION METRICS

Generally, there are two ways for evaluating the performance of BT algorithms. One is the online evaluation strategies and the other is the offline evaluation strategies. Either option has both advantages and limitations. In terms of online evaluation, given a BT algorithm to be evaluated, we directly test its efficacy by testing this live in ad delivery through a real world commercial system or a simulation system. Through this way, we can directly observe the ad Click-through Rate (CTR) and estimated Cost per Impression (eCPI), etc. Though this is a straightforward approach, it is highly costly since the observations come from real world user ad click traffic. The statistical A/B test is generally used in the online evaluation to compare different BT algorithms, which requires considerable amount of impressions and ad clicks to reach statistically significant conclusions. Another limitation is that it is very hard for researchers, who have no support from commercial ad delivery systems, to do online evaluations.

Offline evaluation metrics generally use some previous users' ad click-through behavior to compare the effectiveness of different BT algorithms. Though this kind of evaluation strategy is much cheaper than online strategies, it is likely to be biased by the log data used for evaluation. In this Section, we introduce some offline evaluation metrics, which have been used in recent BT research publications in the BT for Paid Search scenario.

Before introducing the details, we define some mathematical symbols, which will be used throughout this section. Let $A = \{a_1, a_2, \ldots a_n\}$ be the set of n advertisements. For each ad a_i, suppose $Q_i = \{q_{i1}, q_{i2}, \ldots q_{in_i}\}$ are all the queries through which the users have seen or clicked a_i. Through these queries, we can collect all the corresponding users who have seen or clicked a_i. Suppose the group of users who have either seen or clicked a_i is represented by $U_i = \{u_{i1}, u_{i2}, \ldots u_{im_i}\}$

, where m_i is the size of the U_i. We define a Boolean function,

$$\delta\left(u_{ij}\right) = \begin{cases} 1 & if\ u_{ij}\ clicked\ a_i \\ 0 & otherwise \end{cases}$$

to show whether the user u_{ij} has clicked ad a_i. Classical BT aims to group users into segments and deliver different ads to different groups of users. Suppose the users are segmented into K segments according to their behaviors. We use the function,

$$G(U_i) = \{g_1(U_i), g_2(U_i), \ldots, g_K(U_i)\},\ i=1,2,\ldots n$$

to represent the distribution of U_i under given user segmentation results, where $g_k(U_i)$ stands for all the users in U_i who are grouped into the kth user segment. Thus the kth user segment can be represented by,

$$g_{k=} \bigcup_{i=1,2,\ldots,n} g_k(U_i)$$

Ad Click-Through Rate

The performance of online advertising is generally measured by the ad CTR or conversion for Direct Response advertising. Since conversion data is generally difficult to attain, in this Chapter, we propose to modify the classical ad CTR to define the unique user CTR and observe whether BT can improve unique user CTR. The CTR of ad a_i is defined as the number of users who clicked on the ad divided by the number of users who saw it, i.e.,

$$CTR\left(a_i\right) = \frac{1}{m_i} \sum_{j=1}^{m_i} \delta\left(u_{ij}\right)$$

After user segmentation, the CTR of a_i over user segment g_k is,

$$CTR\left(a_i \mid g_k\right) = \frac{1}{\mid g_k(U_i) \mid} \sum_{u_{ij} \in g_k(U_i)} \delta\left(u_{ij}\right)$$

Where $\mid g_k(U_i) \mid$ is the number of users in $g_k(U_i)$. If for a certain ad a_i, we have some user segments whose $CTR\left(a_i \mid g_k\right)$ is larger than $CTR\left(a_i\right)$, it means that these segments successfully find a set of more relevant users for the ad under consideration.

Recall

Even though we can validate the effectiveness of BT by ad CTR, it is not the only measure that is important to look at. For example, suppose we observe that there is a user segment g_k, which satisfies $CTR\left(a_i \mid g_k\right) > CTR\left(a_i\right)$, this segment may be a group of users who are more interested in ad a_i than other users, but we may not have found all users possible who are potentially willing to click a_i; the improvement of CTR after user segmentation can only validate the precision of BT strategies in finding potentially interested users. There is also a user reach aspect that we need to consider. In other words, the recall is not guaranteed. Motivated by this, we can also adopt the classical F-measure (Manning, Raghavan, & Schütze, 2008) for BT evaluation. If we consider the users who clicked a_i as positive instances and consider the users who saw but did not click a_i as negative instances, the recall is defined as,

$$Rec\left(a_i \mid g_k\right) = \frac{\sum_{u_{ij} \in g_k(U_i)} \delta\left(u_{ij}\right)}{\sum_{j=1}^{m_i} \delta\left(u_{ij}\right)}$$

F-Measure

If we define the precision as,

$$Pre\left(a_i \mid g_k\right) = CTR\left(a_i \mid g_k\right)$$

It can be seen that the larger the precision is, the more accurate we can segment the clickers of a_i. The larger the recall is, the better coverage we can achieve in collecting all the clickers of a_i through user segmentation. To integrate these two parts, we propose to utilize the classical F-measure for results evaluation,

$$F\left(a_i \mid g_k\right) = \frac{2Pre\left(a_i \mid g_k\right)Rec\left(a_i \mid g_k\right)}{Pre\left(a_i \mid g_k\right) + Rec\left(a_i \mid g_k\right)}$$

The larger the F measure is, the better performance the user segmentation achieves. Note the F-measure is not only used to evaluate a single user segment, it can be used to evaluate a group of selected user segments if we allow delivery of one ad to multiple user segments.

Ad Click Entropy

Intuitively, if the clickers of an ad a_i dominate some user segments and seldom appear in other user segments, we can easily deliver our targeted ads to them by selecting the segments they dominate. On the contrary, suppose the clickers of a_i are uniformly distributed in all user segments, if we aim to deliver the targeted ads to more interested users, it is very likely that we will deliver the ad to more users who are not interested in this ad simultaneously. Motivated by this, we propose the ad click entropy metric to show effectiveness of different BT strategies. For an ad a_i, the probability of users in segment g_k, who will click this ad, is estimated by,

$$P\left(g_k \mid a_i\right) = \frac{1}{m_i} \sum_{u_{ij} \in g_k(U_i)} \delta\left(u_{ij}\right)$$

According to the definition of Entropy (Baeza-Yates, & Ribeiro-Neto, 1999), given G, we define the ad click Entropy of ad a_i as,

$$Enp\left(a_i\right) = -\sum_{k=1}^{K} P\left(g_k \mid a_i\right) log P\left(g_k \mid a_i\right)$$

Thus the larger the Entropy is, the more uniformly the users, who clicked ad a_i, are distributed amongst all user segments. The smaller the Entropy is, the better results we will achieve.

EXPERIMENTS

In this section, we review some preliminary experimental results to compare different strategies in behavioral targeting. In this chapter, we mainly show the experiments for user segmentation. Detailed experiments for user representation and user to ad matching can be found in (Yan, Liu, Wang, Zhang, Jiang, & Zheng, 2009; Liu, Yan, Shen, Chen, Chen, & Li, 2010). We use one day's ad click-through log records collected from a commercial search engine. There are four properties in the data set that we used. UserId represents a specified user, with different users having different UserIds. Similar to UserId, AdId is used as the unique identification for each advertisement. Query text shows the content of a query used by a user, and we can divide it into terms to adapt to PLSUS, where PLSUS (probabilistic latent semantic user segmentation) is used to represent the semantic user segmentation algorithm introduced in the "User Segmentation" section. ClickCnt is an important property which is used in our evaluation metrics such as CTR. In user segmentation, let $A = \{a_1, a_2, ..., a_n\}$ be the set of ads in our dataset, $U_i = \{u_{i1}, u_{i2}, ..., u_{im}\}$ be the

group of users who have displayed a_i. Thus we define user

$$D(U_i) = \{d_1(U_i), d_2(U_i), ..., d_k(U_i)\}, \quad i = 1, 2, ..., n$$

as the distribution of U_i with our obtained user segments and $d_k U_i$ as the set of users who belong to the *kth* user segment. Apparently, the *kth* segment can be describe as,

$$d_k \bigcup_{i=1,2,...,n} d_k(U_i)$$

We mainly compare PLSUS (for semantic user segmentation) against with traditional clustering methods for BOW user segmentation. CLUTO and k-Means are selected for BOW user segmentation. The results are shown in Tables 3 to 5. Note we exclude the rule based solution for comparative study since different rules have significant variance in terms of BT performance.

CTR is one of the most basic and critical evaluation metrics for online advertising problems. From Table 3, we generally observe that by increasing the number of segments, the improvement of CTR increases simultaneously. In the same dataset, with 20 segments, the PLSUS improves CTR up to 100% against traditional CLUTO.

We compute the average ad click entropy metric over all ads in the dataset we used. The result is shown in Table 4. Generally, all user segmentation approaches' entropy values are almost the same. In this case, entropy has less of an effect on distinction among these methods than CTR. From detailed observations, we discover that the entropy of PLSUS is larger than others. Considering attributes of PLSUS, the reason is understandable. PLSUS allows users to belong to multiple segments Given this, the entropy is naturally larger than those user segmentation approaches which only associate one user with one segment.

Precision, Recall and F-measure are shown in Table 5. Note that the results reported in this table

Table 3. CTR improvement of different user segmentation strategies

	5 segments in 120,000 data records	10 segments in 120,000 data records	10 segments in 150,000 data records	20 segments in 150,000 data records
PLSUS	**0.7876**	**1.3583**	**1.3036**	**2.6549**
CLUTO	0.6444	0.7399	0.7447	1.2076
k-Means	0.5440	0.7761	0.8616	1.0324

Table 4. Ads click Entropy of different user segmentation strategies

	5 segments in 120,000 data records	10 segments in 120,000 data records	10 segments in 150,000 data records	20 segments in 150,000 data records
PLSUS	0.1636	0.1780	0.1824	0.1735
CLUTO	**0.1506**	0.1586	**0.1531**	**0.1540**
k-Means	0.1532	**0.1515**	0.1575	0.1554

Table 5. F-measure of different user segmentation strategies

		5 segments in 120,000 data records	10 segments in 120,000 data records	10 segments in 150,000 data records	20 segments in 150,000 data records
	Precision	**0.9947%**	**1.0628%**	1.0954%	**1.2424%**
PLSUS	Recall	1.3116%	1.3080%	1.3221%	1.3407%
	F	**1.0503%**	**1.1071%**	**1.1414%**	**1.2567%**
	Precision	0.9271%	0.9634%	0.9546%	1.0019%
CLUTO	Recall	**1.3386%**	**1.3718%**	1.3824%	1.3979%
	F	0.9958%	1.0283%	1.0229%	1.0656%
	Precision	0.9196%	0.9197%	0.9663%	0.9833%
k-Means	Recall	1.3122%	1.3708%	**1.3930%**	**1.4083%**
	F	0.9870%	0.9945%	1.0346%	1.0520%

are the averages over all ads. From the table, we see that semantic approaches have better results in Precision. Since we choose CTR as the Precision metric, this result can be predicted by CTR improvement. Another interesting observation is the Recall of BOW clustering approaches is higher than others in our small datasets. On the contrary, semantic user segmentation can improve CTR without building user segments with too large a population. This characteristic is very useful for accurate ad delivery. Integrating Precision and Recall, the F-measure can also be used to evaluate the performance of user segmentation.

In the experiments we ran, high F-measure results of PLSUS showed that semantic user segmentation has better performance than BOW user segmentation.

FUTURE RESEARCH DIRECTIONS

Besides the challenges and solutions introduced in previous Sections, there are also lots of research challenges emerging for BT, with the quick development of the Internet. In this section, we mainly review the BT challenges from four different perspectives, which have not been addressed in previous sections of this Chapter. They are the scalability issues for behavioral targeting, privacy issues for behavioral targeting, user intent for behavioral targeting and impact of social networks on behavioral targeting. All these challenges could be good directions to explore in the future.

Scalability Issues for Behavioral Targeting

For most of the problems on the Web (search, advertising and, etc.), scalability is one of the major issues we have to face. It is particularly critical to behavioral targeting because of the huge space of users and their behavioral data. As reported in Chen, Pavlov, & Canny (2009), Yahoo! logged 9 terabytes of display ad data with about 500 billion entries on August, 2008, which is just a small piece of the whole picture, considering users' behaviors in algorithmic search, sponsored search, social networks and so on. Even more daunting is that with users' behaviors evolving, we have to re-calculate users' segment memberships and even re-train models on a regular basis. All these facts require the behavioral targeting system to be scalable. In Chen, Pavlov, & Canny (2009), the authors designed and implemented a highly scalable and efficient solution to BT using Hadoop MapReduce framework. With their proposed parallel algorithm and the resulting system, they can build models for 450 BT categories from the entire Yahoo user base within one day. In the future, smart approaches to preprocess user data to reduce the feature dimensions can be a promising direction to scale up. Also, efficient parallel algorithms, as studied in Chen, Pavlov, & Canny (2009) is another direction.

Privacy Issues in Behavioral Targeting

Behavioral Targeting on one side can greatly improve the relevance of advertisements presented to users; on the other hand, for this all to work, BT requires access to users' data. Whenever companies have to access users' data, either their self-reported or derived demographic information, search queries, page views, or even their public online behaviors, privacy becomes an issue. As shown in a survey conducted by TRUSTe and TNS, most consumers consider privacy important enough to take steps to protect it. Many individuals know their behavior is being targeted, and they're uncomfortable with being tracked, even with the assurance of anonymity (TRUSTe Survey, n.d). Therefore, solving the privacy problem is urgent for behavioral targeting. One direction is to give the user freedom to make decisions in this space. They can opt-in or opt-out of targeted ads. They can also decide which information to share, or which type of advertisements to receive. Another direction is to move the behavioral data from a central storage server to the user client side. With permission from users, all the computation happens on the client and only the processed information is passed to a server to retrieve proper ads.

Predicting User Behavior in the Future

As we mentioned, the goal of behavioral targeting is to provide the right information to the right user at the right time. Clearly, the right time does not mean that we can only show information to the user according to his/her current needs. Sometimes, presenting advertisements to the user based on future needs is more effective. For example, once we know a user is planning to buy a car, either we can predict this from the user's behaviors (such as she keeps submitting queries like "best SUV", "car dealers in Seattle" and so on), or the user simply tells the system about his needs. With this information, we can not only present advertisements about car dealers for car buyers, but also, we can present advertisements for future needs such as car insurance, car accessories to the end user. It is a precious opportunity for advertisers to be able to catch a user's intention and impress the user with the right message at the right time. Therefore, how to predict users' future needs and figure out the right time to show advertisements will be a challenging yet highly rewarding research direction for behavior targeting.

Targeting on Social Networks

Social networks are becoming very popular, attracting more and more ad spending. In total, marketers will spend $2.2 billion to advertise on social networks worldwide in 2009, with $1.2 billion in spending in the US (Williamson, 2009). Considering the characteristics of social networks, it provides unique advantages for behavioral targeting. First of all, people generate lots of personal behaviors over a social network. For example, people chat with friends through social networks, share their thoughts with friends and post their needs online and so on. All this data provides very good signals to infer the user's need, based on which we can present relevant advertisements. What is more, social networks connect users together. These connections can greatly help solve the data sparcity issue since we can infer a user's needs based on his/her neighbors'/friends' needs or interests. This area has a lot of potential to improve the effectiveness of behavioral targeting. Therefore, behavioral targeting based on social networks is definitely a hot and valuable research direction in the near future.

CONCLUSION

Behavioral Targeting (BT) attempts to deliver the most relevant advertisements to the most interested audiences, and is playing an increasingly important role in the online advertising market. In this chapter, we aim to give an overview of BT related problems with sample solutions. To motivate more BT related research work, we mainly discuss some novel technologies for BT

to address some fundamental BT challenges. For user representation, we highlight the user task based behavioral targeting. As to user segmentation, we introduce a recent proposed work for semantic user segmentation. Regarding user ad matching, we mainly introduce how to leverage the learning to rank approach for user/user segments ranking. We conclude with proposals for evaluation metrics for BT and point out additional research challenges in the area.

REFERENCES

AdLink. (n.d.). Retrieved from http://www.adlink.com/home.shtml.

AlmondNet. (n.d.). Retrieved from http://www.almondnet.com/

Baeza-Yates, R., & Ribeiro-Neto, B. (1999). *Modern Information Retrieval*. Addison Wesley.

BlueLithium. (n.d.). Retrieved from http://www.bluelithium.com/

Brants, T., Chen, F., & Tsochantaridis, I. (2002). Topic-based document segmentation with probabilistic latent semantic analysis. In *Proceedings of CIKM* (pp. 211-218). ACM Press.

Burst (n.d.). Retrieved from http://www.burst-media.com/

Cao, Y., Xu, J., Liu, T. Y., Li, H., Huang, H. Y., & Hon, H. (2006). Adapting ranking SVM to document retrieval. In *Proceedings of the 29th annual international ACM SIGIR conference on Research and development in information retrieval* (pp. 186-193). ACM Press.

Chen, Y., Pavlov, D., & Canny, J. F. (2009). Large-scale behavioral targeting. In *Proceedings of the 15th ACM SIGKDD international conference on Knowledge discovery and data mining* (pp. 209-218). ACM Press.

Davis, H. (2006). *Google advertising tools: cashing in with adsense, adwords, and the google APIs.* O'Reilly Media, Inc.

Deerwester, S., Dumais, S., Furnas, G., Landauer, T., & Hashman, R. (1990). Indexing by latent semantic analysis. *Journal of the American Society for Information Science American Society for Information Science, 41,* 391–407. doi:10.1002/(SICI)1097-4571(199009)41:6<391::AID-ASI1>3.0.CO;2-9

DoubleClick. (n.d.). Retrieved from http://www.doubleclick.com/

Garcia, E. (2006). *Cosine Similarity and Term Weight Tutorial.* Retrieved from http://www.miislita.com/information-retrieval-tutorial/cosine-similarity-tutorial.html

Google's AdSense. (n.d.). Retrieved from https://www.google.com/adsense/login/en_US/

Hallerman, D. (2008). *Behavioral targeting: marketing trends.* Retrieved from http://www.emarketer.com/Reports/All/Emarketer_2000487.aspx

Hofmann, T. (1999). Probabilistic latent semantic analysis. In *Proceedings of Uncertainty in Artificial Intelligence* (pp. 289-296).

Hölscher, C., & Strube, G. (2000). Web search behavior of internet experts and newbies. In *Proceedings of the 9th international World Wide Web conference on Computer networks: the international journal of computer and telecommunications networking* (pp. 337-346). ACM Press.

Hu, J., Zeng, H. J., Li, H., Niu, C., & Zheng, C. (2007). Demographic prediction based on user's browsing behavior. In *Proceedings of the 16th international conference on World Wide Web* (pp. 151-160). ACM Press.

Kanungo, T., Mount, D., Netanyahu, N., Piatko, C., Silverman, R., & Wu, A. (2000). An efficient K-means clustering algorithm: Analysis and implementation. *IEEE Transactions on Pattern Analysis and Machine Intelligence, 24*(7), 881–892. doi:10.1109/TPAMI.2002.1017616

Karypis, G. *CLUTO: A Software Package for Clustering High-Dimensional Data Sets.* University of Minnesota, Dept. of Computer Science.

Liu, N., Yan, J., Shen, D., Chen, D.P., Chen, Z. & Li, Y. (2010). Learning to Rank Audience for Behavioral Targeting. *To be published in Proceedings SIGIR10*, poster.

Liu, T. Y. (2009). Learning to Rank for Information Retrieval. *Foundations and Trends® in Information Retrieval, 3*(3), 225-331.

Manning, C. D., Raghavan, P., & Schütze, H. (2008). *Introduction to Information Retrieval.* Cambridge University Press.

NebuAd. (n.d.). Retrieved from http://www.nebuad.com/

Phillips, J. J. (Ed.). (2003). *Return on investment in training and performance improvement programs.* Butterworth-Heinemann.

Phorm (n.d.). Retrieved from http://www.phorm.com/

Revenue Science. (n.d.). Retrieved from http://www.revenuescience.com/advertisers/advertiser_solutions.asp

Robertson, S. E., Walker, S., & Hancock-Beaulieu, M. (1998). Okapi at TREC-7. In *Proceedings of the Seventh Text REtrieval Conference* (pp. 109-126).

Robertson, S. E., Walker, S., Jones, S., Hancock-Beaulieu, M., & Gatford, M. (1994). Okapi at TREC-3. In *Proceedings of the Third Text REtrieval Conference* (pp. 109-126).

SpecificMedia. (n.d.). Retrieved from http://www.specificmedia.com/

Tacoda (n.d.). Retrieved from http://advertising.aol.com/advertiser-solutions/targeting/behavioral-targeting

TRUSTe Survey. (n.d.). Retrieved from http://www.truste.com/pdf/TRUSTe_TNS_2009_BT_Study_Summary.pdf

White, R. W., & Morris, D. (2007). Investigating the querying and browsing behavior of advanced search engine users. In *Proceedings of the 30th Annual International ACM SIGIR Conference on Research and Development in Information Retrieval* (pp. 255-262). ACM Press.

Wikipedia (n.d.). Retrieved from http://en.wikipedia.org/wiki/Behavioral_Targeting

Williamson, D. A. (2009). *Social Network Ad Spending: 2010 Outlook*. Retrieved from http://www.emarketer.com/Reports/All/Emarketer_2000621.aspx

Wu, X. H., Yan, J., Liu, N., Yan, S. C., Chen, Y., & Zheng, C. (2009). Probabilistic latent semantic user segmentation for behavioral targeted advertising. In *Proceedings of the Third International Workshop on Data Mining and Audience Intelligence for Advertising* (pp. 10-17). ACM Press.

Yahoo Smartads. (n.d.). Retrieved from http://advertising.yahoo.com/smartads

Yan, J., Liu, N., Wang, G., Zhang, W., Jiang, Y., & Zheng, C. (2009). How much can behavioral targeting help online advertising? In *Processing of the 18th international conference on World Wide Web* (pp. 261–270). ACM Press. doi:10.1145/1526709.1526745

ENDNOTES

[1] http://www.dmoz.org/

[2] http://projects.yisongyue.com/svmmap/

Chapter 13
Distributed Technologies for Personalized Advertisement Delivery

Dorothea Tsatsou
Informatics and Telematics Institute, Greece

Symeon Papadopoulos
Informatics and Telematics Institute, Greece

Ioannis Kompatsiaris
Informatics and Telematics Institute, Greece

Paul C. Davis
Motorola Applied Research Center, USA

ABSTRACT

This chapter provides an overview on personalized advertisement delivery paradigms on the web with a focus on the recommendation of advertisements expressed in or accompanied by text. Different methods of online targeted advertising will be examined, while justifying the need for channeling the appropriate ads to the corresponding users. The aim of the work presented here is to illustrate how the semantic representation of ads and user preferences can achieve optimal and unobtrusive ad delivery. We propose a set of distributed technologies that efficiently handles the lack of textual data in ads by enriching ontological knowledge with statistical contextual data in order to classify ads and generic content under a uniform, machine-understandable vocabulary. This classification is used to construct lightweight semantic user profiles, matched with semantic ad descriptions via fuzzy semantic reasoning. A real world user study, as well as an evaluative exploration of framework alternatives validate the system's effectiveness to produce high quality ad recommendations.

DOI: 10.4018/978-1-60960-189-8.ch013

INTRODUCTION

The vast amount of services and products available on the web and channeled to consumers via online advertisements leads to an inevitable end-side overload problem, which can be alleviated by personalizing advertisement delivery for the consuming audience. Particularly on the web, tracing user preferences and channeling the appropriate ads to users can arguably improve the click-through rate (CTR) of advertisements, as well as the ads' impact to the user (ChoiceStream, 2008), (Wang et al 2002). However, given the scarcity and brevity of metadata and descriptions available in multimedia advertisements, a significant challenge for such approaches lies in the extraction and filtering of user preferences.

This chapter discusses such challenges in addition to related issues such as the possibility that the data in the advertisements may not directly match the data collected from the user, as a result of different vocabulary usage, and the potential latency and privacy issues posed by storing, handling and transmitting delicate user information. These issues are described in the context of personalized ad recommendation and a set of distributed technologies is proposed to address them.

The solution proposed herein presents techniques to combine semantic knowledge and statistical terminological information unobtrusively extracted from the content a user consumes in order to match and rank advertisements according to the interest score in the semantic profile of the user.

A typical usage scenario, portrayed in Figure 1, is as follows: the user consumes a content item (ad, article, annotated video, short text). The textual data of the item are unobtrusively analyzed in order to extract its semantic information, based on predefined domain knowledge. This information consists of a set of user preferences which are captured in the semantic user profile through

Figure 1. A graphic illustration of the usage scenario

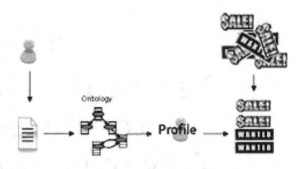

an automated process. User preferences are then matched semantically to a set of supplied ads in order to identify recommendation possibilities, i.e. whether to recommend an ad and to what degree of confidence is the ad useful to the user. The match confidence degree is used to rank recommended ads to achieve more accurate recommendations.

We present a user study on a real world dataset for the soccer domain which indicates the improvement of real world profile-based recommendations in comparison to simple contextual recommendations. In addition, we detail experimental results, evaluating profile convergence and the effectiveness of recommendations presented to different users for three alternatives of the proposed framework. share

The remainder of this chapter is structured as follows. In the next section the background of targeted recommendations is introduced. Following the background section, we next introduce a set of distributed technologies which comprise a framework for ad recommendation. After the presentation of the framework, we present a case study evaluating the performance of the framework for the soccer domain through a real world user study and a set of synthetic experiments. Finally, conclusions on the use of the proposed framework and future work directions are disclosed.

BACKGROUND

This section provides an overview on existing targeted advertising strategies, commencing from simple query and context matching and spanning to the more sophisticated techniques for personalized advertising. Specific reference is made to the value of the use of semantics in recommender systems. The scope of this literature review is to demonstrate the significance of personalized ad recommendation as valued in the prior art while delineating the advantages and disadvantages of the most common personalization strategies. Those strengths and weaknesses have provided the work presented in this paper with the motivation to consider a hybrid approach where a set of interesting features of these strategies are combined in order to overcome their individual limitations. Finally, we introduce an outline of the paradigms used in the literature to assess the effectiveness of an advertising scheme.

Targeted Advertising

Online targeted advertising refers to the delivery of suitable advertisements to the consuming audience by filtering available ads based on either data-driven recommendations, or on user intelligence (otherwise referred to as personalized advertising). Personalized advertising can be based on explicit information about the user (demographic, sex, age, etc.) or on their online behavior. Known personalized recommendation approaches focus on deriving recommendations via inference based on a finite set of user information (rule-based), from users' online content consumption (content-based), the collective behavior of similar users (collaborative), or making inferences based on some kind of underlying domain knowledge (knowledge-based) (Pazzani & Billsus, 2007), (Burke, 2007).

Queries, Bids and Context

Chakrabarti et al (2008) defines two channels of data-driven targeted advertising. Sponsored search (*SS*), taking place in search engines, where sponsored advertisements are matched to a user query and contextual advertising (*CM*) where ads are matched to the web pages' content. Google's AdWords[1] and AdSense[2] are of the most typical examples in data-driven advertising. AdWords targets the advertiser and focuses on defining ad keywords while AdSense provides the framework to utilize AdWords to create contextual matches between ads and web content (Mehta et al, 2007). Yahoo!'s Content Match[3] is another such market paradigm.

Abrams et al. (2007) present a linear algorithm in which query frequency forecasts, advertiser bids and budgets are factored to optimize advertisers' revenues by increasing the click-through probability of a sponsored ad. Feng et al (2007) compare the performance of four sponsored ad slot allocation mechanisms, including the ones used by Google and Overture, aiming to explore the most efficient allocation mechanism with respect to the ad's bidder price and query relevance.

The maximization of ad impact when combined with the context within which the ad is presented has early on been recognized (Wang, 2002). In Anagnostopoulos et al. (2007), contextual advertising is defined as correlation of four factors: the *publisher*'s intention to boost revenue and user experience, the *advertiser*'s marketing campaign requirements, the mediation of an *ad network*, and most importantly the *user*'s response to an ad. Contextualization of ad delivery raises the matter of swift and efficient (Wang et al, 2002) text analysis for on-the-fly ad filtering. Such mechanisms will be further analyzed in the following subsections.

However straightforward and unobtrusive might the contextual matching of ads to content be, the market has quickly realized that efficient advertising relies on delivering "the right message to the right customer at the right time" (Ha, 2004). Prime advertisement publishers such as Google, Yahoo and Microsoft aim in optimizing user experience by delivery of personalized advertisements (Diaz Redondo et al, 2009). Personalizing ad delivery is another form of recommending items to a user and apart of the special textual analysis required, the paradigm follows the strategies of recommender systems (Burke, 2007) (Adomavicius & Tuzhilin, 2005).

Personalized Strategies

The most straightforward way of personalizing advertisement delivery is via explicit information that a user might provide upon registration to a web site/service (Srivastava et al, 2000). Such information would include age, sex, location, work details and other demographic specification or an explicit list of preferences. However, most users are reluctant to disclose personal information on the web, in fear of privacy abuse (Bae et al 2003), (Kobsa 2001). Therefore ad delivery personalization is oriented towards mining user preferences without expecting them to be explicitly expressed (Mulvenna et al, 2000).

Content-based recommendation takes into account features of the available content in combination with the history of a user's transactions with these features (Pazzani & Billsus, 2007). The "Stuff I've seen" system (Dumais et al, 2003) introduced a method for indexing the content seen by a user via linguistic analysis of visited text. The index was used to provide easier access to information already seen by the user and to provide rich contextual information on web searches. Chu & Park (2009) produce predictive bilinear regression models with respect to profiles of content items including updatable features such as freshness and popularity and to user profiles that encompass interaction history with Yahoo! properties. Abrams & Vee (2007) present a novel feature to

take into account on contextual personalization of ads: the *ad fatigue* factor, which refers to the repetition of recommended ads in frequently visited web pages, such as a user's home page. The authors have put forward an approximation tableau algorithm in order to incorporate the ad fatigue factor to the available ad features for an individual user.

Collaborative ad recommendation strategies focus on determining synergy between particular user groups, based on the content ratings or collective user behavior over the delivered items (i.e. ad clicks). The AdROSA system (Kazienko & Adamski, 2007) clusters aggregated user sessions in order to establish user patterns from their navigational behavior. It also clusters ad click-through sessions in order to establish ad visiting patterns. Yang et al. (2006) make use of the connections of users in social networks to determine strong ties between actors and targets ads that have high appearance scores in transaction history of tightly related actors. Ha (2004) implements a self-organizing map (SOM) in web server logs to create ad hoc fuzzy rules for each user cluster, while another *SOM* is used to cluster ads in groups with similar features. The Hamming and the Euclidean distance measures between the clusters are employed in order to result in suitable ad segments for each target user.

It is a fact that the performance of content-based and collaborative based methods in recommender systems depend highly on the existence of an adequate transaction history set for a user of a group of users and on the transaction information for available ads (Burke, 2007). Knowledge-based recommendation techniques aim to leverage the cold-start problem (Middleton et al, 2004) in recommender systems when new items are inserted in the recommendation pool or new users are introduced to the recommendation system. Broder et al. (2007) combine both the semantics (by means of a large taxonomy) and the syntax (bag of words) of advertisements and web pages to define an optimal advertisement-content matching strategy. Sheth et al. (2001) propose a semantic based method that captures and enhances domain or subject specific metadata of digital media content, including the specific meaning and intended use of original content. To support semantics, a World Model is provided that includes specific domain knowledge, ontologies, as well as a set of rules, relevant to the original content. They examine users' queries and try to infer user preferences by gathering data about users' browsing and viewing habits, including sites visited, the time devoted to each site, whether any ad has led to a purchase, etc.

Our proposal is a hybrid approach which combines content feature extraction and expansion with ontological knowledge, essentially encapsulating the advantages of unobtrusive user interest captured in the content-based paradigms with the universal domain information and structure that the knowledge-based paradigms provide. In this manner, high quality ad recommendations can be achieved even for new ads and new users for whom no data are initially available (Sieg et al, 2007).

Text Analysis for Contextual Advertising

A number of techniques have been proposed for the matching of content items (web pages with textual content) with a large pool of textual advertisements. The research community has introduced several approaches trying to deal effectively with the challenges arising from this task. The first work addressing the problem of vocabulary impedance between advertisement and content items was presented by Ribeiro-Neto et al. (2005). The authors describe a set of techniques meant to couple the vocabulary impedance between content and ad items, based on a vocabulary expansion methodology. This involves the exploitation of the vocabulary existing in the landing page an advertisement leads to and the use of a large Bayesian network trained with a significant amount of text corpora as another source of vocabulary enrich-

ment. Further, Lacerda et al. (2006) employ a genetic programming (GP) method to associate web pages with advertisements. The proposed method aims at optimizing a fitness function by means of GP so that the most relevant advertisements end up in the top positions of the consumed web pages. Murdock et al. (2007) tackle the vocabulary impedance problem by means of machine learning technologies originating from the field of machine translation. In our previous work (Papadopoulos et al, 2004a), we employed lexical graphs to improve the effectiveness of the contextual advertising method by mitigating the vocabulary impedance problem.

Another interesting group of contextual advertising systems attempt to tackle the problem of content-ad matching by use of sophisticated text feature selection mechanisms. Yih et al (2008) propose a system that applies several feature selection techniques to extract keywords from web pages for advertising purposes. Li et al. (2007) employ sequential pattern mining in text streams in order to aid the advertising keyword extraction process. Sarmento et al. (2009) mine an ad database to identify local keyword synonyms which are used in an online ad keyword suggestion scheme used for ad targeting. Finally, Yih & Meek (2008) evaluate the effectiveness of several phrase-document similarity measures for ad-web page matching.

Several ad recommendation methods rely on sophisticated text mining and machine learning methods for producing ad placements. A method that uses mixtures of statistical language models to select content-relevant advertisements for personal blog pages is presented by Mishne et al (2006). Shaparenko et al. (2009) make use of word-pair indicator features within a maximum-entropy ranking model to predict the clicks that the recommended ads will attract.

Other text analysis methods focus on the sentiment orientation of web pages in order to recommend appropriate advertising content or prevent inappropriate ad content for being displayed together with the web page. Zhang et al (2008) explore sub-document classification for contextual ad placement, where the desired content appears only in a small part of a multi-topic web document by use of training sub-document classifiers based on page-level labels. The work of Fan & Chang (2009) incorporates a sentiment detection mechanism to prevent the use of ad recommendation for content that contains phrases of negative sentiment, resulting in improved ad relevance scores.

As inferred from the work presented above, two main issues arise in textual analysis for advertising. The difference in vocabularies used between ads and content and the lack of sufficient textual descriptions and metadata in ads to provide meaningful interpretations of the ads. These issues have motivated us to explore a novel approach to extract semantic metadata from text-expressed content and express them in a uniform vocabulary. Our approach uses domain reference ontologies to semantically define the extracted textual information from consumed content and ads. The semantic classification involves a novel combination of linguistic analysis through the use of lexical graphs.

The Use of Semantics for Personalized Recommendation

While the usage of semantics is loosely interpreted in literature as the retrieval of meaningful relationships between content features or user attributes (Zadeh & Moshkenani 2008), this subsection refers to paradigms that employ predefined functional (ontological) knowledge as background base for inferring recommendations or for building structured (semantic) user and content descriptions in the context of knowledge-based recommendations.

Machine learning techniques have been applied in several recommender systems in order to create semantic representations of user profiles, based on underlying semantic knowledge. Song

et al (2005) use a Support Vector Machine (SVM) classifier to map a document's (user transaction) feature space to the vector space of an ontological user profile. These profiles are then used to filter and rank search results of a query from various search engines, again using an SVM mechanism. Similarly, the QuickStep and FoxTrot recommendation systems also (Middleton et al, 2004) employ machine learning techniques to classify research papers to ontological concepts and update user profiles based on transaction history, with the introduction of a time decay factor. The ontological formulation of the profile allows the systems for bootstrapping the recommender to external ontologies.

Kearney et al. (2005) introduce an "impact" factor to measure the influence of ontology concepts to a user based on his/her online transactions. The influential concepts are propagated in an ontology-based user profile and their impact values are used to cluster profiles of similar users in order to trace user behavioral patterns.

In (Trajkova & Gauch, 2004) and (Sieg et al, 2007), spreading activation algorithm variants are employed in order to activate and assess the impact of user preferences, in ontology-*based* user profiles rather than fully semantic user profiles. The population techniques in this chapter adopt the methodology proposed by Trajkova & Gauch (2004) and Sieg et al (2007), where concept vectors are constructed for each ontology concept by indexing a training set of web pages in order to classify an ontological user profile. In these approaches, the user profile is a bag-of-words that are mapped to the ontology, implying a taxonomy-based profile. There is no accounting for relations between terms.

In addition to the structured and finite amount of processing data that the use of ontological knowledge brings to the recommendation process, another major benefit is that it enables the assembly of semantically identical text, expressed in a variety of terms, under a common, machine-understandable vocabulary. Cantador et al (2008), employ advanced lexical filtering to create a common, machine-understandable vocabulary of social tags and then match them to semantic concepts based on domain ontologies, by means of grounding tags based on Wikipedia[4] and the Wordnet lexicon (Miller, 1995). Their filtering approach directly instantiates content items and requires intensive term pre-processing, by lexically filtering concept names, yet it abstains from including other contextual information relevant to a concept.

The aforementioned techniques place the load directly on the server and apply to simple hierarchical structures of underlying semantic knowledge rather than taking advantage of the additional inference possibilities offered by formal semantics (Cann, 1993) in ontologies, possibly due to performance limitations. However, advanced inference capabilities through the use of reasoning over formal semantics have been explored by Kleeman & Sinner (2005), with acceptable performance. This makes profile matchmaking possible on the end-device, even for resource-constraint devices, which can alleviate server load or even eliminate the need to transact with the server whatsoever, thus addressing a major user concern when using personalized services, the interception of private data. Our approach extends the Kleeman & Sinner (2005) technique to fuzziness, enabling us to handle fuzzy annotation and user preference weights.

Internet Advertising Evaluation

The typical research paradigm adopted when attempting to investigate the effectiveness of some advertising scheme involves a forced exposure to some advertising message followed by some measure of consumer response (Pavlou & Stewart, 2000). The assumption behind this paradigm is that advertising has a direct effect to consumers and therefore advertising is considered as the independent variable, while consumer response to advertising is the dependent variable.

Since the inception of internet advertising, a series of operational measures were employed to quantify the effectiveness of advertising campaigns. Common operational measures range from the simplistic number of impressions or exposures (number of times an ad was displayed to users) to the widely established Click-Through Rate (CTR, ratio of the number of click-throughs to the number of impressions). CTR has been considered as the predominant way to measure the performance of online ads. However, there has been a steady decline in the reported CTR levels through the last years; the declined CTR figures (reported to be <0.5%) have been mainly attributed to the fact that online users avoid looking at the ad items during browsing (Drèze & Hussherr, 2003).

A more sophisticated measure of online ad effectiveness is the number of post-impressions, i.e. the number of visits to a website, after exposure to an internet advertisement, without clicking through the advertisement (Rettie et al, 2004). This measure captures both the direct performance of the ad message and the subliminal effects that this message may have on the online user. However, post-impressions are hard to track and miss some aspects of advertising effectiveness, for example the attitudes of users towards the advertised brand.

For the aforementioned reasons (viz. declining CTR and difficulty in tracking post-impressions), traditional memory-based measures of advertising effectiveness have been revived in the context of internet advertising (Papadopoulos, 2009). Such measures reflect the attitudinal response of online users to the ads displayed to them. Unaided and aided recall, brand recognition (Drèze & Hussherr, 2003), purchase intention, as well as purchase consideration sets (Zhang et al, 2008) are suitable measures for quantifying the effect of online ads to the user, assuming that some unconscious ad processing takes place during the pre-attentive webpage viewing (Shapiro et al, 1997). Yoo (2008) differentiates between explicit and implicit memory and notes the different measures that are suitable to quantify the effects of web advertising on them: recall and recognition tests measure the extent to which web advertising affects the explicit memory of consumers, while priming studies quantify the implicit memory effects of advertising.

A FRAMEWORK FOR PERSONALIZED AD RECOMMENDATION

As described earlier, we explored the possibilities of addressing different issues in advertisement recommendation by combining the capabilities of different targeted advertising techniques in order to alleviate their limitations. This exploration led to a framework of distributed technologies that can provide optimal ranked recommendations employing semantic inference to unstructured textual data based on user online behavior. The recommender system proposed herein is comprised by techniques that can be used as standalone strategies for semantic content classification, user profiling and semantic reasoning.

The technologies developed within this framework are an extension of our work presented in (Tsatsou et al, 2009) and dwell on the problem of recognizing and efficiently representing the meaning of multimedia advertisements based on the brief textual metadata available. To achieve this, semantics are extracted from each ad or consumed online content item based on predisposed ontological knowledge, i.e. by mapping textual descriptions to ontological concepts and axioms defined in available domain ontologies.

In order to efficiently address the issues of vocabulary variety and scarcity in textual descriptions, we propose enriching domain ontologies with statistical contextual information on domain knowledge, encompassed in pre-trained lexical graphs (Papadopoulos et al, 2009a). We employ the expanded textual information of the ontology to map user-consumed content and advertisements to ontology concepts and use this classification

to learn ontological user profiles. We then use the ontological mappings to produce semantic annotation for the advertisements, expressed in lightweight structures of manageable knowledge. Finally, we make use of reasoning services to match advertisements to semantic user profiles (Kleeman & Sinner, 2005), while handling classification uncertainty via fuzzy annotation and preference weights (Straccia, 2005), to rank proposed ads and produce high quality, personalized recommendations.

In essence, the framework analyzed in this chapter focuses on:

- Unobtrusively extracting semantic information from the textual metadata of multimedia advertisements (description, keywords, tags) and of the online content consumed by the user (ad, news, article, social content).
- Representing this metadata in a uniform vocabulary expressed in ontological concepts and axioms.
- Using the semantic information to construct and update user profiles, as well as to annotate advertisements.
- Employing semantic reasoning services to match the semantic description of the advertisements against the ontological user profiles while taking into account the uncertainty in metadata classification and using it to rank the recommended advertisements
- Using lightweight knowledge structures and efficient reasoning services that would enable us to manage knowledge and make meaningful inferences even in limited resource devices in order to reduce server load, secure user privacy and insure security safeguarding.

The effectiveness of this system depends on advanced textual analysis used to terminologically enrich the semantic knowledge. We extend our

Figure 2. Overview of the ad recommendation system

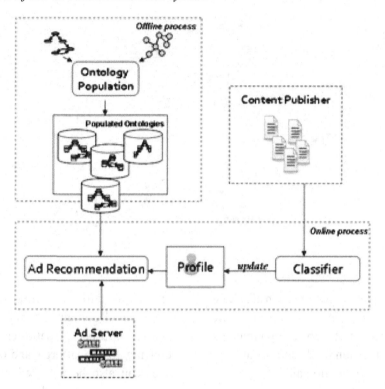

previous work in (Papadopoulos et al, 2009a), where graphs carrying semantic information, such as term frequency and co-occurrence, were employed for content-based recommendation in order to mitigate the vocabulary impedance problem. The expanded linguistic information in lexical graphs prompted the idea to use this kind of information in order to extract semantics from text and produce a robust semantic classifier, as first described in (Tsatsou et al, 2009). Furthermore, using a lightweight knowledge representation and performing the semantic analysis and recommendation in a compact and efficient manner enables us to integrate the technology developed on the end-device, even in resource-constrained devices such as handsets and set top boxes. This approach therefore allows for agile and adaptable deployments which can both satisfy publisher needs to limit server loads and user needs for privacy and security. Figure 2 depicts a simplified overview of the proposed ad recommendation framework.

In extension of the work introduced in (Tsatsou et al, 2009), two alternatives of the framework are examined and presented along with a more detailed description of the original framework.

To the best of our knowledge, this is the first end-to-end framework that can successfully address the scarcity of textual metadata of short texts (i.e. advertisements) by enriching the ontological knowledge in a domain of discourse with expanded lexical data and using them to semantically interpret the consumed text. The transformation of unstructured textual data to formal semantics allows for the inference possibilities and accuracy of semantic reasoning in the final recommendations.

ONTOLOGY POPULATION WITH LEXICAL GRAPHS

Populating an ontology with statistical contextual information is performed in an offline training

Figure 3. Extract of an example soccer ontology

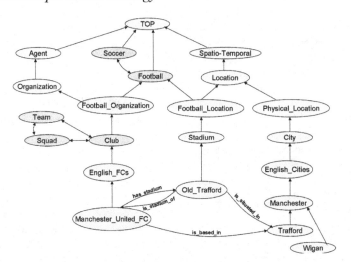

process which involves the construction of at least one lexical graph per topic, based on linguistic analysis over a large set of web corpora relevant to the domain in question, and requires at least one reference ontology per domain.

Ontological Knowledge Modeling

As mentioned earlier, the use of reference ontologies in a personalized recommendation environment presents two advantages: (1) a uniform vocabulary illustrating the semantics of the domain and (2) base knowledge which allows for inferences for new users about whom the system has no data.

The expressivity of the ontologies supported by our system rests within the DLP (Description Logic Programs) fragment as defined in (Grosof et al, 2003). The system can work with any Description Logics (DL) model expressed within this fragment. Figure 3 illustrates a portion of an example ontology for the soccer domain.

The approach does not require extensive ontologies or mapping every detail of the domain. For recommendation purposes, it suffices to identify the domain for the specific recommendation problem and model (or reproduce from existing ontologies) the basic information. Each ontol-

ogy represents a semantic model over fundamental domain information, including its commercial aspects. Spatio-temporal information referring to the offered and/or demanded services can also be modeled with an interest in supporting location and time-aware services.

An ontology O consists of a set of concepts C and roles R and includes axioms that comprise semantic rules by right of the ontology's expressivity. Run-time ontological knowledge in the system follows a variant of Description Logic Knowledge Representation System Specification (KRSS) syntax (Schneider & Swartout, 1993), in order to avoid unnecessary overhead imposed by parsing ontologies and metadata in RDF or OWL. We perform a one-time ontology translation from rdf/xml to KRSS on the server.

Lexical Graph Creation

The lexical graph creation and update process follows the principles in (Papadopoulos et al, 2009a), where the graphs used within our system have the form of a network of connected words (terms) and are progressively built up through processing textual content found on the web. The basic elements of the graph model, denoted by G, are the set of nodes (or vertices) V and the

Figure 4. Extract from the soccer topic graph

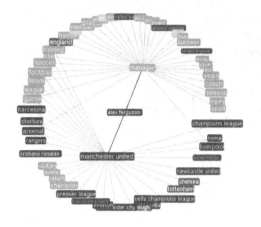

set of edges E, connecting pairs of nodes, which in short can be written as $G \equiv \{V,E\}$. Each node $t_k \in V$ in the graph is thus connected to a set of related nodes $N(t_k) = \{t_1, t_2, ..., t_n\} \subseteq V$, that comprise the term's neighborhood on the graph.

After training the graph from a web-collected training corpus, a set of tokens is derived. Each token, referred to as *lemma*, consists of the graph node, endowed with attributes such as the lemma's part-of-speech (POS) tag, and statistical information such as its term frequency (*tf*), document frequency (*df*) and node degree (*deg*) – i.e. the number of neighbors. The edges of the graph carry the degree denoting the co-occurrence (*cooc*) between a pair of terms in the same sentence. This statistical information is valuable in pruning the graph to eliminate linguistic noise, but also in the population of the ontology and consequently the classification process described further on. A graphic illustration of a graph node and its related terms is portrayed in Figure 4.

Populating the Ontology

The topic graphs serve as enriched dictionaries for each domain and enable us to define contextual relations between the concepts and the terms in the domain. These relations are used to classify text to ontology concepts. Hence, each concept C is terminologically classified to a lemma

in the graph with the *same string* classification method, thus $C \rightarrow V$, and can then be expressed as a vector $\vec{c} = \left\langle t_1 \cdot w_1, t_2 \cdot w_2, ..., t_n \cdot w_n \right\rangle$ of weighted terms, where each term $t_i \in V$ is adjacent to C in the graph and each weight $w_i \in E$ represents the *cooc* of the terms in the neighborhood of C.

Variations Detection

Matching absolute strings to graph nodes leads to loss of valuable information, dispersed in the variations and synonyms of terms represented by different lemmas in the graph. Therefore, we employ a series of advanced linguistic analyses to detect and bring together information on identical data. These techniques are described in the following.

Singular-Plural Inflection. This mechanism involves inflecting the respective grammatical form of a noun or adjective to similar lemmas in the graph, with respect to the particular form of the term in the ontology.

WordNet-based Synonym Detection. This mechanism attempts to identify and merge neighborhoods of semantically identical nouns in the graph. For that purpose, we retrieve all WordNet senses of a concept and then determine a set of components for each. The set of components is comprised by all the terms in the gloss and hyponyms of the given sense. The concept sense is identified based on a list of prominent domain terms which is compared against all the lists of components for each sense. Once the appropriate sense is determined, all synonyms of the reference concept term are retrieved and classified as variations of that term. The initial concept vector is updated with the terms in the neighborhoods of all the synonyms retrieved in the graph.

Wikipedia Named Entities Normalization (NEN). Similarly, we try to group the neighborhoods of all variations of a named entity in the ontology under a single reference name and is illustrated in Figure 5. We accept the Wikipedia

Figure 5. A graphic illustration of the NE variations detection algorithm

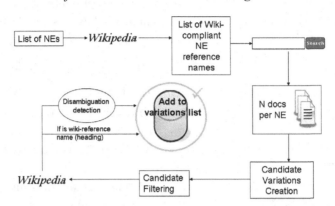

representation of a NE as the reference name for that entity. For example, the terms "Man Utd" and "MUFC" are variations of the English soccer team Manchester United FC. If some or all of these terms are present in the graph, each node representing one of these variations that semantically embody the same entity will be connected to a separate neighborhood of terms. It is essential however that all these variations are merged under a common neighborhood in order to achieve richer and more consistent concept vectors.

To collect all variations for a single NE we begin by assuming that all NEs in the ontology are expressed in or can be converted to a formal reference name retrieved from Wikipedia. Next, a token list (from now referred to as variation candidates) is extracted from a set of texts relevant to the NE. These texts comprise the top N results returned based on querying the reference name to a search engine. The variation candidates are then subjected to further filtering in order to discard linguistically incompatible terms. The heuristic filter used compares the order of letters in the retrieved candidates against the order of letters in the wiki-reference name. For example, the token "MUFC" contains the letters m,u,f and c in the same order as the reference name "Manchester United FC" and is therefore accepted, while "Featured Comic Strips" contains letters found

in the reference name but in the wrong order and is therefore rejected.

Remaining candidates are then queried to Wikipedia. A candidate is finally accepted as a valid variation of the concept only if the query redirects to (a) a page whose header is the original reference name, or (b) a Wikipedia disambiguation page that contains a hyperlink to the original reference name in its body text.

Concept Vector Formulation

After bringing together the variations of semantically identical graph terms, we form a concept vector for each ontology concept which contains the terms that are most relevant to the concept on the lexical graph. Terms which are not as common among different concepts are more likely to be useful for distinguishing individual concepts from each other. So, a lower degree threshold is employed to dispense with the most common terms of the topic, depicted in formula (1). Terms whose degree is higher than this threshold are not reclaimed as part of the concept's relative terms.

$$L \deg_G = avg(\deg_{t \in V}) + 3 \cdot stdDeviation(\deg_{t \in V})$$
(1)

where $L\deg_G$ depicts the lower deg threshold, $avg(\deg_{r \in V})$ depicts the average deg of all terms in the graph and stdDeviation($\deg_{r\in V}$) depicts the standard deviation of the degrees of all terms in the graph.

All terms in the concept vector are assigned a unique weight $w(n_j)\in[0,1]$, n being a term in the vector, representing the confidence degree with which the term describes the concept. All NE variations are assigned with the maximum degree, i.e. 1, of participation to the concept. All synonyms of a noun or adjective are assigned 0.9, to allow some uncertainty with respect to the sense of the particular synonym.

In this volume we examine three different methods of determining the relation between graph terms where different weighting schemes from the relative terms apply.

Immediate Neighborhood Selection (IN). All graph nodes representing variations (or the reference name) of a concept C are assembled in a single vector $\vec{c}$, along with the terms in their joint neighborhood. To avoid circumstantial co-occurrence between two terms, terms whose co-occurrence frequency is lower than the average neighborhood co-occurrence frequency of the examined concept's neighborhood are discarded.

All neighborhood terms are assigned with the normalized co-occurrence frequency of the neighboring term with the concept's name variation term. The normalized weight is calculated based on formula (2). If a term appears in the neighborhood of two or more variations, the maximum of the normalized term degrees is retained.

$$w(n_i) = \frac{co - occurrence(t, n_i)}{tf(t)} \quad (2)$$

Where n is adjacent to the root lemma t, *co-occurrence(t, n)* is the co-occurrence frequency between t and n, and $tf(t)$ is the tf of the root lemma t.

Expanded Neighborhood Selection (EN). We extend the previous approach by spreading our selection to the neighborhoods of the neighbors

of the root term (2-hop neighborhood), with an interest in examining the impact of extended graph relations in the recommendation process. All graph nodes representing variations (or the reference name) of a concept C are assembled in a single vector $\vec{c}$, along with the terms in their joint neighborhood, as well as the terms in respective (joint) neighborhoods of the immediate neighbours (neighbors of neighbors or second hop neighbors). The same cooccurrence filter as before is applied every time we traverse each respective neighborhood.

The weighting scheme follows the paradigm in formula (2) for the immediate neighborhood while the weight of the second hop neighbors is analogous to the weight of their parent neighbor and is inflicted with a penalty value that diminishes the relation of the second hop neighbor to the root term, as depicted in (3)

$$w(n_m) = w(n_i) \cdot \frac{co - occurrence\left(n_i, n_m\right)}{tf(n_i)} \cdot a$$

$$(3)$$

where n_m is adjacent to the immediate neighbor n_i, *co-occurrence(n)* is the co-occurrence frequency between n_i, n_m and $tf(n)$ is the tf of the immediate neighbor n_i, and a is the penalty value, which for the purpose of our experiments was empirically set to 0.7.

Although we are restricted to spreading to just one step off the immediate neighborhood of the root term for the purpose of the current experiment, the method can be extended to further spreading along the graph by propagating the weighting scheme in (3) while increasing the penalty.

Community Detection (CD). In general, the problem of community detection has been defined on generic graphs as the problem of identifying sets of nodes on the graphs that are more densely connected to each other than to the rest of the graph (Newman, 2003). There is an abundance of methods for detecting communities in complex networks. In our proposed personalized ad recommendation framework, we make use of a variant of the method used in (Papadopoulos et al, 2009b) for identifying communities of tags used in folksonomies. The method was shown to produce sets of tags that are semantically related to each other; for that reason, it was considered appropriate for deriving the concept vectors used in our framework.

More specifically, all graph nodes representing variations (or the reference name) of a concept C are assembled in a single vector $\vec{c}$, along with the terms in their graph community. The weighting scheme of the terms in the community of the root term u is depicted in (4)

$$S(u_1, u_2) = \frac{|N(u_1) \cap N(u_2)|}{\sqrt{|N(u_1)| \cdot |N(u_2)|}} \qquad (4)$$

Where $N(u)$ is the set of common neighbours, defined as $N(u) = \{v \mid (u,v) \in E\}$, u_1 is the root term and u_2 its neighbor. When extending the community detection one step further in the graph, the scheme that determines the relevance of the second hop neighbors is defined as $S(u_1, u_2, u_3) = S(u_1, u_2) \cdot S(u_2, u_3)$.

Mapping Text to Concepts

The pre-trained concept vectors are used to classify ads and user consumed content to ontology concepts. A vector of terms is retained for each individual content item or advertisement. Each term is assigned a *tf* value analogous to its appearance to the text, which represents the participation weight of that term to the content item or ad.

The classification process is based on a look-up scheme, where concept mappings for the extracted text terms are retrieved, i.e. each extracted term is looked up in an inverted index scheme in all the concept vectors. The weight w_i of the term t_i in the concept vector and its *tf* in the

text determine the weight of participation $w_i' = w_i *$ *tf* of the concept c_i to the content. If the same concept emerges more than once in a single content item, the concluding weight acquired is the maximum from all occurrences of the concept in the content. After all concept vectors are examined, the set of retrieved concepts and their standing weights constitute the classification set $\{c_1 \cdot w_1', c_2 \cdot w_2', ..., c_n \cdot w_n'\}$ for the particular content item or ad.

Automatic Advertisement Annotation

Raw ads that are available in an ad pool of some remote server can be annotated semantically by the aforementioned process in a pre-processing step on the server or online upon server communication by the following process. Each concept retrieved in the classification step is instantiated automatically with a unique ground value. Then the relations quantifying each concept are assigned with connecting ground values. These ground sentences will constitute the annotation set for the ad. In general, semantic annotation of the ads is automatically generated in the form of instances for every concept involved in the ad. For each concept in the ad, a unique instance of the concept will be automatically generated, i.e. $\langle atom_i : c_i \rangle, c_i \in C$, while following a reasoner-induced semantic processing, a property might be generated relating a unique atom and the atom of the instance of the concept quantified by that property, i.e. $\langle atom_j, atom_i : r_j \rangle, r_j \in R$.

Semantic User Profile Creation

User transactions with web content are tracked through a transaction listener. Refraining from exploring the non-trivial issue of tracking disinterests, we consider as positive transactions, hence interests, viewed content items and clicked advertisements. Upon consumption, the textual content is classified and the emerging concepts are added to the user profile, along with their classification weight. In addition, the profile adapts to fluctuating user interests, so new concepts are incrementally appended, and/or eliminated, or are weight-modified. The user profile stores all positive (or negative) profile concepts, indicating implicit preferences. A semantic rule is created and updated per user expressed as $\bigcup_n \exists hasInterest.Interest_{i\in n} \subseteq \Pr ofile$, where $\bigcup_n$ denotes the disjunction of all preferences n in the user's profile. In a system that disinterests would be traceable, a similar rule would be created to express that every disinterest should not be a part of the profile, expressed analogously as $\bigcup_n \exists hasInterest.Di\sin terest_{i\in n} \subseteq \neg \Pr ofile$. The system can also support explicit preferences, such as user defined requirements or induced spatio-temporal information. The set of explicit preferences is presented as an intersection in the profile, as they represent more strict associations between the concepts, thus producing a semantic role of the form

$$\bigcup_n \exists hasInterest.II_{i\in n} \cap \bigcap_m \exists hasInterest.EI_{j\in m} \subseteq \Pr ofile,$$

where II_i denotes an implicit interest of all implicit interests n and EI_j denotes an explicit interest of all explicit interests m. Concepts are existentially quantified with general descriptor properties of the ontology (where applicable) based on the given property's range, forming complex concepts of the type $\exists \Pr operty_j.Concept_i$. Properties considered as general descriptors are the ontology roles that are not assigned to a specific sub-domain.

Profile concepts might consist not only of individual concepts, but also of persistent combinations of concepts that represent occurrences of atomic concepts with strong correlation. Each concept combination is expressed as a conjunction of the individual correlating concepts in the user profile, such as $\bigcap_k IndividualConcept_{h\in k}$. The combinations for each set of classified concepts

are produced for every set of terms in a consumed item based on formula (3).

$$c_{total} = \sum_{i=1}^{N} c_i^N = \sum_{i=1}^{N} \frac{N!}{i!(N-i)!} \qquad (3)$$

Where N is the number of individual concepts participating in the combination and C_{total} is the sum of all combinations $C_{n,i}$, where i=1,N. Empirical results have demonstrated that N=3 is sufficient to adequately represent plausible persistent combinations.

Profile concepts are updated upon user transaction. The weights of the profile concepts are also decayed by a temporal factor, in the interest of distinguishing long and short term preferences over time. Updating the concept weight due to time decay can take place either upon use of the system or be conducted periodically in predetermined time intervals. The weight of a concept, incorporating the time decay factor, is expressed based on formula (4).

$$w = a \cdot f \cdot e^{-\frac{t-t_{last}}{\lambda}} \qquad (4)$$

where α is the last recorded normalized weight of the profile concept, f is the concept's frequency of appearance in the profile, t is the current timestamp, t_{last} is the timestamp of the last transaction for this profile concept and λ is the mean concept life (in milliseconds). This weight is then normalized in [0,1] with respect to the user's transaction total.

It is possible that the user profile will grow too large, so a scheme is devised to prune the profile concepts when the total number of concepts exceeds a certain count threshold. This threshold might be defined heuristically with regard to the storage capacities of the end-device or be predefined for any use case. The pruning mechanism will remove the lowest-weighted profile concepts below that threshold.

Matchmaking

A semantic reasoning service is employed to match complex semantic user profiles to extracted content annotation. The devised reasoner is an extension of the Pocket KRHyper (Kleeman & Sinner, 2005) mobile reasoner, which allows the recommendation to take place either on the server or on the end-device seamlessly and effectively, while providing slim and meaningful results. The reasoner, called *f-PocketKRHyper[5]*, extends the previous implementation to fuzziness, thus supporting management of annotation and user preferences' uncertainty. The reasoner handles the uncertainty posed by both the annotation degree and the user preference weights, based on Zadeh's fuzzy sets theory (Zadeh et al, 1996) and Straccia's concept weight modifiers (Straccia, 2005) respectively.

Consequently, by appending user implicit information, formulated with formal semantics, in given a domain ontology, *f-PocketKRHyper* can decide whether a given ad item matches the user profile and to what degree, based on the fuzzy annotation metadata that accompany the ad item. In addition, the reasoner supports weighted concepts, thus the participation degree of the produced entailments can be controlled by the confidence weight with which the user preferences participate in the profile.

CASE STUDY: AD RECOMMENDATION FOR THE SOCCER DOMAIN

Experiment Setup and Data Collection

For the implementation of the proposed approach, a single ontology outlining the soccer domain was developed for proof-of-concept purposes. This ontology models the online requirements of the user who is interested in the sport, with an orientation to market aspects over the domain. 547 concepts organized in 552 inclusion axioms and 86 equivalence axioms, 18 relations defined by 18 role axioms and 804 complex axioms represent the soccer world for our system.

A lexical graph has been trained from a set of 112 articles, and a set of 200 soccer ads, crawled from the web. The articles were collected from the BBC[6] website and in particular from the soccer news category. The ads were sorted by the top 10 results of a custom ad scraper built for the Google[7] product services. The graph training set also contained 2200 ad-like content items, retrieved from the ODP[8] taxonomy under the soccer topic, with an interest in analyzing information concerning the supplied content for the ad recommendation problem. By ad-like content we denote the ads and links to websites presented in the database that consequently contain short text descriptions and thus reflect the vocabulary impedance problem in ad recommendation.

For test purposes, we have collected a different corpus of 817 additional soccer news articles and 1860 soccer advertisements which were crawled from the web during various time periods. The articles were collected from the BBC and the official UEFA[9] websites, from a popular soccer news website[10] as well as from assorted Yahoo! search results, collected using the Yahoo! Search BOSS Web Service[11]. The ads were gathered using the custom Google products ad scraper mentioned above, from a manually compiled set of domain relevant keywords, related to the soccer ontology concepts, where we continuously queried the service to extract the final total of the ad items. This real world dataset was used to conduct the two sets of experimental tests described below as well as for the user studies.

User Study

A user study was initially conducted with the use of ontologies populated with the *IN* neighborhood selection strategy in order to validate the efficiency of the use of terminologically populated ontologies in a semantic ad recommendation system.

In this survey, a convenience sample of 38 users was asked to browse a set of articles on the soccer domain and assess ads presented during the browsing process as well as at the end of the study. The dataset used for this study was the complete real world dataset used in our experimental study. The user profiles were progressively learned upon consumption of 20 interesting articles, while next to each viewed article the users were presented with a set of six ads, from which two were selected randomly from the ad pool with respect to removing bias, two were introduced by the content-based recommender described in (Papadopoulos et al, 2009a), and two were introduced by the reasoner-based recommender. The ads were presented in random order and the users were asked to perform two scalar evaluations on each ad: (a) one (1: not relevant – 5: extremely relevant) of the ad's relevance to the article and (b) one (1: extremely dislike – 5: extremely like) of their interest for each ad. Should an ad receive high preference (4-5), its semantic interpretation was aggregated to the user profile. After consuming the 20 articles, the users were presented with their top 10 preferences and with the top 10 ads

recommended by our system. They again were asked to perform a scalar evaluation of their profile (1: extremely dislike – 5: extremely like) and to binary rate the recommendations (Yes/No rating). Finally, they were asked to evaluate their satisfaction over the overall system performance (1: dislike – 5: extremely content).

The users were asked to keep their preferences targeted to 2-3 subtopics within the domain, aiming to simulate a profile of persistent interests from just 20 consumed articles. Results have demonstrated an average percentile success rate of 69.74% over the top 10 final recommendations and of 79.47% over the derived profile. 75.26% was the average satisfaction score over the system's performance on whole. Figure 6 illustrates the percentile frequency of user satisfaction (number of users per score) over the final recommendations and profile formulation respectively. It is important to notice that since the profile was evaluated in a scale of 1 – 5, its percentile representation in the graph lacks contiguousness.

Study of the recommendation results during the course of the trials for each user has indicated significant success in the recommendations in the initial steps of the study, thus demonstrating the utility of domain knowledge in overcoming the

Figure 6. Satisfaction score frequency for top 10 recommendations and top 10 profile concepts

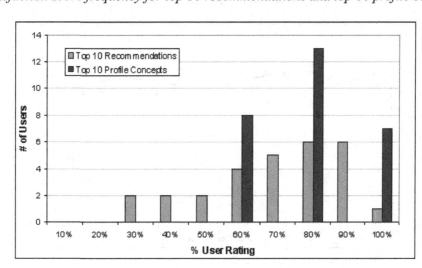

cold-start problem. They have also indicated a considerable improvement in recommendation accuracy compared to the content-based recommender, thus affirming the value of personalizing recommendations. In Figure 7, we present the comparison of the average user rating of the content and reasoner-based recommendations' accuracy (CBR and RBR respectively). Figures 8 and 9 present the comparison of the user-rated ad-to-content relevance with the user rating for each respective recommender. The points denote the actual values, while the colored lines denote the polynomial trendline of the ratings in an order of 5.

Results demonstrate that the RBR performs well from the beginning of the trials, achieving scores comparable to the straightforward CBR, even when no or little user information are available (Figure 7). The recommendation accuracy progressively increases and becomes more stable, as the profile is learned, reaching a peak at article 17, comprising the best score out of both recommenders. We also observe that the CBR's performance depends highly on successfully identifying ads relevant to the text (Figure 8), thus fluctuating significantly in accuracy, whereas the RBR shows steady improvement in user rating independently from the ads' relevance to the text (Figure 9).

Figure 7. Performance and polynomial trendlines for the two recommenders

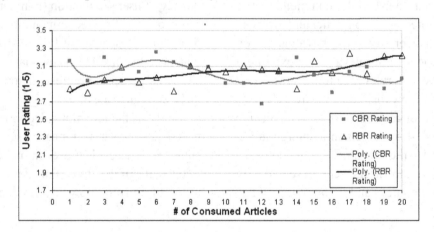

Figure 8. Performance and polynomial trendlines for the content based recommender (CBR)

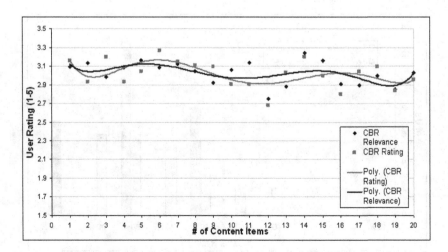

Figure 9. Performance and polynomial trendlines for the reasoner based recommender (RBR)

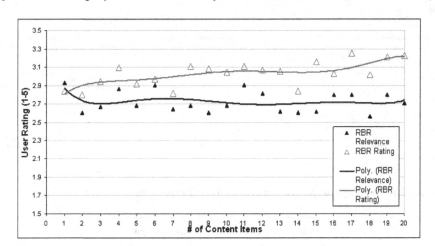

Finally, we notice that the CBR's accuracy score gradually decreases as the user expects targeted recommendations (Figure 7).

Synthetic Experiments

A set of synthetic experiments were conducted in order to validate individual components of the proposed framework, while a comparison of the results for each concept vector creation scheme (*IN, EN, CD*) is performed in order to determine the most efficient populating mechanism for the framework.

In the first test, which explores user profile convergence and accuracy similarly to (Sieg et al, 2007), a single article and a single ad, originally indexed under a specific profile concept, were classified and fed to the profile learning component. The test essentially aims at examining the learning process of a user profile for the particular interest, from now on referred to as *signal concept* (Sieg et al, 2007), This process was repeated for 25 rounds, making it equivalent to learning a profile from 50 consumed content items, for 46 signal concepts, Convergence was verified by measuring the average increase in preference weights, aiming to confirm that the increase rate would eventually decelerate, proving that the

profile becomes more stable over time. Study of the variance in the average interest scores of all the concepts aimed to confirm that the other concepts did not increase in the same rate as the signal concept. The profile accuracy is measured by observing the preference weight scores for the signal concept.

In Figures 10 and 11 we can see that the profile for all three schemes converges, while in Figure 12, a closer examination of the first stages of the profile learning process indicates that the profile converges slightly faster in the *CD* scheme. Variance study in Figure 13 shows that the other concepts' preference weights do not increase analogously to the signal concept, while the higher variance values of the *CD* scheme show higher independence of the signal concept from the res of the concepts, thus rendering the *CD* scheme more efficient in the profile learning process. Figure 14 illustrates the preference weights propagation for the signal concept throughout the profile learning process. The higher weights achieved in the *CD* scheme indicate higher profile accuracy for the mechanism. In contrast, the *EN* mechanism although achieves profile convergence performs poorly in comparison to the other two schemes.

In the second test, evaluating recommendation accuracy with the use of the reasoner-based rec-

Figure 10. Increase in average preference weights for all concepts and in the preference weight of the signal concept

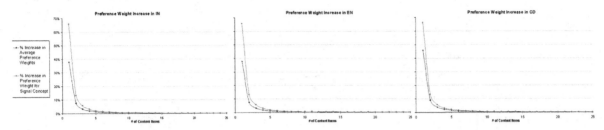

Figure 11. Increase in average preference weights for all concepts

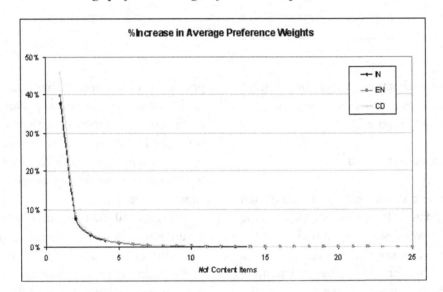

Figure 12. Increase in average preference weights for all concepts: first 5 iterations

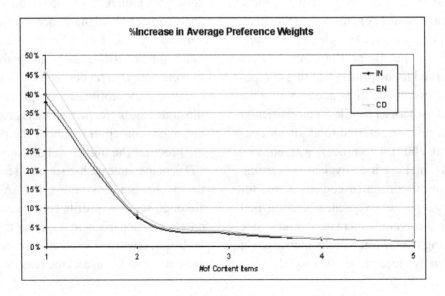

Figure 13. Average variance in preference weights

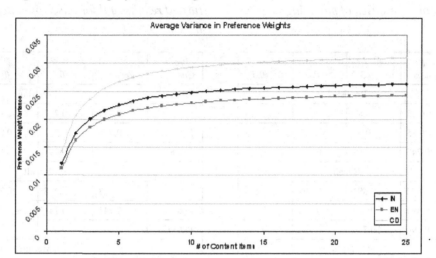

Figure 14. Preference weights for signal concept

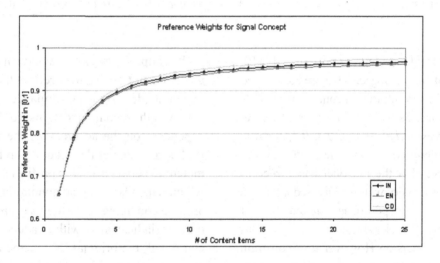

ommender, we have randomly selected 5 of the user profiles derived from the previous experiment and used them to measure the average *Top-n precision* and average *Top-n recall* (Sieg et al, 2007) of the recommended ads for the 5 user scenarios. A subset of 500 ads pulled randomly from our ad dataset was used in this experiment. Relevant ads for each user scenario were manually retrieved and inserted back into the pull of ads. We conducted our experiments for the top 3 profile concepts (denoted as A, B and C respectively for demonstration purposes), aggregated in

3 separate trial sets. Note that for each of the three concept vector creation mechanisms the top concepts are the same since they were the signal concepts in the last experiment, but the rest differ among schemes, since each scheme might classify different terms as being more relative to an ontology concept.

The total *n* is arbitrary and is related to the confidence degree of the recommended ads, thus is defined as the total of ads retrieved that carry a confidence degree above a *degree threshold*. For instance, in a set of recommended ads ranked on

Table 1. Precision and recall metrics for all returned results and for cases of matching degrees in IN

Profile Concepts	All Results	>=0.3	>=0.4	>=0.5
Precision				
A	0.85	0.85	1	1
A+B	0.85	0.85	1	1
A+B+C	0.748	0.888	0.961	0.975
Recall				
A	0.894	0.894	0.894	0.894
A+B	0.894	0.894	0.894	0.769
A+B+C	0.796	0.796	0.796	0.737
F-Measure				
A	0.8715807	0.8716	0.9442	0.94419
A+B	0.8715807	0.8716	0.9442	0.8696
A+B+C	0.7710087	0.8393	0.8706	0.83981

Table 2. Precision and recall metrics for all returned results and for cases of matching degrees in EN

Profile Concepts	All Results	>=0.3	>=0.4	>=0.5
Precision				
A	0.737	0.737	0.908	0.950
A+B	0.705	0.737	0.908	0.950
A+B+C	0.551	0.794	0.866	0.919
Recall				
A	0.758	0.758	0.758	0.644
A+B	0.741	0.741	0.741	0.530
A+B+C	0.696	0.696	0.696	0.596
F-Measure				
A	0.747	0.747	0.827	0.768
A+B	0.722	0.739	0.816	0.681
A+B+C	0.615	0.742	0.772	0.723

the basis of confidence degrees normalized in [0, 1], results that carry a degree < 0.3 are considered semantically irrelevant. Table 1 contains the results of these metrics, as well as for the *F-Measure*, for *degree threshold = {0, 0.3, 0.4, 0.5}*. Profile concepts are denoted in this table as *PC*.

We observe that the reasoner-based recommender performs very well for targeted interests. As more profile concepts are aggregated, the user profile becomes broader and more varied, resulting in a drop of precision. However, if we constrain the top recommendations based on a high degree threshold we observe noteworthy improvement in precision, even for broad user interests. A very high degree threshold however would result in recall decrease, since relevant recommendations are excluded. The *F-Measure* points out that a degree threshold of *0.4* is the best trade-off to achieve optimal results in all concept vector creation schemes. We observe that among the three, the original *IN* scores higher in precision whereas the *CD* achieves slightly better recall scores. The *EN* mechanism has the inferior performance of all.

It is important to note that these high measurements do not necessarily reflect the real world recommender system performance, where the accuracy of the recommendations would be directly dependent on the accuracy of the user profile. Rather they depict the accuracy in the semantic matching between a given profile and a set of ads which depends on the ad annotation correctness and the concreteness of the user profile. The F-measure indicates that with a trade-off in precision and recall, the original IN scheme achieves the most accurate recommendations.

CONCLUSION AND FUTURE WORK

This chapter provided an overview of the textual ad recommendation domain and the different issues that arise in it, extending from the scarcity of textual descriptions problem to the different possibilities of personalized advertisement. A recommendation solution was presented, which combined content information unobtrusively mined from user transactions and explicit domain

Table 3. Precision and recall metrics for all returned results and for cases of matching degrees in CD

Profile Concepts	All Results	>=0.3	>=0.4	>=0.5
Precision				
A	0.735	0.735	0.855	0.855
A+B	0.735	0.735	0.855	0.855
A+B+C	0.726	0.726	0.813	0.838
Recall				
A	0.940	0.940	0.897	0.897
A+B	0.897	0.897	0.852	0.755
A+B+C	0.863	0.863	0.802	0.734
F-Measure				
A	0.825	0.825	0.875	0.875
A+B	0.808	0.808	0.853	0.802
A+B+C	0.789	0.789	0.807	0.783

knowledge structured with formal semantics in an ontology. The approach has indicated that semantic knowledge in combination with the use of statistical terminological data captured in lexical graphs can be beneficial to the recommendation of textual advertisements. The use of community detection in order to infer meaningful relations within the context of a lexical graph has provided evidence that techniques traditionally used on collaborative recommendation approaches are efficient in capturing user preferences in content-based environments. In essence, the method described in this chapter presented a novel hybrid recommendation capable of achieving richer and more meaningful ad recommendations and of producing personal recommendations even when little or no information about the user is available.

Future work can be oriented towards moderating the reliance on manual input, a significant impediment in knowledge based recommendation systems, by extending the developed techniques to automatically induce semantic models extracted from the meaningful connections of augmented contextual data.

REFERENCES

Abrams, Z., Mendelevitch, O., & Tomlin, J. (2007). Optimal delivery of sponsored search advertisements subject to budget constraints. In *EC '07: Proceedings of the 8th ACM conference on Electronic commerce* (pp. 272-278). New York: ACM.

Abrams, Z., & Vee, E. (2007). Personalized Ad Delivery when Ads Fatigue: An Approximation Algorithm. In Proc. *Workshop on Internet and Network Economics (WINE)* (pp. 535-540).

Adomavicius, G., & Tuzhilin, A. (2005). Toward the next generation of recommender systems: A survey of the state-of-the-art and possible extensions. *IEEE Transactions on Knowledge and Data Engineering, 17*(6), 734–749. doi:10.1109/TKDE.2005.99

Anagnostopoulos, A., Broder, A. Z., Gabrilovich, E., Josifovski, V., & Riedel, L. (2007). Just-in-time contextual advertising. In *CIKM '07: Proceedings of the sixteenth ACM conference on Conference on information and knowledge management* (pp. 331-340). New York: ACM.

Bae, S. M., Ha, S. H., & Park, S. C. (2003). Fuzzy Web Ad Selector Based on Web Usage Mining. *IEEE Intelligent Systems, 18*(6), 62–69. doi:10.1109/MIS.2003.1249171

Broder, A., Fontoura, M., Josifovski, V., & Riedel, L. (2007). A semantic approach to contextual advertising. In *Proceedings of the 30th annual international ACM SIGIR conference on Research and development in information retrieval (SIGIR '07)* (pp. 559-566). New York: ACM.

Burke, R. (2007). Hybrid web recommender systems. In *The Adaptive Web* (pp. 377–408). LNCS. doi:10.1007/978-3-540-72079-9_12

Cann, R. (1993). *Formal Semantics: An Introduction*. Cambridge University Press.

Cantador, I., Szomszor, M., Alani, H., Fernández, M., & Castells, P. (2008). Enriching ontological user profiles with tagging history for multi-domain recommendations. In *Proceedings of the 1st International Workshop on Collective Semantics: Collective Intelligence and the Semantic Web (CISWeb 2008)* (pp. 5-19).

Chakrabarti, D., Agarwal, D., & Josifovski, V. (2008). Contextual advertising by combining relevance with click feedback. In *Proceedings of the 17th international Conference on World Wide Web* (pp 417-426).

ChoiceStream. (2008). ChoiceStream Personalization Survey. Retrieved December 28, 2009, from http://www.choicestream.com/pdf/ChoiceStream_2008_Personalization_Survey.pdf

Chu, W., & Park, S. T. (2009). Personalized recommendation on dynamic content using predictive bilinear models. In *WWW '09: Proceedings of the 18th international conference on World wide web* (pp. 691-700). New York: ACM.

Diaz Redondo, R. P., Fernandez Vilas, A., Pazos Arias, J. J., Ramos Cabrer, M., & Garcia Duque, J. (2009). Sponsored advertising for IDTV: A personalized and content-aware approach, In Proc. *International Conference on Computers in Education* (pp. 1-2). Digest of Technical Papers International Conference on Consumer Electronics.

Drèze, X., & Hussherr, F. X. (2003). Internet advertising: Is anybody watching? *Journal of Interactive Marketing, 17*(4), 8–23. doi:10.1002/dir.10063

Dumais, S., Cutrell, E., Cadiz, J. J., Jancke, G., Sarin, R., & Robbins, D. C. (2003). Stuff i've seen: a system for personal information retrieval and re-use. In *SIGIR '03: Proceedings of the 26th annual international ACM SIGIR conference on Research and development in information retrieval* (pp. 72-79). New York: ACM.

Fan, T., & Chang, C. (2009). Sentiment-Oriented Contextual Advertising. In *Proceedings of the 31th European Conference on IR Research on Advances in information Retrieval* (LNCS 5478, pp. 202-215).

Feng, J., Bhargava, H. K., & Pennock, D. M. (2007). Implementing sponsored search in web search engines: Computational evaluation of alternative mechanisms. *INFORMS Journal on Computing, 19*(1), 137–148. doi:10.1287/ijoc.1050.0135

Grosof, B. N., Horrocks, I., Volz, R., & Decker, S. (2003). Description logic programs: combining logic programs with description logic. In *WWW '03: Proceedings of the 12th international conference on World Wide Web* (pp. 48-57). New York: ACM.

Ha, S. H. (2004). *An Intelligent System for Personalized Advertising on the Internet* (pp. 21–30). EC-Web.

Kazienko, P., & Adamski, M. (2007). Adrosa-adaptive personalization of web advertising. *Information Sciences, 177*(11), 2269–2295. doi:10.1016/j.ins.2007.01.002

Kearney, P., Anand, S. S., & Shapcott, M. (2005). Employing a domain ontology to gain insights into user behaviour. In *Working Notes of the IJCAI Workshop on Intelligent Techinques for Web Personalization* (pp. 25-32).

Kleemann, T., & Sinner, A. (2005). User Profiles and Matchmaking on Mobile Phones. In Bartenstein, O. (Ed.), *Proc. of 16th International Conference on Applications of Declarative Programming and Knowledge Management INAP2005*, Fukuoka.

Kobsa, A. (2001). Tailoring privacy to users' needs. In *UM '01: Proceedings of the 8th International Conference on User Modeling 2001* (pp. 303-313). London: Springer-Verlag.

Lacerda, A., Cristo, M., Gonçalves, M. A., Fan, W., Ziviani, N., & Ribeiro-Neto, B. (2006). Learning to advertise. In *Proceedings of the 29th Annual international ACM SIGIR Conference on Research and Development in information Retrieval* (Seattle, Washington, USA, August 06 - 11, 2006). SIGIR '06 (pp. 549-556). New York: ACM.

Li, H., Zhang, D., Hu, J., Zeng, H., & Chen, Z. (2007). Finding keyword from online broadcasting content for targeted advertising. In *Proceedings of the 1st international Workshop on Data Mining and Audience intelligence for Advertising, ADKDD '07* (pp 55-62). New York: ACM.

Mehta, A., Saberi, A., Vazirani, U., & Vazirani, V. (2007). Adwords and generalized online matching. *Journal of the ACM, 54*(5), 22. doi:10.1145/1284320.1284321

Middleton, S. E., Shadbolt, N. R., & De Roure, D. C. (2004). Ontological user profiling in recommender systems. *ACM Transactions on Information Systems, 22*(1), 54–88. doi:10.1145/963770.963773

Miller, G. A. (1995). WordNet: A Lexical Database for English. *Communications of the ACM, 38*(11), 39–41. doi:10.1145/219717.219748

Mishne, G., & de Rijke, M. (2006). Language Model Mixtures for Contextual Ad Placement in Personal Blogs. In *Proceedings of 5th International Conference on NLP, FinTAL* (pp. 435-446), Springer.

Mulvenna, M. D., Anand, S. S., & Büchner, A. G. (2000). Personalization on the Net using Web mining: introduction. *Communications of the ACM, 43*(8), 122–125. doi:10.1145/345124.345165

Murdock, V., Ciaramita, M., & Plachouras, V. (2007). A noisy-channel approach to contextual advertising. In *Proceedings of the 1st international Workshop on Data Mining and Audience intelligence For Advertising (ADKDD '07)* (pp. 21-27). New York: ACM.

Newman, M. E. J. (2003). The Structure and Function of Complex Networks. *SIAM Review, 45*(2), 167–256. doi:10.1137/S003614450342480

Papadopoulos, S. (2009). *Key Success Factors in Internet Advertising: The role of Online User Activity and Social Context.* LAP Lambert Academic Publishing.

Papadopoulos, S., Kompatsiaris, Y., & Vakali, A. (2009b). Leveraging Collective Intelligence through Community Detection in Tag Networks. In *Proceedings CKCaR '09 Workshop on Collective Knowledge Capturing and Representation*, Redondo Beach, California, USA.

Papadopoulos, S., Menemenis, F., Kompatsiaris, Y., & Bratu, B. (2009a). Lexical Graphs for Improved Contextual Ad Recommendation. In *Proceedings of the 31th European Conference on IR Research on Advances in information Retrieval* (pp. 216-227).

Pavlou, P. A., & Stewart, D. W. (2000). Measuring the Effects and Effectiveness of Interactive Advertising: A Research Agenda. *Journal of Interactive Advertising, 1*(1).

Pazzani, M. J., & Billsus, D. (2007). Content-based recommendation systems. In *The Adaptive Web: Methods and Strategies of Web Personalization* (LNCS 4321, pp 325-341).

Rettie, R., Grandcolas, U., & McNeil, C. (2004). Post-impressions: internet advertising without click-through. *Academy of Marketing Conference*, 6-9 July 2004, Cheltenham, United Kingdom.

Ribeiro-Neto, B., Cristo, M., Golgher, P. B., & de Moura, E. S. (2005). Impedance coupling in content-targeted advertising. In *SIGIR '05: Proceedings of the 28th annual international ACM SIGIR conference on Research and development in information retrieval* (pp. 496-503). New York: ACM.

Sarmento, L., Trezentos, P., Gonçalves, J. P., & Oliveira, E. (2009). Inferring local synonyms for improving keyword suggestion in an on-line advertisement system. In *Proceedings of the Third international Workshop on Data Mining and Audience intelligence for Advertising, ADKDD '09* (pp. 37-45). New York: ACM.

Schneider, P. P. F., & Swartout, B. (1993). Description Logic Knowledge Representation System Specification from the KRSS Group. Retrieved from http://www-db.research.bell-labs.com/user/pfps/papers/krss-spec.ps

Shaparenko, B., Çetin, Ö., & Iyer, R. (2009). Data-driven text features for sponsored search click prediction. In *Proceedings of the Third international Workshop on Data Mining and Audience intelligence For Advertising. ADKDD '09.* (pp. 46-54). New York: ACM.

Shapiro, S., Macinnis, D. J., & Heckler, S. E. (1997). The Effects of Incidental Ad Exposure on the Formation of Consideration Sets. *The Journal of Consumer Research, 24*(1). doi:10.1086/209496

Sheth, M., Avant, D., & Bertram, C. (2001) System and method for creating a semantic web and its applications in browsing, searching, profiling, personalization and advertising. US Patent Application 6311194, October 2001

Sieg, A., Mobasher, B., & Burke, R. (2007). Learning Ontology-Based User Profiles: A Semantic Approach to Personalized Web Search. *IEEE Intelligent Informatics Bulletin, 8*(1).

Song, R., Chen, E., & Zhao, M. (2005). *SVM Based Automatic User Profile Construction for Personalized Search* (pp. 475–484). Advances in Intelligent Computing.

Srivastava, J., Cooley, R., Deshpande, M., & Tan, P.-N. (2000). Web usage mining: Discovery and applications of usage patterns from web data. *SIGKDD Explorations, 1*(2), 12–23. doi:10.1145/846183.846188

Straccia, U. (2005). Towards a Fuzzy Description Logic for the Semantic Web (Preliminary Report). In *Proceedings of the 2nd European Semantic Web Conference (ESWC-05)*.

Trajkova, J., & Gauch, S. (2004). Improving ontology-based user profiles. In *Proceedings of RIAO* (pp. 380-389).

Tsatsou, D., Menemenis, F., Kompatsiaris, I., & Davis, P. C. (2009). A semantic framework for personalized ad recommendation based on advanced textual analysis. In *Proceedings of the Third ACM Conference on Recommender Systems. RecSys '09* (pp 217-220). New York: ACM.

Wang, C., Zhang, P., Choi, R., & Eredita, M. D. (2002). Understanding consumers attitude toward advertising. In *Eighth Americas conf. on Information System* (pp. 1143-1148).

Yang, W., Dia, J., Cheng, H., & Lin, H. (2006). Mining Social Networks for Targeted Advertising. In *Proceedings of the 39th Annual Hawaii international Conference on System Sciences vol. 06. HICSS* (pp. 137.1). Washington, DC: IEEE Computer Society.

Yih, W., Goodman, J., & Carvalho, V. R. (2006). Finding advertising keywords on web pages. In *Proceedings of the 15th international conference on World Wide Web (WWW '06)* (pp. 213-222), New York

Yih, W., & Meek, C. (2008). Consistent phrase relevance measures. In *Proceedings of the 2nd international Workshop on Data Mining and Audience intelligence For Advertising. ADKDD '08* (pp. 37-44). New York: ACM.

Yoo, C. Y. (2008). Unconscious processing of Web advertising: Effects on implicit memory, attitude toward the brand, and consideration set. *Journal of Interactive Marketing, 22*(2), 2–18. doi:10.1002/dir.20110

Zadeh, L. A., Klir, G. J., & Yuan, B. (1996). *Fuzzy Sets, Fuzzy Logic, Fuzzy Systems: Selected Papers by Lotfi A. Zedeh*. World Scientific Pub Co Inc.

Zadeh, P. M., & Moshkenani, M. S. (2008). Mining Social Network for Semantic Advertisement. In *Proceedings of the 2008 Third international Conference on Convergence and Hybrid information Technology - Volume 01* (November 11 - 13, 2008). ICCIT (pp. 611-618). Washington, DC: IEEE Computer Society.

Zhang, Y., Surendran, A. C., Platt, J. C., & Narasimhan, M. (2008). Learning from multi-topic web documents for contextual advertisement. In *Proceedings of the 14th ACM SIGKDD international Conference on Knowledge Discovery and Data Mining, KDD '08* (pp. 1051-1059). New York: ACM.

ADDITIONAL READING

Baader, F., Calvanese, D., McGuinness, D. L., Nardi, D., & Patel-Schneider, P. F. (Eds.). (2003). *The Description Logic Handbook: Theory, Implementation, and Applications*. Cambridge University Press.

Bradley, K., Rafter, R., & Smyth, B. (2000). Case-Based User Profiling for Content Personalisation. In P. Brusilovsky, O. Stock, & C. Strapparava (Eds.), *Proceedings of the international Conference on Adaptive Hypermedia and Adaptive Web-Based Systems* (LNCS 1892, pp. 62-72).

Chatterjee, P., Hoffman, D. L., & Novak, T. P. (2003). Modeling the clickstream: Implications for web-based advertising efforts. *Marketing Science*, *22*(4), 520–541. doi:10.1287/mksc.22.4.520.24906

Ciaramita, M., Murdock, V., & Plachouras, V. (2008). Semantic Associations for Contextual Advertising. *Journal of Electronic Commerce Research Special Issue on Online Advertising and Sponsored Search*, *9*(1), 1–15.

Eirinaki, M., Lampos, C., Paulakis, S., & Vazirgiannis, M. (2004). Web personalization integrating content semantics and navigational patterns. In *Proceedings of the 6th Annual ACM international Workshop on Web information and Data Management* (Washington DC, USA, November 12 - 13, 2004). *WIDM '04* (pp. 72-79). New York: ACM.

Eirinaki, M., & Vazirgiannis, M. (2003). Web mining for web personalization. *ACM Transactions on Internet Technology*, *3*(1), 1–27. doi:10.1145/643477.643478

Fortunato, S. (2009). Community detection in graphs. In *Physics Reports, arxiv:0906.0612*

Godoy, D., & Amandi, A. (2002). A user profiling architecture for textual-based agents. In *Proceedings of the Fourth Argentine Sympoisum on Artificial Intelligence*, Sante Fe, Argentina.

Grimes, A., & Kitchen, P. J. (2007). Researching Mere Exposure Effects to Advertising: Methodological Implications & Approaches. *International Journal of Market Research*, *49*(2), 191–219.

Joshi, A., & Motwani, R. (2006). Keyword Generation for Search Engine Advertising. In *Proceedings of the Sixth IEEE international Conference on Data Mining - Workshops* (December 18 - 22, 2006). *ICDMW* (pp. 490-496). Washington, DC: IEEE Computer Society.

Kanth, V. (2004). *Contextual Information Retrieval Using Ontology Based User Profiles*. Master's Thesis, University of Kansas.

Kazienko, P., & Adamski, M. (2004). Personalized Web Advertising Method. In *Adaptive Hypermedia and Adaptive Web-Based Systems* (pp 146-155).

Linoff, G. S., & Berry, M. J. A. (2002). *Mining the Web: Transforming Customer Data into Customer Value*. Wiley.

Mandel, N., & Johnson, E. J. (2002). When web pages influence choice: effects of visual primes on experts and novices. *The Journal of Consumer Research, 29*(2), 235–245. doi:10.1086/341573

Middleton, S. E., Shadbolt, N. R., & De Roure, D. C. (2003). Capturing interest through inference and visualization: ontological user profiling in recommender systems. In *K-CAP '03: Proceedings of the 2nd international conference on Knowledge capture* (pp. 62-69). New York: ACM Press.

Mobasher, B., Cooley, R., & Srivastava, J. (2000). Automatic personalization based on web usage mining. *Communications of the ACM, 43*(8), 142–151. doi:10.1145/345124.345169

Rashid, A. M., Albert, I., Cosley, D., Lam, S. K., McNee, S. M., Konstan, J. A., & Riedl, J. (2002). Getting to know you: learning new user preferences in recommender systems. In *Proceedings of the 7th international Conference on intelligent User interfaces* (San Francisco, California, USA, January 13 - 16, 2002). IUI '02 (pp. 127-134). New York: ACM.

Schafer, J. B., Konstan, J., & Riedi, J. (1999). Recommender systems in e-commerce. In *Proceedings of the 1st ACM Conference on Electronic Commerce* (Denver, Colorado, United States, November 03 - 05, 1999). EC '99 (pp. 158-166). New York: ACM.

Shani, G., Chickering, M., & Meek, C. (2008). Mining recommendations from the web. In *Proceedings of the 2008 ACM Conference on Recommender Systems* (Lausanne, Switzerland, October 23 - 25, 2008). RecSys '08 (pp. 35-42). New York: ACM.

Sheth, A., Bertram, C., Avant, D., Hammond, B., Kochut, K., & Warke, Y. (2002). Managing Semantic Content for the Web. *IEEE Internet Computing, 6*(4), 80–87. doi:10.1109/MIC.2002.1020330

Sieg, A., Mobasher, B., & Burke, R. (2007). Web search personalization with ontological user profiles. In *Proceedings of the Sixteenth ACM Conference on Conference on information and Knowledge Management* (Lisbon, Portugal, November 06 - 10, 2007). CIKM '07 (pp. 525-534). New York: ACM.

Staab, S., & Studer, R. (2004). *Handbook on Ontologies* (1st ed.). International Handbooks on Information Systems. Springer.

Taylor, D. G., Davis, D. F., & Jillapalli, R. (2009). Privacy concern and online personalization: The moderating effects of information control and compensation. *Electronic Commerce Research, 9*(3), 203–223. doi:10.1007/s10660-009-9036-2

Teltzrow, M., & Kobsa, A. (2004). *Impacts of user privacy preferences on personalized systems: a comparative study. Designing personalized user experiences in eCommerce* (pp. 315–332). Norwell, MA: Kluwer Academic Publishers.

Yuan, S. (2003). A recommendation mechanism for contextualized mobile advertising. *Expert Systems with Applications, 24*(4), 399–414. doi:10.1016/S0957-4174(02)00189-6

Zhang, L., Yu, Y., Zhou, J., Lin, C., & Yang, Y. (2005). An enhanced model for searching in semantic portals. In *Proceedings of the 14th international Conference on World Wide Web* (Chiba, Japan, May 10 - 14, 2005). WWW '05 (pp. 453-462). New York: ACM.

ENDNOTES

[1]   http://adwords.google.com/ Google AdWords is a trademark of Google Inc.

[2] https://www.google.com/adsense/ Google AdSense is a trademark of Google Inc.

[3] http://publisher.yahoo.com/sps/cm.php Yahoo! is a trademark of Yahoo! Inc.

[4] http://www.wikipedia.org Wikipedia is a trademark of the Wikimedia Foundation.

[5] Initially developed within the aceMedia project. This work was partially supported by the European Commission under contract FP6-001765. http://www.acemedia.org/

[6] http://news.bbc.co.uk/sport2/hi/football/ BBC is a trademark of the f the British Broadcasting Corporation.

[7] http://www.google.com/products Google is a trademark of Google Inc.

[8] Open Directory Project, www.dmoz.org

[9] http://www.uefa.com/ uefa.com® is a trademark of the Union of European Football Associations.

[10] http://www.soccernews.com/

[11] http://developer.yahoo.com/search/boss/ Yahoo! BOSS is a trademark of Yahoo! Inc.

Chapter 14
Audience Intelligence in Online Advertising

Bin Wang
Microsoft Corporation, China

ABSTRACT

This chapter introduces the fundamentals of audience intelligence's important aspects. The goal is to present what are related to audience intelligence, how online audience intelligence could be done, and some representative methods. In this chapter, the author will first address the fundamentals of the audience intelligence, including the brief introduction of the online ad eco-system, the relationship between audience intelligence and existing online ad types, performance measures and the challenges in this field. Next, some classical methods of audience intelligence on end-users will be introduces, namely, demographic, geographic, behavioral targeting and online commercial intent (OCI) detection. Then, audience intelligence on advertisers will be presented. Finally, related topics of online advertising, such as the privacy issue, will be addressed.

INTRODUCTION

Audience intelligence is to understand the audiences in the online advertising eco-system. There are three roles in this eco-system, and each one could be the study object of the audience intelligence. First of all are the end-users, who browse the web pages, enter search queries, and buy products online. They are the targets of the whole advertising system. Second are the web publishers (or media), who convey the ads/information to end-users through their online channels, such as portals, search engines, IM tools. The third are the advertisers, which are the origins of the eco-system. The study of audience intelligence is to obtain useful knowledge about the roles

DOI: 10.4018/978-1-60960-189-8.ch014

involved in the online advertising eco-system. With this knowledge, advertisement could be delivered "smarter", that is to say, more efficient and effective.

For end-users, audience intelligence helps them to be better understood. Then the information/ads of products which meet their interests and needs will be delivered to them, while those annoying irrelevant ads won't bother them. Thus the end-users will have a friendlier online environment.

For advertisers, their payments of advertisement will hit those who have interests in their products, who are likely to be affected by online ads and who have the desire to purchase. By providing ads to the targeted end-users, advertisers will have higher return of investment.

For publishers, audience intelligence could help them to improve the advertising revenue by delivering the ads in a smarter way. The application of audience intelligence technology, such as behavioral targeting, has demonstrated its power in boosting the ad performance in terms of click through rate (CTR) and other pricing measures. Adopting these kinds of value-adding techniques will increase publishers' profit.

In a word, audience intelligence is a win-win approach for all the participants in the online advertising eco-system.

These years, with the rapid growth of Internet-based e-commerce, audience intelligence has attracted more and more interest from both academic and industrial societies.

The research on audience intelligence combines the efforts on data mining, natural language processing, multimedia, and related fields. The related papers could be found in data mining conferences including SIGKDD (Knowledge Discovery and Data Mining), WWW (World Wide Web Conference) and ADKDD (Workshop on Data Mining and Audience Intelligence) (Belkin, Kelly, Kim, Kim, Lee, Muresan, Tang, Yuan, & Cool, 2003; Conversion rate, n.d.), etc.. Besides, people from traditional advertising and financial fields also send their papers to International Journal

of Advertising. For example, Wharton business school from University of Pennsylvania publishes a lot of reports on their website http://knowledge. wharton.upenn.edu/. After tens of years' research in this field, fruitful results have been achieved. For example, a variety of methods have been proposed to understand the online users. The common approaches include demographic targeting, geographic targeting, behavior targeting and so on.

As for the industrial society, Google, Yahoo!, and Microsoft are major players in this field. comScore, TNS, Tacoda and many other companies also have their shares by devoting in analyzing web users' data. The market of audience intelligence is booming. For example, the market of behavior targeting is expected to explode from 350M in 2006 to 1.7B in 2010.

This chapter is to introduce the fundamentals of audience intelligence's important aspects. The goal is to present what are related to audience intelligence, how online audience intelligence could be done, and some representative methods. In this chapter, we will first address the fundamentals of the audience intelligence, including the brief introduction of the online ad eco-system, the relationship between audience intelligence and existing online ad types, performance measures and the challenges in this field. Next, some classical methods of audience intelligence on end-users will be introduces, namely, demographic, geographic, behavioral targeting and online commercial intent (OCI) detection. Then, audience intelligence on advertisers will be presented. Finally, related topics of online advertising, such as the privacy issue, will be addressed.

1. BACKGROUNDS

1.1 Eco-System

There are three key roles in the online advertising eco-system. They are the end-users, advertisers

Figure 1. Internet advertising eco-system

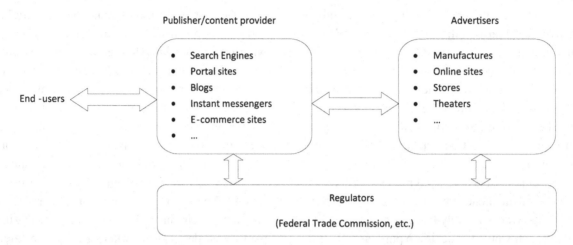

and (online) publishers. Figure 1 illustrates the relationship between them.

When an advertiser wants to deliver ads in the Internet, the advertiser finds an Internet publisher to do that. The advertiser and the publisher negotiate two important issues. One is how to deliver ads through publisher's channels. The other is how to charge. After two sides reach an agreement, the ads will be delivered. Then, web end-users will see these ads when they surf the Internet. Sometimes, end-users not only view the ad, but also click the ads and jump to the URL specified in the advertisement. Whether she/he clicks it or not, the end-user has viewed the ad and got the impression. The goal of advertiser has reached.

In this eco-system, advertisers pay money to publishers and gain end-users' attention or even create purchase. Publishers use the money to deliver the ads and enrich their web sites' contents to attract more end-users. End-users spend their time to view the ads or pay efforts by other activities in advertisers' websites and gain cheap/free contents in the Internet. In this way, three sides depend and benefit each other.

Please note in the figure, there is another role "regulator", which reflects the law or federal regularizations to ensure the whole eco-system running

healthily. This is because there are more and more concerns about the issues such as privacy. People are asking if the publishers/advertisers collect too much (privacy-related) data to deliver their ads.

Next, we'll address some important issues and terms involved in the online advertising.

First, when advertisers want to deliver ads, they may have different goals. There are two main types of advertising goals. One is for branding, and the other is for direct response. Branding ads usually aim to broaden the user acknowledgement of the brand. On the other hand, direct response ads expect to receive end-users' immediate feedbacks. An example for the direct response ad is the promotion of online e-commerce stores.

Second, publishers are in charge of delivery of ads. They can select what channels to deliver. The channels could be:

- **Search engines:** ads could be shown when an end-user enters a search query
- **Instant messengers:** when a user views his/her friend list or open a dialog, the ads could be shown. Besides, ads could also be pushed to the user when he/she is active.
- **Mail lists/RSS feeds:** the mail or RSS content could include the ad information

- **Content websites:** there are quite variety of web sites, including news sites (such as BBC, CNN…), e-commerce sites (eBay, Amazon,…), forums (flickr), blog (Blog, twitter), portal (Yahoo!, MSN) and so many on. These sites have huge amount of browsing from millions of people every day. Each time, when these sites send a web page to the end-user, there are chances to deliver some ads.

Each channel has its strength. For example, users who conduct searches have a clear information requirement at that time. If the search engine can well match this requirement to some ad, there could be good chance the user will click the ad to view the advertiser's page. Direct response ad can expect good performance in search engine channel. On the other hand, a lot of people come to BBS or online forums to watch the discussions or news for entertainment. This is a good chance to show product brands to a large group of people. It works as the similar way as TV: many branding ads are broadcasted in and between programs with high audience rating.

Third one is the pricing mechanism, that is, how to charge for online ads. Typical pricing mechanisms include CPC (Cost Per Click), CPM (Cost Per Mille) and CPA (Cost Per Action). Among them, CPC is preferred by direct response ads and CPM by branding ads. For CPA, the "Action" refers to certain activities end-users do at the advertisers' sites, such as buying a production, registering an account, and subscribing sites' mail list. Some actions, such as buying goods or ticket/hotel booking, are the ultimate goal of the advertising. CPA is a desirable pricing mechanism from advertiser's point.

1.2 Strength of Audience Intelligence

There are many online advertising types available. Some major types include:

- **Sponsored search:** also referred as "paid search". It is to show ads along with search results from the search engines. It is a fast growing advertising type, as there is more and more people use search engine as their web entrance.
- **Contextual advertising:** this kind of advertising is to show the ads which are relevant to the web page content. For example, if a web page's topic is the discussion on travel affairs, it could be benefit show ads for airfare, hotel or other travel-related topics. Contextual advertising are very popular. It is like to show athletic brand ads in sports channels. Usually, because the large amount of web pages, the ads are matched to the web pages using automatic page content (text) analysis methods.
- **Display advertising:** it is to show images, videos or animations embedded in or popped up from the web page that the user is browsing. This is one of the oldest types of online ad and it still holds the largest share of online market now a days.

Audience intelligence is beneficial to all types of advertising, especially to the display advertising. In sponsored search, search engines can use user's query to understand user's intention, while in display advertising, it's not easy to understand user's intention. For example, one of the most common usages of display advertising is to display banner images or videos in the portal page or home page of large web sites. These pages usually contain large amount of different contents. For example, an automobile site's home page might have the news and information for quite different types of cars, ranging from compact to luxury cars. In this case, too much contextual information results in the situation that there is no clear and deterministic indication of the user's intensions. In this usage scenario, audience intelligence would be of great help to provide heuristic information of the individual user, e.g. the user's gender, age, income and past behaviors, and to enable the publisher to make a better "guess" of the user's intention.

Besides audience intelligence, there are also some other techniques aiming to improve the advertising efficiency, such as the common-used contextual advertisement method.

Audience intelligence can be used together with contextual advertisement to achieve better performance. For example, Li, Liu, Yan, Wang, Bai, & Chen (2009) uses behavior targeting together with contextual advertisement and gets larger improvement than using each of them alone. What's more, sometimes audience intelligence can exert its power where contextual ads cannot be applied. For example, in case there is no contextual information. A typical application is the ads in web mail pages. When a user navigates his/her mail through web, contextual ads method cannot be used because the mail content is unseen to the ad publisher. In this case, audience intelligence can provide valuable information to help publishers deliver better ads to users.

From above discussion, we can see that the application of audience intelligence is neither restricted to a certain type of advertising, nor is it repellent to other ad-efficiency boosting technologies. Audience intelligence is actually complementary in that it provides the information about the users/advertisers, while sponsored search reflects user's short-term intention and contextual ads utilize the contents in the web pages. Since they use different knowledge sources, they can be inherently combined together to improve the match among advertisers, ad publishers and online end-users. For example, a web page may discuss on the automobile quality. The contextual advertising will select to present automobile ads. Meanwhile, if the user's past behavior shows she/he is specially interested in a certain brand (e.g., G. M.), the ad selected could be further refined to present this brand's ads or promotion information to the user. Because the selected ad could comply with users' interest, the user will more likely

to click the ad and start exploration. Hence the combination could improve the advertising effect.

1.3 Performance Measures

Since the goal of audience intelligence is to improve the advertising efficiency, it is necessary to have metrics so that people can quantitatively measure whether there is any improvement and how much the improvement could be. Different advertising methodologies may adopt different metrics. After years of development of online advertising technologies, there are some commonly accepted metrics.

Coverage

First of all, an important performance measure is the number of users/advertisers to whom a certain audience intelligence method can be applied. This could be referred as "Coverage" or "Reach". Coverage reflects the scope of a method can reach. Usually, a method with small coverage is regarded as inferior. For publishers, the larger the coverage is, the larger possible improvement on revenue can be got.

Click Through Rate

A popular measure of online advertising is the click through rate (CTR), whose definition is

$$CTR = \frac{\text{number of clicks}}{\text{number of impression}}$$

where "impression" refers to the number of display of an ad in web pages. Usually, an online ad has a hyperlink itself, and a click will lead the users to some other web pages, such as advertisers' home pages, production introductions, online shopping pages, etc. Higher CTR infers there are more people are interested in the ads Therefore, CTR is a very important indicator of the ad delivery quality. Besides, in CPC pricing mechanism, CTR improvement could be directly related to revenue.

CTR for online advertising is usually low. It is around 2-3% for sponsored search, and even lower for display advertising. Research has shown that CTR of banner advertising, which ever dominated the display advertising, is ever decreasing. It's normal for an ad only gains few dozens of clicks. Several clicks could result in large relative change in CTR. It leads to the problem that the precise estimation of CTR is usually very hard. This is even aggravated by click frauds.

A related measure of CTR is the CTR lift, which is to compare two CTRs measured by their relative improvement

$$lift = \frac{CTR_{target} - CTR_{base}}{CTR_{base}}$$

where CTR_{target} and CTR_{base} are two *CTRs* to compared.

CTR could be impacted by many factors. It could change dramatically if the same advertisement is delivered in different channels, ad format (animations abstracts more than text), size, advertisement content (good-looking vs. poor), and many others. How to precisely calculate and predict CTR is still a difficult research problem. For example, (On the Internet, nobody knows you're a dog, n.d.) proposes to categorize the ads with a taxonomy tree, and accumulate the clicks within one taxonomy node to give a better estimation

Conversion Rate

Conversion rate refers to the ratio of a user converting his/her page view to certain desire actions of advertisers (Conversion rate, n.d.). The actions could be very different, such as subscribing a newsletter, registering an account, or buying products. The conversion rate is defined as

$$ConversionRate = \frac{number\ of\ actions}{number\ of\ impressions}$$

As conversion rate is the user actions on advertisers' sites, it could be a direct measure of the advertisement effect. If the action is "user buys something", the conversion rate may well indicate the advertiser's income.

Compared to CTR, the conversion rate will be even lower. The data scarcity problem also impacts the conversion rate calculation. Besides, as conversions are recorded in advertisers' site, there comes a problem of which ads lead to this conversion. The user may have viewed this advertiser's ads at many sites before he/she goes to the advertisers' sites (even without click any ads but by enter the URL himself/herself). How could the advertiser know which ad campaigns are effective and influence the user? A usual model could be last click, which means the ad click right before the conversion is credited. Some other methods are also proposed, such as engagement mapping (Engagement mapping, n.d.). This is also an area need to explore.

1.4 Challenges

Audience intelligence usually depends on large amount of web data to extract valuable information. Like all the online data mining technologies, it faces the challenges of huge amount of data, which usually are TBs and increase every day. This could result in requirements of storage, computational power and etc. Web data could be very noisy, especially when ad clicks or conversions are considered, because invalid clicks/conversions are triggered by the inappropriate purpose, e.g. click frauds could have many clicks while their data won't be really relative to the ads. Besides those common issues, there are some specific requirements for audience intelligence.

Quick Response

The users' interests are not static and they can change very quickly. A user can buy an air ticket online in first half hour, and go to a photo-sharing site (which she/he visits every day) in next half hour. An airfare advertiser needs to catch this user in first half hour to prompt its cheap tickets.

Usually, a user's session, with a consistent interest, lasts for few hours. It is expected that the online audience intelligence could act quickly enough to catch the users' current interest. With the large amount of users and their data, the requirement for quick response needs automatic methods to be well developed and applied.

Multiple Interests

As discussed above, a user could have multiple interests as same time. On the one hand, the behavior of different interests could be mingled together. This increases the difficulty to correctly identify the users and their interests. On the other hand, multiple user interests imply the traditional classification-based modeling methods should be applied carefully. The key point is that each user may belong to several classes and each datum may reflect of combined interests. Therefore, multi-label methods (Tsoumakas, & Katakis, 2007) could be preferred.

2. AUDIENCE INTELLIGENCE ON END-USERS

There could be many different ways to understand the online audience and utilize the information to improve the advertising efficiency. In this section, we focus on our discussion on understand the end-users. The end-users are usually human beings and could have many attributes, such as age, gender, interests, and habits and so on. The audience intelligence on end-users on end users is to collect and analyze these attributes to better serve the ads to those humans.

We will first address the difference between internet users and real human beings. Next a brief introduction on demographic-based user analysis is presented. Then we had more detailed discussions on behavioral targeting, which emerges with the e-commerce. Finally, another kind of effort to understand the user's instant intention is presented.

2.1 User Identification

The users who visit Internet sites are not always real human beings. There is a famous sentence "on the Internet, nobody knows you are a dog" (On the Internet, nobody knows you're a dog, n.d). The programs, e.g. crawler or spiders, could try to visit large amount of sites and store the pages for commercial or academic purposes. Besides, a human may access a web site one day and revisit it few days later. How can the web site recognize this is a same human?

For many web sites, such as facebook or twitter, the human identify themselves by registering an account, with user name (and usually a passcode). This seems to be natural and still be widely adopted. The advantage is that no matter what changes have made to the hardware, software and any other settings, a human can always be identified according to his/her entered account name. But there are also shortcomings. One person can register multiple accounts, or open an account to be used for a program like dialog robot.

Another way is to automatically generate cookie. Those cookies values may correspond to your computer hardware, software and other information on your computer. The expiration dates of the cookies vary greatly, from "end of the session" to "decades of years later". The advantage of long-live cookie is that the site could quickly recognize you when you visit the site several days later.

In short, an "end-user" of the web sites are not necessarily be real human, and a human can be (many) different "users" in different web sites. Any system utilizing the audience intelligence needs to set an appropriate mechanism to identify real humans and their visits in different time.

2.2 Demographic Targeting

Demographic targeting refers to deliver the ads according to users' age, gender information or others in their online demographic profile. The most popular and easiest understanding methods are age/gender targeting and location targeting.

- **Age/gender:** it can be easily figure out that moms are young women, and online game players are more likely to be male students. Although simple, age and gender have their power to distinguish certain sets of people. While gender is relatively fixed, the age is slowly changing. Besides, small age difference (30 vs. 31 years) won't imply large behavior difference. Therefore, ages are usually bucketed. For example, there could be classes as students (<18), young (18-35), and middle (35-65) and old (>65). This information could be entered by humans who register their accounts, or by data mining algorithms (De Bock, & Van Den Poel, 2009).

- **Education level/occupation targeting:** The education or occupation information is usually an option a user can skip during the account registration. If they are filled, it is a good chance for publishers/advertisers to push related contents (e.g. books, seminars) to the user.

Another related topic is the location-based targeting. Location information is very helpful if a user is looking for a restaurant or a subway station. The characteristic could change their places every few hours. Precisely predicting user location is the key. IP-based method is among the earliest methods and is still effective at present.

It could locate the person to a city or a town. It can be expected that location-based targeting has a great opportunity in next few years. The pervasive mobile devices, especially cell-phone, could provide precise location information at any time. This will greatly improve the performance of location-based targeting and attract more and more advertisers such as local stores.

2.3 Behavioral Targeting

The above mentioned demographic targeting manly depends on users static attributes. While users share same background could have very different interests, it is desirable those interests could be identified and appropriate ads are delivered to each user. Obviously, a user's behavior can reflect his/her interest. A sports fan could play several times a week, a photograph enthusiast buys many camera accessories, and a traveler will go overseas often. This is also true for users' online behavior. The photograph enthusiast will visit the photo forum many times, and traveler could search and view information about a lot of different sceneries. Behavioral targeting is to deduce the user interest or patterns to better serve the ads.

In traditional advertisement system, the users' activity cannot be easily obtained. It requires much effort and is very expensive. While for online advertising, a great advantage is that all the online behaviors are conducted in digital and could be recorded with very cheap cost. Hence there could be plenty of user behavior data for analysis. (Rationale to use behavior targeting: research shows past behavior has positive correlation with online activity)

The behavioral targeting was emerged with the Internet, and it receives more and more attention and research in recent years. As discussed above, the audience intelligence should have quick response time. This is more critical for behavior targeting because large volume of user behavioral data. The multi-label character of the user's interest makes it difficult to identify individual interest from mingled behavioral data.

The behavioral targeting could be done with either pattern discovery or data mining methods. For pattern discovery, the ad publishers dig into the user behavioral data and extract some heuristic rules to distinguish a group of users. For example, an automobile buyer may conduct search queries like "car deals" and "sedan price", and navigate a few automobile web sites such as GM and Ford. The pattern could be "conduct x, y, z queries at least m times and visit p, q, r web sites at least n times". These patterns could have clear semantic meanings. But this also requires quite a lot of human effort to study the data, find the patterns, validate the correctness, and maintain the patterns to keep on track of the ever-changing search keywords/ websites. This results in pattern discovery method hard to scale up to huge amount of segments and adapt to fast changing Internet. The data mining method, on the other hand, utilize the machine learning algorithms to automatically discover the patterns. Compared to manual process, the data mining approach has several advantages:

- Most of data mining methods, or major part of the application, could be implemented automatically. It greatly reduces the human effort.
- Easy to scale up. The data mining methods could be easily applied to more and more data given the data processing and learning algorithm are deterministic.
- Could track fast changing behavior. The queries could change over time and there are always new web pages created every day. The automatic data mining algorithms can quickly consume those new data and update their analysis results on user intention.

In the following parts, we will discuss in detail about the data mining in behavioral targeting. The application of data mining for online data usually consists of the following steps:

- **Data pre-processing.** The web data usually contains much noise, for example, page views from crawlers, clicks from click frauds. Those noises should be cleaned first. Other processing may also be required depending on the individual application. For example, query cleaning and keyword stemming.
- **Feature extraction.** This is to convert the raw data into a vector. The feature types also depend on the individual application, and domain knowledge can help to get effective features. The quality of the feature vector is the key for the success of whole data mining tasks. If necessary, dimension reduction is needed to make the data manageable for training.
- **Model training.** There are many algorithms can be applied, including decision trees, association rules, linear regression, SVM and so on (Mitchell, 1997). For online advertising, the model output can be clicks or actions. Validation is needed to evaluate the model performance and tune the model parameters. Besides, if the data has rapid-changing characteristic, the model need to be updated quickly as well.
- **Model application.** The model must be applied in online data for it to take real effect. Because there could be large volume of web data, applying the models in a timely manner is usually required.

Although the process is common to data mining tasks, behavioral targeting has its specific data sources: users' online behaviors. These could include many different types. Among them, the most popular types are search query, page view, online subscription, and clicks:

Figure 2. Poisson distribution with different mean values

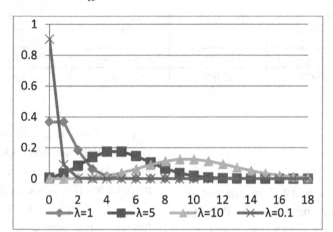

- **Search query.** Search queries are short, concise, user-chosen descriptions of users' intention. Since they are reflection of users interests in text keywords, it facilitate the data processing.
- **Page views.** Most of the time people spent on Internet is to view information pages, forums, blogs and so on. With the consideration that time is a person's critical resource, which pages a person viewed and how long he/she spent on the pages are important clue to show if the user is interested in the content of web pages. If we have ways to understand the pages content, the accumulation of large number of page views can reveal what a user is interested in.
- **Online subscriptions:** This includes news mail list, RSS feeds, online promotion subscription and etc. These subscriptions, like newspapers, reflect the users' interest because users "say" they are willing to read related information. It is also useful to track whether a user opens a news/RSS feed.
- **Clicks:** these clicks include the clicks on search results, hyperlinks in page content, and the advertisements. The clicks on search results are even better indications

than search queries. The click on advertisement, which is strongly connected to CTR, is valuable information. One potential problem is that sometime people click by mistake, so dwell time and bounce rate (Sculley, Malkin, Basu, & Bayardo, 2009) could be used to further improve the analysis of click data.

Due to the large amount of data and the requirement to facilitate the computation, count-based features have advantages because it can be partially calculated and aggregated. Besides, because there could be over millions of (keyword-based) features and billions of online users, it is critical to reduce the feature dimension. A method is to use features with sufficient support (number of users/samples). This method, although simple, is proven to be effective (Barboza, 2008).

Click Through Rate (CTR) usually is the performance measure of behavioral targeting because of its business impacts. For display ads or contextual ads, the CTR are relative low. There are less than 10 clicks for 10,000 ad views. Poisson distribution, which reflects the very rare events in large population, is appropriate to model the click event (Barboza, 2008; Belkin, Kelly, Kim, Kim, Lee, Muresan, Tang, Yuan, & Cool, 2003).

Table 1. CTR lift with different training data size

Percentage of training data	6.25%	12.5%	25%	50%	100%
CTR lift	15.83%	20.03%	22.87%	24.82%	25.98%
ROC area	81.93%	82.16%	82.34%	82.53%	82.67%

$$p(k) = \frac{\lambda^k e^{-\lambda}}{k!}$$

where λ is the parameter, and k is the number of clicks. Both the mean and the variance of Poisson distribution is λ. The following figure shows the Poisson distribution with different λ. It can be seen that when λ is small, the Poisson distribution is largely biased. But when λ is large, Poisson distribution is well approximated by normal distribution.

In click estimation, λ is the expected number of clicks from one user. $\lambda = f(x)$ where x is the user behavior vector. Given certain form of $f(x)$, the λ could be estimated using MLE. The research in Barboza (2008) applies such models to Yahoo! data. During the experiments, four weeks' data are used for training and one successive week is used for evaluation. The baseline system for comparison is a classification-based system using linear regression. The results shown in Table 1 (cited from Barboza (2008)) illustrate the Poisson regression without classification can achieve 25.98% CTR lift.

2.4 Online Commercial Intent

The above two sections address how to understand end-users with their static and long-term attributes. In this section, we introduce the algorithm to detect the users' instant intention by analyzing the pages being viewed and the queries being entered.

With the rapid growth of online e-commerce, there are more and more commercial-related online activities. If a user has an intention to conduct certain online commercial action, such as purchasing, it is said this user has an "online commercial intention" (OCI). Whether the users have intention for a commercial production could be detected (Brandweek, 2008).

As there are two major types of user behavior, namely page view and search query, and have different characteristics, the commercial intention should be detected differently. Overall, the detection is in a supervised leaning framework, that is, the ground-truths are human-labeled and a classifier is trained for either web page or search query. Then, for any unseen web pages and search queries, the trained model will be applied.

2.4.1 Web Page OCI Detection

The web pages are relatively easier to process because they have sufficient keywords. Besides, the HTML tags can provide a lot of information. Given a web page, two kinds of keyword-based features are extracted:

- *Nit(k)*: for each keyword in the "inner" text (text within the HTML tags and can be viewed by web users), it forms one dimension of the feature, and the feature value is its count in the inner text.
- *Nat(k)*: for each keyword in the "tag" of HTML pages, it forms a dimension of the feature and the feature value is its count in "tags".

As there are many different keywords, this could introduce too many feature dimensions and a lot of noisy data. Then feature selection is applied to trim the features to use only "good" keywords. For each keyword, two measures are defined:

$$Significance(k) = \frac{2 * Max(\Pr(k|C_+), \Pr(k|C_-))}{\Pr(k|C_+) + \Pr(k|C_-)} - 1$$

$$Frequency(k) = \Pr(k|C_+ \cup C_-)$$

where $Pr(k|C_x)$ refers to the probability keyword k occurring in web pages belonging to C_x, and C_+ for commercial pages and C_- for non-commercial pages. Both measures have their values between 0 and 1. With manually set thresholds, only few keywords having both measures larger than the thresholds are left. After that, an SVM model is trained with labeled commercial and non-commercial web pages.

2.4.2 Search Query OCI Detection

The process of search query OCI detection is similar as that of web pages. But there are only very few keywords in a search query (Barboza, 2008). The search result information could be used to enrich the information for learning. There are two kinds of enrichment method:

* The search result page from the search engine Given a query, the search engine will return a result page, which shows the information about some (usually 10) related web pages. For each page, the returned information contains the page title, page URL, and snippet exerted from the web page content. The exerted snippets consist of the parts that match the keywords in search query, so they are the informational abstraction. Another advantage of search result page is that its length is relatively constant. This benefits the text processing and learning process. In this way, the OCI detection of search query is converted to

Table 2. Human-labeled data set

	Web pages	Queries
Commercial	4,074	602
Non-Commercial	21,823	790
Confused	289	16
(total)	26,186	1,408

the OCI detection of search result page, whose process has been stated in above section.

* The landing web pages of top search results A further step to enrich the information is to explore the landing pages of search results. Each of those pages could have sufficient information for OCI detection. Suppose the landing pages of top N search results are used and their OCIs forms an N-dimension feature vector

$$(OCI_1, OCI_2, ..., OCI_N)$$

where OCI_n is the predicted value of landing pages of n-th search result. Given the above feature vector, a SVM model is build to predict the search query OCI.

The experiments are conducted on a data set containing 26,186 web pages and 1408 queries. All those pages and queries are identified by human to be either commercial or non-commercial.

The performances are measured by precision/recall measure usually used in information retrieval. Table 2 shows the OCI of queries could be predicted with more than 0.90 precision and recall, while above 0.80 for web pages. Both performances are good.

3. AUDIENCE INTELLIGENCE ON ADVERTISERS

As mentioned in section 1, there are also studies to understand the advertisers, whose investments are

Table 3. The performance of predict web page/ query OCI

	Precision	Recall	F1
Page	0.930	0.925	0.928
Query	0.86	0.82	0.84

the source of whole eco-system. In the following, we will present such study.

3.1 Advertiser Understanding

Web publishers are continuously trying to improve their products or add new functionalities/content types to attract end users, while they also hope to attract advertisers to deliver more ads on their sites. Therefore, it is important to know whether a new function or a new channel will satisfy the advertisers. A usual method is the publishers offer the functions to a few selected advertisers (Pregibon, & Lambert, 2007). These advertisers have the freedom to try the new functions. The publishers thus have to carefully analyze these trials to evaluate if the new functions/content type is effective, and more difficultly, how effective it should be.

From the view point of the ad publisher (search engine in particular), (Pregibon, & Lambert, 2007) proposes a method to study the behavior/business of the advertisers to understand how publishers' functional change can affect the advertisers. It introduces user propensity score and doubly robust estimator to investigate the validity in white-list trials.

The advertisers, which are selected by offering the new function, may not be the random advertisers. Especially, the advertisers who actually use the new module probably share some common characteristic, such as have more advertising budget, be familiar with web the publisher, and so on. Thus, this set of advertisers cannot be regarded as a "random" sample set for granted, and

the effectiveness cannot be simply measure by the difference between two advertiser sets.

To validly get the difference between before and after an advertiser uses the new function, it would be desired to know the outcome Y_1 (after use the function) and Y_0 (before use the function). But because only a few sample advertisers are chosen for the experiment, it is impossible to obtain both Y_1 and Y_0 of one advertiser at same time. Therefore, the effectiveness measured by the outcome difference $diff=E(Y_1)-E(Y_0)$ cannot be obtained directly. Suppose we can form a feature vector X, which contains all the factors associating the outcome and whether an advertiser tried the function, there could be independence between outcomes and the class as depicted as following:

$$Y \perp Z \,|X$$

which means for a given value of feature vector X, the distribution of outcome Y is independent to class label Z. X is called confounders. The effectiveness for a given value of X could be calculated, without the requirement to have both Y_1 and Y_0 for one advertiser. But there is the difficulty to calculate over all possible X values because of its huge value space. In Lunceford & Davidian(2007), it is proved that

$$Y \perp Z \,|p\big(x\big) \; if \; 0 < p\big(x\big) < 1 \, for\, all\, x$$

where $p(x)=P(Z=1|X=x)$ is the conditional probability of the advertisers are selected for trying the new function, which is call propensity score. This could greatly reduce the computation complexity, because p(x) is a one dimensional factor while X may have a lot of dimensions and hard to traverse its value space.

Given a certain propensity score $p(x)$, its difference between the selected/unselected advertisers could be easily computed as $E(Y=1\,|\,p(x))$-

$E(Y=0|p(x))$. The overall expectation of such difference on all $p(x)$ could be calculated as

$$diff_{DO} = \frac{1}{n}\sum_{i=1}^{n}(P\left(Y|Z = 1, x_i\right) - P\left(Y|Z = 0, x_i\right))$$

where n is the number of advertisers and x_i the confounders for an advertiser. This is a direct estimation of the function effectiveness. It is easy to compute, but any mistake in the outcome model may lead to wrong estimation.

Another estimate of the outcome is

$$E\left(Y|Z = 1\right) = E\left\{E\left(Y|Z = 1, X\right)P\left(Z = 1|X\right)\right\}$$

$$= E\left\{E\left(Y_1|X\right)P(X)\right\}$$

where $p(x)$ is the estimate of propensity score.

Both $diff_{ipw}$ and $diff_{DO}$ are valid depending on if the outcome model is correct. The combination of the two estimates can increase the robustness, in that either the output model or the assumed propensity model is not correct. The combined estimate could be written in terms of either $diff_{ipw}$ or $diff_{DO}$:

$$diff_{DR} = diff_{DO} + \frac{1}{n}\sum_{i=1}^{n}\left\{\frac{Z_i\left(Y_i - m_1\left(x_i\right)\right)}{p\left(x_i\right)} - \frac{(1 - Z_i)(Y_i - m_0\left(x_i\right))}{1 - p\left(x_i\right)}\right\}$$

$$= diff_{IPW} - \frac{1}{n}\sum_{i=1}^{n}\left\{\frac{(Z_i - p(x_i))m_1\left(x_i\right)}{p(x_i)} + \frac{(Z_i - p(x_i))m_0\left(x_i\right)}{1 - p(x_i)}\right\}$$

It is shown (Richardson, Dominowska, Ragno, 2007) that for all asymptotic unbiased estimate based of $diff_{ipw}$, $diff_{DR}$ has the smallest asymptotic variance. Pregibon & Lambert (2007) uses this model to explore a sample set of the advertisers of a major search engine. The experiment results show the $diff_{DR}$ could be used to tell which set of advertisers are mostly impacted by a new function of the search engine.

4. RELATED ISSUES

In addition to the problems addressed above, there are many other factors impacting the online advertising. One example is the ad blocking by web browsers. Such ad blocking can lead to wrong estimation of advertising effects. In following parts, we discuss the privacy issue, which receives more attention in current days.

4.1 Privacy Protection

While web publishers and advertisers try their best to understand the users, there is increasing fear from the public on protecting their privacies. The major concern is that the large amount of logged data can eventually record everyone's every activity, so the companies can know your age, home address, occupation, insurance status and other personal information.

A research (Padmanabhan, & Yang, n.d.) shows the behavior on web could provide sufficient information to identify a unique user. It is found that even 3-16 sessions is enough for a small data set. The performance will drop down while the number of users increases. As there are 220M online users in US (Barboza, 2008), it remains difficult to identify each one in such a large user set. However, people are spending more and more time on the web, it is not unusual for a user to have thousands of queries, page views, clicks, postings, and online shopping within a month. It is natural for users to worry about they can be fully tracked/ identified by commercial companies.

As a response to the increasing privacy discussion, the companies including publishers and advertisers began to assure the users they will use the data in a proper way. There is also the governmental regularization effort involved. In November 2007, FTC held a town hall on behavioral advertising, putting special focus on protecting user privacy (Federal Trade Commission, 2007). There are several key issues are raised as well as proposed solution principle. The following are some examples:

- Websites, who collect the user data, should provide clear, concise, and consumer-friendly statement to users, before their activities are recorded.
- Companies who collected data should secure their data and retain them only as long as necessary for legitimate goals
- Expressive consent must be obtained before companies collect any "sensitive" data.

The self-regulatory principles are not fixed, but are under on-going changes to catch-up the fast development of the Internet technologies. The latest change was made in Feb. 2009 (Federal Trade Commission, 2009).

The good news is that according to Forrester data, despite people's concerns about online privacy, they'll trade some of it for relevancy (Brandweek, 2008): 29% of respondents said they would prefer to receive appropriately targeted ads as opposed to random ones (37% of respondents were neutral on this question, and 35% opposed). This suggests the targeting ads may have the potential to relieve the users' repellent to ads, as well as better performance.

5. SUMMARY

In this chapter, we address the online audience understanding, mainly from publishers' viewpoints to study end-users and advertisers. It is critical to understand both of them to achieve the goal: bring proper ads to proper users at proper time.

6. REFERENCES

Barboza, D. (2008, July 26). China Surpasses U.S. in Number of Internet Users. *The New York Times*. Retrieved from http://www.nytimes.com/2008/07/26/business/worldbusiness/26internet.html

Belkin, N. J., Kelly, D., Kim, G., Kim, J.-Y., Lee, H.-J., Muresan, G., et al. (2003). Query Length In Interactive Information Retrieval. In *Proceedings of the 26th Annual International ACM SIGIR Conference on Research and Development in Information Retrieval*, July 28-August 01, 2003, Toronto, Canada

Brandweek (2008, October 20). *Behavior Issues*. Retrieved from http://www.brandweek.com/bw/content_display/current-issue/e3ie08aad-b553c2ade99bd881d67704e566

Chen, Y., & Pavlov, D. (2009). *CIKM 09*. Practical Lessons of Data Mining at Yahoo.

Chen, Y., Pavlov, D., & Canny, J. F. (2009). Large-Scale Behavioral Targeting. ACM Conference on Knowledge Discovery and Data Mining (KDD 2009).

Conversion rate. (n.d.). Retrieved from http://en.wikipedia.org/wiki/Conversion_rate

Dai, K., Zhao, L., Nie, Z., Wen, J.-R., Wang, L., & Li, Y. (2006). Detecting Online Commercial Intention. In *Proceedings of the 15th international conference on World Wide Web* (pp. 829-837). Scotland.

De Bock, K. W., & Van Den Poel, D. (2009). Predicting Website Audience Demographics For Web Advertising Targeting Using Multi-Website Clickstream Data. *Fundamenta Informaticae*, *97*, 1–19.

Engagement mapping (n.d.). Retrieved from http://www.atlassolutions.com/institute_engagement-mapping.aspx

Federal Trade Commission. (2007). Online Behavioral Advertising: Moving the Discussion Forward to Possible Self-Regulatory Principles. Retrieved from http://www.ftc.gov/os/2007/12/P859900stmt.pdf

Federal Trade Commission. (2009). Self-Regulatory Principles For Online Behavioral Advertising: Tracking, Targeting, and Technology. Retrieved from http://www.ftc.gov/os/2009/02/P085400behavadreport.pdf

Li, T., Liu, N., Yan, J., Wang, G., Bai, F., & Chen, Z. (2009). A Markov Chain Model For Integrating Behavioral Targeting Into Contextual Advertising. In *Proceedings of the Third International Workshop on Data Mining and Audience Intelligence for Advertising, Paris, France* (pp. 1-9).

Li, Y., Surendran, A.C., & Shen, D. (2007). Data mining and audience intelligence for advertising. *ACM SIGKDD Explorations Newsletter, 9*(2).

Lunceford, J. K., & Davidian, M. (2007). Stratification And Weighting Via The Propensity Score In Estimation Of Causal Treatment Effects: A Comparative Study. *Statistics in Medicine, 23*, 2937–2960. doi:10.1002/sim.1903

Lyris HQ staff writer (2005). Average Email Click Through Rate. Retrieved from http://lyrishq.lyris.com/index.php/Email-Marketing/Average-Email-Click-Through-Rate.html

Mitchell, T. (1997). *Machine Learning*. McGraw Hill.

On the Internet, nobody knows you're a dog. (n.d.). Retrieved from http://en.wikipedia.org/wiki/On_the_Internet,_nobody_knows_you're_a_dog

Padmanabhan, B., & Yang, Y. (n.d.). Clickprints on the Web: Are there signatures in Web browsing data? Retrieved from http://knowledge.wharton.upenn.edu/papers/1323.pdf?CFID=720523&CFTOKEN=57530247D.

Pregibon, D., & Lambert, D. (2007). Assessing New Features For Online Advertisers. In *ADKDD '07 San Jose*. CA, USA: More Bang For Their Bucks.

Richardson, M., Dominowska, E., & Ragno, R. (2007). Predicting Clicks: Estimating The Click-Through Rate For New Ads. In *Proceedings of the 16th International Conference on World Wide Web, May 08-12, 2007, Banff, Alberta, Canada*.

Robins, J., Rotnitzky, A., & Zhao, L. (1994). Estimation of regression coefficients when some regressors are not always observed. *Journal of the American Statistical Association, 89*, 846–866. doi:10.2307/2290910

Sculley, D., Malkin, R., Basu, S., & Bayardo, R. J. (2009). Predicting Bounce Rates In Sponsored Search Advertisements. In *SIGKDD Conference on Knowledge Discovery and Data Mining (KDD)* (pp. 1325-1334).

Shen, D., Surendran, A. C., & Li, Y. (2008). Report on the Second KDD Workshop on Data Mining for Advertising. *ACM SIGKDD Explorations Newsletter, 10*(2).

Tsoumakas, G., & Katakis, I. (2007). Multi-Label Classification: An Overview. *International Journal of Data Warehousing and Mining, 3*(3), 1–13.

Section 5
Mobile Advertising

Chapter 15
Targeted Mobile Advertisement in the IP Multimedia Subsystem

C. Tselios
University of Patras, Greece

H. Perkuhn
Ericsson Research, Germany

K. Vandikas
Ericsson Research, Germany

M. Kampmann
Ericsson Research, Germany

ABSTRACT

This chapter provides an overview on targeted advertisement in the IP Multimedia Subsystem (IMS). A new entity called Personalization and Advertisement Insertion Logic (PAIL) is introduced, which enables a mobile network operator to exploit contextual data stored in its network for personalized advertisement selection. PAIL combines location information with user profile information in order to select the best match from a pool of advertisement clips. This selection is based on the Vector Space Model. For the evaluation of this framework a series of tests with users were executed. These tests show that using contextual information from the IMS network a subjective better match of advertisement clips with user interests is achievable.

INTRODUCTION

In traditional media such as print media, television or radio, advertisement is one of the main revenue sources. With the rise of the Internet in the recent decades, a new form of media has been established that also relies on advertisement as one of its core

DOI: 10.4018/978-1-60960-189-8.ch015

revenue sources. Compared to traditional media, where advertisements are mostly focused on a specific target group and less to a certain viewer or listener with his or her individual preferences, the Internet allows for a much more targeted i.e. personalized advertisement presentation. Due to increasing bandwidth in mobile networks, the availability of smartphones with higher display resolutions and thus the increasing popularity of the mobile Internet, mobile advertisement is gaining more and more importance. In the case of mobile advertisement, targeted advertisement is even more evident e.g. using the location of a user for a better advertisement selection. Thus the provision of contextual data like location is of high relevance. In mobile networks, a transition towards Next Generation Networks (NGN) is currently happening. The most prominent example for NGN is the IP Multimedia Subsystem (IMS) that is under standardization by 3GPP.

The problem, this chapter is investigating, is how can a network operator leverage intrinsic subscriber information, for instance the subscriber's position or the fashion a subscriber uses the operator's network, in order to provide more meaningful, more relevant advertisements to that subscriber. More specifically, this chapter studies targeted mobile advertising with an application to the IMS, due to its prominence.

This chapter is organized in the following fashion: First of all an overview is provided on mobile advertisement concepts along with an introduction to IMS. Moreover, a solution framework for targeted advertisement in IMS is presented. Later on, a new entity is introduced, the Personalization and Advertisement Insertion Logic (PAIL), which is the core component of the proposed targeted advertisement solution and is presented in detail. Part of the PAIL is the advertisement selection algorithm that is based on a Vector Space Model (VSM). Finally, an evaluation of the advertisement selection is presented which includes user tests.

BACKGROUND

A. Methods of Modern Advertisement

As the advent of Web 2.0 progresses, a new realm of services is spawned; a realm that allows for the application of novel business models that incorporate rich-context based information. A predominant source of such context-based infor-

mation is the direct access that telephony network operators have to their subscribers' personal data. In networks like the IMS, a lot of context data is available today but its potential is not fully used. The momentum on the operator side to exploit this informational wealth is increasing though, manifested in the establishment of lobby groups such as the Subscriber Profile User Group (2009). The exploitation of context data, together with the trusted-provider status in the value chain and the established business and charging relation is a huge potential for establishing business in the new field of personalized advertising; a field that is currently dominated by web companies like Google or Yahoo. Business opportunities enabled by personalized advertisements have gained a lot of attention. Recently a market research in Germany regarding Content Delivery Platforms (2008) revealed that targeted mobile advertisements lead to a response rate of 3.4%, meaning that 34 out of 1000 users e.g. click on a banner displayed to them. Compared to other forms of direct marketing this figure is extremely high, and consequently 74% of the advertisement companies see their expectations of this form of advertisement matched or even exceeded. From the user's point of view, according to the study, users are much more likely to appreciate this new form of advertisement when the content displayed to them actually suits their personal taste and needs. This places the mobile operators into a strong position, because the high response rate and the better customer acceptance leads to a significantly higher price for the cost per thousand impressions (CPM) they can charge to the advertisement companies.

The goal of targeted advertising is to deliver to a user, a set of advertisements for products that the user is actually interested in. The realization of this goal strongly depends on the available information. One can define the following categories of targeting:

- **Behavioral targeting:** Based on e.g. the user's web-browsing behavior

- **Contextual targeting:** Based on the content displayed to the user
- **Demographic targeting:** Based on age, gender, income, mobility, educational attainment, employment status, location

Web site owners that want to target advertisements shown on their site have the possibility to make use of the data that a user produces by surfing the web. Information, such as which sites were visited or what searches were made, is used to select the advertisements shown on the web site. Identifying visitors is usually achieved by assigning unique id cookies to every visitor. In this way a user can be tracked in terms of sites visited in the web.

Contextual targeting is also commonly used by web site owners or content providers. It does not rely so much on the history of visited sites but rather takes the content into account that is currently shown to the visitor. In the case of web site owners, the advertisement is related to the content of the site. In the TV industry this scheme has been used since the early days of TV commercials. The advertisements shown are usually selected for the suspected majority of the audience (e.g. home improvement ads during sports shows etc.). Recently, schemes that try to establish an even closer link between content and related advertisements have come up: e.g. right after a certain scene was shown in a movie, a product is advertised that has some relation to the content of the preceding scene (e.g. "TV in Context" by Turner Entertainment Networks (2009).

Advertising networks (such as e.g. Undertone Networks, Navegg, eXelate) are using this information to make reasonable guesses about the demographic makeup of the audiences. This allows the networks to sell audiences rather than sites as described in IMedia Connection (2004).

Telecom operators are in the unique position to have access to demographic information of their subscribers right away; they do not have to derive it implicitly from any other information.

The subject of mobile advertisement has been taken up also by standardization bodies. Being the biggest standardization body dealing with this matter, the Open Mobile Alliance (OMA) proposes the MobAd Enabler in OMA-TS (2008) with an earlier version already planned in Mobile Advertising Requirements (2007). This concept takes the operator's network and the end device into account for selecting and delivering advertisements. Both network centric and device centric approaches are covered by this proposal. The main functional components of the MobAd Enabler are the Ad Server and the Ad Engine. The Ad Server provides functions for advertisement selection and delivery as well as functions for advertisement metrics data handling and user/ service data management. The Ad Engine provides an advertisement acquisition and delivery function, an advertisement selection function, an advertisement metrics data handling function and a user / service / device data handling function.

The solution proposed in this chapter for targeted mobile advertising in the IMS considers concepts of the OMA specification in the sense that it is designed to use demographic information that are directly available to operators. Therefore, an algorithm is used that matches information about advertisements with demographic information. Since one of the major end-user features that the IMS provides is the Presence framework, it is assumed that users are given the option to convey their preferences regarding leisure time activities, favorite food etc. within this framework. Furthermore, it is assumed that this information is taken into account as input for the matching algorithm - with the full knowledge and consent of the user.

Web pages designers have the option of using the "meta name" HTML tag to provide keywords as well as full text describing the content of an HTML page. This is especially useful if the page represents an advertisement, so that it can be easily categorized and shown to a targeted audience. Within the premises of the proposed solution, it is assumed that an advertisement clip is described by a short text, which is taken as input for the selection algorithm.

The algorithm that performs proper advertisement selection in the proposed solution is called Content Selection Algorithm; it is described in the following and is based on a mathematical model called Vector Space Model.

B. The IP Multimedia Subsystem

The IP Multimedia Subsystem (IMS) is the 3GPP solution for a Next Generation Network (NGN) core.

Defined by the International Telecommunications Union (ITU), an NGN is a "packet-based network capable of providing telecommunication services and of making use of multiple broadband, QoS-enabled transport technologies and in which service-related functions are independent from underlying transport-related technologies" (Knightson, Morita, & Towle, 2005). This set of standards aims to bridge the worlds of the Internet and cellular network technologies bringing a control layer that offers convergence, service provision, fast service creation, and service interconnection based on open standards (Camarillo & Garcia-Martin, 2006).

The convergence provided by IMS gives network operators the chance to take advantage of the combined growth in mobile communications and that of the Internet as mentioned in 3GPP TS 23.228 (2007). Therefore it is sound to estimate that this platform is solid and will play a major role in telecommunication technology in the near future.

There are three compelling reasons given by Camarillo and Garcia-Martin (2006) that explain the momentum IMS has gained towards becoming a widespread telecommunication platform.

- **Quality of Service.** Although Internet services are already present in the packet switched domain of a cellular network, those services do not offer the end-to-end level of Quality of Service, users have

come to expect from circuit switched domain services (Camarillo & Garcia-Martin, 2006). For example, modern multimedia services such as Voice Over IP (VoIP) might encounter operational problems due to lack of resources, and this leads to the necessity for the new platform to include mechanisms that provide a predictable user experience.

- **Charging.** Charging policies based on bulk data transfer are common among carriers when users operate in the packet switched domain. Data stream content remains unknown to all but the final recipient and this might lead to overwhelming expenses since charging is only estimated by the amount of generated traffic, rather than the overall service. Within the IMS-domain, service aware functions do exist, allowing proper service-oriented and more convenient charging.

- **Integration of Different Services.** In a modern competitive telecommunications field, where network operators strive for revenue, operators are very interested in reducing the cost of new service development. A method to achieve this goal is service re-use. In addition to financial benefits, such an action paves the road to the opening of networks to services offered by third parties.

The IMS specification was introduced in UMTS Release 5 and it was refined in subsequent releases of 3GPP TS 22.146 (2006), further enforcing the use of Internet protocols and open standards on the design and development of the new platform. Functionally, the IMS is organized in discrete layers each one in charge of providing different aspects of the overall service.

In a rather abstract depiction of the main architecture there are two different layers: Control Layer and Application Layer. Figure 1 shows the structure and the various components of each one.

Figure 1. The IMS architecture

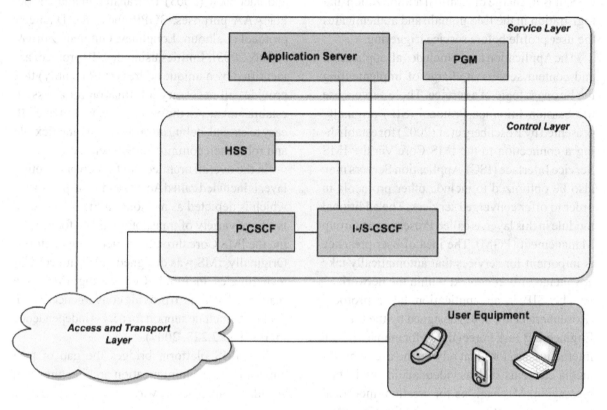

The Control Layer includes all functions operating for a reliable establishment of multimedia sessions. There are functions for Authentication, Authorization and Accounting (AAA), location, negotiation, routing, and charging. The two most important functions are the Home Subscriber Server (HSS) and the Call Session Control Function (CSCF). The HSS is the main user data repository of the IMS domain. All data related to a specific user are stored in the HSS and is used by different nodes for multimedia session handling. Depending on the total number of users a single domain supports, there can be more than one such repository. The CSCF oversees and controls the establishment of sessions, further divided into three separate parts:

The Proxy-CSCF (P-CSCF) is the signaling entry point from any access network described in Ericsson AB (2007). Designed as an inbound/ outbound stateful server, is in charge of establishing a secure connection with the user equipment. The Interrogating-CSCF (I-CSCF) acts as the first point of contact between peer IMS Domains It is in charge of finding the S-CSCF in which a user in the home domain is registered. In addition, whenever there is a case of a roaming user that is entering the local domain, it is responsible for handling signaling between user's home and the current one, but without keeping any state information. Finally there is the Serving-CSCF (S-CSCF) that plays the role of the central node in the control layer, by performing functions related to the actual establishment of multimedia sessions. All signaling traffic is routed through this entity heading towards user devices. By inspecting the so called Initial Filter Criteria (Camarillo & Garcia-Martin, 2006), the S-CSCF determines all possible service invocations. Assisted by the

HSS, it is in charge of terminal authorization and registration in the IMS domain and authenticates the user profile before service triggering.

The Application Layer includes all application and content servers in charge of implementing the business logic of a service. These servers use the Session Initiation Protocol (SIP) originally presented by Rosenberg et al.(2002) for establishing a connection to the IMS Core via the IMS Service Interface (ISC). Application Servers may also be optimized to include other protocols in order to offer converged services. The additional module in this layer, is called Presence and Group Management (PGM). The idea of user presence is important for services that automatically take advantage of user context within the network.

The SIP is an application layer protocol (Rosenberg et al., 2002) designed by the Internet Engineering Task Force (IETF) for managing rich interactive sessions that rely on the use of multimedia elements such as video, audio and instant messaging. Mechanisms for creation, modification and termination of a session are included, while it operates independently of the transport protocol and of the types of sessions established with it. SIP is a text based protocol that imitates a request-response transaction method where a transaction is generated after a client issues a request activating a particular method in the server causing it to respond, while it keeps simplicity and readability at the same time, by inheriting many design principles from the widely used Hypertext Transmission Protocol (HTTP) (Fielding et al., 1999). This protocol is really flexible and able to operate on top of User Datagram Protocol (UDP) as well as Transmission Control Protocol (TCP). It is also used together with several other protocols in a multimedia system. These protocols include Session Description Protocol (SDP) proposed by Handley, Jacobson and Perkins (2006) to describe session parameters like codec, bitrate, etc., and the Realtime Transfer Protocol (RTP) originally introduced by Schulzrinne, Casner, Frederick and Jacobson (2003) to transfer media traffic. For AAA purposes, 3GPP chose the Diameter protocol (Calhoun, Loughney, Guttman, Zorn & Arkko, 2003). Entities using the SIP protocol are identified by a unique address (SIP identity) that provides all necessary information for a session establishment. All the previous features make SIP easy to extend, debug and use for creating flexible and robust telecommunication services.

In the overall architecture framework another layer is included called Access and Transport Layer which is depicted as aa cloud in Figure 1. There is a huge variety of transport methods for accessing the IMS Core through carrier infrastructures. Originally, IMS was designed only with cellular technologies in mind. Considering IMS as a platform that aims to provide convergence, 3GPP decided to include support for access independence (3GPP TS 22.228, 2007).

The IMS platform bridges the gap of past and future telecommunication architectures in a seamless and efficient way.

FRAMEWORK FOR MOBILE ADVERTISEMENT

There are two aspects that are of special interest when introducing mobile advertisement. Using information about the user, e.g. location, raises the question of privacy. Another aspect when introducing such a function in the network is scalability and network impact. Both is highlighted in the following.

Behavioral targeting techniques in advertisement often neglect a rather important user right, the right of privacy. Companies that offer advertisement services, sometimes use monitoring methods that might cause people to feel uncomfortable, provided they are aware of what exactly is happening. User data is scanned with great detail and the results are taken into consideration for discovering patterns revealing human behavior and socialization. The problem of misuse of personal data is gaining attention, also by legislative bodies. But still consumers can not be so sure what is going to happen with their data, once they are given away.

The relationship between users and telecommunication carriers is different than the one mentioned above, in the sense that a legal bond in contract form exists between both parties that regulates the use of personal data. The information that Carriers get could be given to the advertisement companies in anonymous form and could still be used for the benefit of the user - for example by introducing certain business models that lower the usage costs in exchange for personalized advertisements.

In the IMS case user data is stored in the HSS database operated by the network provider. All data regarding a single user including presence and device information is available to the carrier and a module such as PAIL can access and use it for service enhancements. Any network provider considering an extension of its network with this kind of enhancement would like to know about the network impact. A rough estimation of the network load that such an entity would cause on e.g. an HSS shows that the approach scales quite well: Selecting advertisements for an assumed subscriber base of 100.000 within ~20 minutes would cause a signaling load of a little less than 100 requests per second at the HSS. The time frame used in this calculation is taken from a use case scenario where it is assumed that commercial breaks in e.g. a streamed movie (via Mobile TV) take place every twenty minutes. In this time frame the system should be able to choose the best possible advertisement for each user. Carrier grade systems can handle ~10.000 requests per second, which means the additional load would be below 1%. Therefore it can safely be stated that the total number of users such entities can handle would not cause too much extra load.

Advertisement Selection Scheme in IMS

A. The Personalization and Advertisement Insertion Logic

Current mobile advertising approaches focus on the advertisement types and channels that are typically used by most mobile users: text based advertisements delivered via Short Message Service (SMS), Multimedia Message Service (MMS) or Unstructured Supplementary Services Data (USSD) and advertisement banners using the Wireless Access Protocol (WAP) pull channel. There are products, like the Ericsson Ad Orchestrator for example, that enable operators and advertisers to run an advertisement campaign. The advertisements can be targeted according to input the users have to give themselves, like age, gender, income, interests etc.

The "Mobile TV Joint UMTS Forum/GSMA Work Group" discusses and proposes solutions for targeted advertising in Mobile TV. As referred to by OMA, they also suggest terminal based and network based solutions. In a network based advertisement system, they describe three steps for personalization

1. Collect information about users and context
2. Select/modify the advertisement according to this information
3. Deliver the selected advertisement to the user or group of users

Only the selected advertisement is delivered to the user. A terminal based advertisement system would require two steps

1. Deliver all advertisements to all user terminals
2. Each terminal selects and renders the advertisement according to the user and context.

Figure 2. PAIL within IMS architecture

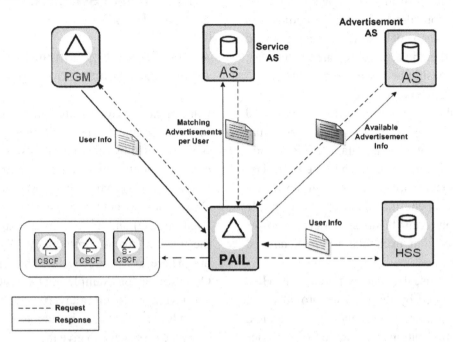

There can also be mixtures of both approaches, where e.g. a regionally relevant set of advertisements is sent to a subgroup qualified by location and on the terminals advertisements are selected based on personal preferences and context (3rd Whitepaper Mobile Advertising).

According to 3rd Whitepaper Mobile Advertising the delivery methods can be broadcast, unicast or a hybrid approach. Unicast delivery allows a very fine grained targeting using the network based approach. When broadcast only is used for delivery, the decentralized, terminal based approach must be followed. A hybrid approach can cater for a compromise of resource-efficient delivery and targeted advertising, e.g. by delivering advertisements to homogeneous as possible subgroups of users.

With the PAIL an entity for enabling the utilization of user-specific information that is available to operators is introduced, in order to offer personalized services such as personalized advertisements. It is meant to enhance different existing services, live and nonlive (e.g. Podcast,

Mobile TV) by controlling the selection of suitable advertisements that are then inserted by other entities. The PAIL design itself is platform independent. As target architecture the IP Multimedia Subsystem (IMS) is chosen, since it is the 3GPP standardized solution for all-IP networks. As shown in Figure 2, the overall architecture spreads across two layers out of the three Layers that exist in the IMS Architecture: the Control Layer, where all modules operated by the network provider are located, and the Service Layer that contains all kinds of Application Servers (AS), some created by the network provider in order to enable fundamental services and others by 3rd party service providers. The third layer, Access and Transport Layer is not included in Figure 2, since PAIL does not introduce any change to its operation or message flow between its components.

The integration of the proposed solution rather deep within the network allows personalization based on user information and enables making decisions about the delivery mode.

Figure 3. PAIL architecture

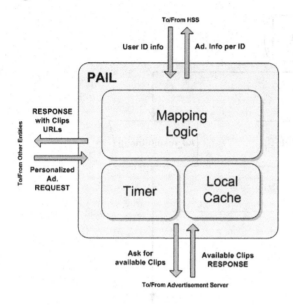

Figure 2 shows PAIL located within the IMS domain where all network nodes are under the control of the network operator. It communicates with the necessary entities for getting user information and it is also connected to two AS of the Service Layer as well as to PGM. The first application server, Service AS, represents an end user service like e.g. podcast while the second, Advertisement AS, is an advertisement clip metadata repository, where information for available advertisement clips is stored. The other two entities located in the IMS domain are HSS and the three types CSCFs. Inside PAIL the Content Selection Algorithm (CSA) takes care of the actual matching process. In addition, PAIL uses a local cache for temporary storage of advertisement meta descriptions. Communication to the network entities PGM, CSCFs and HSS is done via the standardized interfaces these modules use as described in 3GPP TS 29.228 (2004) as well as in OMA-TS(2008). The inner PAIL architecture is presented in Figure 3:

Inside PAIL the correlation of information regarding user profile and advertisement clip metadata takes place, in order for the best possible match of advertisement per user to be chosen.

As shown in Figure 4, this module remains in standby (or idle) status until a request for personalized advertisement arrives from an AS. After issuing the requests, PAIL sets up a Timer and switches to "Wait for Response" mode as depicted in Figure 5.

In case a response arrives, either containing User Profile data or advertisement metadata, the new information is stored in the local cache and the module performs a test to check whether or not all required input has arrived. If yes, the CSA starts. If not, it goes back into "Wait for Response" status. PAIL is designed to wait for all responses until a timer countdown occurs. In such case an error message is generated, that informs the entity that sent the initial request message and the module returns to its original standby status. When all information (about the user and the advertisement metadata) is in place, the mapping algorithm is employed.

The full communication diagram between PAIL and all other network components is presented in the following picture:

According to Figure 6, a series of Requests and Responses takes place before any personalization decision is made.

1. The Service AS issues a Personalization Request to the PAIL, containing a User ID.
2. The PAIL sends a User Data Request (e.g. SIP SUBSCRIBE) to the PGM asking for all available user attributes belonging to the specific ID.
3. PGM responds (e.g. SIP NOTIFY) with all available data, which is stored in PAIL's cache for future use.
4. PAIL sends a User Data Request to the HSS asking for user's location, again based on the User ID.
5. HSS responds and the user location is also saved in PAIL's cache.
6. PAIL sends a request to the Advertisement AS, asking for all available clips in order to select the most suitable ones for the user.

Figure 4. PAIL standby status flow diagram

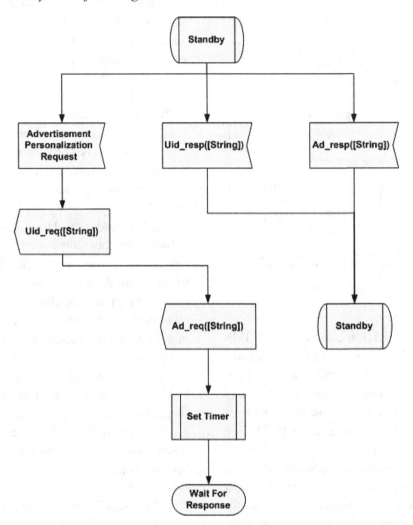

7. Advertisement AS responds by sending a data structure containing a list of all available clips as well as each clip's metadata.
8. The CSA correlates advertisements to user IDs.
9. PAIL responds to the Service AS by sending a data structure that contains a list of matching advertisements for each user ID.

It should be mentioned that the communication between PAIL and the Advertisement AS (steps 6, 7) may also take place in the background, since it is independent from all other request and response

messaging. In steps 2-5 the acquisition of context information is conducted. The provisioning of this information happens earlier or is happening on a constant basis, respectively. Location, for example, is updated all the time. Other information that can e.g. be stored in the PGM like age and gender, is of course more static.

The correlation mentioned in step 8 means that according to the CSA the closest match of user information and advertisement description is found.

Figure 5. PAIL wait for response status flow diagram

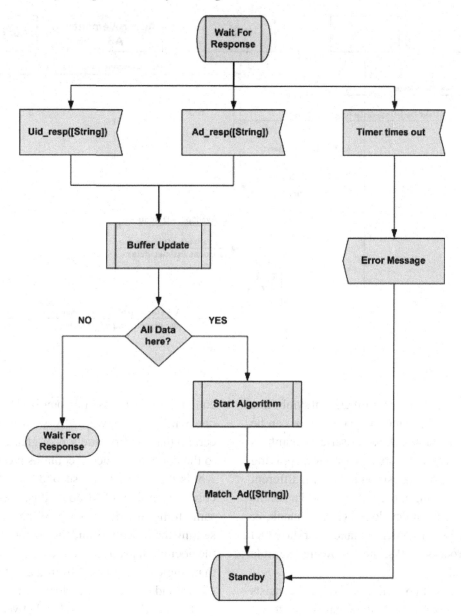

B. Content Selection Algorithm (CSA)

The CSA is part of the Mapping Logic function. It uses a mathematical model called Vector Space Model (VSM) in order to perform the user profile and advertisement metadata correlation.

VSM is an algebraic model for representing text documents as vectors or identifiers (Grossman &

Frieder, 2001). Here a document is considered a plain text file. Documents are represented in such a way that in order to compare their similarity, all it takes is to check the corresponding vectors.

Since all documents consist of words, numbers and a finite variety of symbols there is a way for all components to be expressed mathematically. It is possible to create a list of every single word that exists in a document collection and represent

Figure 6. Signaling diagram for advertisement personalization

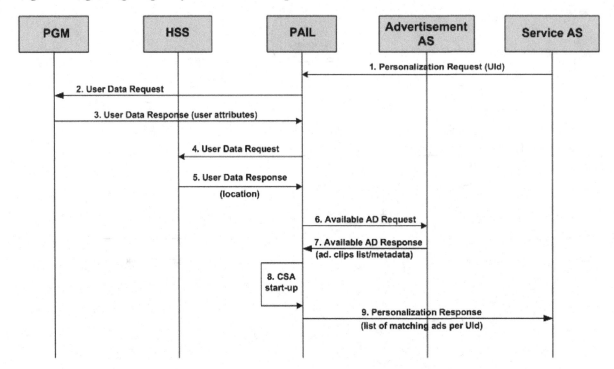

all documents as series of numbers that symbolize the total amount of times a specific term can be found in the document. After the series of numbers is created, it can be treated as a vector, applying all rules of vector analysis on it. Several different ways of computing these values, also known as weights, have been developed (Lee, Chuank, & Seamons, 1997). In order to make clear the exact way this process works, the following example is introduced.

The document collection in Figure 7 consists of a single document that contains the terms "Personalized", "Advertisement" and "Service". This document corresponds to a vector in a three dimensional graph, each axis of which represents a single word. X-axis is the word "Personalized", Y-axis is the word "Service" and Z-axis is "Advertisement". A possible query in this document collection may contain a combination of those three words, therefore can also be represented as a vector in the same way. The two vectors shown in Figure 3, represent two different queries, one

containing the words "Personalized Service" and one with just the word "Advertisement". It is certain that the first query is of greater relevance to the document since it contains more common words with it than the second one. The vector comparison that VSM does illustrates the exact same thing: the dot product of the vector representing the first query and the vector representing the document produces angle β, which is smaller than angle α, originated from the dot product of the second query and the document.

The smaller the dot product between two vectors is, the smaller is the angle, in this case angles α and β, and thus the closer is the match between document and query.

In a true case scenario, the total vector space dimension is equal to the number of different terms existing in the whole document collection but for illustration purposes only three dimensions were used in this picture. In such a scenario e.g. user profiles and advertisement descriptions could be

Figure 7. Vector space model example

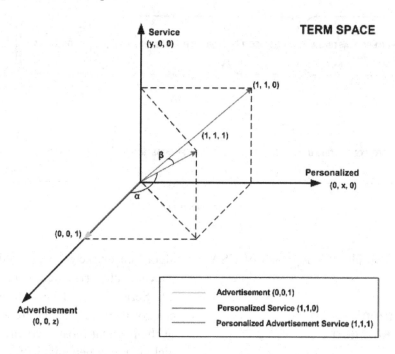

matched. A user profile would contain e.g. information about residence, interests, age, gender etc

A user, whose profile has many identical words with an advertisement description, is more likely to be interested in this advertisement content. This is exactly the clip that CSA is going to match to the User ID. Based on the nature of this scenario, which involves free text description within user presence data, the best VSM approach out of many that have already been implemented in the past (Lee, Chuank, & Seamons, 1997), was considered to be the full Vector Space Model..

Preferences provided by users may be fragmentary or way too explanatory to be properly inserted in the algorithm and provide a valid result. This is the basic reason why a method of additional relevance correlation is needed. More specifically, operator's data that can be retrieved from network nodes can be employed. If an operator is able to select more relevant advertisement clips for a specific user, based on some additional data he has such as location or demographic information,

it is very likely that this advertisement will have more chances actually convincing the user for a potential product purchase.

Another advanced attribute of the CSA over the simple VSM is normalization. The number of times a single term can be found in a document is divided by the total number of document terms. In addition, weight normalization (Lee, Chuank, & Seamons, 1997) is used, where a specific term is divided by the total number of times a term exists in the whole document collection. This method provides more accurate results, and contains benefits when vectors tend to increase in size and common terms are rendered unimportant when compared to unique or rare words that might even define a specific document. For instance, terms like articles or verbs being of minor importance for the document definition compared to nouns or adjectives, get lower weights after normalization.

In conclusion, normal VSM might be capable of performing the correlation task but for optimal

Figure 8. Video session presentation

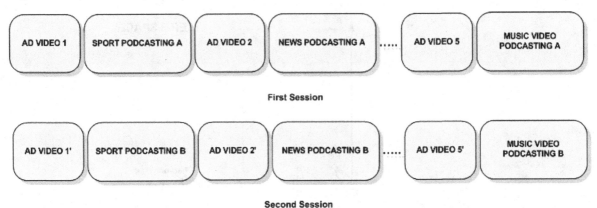

First Session

Second Session

performance and results the approach of CSA prevails.

C. Advertisement Selection Evaluation

In order to properly evaluate the influence of additional data provided by the operator, emphasizing on location as the most important addition to the user profile, two discrete test scenarios are introduced. In the first scenario the input data regarding the user consists of his/her public profile and carrier data (here: location), while in the second scenario the user profile alone was used. The goal is to evaluate if more comprehensive information actually leads to a better match of selected advertisements and user interest. The CSA is based on an implementation of an information retrieval system. For this prototype three parts were implemented. The text database where all documents are located (advertisement metadata), the searching mechanism that performs the query and the user interface where the operator inputs the query words (user profile) and where the results are shown. There is no automated procedure for acquiring user profiles, therefore they must be manually inserted as an input. To measure user satisfaction with the proposed algorithm in a realistic setup, a video podcast playback along with the proposed advertisement clips that the

algorithm extracted, was used. Therefore, five podcast categories were chosen: Sports, News, TV Series, Comedy and Music Video. These categories were selected to span a broad range of themes that most users are interested in. By picking rather general podcasting categories, the influence that this content might have on the subject's impression of the advertisement clips was minimized. During the test, ten video podcasts are needed, two out of each of the previously mentioned categories. These ten videos are the same for all users. In addition, ten advertisement clips were chosen separated into two groups, but this time different clips for each user according to the correlation of user profiles to ad clip metadata performed by the CSA. Figure 8 shows the idea more clearly.

The five advertisement clips used in the first session were selected by the CSA according to scenario 1 using additional operator's data, while the other five were selected according to scenario 2 on which only user preferences and free data have been used for the advertisement selection. Each video podcast and the previously watched ad clip are supposed to be attached together for the user to have a seamless experience of podcast and advertisement combined. After each set of advertisement clip and video podcast, users were asked questions regarding their experience.

A group of eighteen test volunteers was selected and each one provided a description of his/her personal preferences as part of the user profiles. It should be pointed out that no subject is aware of the actual scenario that he/she currently experiences. The CSA selected two series of advertisement clips according to the previously mentioned scenarios and these series were given to users in random order. There is no knowledge of the amount of data used by the CSA to provide the advertisement clips by the users for keeping their answers unbiased. There are four questions per clip and another question for an overall session evaluation. The clip questions were:

1. Was the advertisement clip interesting for you?
2. Would you like to get more information about the product?
3. Would you be willing to buy the product if such chance was given?
4. Was the advertisement clip well-produced?

The question asking users to describe their overall experience was:

5. Did you enjoy the session?

A point system was used to compare the two scenarios. Since a statistical analysis of the collected data is required, certain values are necessary to be assigned to each question. In the questions given to the participants, a scale of five values was offered as answers. For instance, in the first question users may provide an answer scaling from one to five. One stands for worst and escalates to a maximum of five meaning absolute satisfaction. According to the number of the answer the user chooses, the same amount of points is added to the overall points the specific clip and also the session is collecting. The higher the collected point number, the better the clip and the session in total is rated. Figure 9 provides information regarding the points users assigned after answering the first

question. As mentioned earlier, the higher the number of points each user assigns to each clip, the more satisfactory the experience was meaning that the advertisement was somehow closer to his/her preferences. These results indicate a clear user preference for the clips derived in Scenario 1, where additional data was used. Since users were unaware which clip was produced by each scenario, it is correct to assume that all answers were unbiased.

This method of point assignment was used to all questions providing similar results for each question.

Figure 10 shows the result for the first four questions in a more condensed form. On the y-axis the sum of the average scores of the five clips is plotted, divided by the number of clips. Average score means the sum of all scores given by the subjects for one question divided by the number of subjects. E.g. the first pair of columns in Figure 10 compares the sums of average scores for question 1. This yields for example an overall score of

$$S_{q1} = \frac{1}{C} \sum_{j=1}^{C} \frac{1}{U} \sum_{i=1}^{U} S_{j,i} = 3.5$$

for scenario 1, where S_{q1} is the score for question 1, j is the number of the clip, C is the total number of clips, i is the number of the participant, U is the total number of participants and $S_{j,1}$ is the score for clip j given by user i.

As shown in Figure 10 the clip session that includes the additional data from the Operator managed to collect more points in the user evaluation process than the one without any additional data in all four questions previously mentioned. This strengthens the original hypothesis of the extra value of information provided by the network carrier in order to deliver a much better service to the end user. Indeed all users seem to enjoy the first session better than the second one since the selected advertisements considered to be more interesting and closer to their preferences. It is a

Figure 9. First question

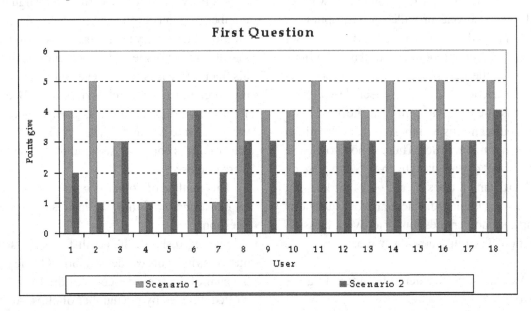

Figure 10. Survey results

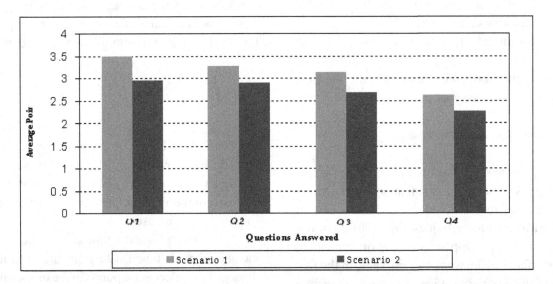

certain achievement of the ads and not the clips because in both cases only advertisement had significant difference between each case, after a careful selection of similar main content clips that didn't attract user focus that much.

In Figure 11 lies the result users provide in the last survey question regarding the overall session satisfaction. This question addresses the whole session instead of individual clips. This means that the y-axis in Figure 11 shows the sum of all session-scores divided by the number of participants. Once again scenario 1 proved to be more popular than scenario 2 since all selected advertisements matched user preferences better

Figure 11. Overall session satisfaction

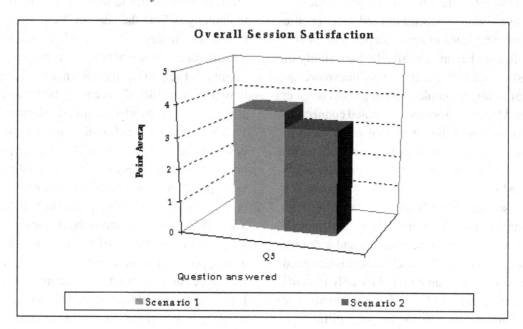

leading to higher satisfaction regarding the whole session experience.

The questions were meant to reach the participants on a more subconscious level. Instead of asking one question like "Did this clip match your interests well?", we asked questions correlating satisfaction and clip-experience indirectly. Question number 5 has a similar purpose. The reasoning is that e.g. a clip about a product that the participant is interested in may be also be regarded as well produced.

FUTURE RESEARCH DIRECTIONS

An attribute of the vector space model that is of great importance for this experiment is relevance feedback firstly taken under consideration by Lee, Chuank and Seamons (1997) after originally introduced by Salton & Buckley, (1990). Relevance feedback can be used from the system in which the service is deployed for providing better and much more useful data of the overall advertisement correlation process as well as user preferences regarding the actual content they received. Relevance feedback in IMS can be accomplished by a variety of modules inside the existing architecture and the retrieved data may include information not only for the advertisement and video combination, but also for the whole process that took place earlier. Issues such as elapsed time between the initial request message that signifies the beginning of the process and the final response that closes the session are rather useful, considering the large number of additional users this service is designed to support and uphold. Before any future upgrade becomes necessary, metrics like these are key aspect that pinpoints abnormalities in the system operation. The vector space model relevance feedback is capable of discovering much more complex correlation problems that include not only implementation sections but also design and architecture related flaws. For instance, user satisfaction over a certain advertisement is way easier to be estimated by using similar methods to the one used in this evaluation, but in a much more generic and automated form. Actual data originated from user device might be included as a certain and reliable way of measuring the degree of an advertisement penetration and if the specific advertisement leads to a product purchase or not. If this feature becomes available, the validity of results is much better, making operators more capable of selling a complete and improved service. The CSA benefits from the integrated connection to the metric and the method of using them in information form that Vector Space Model contains providing an extra way of improving every deployed service.

The second major benefit of the solution is originated in the platform used for realizing the described service of advertisement and user profile correlation. The IMS architecture is designed in such a way that can be rated friendly towards third party services and module deployments. The layered architecture eliminates most difficulties that prevent freelance developers from introducing their own application servers and create services with ease. Creating software as a separate individual rather than behalf of a company gains momentum in modern markets with platforms such as Apple Store from Apple and similar solutions from Deutsche Telecom be a major source of profit for the operating company, not only in terms of pure revenue but also in positive publicity and advertisement. If there is a method for making such services even less expensive to the average user due to some advertisement input, there might be a significant chance of creating a dominant platform not only for IMS but for other next generation networks as well. PAIL module and the CSA within are a winning combination designed to thrive.

The introduction of PAIL in a next generation network framework is about to revolutionize the overall user experience and make operators capable of providing better services. As part of a wider architecture currently under development that will allow decisions to be taken in real time circumstances, this module is the initial step for a more complex solution that will not only correlate advertisement and users but also use network information in order to make decisions on how to actually deliver the content. Being in control of delivery modes such as broadcast and unicast and also being aware of possible user groups that might exist according to preferences and content, it will be capable of executing better delivery services as well as advertisement selection.

The aforementioned architecture solution was designed not only as part of the IMS or just for non-real time services like video podcasting. The same principles apply to other platforms as well and to a wide band of services such as Mobile TV, MMS and telephony advertisement. All it takes is an integration of the new possibilities and opportunities these platforms and services introduce and how exactly problems such as real time operation will be solved. The main concept of using a specific mathematical model for data representation and develop an algorithm that operates in the background extracting results can be the backbone of any type of solution

CONCLUSION

With the advent of mobile Internet services and applications, the market for targeted advertising is constantly gaining momentum. In this chapter, a solution is proposed for a personalization enabler - Personalization and Advertisement Insertion Logic (PAIL) - that has the potential to exploit the unique position that telecom network operators have in the mobile advertisement market. Their subscriber information is a valuable asset to help finding the right advertisement for the right person. The solution presented in this chapter, fits in the IP Multimedia Subsystem (IMS) and uses information available in Home Subscriber Server (HSS) and Presence, Group and Data Management (PGM). However, the concept as such can be applied to other platforms as well.

In a survey, users rate advertisements presented to them, half of which were chosen using preference information while the other half was chosen using location information additionally. The survey strongly supports the thesis that using this additional information results in a greater acceptance of the selected advertisements. The clips selected using additional location information scored an average of 15% better in the users' ratings.

As a next step it is useful to extend the PAIL architecture in order to utilize even more information available to operators such as demographic data, wallet size, service usage data, social network information, attitude survey information or device data. It should be clarified which of these parameters has got the most significant influence on matching the user's interest.

REFERENCES

Camarillo, G., & Garcia-Martin, M. A. (2006). *The 3G IP Multimedia Subsystem (IMS)* (2nd ed.). Wiley.

Ericsson, A. B. (2007). *Introduction to IMS* (Ericsson White Paper).

Fielding, R., Gettys, J., Mogul, J., Frystyk, H., Masinter, L., Leach, P. & Berners- Lee, T. (1999). *Hypertext transfer protocol – http/1.1*. RFC 2616.

3GPP TS 22.146 v7.2.0 (2006). *Multimedia Broadcast/Multicast Service; Stage 1 (Release 7)*.

3GPP TS 22.228 V7.6.0 (2007). *Service requirements for the Internet Protocol (IP) multimedia core network subsystem; Stage 1 (Release 7)*.

3GPP TS 23.228 v7.9.0 (2007). *IP Multimedia Subsystem (IMS); Stage 2 (Release 7)*.

3GPP TS 29.228 v6.5.0. (2004). *IP Multimedia (IM) Subsystem Cx and Dx interfaces; Signalling flows and message contents*.

Grossman, D., & Frieder, O. (2001). *Information Retrieval: Algorithms and Heuristics* (2nd ed.). Springer.

Handley, M., Jacobson, V., & Perkins, C. (2006). *SDP: Session Description Protocol*. RFC 4566.

Hristova, N., & O'Hare, G. M. P. (2004): Ad-me: wireless advertising adapted to the user location, device and emotions. In *Proceedings of the 37th Annual Hawaii International Conference*.

IMedia Connection. (2004). *Behavioral Targeting*. Retrieved from http://www.imediaconnection.com/content/3297.asp

Knightson, K., Morita, N., & Towle, T. (2005). NGN architecture: generic principles, functional architecture, and implementation. *IEEE Communications Magazine, 43*, 49–56. doi:10.1109/MCOM.2005.1522124

Lee, D. L., Chuank, H., & Seamons, K. (1997). Document Ranking and the Vector-Space Model. *IEEE Software*, 0740-7459

Mobile Advertising Architecture. (2007). *Mobile Advertisement in a. mobi World*. Retrieved December 2, 2007 from http://advisorygroup.mobi

Mobile Advertising Requirements. (2007). Open Mobile Alliance Retrieved October 25, 2007 from http://www.openmobilealliance.org/

OMA-TS-Presence_SIMPLE-V1_1-20080627-A (2008).

Content Delivery Platforms: The Next Big SDP Dilemma (2008). *Light Reading Report, 4*(3).

3rd Whitepaper Mobile Advertising, Mobile TV Joint UMTS Forum/GSMA Work Group Calhoun, P., Loughney, J., Guttman, E., Zorn, G., & Arkko, J. (2003). *Diameter Base Protocol*, RFC 3588.

Rosenberg, J., Schulzrinne, H., Camarillo, G., Johnston, A., Peterson, J., Sparks, R., Handley, M., & Schooler, E. (2002), *SIP: Session Initiation Protocol*. RFC 3261

Salton, G., & Buckley, C. (1990). Improving Retrieval Performance by Relevance Feedback. *Journal of the American Society for Information Science American Society for Information Science, 41*(4), 288–297. doi:10.1002/(SICI)1097-4571(199006)41:4<288::AID-ASI8>3.0.CO;2-H

Schulzrinne, H., Casner, S., Frederick, R., & Jacobson, V. (2003). *RTP: A Transport Protocol for Real-Time Applications*. RFC 3550.

Subscriber Profile User Group. (2009). *Reference Architecture Version 1.1*. Retrieved October 3, 2009, from http://www.spugonline.com/

Thawani, A., Gopalan, S., & Sridhar, V. (2004). Event Driven semantics based ad selection. In *ICME '04 Multimedia and Expo* (Vol.3, pp. 1875-1878).

Turner Entertainment Networks. (2009). *TV in Context*. Retrieved May 20, 2009, from http://www.nytimes.com/2009/05/20/business/media/20adco.html?_r=1

ADDITIONAL READING

Asp, K., Badiee, F., Peng, B., Svensson, M., & Wiss, P. (2009). Advertising solutions. *Ericsson Review, 2*, 4–9.

Camarillo, G., Kauppinen, T., Kuparinen, M., & Ivars, I. M. (2007). Towards an innovation oriented IP multimedia subsystem. *IEEE Communications Magazine, 45*(3), 130–136. doi:10.1109/MCOM.2007.344594

Cartas, R., Kampmann, M., Perkuhn, H., & Espinosa, J. M. (2008). An IMS based Mobile Podcasting Architecture supporting Multicast/Broadcast Delivery. In *Principles, Systems and Applications of IP Telecommunications (IPTComm) 2008*, Heidelberg, Germany, July 2008.

Cartas, R. A. (2008). An Enhanced Content Distribution Mechanism for Next Generation Networks. RWTH, Master of Science Thesis

Donovan, S. (2000). The SIP INFO Method. RFC 2976.

Faccin, S. M., Lalwaney, P., & Patil, B. (2004). IP multimedia services: analysis of mobile IP and SIP interactions in 3G networks. *IEEE Communications Magazine, 42*(1), 113–120. doi:10.1109/MCOM.2004.1262170

Harman, D. (1993). Overview of the First Text Retrieval Conference. In *Proceedings of the 16th Int'l ACM/SIGIR Conf. Research and Development in Information Retrieval Pittsburgh* (pp. 36-47).

Hartung, F., Horn, U., Huschke, J., Kampmann, M., Lohmar, T., & Lundevall, M. (2007). Delivery of Broadcast Services in 3G Networks. *IEEE Transactions on Broadcasting, 53*(1, Part 2), 188–199. doi:10.1109/TBC.2007.891711

Hunter, M. T., Clark, R. J., & Park, F. S. (2007). Security issues with the IP multimedia subsystem (IMS). In *Proceedings of the 2007 Workshop on Middleware For Next-Generation Converged Networks and Applications (MNCNA)*. New York: ACM.

International Telecommunication Union (2004). The Portable Internet. ITU Internet Report 2004.

Keen, E. M. (1992). Presenting Results of Experimental Retrieval Comparisons. *Information Processing & Management, 28*(4), 491–502. doi:10.1016/0306-4573(92)90006-L

Knappmeyer, M., Al-Hezmi, A., Ricks, B., & Tönjes, R. (2007). Advanced multicast and broadcast content distribution in mobile cellular networks. 50th IEEE Global Communications Conference.

Leiner, B. M., Cerf, V. G., Clark, D. D., Kahn, R. E., Kleinrock, L., & Lynch, D. C. (2003). *A Brief History of the Internet*. Internet Society.

Light Reading's Services Software insider (2008). Subscriber Data Management: It's Time to Get Personal.

Mas, I., Berggren, V., Jana, R., Murray, J., & Rice, C. W. (2008). IMS-TV: An IMS-based architecture for interactive, personalized IPTV. *IEEE Communications Magazine, 46*(11), 156–163. doi:10.1109/MCOM.2008.4689259

Peltotalo, J., Peltotalo, S., Harju, J., & Walsh, R. (2007). Performance analysis of a file delivery system based on the FLUTE protocol. *International Journal of Communication Systems, 20*(6), 633–659. doi:10.1002/dac.835

Poiksela, M., Mayer, G., Khartabil, H., & Niemi, A. (2006). *The IMS, IP Multimedia Concepts and Services*. Wiley. doi:10.1002/0470031840

Heavy Reading (2008). Mobile Advertising: The service Provider Revenue Opportunity.

Rosenberg, J., & Schulzrinne, H. (2002). Reliability of Provisional Responses in the Session Initiation Protocol (SIP). RFC 3262.

Salton, G., & Buckley, C. (1988). Term-Weighting Approaches in Automatic Text Retrieval. *Information Processing & Management, 24*(5), 513–523. doi:10.1016/0306-4573(88)90021-0

Salton, G., & McGill, M. J. (1983). *Introduction to Modern Information Retrieval*. New York: McGraw-Hill Book Co.

Sparck-Jones, K. (Ed.). (1981). *Information Retrieval Experiment*. London: Butterworth-Heinemann.

Sparks, R. (2003). The Session Initiation Protocol (SIP) Refer Method. RFC 3515

Stanfill C., & Kahle, B. (1986). Parallel Free-Text Search on the Connection Machine System. *ACM Communications,* 1229-1239.

Tsang, M. M., Ho, S.-C., & Liang, T.-P. (2004). Consumer Attitudes Toward Mobile Advertising: An Empirical Study. *International Journal of Electronic Commerce, 8*(3).

Yuan, S.-T., & Tsao, Y.W. (2003). A Recommendation Mechanism for Contextualized Mobile Advertising.

KEY TERMS AND DEFINITIONS

CSA: Content Selection Algorithm. An algorithm designed to correlate advertisement and user profiles based on available information about the user.

IMS: IP Multimedia Subsystem, the 3GPP standardized Next Generation Network.

Mobile Advertisement: Advertisements delivered via mobile distribution channels. This may include SMS, MMS, Mobile TV and other forms of multimedia content.

Next Generation Network: Packet-switched, multimedia-capable telecommunication network.

PAIL: Personalized Advertisement Insertion Logic. A proposed network entity aiming to perform all necessary tasks for achieving optimal advertisement delivery towards users by enabling a mobile network operator to exploit contextual data stored in its network for personalized advertisement selection.

Personalization: Certain method of creating tailor-made content for each user according their preferences and profiles.

SIP: Session Initiation protocol. A signaling protocol used for controlling multimedia communication sessions. Specified in RFC 3261.

VSM: Vector Space Model. An algebraic model that performs vector comparison.

ABBREVIATION LIST

- **3GPP:** 3rd Generation Partnership Project
- **AAA:** Authentication, Authorization and Accounting
- **CSA:** Content Selection Algorithm
- **CSCF:** Call Session Control Function
- **HSS:** Home Subscriber Server
- **HTML:** Hypertext Markup Language
- **HTTP:** Hypertext Transmission Protocol
- **IETF:** Internet Engineering Task Force
- **IMS:** IP Multimedia Subsystem
- **ISC:** IMS Service Interface
- **ITU:** International Telecommunications Union
- **MMS:** Multimedia Message Service
- **NGN:** Next Generation Network
- **OMA:** Open Mobile Alliance
- **PAIL:** Personalized Advertisement Insertion Logic
- **PGM:** Presence and Group Management
- **RTP:** Realtime Transfer Protocol
- **SDP:** Session Description Protocol
- **SIP:** Session Initiation protocol
- **SMS:** Short Message Service
- **TCP:** Transmission Control Protocol
- **UDP:** User Datagram Protocol
- **UMTS:** Universal Mobile Telecommunication System
- **USSD:** Unstructured Supplementary Services Data
- **VoIP:** Voice Over IP
- **VSM:** Vector Space Model

Compilation of References

Aaker, D. A. (1996). *Building strong brands*. New York: Free Press.

Abrams, Z., & Vee, E. (2007). Personalized Ad Delivery when Ads Fatigue: An Approximation Algorithm. In Proc. *Workshop on Internet and Network Economics (WINE)* (pp. 535-540).

Abrams, Z., Mendelevitch, O., & Tomlin, J. (2007). Optimal delivery of sponsored search advertisements subject to budget constraints. In *EC '07: Proceedings of the 8th ACM conference on Electronic commerce* (pp. 272-278). New York: ACM.

Adams, B., Phung, D., & Venkatesh, S. (2006). Extraction of social context and application to personal multimedia exploration. In *Proceedings of the 14th annual ACM international conference on Multimedia* (pp. 987-996). New York: ACM.

Adobe Systems Incorporated. (2008). SWF File Format Specification (Version 10). U.S.A.

Adomavicius, G., & Tuzhilin, A. (2005). Toward the next generation of recommender systems: A survey of the state-of-the-art and possible extensions. *IEEE Transactions on Knowledge and Data Engineering*, *17*(6), 734–749. doi:10.1109/TKDE.2005.99

AdWords InVideo Ads. (n.d.). Retrieved April 27, 2010, from Google AdWords website: http://adwords.google.com/support/aw/bin/topic.py?hl=en&topic=23277

Agarwal, S., & Siddiqui, T. J. (2009). Using syntactic and Contextual Information for Sentiment Polarity Analysis. *ICIS 2009*, November 24-26, Seoul. *Korea & World Affairs*, 620–623.

Agarwal, A., & Triggs, B. (2004). *Learning to track 3D human motion from silhouettes*. ICML.

Agarwal, D., Broder, A. Z., Chakrabarti, D., Diklic, D., Josifovski, V., & Sayyadian, M. (2007). Estimating rates of rare events at multiple resolutions. In *Proceedings of the 13th ACM SIGKDD international Conference on Knowledge Discovery and Data Mining* (pp. 16-25).

Agarwal, D., Chen, B., & Elango, P. (2009). Spatio-temporal models for estimating click-through rate. In *Proceedings of the 18th international Conference on World Wide Web* (pp. 21-30).

Agichtein, E., Brill, E., & Dumais, S. (2006). Improving web search ranking by incorporating user behavior information. In *Proc. the 29th int. ACM SIGIR conf. on Research and development in information retrieval* (pp. 19-26). Seattle, Washington, USA: ACM.

Agichtein, E., Brill, E., Dumais, S., & Ragno, R. (2006). Learning user interaction for predicting web search result preference. In *Proc. the 29th int. ACM SIGIR conf. on Research and development in information retrieval* (pp. 3-10). Seattle, Washington, USA: ACM.

Ahlers, D., & Boll, S. (2008). oh web image, where art thou? *International Conference on Multi-Media Modeling*.

Alcatel-Lucent. (2009, Jul. 29). Three-Screen Advertising: New Ad Revenues for Service Providers.

Allen, C., Deborah, K., & Beth, Y. (1998). *Internet World: Guide to One-to-One Web Marketing*. New York: Wiley.

Ana, M. A., Manuel, E., & Mariano, J. V. (2006). Using principal components for estimating logistic regression with high-dimensional multicollinear data. *Computational Statistics & Data Analysis*, (50): 1905–1924.

Anagnostopoulos, A., Broder, A. Z., Gabrilovich, E., Josifovski, V., & Riedel, L. (2007). Just-in-Time Contextual Advertising. In *Proceedings of the sixteenth ACM conference on Conference on information and knowledge management* (pp. 331–340). New York: ACM.

Aroyo, L., Nack, F., Schiphorst, T., Schut, H., & Kauw AT-joe, M. (2007). Personalized ambient media experience: move.me case study. In *Proceedings of Conference on Intelligent User Interfaces* (pp. 298-301).

Auer, P., Cesa-Bianchi, N., Freund, Y., & Schapire, R. E. (2003). The Nonstochastic Multiarmed Bandit Problem. *SIAM Journal on Computing*, *32*(1), 48–77. doi:10.1137/S0097539701398375

Baccot, B., Choudary, O., Grigoras, R., & Charvillat, V. (2009). On the impact of sequence and time in rich media advertising. In *Proceedings of the Seventeen ACM international Conference on Multimedia* (Beijing, China, October 19 - 24, 2009) (pp. 849-852). New York: ACM.

Bachman, K. (2009). Cracking the set-top box code. *AdWeek*, August 17, 2009. Retrieved December 22, 2009, from http://www.adweek.com/aw/content_display/news/e3i8fb28a31928f66a5893aa9825dee83f2.

Bae, S. M., Ha, S. H., & Park, S. C. (2003). Fuzzy Web Ad Selector Based on Web Usage Mining. *IEEE Intelligent Systems*, *18*(6), 62–69. doi:10.1109/MIS.2003.1249171

Baeza-Yates, R., & Ribeiro-Neto, B. (1999). *Modern Information Retrieval*. Addison Wesley.

Ballan, L., Bertini, M., & Jain, A. (2008). A system for automatic detection and recognition of advertising trademarks in sports videos. In *Proceedings of the 16th ACM International Conference on Multimedia*.

Barnard, K., Duygulu, P., de Freitas, N., Forsyth, D., Blei, D., & Jordan, M. I. (2003). Matching words and pictures. *Journal of Machine Learning Research*, *3*, 1107–1135. doi:10.1162/153244303322533214

Barry, T., & Howard, D. (1990). A review and critique of the hierarchy of effects in advertising. *Journal of Advertising*, *9*(2), 121–135.

Bartholomew, M. (2007). Advertising in the Garden of Eden. *Buffalo Law Review*, *55*(3), 737–775.

Bartle, R. (2003). *Designing Virtual Worlds*. Indianapolis, IN: New Riders Press.

Battelle, J. (2005). *The Search: How Google and Its Rivals Rewrote the Rules of Business and Transformed Our Culture*. New York: Penguin Group.

Bay, H., Ess, A., Tuytelaars, T., & Gool, L. V. (2008). SURF: Speeded Up Robust Features. *Computer Vision and Image Understanding*, *110*(3), 346–359. doi:10.1016/j.cviu.2007.09.014

Berg, A. C., & Malik, J. (2001). Geometric Blue for Template Matching. *Proc. IEEE Conf. on Computer Vision and Pattern Recognition* (pp. 607-613). Kauai, Hawaii: IEEE Computer Society.

Berman, S. J., Battino, B., Shipnuck, L., & Neus, A. (2007). *The end of advertising as we know it*. Somers, NY: IBM Global Services.

Bernardo, J. M. (1976). The Psi (Digamma) function: An algorithm. *Applied Statistics*, *25*, 315–317. doi:10.2307/2347257

Bishop, C. M. (2006). *Pattern Recognition and Machine Learning*. Springer.

Blackwell, R. D., Paul, M. W., & James, E. F. (2001). *Consumer Behavior* (9th ed.). Orlando, FL: Harcourt.

Bogost, I. (2007). *Persuasive Games: The Expressive Power of Video Games*. Cambridge, MA: MIT Press.

Boiman, O., Shechtman, E., & Irani, M. (2008). In defense of Nearest-Neighbor based image classification. In *Proc. 2008 IEEE conf. on Computer Vision and Pattern Recognition* (pp. 1-8). Anchorage, AK: IEEE Computer Society.

Bonsu, S., & Darmody, A. (2008). Co-creating Second Life: Market-Consumer Cooperation in Contemporary Economy. *Journal of Macromarketing*, *24*(4), 355–368. doi:10.1177/0276146708325396

Book, B. (2004). These Bodies are Free, So Get One Now!' Advertising and Branding in Social Virtual Worlds. *Virtual Worlds Review*. Retrieved February 14, 2010 http://www.virtualworldsreview.com/papers/adbrand.pdf

Bosch, A., Zisserman, A., & Munoz, X. (2007). Representing shape with a spatial pyramid kernel. In *Proc. of the 6th ACM int. conf. on Image and video retrieval* (pp. 401-408). Amsterdam, The Netherlands: ACM. *britepic.com*. (n.d.). Retrieved April 29, 2010, from britepic.com: http://www.britepic.com/learnmore.php

Boyd, S., & Vandenberghe, L. (2004). *Convex Optimization*. Cambridge University Press.

Bradley, D. R., & Petry, H. M. (1977). Organizational determinants of subjective contour: The subjective Necker cube. *The American Journal of Psychology, 90*(2), 253–262. doi:10.2307/1422047

Brants, T., Chen, F., & Tsochantaridis, I. (2002). Topic-based document segmentation with probabilistic latent semantic analysis. In *Proceedings of CIKM* (pp. 211-218). ACM Press.

Broder, A., Ciaramita, M., Fontoura, M., Gabrilovich, E., Josifovski, V., Metzler, D., et al. (2008). To swing or not to swing: Learning when (not) to advertise. In *Proceedings of 17th International Conference on Information and Knowledge Management* (pp. 1003–1012).

Broder, A., Fontoura, M., Josifovski, V., & Riedel, L. (2007). A semantic approach to contextual advertising. In *Proc. 30th Ann. Intl. ACM SIGIR Conf. on Research and Development in Information Retrieval* (pp. 559–566).

Broyles, S. (2006). Subliminal advertising and the perpetual popularity of playing to people's paranoia. *The Journal of Consumer Affairs, 40*(2), 392–406. doi:10.1111/j.1745-6606.2006.00063.x

Bruce, V., Green, P. R., & Georgeson, M. A. (1996). *Visual perception: physiology, psychology, and ecology* (3rd ed.). U.K.: Psychology Press.

Burke, R. (2007). Hybrid web recommender systems. In *The Adaptive Web* (pp. 377–408). LNCS. doi:10.1007/978-3-540-72079-9_12

Buss, D. (2003, February 24). Advergaming Scores. *Brand Channel*. Retrieved February 15, 2010 from http://www.brandchannel.com/print_page.asp?ar_id=145&section=main

Caillois, R. (2001). *Man, Play and Games* (Barash, M., Trans.). Urbana: University of Illinois Press.

Calisir, F., & Karaali, D. (2008). The impacts of banner location, banner content and navigation style on banner recognition. *Computers in Human Behavior, 24*(2), 535–543. doi:10.1016/j.chb.2007.02.019

Camarillo, G., & Garcia-Martin, M. A. (2006). *The 3G IP Multimedia Subsystem (IMS)* (2nd ed.). Wiley.

Cann, R. (1993). *Formal Semantics: An Introduction*. Cambridge University Press.

Cannes Lions International Advertising Festival. (n.d.). Retrieved May 2, 2010, from The official website of the international advertising festival: www.canneslions.com/

Cantador, I., Szomszor, M., Alani, H., Fernández, M., & Castells, P. (2008). Enriching ontological user profiles with tagging history for multi-domain recommendations. In *Proceedings of the 1st International Workshop on Collective Semantics: Collective Intelligence and the Semantic Web (CISWeb 2008)* (pp. 5-19).

Cao, Y., Xu, J., Liu, T. Y., Li, H., Huang, H. Y., & Hon, H. (2006). Adapting ranking SVM to document retrieval. In *Proceedings of the 29th annual international ACM SIGIR conference on Research and development in information retrieval* (pp. 186-193). ACM Press.

Chakrabarti, D., Agarwal, D., & Josifovski, V. (2008). Contextual advertising by combining relevance with click feedback. In *Proceedings of the 17th international Conference on World Wide Web* (pp 417-426).

Chambers, J. (2005). The Sponsored Avatar: Examining the Present Reality and Future Possibilities of Advertising in Digital Games. In *Proceedings of DiGRA 2005 Conference: Changing Views – Worlds in Play*, Vancouver, Canada.

Chaney. I., Lin, K., & Chaney, J. (2004). The Effect of Billboards Within the Gaming Environment. *Journal of Interactive Advertising*, 37-45.

Chang, C.-H., Hsieh, K.-Y., Chiang, M.-C., & Wu, J.-L. (in press). Virtual Spotlighted Advertising for Tennis Videos. *Journal of Visual Communication and Image Representation*.

Chang, Y., & Thorson, E. (2004). Television And Web Advertising Synergies. *Journal of Advertising, 33*(2), 75–84.

Chang, C.-H., Chiang, M.-C., & Wu, J.-L. (2009). Evolving Virtual Contents with Interactions in Videos. In *The 1st ACM International Workshop on Interactive Multimedia for Consumer Electronics* (pp. 97-104).

Chang, C.-H., Hsieh, K.-Y., Chung, M.-C., & Wu, J.-L. (2008). ViSA: Virtual Spotlighted Advertising. In *the 16th ACM International Conference on Multimedia* (pp. 837-840).

Chang, C.-H., Hsieh, K.-Y., Chung, M.-C., & Wu, J.-L. (2008). ViSA: Virtual spotlighted advertising. In *Proceedings of ACM Multimedia* (pp. 837–840).

Chang, S.-F., Ellis, D., Jiang, W., Lee, K., Yanagawa, A., Loui, A. C., et al. (2007). Large-scale multimodal semantic concept detection for consumer video. In *Proc. of the int. workshop on Workshop on multimedia information retrieval* (pp. 255-264). Augsburg, Bavaria, Germany: ACM.

Chatterjee, P., Hoffman, D. L., & Novak, T. P. (2003). Modeling the clickstream: Implications for web-based advertising efforts. *Marketing Science, 22*(4), 520–541. doi:10.1287/mksc.22.4.520.24906

Chen, W.-Y., Lee, B. N., & Chang, E. Y. (2006). Fotowiki: distributed map enhancement service. *Proceedings of the 14th annual ACM international conference on Multimedia* (pp. 803-804). New York: ACM.

Chen, X., & Zhang, H.-J. (2001). Text area detection from video frames. In *Proceedings of the IEEE Pacific Rim Conference on Multimedia* (pp. 222–228).

Chen, Y., Pavlov, D., & Canny, J. F. (2009). Large-scale behavioral targeting. In *Proceedings of the 15th ACM SIGKDD international conference on Knowledge discovery and data mining* (pp. 209-218). ACM Press.

Chiang, M.-C., Chang, C.-H., & Wu, J.-L. (2009). Evolution-based Virtual Content Insertion. In *The 17th ACM International Conference on Multimedia* (pp. 995-996).

ChoiceStream. (2008). ChoiceStream Personalization Survey. Retrieved December 28, 2009, from http://www.choicestream.com/pdf/ChoiceStream_2008_Personalization_Survey.pdf

Chu, W., & Park, S. T. (2009). Personalized recommendation on dynamic content using predictive bilinear models. In *WWW '09: Proceedings of the 18th international conference on World wide web* (pp. 691-700). New York: ACM.

Cohen-Or, D., Sorkine, O., Gal, R., Leyvand, T., & Xu, Y.-Q. (2006). Color harmonization. *ACM Transactions on Graphics, 25*(3), 624–630. doi:10.1145/1141911.1141933

Cole, S. (2008). *Creative insights on rich media (Tech Rep)*. DoubleClick Research.

Cole, S. G., Spalding, L., & Fayer, A. (2009). *The brand value of rich media and video ads (Tech Rep)*. DoubleClick Research.

Constantinides, E. (2004). Influencing the Online Consumer's Behaviour: the Web Experience. *Internet Research, 14*(2), 111–126. doi:10.1108/10662240410530835

Content Delivery Platforms: The Next Big SDP Dilemma (2008). *Light Reading Report, 4*(3).

Coulter, K. S. (1998). The effects of affective response to media context on advertising evaluations. *Journal of Advertising, XXVII*(4), 41–51.

Cristianini, N., & Taylor, J. S. (2000). *An introduction to support vector machines and other kernel-based learning*. Cambridge University Press.

Czikszentmihalyi, M. (1990). *Flow: The Psychology of Optimal Experience*. New York: Harper and Row.

Dai, H., Zhao, L., Nie, Z., Wen, J.-R., Wang, L., & Li, Y. (2006). Detecting online commercial intention. In *Proceedings of International World Wide Web Conference*. ACM.

Dai, H., Zhao, L., Nie, Z., Wen, J.-R., Wang, L., & Li, Y. (2006). Detecting online commercial intention. In *Proceedings of International World Wide Web Conference*.

Davis, H. (2006). *Google advertising tools: cashing in with adsense, adwords, and the google APIs*. O'Reilly Media, Inc.

Deerwester, S., Dumais, S., Furnas, G., Landauer, T., & Hashman, R. (1990). Indexing by latent semantic analysis. *Journal of the American Society for Information Science American Society for Information Science, 41*, 391–407. doi:10.1002/(SICI)1097-4571(199009)41:6<391::AID-ASI1>3.0.CO;2-9

Deighton, J., & Grayson, K. (1995). Marketing and Seduction: Building Relationships in Managing Social Consensus. *The Journal of Consumer Research, 21*, 660–676. doi:10.1086/209426

Deshpande, S., Naphade, P., Rao, C. V. K., Bhadada, K., & Rangan, P. V. (2007). *Method and apparatus for including virtual ads in video presentations* (Nos. 7,158,666).

Devitt, A., & Ahmad, K. (2007). Sentiment Polarity Identification in Financial News: A Cohesion-based Approach. In *Proceedings of the 45th Annual Meeting of the Association of Computational Linguistics*, Prague, Czech Republic (pp. 984–991).

Diaz Redondo, R. P., Fernandez Vilas, A., Pazos Arias, J. J., Ramos Cabrer, M., & Garcia Duque, J. (2009). Sponsored advertising for IDTV: A personalized and content-aware approach, In Proc. *International Conference on Computers in Education* (pp. 1-2). Digest of Technical Papers International Conference on Consumer Electronics.

Djurovic, V. (2008, Sep.). *Interactive Media - The New Golden Goose of Branding?* Retrieved Apr. 28, 2010, from http://www.articlesnatch.com/Article/Interactive-Media---The-New-Golden-Goose-Of-Branding-/479306

Drèze, X., & Hussherr, F. X. (2003). Internet advertising: Is anybody watching? *Journal of Interactive Marketing, 17*(4), 8–23. doi:10.1002/dir.10063

Duan, L., Xu, M., Yu, X., & Tian, Q. (2002). A unified framework for semantic shot classification in sports videos. In *Proceedings of the Tenth ACM International Conference on Multimedia*.

Duan, L.-Y., Wang, J., Zheng, Y., Jin, J. S., Lu, H., & Xu, C. (2006). Segmentation, categorization, and identification of commercial clips from TV streams using multimodal analysis. In *Proc. the 14th ACM int. conf. on Multimedia* (pp. 201-210). Santa Barbara: ACM.

Duan, L.-Y., Xu, M., Chua, T.-S., Tian, Q., & Xu, C.-S. (2003). A mid-level representation framework for semantic sports video analysis. In *Proc. of the 11th ACM int. conf. on Multimedia* (pp. 33-44). Berkeley: ACM.

Dumais, S., Cutrell, E., Cadiz, J. J., Jancke, G., Sarin, R., & Robbins, D. C. (2003). Stuff i've seen: a system for personal information retrieval and re-use. In *SIGIR '03: Proceedings of the 26th annual international ACM SIGIR conference on Research and development in information retrieval* (pp. 72-79). New York: ACM.

Edelman, B., Ostrovsky, M., & Schwarz, M. (2007). Internet advertising and the generalized second price auction: Selling billions of dollars worth of keywords. *The American Economic Review, 97*(1), 242–259. doi:10.1257/aer.97.1.242

Ekin, A., & Tekalp, A. (2003). Robust dominant color region detection and color-based applications for sports video. In *The 2003 IEEE International Conference Image Processing, Vol. 1* (pp. 21-24).

Ericsson, A. B. (2007). *Introduction to IMS* (Ericsson White Paper).

Esuli, A., & Sebastiani, F. (2006). Sentiwordnet: A publicly available lexical resource for opinion mining. In *Proceedings of LREC-06, the 5th Conference on Language Resources and Evaluation*, Genova, Italy.

Evangelopoulos, G., Zlatintsi, A., Skoumas, G., Rapantzikos, K., Potamianos, A., Maragos, P., & Avrithis, Y. (2009). Video event detection and summarization using audio, visual and text saliency. In *Proceedings of IEEE International Conference on Acoustics, Speech and Signal Processing.*

Fan, T., & Chang, C. (2009). Sentiment-Oriented Contextual Advertising. In *Proceedings of the 31th European Conference on IR Research on Advances in information Retrieval* (LNCS 5478, pp. 202-215).

Fan, T.-K., & Chang, C.-H. (2009). Sentiment-Oriented Contextual Advertising. In *Proceedings of the 31th European Conference on IR Research on Advances in Information Retrieval* (pp. 202– 215).

Farin, D., & Krabbe, S., & With, Peter H.N. de, & Effelsberg, W. (2004). Robust camera calibration for sport videos using court models. *SPIE: Storage and Retrieval Methods and Applications for Multimedia, 5307,* 80-91.

Feltham, T. S., & Arnold, S. J. (1994). Program involvement and ad/program consistency as moderators of program context effects. *Journal of Consumer Psychology, 3*(1), 51–77. doi:10.1016/S1057-7408(08)80028-9

Feng, J., Bhargava, H. K., & Pennock, D. M. (2007). Implementing sponsored search in web search engines: Computational evaluation of alternative mechanisms. *INFORMS Journal on Computing, 19*(1), 137–148. doi:10.1287/ijoc.1050.0135

Fielding, R., Gettys, J., Mogul, J., Frystyk, H., Masinter, L., Leach, P. & Berners-Lee, T. (1999). *Hypertext transfer protocol – http/1.1.* RFC 2616.

Firat, F., & Dholakhia, N. (2006). Theoretical and Philosophical Implications of Postmodern Debates: Some Challenges to Modern Marketing. *Marketing Theory, 6*(2), 123–162. doi:10.1177/1470593106063981

Fischer, I., & Poland, J. (2004). *New Methods for Spectral Clustering.* Israel: Hebrew University.

Frank, E., Paynter, G. W., Witten, I. H., Gutwin, C., & Nevill-Manning, C. G. (1999). Domain-specific keyphrase extraction. In *Proceedings of the Sixteenth International Joint Conference on Artificial Intelligence.*

Frasca, G. (2007). *Play the Message: Play, Game and Videogame Rhetoric.* Unpublished PhD Thesis. Copenhagen: University of Copenhagen.

Friedman, J., Hastie, T., & Tibshirani, R. (2009). glmnet: Lasso and elastic-net regularized generalized linear models. R package version 1.1-3. http://www-stat.stanford.edu/~hastie/Papers/glmnet.pdf

Gabriel, K. R. (1971). The biplot graphic display of matrices with application to principal component analysis. *Biometrics,* (58): 453–467.

Galloway, A. (2007). A Radical Illusion (A Game Against). *Games and Culture, 2*(4), 376–391. doi:10.1177/1555412007309532

Gangnet, M., Perez, P., & Blake, A. (2003). Poisson image editing, In *The ACM SIGGRAPH '03* (pp. 313-318).

Garcia, E. (2006). *Cosine Similarity and Term Weight Tutorial.* Retrieved from http://www.miislita.com/information-retrieval-tutorial/cosine-similarity-tutorial.html

Geisler, W., & Perry, J. (1998). A real-time foveated multiresolution system for low-bandwidth video communication. *SPIE: Human Vision and Electronic Imaging, 3299*(1), 294–305.

Ghani, J., & Deshpande, S. (1994). Task Characteristics and Experience of Optimal Flow in Human-Computer Interaction. *The Journal of Psychology, 128*(4), 381–391. doi:10.1080/00223980.1994.9712742

Giordano, M., & Hummel, J. (2005). *Mobile Business.* Germany: Springer Science.

Gong, Y., Lim, T., & Chua, H. (1995). Automatic Parsing of TV Soccer Programs. In *Proc. IEEE Int. Conf. on Multimedia Computing and Systems* (pp. 167-174). IEEE.

Google AdSense. (2010). Retrieved from http://www.google.com/adsense

Google AdWords. (2010). Retrieved from http://www.adwords.google.com

Google Blog. (2009, Nov. 5). *Official Google Blog.* Retrieved April 30, 2010, from googleblog: http://googleblog.blogspot.com/2009/11/transparency-choice-and-control-now.html

Google. (2009). What is 'Quality Score' and how is it calculated? Retrieved December 23, 2009, from http://adwords.google.com/support/aw/bin/answer.py?hl=en&answer=10215.

GPP TS 22.146 v7.2.0 (2006). *Multimedia Broadcast/Multicast Service; Stage 1 (Release 7).*

GPP TS 22.228 V7.6.0 (2007). *Service requirements for the Internet Protocol (IP) multimedia core network subsystem; Stage 1 (Release 7).*

GPP TS 23.228 v7.9.0 (2007). *IP Multimedia Subsystem (IMS); Stage 2 (Release 7).*

GPP TS 29.228 v6.5.0. (2004). *IP Multimedia (IM) Subsystem Cx and Dx interfaces; Signalling flows and message contents.*

Green/Red Button advertising. (n.d.). Retrieved Apr. 27, 2010, from www.thinkbox.tv: http://www.thinkbox.tv/server/show/nav.1008

Grosof, B. N., Horrocks, I., Volz, R., & Decker, S. (2003). Description logic programs: combining logic programs with description logic. In *WWW '03: Proceedings of the 12th international conference on World Wide Web* (pp. 48-57). New York: ACM.

Grossman, D., & Frieder, O. (2001). *Information Retrieval: Algorithms and Heuristics* (2nd ed.). Springer.

Guo, J., Mei, T., Liu, F., & Hua, X.-S. (2009). AdOn: An Intelligent Overlay Video Advertising System. In *Proceedings of ACM SIGIR conference on Research and Development in Information Retrieval* (pp. 628–629).

Ha, L. (1996). Advertising clutter in consumer magazines: dimensions and effects. *Journal of Advertising Research, 36.*

Ha, S. H. (2004). *An Intelligent System for Personalized Advertising on the Internet* (pp. 21–30). EC-Web.

Hallerman, D. (2008). *Behavioral targeting: marketing trends.* Retrieved from http://www.emarketer.com/Reports/All/Emarketer_2000487.aspx

Handley, M., Jacobson, V., & Perkins, C. (2006). *SDP: Session Description Protocol.* RFC 4566.

Hartley, R., & Zisserman, A. (2003). *Multiple view geometry in computer vision.* U.K.: Cambridge University Press.

Hauser, J. R., Urban, G. L., Liberali, G., & Braun, M. (2009). Website Morphing. *Marketing Science, 28*(2), 224–224. doi:10.1287/mksc.1080.0459

He, X., Cai, D., Wen, J.-R., Ma, W.-Y., & Zhang, H.-J. (2007). Clustering and searching WWW images using link and page layout. *ACM Transactions on Multimedia Computing, Communications, and, 3*(2).

Hemp, P. (2006, June). Avatar-Based Marketing. *Harvard Business Review,* 48–57.

Hoffman, D., & Novak, T. (1995). Marketing in Hypermedia Computer Mediated Environments: Conceptual Foundations. Working Paper no 1. Retrieved February 14, 2010 from http://www2000.ogsm.vanderbilt.edu

Hofmann, T. (1999). Probabilistic latent semantic analysis. In *Proceedings of Uncertainty in Artificial Intelligence* (pp. 289-296).

Holbrook, B., Chestnut, R., Oliva, T., & Greenleaf, E. (1984). 'Play as Consumption Experience: The Roles of Emotions, Performance and Personality in the Enjoyment of Games. *The Journal of Consumer Research, 11*(2), 728–739. doi:10.1086/209009

Hölscher, C., & Strube, G. (2000). Web search behavior of internet experts and newbies. In *Proceedings of the 9th international World Wide Web conference on Computer networks: the international journal of computer and telecommunications networking* (pp. 337-346). ACM Press.

Holt, D. (1995). How Consumers Consume: A Typology of Consumption Practices. *The Journal of Consumer Research, 22,* 1–16. doi:10.1086/209431

Hoyer, W. D., & Brown, S. P. (1990). Effects of brand awareness on choice for a common, repeat-purchase product. *The Journal of Consumer Research*, *17*(2), 141–148. doi:10.1086/208544

Hristova, N., & O'Hare, G. M. P. (2004): Ad-me: wireless advertising adapted to the user location, device and emotions. In *Proceedings of the 37th Annual Hawaii International Conference*.

Hsu, C., & Lu, H. (2004). Why Do People Play On-line Games? An Extended TAM with Social Influences and Flow Experiences. *Information & Management*, *41*, 853–868. doi:10.1016/j.im.2003.08.014

HTK Speech Recognition Toolkit. (n.d.). Retrieved May 3, 2010, from http://htk.eng.cam.ac.uk/

Hu, J., Zeng, H. J., Li, H., Niu, C., & Zheng, C. (2007). Demographic prediction based on user's browsing behavior. In *Proceedings of the 16th international conference on World Wide Web* (pp. 151-160). ACM Press.

Hua, X., Mei, T., & Li, S. (2008). When multimedia advertising meets the new Internet era. In *The 10th IEEE Workshop on Multimedia Signal Processing* (pp. 1-5).

Huizinga, J. (1971). *Homo Ludens*. New York: Boston.

IMedia Connection. (2004). *Behavioral Targeting*. Retrieved from http://www.imediaconnection.com/content/3297.asp

Interactive Advertising Bureau (IAB) & PricewaterhouseCoopers International. (PwC). (2009). Internet ad revenues at $10.9 billion for first half of '09. Retrieved December 15, 2009, from http://www.iab.net/about_the_iab/recent_press_releases/press_release_archive/press_release/pr-100509

Itti, L., & Koch, C. (2001, Mar). Computational modelling of visual attention. *Nature Reviews. Neuroscience*, *2*(3), 194–203. doi:10.1038/35058500

Itti, L., Koch, C., & Niebur, E. (1998, Nov). A model of saliency-based visual attention for rapid scene analysis. *IEEE Transactions on Pattern Analysis and Machine Intelligence*, *20*(11), 1254–1259. doi:10.1109/34.730558

Jain, A. K., & Farrokhnia, F. (1991). Unsupervised texture segmentation using Gabor filters. *Pattern Recognition*, 1167–1186. doi:10.1016/0031-3203(91)90143-S

Jansen, B. J., & Mullen, T. (2008). Sponsored search: an overview of the concept, history, and technology. *International Journal of Electronic Business*, *6*(2), 114–131. doi:10.1504/IJEB.2008.018068

Jenkins, D. (2006, Nov 6) 'Coke, Pepsi, Nike and Adidas Top-in Advertising Survey', *Gamasutra*. Retrieved February 14, 2010 from http://www.gamasutra.com/php-bin/news_index.php?story=11631

Jin, X., Li, Y., Mah, T., & Tong, J. (2007). Sensitive webpage classification for content advertising. *Proc. The 1st Int. Workshop on Data Mining and Audience Intelligence for Advertising* (pp. 28-33). San Jose, California: ACM.

John, C. (1986). A Computational Approach to Edge Detection. *IEEE Transactions on Pattern Analysis and Machine Intelligence*, *8*, 679–714. doi:10.1109/TPAMI.1986.4767851

Joshi, A., & Motwani, R. (2006). Keyword generation for search engine advertising. In *Proceedings of the Workshops of IEEE International Conference on Data Mining*.

Joshi, A., & Motwani, R. (2006). Keyword generation for search engine advertising. In *Proceedings of the Workshops of IEEE International Conference on Data Mining*.

Kaelbling, L. P., Littman, M. L., & Moore, A. W. (1996). Reinforcement learning: a survey. *Journal of Artificial Intelligence Research*, *4*, 237–285.

Kanungo, T., Mount, D., Netanyahu, N., Piatko, C., Silverman, R., & Wu, A. (2000). An efficient K-means clustering algorithm: Analysis and implementation. *IEEE Transactions on Pattern Analysis and Machine Intelligence*, *24*(7), 881–892. doi:10.1109/TPAMI.2002.1017616

Karypis, G. *CLUTO: A Software Package for Clustering High-Dimensional Data Sets*. University of Minnesota, Dept. of Computer Science.

Kastidou, G., & Cohen, R. (2006). An approach for delivering personalized ads in interactive tv customized to both users and advertisers. In *Proceedings of European Conference on Interactive Television.*

Katz, J. (1987). Playing at Innovation in the Computer Revolution. In M. Frese, E.Ulich, & W. Dzida (Eds.), *Psychological Issues of Human Computer Interaction in the Work Place* (pp 97-112). Amersterdam: North-Holland.

Kazienko, P., & Adamski, M. (2007). Adrosa-adaptive personalization of web advertising. *Information Sciences, 177*(11), 2269–2295. doi:10.1016/j.ins.2007.01.002

Kearney, P., Anand, S. S., & Shapcott, M. (2005). Employing a domain ontology to gain insights into user behaviour. In *Working Notes of the IJCAI Workshop on Intelligent Techinques for Web Personalization* (pp. 25-32).

Kennedy, L., Naaman, M., Ahern, S., Nair, R., & Rattenbury, T. (2007). How flickr helps us make sense of the world: context and content in community-contributed media collections. In *Proceedings of the 15th international conference on Multimedia* (pp. 631-640). New York: ACM.

King, P., & Tester, J. (1999). The Landscape of Persuasive Technologies. *Communications of the ACM, 42*(5), 31–38. doi:10.1145/301353.301398

Kleemann, T., & Sinner, A. (2005). User Profiles and Matchmaking on Mobile Phones. In Bartenstein, O. (Ed.), *Proc. of 16th International Conference on Applications of Declarative Programming and Knowledge Management INAP2005*, Fukuoka.

Knightson, K., Morita, N., & Towle, T. (2005). NGN architecture: generic principles, functional architecture, and implementation. *IEEE Communications Magazine, 43*, 49–56. doi:10.1109/MCOM.2005.1522124

Kobsa, A. (2001). Tailoring privacy to users' needs. In *UM '01: Proceedings of the 8th International Conference on User Modeling 2001* (pp. 303-313). London: Springer-Verlag.

Kullback, S., & Leibler, R. A. (1951). On Information and Sufficiency. *Annals of Mathematical Statistics, 22*(1), 79–86. doi:10.1214/aoms/1177729694

Kullback, S. (1968). *Information Theory and Statistics*. Mineola, NY: Dover Publication, Inc.

Kunert, T. (2009). *User-Centered Interaction Design Patterns for Interactive Digital Television Applications.* Springer.

Lacerda, A., Cristo, M., Gonçalves, M. A., Fan, W., Ziviani, N., & Ribeiro-Neto, B. (2006). *Learning to advertise.* SIGIR.

Lacerda, A., & Cristo, M. Gonsalves., M. A., Fan, W., Ziviani, N., & Ribeiro-Neto, B. (2006). Learning to advertise. In *Proceedings of the 29th Annual International ACM SIGIR Conference on Research and Development in Information Retrieval* (pp. 549–556). New York: ACM.

Lacerda, A., Cristo, M., Gonçalves, M.A., Fan, W., Ziviani, N., & Ribeiro-Neto, B. (2006). Learning to advertise. In *Proceedings of the 29th Annual international ACM SIGIR Conference on Research and Development in information Retrieval* (Seattle, Washington, USA, August 06 - 11, 2006). SIGIR '06 (pp. 549-556). New York: ACM.

Lastowska, G. (2009). Rules of Play. *Games and Culture, 4*(4), 379–395. doi:10.1177/1555412009343573

Lazebnik, S., Schmid, C., & Ponce, J. (2006). Beyond Bags of Features: Spatial Pyramid Matching for Recognizing Natural Scene Categories. In *Proc. of the 2006 IEEE Conf. Computer Vision and Pattern Recognition* (pp. 2169-2178). Washington, DC: IEEE Computer Society.

Lee, D. L., Chuank, H., & Seamons, K. (1997). Document Ranking and the Vector-Space Model. *IEEE Software*, 0740-7459

Lee, T. B., Hendler, J., & Lassila, O. (2001). The Semantic Web. *Scientific American.*

Lekakos, G., Papakiriakopoulos, D., & Chorianopoulos, K. (2001). An integrated approach to interactive and personalized TV advertising. In *Proceedings of Workshop on Personalization in Future TV.*

Li, J., & Wang, J. Z. (2008). Real-time computerized annotation of pictures. *IEEE Trans. Pattern Aanlysis and Machine Intelligence, 30*(6), 985–1002. doi:10.1109/TPAMI.2007.70847

Li, Y., Tian, Y., Duan, L.-Y., Yang, J., Huang, T., & Gao, W. (2011). *Sequence Multi-labeling: A Unified Video Annotation Scheme with Spatial and Temporal Context.* IEEE Trans. Multimedia.

Li, H., Edwards, S. M., & Lee, J. (2002). Measuring the intrusiveness of advertisements: scale development and validation. *Journal of Advertising.*

Li, H., Zhang, D., Hu, J., Zeng, H.-J., & Chen, Z. (2007). Finding keyword from online broadcasting content for targeted advertising. *International Workshop on Data Mining and Audience Intelligence for Advertising.*

Li, S. Z., Zhu, L., Zhang, Z., Blake, A., Zhang, H.-J., & Shum, H. (2002). Statistical learning of multi-view face detection. In *Proceedings of European Conference on Computer Vision* (pp. 67-81). Copenhagen, Denmark.

Li, X., Chen, L., Zhang, L., Lin, F., & Ma, W. (2006). Image annotation by large-scale content-based image retrieval. In *Proceedings of the 14th Annual ACM International Conference on Multimedia.*

Li, Y., Wan, K. W., Yan, X., & Xu, C. (2005). Real time advertisement insertion in baseball video based on advertisement effect. In *Proceedings of the 11th ACM International Conference on Multimedia* (pp. 343–346).

Li, Z., Zhang, L., & Ma, W.-Y. (2008). Delivering online advertisements inside images. In *Proceedings of ACM Multimedia* (pp. 1051-1060). ACM.

Liao, W. S., Chen, K., & Hsu, W. H. (2008). Adimage: video advertising by image matching and ad scheduling optimization. In *SIGIR.*

Liao, W.-S., Chen, K.-T., & Hsu, W. H. (2008). Adimage: video advertising by image matching and ad scheduling optimization. In *Proceedings of ACM SIGIR conference on Research and Development in Information Retrieval* (pp. 767-768). ACM.

Lieberman, N. (1977). *Playfulness: the Relationship to Imagination and Creativity.* New York: Academic Press.

Lim, J., Kim, M., Lee, B., Kim, M., Lee, H., & Lee, H. (2008). A target advertisement system based on TV viewer's profile reasoning. *International Journal on Multimedia Tools and Applications, 36*(1), 11–35. doi:10.1007/s11042-006-0079-2

Lindstorm, M. (2004). Branding is no Long Child's Play. *Journal of Consumer Marketing, 21*(3), 175–182. doi:10.1108/07363760410534722

Ling, H., & Soatto, S. (2007). Proximity Distribution Kernels for Geometric Context in Category. In *Proc. 2007 IEEE 11th Int. Conf. on Computer Vision* (pp. 1-8). Rio de Janeiro, Brazil: IEEE Computer Society.

Liu, T., Sun, J., Zheng, N., Tang, X., & Shum, H. (2007). *Learning to detect a salient object.* CVPR.

Liu, H., Jiang, S., Huang, Q., & Xu, C. (2008). A generic virtual content insertion system based on visual attention analysis. In *Proceeding of the 16th ACM International Conference on Multimedia* (pp. 379–388). New York: ACM.

Liu, H., Jiang, S., Huang, Q., & Xu, C. (2008). A generic virtual content insertion system based on visual attention analysis. In *Proc. the 16th ACM int. conf. on Multimedia* (pp. 379-388). Vancouver, Canada: ACM.

Liu, K., Qiu, Q., Wang, C., Bu, J., Zhang, F., & Chen, C. (2008). Incorporate Sentiment Analysis in Contextual Advertising. In *Proceedings of the First Workshop on Targeting and Ranking for Online Advertising* (In conjunction with WWW'08).

Liu, N., Yan, J., Shen, D., Chen, D.P., Chen, Z. & Li, Y. (2010). Learning to Rank Audience for Behavioral Targeting. *To be published in Proceedings SIGIR10*, poster.

Liu, T. Y. (2009). Learning to Rank for Information Retrieval. *Foundations and Trends® in Information Retrieval, 3*(3), 225-331.

Liu, Y., Jiang, S., Ye, Q., Gao, W., & Huang, Q. (2005). Playfield detection using adaptive GMM and its application. In *The 2005 IEEE International Conference Acoustics, Speech, and Signal Processing, Vol. 2* (pp. 837-840).

Ma, Y., Hua, X., Lu, L., & Zhang, H. (2005). A generic framework of user attention model and its application in video summarization. *IEEE Transactions on Multimedia, 7*(5), 907–919. doi:10.1109/TMM.2005.854410

Ma, Y.-F., & Zhang, H.-J. (2003). Contrast-based image attention analysis by using fuzzy growing. In *Proceedings of ACM Multimedia* (pp. 374-381). ACM.

Ma, Y.-F., Lu, L., Zhang, H.-J., & Li, M. (2002). A user attention model for video summarization. In *Proceedings of ACM Multimedia* (pp. 533–542).

Madambath, M. (2009). The idea of sequential advertising - moving beyond the context. Retrieved May 2, 2010 from http://www.watblog.com/2009/01/30/the-idea-of-sequential-advertising-moving-beyond-the-context

Malaby, T. (2007). Beyond Play: A New Approach to Games. *Games and Culture, 2*(2), 95–113. doi:10.1177/1555412007299434

Malaby, T. (2008). Anthropology and Play: The Contours of Playful Experience. Retrieved February 14, 2010 from http://papers.ssrn.com/sol3/papers.cfm?abstract_id=1315542

Mandal, T., Majumdar, A., & Wu, Q. (2007). Face recognition by curvelet based feature extraction. In *Image Analysis and Recognition* (LNCS 4633, pp. 806-817).

Mandese, J. (2009). Research Rivals Nielsen, comScore, Rentrak, TiVo, TNS Agree to Pool TV Set-Top Data. Retrieved January 14, 2009, from http://www.mediapost.com/publications/?fa=Articles.showArticle&art_aid=105217

Manning, C. D., Raghavan, P., & Schütze, H. (2008). *Introduction to Information Retrieval*. Cambridge University Press.

Marketing Sherpa (Ed.). (2008). *Online Advertising Handbook*. Marketing Sherpa.

Mathieu, B. (2010, January 18). Online Marketing Trends for 2010. *Marketing Daily Commentary*. Retrieved February 14, 2010, from http://www.mediapost.com/publications/?fa=Articles.showArticle&art_aid=120798

Mathwick, C., & Rigdon, E. (2004). Play, Flow and the Online Search Experience. *The Journal of Consumer Research, 31*, 324–332. doi:10.1086/422111

Mccoy, S., Everard, A., Polak, P., & Galletta, D. F. (2007). The effects of online advertising. *Communications of the ACM, 50*(3), 84–88. doi:10.1145/1226736.1226740

Mehta, A., Saberi, A., Vazirani, U., & Vazirani, V. (2007). Adwords and generalized on-line matching. *Journal of the ACM, 54*(5). doi:10.1145/1284320.1284321

Mehta, A., Saberi, A., Vazirani, U., & Vazirani, V. (2007). Adwords and generalized online matching. *Journal of the ACM, 54*(5), 22. doi:10.1145/1284320.1284321

Mei, T., Hua, X., & Li, S. (2009). VideoSense: A Contextual In-Video Advertising System. *IEEE Transactions on Circuits and Systems for Video Technology, 19*(12), 1866–1879. doi:10.1109/TCSVT.2009.2026949

Mei, T., & Hua, X.-S. (2010). Contextual internet multimedia advertising. In *Proceedings of the IEEE*.

Mei, T., Guo, J., Hua, X.-S., and Liu, F. (2010). AdOn: Toward contextual overlay in-video advertising. Multimedia Systems.

Mei, T., Hua, X., & Li, S. (2008). Contextual in-image advertising. In *Proceeding of the 16th ACM International Conference on Multimedia* (pp. 439–448). New York: ACM.

Mei, T., Hua, X., Yang, L., & Li, S. (2007). VideoSense: towards effective online video advertising. In *Proceedings of the 15th ACM International Conference on Multimedia* (Augsburg, Germany, September 25 - 29, 2007) (pp. 1075-1084). New York: ACM.

Microsoft advertising adCenter (2010). Retrieved from http://www.adcenter.microsoft.com

Middleton, S. E., Shadbolt, N. R., & De Roure, D. C. (2004). Ontological user profiling in recommender systems. *ACM Transactions on Information Systems, 22*(1), 54–88. doi:10.1145/963770.963773

Miller, G. A. (1995). WordNet: A Lexical Database for English. *Communications of the ACM, 38*(11), 39–41. doi:10.1145/219717.219748

Minka, T. P. (2003). Estimating a Dirichlet distribution. Retrieved from http://research.microsoft.com/en-us/um/people/minka/papers/dirichlet/

Mishne, G., & de Rijke, M. (2006). Language Model Mixtures for Contextual Ad Placement in Personal Blogs. In *Proceedings of 5th International Conference on NLP, FinTAL* (pp. 435-446), Springer.

Mobile Advertising Architecture. (2007). *Mobile Advertisement in a. mobi World*. Retrieved December 2, 2007 from http://advisorygroup.mobi

Mobile Advertising Requirements. (2007). Open Mobile Alliance Retrieved October 25, 2007 from http://www.openmobilealliance.org/

Molesworth, M., & Denegri-Knott, J. (2007). Digital Play and the Actualization of Consumer Imagination. *Games and Culture, 2*(2), 114–133. doi:10.1177/1555412006298209

Mori, G., Belongie, S., & Malik, J. (2005, Nov.). Efficient Shape Matching Using Shape Contexts. *IEEE Transactions on Pattern Analysis and Machine Intelligence, 27*(11), 1832–1937. doi:10.1109/TPAMI.2005.220

Moriarty, S. E. (1991). *Creative advertising: Theory and practice*. USA: Prentice-Hall.

Mulvenna, M. D., Anand, S. S., & Büchner, A. G. (2000). Personalization on the Net using Web mining: introduction. *Communications of the ACM, 43*(8), 122–125. doi:10.1145/345124.345165

Murdock, V., Ciaramita, M., & Plachouras, V. (2007). A noisy channel approach to contextual advertising. In *Proceedings of the 1st International Workshop on Data Mining and Audience Intelligence for Advertising (AD-KDD'07)* (pp. 21–27).

Naphade, M. R., Kennedy, L., Kender, J. R., Chang, S.-F., Smith, J. R., & Over, P. (2005). *A Light Scale Concept Ontolology for Multimedia Understanding for TRECVID 2005*. IBM Research.

Nelson, M. (2002). Recall of Brand Placements in Computer/Video Games. *Journal of Advertising Research, 42*(2), 80–92.

Newman, M. E. J. (2003). The Structure and Function of Complex Networks. *SIAM Review, 45*(2), 167–256. doi:10.1137/S003614450342480

Nielsen. (n.d.). *Television*. Retrieved May 1, 2010, from en-us.nielsen.com: http://en-us.nielsen.com/tab/measurement/tv_research

Nielsenwire. (2010, March 22). *Americans Using TV and Internet Together 35% More Than A Year Ago*. Retrieved from blog.nielsen.com: http://blog.nielsen.com/nielsenwire/online_mobile/three-screen-report-q409/

Oliva, A., & Torralba, A. (2001). 5). Modeling the Shape of the Scene: A Holistic Representation of the Spatial Envelope. *International Journal of Computer Vision, 42*(3), 145–175. doi:10.1023/A:1011139631724

Oshiba, T., Koike, Y., Tabuchi, M., & Kamba, T. (2002). Personalized advertisement-duration control for streaming delivery. In *Proceedings of the Tenth ACM International Conference on Multimedia* (Juan-les-Pins, France, December 01 - 06, 2002) (pp. 21-28). New York: ACM.

Palmer, S., Rosch, E., & Chase, P. (1981). *Canonical perspective and the perception of objects* (pp. 135–151). Attention and Performance.

Papadopoulos, S. (2009). *Key Success Factors in Internet Advertising: The role of Online User Activity and Social Context*. LAP Lambert Academic Publishing.

Papadopoulos, S., Kompatsiaris, Y., & Vakali, A. (2009b). Leveraging Collective Intelligence through Community Detection in Tag Networks. In *Proceedings CKCaR'09 Workshop on Collective Knowledge Capturing and Representation*, Redondo Beach, California, USA.

Papadopoulos, S., Menemenis, F., Kompatsiaris, Y., & Bratu, B. (2009a). Lexical Graphs for Improved Contextual Ad Recommendation. In *Proceedings of the 31th European Conference on IR Research on Advances in information Retrieval* (pp. 216-227).

Parker, G. R. (1992). *Institutional change, discretion, and the making of modern Congress: An economic interpretation.* USA: University of Michigan Press.

Pascal, V. O. C. (n.d.). Retrieved May 4, 2010, from The PASCAL Visual Object Classes: http://pascallin.ecs.soton.ac.uk/challenges/VOC/

Pavlou, P. A., & Stewart, D. W. (2000). Measuring the Effects and Effectiveness of Interactive Advertising: A Research Agenda. *Journal of Interactive Advertising, 1*(1).

Pazzani, M. J., & Billsus, D. (2007). Content-based recommendation systems. In *The Adaptive Web: Methods and Strategies of Web Personalization* (LNCS 4321, pp 325-341).

Peer39 Semantic advertising solution (2010). Retrieved from http://www.peer39.com/

Phillips, J. J. (Ed.). (2003). *Return on investment in training and performance improvement programs.* Butterworth-Heinemann.

R Development Core Team. (2010). R: A language and environment for statistical computing. R Foundation for Statistical Computing, Vienna, Austria. Retrieved from http://www.R-project.org

Rajani Kanth, K. (2010, January 7). Catch them Young with Advergaming. *Business Standard.* Retrieved February 14, 2010, from http://www.business-standard.com/india/news/catch-them-youngadvergaming/381926/

Ray, A. (n.d.). *Interactive TV audiences.* Retrieved May 1, 2010, from thinkbox.tv: http://www.thinkbox.tv/server/show/nav.1188

rd Whitepaper Mobile Advertising, Mobile TV Joint UMTS Forum/GSMA Work Group Calhoun, P., Loughney, J., Guttman, E., Zorn, G., & Arkko, J. (2003). *Diameter Base Protocol,* RFC 3588.

Rettie, R., Grandcolas, U., & McNeil, C. (2004). Post-impressions: internet advertising without click-through. *Academy of Marketing Conference,* 6-9 July 2004, Cheltenham, United Kingdom.

Revenue Science. (n.d.). Retrieved from http://www.revenuescience.com/advertisers/advertiser_solutions.asp

Ribeiro-Neto, B., Cristo, M., Golgher, P. B., & de Moura, E. S. (2005). Impedance coupling in content-targeted advertising. In *Proceedings of the 28th annual international ACM SIGIR conference on Research and development in information retrieval* (pp. 496–503). New York: ACM.

Richardson, M., Dominowska, E., & Ragno, R. (2007). Predicting clicks: estimating the click-through rate for new ads. In *Proceedings of the 16th international Conference on World Wide Web* (pp. 521-530).

Robertson, S. E., Walker, S., & Hancock-Beaulieu, M. (1998). Okapi at TREC-7. In *Proceedings of the Seventh Text REtrieval Conference* (pp. 109-126).

Robertson, S. E., Walker, S., Jones, S., Hancock-Beaulieu, M., & Gatford, M. (1994). Okapi at TREC-3. In *Proceedings of the Third Text REtrieval Conference* (pp. 109-126).

Rosenberg, J., Schulzrinne, H., Camarillo, G., Johnston, A., Peterson, J., Sparks, R., Handley, M., & Schooler, E. (2002), *SIP: Session Initiation Protocol.* RFC 3261

Rosenkrans, G. (2009). The creativeness and effectiveness of online interactive rich media advertising. *Journal of Interactive Advertising, 9*(2), 18–31.

Rother, C., Bordeaux, L., Hamadi, Y., & Blake, A. (2006). Autocollage. *ACM Transactions on Graphics, 25*(3), 847–852. doi:10.1145/1141911.1141965

Rothschild, M. (1984). Perspectives on Involvement: Current Problems and Future Directions. In Kinnear, T. C. (Ed.), *Advances in Consumer Research* (Vol. 11, pp. 216–217). Provo, UT: Association for Consumer Research.

Rui, Y., Huang, T. S., Ortega, M., & Mehrotra, S. (1998). Relevance feedback: A power tool for interactive content-based image retrieval. *IEEE Trans. on Circuits and Video Technology, 8*(5), 644–655. doi:10.1109/76.718510

Russell, C. A. (1998). Toward a framework of product placement: theoretical propositions. *Advances in Consumer Research. Association for Consumer Research (U. S.), 25*(1), 357–362.

Salton, G., & Buckley, C. (1990). Improving Retrieval Performance by Relevance Feedback. *Journal of the American Society for Information Science American Society for Information Science, 41*(4), 288–297. doi:10.1002/(SICI)1097-4571(199006)41:4<288::AID-ASI8>3.0.CO;2-H

Sarmento, L., Trezentos, P., Gonçalves, J. P., & Oliveira, E. (2009). Inferring local synonyms for improving keyword suggestion in an on-line advertisement system. In *Proceedings of the Third international Workshop on Data Mining and Audience intelligence for Advertising, ADKDD '09* (pp. 37-45). New York: ACM.

Schacter, D. (1987). Implicit memory: history and current status. *Journal of Experimental Psychology. Learning, Memory, and Cognition, 13*(3), 501–518. doi:10.1037/0278-7393.13.3.501

Schneider, P. P. F., & Swartout, B. (1993). Description Logic Knowledge Representation System Specification from the KRSS Group. Retrieved from http://www-db.research.bell-labs.com/user/pfps/papers/krss-spec.ps

Schulzrinne, H., Casner, S., Frederick, R., & Jacobson, V. (2003). *RTP: A Transport Protocol for Real-Time Applications*. RFC 3550.

Schwartz, J. (2006, March 10). Bold New Opportunities in Virtual World. *iMediaConnection*. Retrieved February 14, 2010, from http://www.imediaconnection.com/content/8605.asp

Shani, G., Heckerman, D., & Brafman, R. I. (2005, Dec.). An MDP-Based Recommender System. *Journal of Machine Learning Research, 6*, 1265–1295.

Shaparenko, B., Çetin, Ö., & Iyer, R. (2009). Data-driven text features for sponsored search click prediction. In *Proceedings of the Third international Workshop on Data Mining and Audience intelligence For Advertising*. ADKDD '09. (pp. 46-54). New York: ACM.

Shapiro, S., Macinnis, D. J., & Heckler, S. E. (1997). The Effects of Incidental Ad Exposure on the Formation of Consideration Sets. *The Journal of Consumer Research, 24*(1). doi:10.1086/209496

Shaw, P. (2003). *Multivariate statistics for the Environmental Sciences*. Hodder-Arnold.

Shechtman, E., & Irani, M. (2007). Matching Local Self-Similarities across Images and Videos. In *Proc. of 2007 IEEE Conf. on Computer Vision and Pattern Recognition* (pp. 1-8). Minneapolis, MN: IEEE Computer Society.

Sheikh, H. R., Evans, B. L., & Bovik, A. C. (2003). Real-time foveation techniques for low bit rate video coding. *Real-Time Imaging, 9*(1), 27–40. doi:10.1016/S1077-2014(02)00116-X

Shen, D., Sun, J.-T., Yang, Q., & Chen, Z. (2006). Building bridges for web query classification. In *Proceedings of ACM SIGIR conference on Research and Development in Information Retrieval.* ACM.

Sheth, M., Avant, D., & Bertram, C. (2001) System and method for creating a semantic web and its applications in browsing, searching, profiling, personalization and advertising. US Patent Application 6311194, October 2001

Shih, C. (1998). Conceptualising Consumer Experiences in Cyberspace. *European Journal of Marketing, 32*(7/8), 655–663. doi:10.1108/03090569810224056

Sieg, A., Mobasher, B., & Burke, R. (2007). Learning Ontology-Based User Profiles: A Semantic Approach to Personalized Web Search. *IEEE Intelligent Informatics Bulletin, 8*(1).

Simon, H. A. (1971). Designing Organizations for an Information-Rich World. In Greenberger, M. (Ed.), *Computers, communications, and the public interest* (pp. 37–72). Baltimore, MD: The Johns Hopkins Press.

Simon, H., Morreale, J., & Gronbeck (2001). *Persuasion in Society*. London: Sage Publications.

skymedia. (n.d.). *Green Button Advertising.* Retrieved May 1, 2010, from skymedia.co.uk: http://www.skymedia.co.uk/greenbutton

SkyPlus. (n.d.). Retrieved from radioandtelly.co.uk: http://www.radioandtelly.co.uk/skyplus.html

Smith, J., & Just, S. (2009). Playful Persuasion. *Nordicom Review, 2*, 53–68.

Smith, K., & Rogers, M. (1994). Effectiveness of subliminal messages in television commercials: two experiments. *The Journal of Applied Psychology, 79*(6), 866–874. doi:10.1037/0021-9010.79.6.866

Song, R., Chen, E., & Zhao, M. (2005). *SVM Based Automatic User Profile Construction for Personalized Search* (pp. 475–484). Advances in Intelligent Computing.

Srinivasan, S. H., Sawant, N., & Wadhwa, S. (2007). vADeo: Video Advertising System. In *Proceedings of ACM Multimedia* (pp. 455–456).

Srivastava, J., Cooley, R., Deshpande, M., & Tan, P.-N. (2000). Web usage mining: Discovery and applications of usage patterns from web data. *SIGKDD Explorations, 1*(2), 12–23. doi:10.1145/846183.846188

Sternthal, B., & Craig, S. (1973). Humor in Advertising. *Journal of Marketing, 37*(4), 12–18. doi:10.2307/1250353

Straccia, U. (2005). Towards a Fuzzy Description Logic for the Semantic Web (Preliminary Report). In *Proceedings of the 2nd European Semantic Web Conference (ESWC-05)*.

Subscriber Profile User Group. (2009). *Reference Architecture Version 1.1*. Retrieved October 3, 2009, from http://www.spugonline.com/

Suits, B. (1978). *The Grasshopper: Games, Life, and Utopia*. Toronto, ON: University of Toronto Press.

Sutton, R. S., & Barto, A. G. (1998). *Reinforcement learning: an introduction*. Cambridge, MA: MIT Press.

Sutton-Smith, B. (1997). *The Ambiguity of Play*. Cambridge, MA: Harvard University Press.

Svahn, M. (2009). Processing Play, Perceptions of Persuasion. Breaking New Ground: *Innovation in Games, Play, Practice and Theory, Proceedings of DiGra 2009*.

Sweney, M. (2009, September 30). Internet Overtakes Television to Become Biggest Advertising Sector in the UK. *The Guardian*. Retrieved February 14, 2010, from http://www.guardian.co.uk/media/2009/sept/30/internet-biggest-uk-advertising-sector/

Sweney, M. (2009, Sep. 30). *Internet overtakes television to become biggest advertising sector in the UK*. Retrieved from guardian.co.uk: http://www.guardian.co.uk/media/2009/sep/30/internet-biggest-uk-advertising-sector

Tacoda (n.d.). Retrieved from http://advertising.aol.com/advertiser-solutions/targeting/behavioral-targeting

Tam, K., & Ho, S. (2005). Web Personalization as a Persuasion Strategy: An Elaboration Likelihood Model Perspective. *Information Systems Research, 16*(3), 271–292. doi:10.1287/isre.1050.0058

Tamir, M., Sharir, A., & Wilf, I. (2002). *Method and apparatus for automatic electronic replacement of billboards in a video image* (Nos. 6,384,871).

Taylor, J. (1997). The Emerging Geographies of the Virtual World. *Geographical Review, 87*(2), 172–192. doi:10.2307/216004

Terranova, T. (2000). Free Labour: Producing Culture for the Digital Economy. *Social Text, 18*(2), 33–58. doi:10.1215/01642472-18-2_63-33

Thawani, A., Gopalan, S., & Sridhar, V. (2004). Context aware personalized ad insertion in an interactive TV environment. In *Proceedings of Workshop on Personalization in Future TV*.

Thawani, A., Gopalan, S., & Sridhar, V. (2004). Event Driven semantics based ad selection. In *ICME '04 Multimedia and Expo* (Vol.3, pp. 1875-1878).

thinkbox.tv. (n.d.). *Interactive TV - Executive summary, Facts and Figures*. Retrieved May 1, 2010, from thinkbox.tv: http://www.thinkbox.tv/server/show/nav.1009

Tien, M.-C., Wang, Y.-T., Chou, C.-W., Hsieh, K.-Y., Chu, W.-T., & Wu, J.-L. (2008). Event detection in tennis matches based on video data mining. In *The 2008 IEEE International Conference Multimedia and Expo* (pp. 1477-1480).

timewarnercable.com. (n.d.). Retrieved April 27, 2010, from Time Warner: http://www.timewarnercable.com

Tivo.com. (n.d.). Retrieved from Tivo.com: http://www.tivo.com

Tjondronegoro, D., Chen, Y., & Pham, B. (2004). Highlights for more complete sports video summarization. *IEEE MultiMedia*, *11*(4), 22–37. doi:10.1109/MMUL.2004.28

Tokumaru, M., Muranaka, N., & Imanishi, S. (2002). Color design support system considering color harmony. In *The IEEE Fuzzy Systems, Vol. 1.* (pp. 378-383).

Trajkova, J., & Gauch, S. (2004). Improving ontology-based user profiles. In *Proceedings of RIAO* (pp. 380-389).

TREC Video Retrieval Evaluation. (n.d.). Retrieved May 4, 2010, from trecvid.nist.gov: http://trecvid.nist.gov/

TRUSTe Survey. (n.d.). Retrieved from http://www.truste.com/pdf/TRUSTe_TNS_2009_BT_Study_Summary.pdf

Tsai, M., Liang, W., & Liu, M. (2007). The effects of subliminal advertising on consumer attitudes and buying intentions. *Journal of Management*, *24*(1), 3–14.

Tsatsou, D., Menemenis, F., Kompatsiaris, I., & Davis, P. C. (2009). A semantic framework for personalized ad recommendation based on advanced textual analysis. In *Proceedings of the Third ACM Conference on Recommender Systems. RecSys '09* (pp 217-220). New York: ACM.

Turkle, S. (1995). *Life on the Screen.* New York: Simon & Schuster.

Turner Entertainment Networks. (2009). *TV in Context.* Retrieved May 20, 2009, from http://www.nytimes.com/2009/05/20/business/media/20adco.html?_r=1

Turney, P. D. (2000). Learning algorithms for keyphrase extraction. *Information Retrieval*, *2*(4), 303–336. doi:10.1023/A:1009976227802

Van Der Graaf, S., & Nieborg, D. (2003). 'Together We Brand America's Army', Level Up: Digital Games Research Conference, Utrecht, Holland, Universiteit Holland.

Vargo, S., & Lusch, R. (2004). Evolving to a New Dominant Logic for Marketing. *Journal of Marketing*, *68*, 1–17. doi:10.1509/jmkg.68.1.1.24036

Video Advertising Solutions. (n.d.). Retrieved April 28, 2010, from www.google.com: http://www.google.com/ads/videoadsolutions/advertiser.html

Vilanilam, J. V., & Varghese, A. K. (2004). *Advertising basics! A resource guide.* New Delhi: Response Books.

Viola, P., & Jones, M. (2002). Robust real-time object detection. *International Journal of Computer Vision*, *57*(2), 137–154. doi:10.1023/B:VISI.0000013087.49260.fb

Walther, D., Riesenhuber, M., Poggio, T., Itti, L., & Koch, C. (2002, Apr). Towards an integrated model of saliency-based attention and object recognition in the primate's visual system. *Journal of Cognitive Neuroscience*, *B14*(S), 46-47.

Wan, K., & Xu, C. (2006). Automatic content placement in sports highlights. In *IEEE International Conference on Multimedia & Expo* (pp. 1893–1896).

Wan, K., & Xu, C. (2006). Automatic Content Placement in Sports Highlights. In *Proc. of IEEE Int. Conf. on Multimedia and Expo* (pp. 1893-1896). Toronto, Canada: IEEE Computer Society.

Wan, K., Wang, J., Xu, C., & Tian, Q. (2004). Automatic sports highlights extraction with content augmentation. In *The Pacific-Rim Conference Multimedia* (pp. 19-26).

Wan, K., Yan, X., Yu, X., & Xu, C. (2003). Robust goalmouth detection for virtual content insertion. In *The 11th ACM International Conference Multimedia* (pp. 468-469).

Wang, C., Zhang, P., Choi, R., & Eredita, M. D. (2002). Understanding consumer's attitude toward advertising. In *Proceedings of Americas Conference on Information Systems* (pp. 1143–1148).

Wang, J., Duan, L., Wang, B., Chen, S., Ouyang, Y., Liu, J., et al. (2009). Linking video ads with product or service information by web search. In *The 2009 IEEE International Conference Multimedia and Expo* (pp. 274-277).

Wang, J., Duan, L., Xu, L., Lu, H., & Jin, J. S. (2007). TV ad video categorization with probabilistic concept learning. In *Proc. of the int. workshop on Workshop on multimedia information retrieval* (pp. 217-226). Augsburg, Bavaria, Germany: ACM.

Wang, J., Fang, Y., & Lu, H. (2008). Online video advertising based on user's attention relavancy computing. In *The 2008 IEEE International Conference Multimedia and Expo* (pp. 1161-1164).

Wang, L., & Mueller, K. (2008). Harmonic colormaps for volume visualization. In *The 7th IEEE/EG Symposium on Volume Graphics* (pp. 33-40).

Wang, X., Yu, M., Zhang, L., Cai, R., & Ma, W. (2009). Argo: intelligent advertising by mining a user's interest from his photo collections. In *The 3rd International Workshop on Data Mining and Audience Intelligence for Advertising* (pp. 18-26).

Wang, X.-J., Zhang, L., Jing, F., & Ma, W.-Y. (2006). AnnoSearch:Image Auto-Annotation by Search. In *Proc. of IEEE Conf. Computer Vision and Pattern Recognition* (pp. 1483-1490). Washington, DC: IEEE Computer Society.

Webster, J., Trevino, L., & Ryan, L. (1993). The Dimensionality and Correlates of Flow in Human Computer Interactions. *Computers in Human Behavior, 9*(4), 411–426. doi:10.1016/0747-5632(93)90032-N

Webster, J. G., Phalen, P. F., & Lichty, L. W. (2006). *Ratings Analysis*. Mahwah, NJ: Lawrence Erlbaum Associates.

Weideman, M., & Haig-Smith, T. (2002). *An investigation into search engines as a form of targeted advert delivery*. SAICSIT.

Weinberger, M., & Gulas, C. (1992). The Impact of Humour in Advertising: A Review. *Journal of Advertising, 21*(4), 35–59.

Weiss, Y., Torralba, A., & Fergus, R. (2008). Spectral Hashing. In *Proc. Conf. the Neural Information Processing Systems*.

White, R. W., & Morris, D. (2007). Investigating the querying and browsing behavior of advanced search engine users. In *Proceedings of the 30th Annual International ACM SIGIR Conference on Research and Development in Information Retrieval* (pp. 255-262). ACM Press.

Whitley, D. (1994). A genetic algorithm tutorial. *Statistics and Computing, 4*, 65–85. doi:10.1007/BF00175354

Williamson, D. A. (2009). *Social Network Ad Spending: 2010 Outlook*. Retrieved from http://www.emarketer.com/Reports/All/Emarketer_2000621.aspx

Wu, X. H., Yan, J., Liu, N., Yan, S. C., Chen, Y., & Zheng, C. (2009). Probabilistic latent semantic user segmentation for behavioral targeted advertising. In *Proceedings of the Third International Workshop on Data Mining and Audience Intelligence for Advertising* (pp. 10-17). ACM Press.

Xiao, J., Cheng, H., Sawhney, H., Rao, C., & Isnardi, M. (2006). Bilateral filtering-based optical flow estimation with occlusion detection. In *European Conference on Computer Vision*.

Xu, C., Wan, K., Bui, S., & Tian, Q. (2004). Implanting virtual advertisement into broadcast soccer video. In *The Pacific-Rim Conference Multimedia* (pp. 264-271).

Yahoo Smartads. (n.d.). Retrieved from http://advertising.yahoo.com/smartads

Yahoo. (2009). Writing ads: Ad Quality and Quality Index. Retrieved on December 23, 2009, from http://help.yahoo.com/l/us/yahoo/ysm/sps/articles/writing_ads4.html.

Yan, J., Liu, N., Wang, G., Zhang, W., Jiang, Y., & Zheng, C. (2009). How much can behavioral targeting help online advertising? In *Processing of the 18th international conference on World Wide Web* (pp. 261–270). ACM Press. doi:10.1145/1526709.1526745

Yang, B., Mei, T., Hua, X.-S., Yang, L., Yang, S.-Q., & Li, M. (2007). Online video recommendation based on multimodal fusion and relevance feedback. In *Proceedings of ACM International Conference on Image and Video Retrieval* (pp. 73–80). Amsterdam, The Netherlands.

Yang, J., Li, Y., Tian, Y., Duan, L.-Y., & Gao, W. (2009). Group-sensitive Multiple Kernel Learning for Object Categorization. In *Proc. of the IEEE 12th int. conf. on Computer Vision* (pp. 436-443). Kyoto, Japan: IEEE Computer Society.

Yang, W., Dia, J., Cheng, H., & Lin, H. (2006). Mining Social Networks for Targeted Advertising. In *Proceedings of the 39th Annual Hawaii international Conference on System Sciences vol. 06. HICSS* (pp. 137.1). Washington, DC: IEEE Computer Society.

Yih, W. T., Goodman, J., & Carvalho, V. R. (2006). Finding advertising keywords on web pages. In *Proceedings of WWW.*

Yih, W., & Meek, C. (2008). Consistent phrase relevance measures. In *Proceedings of the 2nd international Workshop on Data Mining and Audience intelligence For Advertising. ADKDD '08* (pp. 37-44). New York: ACM.

Yih, W., Goodman, J., & Carvalho, V. R. (2006). Finding Advertising Keywords on Web Pages. In *Proceedings of the 15th international conference on World Wide Web* (pp. 213–222).

Yoo, C. Y. (2008). Unconscious processing of Web advertising: Effects on implicit memory, attitude toward the brand, and consideration set. *Journal of Interactive Marketing*, 22(2), 2–18. doi:10.1002/dir.20110

Yu, X., Jiang, N., Cheong, L., Leong, H., & Yan, X. (2009). Automatic camera calibration of broadcast tennis video with applications to 3D virtual content insertion and ball detection and tracking. *Computer Vision and Image Understanding*, 113(5), 643–652. doi:10.1016/j.cviu.2008.01.006

Yu, X., Jiang, N., & Cheong, L. (2007). Accurate and stable camera calibration of broadcast tennis video. In *The 2007 IEEE International Conference Image Processing* (pp.93-96).

Yu, X., Yan, X., Chi, T., & Cheong, L. (2006). Inserting 3D projected virtual content into broadcast tennis video. In *The 14th ACM International Conference Multimedia* (pp. 619-622).

Yuan, X., Lai, W., Mei, T., Hua, X.-S., & Wu, X.-Q. (2006). Automatic video genre categorization using hierarchical svm. In *Proceedings of IEEE International Conference on Image Processing*, Atlanta, USA.

Zadeh, L. A., Klir, G. J., & Yuan, B. (1996). *Fuzzy Sets, Fuzzy Logic, Fuzzy Systems: Selected Papers by Lotfi A. Zedeh.* World Scientific Pub Co Inc.

Zadeh, P. M., & Moshkenani, M. S. (2008). Mining Social Network for Semantic Advertisement. In *Proceedings of the 2008 Third international Conference on Convergence and Hybrid information Technology - Volume 01* (November 11 - 13, 2008). ICCIT (pp. 611-618). Washington, DC: IEEE Computer Society.

Zettl, H. (1999). *Sight, sound, motion: Applied media aesthetics.* USA: Wadsworth.

Zhang, H., Kankanhalli, A., & Smoliar, S. (1993). Automatic partitioning of full-motion video. *Multimedia Systems*, 1(1), 10–28. doi:10.1007/BF01210504

Zhang, S., Tian, Q., Jiang, S., Huang, Q., & Gao, W. (2008). Affective mtv analysis based on arousal and valence features. In *Proceedings of ICME* (pp. 1369–1372).

Zhang, Y., Surendran, A. C., Platt, J. C., & Narasimhan, M. (2008). Learning from multi-topic web documents for contextual advertisement. In *Proceedings of the 14th ACM SIGKDD international Conference on Knowledge Discovery and Data Mining, KDD '08* (pp. 1051-1059). New York: ACM.

Zhao, L., Qi, W., Wang, Y.-J., Yang, S.-Q., & Zhang, H.-J. (2001). Video shot grouping using best first model merging. In *Proceedings of Storage and Retrieval for Media Database* (pp. 262–269).

Zheng, Y., Duan, L.-Y., Tian, Q., & Jesse, J. S. (2006). TV Commercial Classification Based on Textual and Visual Semantic Features. *Proc. Asia-Pacific Workshop on Visual Information Processing.* Beijing.

Zigmond, D., Dorai-Raj, S., Interian, Y., & Naveriouk, I. (2009). Measuring Advertising Quality on Television: Deriving Meaningful Metrics from Audience Retention Data. *Journal of Advertising Research*, 49(4), 419–428. doi:10.2501/S0021849909091090

About the Contributors

Xian-Sheng Hua received the B.S. and Ph.D. degrees from Peking University, Beijing, China, in 1996 and 2001, respectively, both in applied mathematics. Since 2001, he has been with Microsoft Research Asia, Beijing, where he is currently a Lead Researcher with the internet media group. His current interests are in the areas of video content analysis, multimedia search, management, authoring, sharing and advertising. He has authored more than 140 publications in these areas and has 40 filed patents or pending applications. Dr. HUA is a member of the Association for Computing Machinery and IEEE. He is now an adjunct professor of University of Science and Technology of China, and serves as an Associate Editor of IEEE Transactions on Multimedia and Editorial Board Member of Advances in Multimedia as well as Multimedia Tools and Applications. Dr. Hua won the Best Paper Award and Best Demonstration Award in ACM Multimedia 2007, Best Poster Award in 2008 IEEE International Workshop on Multimedia Signal Processing. He also won 2008 MIT Technology Review TR35 Young Innovator Award, and named as one of the "Business Elites of People under 40 to Watch" by Global Entrepreneur.

Tao Mei received the B.E. degree in automation and the Ph.D. degree in pattern recognition and intelligent systems from the University of Science and Technology of China, in 2001 and 2006, respectively. He joined Microsoft Research Asia as a Researcher Staff Member in 2006. His current research interests include multimedia content analysis, computer vision, and multimedia applications such as search, advertising, social network, and mobile applications. He is the author of seven book chapters and over 90 publications in these areas, and holds more than 25 filed international and U.S. patents or pending applications. He serves as an Associate Editor for Journal of Multimedia and Neurocomputing. He received the Best Paper and Best Demonstration Awards in ACM Multimedia 2007, the Best Poster Paper Award in IEEE MMSP 2008, and the Best Paper Award in ACM Multimedia 2009.

Alan Hanjalic is an Associate Professor and Coordinator of the Multimedia Information Retrieval lab at the Delft University of Technology, the Netherlands. Research interests and expertise of Dr. Hanjalic are in the area of multimedia signal processing, with focus on multimedia information retrieval. He (co-)authored and (co-)edited more than 100 publications, among which the books titled *Image and Video Databases: Restoration, Watermarking and Retrieval* (Elsevier, 2000) and *Content-Based Analysis of Digital Video* (Kluwer Academic Publishers, 2004) and several journal special issues, among which those in the *Proceedings of the IEEE* and *IEEE Transactions on Multimedia*. Dr. Hanjalic was a keynote speaker at the Pacific-Rim Conference on Multimedia 2007 and is an elected member of the IEEE TC on Multimedia Signal Processing. He has been on editorial boards of several journals in the field of multimedia, among which the *IEEE Transactions on Multimedia* and *IEEE Transactions on Affective*

Computing. He has held key positions in the organizing committees in major multimedia conferences, such as ACM Multimedia (General Chair, Program Chair), IEEE ICME (Program Chair), ACM CIVR (Program Chair), ACM ICMR (Program Chair) and the WWW conference (Track Chair).

* * *

Benoit Baccot is a PhD student at IRIT-ENSEEIHT, University of Toulouse, France. His research is being funded by Sopra Group. He is working on multimedia adaptation and more precisely on website adaptation. The main idea is to modify an existing website according to the user preferences, the network conditions and the terminal capabilities. Contact him at ENSEEIHT Engineering School, National Polytechnic Institute of Toulouse, University of Toulouse, France.

Chia-Hu Chang received the B.S. degree in Electrical Engineering from National Chung Hsing University (NCHU), Taiwan, in 2003 and received the M.S. degree in Communication Engineering from National Central University (NCU), Taiwan, in 2005. He is currently a Ph.D. student in the Graduate Institute of Network and Multimedia, National Taiwan University (NTU), Taiwan. His research interests include multimedia networking (eg., video streaming), multimedia content analysis and applications (eg., multimedia advertising).

Vincent Charvillat received his MEng from ENSEEIHT and PhD in computer science from INPT (National Polytechnics Institute of Toulouse) in 1997. He is currently a full professor in the Department of Computer Science and Applied Mathematics at INPT-ENSEEIHT. His research interests include video processing, interactive visual content, hypermedia content management. He is the leader of the mulitmedia-imaging group (VORTEX) at IRIT-ENSEEIHT. Contact him at ENSEEIHT Engineering School, National Polytechnic Institute of Toulouse, University of Toulouse, France.

Zheng Chen joined Microsoft Research Asia in March 1999 to pursue his wide-ranging research interests in Machine Learning, Information Retrieval, Speech Recognition, Natural Language Processing, Multimedia information retrieval, personal information management, and Artificial intelligence. Now, he is the research manager of machine learning group on Microsoft Research Asia. Dr. Zheng is served as the program committee for several conferences, including AAAI, CIKM, ICDM, PAKDD, IAT, AIRS and APWeb, etc. He has published more than 100 papers on referred conferences and journals, especially, 16 papers on SIGIR conference. He received his bachelor's, master's and PH.D.'s engineering degrees in Computer Science Tsinghua University in 1994 and 1999.

Ying Cui is currently a Scientist at Yahoo! Labs, working on data mining, prediction modeling, and statistical machine learning for online advertising system. Ying received her B.S. in Electrical Engineering from Xi'an Jiaotong University, M.S. in Computer Engineering from North Carolina State University and Ph.D. from Electrical and Computer Engineering Department, Northeastern University, Boston, MA. During her Ph.D. studies, Ying worked on learning multiple non-redundant clusterings and unsupervised feature selection for high dimensional data. Prior to join Yahoo! in 2008, she had been a research fellow in Massachusetts General Hospital and Harvard Medical School from 2005 to 2007, working on applying data mining and machine learning techniques to predict lung tumor motion for medical treatment.

Paul Davis is the Research Manager for the Text Analysis and Processing Lab at Motorola's Applied Research Center. He received his Ph.D. in Linguistics from Ohio State University in 2002, where he specialized in Computational Linguistics, and he received a Master's degree in Linguistics from the University of Wisconsin-Madison and a Bachelor's degree in Business-Economics from Miami University. His research interests include all areas of natural language processing, and in particular machine translation, recommender systems, multimodal dialogue systems, information retrieval, summarization, topic detection, sentiment analysis, and machine learning as applied to natural language processing. He is the coauthor of a number of papers and patents in these areas, and his work has been deployed in several Motorola products.

Sundar Dorai-Raj is a Senior Quantitative Analyst at Google, Inc. His role includes defining metrics for measuring ad quality on both TV and YouTube. He also designs and analyzes experiments for testing ad formats on YouTube. His areas of interests include linear models, data visualization, and statistical computing. He has a Ph.D. and M.S. in Statistics from Virginia Tech as well as a B.S. and M.A. in Applied Math from the University of Alabama.

Ling-Yu Duan received the Ph.D. degree in Information Technology from The University of Newcastle, Australia, in 2007, the M.Sc. degree in Computer Science from National University of Singapore, Singapore, and the M.Sc. degree in Automation from University of Sci. and Tech. of China, Hefei, China, in 2002 and 1999, respectively. Since 2008, he has been with Peking University, Beijing, China, where he is currently an Associate Professor with the School of Electronics Engineering and Computer Science. Before that, he was a Research Scientist in Institute for Infocomm Research, Singapore, from 2003 to 2008. His current interests are in the areas of multimedia content analysis, computer vision, large scale multimedia information mining and retrieval, mobile media computing for multimedia authoring, sharing and advertising. He has authored more than 60 publications in these areas and has 5 filed US patents or pending applications. He is a Member of IEEE and Member of ACM.

Wen Gao received his Ph.D. degree in electronics engineering from the University of Tokyo in 1991. He joined with the Harbin Institute of Technology from 1991 to 1995, as professor, chairman of department of computer science. He joined with Institute of Computing Technology (ICT), Chinese Academy of Sciences (CAS), as professor from 1996 to 2005. During his career at CAS, he served as the managing director of ICT from 1998 to 1999, the vice president of Graduate School of Chinese Academy of Sciences from 2000 to 2004, the vice president of University of Science and Technology China from 2000 to 2003. He is joining with the Peking University as professor since 2006. Dr. Gao is working at the areas of image and video processing, in particular at video coding and video analysis. He is the leader of Chinese National Body for MPEG standard, as well as the founder of AVS standard. He is an IEEE fellow.

Romulus Grigoras is an assistant professor at ENSEEIHT, University of Toulouse, France. His main research field is distributed multimedia systems. He is a member of the VORTEX multimedia research group at IRIT-ENSEEIHT, University of Toulouse. He is also a member of ACM. With his colleagues, they are working on visual objects, from acquisition to modeling, transport over IP networks and usage.

Contact him at ENSEEIHT Engineering School, National Polytechnic Institute of Toulouse, University of Toulouse, France.

Jesse Jin graduated with a PhD degree from University of Otago, New Zealand. He is the Chair Professor of IT in the School of Design, Communication and IT, University of Newcastle. His research interests include multimedia technology, visual information retrieval, medical imaging and computer vision. He has published 297 articles and 13 books. He has also been awarded four patents and is in the process of filing 2 more patents. He established a spin-off company and the company won the 1999 Vice-Chancellor New Business Creation Award in the Australian Technology Park, Sydney. He is/was a consultant of many companies such as Motorola, Computer Associates, ScanWorld, Proteome Systems, HyperSoft, ITIC, etc. He was a visiting professor in MIT, UCLA, HKPU, Tsinghua University, Jilin University, China Academy of Sciences, Tienjin University, Huazhong University of Science and Technology, Beijing Normal University, etc.

Markus Kampmann received a Diploma in electrical engineering from the University of Bochum, Germany, in 1993 and a Ph.D. degree in telecommunications from the University of Hannover, Germany, in 2002. From 1993 to 2001, he was working as a Research Assistant at the Institute of Communication Theory and Signal Processing, the University of Hannover, Germany. Since 2001, he has been working with Ericsson Research in Aachen, Germany, where he is involved in or leading several research projects about multimedia communications funded by the European Union or the German Government. His main research areas are video communications, video streaming and video coding, mobile media transport and delivery, and mobile broadcasting. He is serving as an Associate Editor of IEEE Transactions on Broadcasting and International Journal of Digital Multimedia Broadcasting. He has published more than 70 research papers and holds over 20 granted or pending patents. He is a member of IEEE, VDE, ITG, GI and FKTG.

Ioannis Kompatsiaris received the Diploma degree in electrical engineering and the Ph.D. degree in 3-D model based image sequence coding from Aristotle University of Thessaloniki, Greece, in 1996 and 2001, respectively. He is a Senior Researcher (Researcher B') with the Informatics and Telematics Institute. His research interests include semantic multimedia analysis, indexing and retrieval, Web 2.0 content analysis, knowledge structures, reasoning and personalization for multimedia applications. He is the coauthor of 39 papers in refereed journals, 20 book chapters, 4 patents and more than 150 papers in international conferences. He has served as a regular reviewer for a number of international journals and conferences. He is a member of IEEE and ACM.

Yasmin Ibrahim is a Reader in International Business and Communications at Queen Mary, University of London. Her ongoing research on new media technologies explores the cultural dimensions and social implication of the diffusion of ICTs in different contexts. Beyond new media and digital technologies she writes on political communication and political mobilisation from cultural perspectives. Her other research interests include globalization, visual culture and memory studies.

Yannet Interian is a Quantitative Analyst at Google, Inc. Her work includes defining and analyzing quality metrics for videos and ads on YouTube and TV. She has also works on Sell Through Rate models for ads on YouTube. Her areas of interests include data mining and machine learning. She has a Ph.D. in Applied Mathematics from Cornell University.

Lusong Li received the Ph.D. degree in Computer Software and Theory from Beihang University (formerly Beijing University of Aeronautics and Astronautics), Beijing, in 2010. Since 2002, he has been with State Key Laboratory of Software Development Environment, People's Republic of China. His current interests are in the areas of multimedia networking, multimedia content analysis, multimedia information retrieval, multimedia advertising, social network, semantic web and web service. He is also an information technology professional with particular experience of system design and software development. He has authored more than 20 publications, including five books, one book chapter, and over 10 journal and conference papers.

Shipeng Li joined Microsoft Research Asia in May 1999. He is now a Principal Researcher and Research Area Manager at MSRA. His research interests include Signal and Image Processing; Content-based Analysis; Image and Video Coding; HDTV Technology; Multimedia Streaming and Communications over Internet and Wireless Networks; Scalable Multimedia Representation; Application Level Multicast; Digital Right Management; Wireless Communication and Networking; P2P Networking; New Media Formats and Systems; Media Advertisement. From Oct. 1996 to May 1999, Dr. Li was with Multimedia Technology Laboratory at Sarnoff Corporation (formerly David Sarnoff Research Center, and RCA Laboratories) as a member of technical staff. He has authored and co-authored over 200 journal and conference papers and holds 60+ granted and 70+ pending US patents in image/video processing, compression and communications, digital television, multimedia and wireless communication. He has co-authored 3 book chapters on multimedia coding and standards and co-edited 2 multimedia conference proceedings.

Wei Li is a Scientist in the Contextual and Display Advertising Sciences department at Yahoo! Labs. She joined Yahoo! in August 2007. Wei's research focuses on machine learning, information retrieval and large scale data mining. Wei received her M.S. and Ph.D. degrees in computer science from the University of Massachusetts, Amherst and her B.S. degree from Peking University (Beijing, China). For her Ph.D. studies, Wei worked with Prof. Andrew McCallum and Prof. Bruce Croft on statistical topic models, semi-supervised learning, information extraction and question answering.

Xu Liu is currently working at Microsoft Ad Platform China. He received the BE degree in computer science, focusing on network, from Beihang University, P.R. China, in 2004, and the MS degree in computer software enginerring from Beihang University, P.R. China, in 2007. He has been working at Microsoft for 3 years as a research developer, research topic includes computer graphics, visual codec, online commercial intent, and live A/B experiment in online ads business. From 2008 to 2010, his team delivered several products and he has been a core member of team. These products has been or will be helping Microsoft to win online business.

Hanqing Lu received his B.E. degree in 1982 and his M.E. degree in 1985 from Harbin Institute of Technology, and Ph.D. degree in 1992 from Huazhong University of Sciences and Technology. Currently, he is a deputy director of National Laboratory of Pattern Recognition, Institute of Automation,

Chinese Academy of Sciences. His research interests include image and video analysis, medical image processing, object recognition, etc. He has published more than 100 papers in these fields.

Wei-Ying Ma. Dr. Wei-Ying Ma received the B.S. degree in electrical engineering from the National Tsing Hua University in Taiwan in 1990, and the M.S. and Ph.D. degrees in electrical and computer engineering from the University of California at Santa Barbara in 1994 and 1997, respectively. From 1997 to 2001, he was with HP Labs and then joined Microsoft Research Asia in 2001. Since then, he has been leading a research group to conduct research in the areas of information retrieval, web search, data mining, mobile browsing, and multimedia management. He has published 5 book chapters and over 100 international journal and conference papers.

Jianchang (JC) Mao is a Vice President and the head of Advertising Sciences in Y! Labs, overseeing the R&D of advertising technologies and products, including Search Advertising, Contextual Advertising, Display Advertising, Targeting, and Categorization. He was also a Science/Engineering director responsible for development of backend technologies for several Yahoo! Social Search products, including Y! Answers and Y! MyWeb (Social Bookmarks). Prior to joining Yahoo!, Dr. Mao was Director of Emerging Technologies & Principal Architect at Verity Inc., a leader in Enterprise Search (acquired by Autonomy), from 2000 to 2004. Prior to this, Dr. Mao was a research staff member at the IBM Almaden Research Center from 1994 to 2000. Dr. Mao's research interest includes Machine Learning, Data Mining, Information Retrieval, Computational Advertising, Social Networks, Pattern Recognition and Image Processing. He received an Honorable Mention Award in ACM KDD Cup 2002, IEEE Transactions on Neural Networks Outstanding Paper Award in 1996, and Honorable Mention Award from the International Pattern Recognition Society in 1993. Dr. Mao served as an associate editor of the IEEE Transactions on Neural Networks, 1999-2000. He received his Ph.D. degree in Computer Science from Michigan State University in 1994.

Igor Naverniouk is a Senior Software Engineer at Google, Inc. His role includes designing distributed algorithms for analysing TV viewer behaviour. He also works on ad quality in Google's TV ads auction. His areas of interest include combinatorial optimization, machine learning, and distributed computing. He has an M.S. in Computer Science from the University of British Columbia.

Huazhong Ning received PHD degree in electrical engineering at University of Illinois at Urbana-Champaign, 2008, MSc degree in pattern recognition and intelligence systems from the Institute of Automation, Chinese Academy of Sciences, Beijing, China in 2003, and the BSc degree in computer science from University of Science and Technology of China, Hefei, China in 2000. Now he is a research scientist in AKiiRA Media Systems Inc. He has been an applied researcher in Microsoft AdCenter Labs and worked as a 3G Software Engineer in Alcatel Shanghai Bell, China. His current research interests include video/image processing, machine learning, clustering, audio analysis, data mining, etc.

Symeon Papadopoulos received the Diploma degree in Electrical and Computer Engineering in the Aristotle University of Thessaloniki (AUTH), Greece in 2004. In 2006, he received the Professional Doctorate in Engineering (P.D.Eng.) from the Technical University of Eindhoven, the Netherlands. His P.D.Eng. thesis concerned the improvement of Digital Subtraction Angiography by means of real-time motion compensation. In July 2009, he received an MBA degree from the Blekinge Institute of Technology, Sweden; his MBA thesis focused on online advertising. Since September 2006, he has been working as a researcher in the Informatics and Telematics Institute. His current research interests pertain to community detection in large networks and mining of social media data. He is currently a Ph.D. candidate in the Informatics department of AUTH under the supervision of prof. Athena Vakali.

Heiko Perkuhn was born in Bonn, Germany in 1976. He received his Diploma in electrical engineering from the RWTH (Rheinisch-Westfälische Technische Hochschule) Aachen University, Germany, in 2005. His diploma thesis topic was "Implementation and Performance Evaluation of a WLAN - GPRS Inter-System Handover". Since 2006 he has been working with Ericsson Research in Aachen, Germany. His research areas include content delivery and media control in managed and unmanaged networks, mobile advertising, mobile push technology and device connectivity. He holds several patents in these areas.

Ying Shan is currently a Lead Applied Researcher at Microsoft. He received the BE degree in chemical engineering, focusing on automatic process control, from Zhejiang University, P.R. China, in 1990, and the MS and PhD degrees in computer science from Shanghai Jiaotong University, P.R. China, in 1993 and 1997, respectively. His research interests include Computer Vision, pattern recognition, machine learning, and computer graphics, with applications in online video ads, video surveillance, object/face detection, image registration, and 3D reconstruction. Until 2006, he was a Senior Member of Technical Staff in Sarnoff Corp.'s Vision and Learning Laboratory, where he initiated, led, and contributed to a number of government and commercial projects. Ying has published more than 25 peer reviewed papers, holds 19 US patents, and has 10 others pending. He is an active reviewer of top journals such as the IEEE Transactions on Pattern Analysis and Machine Intelligence and the International Journal on Computer Vision. He was on the program committee of major international conferences such as the European Conference on Computer Vision, Computer Vision and Pattern Recognition, and International Conference on Computer Vision. He was a Program Co-Chair for the First and Second IEEE Workshop on Internet Vision in 2008 and 2009.

Tanveer J. Siddiqui received her M.Sc. and D. Phil. degrees in Computer Science from University of Allahabad. Her thesis work was in the area of information retrieval. She worked as scientific officer in DRDO project, as lecturer in University of Allahabad and as Assistant Professor at Indian Institute of Information Technology. Currently she is senior lecturer in computer science at University of Allahabad. Her major research interests include Information Retrieval and Natural language Processing. She has authored and/or edited three books and published more than 15 research papers in these areas.

Dorothea Tsatsou received the Diploma degree in Applied Informatics from the University of Macedonia (UOM), Greece in 2003. She received the Master of Science (M.Sc.) degree in Multimedia Applications and Virtual Environments from the University of Sussex, UK in 2004. Since July 2007 she has been working as a researcher in the Informatics and Telematics Institute (ITI), Greece where she was involved as a research associate and manager in domestic and international projects. Her research interests include extraction and management of semantic knowledge, personalization strategies for the Semantic Web and Web 2.0 and recommender systems as well as mobile integration of advanced multimedia.

Christos Tselios was born in Athens, Greece, in 1981. He received his Diploma in Electrical and Electronic Engineering from Polytechnic School of University of Patras (2009), Greece. Currently, he is a research associate of Wireless Telecommunications Laboratory at the Department of Electrical Engineering and Computer Engineering in the University of Patras, Greece, and he is working towards the PhD degree. He is also participating in EU-funded R&D projects as engineer and developer. His research interests include but are not limited to Network Security, Mobile Telecommunication platforms, services and applications as well as All-IP Networks, B3G, NGN and P2P architectures. He is a member of the IEEE, FITCE and the Technical Chamber of Greece.

Konstantinos Vandikas was born in Kozani, Greece in 1982. He received a Diploma in Informatics from the Aristotle University of Thessaloniki, Greece in 2004 and a Masters in Computer Science from the University of Crete, Greece in 2007. While pursuing his Masters, he was working as a Research Assistant at the Institute of Computer Science (ICS) of the Foundation for Research and Technology – Hellas (FORTH) with a focus in the areas of software engineering and parallel and distributed systems from 2004 to 2007. In 2007, he joined Ericsson Corporate Research in the Service Layer Technologies group in Aachen, Germany, where he is currently working in the area of software research and service oriented architectures. In parallel he is pursuing a PhD from the RWTH Aachen University of Technology. He is a member of IEEE.

Bin Wang received Ph.D. degree from the University of Science and Technology of China (USTC) in 2007. Since then, he joined Microsoft as a research software developer. His focus is on the large-scale web data mining, especially internet advertising and behavioral targeting.

Jinqiao Wang received the B.E. degree in 2001 from Hebei University of Technology, China, and the M.S. degree in 2004 from Tianjin University, China. He received the Ph.D. degree in pattern recognition and intelligence systems from the National Laboratory of Pattern Recognition, Chinese Academy of Sciences, in 2008. He is now an Assistant Professor with Chinese Academy of Sciences. His research interests are pattern recognition and machine learning, image and video processing, mobile multimedia, and intelligent video surveillance.

Junxian Wang is currently an Applied Researcher at Microsoft. She received a Ph.D. degree in Electrical and Electronic Engineering from Nanyang Technological University, Singapore (NTU, 2003), with a specialization on signal & media processing. She served as a postdoctoral research fellow from 2004 to 2006, at the Laboratory of Computer Vision, College of Engineering, University of Nevada, Reno. After her post-doctoral research, she was a Senior Research Scientist in UtopiaCompression Corporation. Her research activities include computer vision, pattern recognition and machine learning, with applications in online video ads, video surveillance, image/video compression and content-based indexing/retrieval. She is an IEEE member and has authored and/or coauthored more than 18 journal and conference papers. She is an active reviewer for several journals and conferences including IEEE Trans on Automation Science and Engineering and IEEE Advanced Video and Signal based Surveillance. She was a member of the technical program committee of several international conferences, such as IEEE International Conference on Computer Vision Theory Applications.

Xin-Jing Wang. Xin-Jing Wang received her PhD degree in Electronic Engineering from Tsinghua University in 2005. She is now with Microsoft Research Asia. Her primary research interests include image retrieval, image understanding, pattern recognition and machine learning.

Xuerui Wang is currently a Scientist at Yahoo! Labs, working on machine learning for online advertising. In the early 2000's, he was a Research Scientist at UtopiaCompression Corporation, working on image/video/text compression and mining. Wang received the Best Foundational Paper Award from American Medical Informatics Association in Nov. 2003. Wang got his Ph.D. in Computer Science at University of Massachusetts, Amherst. During his Ph.D. studies, Wang worked on structured topic models on text and its accommpanying modalities. He also holds an M.S. in Knowledge Discovery and Data Mining from Carnegie Mellon University, an M.E. in Control Theory and Its Application and a B.E. in Automation from Tsinghua University where he graduated with honor.

Ja-Ling Wu received his Ph.D. degrees in electrical engineering from Tatung Institute of Technology, Taipei, Taiwan, in 1986. He is currently a professor in the Department of Computer Science and Information Engineering, National Taiwan University. Professor Wu was selected to be one of the lifetime Distinguished Professors of NTU, November 2006. He has published more than 200 technique and conference papers. His research interests include digital signal processing, image and video compression, digital content analysis, multimedia systems, digital watermarking, and digital right management systems. Prof. Wu has been elected to be IEEE Fellow, since 1 January 2008, for his contributions to image and video analysis, coding, digital watermarking, and rights management.

Changsheng Xu is Professor of National Lab of Pattern Recognition, Institute of Automation, Chinese Academy of Sciences. He is also Executive Director of China-Singapore Institute of Digital Media. His research interests include Multimedia Content Analysis, Image Processing, Pattern Recognition, and Computer Vision. He has published over 180 refereed book chapters, journal and conference papers in these areas. He is an Associate Editor of ACM/Springer Multimedia System Journal and is on the Editorial Board of International Journal of Multimedia Intelligence and Security. He served as Program Co-Chair of ACM Multimedia 2009, Program Co-Chair of 2009 International Conference on Internet Multimedia Computing and Services, General Co-Chair of Pacific-Rim Conference on Multimedia (PCM) 2008, Short Paper Co-Chair of ACM Multimedia 2008, General Co-Chair of 2007 Asia-Pacific Workshop on Visual Information Processing, Program Co-Chair of Asia-Pacific Workshop on Visual Information Processing, Industry Track Chair and Area Chair of 2007 International Conference on Multimedia Modeling. He is on Organizing committees and program committees in many prestigious multimedia conferences including ACM Multimedia, ICME, PCM, CIVR, MMM, among others. He is Director of Programs of ACM SIG Multimedia Beijing Chapter. Dr. Xu is a Senior Member of IEEE and Member of ACM.

Jun Yan received the Ph.D. degree in digital signal processing and pattern recognition from the department of information science, school of mathematical science, Peking University, P.R. China. He has been a research associate at CBI, HMS, Harvard, Cambridge, MA, in 2005. He joined Microsoft Research Asia (MSRA) from 2006 as an associate researcher. Currently he is working in the machine learning group of MSRA. His research interests are on online advertising, large scale data mining, data preprocessing, information retrieval and text mining. So far, he has more than 50 quality papers published in referred conferences and journals, including SIGKDD, SIGIR, WWW, ICDM, TKDE, etc.

Mo Yu received his B.S. in Computer Science from Harbin Institute University in 2009. He was an intern in Microsoft Research Asia from Mar. 2009 to Nov. 2009. He is currently a master student in the Computer Science from Harbin Institute University.

Lei Zhang is a researcher and a project lead in Microsoft Research Asia. He received his B.S. and M.S. degrees in Computer Science from Tsinghua University in 1993 and 1995 respectively. After two years of working in the industry, he returned to Tsinghua University and received his Ph.D. degree in Computer Science in 2001. Then he joined Microsoft Research Asia. His current research interests are search relevance ranking, web-scale image retrieval, social search, and photo management and sharing. He is a member of IEEE and a member of ACM.

Ruofei (Bruce) Zhang is a Senior Scientist in Advertising Sciences department at Yahoo! Labs. He currently manages information retrieval modeling, response prediction and optimization group that applies statistical machine learning and time series analysis techniques for solving problems in contextual and display advertising. His research fields are in machine learning, large scale data analysis and mining, optimization, time series analysis, image/video processing and analysis, and multimedia information retrieval. He has co-authored a monograph book on multimedia data mining, published over two dozen peer-reviewed papers on leading international journals and conferences. He has filed 15 patents on search relevance, ranking function learning, and multimedia content analysis. He received a Ph. D. in computer science with Distinguished Dissertation Award from State University of New York at Binghamton; a M.E. and B.E. from Tsinghua University and Xi'an Jiaotong University, respectively.

Dan Zigmond is an Engineering Manager of Google, Inc. He leads the Video Data Infrastructure, Reporting, and Analysis team and overseas quantitative aspects of Google's TV and online video advertising efforts. He holds a BA in computational neuroscience from the University of Pennsylvania.

Index

A

ad-blindness effect 123, 143
ad branding 264, 265
Ad delivery engine 106
ad fatigue 236
ad impact 235
ad insertion points 65, 197, 199, 201, 203, 205
ad location 194, 197, 198, 199, 200, 201, 202, 204, 205, 206, 207, 208
ad location, banner 197
ad location, midroll 197
ad location, post-roll 197
ad location, pre-roll 197
ad network 33, 53, 235
ad overload problem 14
ad relevance 104, 120, 199, 206, 207, 208, 214, 215, 217, 221, 222, 223, 229
ad revenue 214, 221, 222
ads and keywords (AAK) 40
ads, direct response 264, 265
AdSense 33, 35, 46, 135, 195, 199, 207, 208, 209, 235, 261
Ad Sitelinks 167, 192
ad spending 213, 230
ad spending, behaviorally targeted 213
Ad-Template Compatibility 111, 116
advertisement overload 234
advertisers 262, 263, 264, 265, 266, 267, 269, 273, 274, 275, 276
advertising policy 13
advertising theory 122, 123, 127, 144
ad-video association 199
AdWords 135, 235, 260
AdWords Sitelink (Ad Sitelinks) 167
AIDMA model 127, 147,

Amazon.com 67, 70, 81
applied media aesthetics 123, 144
Argo system 67, 68, 70, 72
ARIMA model 7
Arista 74, 75, 79
attractiveness 101, 102, 103, 105, 110, 118, 119, 121
audience intelligence 196, 262, 263, 265, 266, 267, 268, 269, 277
audio scene change (ASC) 178, 180
audio scene change indicator (ASCI) 175, 178
authentication, authorization and accounting (AAA) 284, 300,
automatic speech recognition (ASR) 176
Average Precision (AP) 78, 79, 80

B

Bandit-based adaptation strategy 27
Bandit Problem 16, 20, 21, 24, 26, 27, 30
banner 33, 34, 37
Basic Model 154
beam forming matrix module (BFMM) 202, 205, 206
behavioral targeting (BT) 213, 214, 215, 216, 217, 218, 219, 220, 225, 226, 227, 228, 229, 230, 231, 232, 263, 266, 269
behavioral targeting detection 262, 263, 268, 269, 270, 271
behavioral user profiling 217
Bernardo's algorithm 6
brand advertising 34
budget planning 1

C

call session control function (CSCF) 283, 300

candidate replacement space 134, 135

click-through rate (CTR) 1-12, 14, 17, 150,
    214, 222-228, 234, 239, 263, 266, 267,
    271, 272

closed-loop framework 16, 17

cluster importance (CI) 74

Collaborative Business Solutions 21

Color Harmonization 136

Combined Smoothing 9

Communication Effect Mapping 132

community-contributed photo sites 50

consumer empowerment 84, 88

content-based targeting 103

content-match 34

content selection algorithm (CSA) 287, 288,
    289, 290, 291, 292, 293, 295, 296, 299,
    300

content-targeted advertising 34, 35, 104, 120

context-based heuristics 32

contextual ads 1, 2, 3, 8, 11, 12, 13, 14, 32, 33,
    34, 35, 36, 37, 38, 39, 41, 42, 46, 47

contextual in-image advertising strategy 49

contextual marketing (CM) 235

cost per mille (CPM) 37

creative placement 124

cross-media marketing campaigns 166

Csikszentmihalyi, Mihalyi 91, 92

D

Data Continuity 4

Data Hierarchies 4, 5, 7, 8, 12

data mining 263, 267, 269, 270

demographic detection 262, 263, 268, 269

demographic profiling 215, 216, 217, 218, 229

demographics 214, 218

Demographics Model 154

demographic targeting 263, 269

Devoe, Merrill 127

difference of Gaussian (DOG) 108

digital capture devices 50, 194

digital environment 85, 90

digital video recorder (DVR) 123, 168, 169,
    174

direct marketing 34

direct match model (COS) 77, 79, 80, 81

direct-response (DR) 214

display ads 1, 2, 3

dissatisfaction oriented advertising framework
    (DASA) 42

DoubleClick 216, 231

Dynamic overlay ad 106

E

effective advertising system 54

Efficiency 36

Empirical Bayes Methods 5, 12

end-users 262, 263, 264, 265, 266, 268, 272,
    276

Exponential Smoothing 3, 4, 5, 7, 9, 10, 12

F

fixed-point iteration 6

Flickr 67, 68, 69, 78, 81, 82, 83

FoxTrot recommendation system 238

Frame Marked with Product Information
    (FMPI) 174, 175, 178, 181, 182, 183

Front-End System 106

fuzzy semantic reasoning 233

G

GameSense 49, 58, 59, 60, 63, 64

Gamma-Poisson 4, 11

generalized second price auction (GSP) 38

genetic programming (GP) methods 76, 237

geographic detection 262, 263

geographic profiling 217

geographic targeting 263

Gestalt effect 129

Gestalt theory 128

global motion estimation (GME) 126

Global textual relevance 62

Google 33, 34, 35, 36, 38, 46, 167, 169, 170,
    171, 173, 183, 188, 190, 192

Google AdWords 33, 46

Google Video 195, 209

Grasshopper 91, 97

Green Button Advertising 167, 172, 192

Group-Sensitive Multiple Kernel Learning
    (GS-MKL) 180, 181

H

harmonic degree (HD) 170, 180
Hidden Markov Model (HMM) 178
high attentive (HA) 109, 114
higher attractive shots (HAS) 126
home subscriber server (HSS) 283, 284, 285, 287, 296, 297, 300
Homo Ludens 91, 96
Ho, Shuk Ying 90, 91, 97
Huizinga, Johan 84, 91, 96
Hulu 167, 173, 190
human visual system (HVS) 126, 133, 134
hypertext markup language (HTML) 281, 300,
hypertext transmission protocol (HTTP) 300,

I

IAR Residual 151
IBM Institute for Business Value 169
image advertising 49, 66, 124, 125, 137, 145
image salience 49
ImageSense 33
impedance coupling strategies 104
improved BFMM (iBFMM) 202, 205, 206
IMS service interface (ISC) 300,
information retrieval (IR) 33, 39, 46, 170
Informative Advertising 66
in-image advertising 49, 50, 51, 53, 54, 55, 58, 59, 60, 62, 63, 64, 104, 120
in-image advertising platform 49, 53
in-image advertising system 53, 55
initial audience retained (IAR) 150, 151, 152, 153, 154, 157, 158, 159, 161, 162, 163
in-line advertising 33
inline text 34
Insertion Point Detection 55
Interactive Advertising Bureau 2, 11
Interactive television (iTV) 167, 172, 173
international telecommunications union (ITU) 298, 299, 300
Internet ads 166, 167, 168, 169, 174, 176, 177, 178, 181, 182, 183, 186, 187
Internet advertising 168, 169, 172, 173, 174
Internet Advertising Bureau (IAB) 86
Internet engineering task force (IETF) 300,
Internet Protocol television (IPTV) 173, 177

Internet revolution 2
Intrusiveness 103, 121
inverse webpage frequency (IWF) 73
IP multimedia subsystem (IMS) 280, 281, 282, 283, 284, 285, 286, 287, 295, 296, 297, 298, 299, 300
IR approach 39

K

K-Armed Bandit Problem 20
Keyword extraction 104, 106
keyword match 34, 39
Keyword Selection 35
keyword-targeted advertising 104
Kullback-Leibler Divergence 8, 9, 10, 11, 12, 57

L

LAR detection 104, 105, 106, 107
LAR map 107, 108, 109, 110
LastEvent 157, 159
latency issues 234
Latent Dirichlet Allocation (LDA) 56, 58
leaf category 78
less informative region (LIR) 125
LiveRail 102
look-alike modeling approach 215
low attentive regions (LAR) 103, 104, 105, 106, 107, 108, 109, 110, 113, 114, 115, 126
low attentive score (LAS) 106, 107, 109, 110, 111, 114, 115, 116

M

Machine Learning 12, 158, 163, 164
machine learning technologies 237, 238
machine translation 237
machine-understandable vocabularies 233, 238, 239
Markov Decision Processes (MDP) 14, 19, 21, 22, 24, 25, 28, 30
Mean Average Precision (MAP) 181, 183, 184, 185, 186, 187
mean squared error (MSE) 7, 8, 9, 10
media literacy 86

Mel-frequency cepstral coefficients (MFCC) 179

Metacafe 195, 210

Microsoft 170

mobile advertisement 284, 297, 298, 299

Multi-Armed Bandit Problems (MABP) 16, 19, 20, 21, 23, 28, 30

Multi-Armed Problems 14

Multimedia advertising 84

multimedia community 101

multimedia message services (MMS) 296, 297, 299, 300

Multimodal Relevance 66

multiple kernel learning (MKL) 180, 181

N

Naïve Bayes Nearest Neighbor (NBNN) 182, 183

natural hierarchy 4

natural language processing (NLP) 263

Nearest-Neighbor (NN) 181, 182, 184

next generation network (NGN) 282, 297, 298, 299, 300

Nielsen, Arthur 149, 165,

Nielsen Company 165, , 167, 168, 172, 173, 191

Nikon 53

non-intrusive metric 101, 103

non-intrusiveness (NI) 101, 103, 110, 112, 118

O

ODP ontology 67

Offline Data Preparation 178

online ad ecosystem 262, 263, 264, 274

online ads 262, 263, 265, 266

online ad types 262, 263

online advertising 13, 14, 30, 32, 33, 34, 35, 37, 84, 85, 148, 149, 165

online commercial intent (OCI) detection 262, 263, 272, 273, 274

online environment 85, 90

online targeted advertising 233, 235

online video 194, 195, 198, 199, 204, 210

online video advertising 101, 102, 118, 120, 194, 195, 210

on-set placement 124

Open Directory Project (ODP) 67, 71, 72, 73, 74, 76, 77, 78, 81

open mobile alliance (OMA) 281, 285, 287, 297, 298, 300

optical character recognition (OCR) 174, 175, 176, 198, 200

optimal policy 16, 20, 29

overlay ad creative 105

P

paid listing and content match 34

Partially Observable Markov Decision Processes (POMDP) 30

Payment model 37

pay-per-action 33, 34, 37, 71

pay-per-click 33, 34, 37, 38, 71

pay-per-impression 34, 37

performance evaluation 1

personalization 37, 279, 280, 285, 287, 296, 299

personalized ad delivery 197

personalized advertisement delivery paradigms 233, 234, 236

personalized advertisement insertion logic (PAIL) 279, 280, 285, 286, 287, 288, 289, 296, 297, 299, 300

personalized advertisements 236

plot placement 124, 125, 126, 144

pop-up 33, 34

predictive power 160, 162, 163, 164

presence and group management (PGM) 287, 288, 290, 296, 300

PricewaterhouseCoopers 2, 11

pricing mechanisms 265, 267

pricing mechanisms, cost per action (CPA) 265

pricing mechanisms, cost per click (CPC) 265, 267

pricing mechanisms, cost per mille (CPM) 265

principal components analysis (PCA) 154, 155

privacy 234, 236, 240, 241, 256, 260, 262, 263, 264, 275, 276

product placement 122, 123, 124, 125, 126, 127, 132, 142, 144, 146

proximity distribution kernel (PDK) 180

pyramid histogram of orientated gradients (PHOG) 180

Q

Q-Learning algorithm 19, 20, 25, 27
QuickStep recommendation system 238

R

realtime transfer protocol (RTP) 298, 300,
receiver operating characteristic (ROC) 114
region of interest (ROI) 51
regulators 264
Reinforcement Learning Framework 18
reinforcement learning (RL) 13, 15, 16, 17, 18,
        19, 21, 28, 29
Relevance 36, 53, 56, 57, 58, 62, 66
Renderer 107
replacement space 132, 134, 135, 136
retentions scores (RS) 150, 151, 155, 162, 163,
        164
return on investment (ROI) 214, 222
Revver 195, 207, 210
rich media 166, 170, 171, 174
Rich-media banners 29

S

salience /LAR detection 104
salience map 104, 107
scalable 101, 102, 103
screen placement 124, 126, 144
script placement 124
Search Engine Auction 38
search engine (SE) 37, 38
Second Life 93, 95, 99
self-organizing map (SOM) 236
semantic knowledge 234, 238, 239, 240, 255
SemanticMatch 41
semantic user profiling 217
sentence importance (SI) 73
SentiWordNet 32, 43, 45
sequential multi-labeling (SML) 181
session description protocol (SDP) 297, 298,
        300
session initiation protocol (SIP) 284, 287, 297,
        298, 299, 300
set-top boxes (STBs) 149, 150, 152, 153, 154,
        155, 156, 157, 160, 172, 177, 187
Shih, Chuan-Fong 90, 97

short message service (SMS) 299, 300
short time energy (STE) 179
smoothing techniques 7, 9, 10, 11
social media 194
spatial optimization 29
spatial pyramid kernel (SPK) 180
spectrum flux (SF) 180
sponsored search 1, 2, 3, 10, 33, 34, 35, 37, 39,
        215
stochastic models 14, 15, 18, 19, 25, 29
subliminal advertising 124, 129, 140, 146
subliminal perception 124, 129
Support Vector Machine (SVM) 58, 108, 109,
        110, 114
Synergy 168

T

Tam, Kar Yan 90, 91, 97
Temporal Smoothing 7
Term Frequency Inverse Document Frequency
        (TFIDF) indexing 218, 223
Text-Based Contextual Advertising 215
TF-IDF-weighted 74, 76
third generation partnership project (3GPP)
        282, 284, 286, 287, 297, 299, 300
Three Screen Report 167, 172
Topic Bridging Model (TB) 77, 79, 80
Traditional Media 37
transmission control protocol (TCP) 300,
trial-and-error 13, 16, 17, 28
Turkle, Sherry 90, 98
TV ad consumption 148
TV ads 166, 167, 168, 169, 172, 173, 174, 175,
        176, 177, 178, 180, 182, 183, 186, 187
TV-style ad 102

U

ubiquitous pursuit 85
underperforming airings 151
universal mobile telecommunication system
        (UMTS) 285, 297, 298, 300
University of Bochum 93
unstructured supplementary services data
        (USSD) 300,
Upper Confidence Bound (UCB) 20, 21, 23, 28
user attention 202, 210

user-based targeting 103

user datagram protocol (UDP) 300,

user-generated content (UGC) 68, 169

user groups 214

User Interest Mining 75

user preferences 233, 234, 236, 237, 238, 248, 255, 260

user representation 217

user segmentation, bag of words (BOW) based 217, 218, 219, 227, 228

user segmentation, rule-based 217

user segmentation, semantic user based 214, 217, 218, 219, 227, 228, 230, 232

user segments 214, 215, 216, 217, 219, 220, 221, 222, 223, 224, 225, 226, 227, 228, 230

V

vADeo system 197

vector space model (VSM) 200, 289, 290, 291, 292, 299, 300

Vibrant media 33

video advertising 101, 102, 103, 104, 115, 118, 120, 194, 195, 196, 197, 198, 199, 200, 207, 210

video content 194, 195, 197, 198, 199, 200

video on demand (VOD) 169, 174

video overlay ad 101, 110

VideoSense 33, 47

VideoSense system 194, 196, 197, 199, 205, 206, 207, 210

viewer relevance measure (VRM) 126

virtual content insertion (VCI) 102, 104, 124

virtual product placement 122, 124, 125, 126, 127, 132, 142, 144

virtual spotlighted advertising (ViSA) 122, 124, 127, 129, 136, 139, 140, 141, 142, 143, 144, 145, 147

Virtual worlds 92, 93, 94

Visual Acuity Estimation 132

visual communication effect 132

visual systems 104

vocabulary impedance 68

voice over IP (VoIP) 300,

W

Web 2.0 84, 85, 90, 194

Web-based technologies 166, 169

web-browsing behavior 103

Web publishers 262, 275

Weighted Average Precision (WAP) 78, 79, 80

WordTracker 76, 83

Y

Yahoo! 1, 2, 8, 33, 34, 41, 1

Yahoo! Smart Ads 216

Yahoo! Video 195

YouKu 167

YouTube 33, 167, 169, 170, 193, 195, 207, 211

Z

zero-crossing rate (ZCR) 179